FRONTISPIECE. Sir Francis Bacon, by Henry Weekes. Trinity College Chapel, Cambridge University.

(By courtesy of The Courtauld Institute of Art, London.)

Modern European Thought

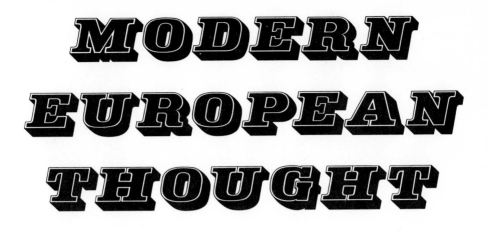

MODERN EUROPEAN THOUGHT

Continuity and Change in Ideas, 1600–1950

Franklin L. Baumer

Macmillan Publishing Co., Inc.
NEW YORK

Collier Macmillan Publishers
LONDON

Copyright © 1977, Franklin L. Baumer

Printed in the United States of America

All rights reserved. No part of this book may be reproduced or
transmitted in any form or by any means, electronic or mechanical, including photocopying, recording, or any information
storage and retrieval system, without permission in writing from
the Publisher.

Macmillan Publishing Co., Inc.
866 Third Avenue, New York, New York 10022

Collier Macmillan Canada, Ltd.

Library of Congress Cataloging in Publication Data

Baumer, Franklin LeVan.
  Modern European thought.

  Bibliography: p.
  Includes index.
  1. Philosophy, Modern—History. 2. Europe—
Intellectual life. I. Title.
B791.B36   190   77–4243
ISBN 0–02–306500–1
ISBN 0–02–306450–1 pbk.

Printing: 1 2 3 4 5 6 7 8   Year: 7 8 9 0 1 2 3 4

To my students

Foreword

This book is for anyone interested in ideas and their history. Despite its comprehensiveness, it is not primarily a survey or synthesis but rather an interpretation of modern intellectual history. Its specific purpose is to trace the development of one intriguing theme—perhaps the major theme—in modern man's way of thinking about himself and his universe. That theme is the sense of *becoming* rather than *being.* I have tried, through the study of a number of thinkers in Europe from the last four or five centuries, to pin down what it means to be "modern"—detailing the perception, ever increasing in intensity from Bacon on through Nietzsche and Bergson and beyond, that there is an essential and continuous flux in the order of things, as opposed to man's earlier view of a world of static entities or absolutes. Although here worked out on the European stage and with particular reference to England, France, and Germany because the key ideas discussed come mostly from these nations, the theme has important applicability to modern man in general. Dutch, Italian, Swiss, Spanish, Russian thinkers appear when reference to them is warranted or is necessary to the argument.

I have organized the work around large fundamental questions— our evolving views of God, nature, man, society, and history—rather than around individuals or fields of knowledge. There is no "age of Newton" and no discussion of philosophy or of science *per se.* The necessary periodization is, nevertheless, by centuries, probably the simplest way of managing the mass of material. The nineteenth century runs somewhat longer than the others because it is so crucial to the central thesis, albeit not more crucial for consideration of our five questions. There is copious quoting, since I believe in the all-importance of letting men of the past speak for themselves, and in their own idiom, and of then analyzing what they have said. For quotations I have availed myself of good published translations wherever possible, but it has obviously been necessary to make frequent translations of my own. Important use is also made of visual materials. The forty-three illustrations give poignance to a number of the ideas discussed. They also show, I believe, that artists and writers do not live in worlds apart, as they and others may sometimes like to think, but often share a common world of ideas.

Both the theme of the book and the five paramount questions are described at length in the Prologue, and discussion is devoted to each question in each chronological division of the book. Read in its entirety, undoubtedly the best way, the book yields a leisurely development of the overall theme; but it may be read topically by following any one of the basic questions and its answers through appropriate chapters. It may also be read for the content of a single century, for each division is largely self-contained.

I have assumed that the reader has some familiarity with the historical setting of modern Europe. The nonspecialist may, however, wish to do some collateral reading in both general works in the history of European thought and in the sources. A brief bibliography at the end makes some suggestions for further reading, and many other good books are mentioned in the course of the work. The bibliography does not include the original sources, which are discussed throughout the main text. The specialist will be interested, I hope, in some of the formulations, in the references to fields of knowledge other than his own, and in "new" materials used in some chapters. The same specialist, too, may say, as has been said, that my approach to intellectual history is more "classical" and "ideational-historicist" than sociological or psychological. I agree, if I may take this to mean that I place emphasis on ideas themselves, on how they were generated and became crucial in a particular historical context, and on their historical development. I would not wish it otherwise, although there is no gainsaying that intellectual history can, of course, be written in other ways.

Finally, a statement by Steven Runciman, called to my attention several years ago by Jaroslav Pelikan, seems peculiarly appropriate to this work, covering, as it does, four centuries and crossing numerous intellectual disciplines.

A single author cannot speak with the high authority of a panel of experts, but he may succeed in giving to his work an integrated and even an epical quality that no composite volume can achieve. . . . [The specialized historian's] work can be of the highest value; but it is not an end in itself. I believe that the supreme duty of the historian is to write history, that is to say, to attempt to record in one sweeping sequence the greater events and movements that have swayed the destinies of men. The writer rash enough to make the attempt should not be criticized for his ambition, however much he may deserve censure for the inadequacy of his equipment or the inanity of his results.

STEVEN RUNCIMAN
A History of the Crusades, Cambridge University Press,
1951–54, Vol. I, Preface.

*   *   *   *   *

My thanks go to Bruce Mazlish of M. I. T., W. Warren Wagar of the State University of New York, Binghamton, and John R. Hubbard of the University of Southern California for reading the manuscript with great care and making suggestions, some of which I have acted on. Thanks go also to my wife and daughter for their help in preparing the manuscript for publication and, especially in the case of my wife, for giving me excellent advice about both style and content. Charles Early read several of the chapters and made useful comments on them. Frank Turner and John Merriman, Yale colleagues, went out of their way to help me find copies of several of the more esoteric pictures I wanted. I owe a special debt to A. H. McLeod at Macmillan. Rarely does an author have the good fortune to work with an executive editor as generally helpful and meticulous. Of course, I could not have written this book without the use of Yale's Sterling and Beinecke Libraries and without access to many of Europe's, as well as America's, art museums.

I have dedicated this book to my students of many years, both graduate and undergraduate, who have listened to me patiently while I expounded some of the ideas discussed herein but who have also challenged, stimulated, and even corrected me at times. I consider it a privilege to have taught them and to have had the chance to help some of them get started in their scholarly careers. Books by several of my former students are cited in the footnotes and bibliography. To some of my more recent students, especially Clark Dougan and Dwight Barnaby, I owe particular suggestions for the nineteenth-century section of the book.

FRANKLIN L. BAUMER

Pierson College
Yale University

[ix]

Contents

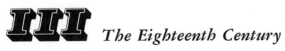

The Nineteenth Century

 *The Twentieth Century*

VI *Epilogue*

Illustrations

Modern European Thought

What is that which always is, and is never becoming?
What is that which is always becoming and never is?

PLATO, Timaeus

PART I

Prologue

The History of Ideas

The Perennial Questions

From Being to Becoming

1

The History of Ideas

"The great object, in trying to understand history," Lord Acton wrote to Mary Gladstone in 1880, "is to get behind men and to grasp ideas. Ideas have a radiation and development, an ancestry and posterity of their own, in which men play the part of godfathers and godmothers more than that of legitimate parents."[1]

Acton had been reading Sir John Seeley's lectures on British imperial history, "with improvement," Acton says, "but with more indignation." What aroused Acton's indignation, and prompted his remark, was Seeley's penchant for the idiosyncratic and purely political side of history. Seeley discerned Whigs but not Whigism. Seeley failed to see the importance of "the impersonal forces which rule the world," that is, the doctrines or ideas that "push things towards certain consequences without help from local or temporary or accidental motives." Acton expatiated on this theme after becoming Regius Professor of Modern History at Cambridge University, a post to which he was named, ironically, as Seeley's successor. "It is our function," Acton said in his Inaugural Lecture of 1895, "to command the movement of ideas, which are not the effect but the cause of public events." If Acton had had his way, the *Cambridge Modern History,* of which he was the first editor, would have been largely devoted to demonstrating this thesis.

---

[1] *Letters of Lord Acton to Mary, daughter of the Right Hon. W. E. Gladstone,* Herbert Paul (ed.), George Allen, London, 1904, p. 6.

Acton did not invent the history of ideas. The modern origins of the history of ideas can be traced to the Enlightenment of the eighteenth century, to "philosophic" historians such as Voltaire who tied progress to the growth of "reason," or the triumph of the human mind over superstition. But through most of the nineteenth century interest in the history of ideas lagged behind that in other kinds of history, particularly political history.[2] The dominance of political history in the nineteenth century reflected the increasing importance, in the era following the French Revolution, of politics and the state, and the concomitant belief, conspicuous in the land of Hegel, in the state as a great moral and cultural power. It became common to speak of history as past politics, or the biography of states. Seeley called political history a "school of statesmanship."

Interest in the history of ideas rose appreciably toward the close of the nineteenth century, for several reasons. First, it profited from the quarrel between the cultural and political historians. The former were calling for a wider sort of history, less restricted to politics, including all sides of "civilization," intellectual as well as material and political. Some like Jacob Burckhardt were also distrustful of state power. In his lectures on world history, delivered just before and during the Franco-Prussian War, for instance, this master of *Kulturgeschichte* depicted "Culture" (defined as "the sum total of those developments of the mind that occur spontaneously") as an independent entity engaged in eternal conflict with State and Church. The latter two "powers," he thought, frequently forestalled ethical goals and tried to suppress the free development of ideas. Acton, it should be noted, shared Burckhardt's views about both the narrowness of political history and the corrupting nature of political power.

The history of ideas also profited from the contemporary "revolt against positivism." In France, the "idealist" philosopher Alfred Fouillée, in defiance of the reigning scientific determinism, affirmed the decisive influence on human action of ideas freely conceived by the mind. In Germany, another philosopher, Wilhelm Dilthey, who was named to Hegel's chair at the University of Berlin in 1882, fought to establish the autonomy of the "cultural" or "human" sciences. In Dilthey's

---

[2] Not that there wasn't any history of ideas written in the nineteenth century prior to Acton or Dilthey. One has only to think of the important, and still useful, studies by Sir Leslie Stephen on English thought in the eighteenth century, and the Utilitarians; Lord Morley on the French *philosophes;* and W. E. H. Lecky on the growth of the spirit of rationalism. Both Stephen and Morley saw a close connection, as did J. S. Mill, between the ideas men hold and their politics.

view, the "human" sciences provided a far better way of understanding historico-social reality, hence also the nature of man, than the natural sciences. Dilthey, called "the father of the modern history of ideas," made history preeminent among the *Geisteswissenschaften,* and made the human mind and its ideas history's fulcrum. He did much, more than anyone else up to that time, to establish a methodology for the study of the history of ideas. He also broadened its scope to include, not only rational thought, so much emphasized by the Hegelian tradition, but also the products of the human imagination and will, as embodied in literature, art, and religion, as well as philosophy and science. Acton and Dilthey both wanted a new kind of history centering in ideas. But it was the Englishman's function, since he wrote comparatively little himself, mostly to trumpet its virtues, and the German's to practice the virtues of the history of ideas in a series of impressive studies of historical "world views."

The history of ideas became firmly established, and even popular, in the twentieth century. Dilthey's influence had something to do with this increasing vogue, especially after the publication of his collected works in the 1920's. So, doubtless, did the charged political climate of the 1930's and 1940's, in which ideas clashed as violently as at any time in history, and obviously moved men and armies. How could big history be written any longer without reference to ideas and ideologies? The further progress of the history of ideas owed most, however, to the continuing fragmentation of knowledge in Western culture, which by now had reached alarming proportions. From the first, but now much more consciously, the history of ideas represented an attempt to stem this trend, to see whether it was not still possible to view cultures as wholes, to interrelate their parts. "The history of ideas," wrote one of its chief exemplars, "is no subject for highly departmentalized minds." It "put[s] gates through the fences" that specialization has set up between departments of knowledge "whose work ought to be constantly interrelated."[3] Mainly for these reasons the history of ideas has had the power to attract some of the best minds among the historians, philosophers, and sociologists of the twentieth century. Among the historians, Ernst Cassirer (who was also a creative philosopher) and Friedrich Meinecke enlarged on Dilthey's vision, Meinecke by extending Dilthey's vision into the field of political thought.[4] Arthur

[3] Arthur O. Lovejoy, *The Great Chain of Being,* Harvard University Press, Cambridge, 1936, pp. 16, 22.
[4] Notably in *Die Idee der Staatsräson* (1924). Cassirer also, of course, dealt with political ideas, as in his well-known *The Myth of the State* (1946). Among

Lovejoy, professor of philosophy at Johns Hopkins University, did more than anyone else to get the history of ideas started in the United States, and to define it as a discipline. Sociologists of knowledge such as Karl Mannheim further enriched the history of ideas by drawing it out of the abstract, and relating it to social history. The sociology of knowledge, said Mannheim, "seeks to comprehend thought in the concrete setting of an historical-social situation out of which individually differentiated thought only very gradually emerges."[5] There are by now courses, textbooks, and programs in the history of ideas in many universities, particularly in the United States. The history of ideas even has its own journal, founded in New York in 1940, and a dictionary bearing the same title. It has been said that the history of ideas is less popular in England and continental Europe. But this is true only in the sense that the "straight" historians, emphasizing political and social history, have not been especially hospitable to it. In fact, much of the best intellectual history in the twentieth century has been written by Europeans. One thinks of distinguished work by Bernhard Groethuysen and Federico Chabod, Daniel Mornet and Paul Hazard, and Herbert Butterfield and Basil Willey.

Thus, it seems fair to say that the history of ideas—or intellectual history, as some prefer to call it—has won a secure place for itself among the "cultural sciences." Yet it still lacks clear definition. Despite the efforts of Dilthey and others, the subject matter, methodology, and perhaps especially the assumptions about the historical process of the history of ideas remain rather nebulous. What, precisely, is meant by "ideas"? Do these ideas pertain only to intellectuals? Are the protagonists of this kind of history trying to say that ideas, however defined, play the major role, or at least *a* major role, in history? And, if not, why then is the subject worth pursuing? The author's answers to these questions should emerge clearly enough in subsequent pages, but it would seem useful also to touch on these questions here, both for their own sake and to avoid possible misunderstanding.

It is not hard to see how the history of ideas differs from political, social, or institutional history. It focuses on men's ideas, on "the inner world of thought," whereas they dwell largely in "the external world of action." *Ideas,* however, is an elastic term that might refer to almost anything from the thought of a small elite to that of Everyman. On

---

American historians James Harvey Robinson and Carl Becker were some of the first to focus attention on men's ideas and on the role played by ideas in history.

[5] Karl Mannheim, *Ideology and Utopia,* Harcourt Brace, New York, 1936, p. 3.

this score, the history of ideas belongs somewhere between the history of philosophy and cultural history. That is, the range of the history of ideas is considerably wider than that of the history of philosophy, yet is not so wide as to include, at least not centrally, popular culture. The history of ideas is not restricted to the thoughts of the few, the specially talented, those whom one commonly encounters in histories of philosophy. As Lovejoy put it, the history of ideas "is most interested in ideas which attain a wide diffusion."[6] Diffusion may be taken here in two ways: first, as diffusion beyond one department of thought, even so broad a department as philosophy; and second, as diffusion beyond individuals through larger groups and movements of men. The history of ideas is the interdepartmental discipline *par excellence.* It pursues ideas into whatever "department" they are to be found: such an idea as organic evolution, for example, which although it originated among biologists, soon spread into nearly every nook and cranny of late nineteenth-century thought, affecting profoundly, not only scientists and philosophers but also theologians, historians, and even writers and artists. Obviously, the history of ideas, unlike the history of philosophy, tries to get beyond private into public thought, beyond the unique and idiosyncratic to shared ideas, to collective states of mind. It is interested not only in the creative thinkers but also in the popularizers who, like a Voltaire or a Leslie Stephen, were concerned with the dissemination of knowledge to a wider public. Yet even this broad range hardly extends so far as the endeavor of cultural history that reaches down into the folkways, habits, myths, and, so to speak, the ideas of the great mass of people. I will not say that the history of ideas entirely ignores, or can afford to ignore, popular culture. Nevertheless, its main interest is in the ideas of the higher rather than the lower culture. These ideas, however, may be exemplified in the arts as well as the sciences, in painting, for example, as in philosophy, in styles of gardening as in physics, and at different levels of sophistication.

I hasten to add, moreover, that the history of ideas does not concern itself exclusively, like René Descartes, with clear and distinct ideas, that is, rational or "methodical" thought, nor even with consciously held ideas. Indeed, it is vital to understand that the history of ideas, again in contradistinction to the history of philosophy, has as one of its foremost aims the uncovering of a certain class of ideas that might be said to underlie and condition nearly all formal thought. These are the fundamental assumptions, the *pre*conceptions, the *pre*suppositions,

---

[6] Lovejoy, *The Great Chain of Being* (see note 3), p. 19.

which men absorb almost by osmosis from their mental environment, of which they are frequently not fully aware, or in any case seldom mention since they take them for granted. Professor Cornford appropriately named this subterranean species of thought "the unwritten philosophy," and cited as examples the ancient Greeks' assumption, largely unexpressed or "unwritten," that the world was intelligible and rational, and that the human reason was capable of deducing a complete system of truth.[7] Thus, the history of ideas, though it necessarily operates largely within the orbit of rational thought, nevertheless also deals with ideas that may more properly be called beliefs or convictions. As expressed by Ortega y Gasset, there are ideas "which are merely thought" and "ideas in which one also believes."[8] The latter, because they engage not merely the "intellectual mechanism" but the whole personality, provide the key to the inmost thought of a people or an epoch.

Inevitably, intellectuals play the major role in the history of ideas, and since this is the case, many, myself included, prefer to call it intellectual history.[9] But this role must be properly understood. It involves the relationship of the intellectual to the rest of society. On the one hand, the intellectuals do constitute a distinctive class, a sort of classless class, relatively detached from the everyday struggles of the marketplace or forum, doing much of society's original, creative, and critical thinking for it. On the other hand, this "philosophic class," as Samuel Taylor Coleridge called it, is never so detached that it does not intersect with other classes or share the common concerns of its epoch. Seen in this light, this intellectual class resembles more a mirror than a vacuum (or ivory tower), a mirror that reflects the life experience of larger groups, and even at times of a whole society. There is no idea so esoteric or "intellectual" that it does not do this sort of reflecting in some de-

---

[7] See F. M. Cornford, *The Unwritten Philosophy and Other Essays,* Cambridge University Press, Cambridge, England, 1950.

[8] Ortega y Gasset, *Ideas y Creencias,* translated as "History as a System," in *Philosophy and History,* R. Klibansky (ed.), Harper & Row, New York, 1963, p. 284.

[9] Neither term, *history of ideas* or *intellectual history,* is completely satisfactory. The trouble with history of ideas as a descriptive term is that everybody has ideas, even the most unthinking people. On the other hand, intellectual history, although a somewhat more precise term, may give the opposite impression, of being confined to the thought of a small elite, as in the history of philosophy. The German term *Geistesgeschichte* more nearly fits this sort of "esoteric" intellectual history. As may be gathered from my remarks in the text, and elsewhere, I conceive intellectual history (or the history of ideas) more broadly, to include popularizers of ideas as well as the creative thinkers.

gree. For instance, the existentialist idea, quite abstract on the fact of it, that "Existence precedes essence," distills in one phrase a whole society's disenchantment with tradition and all the traditional absolutes or "essences." The mirror metaphor, however, is not entirely exact because the intellectual never merely reflects common ideas. He takes them in their raw state, often hardly more than mere gropings, poorly understood, and gives them eloquence, a structure, and a more general meaning. In this way the intellectual is able, by means of essay, play, poem, or painting, to sharpen other people's awareness of what they have experienced and are endeavoring to say. The intellectual reflects other people's ideas, but also refines and clarifies them. Hence, the history of ideas properly concentrates largely on the intellectuals, for they articulate best the ideas and beliefs that circulate widely in a society.

What role do ideas play in history? Historians of ideas have been accused, with some justice, of presupposing "that mind or spirit is the ultimate force behind the whole development of history."[10] But rightly understood, the history of ideas mediates between "idealistic" and "mechanistic" explanations of history. The idealist holds that an idea is not simply a reproduction of objects existing outside the mind; it is a "force" in its own right, originating in the mind, and seeking to manifest itself in the material world. The philosopher Fouillée actually labeled ideas "idées-forces," citing as example the idea of liberty, which in his view was father to the wish, which in turn impelled individual and collective action.[11] "Thought," said Heinrich Heine, "strives to become action, the word to become flesh, and, marvelous to relate, man, like God in the Bible, needs only to express his thought and the world takes form."[12] Heine saw Rousseau's thought embodied in the French Revolution, as Fouillée saw the idea of liberty forcing itself on modern society. The mechanist, on the other hand, descending from heaven to earth, as Marx would say, demotes ideas as principal determinants in history. Ideas become superstructure, or "ideological reflexes" of deeper social and psychological realities. "Thinking," said Freud, "is indeed nothing but a substitute for the hallucinatory wish; . . . nothing but

[10] Thus, Hajo Holborn, "The History of Ideas," *American Historical Review,* February, 1968, p. 691.

[11] Fouillée developed this idea, central to his philosophy, in a series of books commencing with *La liberté et le déterminisme* (1872) down to *La morale des idées-forces* (1907).

[12] Heinrich Heine, *Religion and Philosophy in Germany,* John Snodgrass (trans.), Beacon Press, Boston, 1956, p. 106.

a wish [emanating from "the unconscious"] can impel our psychic apparatus to activity."[13] Likewise, the sociologist of knowledge thinks of knowledge as ideology, that is, socially determined, by the economic system, class interest, and the like.

The history of ideas need not, and indeed ought not to, take either of these extreme positions. It by no means denies that other forces, "senseless agencies" even, such as natural disasters or population change, play a major role in history, or that thinking itself is environmentally conditioned. But it affirms that ideas, too, move history; that history cannot be reduced to mechanistic causes; that men seldom act decisively in history save under the stimulus of general ideas expressing values, aims, and utopias.[14] Substract from history these "formulated aspirations," and what would be left?—God perhaps, or matter in motion, but scarcely human beings. To this degree the idealists are surely right. Lord Acton and Fouillée were also right. It is simply not possible to imagine modern history without the idea of liberty and equality, which, ever since the French Revolution, has incited all sorts of people—liberals, nationalists, and socialists, black as well as white—to all sorts of action. Without reference to Philip II's ideas, to his scheme of values derived from the Counter Reformation, could one explain many of the great events of the sixteenth century, or even possibly the "decadence" of Spain itself? Heine exaggerated when he said "the thought precedes the deed as the lightning the thunder." Patently, however, ideas do move armies and men, do affect, sometimes profoundly, institutions, the law, administrative practice, and property arrangements.

To call attention to the role of ideas in history, to "spiritual-moral" causes, is surely important. The history of ideas, however, has a still more important function, to assist in the search for truth. As Friedrich Meinecke said, the history of ideas is worth studying for its own sake, quite apart from its bearing on "causalities." He meant that the history of ideas involved the search for "values" (the good, the true, the beautiful), as well as "causes." It "gives us the content, wisdom, and signposts of our lives," he wrote. "And it is the need for this, along with and beyond the pure will to causal knowledge, which at bottom has

---

[13] Sigmund Freud, *The Interpretation of Dreams*, in *Basic Writings*, A. A. Brill (ed.), Random House (Modern Library), New York, 1938, p. 510.

[14] Of course, ideas incite to action only when they constitute a "living faith" and not a merely "sluggish faith," only half believed in, as is frequently the case. Ortega makes this distinction in his essay "Ideas y Creencias" (1934), as J. S. Mill had done in the second chapter of *On Liberty*.

drawn men to history in every age, and in modern times especially."[15]
How is the history of ideas "relevant?", as the young rightly asked, not
so long ago, of every academic discipline. Above all, because, as I prefer to put it, it has to do centrally with man's search for answers to
"the perennial questions," that is, questions concerning his nature and
destiny. The past reveals answers, subtly or even radically different
from our own, to these questions in which we necessarily retain a vital
interest. Despite our superior knowledge in many areas, we see ourselves and the world only from our own perspective. This perspective
is inevitably somewhat special, partial, and limited. Hence, we need
to learn what others, situated in different times and places, have sensed
and thought. These earlier thinkers may have something immensely
valuable to tell us, especially in those areas in which, because of the
peculiar texture of their world, they developed a special sensitivity and
special skills. The history of ideas gives us access to their insights and
answers.

Thus, in the last analysis the history of ideas is a contemplative subject. It might be said to occupy the frontier between history and philosophy, partaking of the purposes of both, providing "values" from the
past for present scrutiny, yet also throwing light on historical "causes."
The two, in truth, the values and the causes, might be said to complement each other, the former by identifying ideas and ideals that have
had appeal for past generations, the latter by showing how men came
to have them, and how they affected their civilization. The history of
ideas is interested in both the historical origin and the validity of ideas.

[15] Friedrich Meinecke, "Values and Causalities in History," in *The Varieties of
History,* Fritz Stern (ed.), World Publishing Company (Meridian Books),
Cleveland, 1961, p. 272.

The Perennial Questions

The history of ideas boils down essentially to answers to perennial questions. But what, more precisely, are these perennial questions? It is important to be precise, for these questions will furnish the structure, just as various answers to them will furnish the major content, of this book. In general, they signify the questions that man raises more or less continuously through all generations and epochs. They are to be distinguished from merely temporary or timely questions, which have their day and then pass into oblivion, either because they are "solved" or else no longer seem relevant. The difference between these two types of questions, the timely and the timeless, is illustrated by the debates over Copernicanism and the divine right of kings. The Copernican system of the universe, which had aroused furious controversy during Galileo's lifetime, ceased to be a lively issue after Newton solved its mechanics. The question of nature, however, persisted. Similarly, divine right, revived as an issue during the Reformation, lost its capacity to make men apoplectic, and began, in fact, to seem somewhat ridiculous by the eighteenth century. Nevertheless, the question of how best to organize society persisted, and still persists. The perennial questions, then, are the deepest questions man can ask about himself and his universe. They are perennial because man cannot help asking them; they are fundamental to his whole cosmic orientation. How could man not inquire continuously about God, nature, man, society, and history?

These five areas of man's intellectual concern are all closely interrelated and interlocked, and are, in a sense, the same, so that it is difficult to speak of one without begging all the others. For the immediate purpose of definition, however, it would seem best to take them up one by one. I shall not only define them but also anticipate some of the main answers to be encountered in more detail in the body of this work. The answers, of course, have varied greatly in European history, whereas the questions, though the modes of stating them have also varied, have remained essentially the same.

1. The question of *God,* traditionally ranked first, concerns man's religious ideas. Does God exist? How do we know he exists? and if he exists, what are his attributes? In particular, how does he relate to man?—This was the traditional way of posing the question from St. Thomas Aquinas to Immanuel Kant. But this question may, and should be, stated more broadly. Essentially, it delves into first and last things. It asks whether naturalistic categories alone can explain the world and man; whether there is not also a transcendental or "extra" dimension to human life; whether man, indeed, lives in a meaningless universe (save for such meaning as he may be able to impose upon it himself), or whether, after all, the universe cares for man and in some fashion orders and decrees his fate.

The history of the idea of God since the Reformation is seismographic, recording both births and deaths and one tremendous earthquake. So much attention has been paid to the earthquake that one tends to forget Europe's ability to give birth to new gods; or, if one prefers, its ability to endow God with ever new characteristics, or new combinations of old characteristics, as the need arose. Among these new gods were the "absentee" god of the eighteenth-century deists, and the immanent-evolutionary god of the nineteenth century, both so different from the transcendent, almighty God of "orthodox" tradition. By far the most disrupting and disturbing upheaval yet noted on the religious seismograph, however, has been "the death of God" in more recent years. This event, prophesied by Nietzsche, signifies the demise (in men's minds) not merely of one god, needing perhaps only to be brought up to date, but of the whole pantheon. It signifies the trend in European thought, strong from the seventeenth century on, but wildly accelerating as one approaches the present, toward religious skepticism and indifference. The end product of this trend, still fully visible, has been the most secular society that the Western civilized world has ever seen.

2. *Nature,* a complex term at best, requires especially careful definition. As understood in the Middle Ages, nature had a comprehensive

meaning. It signified the whole order of creation, which was divided into three parts, the cosmos of planets and stars, the earth and all its creatures, and the state. But as used in this study, it refers only to non-human nature. More specifically, it denotes the world around man, the physical but not the cultural world, including, however, living creatures, animals and plants as well as inanimate objects.[1] No dualism is intended, incidentally, in the exclusion of man (human nature) from the definition since the relationship between man and nature has always constituted an important part of the question of nature. That question, then, comes down to this: what is physical nature made of, and by what principles does it operate? There is a myriad of possibilities. Nature may be regarded, for example, as teleological, that is, as designed for a purpose, mechanistic or evolutionary. The three imply radically different types of causality. Or, to use Collingwood's categories,[2] nature may be (and, indeed, often has been) explained in terms of mind, matter, or life, and "matter" itself is understood differently in different systems. Or it may be thought of as "fallen" or decayed, or, alternatively, as in some sense divinized. The conceptions elicit in each case a corresponding metaphor, as in the mechanistic hypothesis in which nature is said to be like a machine. More importantly, these conceptions inspire diverse attitudes and emotional responses ranging from reverence to arrogance, and from love to loathing and fear.

Largely as a result of the growth of science, the picture of nature has changed drastically at least three times since the age of Galileo. First, the Aristotelian-Christian conception, teleological and symbolic, gave way, though stubbornly, to the Newtonian machine. The latter was then temporalized with the idea of evolution and further modified by the scientific revolution of the twentieth century, particularly by the new quantum and relativity physics. The main trend has been toward an increasingly mathematical and abstract picture, more and more remote from man's everyday experience, comprehensible perhaps only to trained scientists and computers. Predictably, the reactions to this trend have been contradictory and ambiguous. Some, by no means only

---

[1] Of course, it has other meanings as well. Indeed, no word, it seems safe to say, has acquired a wider range of meaning, or been more ubiquitous or "sacred" in the history of Western ideas. It is often used, for example, as a synonym for norm or standard of excellence, whether in politics, morals, or art, or to indicate universal and general, as opposed to particular and provincial, qualities (for example, "natural" *versus* "positive" laws).

[2] See R. G. Collingwood, *The Idea of Nature,* Oxford University Press (Galaxy Book), New York, 1960.

the scientists, have rejoiced in it as a great humanistic triumph since it shows man at the controls, victorious *over* nature, manipulating nature for "the relief of man's estate," wresting from it life's deepest secrets. Others, however, have periodically protested against the dehumanization of nature by "mechanistic" science, as happened, for instance, in the Romantic Movement, and against scientific imperialism, as in the "revolt against positivism" beginning in the late nineteenth century. Still others, accepting the modern picture, but revolted by it, feel alienated from nature as well as from God.

3. What, then, is *man?* Thomas Henry Huxley, writing at the height of the furor over Darwinism, called this "the question of questions," ever presenting itself anew, and with undiminished interest "to every man born into the world." But it is much more than a question of human nature alone, at least as David Hume understood that term. " 'Tis evident," Hume said, referring to man's cognitive faculties, "that all the sciences have a relation, greater or less, to human nature."[3] Obviously the question involves, in a still larger sense, not only human nature but human stature, not only the reaches of human cognition (admittedly an important problem) but also the extent of man's freedom (freedom of will), his moral propensities, ultimately his power to shape his own destiny. "The question of questions" might be broken up into a number of subsidiary questions, as follows. Is man *sui generis,* or is he best understood as assimilated to nature and nature's laws, like the lower animals?—Darwinism, of course, fanned new life into this old query. In deciding what man is at any particular moment, which is more important, nature or nurture? That is, does man have a fixed nature, or is he malleable, like soft wax or clay, conditioned, possibly even determined, by his environment? Assuming some sort of raw human nature, what is its chief mark? Is it reason or unreason, spirit, will, love, aggression, sin, sex, the death wish—or freedom, as the Renaissance humanist Pico della Mirandola believed? And if it is freedom, the godlike freedom "to be whatever he wills," could man then conceivably become someday master of his soul, and lord of both nature and history?

The replies to the question of man over five hundred years oscillate between optimism and pessimism. The traditional Christian view was, on the whole, pessimistic as to human nature, though extremely complimentary to man's cosmic stature, making him the darling of creation. Since the Renaissance this view, never totally eclipsed, gave way gradu-

[3] David Hume, *A Treatise of Human Nature* (1739–1740), Introduction.

ally to a new anthropology that explained man in terms of human knowledge, science, culture, or history, rather than by religion or metaphysics. The results are confusing and ambiguous. Nevertheless, two major trends are discernible. One, descended from Greek rationalism, but largely the by-product of modern science, is strongly narcissistic, exalting man's reason, exulting in his power, vastly extended by the tools and machines that he himself has created. This "modern" view, foreshadowed by Francis Bacon and Descartes, probably peaked in the nineteenth century. It has been seriously challenged by another trend, which discerns the dark side of human nature, the underground, the irrational, the barbaric; also modern man's hollowness and sense of alienation. The product of disenchantment with modern man and his works, this "realistic" view runs all through twentieth-century literature. Sigmund Freud also emphasized severe "blows to man's narcissism." No wonder Max Scheler said man had become "problematic" to himself as never before in history. These two answers to the question of man, the Apollonian and the Dionysian, as we may call them, stand side by side, unreconciled and perhaps unreconcilable.

4. Whereas the question of man focuses largely on the individual, that of *society* deals with communities of men. This is much more than a question of forms of government. It asks how society, or the state, should be conceived in the first place. Is society to be thought of as static or dynamic?—as fundamentally unalterable because sanctioned in its present, or in some ideal, form, by God, tradition, natural law, or reason—or as alterable, and, in fact, necessarily changing all the time to meet new conditions. Is it more like a machine or an organism?[4] A machine is "made," whereas an organism "has grown" to be what it is. A machine may be dismantled at any time, or radically altered because it is the product of rational engineering. An "organic" society, on the other hand, reveres tradition, postulates a fundamental inequality between men (on the analogy of more or less important organs of the body), and emphasizes community, the duties owed by individuals to the life of the whole. Which is more real, then, society or the individual? And how is freedom to be conceived, as something that society confers on the individual, or as something that he has by "right" and that affords him some real measure of privacy?

Modern Europe very nearly destroyed itself over these questions.

---

[4] According to J. S. Mill (*Representative Government,* Introduction), these are the two basic ways of conceiving society and its political institutions. *Cf.* Ferdinand Tönnies' conception of *Gemeinschaft* and *Gesellschaft* (roughly equivalent to the organic and machine theories).

Through the smoke of conflict, however, it is possible to distinguish several common trends. Secularization, for example, set in quite early, as did the machine idea, gradually displacing "the idea of a Christian society." The machine idea took two main forms. The first, propounded by rationalists, aimed to substitute a new and more perfect model of statecraft for the old, to be based on a "social physics" rather than religious dicta. The other, descended from Locke's empiricism, emphasized utilitarian and pragmatic experimentation. Either form could take a liberal or authoritarian, an individualistic or a collectivistic, turn. The nineteenth century saw the high-water mark of middle-class liberalism with its emphasis on "negative" freedom for the individual. Just as nineteenth-century liberalism challenged an older absolutism, however, so it in turn has been challenged many times by systems—nationalism, socialism, even a new liberalism—calling for a "positive" freedom, or the subordination of the individual to a "higher," collective self. And in a time of rapid industrialization and population increase the demand for root-and-branch social reform, as distinguished from mere political change, has been insistent.

5. The last of the questions, that of *history,* asks, first of all, about attitudes toward the past. How significant is the past? Should the present look up to it (or to significant portions of it) as to a great teacher, or should it try to break free of it in its search for identity and truth? But the question of history also tries to read the future as well as the past and present. That is, it encompasses the whole historical process, tries to make sense out of it, to see whether it has any "meaning." Does history move in any visible direction, round in a circle, as the ancients thought, or perhaps in a spiral or straight line? Does it appear, then, to have some sort of design, to be subject to law, to be moving toward a goal? And what are its chief driving forces: Fate or free will? the will of God or the will of man? the "cunning of reason" or certain impersonal forces such as economic systems, technology, and the like?

In the modern world the philosophy of history, as this inquiry may be called, centers on the idea of progress. This idea, emerging strongly in the seventeenth and eighteenth centuries, drove out the Christian or theological interpretation of history whose classic statement was by St. Augustine. Though it too preached a linear progression, the idea of progress was not toward the City of God, which is beyond history, but toward a secular city, created by man himself on earth. Though it continued to have supporters well into the twentieth century, this secular faith was seriously eroded in more recent times, chiefly by two other ideas, one more or less optimistic, the other pessimistic. "Historicism," largely a nineteenth-century product, exulted in the infinite variety of historical phenomena, in the uniqueness of each successive age and culture. Thus, it stressed the profound difference between history and philosophy, the former resisting, in its rich complexity, any sort of abstract generalization, including a law of progress. More recently still, history came to seem meaningless and even nightmarish. The "unreason" of contemporary events appeared to reveal all too clearly the "illusion" of historical progress. Already in the late nineteenth century, Friedrich Nietzsche was talking about the sickness of modern man and his complacent views about history. The ancient idea of cycles, or eternal recurrence, in history seemed to him more nearly to fit the facts.

It is not contended that these five questions are raised with equal intensity in all periods of history. This is certainly not the case. Now one question, now another, assumes a special prominence, depending on the state of knowledge and the felt needs of the times. The question of nature, for example, caused extraordinary excitement in the sevententh century, just as the question of man has prompted inordinate concern in the twentieth. Commenting on the latter, the psychiatrist Franz Alexander observes that in periods of relatively acute "pain" and social distress the intellect focuses "upon the center of the trouble, man himself."[5] Moreover, the degree of interest generated by one or another of the questions controls the prestige of certain types of study or intellectual work. The historian Edward Gibbon remarked on this interrelationship in a youthful, but perceptive, essay. "In our day," he wrote, "physics and mathematics sit on the throne" (though their fall, he thought, might not be far off), whereas politics and eloquence ruled supreme in republican Rome, history and poetry in the century of Caesar Augustus, and scholastic philosophy in the thirteenth century.[6]

The fact that one question stands out at a particular time does not, however, mean the eclipse of the others. The others, too, continue to be raised right along, and if relatively slighted at one time, come back into prominence at another. Is the religious question an exception? I do not think it is, especially not as I have defined it. The twentieth century is a test case in this respect. Age of advanced secularism though it assuredly is, it has nevertheless witnessed the rise of vigorous new

[5] Franz Alexander, *Our Age of Unreason,* J. B. Lippincott Company, Philadelphia, 1942, p. 25.
[6] Edward Gibbon, "Essai sur l'Etude de la Littérature" (1759), in *Miscellaneous Works,* John Murray, London, 1814, pp. 16–17.

theologies, as well as a literature full of religious longing, if not belief. The reason why all of these questions continue to be raised simultaneously is because it is in man's nature to raise them, and because they do interlock. The Elizabethans assumed that there were correspondences between the three domains of the created world, the cosmos, the individual soul, and the political state, so that what happened in one inevitably had repercussions in the other two. If Caesar seized an illicit crown, there would be "civil strife in heaven" as well as in the state, and he himself would suffer pangs of conscience. It is the same with the five questions. They are constituents of a whole, of a *Weltanschauung*, or general view of life. Consequently, it is not really possible to ask one question without drawing in, or at least inferring something about, all the others. How could one say, for instance, what society is or ought to be like without having some notions, perhaps partially "unwritten," about human nature and history? Does not disbelief in God, or a certain kind of God, react back on ideas of nature and man, and so on? Actually, this interconnectedness is borne out in the history of ideas. Correspondences do not exist merely as logical possibility, but in actual historical fact. To ask the question of nature in the age of Galileo (and to answer it in radically new ways) was to play havoc, within a fairly short time, with ideas about divine and human government, and the course of history and man's control over it.

These are the reasons why, in spite of the ebb and flow of fashion, I call these questions perennial. The philosopher-historian R. G. Collingwood, who thought much about these things, appears to disagree. In his *Autobiography* Collingwood tells about his quarrel, early on, with the philosophical "realists" of his time. "The 'realists' thought that the problems with which philosophy is concerned were unchanging. They thought that Plato, Aristotle, the Epicureans, the Stoics, the Schoolmen, the Cartesians, etc., had all asked themselves the same set of questions, and had given different answers to them."[7] By degrees, interestingly after meditating on Einstein's theory of relativity, Collingwood came to the conclusion that this thought was false, that the questions as well as the answers were relative to the times, that there were no "eternal problems" or questions. The difference between his and my position, however, is more apparent than real. Collingwood had in mind a more limited kind of question, whether, for example, Plato and Thomas Hobbes were talking about the same thing when

[7] R. G. Collingwood, *An Autobiography,* Oxford University Press, London, 1939, p. 59.

they discussed "the State." I agree that they were not, that Plato, of course, had in mind the Greek Polis, and Hobbes the absolute state of the seventeenth century. But judging by two of his other books,[8] Collingwood would certainly agree that the wider problem of society (as previously defined) and man was common to both Plato and Hobbes, and was, indeed, "eternal." And so, from the fact that some questions do get raised continuously, and to some extent simultaneously, I conclude that there is, after all, an element of permanence in the midst of historical change.

---

[8] *The Idea of Nature* (1945), cited in note 2, and *The Idea of History* (1946), in which Collingwood discusses various answers in a historical series to the same question.

From Being to Becoming

But in the end flux is king, as Heraclitus said, or at any rate has become king in the thought of modern Europe and the West. This is the major theme running through these pages, namely that becoming has superseded being as the major category in European thinking between the times of Francis Bacon and Henri Bergson (and down to the present). Ernest Renan caught this Heraclitean movement in words written over a hundred years ago. The big new step taken in modern criticism, he said, has been "to substitute the category of *becoming* for the category of being, the conception of the relative for that of the absolute, of movement for immobility."[1]

"Becoming," it should be made clear, does not refer here merely to new and changing answers to perennial questions, which may be taken for granted, nor even to great revolutions in ideas. It refers instead to a mode of thinking that contemplates everything—nature, man, society, history, God himself—*sub specie temporis,* as not merely changing, but as forever evolving into something new and different. It disbelieves in all fixities, absolutes, and "eternal" ideas. Historically speaking, its essence, as John Dewey observed apropos of the impact of Darwinism on philosophy, consisted in a remarkable "transfer of interest from the permanent to the changing."

[1] Ernest Renan, *Averroes et l'Averroisme*, A. Durand, Paris, 1852, p. ii.

. . . The conceptions that had reigned in the philosophy of nature and knowledge for two thousand years, the conceptions that had become the familiar furniture of the mind, rested on the assumption of the superiority of the fixed and final; they rested upon treating change and origin as signs of defect and unreality. In laying hands upon the sacred ark of absolute permanency, in treating the forms that had been regarded as types of fixity and perfection as originating and passing away, the "Origin of Species" introduced a mode of thinking that in the end was bound to transform the logic of knowledge, and hence the treatment of morals, politics, and religion.[2]

This sense of becoming is at the heart of what we mean by modernity, or "the modern mind." This sense did not originate with Darwin, as Dewey knew very well. It was already germinating in the sixteenth and seventeenth centuries, in the conception, fomented by the overseas discoveries and the *scienza nuova,* of an ever expanding body of knowledge. However, there was still much being in Western thought far down into the eighteenth century and beyond, as we shall see. Reform itself, pushed on all fronts during an age of revolutions, postulated, more often than not, simply a new form of being, allegedly more perfect than the old. But by the time of Renan the tide had turned, and a world that had seemed more or less static, at least in terms of ultimate goals and eternal frames of reference, now began to look endlessly dynamic. "The most obvious attribute of the cosmos is its impermanence," said Thomas Henry Huxley, who was the spokesman for a whole generation on this subject. The historicist-evolutionary point of view, as it may be called, now impregnated nearly every department of thought, including theology, ethics, and social philosophy. It culminated in an extreme relativism, which dared to assault even the inner citadel of the self, as in the philosophy of Henri Bergson. Bergson, though he mixed being with becoming in his own peculiar way, is the philosopher of becoming *par excellence.*

I find, first of all, that I pass from state to state. . . . I change, then, without ceasing. But this is not saying enough. Change is far more radical than we are first inclined to suppose. For I speak of each of my states as if it formed a block and were a separate

---

[2] John Dewey, *The Influence of Darwin on Philosophy,* Henry Holt and Company, New York, 1910, pp. 1–2.

whole. . . . The truth is that we change without ceasing, and that the state itself is nothing but change.[3]

Bergson's picture of impermanence should be compared with another French philosopher's famous affirmation about the self. "I think, therefore I am": René Descartes, though he too heralded a revolution in thought, knew who he was at all times, namely a thinking substance, which, moreover, contemplated a stable (though not in all respects a traditional) universe guaranteed by God. Bergson, on the other hand, was aware primarily of "duration," or ceaseless change throughout the universe and even in his own self.

This whole trend from being to becoming, greatly accelerating in the nineteenth and twentieth centuries, would be inconceivable without the great convulsions of modern times—the French Revolution, the Industrial Revolution, the technological revolution, both mechanical and "electric"—which loosened the traditional social fabric of Old Europe, quickened the pace of living, and bombarded the senses with innumerable new stimuli. It also owed much, however, to an earlier revolution that began in the mind. The scientific revolution of Galileo and Newton, to be sure, produced its own special kind of being; it taught people to think in terms of invariable laws and "perfect," mechanical models. But it also fostered a type of mind that was destructive of traditional "Idols," including its own. The scientific mind, ever restless and restive, never content with present truths, insisted on subjecting its own hypotheses to constant re-examination, and on changing them, when necessary, in the light of new evidence.

"Becoming," it seems clear, is an explosive conception that breaks up worlds, or in its most advanced modern form, does not even allow worlds to form. As such, it has understandably had diverse psychological effects. It can be, and to many has been, an exhilarating idea, enabling "free spirits," as Nietzsche said, to ply their ships in the "open sea." To others, the idea of living in an endlessly changing world is depressing. Heraclitus was known for good cause as the Weeping Philosopher. He wept because he thought fire, the symbol of change, was the ultimate ground of the universe, and fire is born from the death of something else. Here we have two types of "modern mind," one excited by change, filled with "astonishment, presentiment, and expectation" at the prospect of it; the other weary from having con-

---

[3] Henri Bergson, *Creative Evolution* (1907), Arthur Mitchell (trans.), Random House (Modern Library), New York, 1944, pp. 3-4.

stantly to adapt to it, and perplexed by the total lack of stability and certainty.

What is the bearing of all this on civilization? I return to this question in a concluding section. Suffice it to say here that it is hard to see how a civilization can long endure on becoming alone. Civilization demands, surely, a healthy mixture of becoming and being, the former to guarantee, not merely continuing criticism, but fresh forms of creativity; the latter to provide continuity and direction. But how to find being again, at least in any widely accepted sense, in an age of becoming is a puzzlement. This is the supreme problem of the twentieth century.

PART II

The Seventeenth Century

Being over Becoming

A New Nature

Faith and Reason

The Greatness and Wretchedness of Man

The Mortal God

Ancients and Moderns

1

Being over Becoming

Attempts to categorize seventeenth-century thought have not proved very successful. This is not surprising, since the seventeenth century was a period of great contrasts, even of polarities. Catholic and Protestant Europe, now permanently divided; mystic Spain and the down-to-earth Dutch Republic; "classical" France and "baroque" Italy; a dismembered and distracted Germany, its intellectual life dealt a severe blow by the Thirty Years' War; and Bourbon France, successful in its search for unity, law, and order; English empiricism and continental rationalism, not to speak of the eternal feuding among the sects, religious, philosophical, and political, of every country, and, in the minds of many individuals, the tension between science and superstition. A "double-faced age"? More like a hydra-headed age; at any rate, hardly a promising field for the combinative arts of even such a master reconciler as the German philosopher Leibniz.

Yet there were unities, too, and a case can be made for calling the seventeenth century the first "modern" century, ushering in a new Modern Age that, in certain respects, has still not run its course. The grounds for giving the seventeenth century a modern label are partly psychological, namely that during those years educated people in increasing numbers began to think of themselves consciously as "Moderns," as distinguished from "Ancients";[1] or, if they did not actually

[1] Moderns and Ancients are capitalized in this and succeeding chapters only when they refer to a specific party of men, identified as such at the time.

use the term modern, to think of themselves as doing something historically new, hence of inaugurating a new era of thought. Also, and more important, however, thought itself, regardless of how it was understood at the time, did in fact now begin to take on what we should call a "modern" (as distinguished from, let us say, a "medieval" or "ancient") look. This, incidentally, was the way Voltaire viewed the century of Louis XIV—by which Voltaire meant, at least as applied to thought, the whole seventeenth century, and Europe as well as France. In the ground-breaking chapters on the sciences and beaux arts in *Le Siècle de Louis XIV,* Voltaire singled out for special comment the achievements of the "Moderns" who, he said, in spite of opposition, had already won a "prodigious superiority," especially in philosophy.

It used to be thought proper to begin a discussion of modern European thought with the Renaissance and Reformation. But Renaissance humanists and Protestant reformers did not for the most part think of themselves as moderns, except in opposition to the Middle Ages. Both were at core "fundamentalists," seeking to revive, and to rival, primitive or ancient models of thought and civilization, ancient Greece or Rome, or the early Christian Church. This is not to deny in the least that the Renaissance, centering in a new sort of humanism, and the Reformation, defiant of traditional doctrines and authorities, were mighty movements in thought, or that they had important implications for modern ways of thinking. Psychologically, however, these movements tended to look to the past for inspiration and guidance. This was not true of the Moderns of the seventeenth century who looked more to the future and present. Sir Francis Bacon (see Frontispiece), a product of the Renaissance and Reformation, but also of the scientific revolution, was both prototype and epitome of this new sort of modernity.

To be sure, this characterization of a century, and of an age, poses some problems. The first is a semantic problem, which can be disposed of very quickly. The word "modern" requires definition. It may mean simply recent or present, in which case there are obviously "moderns" in every generation. On the other hand, the term may refer to a body of quite specific ideas and attitudes. It is obviously in this latter, and less neutral sense, that the word is used here. But, even so, the connotations of the word change, sometimes radically, in different periods of history. Later on we encounter other kinds of modernity, as, for example, romantic modernity and twentieth-century modernities, which actually clash with the modernity observed to surface in the seventeenth century. Suffice it to say that "modern" here refers to this latter type, to the "Moderns" mentioned in Voltaire's account, and to the new world-view they helped to sponsor, and which eventually became a dominant force in European civilization. In those early days the word modern had a polemical ring and was very much tied up with brash new conceptions of history and knowledge. The opening lines of Charles Perrault's poem, also on *Le Siècle de Louis le Grand* (1687), and read before the French Academy, strikes the note of the whole movement:

> *Beautiful Antiquity was always venerable*
> *But I never believed it was adorable*
> *I see the Ancients without bending the knee.*[2]

And one could compare, Perrault went on to say, the century of Louis XIV, that is, the modern world, with the century of Caesar Augustus without disadvantage to the former. "Moderns, take courage," a contemporary wrote, "you will carry away the advantage." Afterward, as they saw their views do just that, modern-looking people could drop their contentiousness and simply assume the "prodigious superiority" of their position. Just what that position was, and what it implied, will appear in due course.

Another problem, somewhat more serious, is that in the seventeenth century the "moderns" were by any definition still in the minority. However, their number was certainly considerable, and constantly growing. By the end of the seventeenth century they had won some notable victories, as, for example, in the French Academy itself, which in 1691 elected Fontenelle, bright young star of the self-styled Moderns, to membership over the protests of the literary elite of France. During the reign of Louis XIV, says Voltaire again, "one saw established imperceptibly in Europe a literary republic (*une république littéraire*), in spite of wars and religious strife." Voltaire's reference was mainly to the Moderns or, as they were sometimes called, the "Virtuosi," that is, to those who everywhere favored "New Philosophy" in whatever form; also to those who, especially in France, championed new developments in literature and art and even morals. These included the leading scientists and philosophers of the time, but, significantly, many amateurs as well as professionals. "All Conditions of Men," says Bishop Sprat, were admitted to England's new Royal So-

---

[2] La belle antiquité fut toujours vénérable
Mais je ne crus jamais qu'elle fut adorable
Je vois les anciens sans plier les genoux.

ciety, nobles, businessmen, and divines as well as "philosophers."[3]
"Though the Society entertains very many men of particular profes-
sions, yet the far greater number are gentlemen, free and unconfined."
Sprat also testifies, in this first history of the Royal Society (1667),
to the mounting enthusiasm for experimental science in seventeenth-
century England. Critics had objected that there would not be enough
"men of philosophical temper" to fill up the Society. To which Sprat
replied that the scruple had no force in respect of "the Age wherein
we live." "For now the genius of experimenting is so much dispersed,
that even in this nation, if there were one or two more such assemblies
settled, there could not be wanting able men enough to carry them on.
All places and corners are now busy and warm about this work. . . ."[4]
In France, neither the literary Academy, previously mentioned, nor
the new *Académie des sciences* could reflect anything like such a broad
social base since their membership was strictly limited to professionals
by royal decree. On the other hand, we hear of mixed and enthusiastic
audiences at public debates on Cartesianism in the provinces, and of
scientific demonstrations and lecture courses attended by all sorts of
people. And in Paris itself the new popular journals, and many young
writers and even women, were often to be found on the side of the
"Moderns." The Perraults were typical of this new modernity: four
brothers, all of them distinguished in one or more lines of intellectual
work, or else prominent in public life, three of the four interested in
the sciences and belonging to the Modern party.[5] The intention here
is not to exaggerate the numbers or the unity of this party in seventeenth-century Europe, but merely to point out that it was not only
increasing in size but also attracting public attention, and that it represented an important thrust in seventeenth-century thinking.

Did this thrust amount to a revolution, as Voltaire said it did? This,
too, is something of a problem. No one doubts that the seventeenth
century witnessed important changes in the way many people thought
about the world. But how far-reaching really were these changes? Did

[3] That this was in fact the case is clearly indicated in the original roster of the
Royal Society. Of the original hundred odd Fellows of England's first chartered
scientific society, the great majority were "gentlemen" or amateurs.

[4] Thomas Sprat, *The History of the Royal Society of London,* Pt. I, Sects. VII,
VIII.

[5] Claude Perrault was, among other things, one of the architects of the famous
new colonnade of the Louvre, and interested in anatomy and physiology. Pierre, a
financier, translated Tassoni and developed many of the ideas about modern and
ancient knowledge that were later presented by his brother Charles to the French
Academy.

they shake the foundations, as the Christian Revolution of an earlier age had done, or, as the twentieth century—call it what you will—is almost certainly doing today? Or were they somewhat more moderate, comparable, say, to the new awarenesses that developed in the Renaissance, but hardly disturbing, at least for any appreciable number of people, traditional assumptions? The position taken here is that there was a revolution indeed, but that it was not so drastic as has sometimes been suggested. In terms of the major theme of this book, becoming did not dislodge being in the seventeenth century, nor even seriously challenge it as a major category of thought, even though the latter assumed some markedly different modes. In other words, along with the innovations there were significant continuities, not to speak of atavisms, even in the thought of the "moderns" themselves.

The revolution, however, is not in doubt. That there was a revolution is hardly surprising in view of the new and powerful pressures building up on thought, and coalescing in the seventeenth century. The pressures came from many directions: from the explosion of scientific ideas in the age of Galileo and Newton; from the Renaissance, which, among other things, revived knowledge of the ancient skeptics; and from the Reformation, which, like science, though in a different way, challenged traditional authorities. Pressures also came from the world of action, from the religious wars, the commercial revolution, and expansion overseas that confronted Europeans with alien cultures. Philosophy had no choice but to respond to, and to absorb as best it could, the new ideas, the new information, and the new realities. "This is the Age," an Englishman wrote in 1663, "wherein philosophy comes in with a spring-tide. . . . Me-thinks, I see how all the old rubbish must be thrown away, and the rotten buildings be overthrown, and carried away with so powerful an inundation."[6] To put it another way, out of this milieu ineluctably came new answers to the perennial questions, as well as a new ranking of these questions in order of interest. The question of nature became central, as witness philosophy's preoccupation with it, and the power it had to galvanize thought on all the other questions. Nature took on a radically new look in consequence of a succession of "revolutions," Copernican, Galilean, Cartesian, and Newtonian. This "New Nature," in large part the creation of an *esprit géométrique,* in turn raised problems about human nature; yet at the same time it roused man's sense of his own power, not only to read

[6] Henry Power, *Experimental Philosophy,* Johnson Reprint Corporation, New York, 1966, p. 192. This is a reprint of the enlarged edition of 1664.

and control nature but also to organize society on a more rational plan, and possibly even to bend history to his purposes. Meanwhile, religious questions continued to excite interest and controversy, and God figured importantly in nearly all the new philosophical systems. The idea of God, however, was transformed in these systems. Theology, once queen of the sciences, had lost its power to dominate thought, thought about God as well as nature and man.

In retrospect, the most radical aspect of this seventeenth-century revolution might now seem to be the new conception of knowledge it produced. This conception, quintessentially modern, has long since been taken for granted. It was a dynamic conception, consisting above all in a shift from a contemplative to a utilitarian and activist goal. Sir Francis Bacon, as is well known, called for a conjoining of contemplation and action, and was always talking about knowledge for "the relief of man's estate," and for "the enlarging of the bounds of human empire, to the effecting of all things possible." Likewise, René Descartes who, one might have thought, resembled less one of Bacon's bees at work making honey, than a spider spinning, for its own sake and out of itself, a web of pure reason. But Descartes too wanted knowledge that would be of "much utility in this life." "Instead of the speculative philosophy now taught in the schools," he wrote in the *Discourse on Method* (1637), "we can find a practical one" whereby, learning to know how nature works, we can "make ourselves masters and possessors of nature." This utilitarian perspective was at variance with traditional, Aristotelian and Augustinian, conceptions of knowledge emphasizing knowing or "wisdom" for its own sake.[7] However, it was the product, not merely of revulsion against a by-now arid and academic scholasticism but of an increasingly commercial and urban society that was interested in "works." The Royal Society, said Bishop Sprat, intended a philosophy "for the use of cities, and not for the retirement of schools,"[8] and had as one of its projects a history of trades, advocated by Bacon. Another instance of this shift in focus was the debate (another *querelle*) in late seventeenth-century France over the contemplative life, as exhibited particularly by monks. A "public opinion" was developing that called on monks to join action to contemplation, to orient their contemplation more toward practical ends such as the

---

[7] See on this subject John Herman Randall's excellent chapter on "Knowledge as Power," in *The Career of Philosophy*, Columbia University Press, New York, 1962, Vol. I.

[8] Sprat, *Royal Society* (see note 4), Pt. I, Sect. VIII, and *passim*.

study of "science," to be less removed from the world and more useful to society.[9]

Bacon also frequently stressed the "advancement of learning," which he urged on everybody, including the king of England. This phrase, a favorite among seventeenth-century *Virtuosi,* strikes the new dynamic note in the conception of knowledge. Drawing on the imagery of the voyages to the New World,[10] Bacon expressed his hope of a great expansion of knowledge, surpassing by far anything the ancients or scholastics, proceeding by a false method, had ever discovered. Bacon aimed, he said, to be the Columbus of a "new intellectual world," to sail through the Pillars of Hercules, symbol of the old world, into the Atlantic Ocean of new discovery. And others could do the same if only they shook off undue reverence for antiquity and "the authority of men accounted great in philosophy," and adopted his "novum organum," or new inductive method of thinking. This dynamism, this sense of a cumulative science, was by no means limited to Baconians or experimentalists. But it was they who expressed this mode of thinking most vigorously, doubtless because they were so conscious of the day-by-day, patient collection of new facts that gave the lie to old notions. How indebted we are to "modern industry," says Henry Power in *Experimental Philosophy* (1663), for the discovery of the microscope, which promised to reveal the whole world of small objects until now invisible to the eye. And who could tell how far such industry might go? "For the process of art is indefinite, and who can set a *nonultra* to her endeavours?" Power, like Bacon, thought the scientific endeavor heroic, and heaped praise on "the enlarged and elastical souls of the world, who, removing all former rubbish, and prejudicial resistances do make way for the springy intellect to fly out into its desired expansion."[11] Power and others like him obviously had a keen sense of forward movement, of "becoming" in the sciences.

[9] See on this subject Gustave Lanson, "L'Esprit philosophique dans la littérature française de 1675 à 1748," *Revue des Cours et Conférences,* Paris, 1907–08, pp. 723–725.

[10] The voyages had already seized the imagination of artists. The Flemish painter Jan van Kessel's *America* (Plate 1), executed between 1664 and 1666, is a wonderful pictorial example of what the discoveries were coming to mean to many Europeans by the seventeenth century. Though not accurate in detail, and mixing up the two Indies, this painting celebrated visually the advancement of learning, the new information about geography and plant and animal life, as well as man in the "state of nature."

[11] Henry Power, *Experimental Philosophy* (see note 6), Preface, and pp. 190–92. Power was a provincial physician and Fellow of the Royal Society. *Experimental Philosophy* was the first English book on microscopy.

PLATE 1. *America,* by Jan van Kessel.

So much for the revolution. A word now on the survivals and continuities that are equally important for understanding seventeenth-century thought. By survivals I do not only mean the sort of credulity or superstition exhibited, for example, by the witchcraft mania in Germany during the Thirty Years' War, or the spasmodic belief in evil spirits by even such an advanced thinker as Thomas Hobbes. I also mean something more subtle, of which one becomes acutely aware from looking at contemporary art and architecture. Consider, for instance, the *vanitas* motif in seventeenth-century painting, strong not only in the Spain of the Counter Reformation where it might be expected but also in Holland where the new still lifes glorifying the senses did not succeed altogether in elbowing it out (Plates 2 and 3). Consider also the many representations of religious ecstasy by some of the greatest artists of the day, again not only Spaniards such as Juan de Zurbarán but also Bernini and the French portraitist Philippe de Champaigne. The latter's fine votive painting of 1662 (Plate 4) depicts two nuns of the Jansenist convent of Port Royal waiting ecstatically for the miracle that will cure Sister Catherine, the daughter of the painter, of her lameness. Was life a dream? This was a recurring theme in both art and literature, the subject of plays, sacred as well as profane, by Calderón de la Barca, and taking up a large part of one of Blaise Pascal's longer *pensées*. "Is not life itself a dream on to which other dreams are grafted from which we awake at death . . . ?" If the tide was running strongly toward earthly "utility" in philosophical thought, there remained nonetheless a stubborn residue of otherworldly sentiment that could still evoke great art. To be sure, the latter weakened toward the end of the century. On the other hand, admiration for classical architecture, if not classical science, grew stronger, especially in France and England. Claude Perrault's famous east front colonnade at the Louvre,[12] the Palladian vogue in English public and private building, and the like indicate the abiding influence of classical Renaissance taste.

But by far the most important survival was the continuing disposition to think about the world predominantly in terms of being—or, in Paul Hazard's phrase, of "stability"—as opposed to becoming or "movement." Not even a revolution of the magnitude described previously could upset this disposition, which had been ingrained by centuries of thinking. Habit, however, does not adequately explain its

---

[12] It is now believed that others including LeVau, one of the architects of Versailles, collaborated on the colonnade, which was begun in 1665.

persistence and strength in the seventeenth century. It also reflected an intense desire to overcome the current disorder in the world of thought as well as action. The intellectual crisis of the early seventeenth century has already been remarked on, a crisis that seemed to some to put all in doubt, both macrocosm and microcosm, the body politic, and knowledge itself. The response to the crisis was not only *new* philosophy but philosophy that could at the same time restore and reconcile; provide permanent and universal principles, new ones if necessary, on which men could count and agree after a century, the century of the Reformation, of bitter religious and philosophical debate. This need to conquer doubt and "transcend controversy" explains much in seventeenth-century thought: the search for objective truth transcending merely subjective certainties; the appeal to "reason," not merely in order to doubt, but to put the world together again; the attempt to impose rules and laws on everything from nature to society and art.

Both the new classicism and rationalism exemplify these trends. In fact, in this one respect, in their mutual taste for a changeless order, there is a remarkable parallel between them. Classicism, of course, was much the more conservative in spirit. Nicolas Boileau, France's foremost arbiter of literary taste under Louis XIV, summed up the classical doctrine in his didactic poem *L'art poétique* (1674). Let the writer, Boileau wrote, be guided, above all, by "reason" and "good sense." These two words, obviously *mots d'ordre,* sprinkle nearly every page of Boileau's text. The writer is to avoid at all costs the "caprice" and "excess" exhibited by earlier French writers such as François Villon and Ronsard, and learn the "right rules" (*règles de devoir*), first laid down by the ancients. Let the writer study the ancients, especially the likes of Horace and Vergil, for precisely this reason, because they were the first to perceive what is general and eternal, as distinguished from what is merely adventitious, in human nature, and to express themselves in forms never since surpassed for clarity and beauty.[13] Another Nicolas, the painter Poussin, whom Boileau praised, shared these sentiments. "My disposition," Poussin wrote to a friend in 1642, "constrains me to seek and love things well ordered, fleeing confusion. . . ." In his landscapes, especially those painted in midcareer, this most "classical" and most intellectual of all French painters also tried, in

[13] Though a leader of the Ancients, Boileau was willing to concede, toward the end of his life, modern superiority in some genres of literature and art, as well as science. In his rhymed *Lettre à Perrault* (1701) Boileau took the position that Louis XIV's century was gerater than any other single century, but not equal to all the other centuries combined.

Museum Boymans–van Beuningen, Rotterdam.

PLATE 2. *Still Life*, by Willem Claesz. Heda.

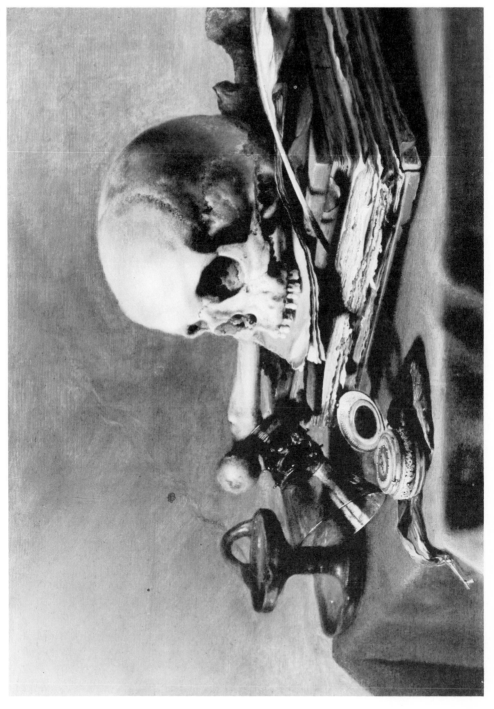

PLATE 3. *Vanitas*, by Pieter Claesz.

Musée du Louvre, Paris. (Cliché des Musées Nationaux.)

PLATE 4. *Artist's Daughter with Mother Agnes Arnauld* (Ex-Voto of 1662), by Philippe de Champaigne.

Kenneth Clark's words, to give to nature "an air of order and permanence."[14] There is no movement in a painting such as *The Funeral of Phocion* (1648). (Plate 5). Nature is geometrized, showing a harmonious balance between horizontal and vertical elements. To achieve the latter effect, Poussin has introduced architecture, chiefly of antique design, a temple, and the like, intended, doubtless, to heighten the sense of ideality and timelessness.

The world of René Descartes, rationalist *par excellence,* was different from Boileau's or Poussin's in important respects. Descartes was a modern who was disrespectful of past systems of philosophy, Aristotelian or scholastic, a protagonist of Galilean science. Yet he too wanted order and clarity, in order to combat a resurgent Pyrrhonism or skepticism, and ended by finding "rules" and "principles" (the titles of two of his most important books) for governing, respectively, thinking and the universe. Descartes, and the whole rationalist family of philosophy to which be belonged, might be said to have created an up-to-date "classical" universe: harmonious, rational, geometrized, explicable ultimately in terms of eternal essences or substance. The rationalist philosophers quarreled about the number and nature of substance, whether, for instance, there were two substances, as Descartes said, or only one (Spinoza), whether body or extension was a substance as well as mind, and so on. But none doubted the existence of some sort of essential order to which all phenomena, cosmological, psychological, or social could be referred. Like classicism, then, rationalism —or at least the great rationalist philosophies of the seventeenth century—stood for a timeless system of things.

This timelessness is not nearly so clear in empiricism, that other mainstream of seventeenth-century philosophy, or in classicism's opposite, the "baroque."[15] The baroque delighted in curves, movement, tension, expansive spatial effects—in a word, dynamism—as in the

---

[14] Kenneth Clark, *Landscape into Art,* Beacon Press, Boston, 1961, p. 66. The letter referred to, from Poussin to M. de Chantelou, is quoted in Henri Peyre, *Le classicisme français,* Editions de la Maison Française, New York, 1942, p. 162.

[15] Of course, these terms, classical and baroque, represent ideal types. In practice, the two often coexisted in the same author or mind. As Pierre Clarac remarks (*L'Age classique,* Arthaud, Paris, 1969, Vol. II, p. 69), "entre 1660 et 1680, on ne saurait citer un seul écrivain, un seul personnage dont on puisse dire que le goût ait été exclusivement classique ou exclusivement baroque." Louis XIV, for example, had baroque as well as classical tastes, if by baroque is meant not only excess but also movement and change. Witness the ceaseless modifications and embellishments at Versailles, and especially the enlarging of perspectives, as in Le Nôtre's gardens.

PLATE 5. *The Funeral of Phocion,* by Nicolas Poussin.

great churches of Bernini and Borromini in Rome. As we have seen, empiricism, and its ally experimental science, was similarly dynamic, at least in its conception of knowledge. Nor, since it counseled sticking to hard facts and to hypotheses subject to future correction, could empiricism claim certain or complete knowledge at any point. Yet seventeenth-century empiricism was by no means unadulterated with rationalism. Admittedly, John Locke's metaphysics was more modest than Descartes'. Locke too, however, clearly believed in substances—particular bodies in space, for example, the idea of causality, God himself—which could not be objects of direct experience. It should also be remembered that baroque art, although explosive in its visual effects and defiant of classical canons, was nevertheless usually to be found in the service of the Roman Church and its verities. Bernini, possibly the greatest artist in Europe, was a genuinely devout man, who not only recreated St. Peter's but practiced the spiritual exercises of St. Ignatius Loyola.

No doubt, many of the new movements in thought, the new empiricism included (especially when expounded by a philosophic nominalist such as Thomas Hobbes) were upsetting to many people throughout the seventeenth century. Nevertheless, as appears from evidence already cited, belief in a substantial world underlying appearances, in a stable universe, stood firm, even though it sometimes assumed new guises, as in Cartesianism and Newtonianism. By and large, being still maintained superiority over becoming as a major assumption of European thought. Any examination of seventeenth-century answers to the perennial questions reveals this fact.

In conclusion, a word should be said about leadership in the "republic of letters," or "commonwealth of learning" (as Locke called it), both with regard to nations and institutions. On the matter of national hegemony, it depends somewhat on whether one chooses to focus on the revolutionary or conservative aspects of seventeenth-century thought. Both Bishop Sprat and Voltaire did the former, for obvious reasons. Yet their histories were remarkably broad for all that, especially Voltaire's, and observant, and if we allow for their biases we can follow them with profit. There is striking agreement between them on one thing, namely that England was coming up fast in the intellectual world. We would expect Sprat, an English patriot, to boast about England's heading a "philosophical League, above all other countries in Europe." But Sprat was also a good European, and often talked about the superiority of Europeans in general to "the Barbarians," or to "the unlearned parts of the present world," by which he meant the

Turks, Moors, and primitive peoples overseas. His point about the English, debatable but not so far from the mark, was that they had advanced farthest in experimental science. And this they had done, not only because of "natural genius" but because they sat astride the ocean and had built an empire overseas from which all sorts of new discoveries could be expected.[16] Voltaire, writing several generations later and therefore profiting from hindsight, concurred.[17] He was willing to call the seventeenth century "le siècle des Anglais," as well as that of Louis XIV. It was especially in "philosophy" that the English displayed their superiority over other nations. By philosophy, Voltaire meant a mixture of philosophy and science, which was the way most people still thought of it in his own time; he was thinking of Newton as well as Locke, of physical scientists such as Robert Boyle and Edmund Halley as well as Francis Bacon. But in overall intellectual achievement Voltaire, of course, gave the palm to the French. France had at last become the cynosure of Europe, intellectually as well as politically. She might lag slightly behind England in the sciences, but in everything else, in eloquence, language, literature, and the arts, the French, Voltaire said, "were the legislators of Europe." But for his prejudice against Descartes, who "disdained experience" and built his system on air, Voltaire might also have talked up France's new preeminence in philosophy. He depicted Italy, the intellectual mistress of Europe during the Renaissance, as on the downgrade. The Italians still did respectable work in the sciences, but largely on the momentum provided by Galileo and Torricelli. And as for the arts, although Italy had conserved some of her ancient glory, there were no new Tassos or Raphaels. "It is enough to have produced them once." Voltaire thought of Italy as generally priest-ridden, and, consequently, as deprived of that freedom of thought upon which great philosophy depended. He seems not to have grasped Italy's continuing importance, not merely as a museum of "monuments" but as a generator of exciting new ideas in the arts. Voltaire mentions Bernini only in passing, and Caravaggio not at all. Nevertheless, Voltaire was basically right. Except in the arts Italy had fallen from her intellectual pedestal and now ranked distinctly lower than either France or England.

[16] Sprat, *Royal Society* (see note 4), Pt. II, Sects. X, XIII, and XX.
[17] Voltaire's bird's-eye view of intellectual Europe in the seventeenth century is to be found in Chapters 30 (on the sciences) and 32–34 (on the beaux arts) of *Le Siècle de Louis XIV* (1751).

One serious defect in this first survey of the European mind is that it slights the Dutch. Yet for a time, all too brief, the Dutch Republic occupied a unique and very important position in European intellectual life. It is fascinating to compare the Dutch with the Spanish, their arch rivals, during and immediately after their heroic struggle for independence (won *de facto* in 1609). Both were experiencing "golden ages" of culture. The former, however, represented the future (in the sense of the previously described intellectual revolution), the latter the past. Spain, champion of the Counter Reformation since the time of Philip II, explored "God's Indies," as one of her mystics put it, as well as the West Indies. Capable of producing one of the greatest schools of courtly painting in Europe, and a great drama imitated elsewhere, Spain in large part neglected the sciences. Though ecclesiastical power declined under Philip IV, much of Spain's intellectual and cultural effort continued to be church- and monastery-based, as witness the efflorescence of mysticism, and the work of artists like Zurbarán, painter *par excellence* of monks and friars, and Juan Martinez Montañes, sculptor of vanities and saints at prayer. The Dutch, on the other hand, had entered a period of "realism" (not, however, necessarily unreligious) reflecting a new bourgeois culture. Observation of worldly phenomena is the keynote of the new Dutch culture: not only in painting, which is well known, but in the sciences, anatomy, astronomy, microscopy, optics, and technology at which the Dutch excelled. Holland also became a haven for intellectuals in the seventeenth century, attracting, because of her relative intellectual freedom, the likes of Descartes, Pierre Bayle, and Locke, and tolerating the philosopher Spinoza. Although certainly admiring Amsterdam's culture in general and singling out several Dutch scientists for particular mention, Voltaire rather underestimated the Dutch achievement, perhaps because by the time his account ended Holland had declined to a second-rate power, eclipsed by "la grande nation," and already imitative of the latter's culture.[18] Nor did Voltaire dwell long on Germany and the Germans, though here he was on firmer ground. Thanks partly to the Thirty Years' War, Germany did not compare philosophically with France and England, nor did any influential new waves of thought come out of Germany until a much

---

[18] On the other hand, in his *Essai sur les moeurs et l'esprit des nations,* a work of much broader scope, Voltaire talks of the "frugality, simplicity, and grandeur" of the Dutch, and praises them for their religious tolerance. But here (in Chapter CLXXXVII) he is not concerned with their intellectual achievements.

later date. Leibniz was an exception. Voltaire, who deplored his metaphysics, called Leibniz "the most universal savant of Europe," prominent in mathematics, law, and Latin poetry as well as philosophy.

In Germany the universities deteriorated as centers of intellectual life. To a lesser extent this also happened elsewhere except in the Dutch Republic and possibly England.[19] One remembers Bacon's famous attack on the "colleges in Europe" as deficient in new philosophy and "universality," and badly needing reformation.[20] This was a common complaint, reiterated by educational reformers all through the century, and though exaggerated, was substantially true. "Modern" philosophy developed almost entirely outside academic circles. Among the scientists of note some were university professors—for example, Galileo at Pisa and Padua, and Newton at Cambridge—but the majority were not. The University of Leyden, founded in 1575 to commemorate a great victory over the Spanish, encouraged the study of anatomy, astronomy, and botany, as well as Oriental languages. On the other hand, Holland's greatest scientists, Huygens, Leeuwenhoek, and Swammerdam, did not teach there or in any other university.

The conservatism (or positive decline, as in Germany) of the universities made almost inevitable the development of supplemental or alternative centers of learning and intellectual discourse. The seventeenth century was a century of academies. Among them were the Ritterakademien of Germany and the dissenting academies of England that taught "modern" subjects; the French Academy, only the best known of a number of literary academies; and, especially, the new scientific societies. Like the universities in the Middle Ages, these academies and societies were founded in every country, with the exception, curiously, of Holland. France gave birth to four important provincial academies at Blois, Montpellier, Toulouse, and Caen, as well as the famous *Académie des sciences* of Paris, given official status by the king in 1666. (Plate 6, a reproduction of a painting by Henri Tesselin, depicts Louis XIV visiting the *Académie* and surrounded by scientists, with his minister Colbert on his left.) Though not devoted exclusively to the natural sciences, the main thrust of these institutions was principally in that direction. The motley membership of the aca-

---

[19] Though suffering much from the political commotions of the times like their continental counterparts, the English universities always had the advantage of a tutorial system that could foster "modern" studies even while the public lectures must follow strictly traditional patterns. See on this point, Mark Curtis, *Oxford and Cambridge in Transition, 1558–1642*, Oxford University Press, Oxford, 1959.
[20] In *The Advancement of Learning* (1605), Bk. II.

PLATE 6. *Louis XIV Visiting the Academy of Sciences*, by Henri Tesselin.

demies and societies has already been remarked on. In their places of meeting scientists rubbed shoulders with amateurs of the upper and middle classes. These institutions reached an even wider audience through the publication of learned journals such as the *Journal des savants* of the Paris academy, which included news about literature and history as well as "science," and the *Philosophical Transactions* of the Royal Society, which was more specialized. The type of knowledge on display in these new intellectual institutions marks the advent of what some contemporaries were already calling a new Modern Age. How this knowledge blended with traditional knowledge to produce new answers to old questions is the subject of the succeeding chapters.

A New Nature

Natural philosophy, Francis Bacon said in the *Novum Organum* (1620), ought to be esteemed as "the great mother of the sciences," as the stem or trunk of the tree of knowledge, from which the other branches gain sustenance and grow. Yet, of the twenty-five centuries of the history of civilization, scarcely six, Bacon thought, "can be culled out as fertile in sciences, or suitable to their improvement." The Greeks, after a promising start under Thales, applied themselves to the study of morality and politics, thus diverting men's minds from natural philosophy. The Romans did likewise, owing to the needs of their great empire. And in the third period of Western European history, the one beginning with the reception of Christianity, the greatest geniuses applied themselves to theology to which the greatest rewards were attached. "The Middle Ages of the world were unhappy, as to any plentiful harvest of the sciences." During that period, and up to the seventeenth century, natural philosophy had been degraded to the office of handmaiden, administering to lesser sciences, or other kinds of learning. The new century, however, seemed to augur well for the spreading and flourishing of this plant; "as if," Bacon wrote in 1603, "the opening of the world by navigation and commerce and the further discovery of knowledge should meet in one time or age."[1]

---

[1] Sir Francis Bacon, *Novum Organum,* Bk. I, Aphorisms 78–80; *Valerius Terminus* (1603), in *The Works of Francis Bacon,* James Spedding (ed.), Taggard and Thompson, Boston, 1863, Vol. VI, p. 32.

In effect, Bacon made natural philosophy the new queen or mother of the sciences. In his reclassification of knowledge, outlined in *The Advancement of Learning* (1605) and the *De Augmentis Scientiarum* (1623), natural philosophy stands at the center, superior to history and poetry (though not to revealed theology), and nourishes the other sciences, including moral and political philosophy, and the study of human nature itself. In general, natural philosophy, as understood by Bacon, referred to the "human kingdom of knowledge," or knowledge that man could acquire through his senses, and sometimes also to science in general, as distinguished from the particular sciences, that is, a "first philosophy," consisting of principles common to two or more of the sciences. More particularly, however, natural philosophy had "nature" as its object, and was therefore principally concerned with physics and mechanics (and also with metaphysics, though in Bacon's view, it should be noted, metaphysics signified only a generalized physics, dealing with the most general laws of nature). In short, Bacon, following in the wake of the Renaissance nature philosophers, put the question of nature once more to the forefront. What is nature? Before the century was out the age-old question, raised to such prominence by England's Lord Chancellor, had engaged the attention, not only of minds of the first rank, professional scientists and philosophers, but also of a host of amateurs, poets, satirists, clergymen, courtiers, gentlemen, and even ladies. Not since the days of the Ionian philosophers had "nature" been so all-absorbing, or stirred such debate. It very nearly became *the* question of the age, especially when it was realized that upon its answer hinged answers to still other questions concerning man and his world, and even God himself.

Out of this far-flung inquiry came a startling new picture of nature. "Is it not evident," remarked the poet and dramatist John Dryden in 1668, "in these last hundred years (when the study of [natural] philosophy has been the business of all the Virtuosi in Christendom), that almost a new Nature has been revealed to us?"[2] This "new Nature," not yet complete in all its lineaments—Newton was still to come—was the joint creation of science and philosophy, of a particularly brilliant succession of astronomers and physical scientists, from Copernicus to Galileo, and of philosophers in the line from Descartes to Spinoza, but also including Neoplatonists such as Giordano Bruno. This theory was subsequently called the mechanical, or, more techni-

---

[2] John Dryden, *An Essay on Dramatic Poetry* (1668), in *Essays,* W. P. Ker (ed.), Oxford University Press, Oxford, 1926, pp. 36–37.

cally, the corpuscular-kinetic theory of nature. It displaced, though by no means abruptly, the Greek-Christian theory, which had dominated thought, and had been presupposed in art and literature, from the Middle Ages down to the seventeenth century.

The chief tendency of the new "world system," as Galileo also called it, was to read out of nature all or most of its "spiritual" and human characters. Nature remained pictorial, but it was now pictured, increasingly, not as an organism, but as a machine, engine, or clock. Thus originated the famous clockwork universe, which captured the European imagination for the next two hundred years. Nature, said the philosophical chemist Robert Boyle, is not as the peripatetics or Aristotelians "vulgarly conceive it," that is to say, as a puppet whose "almost every particular motion" derives from its artificer's pulling upon its wires and strings. On the contrary, nature

> is like a rare clock, such as may be that at Strasbourg, where all things are so skillfully contrived, that the engine being once set a moving, all things proceed, according to the artificer's first design, and the motions of the little statues, that at such hours perform these or those things, do not require, like those of puppets, the peculiar interposing of the artificer, or any intelligent agent employed by him, but perform their functions upon particular occasions, by virtue of the general and primitive contrivance of the whole engine.[3]

Natural phenomena, Boyle says in another place, "may be solved mechanically, that is, by the mechanical affections of matter, without recourse to nature's abhorrence of a vacuum, to substantial forms, or to other incorporeal creatures."[4] These lines express well the seventeenth-century natural philosopher's rejection of teleology, at least as applied to the workings of nature subsequent to the first creation. Boyle now talked more of efficient than of final causes, less of spirits and intelligences moving bodies toward appointed ends than of the "natural" motion of bodies, and of "forces" acting upon them whether by touch or at a distance. The modern law of inertia, as stated by Sir Isaac Newton in his first law of motion, is a classical example of the new mechanistic, as opposed to the inherited teleological, conception of nature: "Every body continues in its state of rest, or of uniform motion in a

---

[3] Robert Boyle, *Works*, J. & F. Rivington, London, 1772, Vol. V, p. 163. The famous clock at Strasbourg, which Boyle probably saw, was constructed in 1574 according to the plans of a Strasbourg mathematician.

[4] Ibid., Vol. III, pp. 608–609.

straight line, except so far as it may be compelled by force to change that state." The whole conception of causation had changed. The "motions of the little statues" in the clock did not require causes— intellectual substance, a built-in *nisus,* an unmoved mover, as in the Aristotelian system—more perfect than themselves. Effects were now equivalent to causes. Both were reducible to the movements of bodies in time and space.

Boyle, since he was not a mathematician, failed to emphasize the mathematical structure of the new nature. Yet this was perhaps its most conspicuous feature. Galileo, in *The Assayer* (1623), which has been called his scientific manifesto states:

> Philosophy is written in this grand book, the universe, which stands continually open to our gaze. But the book cannot be understood unless first learns one to comprehend the language and read the letters in which it is composed. *It is written in the language of mathematics,* and its characters are triangles, circles, and other geometric figures without which it is humanly impossible to understand a single word of it; without these, one wanders about in a dark labyrinth.[5]

Behind this remark lay a century of extraordinary mathematical activity, the rediscovery of ancient Greek mathematics in the Renaissance, especially Archimedes of Syracuse whom Galileo studied; the work of the Renaissance artists on perspective; the practical geometrizing of men such as Niccolò Tartaglia, who was the first translator of Archimedes; and the philosophizing of Leonardo da Vinci. Galileo, who taught mathematics at the universities of Pisa and Padua, also grew up in a world in which navigators, merchants, and princes were calling for a more quantitatively exact treatment of their practical problems. Thus, when Galileo reduced nature to "geometric figures" he was only carrying to its logical conclusion a way of thinking that had already become widespread. Understandably, Galileo was accused, as was Descartes, of abstraction,[6] that is, of selecting and isolating for study only those elements of nature that could be quantified and measured. But Galileo and Descartes each denied that they misrepresented nature, as becomes clear

[5] Galileo, *The Assayer,* in *Discoveries and Opinions of Galileo,* Stillman Drake (trans.), Doubleday & Co., Garden City, New York, pp. 237–238.

[6] In Galileo's *Dialogue concerning the Two Chief World Systems* (1632), for example, "Simplicio," defender of Aristotle's "system," accuses his opponents of forcing geometry on nature: "these mathematical subtleties, Salviati, are true in abstract, but applied to sensible and physical matter they hold not good."

in their doctrine, reiterated by Newton and Locke, of the primary and secondary qualities. Only the former—figure, magnitude, position, and motion—could be said to be *in* or to belong to material bodies. The latter—light, color, smell, sound—are purely subjective, the effects of false appearances to the senses, and falsely projected back into nature by the human mind. "Hence I think," said Galileo, "that tastes, odors, colors, and so on are no more than mere names so far as the object in which we place them is concerned, and that they reside only in the consciousness."[7]

Galileo was close to stating the famous two-substance theory, or dualism, of the seventeenth century. This theory, developed more fully by Descartes, soon became orthodox in scientific circles. It divided the world into two great realms of mind and matter, or of thought and extension. Mind—as signified by final causes—was ejected from nature. So also were all the qualities that had formerly kept nature close to man: the fragrance of flowers, the songs of birds, the color in everything, including light itself. Mind, soul, purpose belonged to man's world, no longer to nature's. Nature, it now appeared, was like a great machine or clock, made of dead matter, possessing fundamentally mathematical characteristics, functioning mechanistically rather than teleogically, obedient to invariable natural laws. This dualism, a triumph of simplification, allowed scientists to pursue their inquiries without paying more than passing attention to theology and metaphysics. Though it created some formidable philosophical and epistemological problems, dualism provided the conceptual framework for a spectacular advance in the sciences.

Before passing on to the other features of the new nature—the rearrangement of the heavens and the space revolution—it should be noted that the mechanistic model existed almost nowhere in an absolutely pure state, not even in Galileo and Descartes. The irresistible and irreversible trend in seventeenth-century natural philosophy was, in general, as stated. But in actual historical fact finalism (teleology) died hard, and was nearly always mixed in with the mechanism in some form or other. Not counting the traditional Aristotelians and Platonists, who were still numerous but hostile to mechanistic presuppositions, it is possible to discern four major types of mixture. At the extreme left were the philosophical materialists such as Bacon, who found only matter and local motion in nature. Bacon, as will be seen, urged a rigid separation between theology and natural philosophy. He

[7] Galileo, *The Assayer* (see note 5), p. 274.

likewise separated nature from God. Nature was neither the image of God, as some heathen philosophers had said, nor related to God. Nature was like Cupid in the fable: without parents (having no cause outside itself), blind (comprised of atoms that move blindly), naked (material atoms can be described in no other way), and skilled in archery (representing the action of matter through space).[8] As a Christian, Bacon did not doubt that God had created nature, or that the works of nature revealed the power and skill of the great artificer. However, this truth one could learn only from revealed theology, not from philosophy or science. Pierre Gassendi, though also a materialist, differed from Bacon in his greater Pyrrhonism. The corpuscular theory of nature, derived by him from Epicurus and Lucretius, but with the addition of mathematics, was only a hypothesis for organizing knowledge. Man, because of his limited mental endowment, could never have more than a science of appearances. But Gassendi, who was a priest with sincere religious convictions, also believed that behind the appearances stood the Christian God, who set the atoms in motion and decreed the laws of nature. The Cartesians display still another mixture. Descartes, as noted, propounded a dualism, which freed nature from nonmechanistic features. Strictly speaking, however, his dualism was not a two-substance theory, for mind and matter had a common source in God to whom alone, therefore, the term *substance* properly applied. In other words, Descartes, too, derived nature from God.

These three types, however much their exemplars might differ in other respects, had one thing in common. Though continuing to believe in the First Cause, they pushed final causes out of the world, which was allowed to run on substantially different, that is, mechanistic, mindless principles. A fourth type brought finalism back in, though always somewhat hesitantly and in novel forms. In this group are to be found some of the great names in seventeenth-century philosophy and science: Spinoza, Newton, Leibniz, and Boyle, strange bedfellows in that they frequently quarreled among themselves, but also agreeing, in their several ways, in a kind of divinization of nature. Spinoza is perhaps the most equivocal name in the list, since he was uncompromising in his rejection of providential teleology and in his description of nature (carrying Galileo to his logical conclusion, and understanding Galileo better than anyone else) as a mathematical order indifferent to man's

---

[8] For Bacon on "Cupid, or the Atom," see *De Sapientia Veterum* (*Concerning the Wisdom of the Ancients,* 1609), XVII. Bacon's favorite philosopher was the ancient atomist Democritus.

salvation. Yet Spinoza made a mighty attempt to overcome Descartes' dualism by uniting matter with mind as two attributes of one substance, which he called God *or* Nature. Because he identified nature with God, it is easy to see why Spinoza was thought to be a pantheist, and why, much later, the romantic nature mystics took him up. Spinoza was not, in fact, a pantheist, but his monism did keep finalism, though only indirectly, in the picture. Strange that the German philosopher Leibniz should have berated Spinoza for rejecting teleology, but should have attacked Newton for just the opposite reason, for wanting to make God, as Leibniz said, *"intelligentia mundana; that is, the soul of the world."* Leibniz was right about Newton, however. There is much finalism left in the great English scientist's system. Not only did Newton conceive of space as God's *sensorium* but also, much to Leibniz's disgust, kept God in the wings to clean and mend the world clock when it became necessary, and even to assist the motion of bodies as though their natural *"Vis Inertiae"* was not enough. A few lines from Newton's *Optics* (1704) makes his position clear.

> The main business of natural philosophy is . . . to deduce Causes from Effects, till we come to the very first Cause, which certainly is not mechanical. . . . [The wonderful order of nature] can be the effect of nothing else than the Wisdom and Skill of a powerful ever living Agent, who being in all Places, is more able by his Will to move the Bodies within his boundless uniform Sensorium, and thereby to form and reform the Parts of the Universe, than we are by our Will to move the Parts of our own Bodies.[9]

And where did Leibniz himself stand? He too retained finalism in his system, except that God figures therein only as *"intelligentia supramundana,"* who makes the clock so perfectly that it can run thereafter without his special assistance.[10] But Leibniz's clock is not a completely mechanical clock like Galileo's or Spinoza's, for it consists ultimately of "monads," which are more like souls than bodies, and which behave purposively. The conclusion is ineluctable that natural philosophy in the seventeenth century was still not fully naturalistic, though it was tending to be so, and was so by comparison to medieval scholasticism.

[9] Sir Isaac Newton, *Opticks,* W. & J. Innys, London, 1721, p. 344, 375–381. Boyle's position on final causes was, in general, similar to Newton's.

[10] See on this, and on Leibniz's criticism of Newton's position, the famous exchange of letters in 1715 and 1716 between Leibniz and Dr. Samuel Clarke, the philosopher-theologian, who defended Newton.

Spirit or mind still adhered to the new nature, though to a lesser degree, in many shapes and forms.

The new nature also involved a drastic rearrangement of the heavens and a new conception of space. This space revolution, as we may call it, is usually described as coming in two phases, the first or Copernican phase, and the second, proposing the infinity of the universe, spearheaded by the Italian philosopher Giordano Bruno. Of the two phases, it is sometimes contended that the latter was far more revolutionary than the former. This is debatable, for it overlooks the truly radical innovation introduced by the Copernican cosmology, namely its destruction of the old dualism of earth and heavens. The Copernicans, by making the earth a planet, and ultimately applying terrestrial dynamics to the heavens, reduced all nature to one system, homogeneous in substance, and subject to the same laws. They dismantled Aristotle's "Sky," which, unlike "Nature" below the moon, was supposed to be inalterable, immutable, and immortal. "We possess a better basis for reasoning about celestial things than Aristotle did," Galileo said in his great defense of the Copernican system. Were Aristotle alive today, would he not have to change his mind, after seeing sunspots through the new telescopes and hearing about the new stars and comets, which had appeared recently in the supposedly changeless heavens? But the most remarkable thing in Galileo's statement is his own personal preference for alterability, as compared to inalterability. Galileo has one of his protagonists say, in the course of the argument with "Simplicio," who defends the Aristotelian position:

> I cannot without great astonishment—I may say without great insult to my intelligence—hear it attributed as a prime perfection and nobility of the natural and integral bodies of the universe that they are invariant, immutable, inalterable, etc., while on the other hand it is called a great imperfection to be alterable, generable, mutable, etc. For my part I consider the earth very noble and admirable precisely because of the diverse alterations, changes, generations, etc. that occur in it incessantly.[11]

Evidently, becoming was beginning to displace being, not only in the heavens but in men's system of values as well.

Becoming was pressed still farther in the second phase of the space revolution, in which the "world" perceived by the senses was trans-

[11] Galileo, *Dialogue concerning the Two Chief World Systems,* Stillman Drake (trans.), University of California Press, Berkeley, 1953, p. 58.

formed into a vast "universe," spatially infinite, infinitely populous, without any center. This transformation, complete in the sense of being widely accepted in the seventeenth century, was only partially the work of the new science. It owed as much to philosophical speculation, rife in the late Middle Ages and the Renaissance, on the Platonistic principle of plenitude, and to the revival of certain other Greek philosophies, which postulated an infinite universe. The Copernican hypothesis undoubtedly stimulated thinking about infinity, by increasing the distance to the fixed stars, and enlarging their diameters, and by suggesting an indefinite eighth sphere or heaven. Giordano Bruno, however, in his *De l'infinito universo e mondi* (1586) did not rely primarily on Copernicus but drew from a variety of philosophical sources, including Plato's *Timaeus*, Nicholas Cusanus, and—though Bruno himself was no materialist—Lucretius, Epicurus, and Democritus. The ex-Dominican friar argued that an infinite cause must have infinite effects; that since God was an infinite substance, and since in him possibility and actuality were identical, there must therefore be an infinity of beings and worlds. "Thus is the excellence of God magnified and the greatness of his kingdom made manifest; he is glorified not in one, but in countless suns; not in a single earth, a single world, but in a hundred thousand, I say in an infinity of worlds." Bruno's nature, saturated with God, was obviously fecund, a continuing process, ever producing new effects, ever changing its aspect. "Therefore the earth and the ocean thereof are fecund. . . . For from infinity is born an ever fresh abundance of matter."[12] It is easy to see why Bruno was, and has been adjudged, more radical than Copernicus. Bruno did not merely move the fences of man's cosmos farther out; he tore them down and filled up the universe beyond with a plurality of worlds. Bruno and those who followed him—Descartes; the Cambridge Platonist philosopher Henry More; Fontenelle, author of the popular *Entrétiens sur la Pluralité des Mondes* (1686); and others—destroyed the finite world of the Middle Ages, the world in which Dante and Shakespeare lived, not to speak of Aristotle, and projected a radically different sort of infinite universe.

What was the subjective response to this new picture of nature that was coming into focus in the seventeenth century? Did nature now seem more remote to man, less correspondent to his psychic needs? How did this picture of nature affect the human imagination? The reactions varied greatly, of course, as did the scientific and philosophical

[12] Giordano Bruno, *On the Infinite Universe and Worlds,* Dorothy Singer (trans.), Henry Schuman, New York, 1950, pp. 245–246.

theories themselves. But they were, perhaps, not quite as severe as one might expect, for several reasons. First, because the new nature was only imperfectly understood, hence its full implications—for instance, what a mechanistic universe might imply for conceptions of man or God—passed over the heads of all but an informed few. Second, as stated, the natural philosophers themselves lived partially within an older intellectual world, and hence went out of their way to blunt the contrasts between old and new. Finally, the new nature, at least in several of its aspects, also opened up exciting prospects, and thus served, not merely to dampen but also to fire the imagination.

Understandably, many people expressed consternation. For the poet and Anglican clergyman John Donne, writing in 1611, "new philosophy" called "all in doubt." Reared in the Aristotelian-Christian universe, Donne was confused and depressed by the Copernican astronomy. The macrocosm seemed to him to have dissolved into a chaos, in which the sun, and the earth too, was lost, and no man's wit could "well direct him where to look for it." " 'Tis all in pieces," Donne lamented, "all coherence gone."[13] The new cosmology also drove home to Donne the decay of nature, as well as of man and government. For did it not show that the realm above the moon, the celestial world, formerly thought to be so perfect, was subject to change and corruption, just like the sublunary world? Donne's was a typical attitude, especially in the early part of the century. Blaise Pascal's response was more extreme, and less typical.[14] Reacting more to the new notion of infinity, than to the Copernican hypothesis (which in fact he did not accept), Pascal felt lost in nature's immensity. "Man's disproportion" is the subject of one of his greatest meditations. Disproportion to what? Disproportion to nature, which defies both the imagination and reason. Nature, he wrote, "is an infinite sphere, the center of which is everywhere, the circumference nowhere." What is man in this Infinite? "We sail in a fast sphere, ever drifting in uncertainty, driven from end to end."[15] In the end, Pascal, though a great scientist as well as religious thinker, could find certainty and stability only in supernatural revelation. Para-

---

[13] John Donne, *The First Anniversary*, lines 205–213.

[14] But Pascal was not the only one who felt this way. In his book on the plurality of worlds, Fontenelle has the Countess chide him (Joseph Glanvill, trans., R. Bently, London, 1695, pp. 125–126): "You have made the Universe so large that I know not where I am, or what will become of me. . . . I protest it is dreadful."

[15] Blaise Pascal, *Pensées* no. 72, W. F. Trotter (trans.), from Brunschvieg edition.

doxically, however, Pascal may have felt somewhat closer to nature than Descartes. For although he thought man disproportionate to it, Pascal, on the other hand, rejected Descartes' closed mechanical system. "I see plainly," he wrote, no doubt with Descartes in mind, "that there exists in nature a necessary Being, eternal and infinite."[16]

Others, particularly churchmen, worried about the threat to anthropocentric theology. This worry increased in proportion as the principles of the new nature came to be more widely understood. The Protestant reformers had denounced the Copernican system from the beginning. The Roman Catholic Church was slower to react, but eventually also came down hard on it, significantly after Bruno had gone up and down Europe winning converts for the infinity-plurality idea. The threat was real. "Only one bereft of his reason could believe," said Bruno, "that those infinite spaces, tenanted by vast and magnificent bodies, are designed only to give us light."[17] Let man be not puffed up, Descartes wrote, for now that we know an infinitude of things exists in the universe, it is by no means certain that they "have been created for us in such a manner that God has had no other end in creating them."[18] What was at stake was considerably more than Aristotelian physics. It was nothing less than the idea that nature had been created especially and exclusively for man. To accept a plurality of worlds, the Lutheran theologian Philip Melanchthon had suggested years before, was to make a mockery of the Atonement, of Jesus Christ's special mission on earth. *Gulliver's Travels,* published somewhat later (1726), mirrored many of the contemporary misgivings about nature in its depiction of man as a lonely mite, infinitely small by comparison with the inhabitants of greater worlds, and unable to comprehend so vast a universe.

Yet this was not the only or even the dominant response. The new nature could also inspire reverence, exhilaration, and a sense of power. It could inspire reverence because, as suggested, remnants of the old finalism still adhered to it. Nature, said Francis Bacon, reveals the power and wisdom of God, just as the Bible reveals his will. This doctrine of the two Scriptures was axiomatic among the seventeenth-century Virtuosi. Hence, when one contemplated nature, it was natural to be awed by its "wonderful order, law, and power," and to connect it somehow with divine providence. "Whence is it that Nature doth nothing in vain; and whence arises all that order and beauty which we see

---

[16] Ibid., no. 469; see also no. 76 and no. 77.

[17] Giordano Bruno, quoted in I. Frith, *Life of Giordano Bruno,* Trübner & Co., London, 1887, pp. 43–44.

[18] René Descartes, *Principles of Philosophy,* Third Part, Principle III.

in the world"? To Newton and most of his contemporaries the answer was obvious. It was the effect of design, though not necessarily of an anthropocentric design. One senses the same sort of reverence in the new landscape art of the Dutch, notably in Jacob van Ruysdael. For all its "realism," this art frequently had religious and poetic undertones.

A heady exhilaration was added to reverence among the enthusiasts of outer space. Bruno got drunk on space, or, to use his own metaphor, he felt released from prison. The Ptolemaic universe had shut the human mind up in "a most narrow kingdom," like a parrot in a cage. But now it was set free to fly and expand in the spacious ether.

> *Henceforth I spread confident wings to space;*
> *I feel no barrier of crystal or of glass;*
> *I cleave the heavens and soar to the infinite.*[19]

Seventeenth-century literature was full of this "aesthetics of infinity," as Marjorie Nicolson calls it. "Th'infinite I'll sing," exclaimed Henry More in his poem *Infinity of Worlds* (1646). Like Bruno, More believed in a plastic nature, and in tune with nature, could feel his own personality expand and grow. Thomas Traherne, another "poet of aspiration," and deeply religious, felt the same way. He wrote poems bearing titles such as "On Leaping over the Moon," "Insatiableness," and "Nature." "How often did I lift mine Eys/ Beyond the Spheres!/ Dame Nature told me there was endless Space/ Within my Soul": thus did Traherne couple the two thoughts of outer and inner infinity in his poem "Felicity."[20] Traherne's idea of nature, and his personal response to it was, we might say, "romantic" rather than classical.

Scientists and poets were obviously expanding together in this new nature. Among the scientists and natural philosophers, however, the emphasis was more on power—the sense of power that their new concepts and methods were giving them. Thus, at the same time that they were expressing reverence for nature as God's handiwork, they were also talking about "the Kingdom of Man," of man's "empire" *over* nature. They did not see this as a contradiction. Had not God created man in his image, and nature for man's use? The "empire" idea, however, conveyed a stronger message than that. Bold and aggressive, it was rooted in the new Renaissance doctrine of man's creativity and in

---

[19] Giordano Bruno, *On the Infinite Universe and Worlds* (see note 12), p. 249.
[20] Thomas Traherne, *Poems of Felicity*, H. I. Bell (ed.), Clarendon Press, London, 1910, p. 22. For further examples, see Marjorie Nicolson, *The Breaking of the Circle*, Northwestern University Press, Evanston, 1950, Chap. V.

the confidence generated by recent human technological achievements, navigation and exploration, and inventions. Though he warned against the lust of power that caused the fall of the angels, Bacon nevertheless urged the reassertion of man's "right over nature" and the extension of "the power and dominion of the human race over the universe."[21] "The end of our foundation," says the head of Solomon's House, the scientific academy in New Atlantis, Bacon's utopia, "is the knowledge of causes and secret motions of things, and the enlarging of the bounds of human empire, to the effecting of all things possible."[22] This is not the language of traditional Christianity or of romantic primitivism. It is Promethean language, pointing toward the more secular and exploitative attitude toward nature of the new Modern Age.

Thus, ideas of, and attitudes toward, nature were changing rapidly in the seventeenth century. Yet to its beholders nature still certainly exhibited being as well as becoming. It was not just that parts of the old system survived, even in the most advanced and sophisticated minds. The new system itself, like a well-built house, stood on permanent foundations that did not change. In the new nature of Galileo, Descartes, and Newton, both space and time were absolute, in the sense of existing objectively and of being completely independent of any physical content. Matter, to be sure, occupied, and moved in, space, but space itself remained, as Newton declared in Scholium II of the *Principia* (*Mathematical Principles of Natural Philosophy,* 1687), "always similar and immovable." For that reason, Henry More could describe space as, like deity, "one, eternal, independent, Being in essence (*Ens per essentiam*), Being in act."[23] Likewise, changes occurred *in* time, but time itself did not change but merely flowed. In Scholium I of the *Principia,* Newton distinguished between "absolute, true, and mathematical time" and "relative, apparent, and vulgar time," the latter measured by the motion of bodies, as, for example, an hour, day, or week. Newton may have learned this distinction from his tutor Isaac Barrow, who similarly spoke of a "distinction between time and con-

[21] See especially the famous aphorism in the *Novum Organum* (Bk. I, no. 129), which discusses the three kinds of human ambition.

[22] Sir Francis Bacon, *New Atlantis* (1627), in *The Works of Francis Bacon* (see note 1), Vol. V, p. 398. And Descartes to the same effect: by means of scientific knowledge "we can make ourselves the lords and masters of nature" (*Discourse on Method,* Pt. VI; see also p. 31).

[23] Henry More, *Enchiridion Metaphysicum* (1671), quoted in Milič Čapek, *The Philosophical Impact of Contemporary Physics,* D. Van Nostrand, Princeton, 1961, pp. 9–10. The quotation is slightly abbreviated.

crete becoming."[24] Even matter did not change, at least not in its ultimate elements, in mass, volume, and shape. In this system, time was
obviously subordinate to, less real than, space, because such changes as
occurred were conceived as taking place in a changeless context, and
without affecting the basic material reality. In other words, the universe
had no history, as Henri Bergson was later to say of it. It was a deterministic system, always basically the same, whose future operations could
be predicted on the basis of knowable causes. Of course, there was the
incipiently rival conception, urged by the Brunonians, and sensed even
by some biologists, of a plastic nature, forever producing fresh and
variable effects. But here, too, it seems clear, becoming rested on being.
It had its source in the God of plenitude.

Contemporary biologists lived and worked in the same sort of am-
phibious thought world. There was much that was "modern" in what
they were doing. This was the great age of collection, classification, and
description. A new breed of naturalists upset ancient notions, exploded
old fables, observed with a keen eye, or with the help of the microscope, species and varieties of previously unknown species (some from
the New World, and some extinct, revealed by fossils), and creatures,
or parts of creatures, never before seen, insects, protozoa, bacteria, and
the like. The effect of this "biological revolution," if such it may be
called, was to dispel mystery and to come to rely henceforth, not on
authority, but, in the words of Sir Thomas Browne, on "the solid reason
or confirmed experience." What is more, the biologists also adopted the
mechanical model of nature and used mechanics to explain organic
functions. On the other hand, a vital principle was frequently deemed
necessary to account for many of nature's operations, and all of nature,
however it was thought to operate, was assumed to depend ultimately
on God's design. Above all, there was scarcely a hint in their writings
of the notion of evolution. "Nature is the art of God," Browne said.[25]
That is, God created nature as it is, and that was also the view of John
Ray, perhaps the greatest naturalist of the seventeenth century. In *The
Wisdom of God Manifested in the Works of Creation* (1691), Ray
portrayed a world fully made, or developed, at the time of the Creation.
"The 17th century," says Richard Westfall, "may be excused for leav-

---

[24] See on all this, ibid., Pt. I, "The Classical Picture of the Physical World."
[25] Sir Thomas Browne, *Religio Medici* (1642), Pt. I, Sect. XVI. For Browne
on the authority of the ancients, see his "Enquiries into Vulgar and Common
Errors." He sounds like Bacon when he says: "But the mortalest enemy unto
knowledge . . . hath been a peremptory adhesion unto authority, and more
especially the establishing of our belief upon the dictates of antiquity."

ing evolution to a later age; it discovered enough."[26] To put it another way, the world of seventeenth-century biology was obviously no more a world of becoming than the world of seventeenth-century physics.

That is probably the main reason why the new nature, initially so disturbing, eventually generated an optimistic response. It provided a framework of stability within which to see change. But there were other reasons too. Nature, whether pictured as machine or organism, was patently not fallen or decaying, as some were still saying early in the century. Especially to the mechanists, nature appeared to be lawful and ordered throughout, its harmony to be guaranteed by God himself. Leibniz, who was one of those who fancied the clock metaphor, spoke of a pre-established harmony whereby God constructed two clocks, soul and body, in the beginning, and then synchronized them to run perfectly together in the phenomenal world of nature. There was also ground in the new nature for religious worship, even if one no longer believed in anthropocentric design, as some did not. The immateriality of the new absolutes made it possible to divinize nature, though in new ways. In Newton's system, for example, space and time could be viewed as attributes of God.

Yet the erosion had begun. It is a matter of degree, of course. It is not true that men were cut off from nature in the seventeenth century, or that nature was dehumanized. All the same, with the elimination of the secondary qualities, nature inevitably began to seem less like the setting for man's spiritual pilgrimage and more like a field for the exercise of human power. But where this was understood, it prompted, on the whole, more optimism than pessimism.

[26] Richard S. Westfall, *Science and Religion in Seventeenth-Century England,* Yale University Press, New Haven, 1958, p. 66.

Faith and Reason

Despite the increasing fascination with "nature," religious questions and considerations remained to the fore in men's minds all through the seventeenth century, as shown in the previous chapter. The new crop of scientists and "Virtuosi" were neither hostile nor indifferent to religion. On the contrary, they went out of their way to represent science as a religious enterprise. The Royal Society, says Bishop Sprat, took as its province matters pertaining to God, man, or nature. But as to "divine things"

> they meddle no otherwise than only as the power and wisdom and goodness of the Creator is displayed in the admirable order and workmanship of the creatures. It cannot be denied, but it lies in the natural philosopher's hands, best to advance this kind of divinity. . . . This is a religion which is confirmed by the unanimous agreement of all sorts of worships, and may serve in respect to Christianity, as Solomon's porch to the temple; into the one the heathens themselves did also enter. . . .[1]

As for the philosophers, the case is even more conclusive. The continental rationalists, combatting Renaissance skepticism or Pyrrhonism, made God the linchpin of their systems. Though hardly doing that, the

---

[1] Thomas Sprat, *The History of the Royal Society of London,* Pt. II, Sect. XI.

empiricists also (always excepting Hobbes)[2] concerned themselves with religious problems. Locke, for example, devoted much of the fourth book of his major philosophical treatise, the *Essay Concerning Human Understanding* (1690), to showing how to prove the existence of God, which he thought was "not hard to do," and discussing God's attributes and "the measures and boundaries between faith and reason in religion." A later work by Locke demonstrated the "reasonableness" of Christianity. Clearly, there was an entente, if not a formal alliance, between philosophy and religion, and between science and religion, in the seventeenth century. Seventeenth-century art similarly records a deep religious conviction and concern. As noted in the first chapter of this section,[3] some of the foremost artists, not to speak of many lesser ones, addressed themselves to religious as well as secular themes. This was by no means merely a matter of convention or ecclesiastical patronage. Bernini's mystical *Saint Teresa,* though commissioned by the Cornaro family, was the work of a genuinely devout Catholic. So, likewise, was the remarkable tableau entitled *The Triumph of the Eucharist,* by Peter Paul Rubens (Plate 7). In this symbolic canvas, Rubens, now the artistic champion of the Counter Reformation, depicted Religion seated in a triumphal chair, with Science (represented as a young man), Philosophy (a bearded old man leaning on a staff), and Nature immediately behind Religion on the chariot; and behind them, two more figures, an American Indian and a black, who personify the new world recently won to the true religion by the missionaries. As I have written elsewhere, the picture "obviously symbolizes theology as queen of all the sciences, the new sciences as well as the old."[4] In the great works of his later life, Rembrandt, a Protestant artist of equal stature, deliberately used Dutch realism to explore man's inner life, especially the world of religious feeling, mystery, and destiny. The debates, bitter and sometimes leading to persecution and war, between Christians, both Catholic and Protestant, over the sources of religious truth, free will and predestination, the doctrine of the Trinity, moral casuistry (inspired by the Jesuits), and toleration, also testify to continuing interest in the religious question. All this is not to say that the seventeenth

---

[2] Hobbes, of course, concerned himself very much with questions of church and state and ecclesiastical power. But I am speaking here of religious faith and doctrine.

[3] See p. 34.

[4] Franklin L. Baumer, *Religion and the Rise of Scepticism,* Harcourt Brace, New York, 1960, p. 113. Henri Busson sees Rubens' painting as a symbol of the retreat from "incredulity," and the renewal of Christianity in the early seventeenth century (see *La pensée française de Charron à Pascal,* Paris, 1933).

Musées Royaux des Beaux-Arts, Brussels.

PLATE 7. *Triumph of the Eucharist*, by Peter Paul Rubens.

century was an age comparable in religious intensity to the preceding century of the Reformation. Obviously, theology, *pace* Rubens, no longer stood at the very center of thought, as in the days of Martin Luther and John Calvin. On the other hand, interest in theology had not yet become purely peripheral either, nor had it been forced wholly on the defensive, as was to happen later in the eighteenth-century Enlightenment. It continued to exercise a considerable influence on thought in general, by remote if not always by direct control.

Nevertheless, religious doubt was growing, foreshadowing the Enlightenment, and there were also important changes within religious thought itself with respect to the sources and extent of religious knowledge, and the idea of God. Since the mental climate still did not countenance frontal attacks on religion, the evidence of religious doubt comes mostly from the many books and diatribes written against it. Hobbes was the one major thinker who, despite a native timidity, expressed his doubts openly. Though choosing his words carefully, the "atheist of Malmesbury" traced the origins of religion back to human fear and ignorance, and pretty clearly thought of religion as superstition or else as the decree of the sovereign in the interest of public order. Usually, however, we have to infer the existence of libertines, *esprits forts,* deists (all neologisms), skeptics, and atheists from what Blaise Pascal and many others said about them. The *Pensées,* actually notes for a book never completed, were written expressly to confute the "fashionable unbelief" of the times. Of this unbelief Pascal had firsthand knowledge since he numbered among the friends of his "worldly period" such *libertins* as Damien Mitton, who doubted the immortality of the soul, and the Chevalier de Méré, a gambler and man-about-town. Pascal could put himself imaginatively in the position of the more serious *libertins* and write:

> I look everywhere and everywhere I see only darkness. Nature offers me nothing that is not a source of doubt and anxiety. . . . Seeing ·too much for denial and too little for certainty, I am in a state which inspires pity, and in which I have wished a hundred times that, if there is a God who preserves it, it should reveal him unequivocally. . . .[5]

As a scientist, Pascal well understood how the "new nature" could disturb traditional belief and make men deists, atheists, or skeptics.

[5] Pascal, *Pensées,* no. 13, Martin Turnell (trans.), from Lafuma edition.

That was why, in his own defense of Christianity, Pascal abjured metaphysical proofs and relied on reasons of the heart and history. The satirist Jean La Bruyère, who devoted a whole section to freethinkers in his *Characters* (first edition, 1688), calls attention to another important source of religious doubt: the overseas voyages. "Some men complete their corruption by long voyages, and lose what religion they still retained. They see a new form of worship every day, other customs, various ceremonies." The multiplication of sects within Christian Europe, especially in the Protestant countries, militated in the same relativistic direction. How could one know where the truth lay, when one considered the rival claims of Lutherans, Calvinists, and Anglicans, not to speak of Roman Catholics, and all the separatists and dissenters? No wonder Bishop Bossuet, writing toward the end of the century, feared the coming of a new age of "intemperance of mind," following an age of obedience to God and king. Bishop Bossuet still lived in an orthodox society, which had only recently, in 1685, closed religious ranks with Louis XIV's revocation of the Edict of Nantes.[6] But there were already fissures in that society, religious as well as political, and the king's chief spiritual adviser was well aware of that fact. Bossuet blamed the "great battle being prepared against religion" chiefly on the Cartesians, who, though ostensibly religious, made God conform to their own "reason," and thus showed others how to banish the supernatural entirely.[7] Despite state orthodoxy, enforced by an absolute monarch in his own pious phase of life, free thought had probably progressed farther in France than anywhere else in Europe.

Secularism also made headway in the seventeenth century. Secularism, unlike free thought, posed no threat to particular theological tenets. What it did was to outflank theology by staking out autonomous spheres of thought. The tendency was, more and more, to limit theology to the comparatively restricted sphere of faith and morals. This statement does not contradict what was said previously about theology's continuing influence. Bacon's views on science show this to be the case. Like the Virtuosi of the Royal Society later on, Bacon thought of the scientist as studying the Bible of nature, and of science as having religious overtones, that is, as revealing God's power in his created works. But this conviction did not prevent Bacon from trying to seal science

---

[6] The Edict of Nantes of 1598, issued by Henry IV, had extended limited toleration to the French Huguenots.

[7] Bishop Bossuet, Letter to a disciple of Malebranche, May 21, 1687, quoted in Paul Hazard, *La Crise de la conscience européenne,* Boivin & Cie, Paris, 1935, Vol. I, p. 286.

off from theological interference. His stance on theology itself was traditionally correct. To theology, and theology alone, belonged knowledge of God's nature and will, of the moral law and of man's rational soul, as revealed in prophecy, parable, and doctrine. At the same time, Bacon warned against "the wild mixture of divine things with human." One of the chief reasons why science had made so little progress through the ages was the ignorance and meddling of scholastic divines who tried to base science on sacred writ. Hence, Bacon's counsel "to give to faith no more than the things that are faith's."[8] In Bacon's system, theology, though still prestigious, had lost its hold over science. Galileo took essentially the same line in his famous letter of 1615 to the Grand Duchess Christina of Tuscany, which might be called science's declaration of independence. Galileo too conceded theology's title to queenship, but only in the sense that theology excelled the other sciences in dignity and ruled over "supernatural things which are matters of faith." He denied the right of theology to interfere in "purely physical matters," which would mean delivering science up to persons who knew nothing about it, thus hindering the progress of knowledge. Galileo had in mind certain contemporary theologians who had recently condemned the Copernican theory of the universe, even though the latter had nothing to do with Christian faith or morals. It was as if an absolute despot, neither physician nor architect, should prescribe medicines and architectural rules, to the detriment of both patients and buildings.[9]

The philosophers, though not so outspoken, also went their own independent way. Although frequently calling on theology for support, philosophy's main task was now to understand and explain the new nature revealed by science. The philosophers themselves were not professional theologians, as had generally been the case in the Middle Ages, and the theology they invoked was of their own choosing, and not always orthodox. Pierre Bayle, anticipating the Enlightenment, even tried to establish a secular morality and to secularize history, including the "sacred" history of the Bible and Christianity. In political thought, too, religious considerations inevitably faded as ideas such as state sovereignty and *raison d'état* gained ground. In France, a theologically based theory of kingship continued to show strength until well through the reign of Louis XIV. But Locke, a contemporary of Bishop Bossuet, expressly refuted the divine right of kings, and dis-

[8] Sir Francis Bacon, *Novum Organum*, Bk. I, Aphorism 65.
[9] Galileo, Letter to the Grand Duchess Christina of Tuscany, in Stillman Drake (ed.), *Discoveries and Opinions of Galileo*, Doubleday & Company, Garden City, New York, 1957, pp. 191–193, and *passim*.

cussed politics in an almost exclusively secular context, as also did most of the critics of French absolutism.

Meanwhile, religious thought itself was not standing still. There were two new developments of special importance in this sphere, one in epistemology, the other in metaphysics, that is, concerning the idea of God. The epistemological problem became acute in consequence of the Renaissance and Reformation, which created confusion about the criteria of religious knowledge. It was certainly not the intention of the Protestant Reformers, Luther, Calvin, and others to cause uncertainty on that score. That, however, was one of the effects of the interminable debates over Bible, Church, and individual conscience as sources of religious truth. The problem was compounded by the revival of Greek skepticism, made available chiefly through Latin translations of works by Sextus Empiricus in 1562 and 1569. Sextus, like his master Pyrrho of Elis (hence the term Pyrrhonism for the whole movement), questioned the reliability of either the senses or reason to prove the existence of God. The result of this skeptical crisis, brought to a head in the *Essays* of Michel de Montaigne, was to drive religious men to ask bedrock questions all over again: How do we know God exists? Can we prove his existence? What sort of proofs can we accept? How much can we know about God over and above the fact that he exists? The answers varied greatly, ranging from extreme fideism to extreme rationalism, but with many, such as Pascal and Locke, taking up intermediate and sometimes novel positions.

Fideism, emphasizing faith rather than reason in religion, was an important weapon of Roman Catholic apologetics in the seventeenth century. There is considerable irony in this fact, as it was the Protestants who had insisted on *"fides sola"* at the start of the Reformation. But now the tables were turned as more and more Protestants appealed to reason, at least as a guide to faith, whereas the Catholics, in effect abandoning their own Thomist tradition, fell back on faith—faith in a supernatural revelation that was utterly incomprehensible by reason. Hardly new, the novelty of this seventeenth-century fideism, whether Catholic or Protestant,[10] lay in its alliance with philosophical skepticism. That is, it started from the Pyrrhonist proposition that human reason was incompetent to discover truth, especially religious truth. Fideism

---

[10] There were Protestant as well as Catholic fideists in the seventeenth century (witness, for instance, the religious "enthusiasm" or "immediate revelation" scored by Locke in Book IV of *An Essay concerning Human Understanding*). Comparatively few, however, based their fideism on skeptical arguments. Sir Thomas Browne and John Dryden were among those who did.

further argued that religious anarchy could be avoided only by submitting the individual reason, defective in any case, to Church authority.
Both of these arguments, already to be found in Montaigne's "Apology
for Raimond Sebond," were repeated over and over again by a long
line of French fideists from Father Charron to Bishop Huet. The latter's
Weakness of the Human Mind (written about 1690) is the classic
statement. Huet preferred the skeptics to all other philosophers. Affirming nothing positive about either divine or human things, the skeptics
could not be deceived like the "dogmatic philosophers." Skepticism
prepared the way for faith, by instilling in men a proper intellectual
humility. Faith, Huet asserted, "confirms the staggering reason, and
corrects the doubts which men bring to the knowledge of things."[11]
Fideism reached a more popular audience in poems by John Dryden,
Poet Laureate of England and Historiographer Royal. In his *Religio
Laici* (1682), written while he was still technically an Anglican,
Dryden described himself as "naturally inclined to scepticism in philosophy." By this he meant, not only that reason could never discover
religious truths but that once ensconced in power, as with the Socinians
and deists, it would dilute or destroy such truths entirely. "How can the
less the greater comprehend?/ Or finite reason reach Infinity?" The
answer was obvious, for Dryden as for Huet: faith alone could give
what reason could not supply.

> *Rest then, my soul, from endless anguish freed:*
> *Nor sciences thy guide, nor sense thy creed.*
> *Faith is the best ensurer of thy bliss;*
> *The bank above must fail before the venture miss.*[12]

By the time Dryden wrote these lines in 1687 he had been converted
to the faith of the Hind, that is, Roman Catholicism, which tried even
the Scripture[13] "by tradition's force." One senses in Dryden the fear of

[11] Huet, *Traité philosophique de la faiblesse de l'esprit humain* (not published
until 1723, in Amsterdam). See especially Bk. I, Chap. XV, and Bk. II, Chap. II.
In the latter chapter, it should be noted, Huet quotes St. Thomas Aquinas frequently to support the fideist position. Peter Daniel Huet, an important scholar
and ecclesiastic in Louis XIV's France, was consecrated Bishop of Avranches in
1692.

[12] John Dryden, *The Hind and the Panther,* lines 290–294. On "reason," see
also lines 248–249, and *Religio Laici* (called "A Layman's Faith"), Preface,
passim, and lines 421f, 461–462. *The Hind and the Panther* was Dryden's apology
for Roman Catholicism.

[13] Dryden especially distrusted Scripture as the final religious authority after
reading, in English translation, Father Richard Simon's *Histoire critique du Vieux*
(*Continued*)

religious chaos, engendered partly by memory of the Civil Wars period when England swarmed with sects, but also by the threat posed by deism and free thought in general. Like the French fideists, Dryden felt the need of a "solid rock" on which to stand, an omniscient church "not built with mortal hands," given authority from on high to fix the faith and settle all controversies. "One is the Church, and must be to be true." And this religious oneness also guaranteed political oneness. As Dryden had already written in *Religio Laici:*

> *And after hearing what our Church can say,*
> *If still our Reason runs another way,*
> *That private Reason 'tis more just to curb,*
> *Than by disputes the public peace disturb.*[14]

The rationalist philosophers came to exactly opposite conclusions about the way to religious knowledge. It was immensely important to them to prove God's existence—their systems depended upon so doing —but it must be done, and it could be done, by rational demonstration. Contrary to the fideists, the rationalists professed complete confidence in the capacity of "finite reason" to comprehend "Infinity." Descartes, who was familiar with the skeptical arguments,[15] affirmed this faith in reason in the prefatory letter to the *Meditations concerning First Philosophy* (1641). "I have always thought," he wrote to the theologians of the Sorbonne, "that the two questions, of God and of the soul, were the principal questions among those that should be demonstrated by rational philosophy rather than theology." For whereas faith sufficed for the faithful, not everybody had faith, and if those without faith were to be persuaded of these two things, it would have to be done "by means of natural reason." Scripture itself supported the rationalist claim that all that may be known of God can be demonstrated by reasons "that we do not need to seek elsewhere than in ourselves, and that our minds alone are capable of furnishing us."[16] Descartes then went on to de-

---

Testament (1678). This famous early work of "Higher Criticism" emphasized the obscurity and difficulties of the Biblical text.

[14] John Dryden, *Religio Laici*, lines 867–870. See also *The Hind and the Panther*, lines 637–639, 1245f.

[15] Descartes desired certainty, above all. He complained about the lack of it in his education at the Jesuit college of La Flèche. But contemporary Pyrrhonism posed the greatest threat of all to certainty, and Descartes set out to refute it, by appeal, not to dogma or authority, but to the power of reason, of clear and distinct ideas.

[16] Descartes, *Philosophical Essays*, L. J. Lafleur (trans.), Bobbs-Merrill, Library of Liberal Arts, Indianapolis, 1964, pp. 61–62.

velop these reasons in the main body of the *Meditations*. The *Cogito*, or thinking self, whose existence Descartes had already proved, could not be deceived, not even by a supposititious demon, provided it was careful to admit only clear and distinct ideas. God is such an idea. Although not disdaining a posteriori proofs, Descartes turned ultimately to the famous ontological argument to prove God's existence. The idea of God, he said, "is in us." That is, it is innate in the sense of being evident to the mind a priori, in advance of sense experience. "I find in my mind the idea of God, of a supremely perfect Being, no less than that of any shape or number whatsoever."[17] From this statement about God's essence, Descartes argued God's existence. For was not existence itself a quality of essence or supreme perfection? This argument could hardly have seemed very convincing to unbelievers. Hence, Descartes supplied other arguments, more easily grasped, such as the contingent nature of the mind, God as source of the finite mind's ideas of the infinite, and the like. The "proofs" to be found in other rationalists varied somewhat, but were substantially of the same order. Spinoza, for example, though his God differed radically from Descartes', also deduced God's existence from his essence. God, defined as substance (or the substantial essence of all things in nature) existed because "essence necessarily involves existence." Liebniz spun off any number of proofs, including the a posteriori proof from the "perfect harmony" of the many substances of nature, which required a common cause. The rationalist philosophers all exuded confidence in reason's power, both to prove God's existence and to probe his essence.

Pascal had no such confidence. Yet neither was he a complete or typical fideist. Natural knowledge of God was possible, for pagans as well as Christians. It was essential, moreover, to show unbelievers that religion was "not contrary to reason." All the same, Pascal distrusted "metaphysical proofs" profoundly, not only because, like the fideists, he thought them inadequate but because they could never lead to the living God, as distinguished from the God of the philosophers. They were too abstract, too remote from ordinary human experience. What had the arguments in Descartes' *Principles of Philosophy* to do with the God of Abraham or St. Paul? In the end Pascal fell back, not simply on blind faith, but on human psychology. This sort of psychological, as opposed to metaphysical reasoning, is in fact Pascal's chief claim to originality in this area and marks him as a forerunner of such religious apologists as Kierkegaard and Bergson.

[17] Ibid., p. 120. This is from the Fifth Meditation.

Up to a certain point Pascal reasoned like the fideists. The human mind, beclouded by the Fall, was in no way commensurable with God. "We therefore know the existence and nature of the finite because we are finite and like it consist of extension in space. . . . But we do not know either the existence or the nature of God because he has neither extension nor limits."[18] Not for Pascal was the rationalist's argument from God's essence to his existence. But what, then, if not reason, could know "infinity"? The heart could, was Pascal's answer. "The heart has its reasons which are unknown to reason." The heart, relatively untainted by original sin, loved the universal being "naturally." "It is the heart which is aware of God and not reason. That is what faith is: God perceived intuitively by the heart, not by the reason."[19] But the heart, as Pascal understood it, involved much more than mere sentiment or feeling. It combined knowledge, feeling, and will in establishing a vivifying personal relationship with God. To persuade the worldly, Pascal also advanced the famous wager argument. Either God existed or he did not. Why not bet on his existence, since there was so much at stake, nothing less than our eternal happiness. The mathematics of probability dictated risking the finite, in a game in which the odds were even, in order to win the infinite. But Pascal, though himself a great mathematician, never said God was amenable to mathematical demonstration. God always remained largely "hidden" for him, accessible only to the heart in rare moments of faith.

Actually, Locke, who was not a mathematician, pushed mathematical demonstration in this area much farther than Pascal. Evidence for God's existence, he affirmed, was "equal to mathematical certainty," and could be had simply by making mathematically correct deductions from self-evident facts and propositions. This sort of statement places Locke securely among the religious rationalists of the seventeenth century. Yet he was no more the complete rationalist than Pascal was the complete fideist. Locke differed from the continental rationalists in important respects. First of all, as an empiricist as well as a rationalist, he rejected innate ideas. Proofs of God's existence, therefore, had to be strictly demonstrative rather than intuitive, that is, derived from sensation and reflection, and thus entirely a posteriori. Further, Locke continually stressed the disproportion between man's understanding and God's. The former was incapable of grasping "infinity," or fathoming God's essence, as the Cartesians said it could. In opposition to Male-

[18] Pascal, *Pensées*, no. 343 (see note 5).
[19] Ibid., nos. 224–225.

branche, Locke confessed himself in the dark, "having no notion at all of the substance of God."[20] This is not to deny for a moment that Locke favored reason in religion as opposed to blind faith or "enthusiasm," which he berated, over and over again in the fourth book of *An Essay concerning Human Understanding.* To give in to enthusiasm (he might have said "the heart") would be to open the door to chaos and credulity. "Reason," Locke asserted, "must be our last judge and guide in everything." All the same, his emphasis, at least when he was not confronting the enthusiasts, was on the weakness of reason with regard to supernal things. Reason was more than adequate for "knowledge proper for the use and advantage of men in this world." Nature, however, never intended reason to venture into "the vast expanse of incomprehensible verities."[21] Some truths were clearly "above," though never "contrary to," reason, and therefore had to be accepted on faith. Locke has rightly been called a supernatural rationalist since he still regarded supernatural revelation through the Bible as an important, even if supplementary, source of religious truth. It seems clear that Locke, coming at the end of several centuries of religious warfare in England and Europe, wanted to support traditional Christianity, and yet make as few dogmatic statements about it as possible for the sake of peace. This desire for peace partially explains why he came down hard on both enthusiasts and rationalists, and preached a "reasonable," yet, in addition, also "minimal," theology.

To sum up, the *existence* of God stood firm in seventeenth-century thought despite the skeptical challenge. Major thinkers debated how best to prove it, whether by faith or reason, or some mixture of both. But what of God's *nature?* There was much disagreement, of course, and some wavering, too, over such matters as divine transcendence and immanence, freedom and determinism, personality and impersonality. All the same, it is possible to discern, amidst the disagreement, certain new developments that changed rather drastically the conception of deity as traditionally held in Christian Europe. To put it another way, God, still identified by most with the God of Christian revelation, now acquired new attributes (and lost others) in response to, not only the

[20] Locke, *An Examination of P. Malebranche's Opinion of Seeing all Things in God* (written 1694–95, published posthumously), Sect. 6. Locke attacked Malebranche, Descartes' most illustrious disciple, for thinking "he knows God's understanding so much better than his own, that he will make use of the divine intellect to explain the human" (Sect. 23).

[21] From Locke's Journal (February 8 and March 6, 1677), reprinted in Peter King, *The Life of John Locke,* H. Colburn, London, 1830, Vol. I, pp. 163, 197.

skeptical crisis and the desire for religious peace but also the new cosmology.

One such development has already been alluded to, that toward a minimal theology that was the work of latitudinarians from Erasmus and Sebastian Castellio in the sixteenth century down to Locke. The latitudinarian, whether to minimize differences for the sake of religious peace in the community, or because he was genuinely skeptical of theology, said as little as possible about God's nature, preferring to stress ethics. Locke did affirm that God was eternal, omnipotent, omniscient, and good. But these were superlative qualities that man in his ignorance attributed to God. Of God "in his own essence" man could know nothing, any more than he could know the real essence of a pebble, a fly, or his own self. Hence, salvation did not depend on the "speculations and niceties, obscure terms, and abstract notions" insisted upon by the writers and wranglers in religion. Like the Dutch Arminians and the Latitudinarians of his own country, John Hales of Eton, William Chillingworth, and especially Archbishop Tillotson, from whom he learned so much, Locke distinguished between essentials and nonessentials in religion. To achieve eternal life one had only to believe in Jesus as the Messiah, sent by a compassionate God, and, with his assistance, to lead a good life.[22] No wonder Locke was accused of Unitarianism and worse in his own day, and regarded as a threat to the Christian faith. Yet in truth he was no deist, but, as previously stated admitted truths "above reason" in religion, believed in the Biblical miracles, and stayed within the Church of England while trying to broaden it. What Locke did do—and this was characteristic of the whole latitudinarian movement—was to shift the center of gravity in religion from theology to ethics. If God's essence was forever unknowable, as was the real essence of bodies, at least one could know— "perfectly," Locke says—"the precise real essence of the things moral words stand for." That was what man's mind was fitted for, not for the "niceties" and "notions" of theological speculation but for moral knowledge, which, Locke concluded, was "the proper science and business of mankind in general,"[23] and which, if properly pursued, could enable men to agree tolerably well and live in peace with one another.

There were two other developments of great importance in which Locke also participated to some degree. Though contradictory, both

---

[22] This is the conclusion of *The Reasonableness of Christianity* (1695). See especially Sects. 172 and 252.

[23] Locke, *An Essay concerning Human Understanding*, Bk. III, Chap. XI, Sect. 16; Bk. IV, Chap. XII, Sect. 11.

developments were the effect of the scientific revolution, of the new ways of arranging and visualizing space, and the movement of bodies in space. One, referred to in the previous chapter, was to push God out of the universe and thus to turn him into a superior clockmaker or, in Alexandre Koyré's expression, a "God of the Sabbath," resting and in large part absenting himself from the world after the original act of creation. This development, never quite complete in any of the foremost thinkers, pointed in a deistic direction. The other development pointed the opposite way, affirming God's omnipresence in the world, and even identifying him with it in certain respects. This latter development, one might say, led in a "romantic" direction. Combinations of both views, of an absentee God and an immanent God, are not infrequently to be found in the same person. In an age of theological innovation there were inevitably shades and grades of opinion, not always strictly logical, about God's relative transcendence and immanence, or providentialism. There was also some misunderstanding, some of it perhaps deliberate, of what certain thinkers did in fact say, or were trying to say, about God.

Descartes, enamoured as he was of Galilean science, inclined toward the first view. Pascal is supposed to have said of Descartes that he would have been quite willing to dispense with God except that he needed him to "give a fillip to set the world in motion; beyond this, he has no further need of God."[24] This certainly did not do justice to Descartes. Descartes, who was a practicing Catholic, kept a good deal of the traditional theism in his system. "By the word 'God' I mean," he wrote in the *Meditations,* "an infinite substance, eternal, immutable, independent, omniscient, and that by which I myself and all other existent things . . . have been created and produced."[25] This is the traditional list of divine attributes, as noted also in Locke. Descartes also speaks of God's continuing conservation of the world, and even perpetual recreation of motion and time to keep the world going. All the same, there is something to what Pascal said. In the interest of science Descartes clearly reduced, though he did not eliminate entirely, divine activity in the world. The picture he paints in the fifth part of the *Discourse on Method* is of a universe running by itself, once God had originally created matter and motion, and the natural laws, including the law of inertia. In Descartes' philosophy God has primarily the function of guaranteeing the world-machine, of giving it certainty and depend-

[24] Pascal, *Pensées,* no. 77 (Brunschvieg edition; omitted in Lafuma edition).
[25] Descartes, *Philosophical Essays* (see note 15), p. 101. This statement is from the Third Meditation.

ability. After the creation, the Cartesian God continues to conserve the world, and even in a sense to re-create it, but he does not change, or interfere, with the ordinary processes of nature. The latter, in fact, made the world as we see it today, starting with original matter and the vortices set in motion by the First Cause.

In Newton more was left of the Biblical God, who was "Lord over all," and who exercised "dominion." Yet Newton's God resembled Descartes' God more than might appear on the surface. There is no question, of course, that Newton thought of God as conserver as well as creator of the universe. From the ordered motions of the planets Newton deduced that the First Cause of it all must have been "an intelligent agent," "well skilled in mechanics and geometry." Moreover, subsequent to the creation God, in the words of the General Scholium added to the *Principia,* "governs all things," in the sense of holding the universe together, and even repairing parts of it when needed. God's function as repairman, was, indeed, the basis for Leibniz's famous jibe, mentioned in the previous chapter, that according to Newton and his friends, the world-machine of God's making was so imperfect "that he [God] is obliged to clean it now and then by extraordinary concourse, and even to mend it, as a clockmaker mends his work." Leibniz, claiming to have a higher opinion of the divine wisdom, depicted God as a "supra-mundane intelligence," who freely created the best of all possible worlds, but who thereafter, though he might indeed work miracles, did so not "in order to supply the wants of nature, but those of grace." Dr. Samuel Clarke, taking up the cudgels for Newton, shied away from this formulation, fearing that it tended "to exclude providence and God's government in reality out of the world," thus implying the notion of materialism and fate.[26] A close reading of Newton's language, however, reveals that in reality Newton stood closer to the Cartesian conception than either Clarke or Leibniz supposed. Save for occasional tinkering required, for example, to overcome noted irregularities in the motions of the planets, and to prevent the fixed stars from collapsing together in space, Newton's God left the world pretty much to its own devices. "Being once formed," Newton wrote in the *Optics,* "it [the world] may continue by those laws for

---

[26] Dr. Samuel Clarke, philosopher-theologian, Boyle Lecturer, and Rector of St. James, Westminster, was Newton's pupil and friend. The quotations from Leibniz and Clarke are from the lengthy correspondence between them: *A Collection of Papers which passed between the late Learned Mr. Leibnitz and Dr. Clarke,* James Knapton, London, 1717, pages 5–7, 15–17. The term "supra-mundane intelligence" was Clarke's, not Leibniz's.

many ages." Newton's God did exercise dominion, but by dominion was usually meant nothing much beyond the creation and organization of the world, and, subsequently, concurrence in the world-order.[27] The natural philosophers of the seventeenth century, including Newton, wanted to have the best of two worlds: to keep God as creator and guarantor of scientific certainty; yet at the same time to reduce his providentialism, his infra-mundane activity, in the interest of scientific reliability and predictability. Hence, the popularity of God's new image as clockmaker (also occasional clockmender) and geometer.

But, as stated previously, this was not the only new image, not even in Newton. Newton, who exhibits considerable tension in his conception of deity, also visualized God as spread out in space which, indeed, he called God's "sensorium." This image of God, as immanent as well as transcendent, and as endowed preeminently with the attributes of plenitude and infinity, was the effect of the space revolution of the seventeenth century. Infinite space, especially when viewed as possibly indifferent to man and man's purposes, terrified Pascal earlier in the century.[28] But by putting God into space, by representing space as a substance extended but not corporeal, by thus joining God and nature, men could be reassured and take comfort again. This drive to divinize space, or to spatialize divinity, began at least as early as Giordano Bruno, as we have seen.[29] By Newton's time the new God of Plenitude, as Marjorie Nicolson calls him, was almost a commonplace, admitted to the pantheon, paradoxically, at about the same time as the Clockmaker (and coinciding in time also with Leibniz's Chief Monad, who in addition to being clockmaker, that is, principle outside and above the system of the world, was also linked to the world as the highest term in the hierarchical system of monads). Men spoke increasingly of God's "omnipresence," and of his "filling" space. God, said Newton, is "omnipresent not virtually only, but substantially." "God, everyone easily allows, fills eternity," Locke wrote, "and it is hard to find a reason why any one should doubt that he likewise fills immensity."[30]

---

[27] On the meaning of "dominion" in Newton, see Richard S. Westfall, *Science and Religion in Seventeenth-Century England,* Yale University Press, New Haven, 1958, pp. 202–203.

[28] See p. 56.

[29] See p. 57.

[30] Locke, *An Essay concerning Human Understanding,* Bk. II, Chap. XV, Sect. 3. See also to the same effect, Henry More's *Essay upon the Infinity of Worlds out of Platonick Principles* (1646), and Thomas Traherne's *Thoughts.* Thus Traherne:

His [God's] *omnipresence is an Endless Sphere,*
Wherein all Worlds as his Delights appear . . .   (*Continued*)

Spinoza, though using mostly traditional language, carried this immanence to its logical extreme. "God is the immanent, and not the transitive [that is, coming from the outside] cause of all things"; "Whatever is, is in God, and nothing can either be or be conceived without God," and so on: thus read several of the propositions of the *Ethics*.[31] God, in other words, did not exist outside his modes or creatures, but lived and moved in them. Spinoza abolished God's transcendence, identified him with the whole of nature. In the process Spinoza also denuded God of all personal features such as will, understanding, goodness, and freedom of choice. This was, in fact, the basis of Leibniz's quarrel with Spinoza; Leibniz thought Spinoza had completely depersonalized God, as indeed he had. Pascal also would have abominated Spinoza's diety, as he already abominated Descartes'. From his Christian point of view, both, though they were poles apart in conception, were merely metaphysical gods, impersonal constructs, having nothing to do with the "hidden God" of the Scriptures or with the human heart.

One other attribute of deity, hitherto unmentioned, needs to be stressed in view of the thesis of this book. Whatever else he might be, God remained above all "immutable" for most people in the seventeenth century. There is, to be sure, a suggestion in the idea of plenitude, of God's acting in new and different ways, of a fecund God lavishly creating an infinity of beings and worlds. But for anyone who took the new order of nature seriously it was essential not to have God himself change, as the Hegelians were later to have him do. Descartes insisted on the "immutability of God" in *The Principles of Philosophy*. We know, Descartes wrote, not only that God "is immovable in his nature" but that "he acts in a manner which he never changes." "From the fact that God is in no way subject to change and that he acts always in the same manner we can arrive at the knowledge of certain rules which I call the laws of nature."[32] The connection in Descartes' mind between the two, between God and the laws of nature, is obvious. God's immutability guaranteed the dependability of nature (thought of as God's works) and therefore scientific certainty. This interconnection was true also for Spinoza and Leibniz even though, as we have seen, they had different ideas about God and his relation to nature. As yet, the emphasis was still clearly on God's being rather than becoming.

His Glory Endless is, and doth Surround
And fill all Worlds, without or End or Bound.

[31] Propositions XV and XVIII of the First Part of the *Ethics*. The *Ethics* was published posthumously.

[32] Descartes, *The Principles of Philosophy*, Pt. II, nos. 36 and 37.

The Greatness and
Wretchedness of Man

Men of insight, Pascal wrote, "find both greatness and wretchedness in man. In a word, man knows that he is wretched; he is therefore
wretched because he is so; but he is very great because he knows it."[1]
Pascal's famous conundrum epitomizes seventeenth-century thought on
man. On the one hand, man was viewed as wretched in the extreme—
as controlled by sin; or, in a more secular vein, as generally deceitful,
vain, and unjust, unable to control his passions and to direct them to
good ends. Calvinists and Jansenists, French moralists from La Rochefoucauld to La Bruyère and La Fontaine, and even acute scientific observers such as Thomas Hobbes and Pierre Bayle, rang changes on
these and other pejorative words all through the century. On the other
hand, there was increasing recognition of man's greatness or potential
greatness, not only in Pascal's sense of self-consciousness but especially
in the sense of rational power and of power over nature. The weight of
the Pauline-Augustinian tradition, strengthened by the Reformation
and the events of recent political and religious history, supported the
pessimistic view. Science, though raising some new problems about
both human nature and the human condition, encouraged a more op-

---

[1] Pascal, *Pensées,* no. 237, Martin Turnell (trans.) from Lafuma edition.

timistic view. Of the two views, the former predominated. But just as new gods were born in the seventeenth century, so were new men—or new images of man—and for somewhat the same reasons. Augustinian Man, still favored by many, did not entirely fit the scientific euphoria of the new "modern" age.

Before examining these two very different anthropologies more closely, it is important to note one thing they had in common, which was widely characteristic of seventeenth-century, as of earlier, European thought. Both took what might be called a classical, as opposed to a historicist, view of their subject. That is, they both assumed that human nature did not change but was fundamentally the same in all times and places. To assume this sameness was by no means to deny varieties of human behavior according to temperament (sanguine, choleric, or whatever), or a plurality of customs as between different societies and peoples. Indeed, as Paul Hazard points out, the lesson of relativity was being learned rather quickly through travel overseas and through the literature of travel.[2] However, this relativity applied mainly to a recognition of "infinite varieties to be found in the laws and usages of nations," and not to any fundamental difference in human nature. As Bayle went on to say in the passage just quoted from his *Historical and Critical Dictionary* (1697), one recognizes without difficulty "vices which are of every country and religion, and of every century," as well as "good actions" to be found everywhere.[3] Hobbes, it is true, expressly denied there was any such thing as "man in general." The nominalist in him protested that "man" was only a name, and that only particular men were real, hence that the diversity among them as to passions, knowledge, opinions, and manners was enormous. But this did not prevent Hobbes from going ahead and generalizing to his heart's content about "man," which is indeed the heading of a major section of the *Leviathan* (1651). "So that, in the first place," he wrote, "I put for a general inclination of all mankind a perpetual and restless desire of power after power that ceases only in death."[4] Certainly Hobbes had no sense of man as a product of history, of a human nature being made and remade ceaselessly in time and space. Nor did Bayle, who explicitly stated his belief in a "general notion of man." Jew, Mohammedan, and Christian, Indian and Tartar, inhabitant of mainland

---

[2] Paul Hazard, *La Crise de la conscience européenne*, Boivin & Cie, Paris, 1935, Vol. I, pp. 14–15.

[3] Pierre Bayle, *Dictionnaire historique et critique*, "Averroès," Remarque P.

[4] Thomas Hobbes, *Leviathan*, Pt. I, Chap. 11. See also his *The Elements of Law*, Ferdinand Tönnies (ed.), Cambridge University Press, Cambridge, 1928, p. 15.

and islander, noble and commoner, all kinds of people who in everything else disagree, "are so similar with respect to the [basic] passions that one might almost say they copy one another."[5] Christians of all persuasions were similarly talking about a universal nature of man, as were the secular moralists, as we shall see. Clearly, becoming was as yet scarcely more characteristic of the European's conception of man than of his conception of God.

Returning to Pascal's opposites, we may take up the wretchedness first. The wretchedness, it should be emphasized, was never wholly unmitigated. No Christian, least of all Pascal, questioned man's special moral and religious status in the universe, which lifted him far above the beasts. Pascal, in addition, praised human thought, and especially the heart which, as we have seen, could apprehend God intuitively. Yet it is man's wretchedness that commands attention in the *Pensées,* and is the basis for Pascal's apology for Christianity, for his conviction, not only that man was wretched without God but that he desperately needed God's special assistance, that is, "efficacious" in addition to "sufficient" grace, to be saved. Man, according to Pascal, had two natures, one good, the other bad. Created good, in God's image, man was corrupted by original sin. Original sin, the sin committed by Adam and transmitted to his posterity, is the key to Pascal's anthropology. By this original sin man lost his "first nature" and became, as it were, a "fallen monarch," his reason dimmed, given over to concupiscence, living in a dungeon under sentence of eternal death.[6] This conception of fallen humanity was, of course, a commonplace of Christian anthropology. But in its extreme Augustinian form it received fresh emphasis at the Reformation, not only by Protestants (conspicuously Calvin) but also by some Roman Catholics reacting against Jesuit license. Pascal learned it from the Jansenists whose teaching derived from the *Augustinus* of Cornelius Jansenius, erstwhile bishop of Ypres. Jansenius' *The Augustinus, or, The Doctrine of St. Augustine on the Health, Sickness, and Medicine of Human Nature,* published posthumously in 1640, and later condemned by the pope, attacked Pelagianism, both old and new, affirming, against the Jesuits (stigmatized as modern Pelagians), the utter ruin of human nature at the Fall, man's loss of "the liberty of indifference," and predestination.[7] To the contrary, the Spanish Jesuit

---

[5] Bayle, *Pensées diverses sur la comète* (1682), Sect. 137.

[6] Pascal, *Pensées,* no. 220, 395 (see note 1), and *passim.*

[7] Pelagianism refers to the British monk Pelagius, who, in opposition to St. Augustine, affirmed man's freedom of will. The "liberty of indifference," or inde-

(*Continued*)

Luis Molina, and his follower Lessius, gave man freedom, based on what was called "sufficient grace," to choose good as well as evil, and hence the power, at least in some measure, of contributing to his salvation. Pascal, coached by the Jansenist theologian Antoine Arnauld, expressly denounced the Jesuit theology of grace—and hence, Jesuit anthropology—as well as Jesuit morality, in the *Provincial Letters* (1656–1657).

This severe doctrine was by no means an anomaly in seventeenth-century Christian thought. It was paralleled to a remarkable degree in contemporary Calvinism and Puritanism, to which indeed Jansenism has often been compared, and even among some Anglicans, especially of the late Elizabethan and early Jacobean period. If anything, Puritanism went farther than Jansenism, certainly farther than Pascal, in insisting on man's total corruption. This was the chief difference between Anglican and Puritan. The Puritans would permit no "intermediate nature," halfway between angels and animals, such as the Anglicans, like the Jesuits, contemplated. The Puritans, in order to preserve God's absolute sovereignty, put an unbridgeable gulf between nature and grace. Not only could man not earn his own salvation (the Anglicans did not deny this) but he could not reason clearly or make free choices even on the natural level. "Original sin," said William Perkins, the most systematic of the Puritan theologians, is "the corruption engendered in our first conception, whereby every faculty of soul and body is prone and disposed to evil."[8] The Synod of Dordrecht (or Dort) in Holland (1618), summing up "official" Calvinist doctrine on the subject, declared that God, while "electing" some, condemned others to eternal wretchedness, some said even before *any* sin had been committed.[9] Not only the Remonstrants in Holland but also Anglicans in general drew back from this sort of extreme Augustinianism, which in its concern to preserve God's freedom and justice, appeared to deny his mercy. None, however, disputed that man was in bad plight, and

---

termination, meant the ability to choose good as well as evil. St. Augustine, and Jansenius after him, held that man lost this liberty at the Fall, but not free will. Fallen man's will remained free—to choose evil (*posse peccare*).

[8] William Perkins, *A Golden Chain or Description of Theology* (first published in 1590; went through many editions), in *Works,* John Legett, London, 1612, Vol. I, p. 20. Three chapters deal with "Sin," "Man's Fall and Disobedience," and "Original Sin."

[9] The Synod wavered, as did Calvinists in general, between supra- and infralapsarianism, the former holding that election was consequent upon God's free choice before the creation of the world, the latter that nonelection or eternal damnation was pronounced by a just God as the result of original sin.

some Anglicans, depressed, as we saw earlier, by the intellectual and religious chaos of the times, harped incessantly on the evil in human nature. Such a one was John Donne, who in a Christmas Day sermon of 1629, exclaimed: "How poor and inconsiderable a thing is man . . . : man, who, if they were all together, all the men that ever were, and are, and shall be, would not have the power of one angel in them all . . . ; man [who] is so much less than a worm" which shall, indeed, feed upon his dead body in the grave and upon his conscience in hell.[10] Another such Anglican was Godfrey Goodman, chaplain to the Queen of England and future bishop, who in *The Fall of Man* (1616) showed how original sin had tainted nature and the state as well. Since man was a microcosm, the whole world in little, and since the world was made for him, his corruption could not help but bring the inter-related orders down with him. All these views, though they differed in degree of pessimism and in faithfulness to the original, were in the very best Augustinian tradition.

A secular Augustinianism, equally emphatic about man's wretched-ness, developed side by side with this religious Augustinianism. The term *secular Augustinianism* is not inappropriate since, though it sel-dom talked religious language, it had its source partially in the religious tradition. Pierre Bayle, brought up a Huguenot, admitted as much when he wrote that his principles "emanated from those of St. Augustine on the corruption of man."[11] But it is also traceable to the "counter Renais-sance," which might be said to have begun with such figures as Machia-velli and Montaigne, and to disillusionment with recent history. The early Renaissance, Theodore Spencer once said, compared man with the angels, whereas the later Renaissance compared him with the animals (for example, Montaigne did so, in the "Apology for Raymond Se-bond," the longest of his essays). In the seventeenth century, both La Rochefoucauld and La Bruyère illustrate this later or "counter" Renais-sance attitude in their reaction against the ancient Stoic ideal of man, as discussed later in greater detail. But it was perhaps chiefly the contem-plation of contemporary events that gave all these people their less ideal view; the French religious wars in the case of Montaigne, the English civil war and its disorders for Hobbes, the humiliation of a proud aristocracy by the French crown for La Rochefoucauld, religious fanaticism for Bayle, and for La Bruyère, life at Chantilly and Ver-

[10] John Donne, *Sermons,* Evelyn Simpson and George Potter (eds.), University of California Press, Berkeley, 1958, Vol. IX, p. 136.
[11] Bayle, *Continuation des Pensées diverses sur la comète* (1704), quoted in Elizabeth Labrousse, *Pierre Bayle,* Martinus Nijhoff, La Haye, 1964, p. 80, note 36.

sailles, which opened his bourgeois eyes to an unjust and corrupt social system. La Rochefoucauld, veteran of the Fronde and personally involved in its aftermath, the fall of the French nobility, describes some of these events in his *Reflections* (1659–1680), and concludes on a sour note, that if the present century had produced no fewer extraordinary events than past centuries, it surpassed them all "in the excess of crimes." "France," he wrote, "is today the theatre in which one sees on display all that history and fable have told us of the crimes of antiquity." And he, like the others, traced the crimes back to human nature: "Vices are of all times, men are born of cruelty and debauchery."[12]

The wretchedness of man was, then, the theme of secular as well as religious "Augustinians," frequently also of the new drama of both England and France, and above all of the many writers of maxims, reflections, satires, and fables that had such a great vogue in the seventeenth century. There are traces in all these writers of a nobler image of man, of the "courtier" and *honnête homme* of the Renaissance, and the bourgeois *homme de mérite* whom La Bruyère compared favorably with the *parvenus,* the financiers, profiteers, and tax-farmers who were preying on France. But in the main the image of man that carried conviction with them was a decidedly unheroic one, of man ruled by egoism and passion, morally flawed, in no sense captain of his soul. And since he was nearly always pictured as born that way, not much was to be hoped for in the way of improvement over "nature"—unless by a special act of God, which was what the religious Augustinians were saying. That man was more drawn toward evil than good was, for Bayle, "as certain as any principle of metaphysics."[13]

In French literature, discussions of human nature centered on the conflict between reason and the passions. Pierre Corneille, father of the new French drama, upheld the "classical" view that reason or will stood a good chance of curbing "les sens." That was, in fact, what made character, when heroes such as the Cid (*Le Cid,* 1636, Corneille's most popular play) put honor above love, and thus, so to speak, imposed a principle of order on the chaos of instincts and desires. But in a classical age when men were very much concerned to restore and maintain order, not many, at least among the *littérateurs,* believed in the Corneillean image. Certainly Racine did not, nor Molière, nor perhaps always

---

[12] François de La Rochefoucauld, *Réflexions diverses,* Sect. XIX, "Des Evénements de ce siècle."

[13] Bayle, *Nouvelles Lettres sur l'Histoire du Calvinisme,* quoted in Labrousse, *Pierre Bayle* (see note 11), p. 82.

Corneille himself. Racine, who was educated by the Jansenists,[14] put tragic figures on stage, like Phèdre, who are swept off their feet by "amour," over which reason has lost control, thus throwing everything, the community included, into disorder (*désordre*). "My feeble reason no longer rules over me": Phèdre, unable to put her house in order, is forced to live under the "shameful" yoke of her passion for Hippolyte. It has been pointed out that Racine increasingly portrayed a dark hinterland of human nature, in which men deliberately contrived their own and others' death and destruction.[15] It was, of course, the discovery of this hinterland, and of the disparity between the appearance and the reality of human nature that had made Hamlet melancholy. "Paragon of animals," "how like a god"—in a word, the ideal man of the Renaissance—delighted Hamlet no more after he discovered the crimes, the perfidy, incest, and murder, of which man was capable.

The point usually made by the seventeenth-century moralists, however, was not so much that reason was feeble as that reason did not commonly influence conduct. Bayle makes this point over and over again in his *Pensées diverses sur la comète* (1683) where he is trying to show the lack of conformity between religious beliefs (belief, for example, in a righteous God, and in a paradise and hell after death) and moral practice. "Let man be as rational as you please, but it is no less true that he almost never acts comformably with his principles."[16] Man reasons well enough,[17] and what is more, knows the difference between right and wrong. Yet at the point of action he is ruled "almost always" by passion, temperament, or force of habit. La Bruyère says much the same thing when, in his famous *Characters,* he discusses the three ages of man. In the first age, the age of childhood, men live by instinct like animals.

> (But) there is a second age when reason develops, when it matures, and when it might act, if it were not clouded and, as it were, extinguished by our constitutional devices and by a chain of passions

[14] Whereas Racine was educated by the Jansenists (and later wrote a history of Port Royal, the Jansenist monastery), Corneille was educated by the Jesuits and, like the latter, believed in free will.

[15] See on this, Martin Turnell's penetrating remarks in *The Classical Moment,* New Directions, New York, 1948.

[16] Bayle, *Pensées sur la comète,* Sect. 136.

[17] Bayle could as easily comment on the weakness of reason, on its propensity to mislead, but his point in the *Pensées* is that once given first principles (which, however, may be false), reason can be counted upon to draw logical conclusions from them.

which succeed one another and lead us into the third and last age. Reason, then, is ripe and should bear fruit; but it has been chilled and slowed down by age, sickness and suffering, and then thrown out of gear by the breaking-down of our worn-out machine; and yet these ages make up the whole life of man.[18]

"We haven't enough strength to follow our reason":[19] It was La Rochefoucauld's genius to be able to boil down to a maxim what was obviously a common sentiment among all the French moralists.

There is in all this moralizing more than a hint of determinism, even of corporal determinism. Both La Rochefoucauld and Bayle believed in a theory, very popular just then in medical circles, which traced human inclinations back to the "humours" of the body. The individual's course was largely set for him in advance, not merely by his passionate nature, which he shared with others, but by the particular humour, or mixture of humours (blood, phlegm, black and yellow bile) that he also had at birth. The passions, the humours—and, La Rochefoucauld would add, fortune—corresponded to original sin in their effects. They exercized a tyranny over the will, and, hence, over conduct.

> The humours of the body have an ordinary and ruled course which moves and turns our will imperceptibly; they move together and exercise successively a secret empire over us. . . . Although men flatter themselves on their great actions, they are not often the result of a great design, but of fortune [*hasard*]. . . . Fortune and humour [*humeur*] govern the world. . . . Man often believes himself leader when, in fact, he is led; and while by his mind he endeavours to reach one goal, his heart draws him insensibly toward another.[20]

In these and many other maxims La Rochefoucauld not only punctured man's self-esteem but took away his autonomy. So much for the Stoic image of the wise man, praised by Renaissance humanists, who could defy fortune and control his own thoughts and actions, even if he could not control the universe. "Stoicism is a flight of fancy, an idea like Plato's Republic," said La Bruyère.[21] Not that education and laws

---

[18] La Bruyère, *Caractères,* "De l'homme" (no. 49, in the English translation of Jean Stewart, Penguin Books, Harmondsworth, England, 1970).

[19] La Rochefoucauld, *Maximes morales* (1678 ed.), no. 42.

[20] Ibid., no. 43, 57, 297, 435.

[21] La Bruyère, *Caractères,* "De l'homme," no. 3. La Rochefoucauld also frequently derided the Stoic philosophers, especially Seneca.

could do nothing to civilize man, to restrain his instincts, and turn them to social uses by instilling fear of punishment or the desire for praise and glory. But, according to Bayle, education, in addition to its possible beneficial effects, could also have the bad effect of subjecting men to the passions of the educators and the community, as in the case of religious fanaticism and persecution. And in any event education could not remove "the germ of corruption in man's soul," which Bayle compared to a fire attached to a combustible matter.[22] That being so, why rail against man's faults, seeing that they are fundamental to his nature? The worldly-wise Philinte, who may also speak for Molière, counsels his splenetic friend Alceste, in *The Misanthrope* (1666), to "take men as they are, or let them be." A wise man will accept the situation, and there is no greater folly "than trying to reform society"—or human nature, which is "beastly," yet also capable, in some instances, of virtuous action.[23]

Compared to the "wretchedness," emphasized by these and other writers, reflections on man's "greatness" occupied much less space and carried less conviction. But a more optimistic anthropology was definitely now in the making, and indeed it would be impossible to understand some of the new emergent ideas about society and history without it. Pascal, it will be recalled, often talked of the greatness of man, but his reference was always either to Adam's original state in the Garden of Eden, or to the remnant of that state in fallen humanity. When, however, Francis Bacon declared his intention, in the *Magna Instauratio,* of extending "more widely the limits of the power and greatness of man," a new note had obviously been struck. Bacon spoke for a new age of science, which opened up a new prospect for man's control and mastery of the world, and hence shifted the emphasis from human corruption to human power. It was chiefly among those persons prominently connected with the scientific movement, and among the rationalists, that newer and more "modern" images of man—we might call them Rational Man and Promethean Man—began to form.

But before examining these new images, brief notice should be taken of the persistence into the seventeenth century of several other, also less harsh, images, left over from the Renaissance, or else generated within, or in opposition to, the Reformation. One such image was the gentleman or *honnête homme,* a watered-down version of the Renais-

---

[22] Bayle, *Pensées sur la comète,* Sect. 238.
[23] Philinte's counsel follows Alceste's famous diatribe against human nature in Act I, Scene I: "I include all men in one dim view, etc."

sance "courtier," of which there was a considerable literature and that assumed a "nobility in man" that could be developed by training and education. Examples of this genre are books by Henry Peacham (1622), Richard Brathwaite (1630), and Nicolas Faret (1630), all of which, though exhibiting important differences, stressed moral goodness, as well as manners and the cultivation of the arts.[24] The influence of Stoicism, derided by the French moralists, is apparent in all of these works.

Another traditional image was the one projected concurrently by the Jesuits, and by the Arminians or Remonstrants of Holland. Both, as previously noted,[25] rejected the extreme Augustinian interpretation of the Fall, and spoke up for free will, and hence man's ability to do good, and even (with God's aid, of course) to do good works leading to salvation. The parallel between the teachings of Molina, the Spanish Jesuit, and the Dutch Calvinist Jacob Arminius at this point is striking. Arminius, professor of theology at the University of Leyden, began as a Calvinist but recoiled from the Calvinist view of election. His antipredestinarian views inspired the Great Remonstrance of 1618, which, although voted down at the Synod of Dordrecht, stood as a beacon to Protestant latitudinarians in all countries. John Milton's anthropology was not dissimilar. Though not a follower of Arminius—he might be described as a Calvinist Independent—Milton interpreted the Fall humanistically. The Fall, for Milton, represented the surrender of reason to the passions, after God had created man in his image. But even after the Fall, as Milton tells us clearly enough in his book on Christian doctrine, "remnants" of the divine image still existed in man, being visible in both human reason or understanding, and the will, and making possible "renovation" whereby "the natural mind and will of man being partially renewed by a divine impulse, are led to seek the knowledge of God, and for the time, at least, undergo an alteration for

[24] All these "courtesy" books owed much to Castiglione's *Courtier* (first published in 1516), the classic of the genre, but in varying degrees. Peacham, schoolmaster and tutor to nobility, more or less followed Castiglione's aristocratic line, emphasizing the perfection of the individual, though mixing it with English nationalism. Faret, though also aristocratic in tone, is more practical, stressing, as did all the French works, "the art of pleasing the Court," that is, the qualities needed by the courtier to rise and make himself agreeable to the prince. Faret, a historian and man of letters, was one of the first members of the French Academy. Brathwaite, who was a Puritan, is more bourgeois in his stress on useful activity and the development of moral character.

[25] See pp. 81–82.

the better."[26] Despite his Calvinism, Milton came close to saying that virtue was knowledge, acquired through education.

Perhaps there was nothing absolutely new about the image of Rational Man projected by the philosophers of the seventeenth century. Its lineage clearly goes back to Platonism and Neo-Platonism, to Aristotle, and the Stoics, and in some respects to the medieval scholastics, as well as to the Renaissance humanists. But it was now restated with great vigor, and with additional embellishment, by the Cartesians, and by Spinoza, Leibniz, and others. We have already seen how the system builders, in opposition to the skeptics, expanded the human mind's capacity to attain metaphysical and theological truth.[27] Contrary to the moralists cited previously, they also expressed considerable confidence in the ability of reason to control the passions. Hugo Grotius, Locke, and other political thinkers, further insisted on man's social nature, and hence on his ability, by means of judicious agreements, to build a more rational society.

The continental philosophers all had an exalted view of man. Descartes, refusing to follow Montaigne's line in the "Apology for Raymond Sebond," differentiated sharply between men and animals.[28] Man, though saddled with a body, is unique, possessing, as animals do not, a soul or mind, and hence belonging to a world of spirit as well as matter. Among other things, possession of mind meant that man had free will, though Descartes was not wholly consistent or clear about this. Like so many others in the seventeenth century, Descartes got himself entangled in the theological problem of how to reconcile human freedom with divine foreknowledge. Yet he clearly believed, with the Jesuits who educated him, and with the dramatist Corneille from whom he also may have learned something, in the sort of free will that enables man, like the traveler, to set his own course within certain limits: to think clearly about moral goals; to follow the best, or the probably best, goal, not permitting the passions to deflect him from it; and, like the Stoic sage, to regulate his desires, rejecting those that nature has

---

[26] John Milton, *De Doctrina Christiana* (finished by the early 1660's, but not published until 1825), Bk. I, Chap. 17. On Milton's humanist anthropology, see Basil Willey, *The Seventeenth Century Background*, Doubleday & Co., Garden City, New York, 1953, Chap. X, Sect. 2, iii.

[27] See p. 70.

[28] There were also those who, like Montaigne and Pierre Charron, maintained the superiority, in important respects, of animals to men. Descartes' assertion that animals lacked a soul, their acts being purely mechanical, was in part a rebuttal of this sort of theriophilic "primitivism."

put beyond his control. "I think that this [this last "maxim," as he calls it] must have been the principal secret of those philosophers of ancient times who were able to rise above fortune, and, despite pains and poverty, to vie with the gods in happiness."[29] The passions, Descartes thought, though "all good in their nature," nevertheless needed to be, and could be, controlled by reason. "There is no soul so feeble," Descartes wrote in his treatise on *The Passions of the Soul* (1649), "that it cannot, if well directed, acquire an absolute power over its passions." "The principal use of prudence or self-control is that it teaches us to be masters of our passions."[30] Not for nothing did Jacques Maritain accuse Descartes of "angelism," that is, praising Rational Man to the skies.

Spinoza and Leibniz similarly put rational man high in their systems, though they did so in different ways. At first glance, Spinoza might not appear to do this, for his language is frequently deterministic. Spinoza denied that man constituted any sort of "kingdom within a kingdom," and made him a part of nature, as, of course, Descartes only partially did. Yet despite his denial of Cartesian free will, Spinoza's moral goal was exactly the same as Descartes': to establish, as he said in the conclusion of the *Ethics* (published posthumously in 1677), "the mind's power over the emotions and the mind's freedom." "Whence it appears, how potent is the wise man, and how much he surpasses the ignorant man, who is driven only by his lusts."[31] Spinoza inveighed against those who "bemoan, deride, despise, or abuse" human nature, invoking against them "the power of the mind" to restrain the passions. By means of reason it was possible, first of all, to understand human actions and desires in the same way that one would consider "lines, planes, and solids" in geometry; then, in possession of such knowledge, to convert what he called "passive" into "active" passions (such as courage and nobility) that do not merely reflect bodily changes. One should also remember that Spinoza equated nature with God, and that in making man part of nature, he therefore meant only to say that man shared the divine substance. "Hence it follows, that the human mind is part of the infinite intellect of God."[32] However one explains the dilemma of freedom and determinism in Spinoza's ethics, it is at least clear that Spinoza thought man was essentially rational, and that reason could liberate him and give him happiness.

[29] Descartes, *Discourse on Method,* Pt. III.
[30] Descartes, *The Passions of the Soul,* Pt. I, Article L; Pt. III, Article CCXXII.
[31] Spinoza, *Ethics,* Pt. V, Note to Proposition XLII.
[32] Ibid., Pt. II, Proposition XI, Corollary.

Leibniz, optimist *par excellence,* described men[33] as sensitive souls raised by God to the rank of "rational souls" in whom "spirit" predominated. To account for the evil in the world, Leibniz conceded "an original imperfection of creatures," caused, however, not by "original sin" but by the mere fact of having been created, which necessarily involved limitations and imperfections, making "human nature" liable to error and the commission of sin. Nevertheless, by a special act God gave men reason, thus elevating them above "ordinary souls" or animals, and enabling them to reflect on "self," and to have knowledge of necessary and eternal truths, even of God. "Spirits," Leibniz wrote in the *Monadology,* a late work (1714), but following earlier ideas, are "images of the Deity itself," constituting all together "a moral world within the natural world," striving toward moral perfection.[34] The gift of reason also implied freedom, making men in that respect like God himself. But in Leibniz, as in Descartes and Spinoza, just what it meant to be free is not at all clear. Although Leibniz apparently denied the "liberty of indifference" in men, he clearly meant to make them morally responsible and to apportion rewards and punishments in a future life in consequence of acts freely committed. In any case, Leibniz assumed, not only that men were sufficiently rational to have metaphysical knowledge and to behave morally but to adjudicate all their outstanding disputes. A great harmonizer in a century of harmonizers, Leibniz was full of projects for achieving Christian reunion and a union of Christian princes, all predicated on mutual agreement to rational propositions.

Others, notably Grotius and Locke, especially emphasized man's social nature as the basis for social peace. This was contrary to what Hobbes said, in *Leviathan,* about man in "the state of nature." For Hobbes, who belongs among the secular Augustinians,[35] the state of nature was equivalent to a state of war, "such a war as is of every man against every man." Man was by nature an individualist, seeking "power after power" to achieve security and avoid death, inevitably behaving therefore as a wolf to his fellow men. From this unhappy state of affairs men could be delivered only by submitting to a "mortal

[33] Strictly speaking, Leibniz spoke of "men," or of "a man," rather than "man" as a genus, since he believed that each man was a concrete being, having special qualities and pursuing his own individual destiny.

[34] Leibniz, *Monadology,* No. 82–86; also 29–30, and on "original imperfection" the *Essays in Theodicy* (1710), V. Answer to Objection.

[35] J. H. Randall calls Hobbes a "rational Calvinist," and his anthropology a "secularized version of the Calvinistic doctrine of 'original sin'." See *The Career of Philosophy,* Columbia University Press, New York, 1962, Vol. I, Bk. III, Chap. 9.

God," or sovereign political power, which could restrain their passions and thus keep the peace.

Grotius had a very different idea about the state of nature.[36] For him it was a prepolitical but not a presocial state. Following the Stoic tradition of natural law, he defined man as "an animal of a superior kind," characterized by "an impelling desire for society" or social life. All law, including international law, of which Grotius was the chief advocate in the seventeenth century, was based on this sociableness. A disposition to do good to others, that is, sociableness, could be observed, Grotius thought, in children "even before their training has begun."[37] It is instructive to compare Grotius' opinion with what Bayle and La Bruyère had to say about children. The latter saw mostly the self-seeking motives, as Hobbes did. "One perceives only bad inclinations in children," Bayle wrote: among other things, pride, anger, jealousy, envy, and the desire of vengeance. Children, said La Bruyère, are "envious" and "self-seeking." "They wish not to be hurt, but they like hurting others: they are men already."[38]

Locke steered a course somewhere between Grotius and Hobbes. He was somewhat less sanguine than Grotius about the state of nature. "The corruption and viciousness of degenerate men" drove men to form civil societies for their mutual protection. Yet Locke did not for a moment equate the state of nature with the state of war, as he said "some men," that is, the Hobbists, had done. Man was social by nature, and rational and free. Quoting the judicious Hooker,[39] Locke affirmed "a natural inclination, whereby all men desire sociable life and fellowship." The real trouble with the state of nature was not, then, so much human nature, as it was the lack of any sort of judge of controversies

---

[36] Some of this talk about the state of nature, and of man in the state of nature, was stimulated by the overseas discoveries. Many, including Grotius, wrote books about the American Indian, endowing "the noble savage," a phrase invented by John Dryden in 1670, with all sorts of "natural" virtues, both social and moral.

[37] Hugo Grotius, *De Jure Belli ac Pacis* (1625), Prologomena, Sect. 5–8. The German jurist Samuel Pufendorf expounds the same view of the state of nature in his *De Jure Naturae et Gentium* (1672). Grotius, it should be noted, was an Arminian who did not believe in the extreme Calvinist view of original sin.

[38] Bayle wrote a lot about children. See on this Labrousse, *Pierre Bayle* (see note 11), pp. 77, 79; La Bruyère, *Caractères*, "De l'homme," no. 50.

[39] Richard Hooker, the great Elizabethan divine, is Locke's chief authority on the natural law tradition. He quotes *The Laws of Ecclesiastical Polity* (first four books, 1594) throughout the *Essay concerning Civil Government* (1690). Hooker engaged the Puritans in debate, not only about church government but also about the nature of man, upon which he believed the former should be based, and not only on the Bible, which was largely silent on the subject.

other than individuals pursuing their own objectives. To interpret and execute the law of nature fairly, and thus to protect their freedom and their property, men needed an "umpire," "a common established law and judicature."[40] Locke built his politics, it seems clear, on a relatively optimistic anthropology.

From science or "New Philosophy" came still another image of man's greatness. Actually, science inspired two new images, one of man in nature, another of man over nature. It was only natural that in a great age of science some men should have aspired to a science of human nature. But to achieve such a science in the seventeenth century meant, at least if one followed the Galilean model, to think of man as a machine; to reject the Cartesian dichotomy of mind and body, to explain human behavior (and human thought) in terms of "body," that is, in terms of mechanical rather than teleological or conative causes. This was the way taken by Hobbes who was a disciple of Galileo. Hobbes, extending the principles of Galilean mechanics to man himself, described men as bodies in motion, responding to external stimuli by attraction or repulsion, according to the ruling instinct of vitality or self-preservation. Thus, in the end Hobbes reduced behavior to physiology, ruling out free will. "I conceive," he wrote apropos of liberty and necessity, "that nothing taketh beginning from itself, but from the action of some other immediate agent without itself. . . . Voluntary actions have all of them necessary causes, and therefore are necessitated."[41] This was hardly a picture of human greatness, and it did not recommend itself to many people in the seventeenth century. It contrasted sharply with Descartes' view,[42] but also with Bacon's.

For Bacon—and most lovers of science—chose to emphasize man's power over nature, rather than his subjection to it. So also did Hobbes' mentor Galileo. When Galileo turned his attention to man, it was not to bind him to mechanical laws, but, in the manner of Renaissance humanism, to extol his godlike mind and "admirable inventions." But he went beyond the conventional Renaissance glorification of man in his praise especially of the scientific intellect, which he thought coincided with the divine mind in its ability to think mathematically. To

---

[40] For the quotations from Locke, see the *Essay concerning Civil Government,* sometimes called the *Second Treatise of Government,* Chap. IX, Sect. 15; Chap. III, Sect. 19; Chap. VII, Sect. 87; Chap. IX, Sect. 128.

[41] Hobbes, *Of Liberty and Necessity* (1654), in *English Works,* Sir William Molesworth (ed.), John Bohn, 1840, Vol. IV, p. 274. For Hobbes' anthropology, see his *Human Nature* (1650), and *Leviathan,* Pt. I.

[42] Descartes, however, thought of the human body, as well as animals, as a machine or automaton, governed by mechanico-materialistic principles.

Sagredo's plaint, in the *Dialogue on the Great World Systems,* against man's "vain presumption of knowing," Salviati (Galileo's mouthpiece) replies "that human wisdom understands some propositions as perfectly and is as absolutely certain thereof, as Nature herself; and such are the pure mathematical sciences, to wit, Geometry and Arithmetic." Though, obviously, divine wisdom far surpassed human wisdom in breadth and depth, in respect of such propositions at least "human understanding equals the Divine."[43] Thus, with respect to scientific knowledge Galileo put no limits to the human mind and foresaw steady progress in comprehending nature's laws.

Bacon's emphasis was more Promethean—and less mathematical, since mathematics was not Bacon's long suit. Like Descartes, Bacon put man both in and above nature. Man had both a rational and irrational soul. The latter, described as a "corporeal substance" and possessed in common with the brutes, could be the object of scientific study. The former, however, could not, since it was made in God's image and was therefore established "as the center of the world" for whose service nature had been created. This was, of course, the traditional Christian teaching, but Bacon improved on it. In his reading of the fable of Prometheus, Bacon explained that Prometheus signified Providence and that when Prometheus created man he bequeathed to him his own providential powers. In other words, man, like God, could act providentially in nature. With the additional gift of fire man could effect new operations and further immensely the mechanical arts and the sciences.[44] Bacon also believed that science had put into men's hands new tools—the art of scientific experiment and the new logic of induction—which could correct the obvious fallibility of his senses and intellect. It was Bacon's constant endeavor to remove cause for despair, and to raise men's hopes in their power, not merely to acquire new knowledge, but to put that knowledge to work for man's use. As previously noted,[45] Bacon was always talking about "human power," and by so doing diverted attention from the problems of the soul to the enlargement of the "Kingdom of Man" on earth.

After Bacon, praise of man along these Promethean lines became increasingly common, especially among the Virtuosi. "And, certainly, there is no truth so abstruse, nor so far elevated out of our reach, but

[43] Galileo, *Dialogue on the Great World Systems,* Giorgio de Santillana (ed.), University of Chicago Press, Chicago, 1953, p. 114.

[44] Sir Francis Bacon, *De Sapientia Veterum* (*Concerning the Wisdom of the Ancients,* 1609), XXVI, "Prometheus."

[45] See p. 58.

man's wit may raise engines to scale and conquer it": so wrote the scientist Henry Power in a typical statement. "The enlarged and elastical souls of the world" is how Power described the new men of experiment,[46] just as the poet Thomas Traherne spoke of the "new infinite man" who had discovered new capacities in himself with the enlargement of space. But the chief accomplishment of the Virtuosi was to combat the notion of man's degeneration by comparison with the ancients. In effect, what they all said was that modern men were equal to ancient men by nature, and that they surpassed them in certain areas by virtue of superior knowledge and skills. Both Power and Joseph Glanvill extolled the "modern hero" for inventions—gunpower and printing, decimals, logarithms, and analytical geometry, the telescope and microscope, and the like—unknown to the ancients. In Fontenelle's words, "nature uses a certain paste which is always the same" when it forms men, animals, and plants. Ergo, Plato, Demosthenes, and Homer were not made of finer clay than the philosophers, orators, and poets of today. By a like token, however, modern men were not more virtuous than the Greeks and Romans. In this belief Fontenelle reflected, better than most, what in the round the seventeenth century had come to think about man. The permanence of the forces of nature guaranteed the progress of knowledge, which, however, did not necessarily profit man, make him better, or add to his pleasure. Fontenelle combined the optimism of the Virtuoso, enthusiast of science, with the skepticism of the French moralists.[47] He also reflected the traditional, and still prevailing, view that human nature *per se* did not change, was not changing, and could not change.

[46] Henry Power, *Experimental Philosophy*, Johnson Reprint Corporation, New York, 1966, pp. 190–191.

[47] See especially on this combination of optimism and skepticism, the dialogue between Montaigne and Socrates in Fontenelle's *Dialogue des Morts* (1683).

The Mortal God

The seventeenth century was crucial for the development of "modern" political thought in the West. Out of the conflicts of the times arose radically new ways of considering the whole social and political question, and novel ideas such as sovereignty, the secular state, individual rights, and government as a rational construct. These ideas were integrally related to contemporary conceptions of the nature of man and the nature of nature, which we have already considered. However, they also reflected contemporary events: the religious wars consequent to the Reformation, the power struggle between the great nations, and between monarchs and monarchomachs, and, as James Harrington perceived, the new balance of property since the Reformation. These new political ideas may be conveniently discussed under three main heads: absolutism, which reached its apogee in Bourbon France; the protest against absolutism, carried farthest in England, but beginning to gain momentum also in France toward the end of the century; and, observable in all countries, but only in its infancy, the idea of politics as a science, or, more generally, of a social science.

But before pursuing these trends, all of them significant departures, we should note one very important carry-over from past modes of thinking. This was the assumption, cutting across parties and doctrines, that politics should be viewed *sub specie aeternitatis*, that is, that there were eternal ideas of politics, which, if not necessarily innate, were at least deducible by right reason. No doubt the idea of a political relativity was catching on more and more as opportunities to observe other countries, both inside and outside Europe, increased and stimulated the comparative study of constitutions and mores. Even Bishop Bossuet, staunch advocate of the divine right of kings, respected "in each people" that form of government, monarchy, republic, democracy, or whatever, which he said, custom had consecrated and experience found to be the best.[1] No doubt empiricism also, as notoriously in Locke, dictated a course of political action based largely on experience rather than "certain knowledge or demonstration." But the relativism and the empiricism had to make headway against the reigning rationalism that assumed, in the words of Hugo Grotius, "fundamental conceptions that are beyond question, so that no one can deny them without doing violence to himself." This was, of course, sheer Platonism, dressed up (in Grotius' case) in the language of contemporary rationalism and contemporary science. Grotius, like so many others in the seventeenth century, wanted clear and distinct ideas in politics and international law, as in mathematics and physics. That there was a range within which positive law could vary was taken for granted, as in Aristotle it was assumed that there are different forms of government, and that possibly one certain form was better suited to a particular people. But Grotius distinguished between the positive law, which he attributed to man's free will, and natural law, which was grounded in the order of things. The former, or elements thereof, he said, "often undergo change and are different in different places." The latter alone, therefore, was subject to systematic treatment. This, indeed, was the main purpose of the *De Jure Belli ac Pacis:* to treat "the natural and unchangeable philosophy of law," after having removed everything that had its origin in man's free will.[2] The *esprit géométrique,* or contemporary rage for mathematics, reinforced this same tendency, to find universal truths in politics, as in mathematics itself.

Harrington offers an interesting variation on this universalist theme in his combination of historical and rationalistic argument in his republican utopia, *Oceana* (1656), dedicated to Oliver Cromwell. Historical necessity, Harrington believed, as manifested chiefly in economic and social change, required new forms of government. Yet

---

[1] Bishop Bossuet, *Politique tirée de l'Ecriture sainte,* Bk. II, Propositions 6 and 12, and Conclusion. Bossuet began this work, never finished, while he was tutor to the dauphin, and added further chapters later. It was not published until 1709.

[2] Hugo Grotius, *De Jure Belli ac Pacis,* Prologomena, Sects. 30–31, 39.

despite the profound change he observed in this regard in England from the time of the early Tudors down to the Protectorate, Harrington contemplated the establishment of an "immortal" republic based on the eternal principles of reason. "A commonwealth rightly ordered, may for any internal causes be as immortal, or longlived as the world," he makes the Archon say in his harangue to the lords and patriots of his imaginary state. And again, commenting on Plutarch's story of Lycurgus, Harrington observes that the Spartan lawgiver, having completed his work, fell into deep thought "how he might render them [his laws], so far forth as in human providence, unalterable and immortal."[3] Grotius and Harrington were spokesmen for a still widely accepted view. Whether the appeal was to Scripture, reason, nature, or history, there continued to be widespread belief in ideal models and final solutions to political problems—a belief that persisted into the eighteenth century.

One of these models was absolutism. Absolutism, to take it first in its more general signification, was closely identified with the idea of sovereignty, which stressed the centralization of power, however initially derived, in one individual or assembly—as opposed to the division of powers among king, church, and feudality, as in medieval political theory. This idea was not only new but fundamental in seventeenth-century political thought, not only among royalists but also among advocates of other forms of government. The idea of sovereignty had had earlier formulations, of course, by the champions of Empire and Papacy in the Middle Ages, and, more recently, by the French *Politique* Jean Bodin, whose *Republic* (1576) was widely known and cited in the seventeenth century. But by the time Grotius wrote his great work on international law it was by way of becoming a general assumption, as had certainly not been the case during Bodin's lifetime. The *De Jure Belli ac Pacis* simply assumes the breakup of medieval Christendom into sovereign states, each headed by a sovereign power—hence the need for agreement on a law binding the relations between states. Grotius, in the manner of Bodin, defined sovereignty as "the supreme political power vested in him whose acts cannot be rendered void by any other human power." Spinoza, who favored democracy, likewise stressed sovereign power, whether its possessor was "one, or many, or

---

[3] James Harrington, *Oceana,* S. B. Liljegren (ed.), Carl Winters Universitäts-buchhandlung, Heidelberg, 1924, pp. 184, 207. Paradoxically, this spokesman for republicanism had remained personally loyal to King Charles I up to the time of the latter's execution.

the whole body politic."[4] Absolutism, in this sense of a sovereign authority in a society, was the answer to anarchy, so much feared by Europeans in an era of religious and civil wars. It also reflected the growing power of the state at the expense of the church during the Reformation, and in England during the Civil War period, of Parliament in its struggle with the crown. Parliamentarians like Henry Parker and William Prynne came close to asserting "the sovereign power of parliaments" (which was the title of a book by Prynne) to offset royal sovereignty.

In the seventeenth century, however, only the advocates of monarchy *jure divino,* and Thomas Hobbes, advocate of a *de facto* Leviathan state, pushed this idea to its farthest extreme. Hobbes' views, though they stirred up much thought and debate, were too unconventional to command a wide audience. The divine right of kings, on the other hand, became the reigning political philosophy on the continent, with France and French thinkers setting the pattern for the rest of Europe. Rubens celebrated its enhanced prestige in his many canvases of the ruling sovereigns of Europe. The painting reproduced here (Plate 8) shows the triumphal entry into Paris of Henry IV of Navarre, bright new star of the Bourbon dynasty in France. Divine right fared less well in England, though there, too, it had a certain vogue, during the Civil Wars, but especially in the 1680's when Sir Robert Filmer's *Patriarcha, or the Natural Power of Kings* was resurrected to defend the Restoration monarchy against attack by the Whigs. Filmer, along with King James I of England and Bishop Bossuet, was the chief expounder of the divine right theory in its modern form. Strictly speaking, the theory was not new. But it was now made to assert, not merely that kings ruled by God's grace[5] but that "kings were the authors and makers of the laws, and not the laws of the kings,"[6] that they alone had sovereign power, and could not give it away to others, and that they might not be resisted under any circumstances. Furthermore, the divine

---

[4] Grotius, *De Jure Belli ac Pacis,* Bk. I, Chap. III, Sect. 7; Spinoza, *Tractatus Theologico-Politicus* (1670), Chap. XVI. Both Grotius and Spinoza limited sovereignty, if it is possible to say that. In Grotius it is always understood that sovereignty is subject to natural and divine law. Spinoza, while emphasizing power, wanted a commonwealth based on reason and freedom of thought.

[5] In medieval theory, kings were also usually believed to rule by the combined right of election and inheritance.

[6] James I, *The True Law of Free Monarchies* (1598), in *The Political Works of James I,* C. H. McIlwain (ed.), Harvard University Press, Cambridge, 1918, p. 62. This book was written while James was still king of Scotland.

PLATE 8. *Triumphal Entry of Henry IV into Paris,* by Peter Paul Rubens.

right theory now emphasized the duties rather than the rights of individuals.

The arguments advanced to support "free monarchy," as James I called it, were a blend of the old and new. Appeal was made simultaneously to the Bible, natural law, and secular history. Of these, the first was certainly the most important. Bossuet's treatise on politics is significantly entitled *La Politique tirée de l'Ecriture sainte,* and James I and Filmer likewise repeatedly cited Biblical texts, chiefly from the Old Testament and *Romans* 13, as authority for absolute monarchy. The divine righters, despite their new notions about sovereignty, continued to think of politics as a branch of theology, as in the Middle Ages, and of political rules as made in heaven, not by man, and as therefore irrevocable. But Biblical politics was no longer clerical politics. Even Bishop Bossuet represented the king as free of clerical, and especially papal, interference in his domain, though the king must, of course, be a Christian and stamp out heresy.

The law of nature agreed with the law of God in making kings supreme. This was supposedly proved by the patriarchal argument, which all three theorists used, but which Filmer made central to his argument. "The king towards his people is rightly compared to a father of children," said James I. Filmer, however, not merely compared the family and the state, he made them identical. "This subordination of children [in families]," he wrote in *Patriarcha,* "is the fountain of all regal authority, by the ordination of God himself."[7] Adam was at one and the same time the first king and the first *paterfamilias.* He had absolute power from God over his household, which was then the only kingdom on earth, and an absolute ownership over all property. All present-day monarchs were descended from Adam. What Filmer was trying to say, in his roundabout way, was that society in general, and patriarchal society in particular, was natural to man; that there had never been a time when men had not lived in subjection, or had had any choice, or right of consent, as to the kind of government they wanted to live under. The patriarchal argument, as Peter Laslett has pointed out, reflected rather well the actual structure of European society at that time, built as it still was on the family in which the father or patriarch was all-powerful. But behind Filmer's argument was also a deep-seated conviction, shared by James I and Bossuet, that

---

[7] Sir Robert Filmer, *Patriarcha and Other Political Works,* Peter Laslett (ed.), Basil Blackwell, Oxford, 1949, p. 57. *Cf.* James I, *The True Law* (see note 6), p. 64. Filmer's book was probably written in the late 1630's or early 1640's, but was not published until 1680.

absolute monarchy constituted the only real alternative to anarchy. Any other form of government lacked the power or the sanctity to restrain men's evil passions. Democracies especially, resting as they did on consent, ended only in misery and tyranny, as history showed. "There is no tyranny to be compared to the tyranny of a multitude."[8] When Filmer said this, he was doubtless thinking of what might soon befall England as Parliament and king headed toward collision in the late 1630's and early 1640's.

Bishop Bossuet, on the other hand, wrote not so much to defend, as to glorify, absolute monarchy, for by the end of the seventeenth century the threat of rebellion had long since subsided in France, and "Louis le Grand" had achieved the pinnacle of his power and fame. The *Politics,* written by Bossuet to instruct the dauphin in his future prerogatives and duties, helped to put a high gloss on absolutism as it was actually practiced by the king. "Princes act then as ministers of God on earth"; "kings were made on the model of fathers"; "let authority cease in the kingdom, and everything will be in confusion"; "the royal authority is absolute": these and other asseverations only repeated what others had said earlier and often. When, however, Bossuet wrote that "kings are gods and participate in the divine independence," that "the whole state is in the prince. . . . What grandeur that a single man contains so much power!", he was joining in the apotheosis of the Sun King. Even so, he did not go so far as Louis XIV himself, or the artists in Louis' service, the Premier Peintre and the architects of Versailles. As a prince of the Church, Bossuet also constantly reminded the king (and the dauphin) of the strict accounting God would demand of him in the performance of his duties, and of the distinction between absolute and arbitrary government. The artists, on the other hand, Charles Le Brun in his famous series of "l'histoire du Roi" and the king's conquests at Versailles, and Hyacinthe Rigaud, the portrait painter, put the king, and not God, at the center of their conceptions. In Rigaud's celebrated portrait (1701; Plate 9), Louis stands alone in all his majesty, without visible reference to either God or man. And, at least so far as man was concerned, Louis did, in fact, put a great gulf between himself and the privileged orders, the Church and the aristocracy, which had once challenged the king's right to absolute power.

Ironically, Thomas Hobbes, the greatest of all seventeenth-century theorists of absolutism, was *persona non grata* at both the French and English courts (though he later made his peace with Charles II), and

[8] Filmer, *Patriarcha* (see note 7), p. 93.

PLATE 9. *Louis XIV*, by Hyacinthe Rigaud.

among the divine righters. Filmer tells us why. "I consent with him [Mr. Hobbes] about the rights of exercising government, but I cannot agree to his means of acquiring it."[9] It was, above all, the "liberal" element in Hobbes' political philosophy that they objected to, the deriving of government from consent by individuals with rights in nature, preeminently the right of life and self-protection. Filmer thought Hobbes' theory was full of contradictions, and probably he was right. Indeed, there is in Hobbes' contractual theory the germ of a later liberalism, which he himself would not have countenanced. The absolutism that Hobbes upheld was also objected to because there was no divine right in it, nor anything to say it could not be applied to any form of government, monarchy or otherwise. Hobbes based his argument for absolutism on the nature of man without reference to God, or any sort of transcendent order. His sovereign, called indifferently "one man as in a monarchy" or an "assembly of men," had no sanctity or mysterious aura about it such as had always infused divine right theory.

Nevertheless, Hobbes' intention was certainly not to stress individual rights, but rather the "rights of sovereigns by institution," and here he stood on common ground with the divine righters, as Filmer observed. Hobbes wanted to prevent anarchy, the evil effects of which he observed around him, and give men the security that he believed only sovereign authority could provide. To this end Hobbes annexed to his sovereign or "Mortal God" rights such as not even a James I or Filmer could imagine: in addition to power to preserve the peace, make laws, and settle controversies, the right to be the sole judge of what the truth was, of what constituted right and wrong action, good and evil, and the like. "It belongeth therefore to him that hath the sovereign power, to be judge, or constitute all judges of opinions and doctrines, as a thing necessary to peace; thereby to prevent discord and civil war."[10] Thus, Hobbes set aside natural law as traditionally understood, that is, as the unwritten moral law to which all man-made law must conform, and equated it effectively with human reason—or the reason of the sovereign. "A Law of Nature (*Lex Naturalis*)," he declared in *Leviathan* (1651), "is a precept, or general rule, found out by reason, by which a man is forbidden to do, that, which is destructive of his life, or taketh away the means of preserving the same." There might be a higher moral law, but only the sovereign, acting on behalf of the

---

[9] Filmer, *Observations concerning the Originall of Government,* in ibid., p. 239.
[10] Hobbes, *Leviathan,* Pt. 2, Chap. 18.

multitude of men, could say precisely what it was and make it operative. That was what Hobbes meant when he said that "it is by the sovereign power that it [natural law] is law."[11] Hobbes even made the divine law, or religion, rest on the sovereign's will. He did not, as some have said, have in his mind's eye a fully secular state. Two of four parts of *Leviathan* are devoted to "power ecclesiastical" and who should have it. But Hobbes did subordinate the church, as he subordinated everything else, to the state, thus making ecclesiastical power, which included belief, or the public expression of belief, dependent on the civil law. In this Erastianism,[12] as it came to be called, Hobbes was joined by others including his friend, the renowned lawyer and historian John Selden. Selden, an inveterate foe of clerical independence and a religious skeptic, went as far as it was possible to go on the Erastian road. "They are mad," he was reported as saying, "who say bishops are so *jure divino* that they must be continued. . . . All is as the state likes." "There's no such thing as spiritual jurisdiction; all is civil, the church's is the same as the lord mayor's." Was the church or scripture the judge of religion? "In truth neither, but the state," said Selden.[13] It followed, at least from Hobbes' premises, that the sovereign might not be removed for any reason. For to remove him would be, of course, to open the door to anarchy all over again. But removal would also be illegal and "unjust," since the grant or possession (by conquest) of sovereignty was irrevocable, incommunicable, and inseparable. The sovereign could not break the contract, agreed to by individuals in the state of nature, because he was not a party to it. The contractors had delivered over to him their right to govern themselves once and for all—for a good reason, so that the state of war that characterized the state of nature might be aborted. Clearly, Hobbes' sovereign was, indeed, a "Mortal God," more powerful (and more secular) by far than even Bossuet's Sun King who, though he ruled by divine right, must uphold, on pain of eternal damnation, religion and justice as decreed by a higher law.

[11] Ibid., Pt. 1, Chap. 14; Pt. 2, Chap. 26.

[12] Erastianism is derived from Erastus, a Swiss Zwinglian and medical doctor, who became, first, professor and, later, rector of the University of Heidelberg. Actually, Erastus was not a full-fledged Erastian, but since he said that all coercive power was vested in the state, his name was linked to those who, like Hobbes and Selden, vested all so-called spiritual as well as temporal authority in the state.

[13] John Selden, *Table Talk*, S. H. Reynolds (ed.), Clarendon Press, Oxford, 1892, pp. 26, 88, 162. *Table Talk*, not published until 1689, comprises Selden's reflections in later life on politics and religion.

While stressing the emergence of new absolutist theories in the seventeenth century, it is important to bear in mind what Filmer said in 1652, namely that the counter theory of government by consent (present as well as original consent) had become "an axiom of late," and now passed almost without contradiction.[14] In other words, along with absolutism, whether of the divine right or Hobbist variety, went protest against absolutism. This was, of course, especially the case in England, known as the land of revolution in the seventeenth century. There was also protest in the France of Louis XIV, as we shall see, but it was mild by comparison, and almost never rose to the level of a fully articulated theory, calling more for the reform of specific abuses within the framework of the existing monarchy. Nevertheless, there were some anticipations, in the last decades of the seventeenth century, of the more drastic criticism to come in the next century.

The English protest broke wide open during the Civil War period and the interregnum. Filmer's remark could have referred to the famous army debates of the late 1640's, and to the Leveller manifestos of John Lilburne and others, or to less radical works by champions of Parliament and the common law. The same year 1652 also saw the publication of Gerald Winstanley's communist utopia, *The Law of Freedom,* and Harrington's republican utopia, *Oceana,* came four years later. These are only a few choice samples of a vast literature dealing with fundamental issues of political and social philosophy, and nearly all of it protesting against any sort of absolutism. Spawned in the struggle between king, Parliament, and army, this literature drew heavily, for its ideas, on the Protestant Reformation and the natural law tradition.

The English protest, largely abortive in the short run (since it was followed by the Cromwellian dictatorship and Stuart Restoration), charted the course for modern liberalism. Despite the great variety of proposals that were put forward, some calling for mainly political reform, and others calling for far-reaching economic and social reform, there was general agreement that government should be by the consent of individuals; that individuals had fundamental rights; that, in short, all government, regardless of its form, was limited by nature. Even Harrington's parliament, endowed by him with sovereign power, might not contravene an agrarian law that restricted the annual income of a landowner to two thousand pounds per annum. Government *de jure,* as distinguished from government *de facto,* Harrington described as

[14] Filmer, *Observations upon Aristotle's Politics touching Forms of Government,* in op. cit. (see note 7), p. 226.

"the empire of laws, not of men." Lilburne the Leveller, who grew up among Protestant separatists, traced limits on government back to an original covenant or contract between government and people. In his version of the contract myth, which contrasts sharply with Hobbes' version, the people reserved certain rights or "natural liberties," which, in fact, could never be transferred to king or Parliament. Sustaining all this radical theorizing, it should be noted, was an optimistic anthropology, which again contrasts sharply with Hobbist or divine right ideas. Lilburne, though he believed in original sin, began more and more to speak of the difference between men and beasts, of the reason and liberty that were man's birthright, of the "glorious image that God made man in." Harrington, an incipient environmentalist, thought that bad government was what made man a sinner. "Give us good orders [laws], and they will make good men," he said.[15] Likewise, Winstanley the Digger discovered the root of all evil, of greed and covetousness, in private property. Abolish private property, and man's better nature—Winstanley called it reason and identified it with an immanent God—would then grow and bring freedom on earth.

Echoes of this Civil War liberalism, especially Leveller, can almost certainly be heard in Locke's *Two Treatises of Government* (first published in 1690). Drawing upon that, as upon other sources, Locke was able, later in the century, to state the classic case for liberalism[16] (it became classic in the eighteenth century) and against absolutism. He did so in opposition to Filmer, and in order to help his patron and friend, Lord Shaftesbury, in his fight to exclude James II from the throne of England. Locke began by trying to answer, one by one, the specific arguments of the *Patriarcha.* Soon, however, in the *Second Treatise,* he broadened his scope to lay down the universal principles of politics according to natural law, or reason.

The individual, not the family with its authoritative structure, was Locke's point of departure. This is not to say that Locke preached a radical individualism, or an atomic view of society corresponding to the atomic view, currently fashionable, of the universe. Yet he did clearly build political society on a basis that was radically different from that of divine right monarchy, which assumed the subjection of individuals

---

[15] Harrington, *Oceana* (see note 3), p. 56; John Lilburne, *The Charters of London* (1646), quoted in Perez Zagorin, *A History of Political Thought in the English Revolution,* Routledge & Kegan Paul, London, 1954, p. 13.

[16] Doubts have been raised about Locke's liberalism. It is true that he himself did not use the word, and that he gave his executive considerable legislative power. In calling Locke a liberal, I simply mean that he was opposed to tyranny and that he put individual rights under the protection of natural law.

to paternal rulers. While still an Oxford don, Locke had written in favor of "the largeness of the governor's power." At that time, soon after the Restoration, he feared the "beasts," who made up the majority of men, more than "those whom the Scripture calls Gods," that is, princes.[17] But later, when tyranny again threatened, Locke wrote, like the Levellers, mainly to safeguard individuals and individual rights. He did not defend these rights by reference primarily to history, but to nature. "In the beginning all the world was America." This statement in the *Second Treatise* comes in the middle of a passage to do with property and money. But it implied, more widely, that behind all organized political life was a "state of nature," in which each individual, born rational and free, was his own master, and had equal rights with other individuals. Government was not there in the beginning, as Filmer said. Government was created by a compact among individuals, and thereafter trusted by them (for government in Locke is a fiduciary power) to protect their rights, which included self-preservation and private property. Locke put increasing emphasis on the latter right. "The great and chief end therefore of men's uniting into commonwealths, and of putting themselves under government, is the preservation of their property"—as much property as they mixed their labor with.[18] Here, of course, Locke diverged sharply from the Levellers, who in economics reflected more lower middle-class interests, as well as the communists. His theory was not "capitalist" in the sense of egoist, as has sometimes been said. His individuals are pretty sociable even in the state of nature, and see the value of community and the state. All the same, Locke was in the main individual-oriented in his political thought, as in his philosophy in which, it will be remembered, his focus was on individual psychology and epistemology. In this respect, Locke was a true son of the Reformation, even of the radical Reformation, and of radical (though not the most radical, economically speaking) English political thought of the seventeenth century.

Locke's theory of religious toleration followed logically from his political theory, and may, indeed, be said to have been a corollary of it. The civil government, he argued in successive "letters" on the subject, might not interfere with the practice of religion save to preserve public order. Religion—here again Locke's individualism shows through—was the concern of the individual, of the "inward persuasion

---

[17] From a tract on the civil magistrate, quoted by Peter Laslett (ed.), *John Locke. Two Treatises of Government,* Cambridge University Press, Cambridge, 1960, p. 20.
[18] Locke, *Second Treatise,* Chap. 9, Sect. 124. See also Chap. 5, Sects. 27, 49.

of the mind," which could not and should not be coerced. Reflecting Protestant separatist views, Locke distinguished "exactly the business of civil government from that of religion," thus converting the state into a purely secular power without jurisdiction over the salvation of souls. Nor, thought Locke, should an individual be constrained by an established church, for one was not born a member of a church, but joined a church freely. It is illuminating to compare Locke's definition of a church as "a free and voluntary society" with Hobbes' definition. "I define a 'Church'," the Erastian Hobbes had said, "to be 'a company of men professing Christian religion, united in the person of one sovereign, at whose command they ought to assemble, and without whose authority they ought not to assemble'."[19] Nevertheless, Locke did not preach an absolute liberty in religion. Like England's Act of Toleration of 1689, for which his *Letter* published in the same year provided a philosophical basis, Locke outlawed those who paid allegiance to a foreign power (the Roman Catholics) and those who professed not to believe in God (atheists). "The taking away of God, though but even in thought, dissolves all," he said, including morals and the very bonds of society that depended on covenants and oaths.

As stated previously, protest against absolutism was also building in France. However, it was neither as far-reaching, nor as immediately successful, as the English protest before, during, and after the Glorious Revolution. Moreover, the French protest had no real unity, unless it was opposition to Louis XIV's policies. Mounting in the 1680's and 1690's, this opposition came alike from great ecclesiastics who wanted to free the Gallican Church from slavish dependence on the crown; from Protestant refugees, persecuted by both church and state, and fighting for their very existence in France; from aristocrats such as the Duc de Saint-Simon who wanted to restore the historic privileges of the *haute noblesse,* leveled down and humiliated by the king; from merchants and their champions who criticized the mercantilist system; and from bourgeois critics such as La Bruyère who impeached the whole society, but especially the upper echelons, not excluding the king himself. "There is an exchange, or reciprocity, of duties between a sovereign and his subjects," La Bruyère wrote in *Characters,* which was widely read; ". . . to add that he is absolute master of all his subjects' possessions, without discrimination, without argument or account rendered,

---

[19] Hobbes, *Leviathan,* Pt. 3, Chap. 39. *Cf.* Locke, *A Letter concerning Toleration* (1689; originally written in Latin while Locke was in exile in Holland), in *Works,* Ward, Locke, & Co., London, 1888, Vol. III, p. 7.

is the language of flattery."[20] Perhaps Bishop Fénelon, appointed tutor to the king's grandson but soon fallen from favor, came closest to formulating a general theory of protest. In *Télémaque,* a French classic written for the young Duke of Burgundy's entertainment and edification, Fénelon dreamed of an ideal society in which the people were all free and equal; in which there were no hampering restrictions on commerce as under Colbert, Louis XIV's comptroller general of finances; in which the nation was not addicted to luxury, waste, and wars of conquest; and the king's actions were subject to law. After forced retirement to his bishopric of Cambrai in 1697, Fénelon made more definite proposals, calling for, among other things, the establishment of provincial parliaments as well as a re-established *Etats Généraux* with new and enlarged powers over economics and foreign affairs. Fénelon was obviously and openly advocating a constitutional monarchy.

The Protestant refugees naturally reacted primarily to Louis XIV's repressive religious policy, which came to a head with the Revocation of the Edict of Nantes in 1685. The two most famous of these, Pierre Jurieu, pastor and professor of theology, and Pierre Bayle, were originally friends and academic colleagues, but soon fell out after emigrating to Holland. Jurieu was, in fact, responsible for Bayle's dismissal from his post as professor of philosophy and theology at the Ecole Illustre, Rotterdam's new municipal academy. Jurieu, despite his ultra-conservatism as a theologian, had very liberal political views, derived partly from England's revolution, which he admired greatly, partly from Grotius and his own Calvinist tradition. The antithesis of Bossuet, he preached, in *Lettres pastorales* (1686–1689), addressed to the French Huguenots "groaning under the Babylonian captivity," both popular sovereignty and rights anterior to the establishment of government. But this paladin of Protestant orthodoxy was less individualistic than Locke, advocating more the rights of groups and sects than of individuals. For instance, while demanding religious toleration for French Calvinists, Jurieu withheld it from those holding "false" views, whether Catholic or Protestant.

Bayle was just the reverse of Jurieu, rather conservative politically, but liberal on toleration. In this respect Bayle was more like Spinoza who, it will be recalled, championed sovereignty in the name of law and order, yet affirmed man's "natural right of free reason and judgment." Hobbes to the contrary, man could not abdicate this right

---

[20] La Bruyère, *Caractères,* "Du Souverain ou de la république" (no. 28).

even with his own consent. Spinoza, with the example of Holland in mind, justified toleration partly on practical grounds; compare, he said, the beneficial effects of toleration in the prosperous city of Amsterdam, with the baneful effects of persecution, as when the orthodox party tried to suppress the Remonstrants. But mainly Spinoza defended toleration—or more properly, freedom of thought and speech—in terms of his large vision of a rational and free society.

> No, the object of government is not to change men from rational beings into beasts or puppets, but to enable them to develop their minds and bodies in security, and to employ their reason unshackled. . . . In fact, the true aim of government is liberty. . . . Such freedom is absolutely necessary for progress in science and the liberal arts: for no man follows such pursuits to advantage unless his judgment be entirely free and unhampered.[21]

This was also Milton's vision, expressed years earlier in the *Areopagetica* (1644), which was written to protest censorship of the press by a presbyterian Parliament. Milton and Spinoza both had faith that truth was strong, that it would surely triumph, if set free to grapple with falsehood, that it might assume more shapes than one, particularly with regard to "things indifferent." Therefore, so Milton argued, it was both more prudent and more Christian, "that many be tolerated rather than all compelled."

Though less generally sanguine than Milton and Spinoza, Bayle carried toleration about as far as it could go in the seventeenth century. In *Compelle intrare* (1686–1687), his chief philosophical work on the subject, Bayle excoriated the intolerance of both Catholics and Protestants, demanding freedom of worship for Unitarians, Jews, and Moslems, excluding only atheists whom he regarded as a threat to public security.[22] An Augustinian in his conception of human nature, as we have seen, Bayle here attacked St. Augustine as the chief architect of the Christian theory of persecution. By way of rebuttal, Bayle em-

---

[21] Spinoza, *Tractatus Theologico-Politicus,* in *Chief Works,* R. Elwes (trans.), G. Bell (Bohn's Library), London, 1917, Vol. I, pp. 259, 261. This whole chapter deals with freedom of thought and speech.

[22] Bayle was ambivalent on atheism. In his book on the comet of 1680, Bayle argued that there was no necessary connection between religion and morals, that a society of moral atheists was possible. Yet in the *Compelle intrare* (full French title: *Commentaire philosophique sur ces paroles de Jésus-Christ, Contrain-les d'entrer*), he argued against toleration of atheists on the ground that disbelief in divine providence and fear of divine justice threatened the laws of the state.

phasized the limits of reason vis-à-vis metaphysical and religious truth, which, to his mind, precluded the making of any sort of absolute judgment. Bayle was also aware that the particular convictions that an individual held depended on the education he had received and the environment in which he was brought up. That being so, nobody, least of all the state, should presume to judge another man's conscience. Bayle also believed, with Spinoza, that a multiplicity of sects did not necessarily endanger the state, and that a forced unity, as in Louis XIV's France, could, in the end, only lead to bad faith, violence, and disillusionment with religion itself.

It remains to take note of one other movement in political thought, which cut across party lines, and which, though still groping and crude, became increasingly assertive in the course of the century. This was the movement, satirized a bit later in *Gulliver's Travels,* to assimilate politics to mathematics and natural science. Tongue in cheek, Swift has Gulliver comment on the ignorance of the Brobdingnagians, "they not having hitherto reduced politics into a science, as the more acute wits of Europe have done."[23] Among the seventeenth-century "wits" who tried to do just that were Hobbes, Sir William Petty, who coined the term "political arithmetic," and Locke, among Swift-Gulliver's own countrymen; and Grotius, Leibniz, and the Comte de Boulainvilliers on the continent. The political science of these and others varied considerably as to method and models. All, however, wanted to make government more rational, to ground it in rules and laws that could be shown to be "natural," and thus to free it from superstition and caprice. Their inspiration undoubtedly came in large part[24] from the science of the day, particularly from the exact sciences, but also to some extent from empirical medicine, as in the case of Locke.

Hobbes exemplifies this endeavor best. He actually claimed to have invented political science, the Greeks and Christian doctors having done nothing but dispute and determine political as well as philosophical questions "according to their own fancies." "Natural philosophy," Hobbes wrote, "is therefore but young; but civil philosophy yet much younger, as being no older . . . than my own book *De Cive.*"[25] His methodological model was mathematics, as he makes explicit in many

---

[23] Jonathan Swift, *Gulliver's Travels* (1726), Pt. II, Chap. 7.

[24] Of course, there was also the other natural law tradition, derived from the Stoics and the Roman jurists, which likewise stressed fixed and general laws.

[25] Hobbes, *De Corpore* (1655), published in English as *Concerning Body* (1656), Epistle Dedicatory.

places. Hobbes stumbled on Euclid's *Elements* in middle age, but it left on him an indelible impression. Geometry signified to Hobbes, as it signified to Descartes and to so many others in the seventeenth century, certainty of demonstration, proceeding step by step from the simplest to the most complex problems. Descartes did not try to carry this method over into politics, but Hobbes did. This method represented, in Hobbes' opinion, the only way to avoid building commonwealths on the sand. To do this, to try to apply mathematical reasoning to social and political phenomena, became fairly common after Hobbes. It was the basis for Sir William Petty's "political arithmetic," though Petty combined Baconian with mathematical reasoning. Petty took as his motto a passage from the *Book of Wisdom* where it was said that God had ordered all things by number, weight, and measure. By means of quantitative analysis, of population statistics, ownership of the land, trades, climate, and the like, Petty hoped to provide precise information for making policy decisions.[26] Mathematics was the basis also for Leibniz's many political and quasi-political projects. Leibniz, inventor of the infinitesimal calculus, probably had greater faith in mathematics than anyone else who lived in the seventeenth century. "Everything in the whole wide world proceeds mathematically," Leibniz said, and he employed mathematics, or the mathematical method, not only to establish the most general truths, for example, of jurisprudence and international law but also to solve everyday political problems, such as establishing procedures for the election of the king of Poland and uniting the Christian churches and Christian states in a general peace. All these combinatory projects were tied up with Leibniz's search for a "universal characteristic," which would reduce language to its simplest terms, which could then be represented by mathematical symbols. In this way, men of all nations would learn what they had in common, and be able to eliminate disputes. Fontenelle obviously only spoke the truth when he said, at just about the same time, that "the *esprit géométrique* spreads more than ever"; that "the order, clarity,

---

[26] Petty's *Political Arithmetic*, written against the decay of British trade, was published posthumously in 1690, but written in the 1670's. In a letter of 1687, Petty claimed to have applied algebra "to other than purely mathematical matters, viz: to policy by the name of political arithmetic, by reducing many terms of matter to terms of number, weight, and measure, in order to be handled mathematically." (*The Petty-Southwell Correspondence*, Marquis of Lansdowne (ed.), Constable and Co., London, 1928, p. 322). In these and other writings, Dutch as well as English (by William Graunt, Petty's friend; Sir Dudley and Roger North, John Collins, and others), are to be found the origins of the science of economics.

precision, and exactitude" that were characteristic of geometry were being communicated contemporaneously to other fields of knowledge, in politics, as in morals, criticism, and even eloquence.[27]

Hobbes, however, coupled mathematics with "body," and indeed a philosophy of body (or matter) lay at the heart of his political science. Politics, he thought, could conceivably be learned simply by experience, but he himself, using what he called the "synthetical method," saw an inseparable connection between physics, psychology, and politics. From Galileo and the physiologist William Harvey he learned that everything in creation consisted of bodies in motion, of mechanical cause and effect. The state, then, like nature, and like man, was a body, a political body, moved by the natural desires and endeavors, that is, the motions, of men. But it was a body more like a machine than an organism, as is made clear in the frontispiece to *Leviathan,* and especially in the introduction to that work. The frontispiece (Plate 10) portrays a giant, crown on head, whose body is composed of innumerable smaller bodies of men. This Leviathan, or commonwealth, is said to have a soul, joints, nerves, reason, will, and so on, just like any "body natural." But, in addition to this traditional sort of metaphor, Hobbes employed another more in keeping with the new mechanical science. The body politic, he said, is like an automaton or engine, moving itself by means of springs, strings (comparable to the nerves of the body), and wheels.

Hobbes also called the state "an artificial man," and this metaphor, perhaps more than any other strikes the truly modern note of his political science. That is, Hobbes thought of the state as a rational construct, made neither by God or history, but by man (though man could not avoid doing so, because of his imperative needs or "motions"). "There be two ways of erecting a body politic," Hobbes wrote in *De Corpore Politico* (1650); "one by arbitrary institution of many men assembled together, which is like a creation out of nothing by human wit; the other by compulsion, which is as it were a generation thereof out of natural force."[28] Locke, the liberal, shared this conception with Hobbes, the absolutist—to a degree, for Locke is somewhat ambiguous on this point. Locke derived political arrangements, not only from rational men agreeing together but also from the law of nature, between which and the human will he made a distinction. The law of nature,

---

[27] Fontenelle, *Préface sur l'utilité des mathématiques et de la physique,* in *Oeuvres diverses,* Gosse & Neaulme, La Haye, 1729, Vol. III, p. 6.

[28] Hobbes, *De Corpore Politico* (1650), Chap. I, Sect. 1. See also *Leviathan,* Introduction.

PLATE 10. *The Great Leviathan or State. Frontispiece to Leviathan by Thomas Hobbes* (1651).

to be sure, could be known only by "the light of nature," that is, a combination of man's sense impressions and reason. But it was there to be found, not made; God was its author. This was the traditional conception of natural law, which made modern sovereignty, or at least the idea of law as the sovereign's fiat, impossible. In my opinion, Locke comes closest to Hobbes' conception of "artificial man" on the empirical side of his politics where, as has been pointed out, his model may have been empirical medicine. In an often quoted, but very significant passage in his journal for 1681 Locke wrote:

> But whether this course in public or private affairs will succeed well, whether rhubarb or quinquina cure an ague, is only known by experience, and there is but probability grounded upon experience, or analogical reasoning, but no certain knowledge or demonstration [as contrasted with mathematical knowledge, which is "infallibly true"].[29]

That is, in the everyday workings of politics, neither God nor natural law could be of much help. Man had to learn about such things by experience, and could never hope to have the certain knowledge vouchsafed by mathematics. For Locke, then, politics was a human art, as Hobbes said it was, but it was more an empirical art.

---

[29] Locke, Journals, June 26, 1681, printed in *An Early Draft of Locke's Essay,* R. I. Aaron (ed.), Clarendon Press, Oxford, 1936, pp. 117–118. This passage is quoted by Laslett, op. cit. (see note 16), and by C. H. Driver, "John Locke," in F. J. C. Hearnshaw (ed.), *Social and Political Ideas of the Augustan Age.* To understand its full force, it should be compared with statements by Locke in his early essays on natural law (1660–1664).

Ancients and Moderns

As hinted earlier,[1] the seventeenth century witnessed a particularly important change in outlook regarding history. This is the last of the great questions to be considered in this section: how past, present, and future were regarded, and for what reasons. Older philosophies of history continued in strength throughout the century, as witness Bishop Bossuet's *Discours sur l'histoire universelle* (1679f.), written, like his *Politics,* for the instruction of France's heir to the throne, or the not dissimilar and many attempts made by Sir Isaac Newton to weave together the sacred and profane history of mankind since the Creation. Nevertheless, a new outlook was now obviously in the making, more secular, more critical of past epochs, more optimistic about present and future. This outlook, which adumbrated the idea of progress, would have been inconceivable without the scientific revolution. But it also owed much to contemporary Pyrrhonism, which questioned historical as well as metaphysical certainties, and to the religious revival, both Catholic and Protestant. It climaxed in the famous *Querelle* between the Ancients and Moderns, or, as Jonathan Swift called it, the Battle of the Books, during the closing decades of the century.

To reach the position taken by the Moderns, that is, to form and to formulate a conception of history that was in any sense developmental,

---

[1] See pp. 26–27.

it was necessary first to overcome two ideas of very ancient vintage. These were the ideas of historical degeneration or decay, and of historical cycles. Both enjoyed a renaissance in the sixteenth and early seventeenth centuries. "The opinion of the world's decay," wrote an English ecclesiastic in 1627, "is so generally received, not only among the vulgar, but of the learned, both divines and others, that the very commonness of it makes it current with many, without any further examination."[2] As we shall see, the Reverend Mr. Hakewill wrote, not to praise but to blame this "opinion," which he found full blown in a contemporary work by another ecclesiastic, Godfrey Goodman's *The Fall of Man, or the Corruption of Nature* (1616).[3] By that time the idea of degeneration had, indeed, become commonplace, expressing the pessimism of the early Reformation and the late Renaissance. Put quite simply, this idea postulated a Fall, involving the whole universe, from an original perfect state created by God to the decay of old age, and a possible final dissolution. The cause of the Fall was man, who by his sin brought death to nature as well as to himself. According to the melancholy Burton, who was, ironically, a critic of Goodman's particular brand of churchmanship, all God's creatures, the stars, heavens, elements, beasts, and the like, "once good in themselves," had changed for the worse, and become hostile to man.[4] And mankind itself had visibly decayed, in Hakewill's words, paraphrasing Goodman, "in regard of age and duration, of strength and stature, of arts and wits." This sort of primitivist bias flourished, however, not only in a certain kind of religious thought, chiefly Protestant, but also among those who looked up to the pagan Greeks and Romans as paragons. Thus, even Grotius, himself very much a "modern" in other respects, preferred "ancient" examples, Greek and Roman, to others, since, as he said, illustrations from history had greater weight in proportion as they were taken "from better times and better peoples."[5]

Hakewill put over against the idea of degeneration a cyclical theory of history, which was more hopeful, at least in the short run. This

[2] George Hakewill, *An Apologie of the Power and Providence of God in the Government of the World,* 3rd ed., London, 1635, p. 1. Hakewill was chaplain to Prince Charles, afterwards Charles I, for a time, but then fell into disgrace because of his antisacerdotal views and his opposition to Charles' projected Spanish marriage. *The Apology,* however, was an influential book.

[3] See p. 83.

[4] Robert Burton, *The Anatomy of Melancholy* (1621), Pt. I, Sect. 1, member 1, subsection 1. Burton, along with others, accused Goodman of popish practices.

[5] Grotius, *De Jure Belli ac Pacis,* Prologomena, Sect. 46.

theory, popular in the ancient world but submerged during the Middle Ages, had recently surfaced again in works by Machiavelli, Jean Bodin, and Le Roy, among others. "They are mistaken who think that the race of men always deteriorates," Bodin wrote in a pioneering work on historical method and philosophy of history. "By some eternal law of nature the path of change seems to go in a circle. Nature has countless treasures of knowledge which cannot be exhausted in any age."[6] Hakewill, who had been reading Bodin, expatiated on these ideas. His primary concern was to argue, against Goodman, the permanence of the forces of nature, in spite of original sin. How, in view of mankind's recent great achievements, could one possibly believe in the senescence of nature, even including human nature? Hakewill saw progress on all fronts since the Middle Ages, and also since ancient times in certain respects; in religion, now restored by the Reformation to its primitive brightness, and therefore also in morals, as well as in learning and the arts. And although it is true that Hakewill's main emphasis was not on science, he also made much of such modern inventions as printing, the compass, and gunpowder, and improvements, particularly in the arts of navigation and medicine. As he saw it, then, the present age was on the upswing, and Hakewill sounds almost Baconian as he expresses the hope that contemporary Europeans might do as well or better than their forebears. It was clearly wrong to think of contemporary Europeans as dwarfs standing on the shoulders of giants. "It is not so, neither are we dwarfs nor they giants, but we are all of one stature save that we are lifted up somewhat higher by their means."[7] This statement or its equivalent would be repeated many times over by Moderns throughout the century. It became, in fact, the core of the Modern argument.

Yet Hakewill's was no theory of linear progress. He reminded his readers repeatedly of the "wheeling about of all things" in history. Like the turning wheel that eventually brings all its spokes back to the same point, just so did all the cultures of the world flourish, fade, and then perhaps flourish again. Actually, Hakewill preached, in his own words, "a kind of circular progress." That is, civilization moved from one area or nation to another in different ages, so that while some members suffered, "yet the whole [was] in no way thereby endamaged

[6] Jean Bodin, *Methodus, ad Facilam Historiarum Cognitionem* (1566), Chap. VII, last paragraph (*cf.* translation by Beatrice Reynolds, Columbia University Press, New York, 1945, p. 302). I have inverted the order of the sentences quoted.
[7] Hakewill, op. cit. (see note 2), Preface, page b3ᵇ.

at any time." The Greeks succeeded the Persians, Egyptians, and Chaldeans as leaders in the arts and sciences, and were in time succeeded by the Romans and Arabs, and now by the northern Europeans, who were able to improve upon all of them. Bodin had said the same thing. But Hakewill, writing in the Christian apocalyptic tradition, also predicted a final consummation when the world would be destroyed by fire, and history cut off abruptly.

The Moderns, though appropriating some Bodinian arguments, worked out an essentially different—a much more progressivist—conception of history. There were, however, two separate strands of progressivist thinking in the seventeenth century, one predominantly religious and apocalyptic, and in evidence chiefly in England; the other predominantly secular, representative of Europe as a whole, and centering more on present achievements than on future prophecy. The former, we might say, was less modern since it turned on the interpretation of certain key Biblical texts, and had its roots in Christian providentialism. Providentialism, of course, was an old story, and in its medieval, Augustinian version told no tale of secular progress. St. Augustine, it is true, had attacked the cyclical theory, but had simultaneously attacked the millenarians of his time, who predicted a utopia on earth, following the binding of Satan and the second coming of Christ. In St. Augustine's view, there was spiritual meaning in history, and divine judgment in history, but no City of God in a temporal sense. The Augustinian conception lived on into the seventeenth century in such a work as Bossuet's *Discours* and also, rather surprisingly, in the mind of a skeptic such as Pierre Bayle, who in other respects treated history as a wholly naturalistic discipline. Bossuet sounds very much like St. Augustine when he warns against speaking of chance or fortune in history; these were nothing but names to cover human ignorance. "Remember, Monseigneur," he concluded, "that this long chain of particular causes which makes and unmakes empires depends on the secret orders of divine Providence."[8] Bayle certainly did not believe, as Bossuet sometimes appears to do, in God's intervention in particular historical events. But Bayle did clearly think of Providence as working for order in history. Providence was what made society possible in spite of human corruption and prevented individuals and states from ever becoming too powerful. Bayle once described Providence as "a restraining grace (*grâce réprimante*) which, like a strong dike, holds back the

---

[8] Bossuet, *Discours sur l'histoire universelle*, Pt. III, Chap. 8. "Monseigneur," of course, is the dauphin.

waters of sin as much as is necessary to prevent a general inundation."[9]

The new thing in seventeenth-century providentialism was that it came to be used more and more, especially by English Protestants, to support an updated millenarianism.[10] To do this required a different and more optimistic reading of the familiar prophetic passages in the Bible (Revelation 15–17 and 20:1–5; Daniel 12:2; II Peter 3), and this began to happen in England during the period 1624–1660, when hopes of "a general reforming," religious and educational as well as political and economic, ran high and anything seemed possible. By then, too, it was possible to think of the Reformation itself more optimistically, as being now firmly established and winning the battle against the Antichrist on earth. The most eloquent as well as the most learned exponents of this new providentialism were the Cambridge Platonists, beginning with their mentor, the great Biblical scholar Joseph Mede. Mede, breaking with the Augustinian (and Lutheran) tradition, confidently predicted the coming of an earthly millennium in his *Clavis Apocalyptica* (1627; English translation 1642 by order of Parliament). Indeed, the pouring out of the seven vials described in the Revelation of St. John signified to Mede that there had already been great progress in history, especially since the Reformation, intellectual as well as spiritual and moral. As an amateur of science, Mede developed some doubts about the final consummation of the universe, including the earth. Could the conflagration predicted by St. Peter refer, perhaps, to some sort of social revolution, in which the wicked would be put down once and for all? At any rate, for Mede, God's plan for history, spelled out in the prophetic books, dictated neither permanent degeneration nor cycles, but progress toward a new Eden. From Eden to Eden, with a long fall in between: such were the major periods of history denoted also by Mede's successors in the Platonist group, by Henry More the philosopher, and above all by Thomas Burnet, theologian, scholar, and Virtuoso. In his *Theory of the Earth* (1681–1689),[11] which purported to describe "the great turns of fate," "the hinges upon

---

[9] Quoted in Elizabeth Labrousse, *Pierre Bayle,* Martinus Nijhoff, La Haye, 1964, p. 463. Strictly speaking, Bayle was not an Augustinian in his conception of history since he also believed in historical cycles and thought he lived in an ascending cycle of history.

[10] See on this subject, Ernest Lee Tuveson, *Millennium and Utopia,* University of California Press, Berkeley, 1949.

[11] Like Mede's book, Burnet's *Theory* first appeared in Latin, but was later expanded in English editions. Burnet's orthodoxy was somewhat suspect, chiefly because of his attempt to reconcile Scripture with reason and the latest science. Tuveson calls Burnet "a catastrophic evolutionist" (ibid., p. 130).

which the Providence of this earth moves," Burnet did not wholly reject the degeneration theory. Created perfect by God, the earth, he believed, had degenerated after the Flood (partly but not wholly, one gathers, as the result of man's sin), and this degeneration, which affected both the natural and human worlds, had continued up to the present, with some "melioration" since the Reformation. But this fallen state would be succeeded at the appointed hour by, successively, "the burning of the world" and "the Apocalyptical Millennium," the latter to be ruled over by Christ. This new Eden would have for its setting a new heaven and earth, qualitatively superior in every way to the ruined earth after the Flood. And in this Eden would live a superior breed of men, capable of exercising the powers originally bestowed on man at the first creation, that is, of worshiping and contemplating the divine without stint, and of exercising the intellectual faculties fully in scientific study. All of these blessings would come about through what Burnet called "a system of Natural Providence." Natural Providence, expounded in the eleventh chapter of the second book, was Burnet's concession to the science of the day, which, as we have seen, stressed second or mechanical causes.[12] Thus, Burnet's philosophy of history, like Mede's, combined old and new elements. Providence still ruled the world, but it worked through the ordinary laws of nature and decreed a great leap forward of both physical and human nature.

Providentialism entered hardly at all into the *Querelle* between the Ancients and Moderns, which broke out almost simultaneously with the publication of Burnet's book. The *Querelle* did not, of course, begin in the seventeenth century. Its origins go back to Quattrocento Italy when humanists debated imitation of the ancients, and the degree to which they might equal, or even surpass them. But it was not until the seventeenth century that the battle lines were distinctly drawn—or could be drawn, since the Modern stance depended to a large extent on the development of modern science, and since "classicism" needed institutional embodiment, such as that provided by the new academies of Bourbon France,[13] to define and harden its doctrine. The reading of Charles Perrault's poem *Le Siècle de Louis le Grand* (1687) before the French Academy might be said to have precipitated open warfare between the two camps. This event was followed the next year by the

---

[12] See pp. 49–50.
[13] The *Académie française* (1635), founded by Cardinal Richelieu for the cultivation of the French language and literature, was the most famous. Others were the *Académie royale de peinture et de sculpture* (1648), and academies established for architecture, music, and the ballet.

publication of Fontenelle's short but suggestive "digression" defending
the Moderns, and by the first volume (three more were still to come)
of Perrault's massive "parallel" of the Ancients and Moderns, a systematic prose defense of the position established in his poem. An in-
dignant Boileau hastened to refute Perrault, notably in the *Réflexions
sur Longin* (1694), just as in England Sir William Temple, though
recently retired, took up his pen to answer Fontenelle and, incidentally,
also Burnet. Temple was in turn replied to by the learned William
Wotton, and defended by his own secretary and protégé, Jonathan
Swift. These were only the best-known warriors in the Battle of the
Books. Swift mentions others, including some philosophers as well as
literary men, mostly on the side of the Moderns, for he does say that
"the army of the ancients was much fewer in number." Incidentally,
Boileau appears on Swift's list as a Modern, by which was meant, however, only that Boileau was a distinguished contemporary writer. But
it is also true that in the end there was a partial reconciliation, ne-
gotiated by the philosopher Antoine Arnauld, between the two chief
French antagonists, Boileau and Perrault. This is apparent from
Boileau's *Lettre à Perrault* of 1701 in which he conceded superiority to
the Age of Louis XIV in certain areas, especially the scientific, while
continuing to give the palm to Roman antiquity in others. Neither side
won a clear-cut victory, as perhaps Swift meant to say by purposely
leaving his "manuscript" unfinished. "We cannot learn to which side
the victory fell," says the advertisement to *The Battle of the Books*
(published 1704, but written in 1697). Actually, the *Querelle* simply
petered out in the early eighteenth century after a final skirmish over
Homer. But out of it came a new view of history.

How did the seventeenth-century Ancients view history? It might
be said of them that they taught a version of the degeneration theory,
or sometimes a combination of degeneration and cycles. It would be
truer to say that they did not normally think historically at all, that in
a certain sense they even repudiated history. In this respect they were
not alone in the seventeenth century, as we have seen.[14] Like those who
found a sameness in human nature in all ages, or who aimed to establish
universal principles of law and politics, the Ancients sought, and
usually found, permanent canons of artistic taste and execution, good
for all times and places. Their range of interest was rather narrow.
They were not primarily interested in the sciences, that is, in natural
philosophy, but in art, language, and literature, and somewhat in

[14] See note, pp. 35, 39.

morals. Hence, change could be more easily viewed as simply lapse from a standard of perfection, or alternatively as an approximation to it, than as genuine movement toward something better, or different, and perhaps unique in history. Standards did not change though human taste unfortunately did. But there was really only good and bad taste, and rules were either right or wrong. The important thing, as La Bruyère pointed out, was not to try to keep up with changes of taste but to fix the "point of perfection." "There is in art a point of perfection as there is in nature a point of excellence or of maturity. . . . So there is good taste and bad taste, and we rightly argue about our tastes."[15] By this criterion not only individuals but whole epochs could be, and often were, judged according to their perception, or lack of perception, of "ideal Beauty," and by their ability to embody it in suitable works of art. Fréart de Chambray, for example, director of the newly founded royal academy of architecture, denounced the modern age, and especially modern libertines, for holding that "art is an infinite thing, growing everyday to more perfection, and suiting itself to the humor of the several ages and nations, who judge of it differently, and define what is agreeable, everyone according to his own mode" (*définissent le Beau chacune à sa mode*).[16] This was historical relativism, and the Ancients could not abide it. But how then did one distinguish between good and bad taste? By what means could one define the beautiful? By "reason," of course. "Love reason," Boileau pontificated; "let your writings always borrow from it both their lustre and their worth." "The arts," said Father Le Bossu, "have this in common with the sciences, that they are, like them, founded on reason."[17] But the reason meant, in these and many similar statements, was not individual reason, or the critical reason that overturns authority, but a faculty, common to all men, for perceiving beauty and the rules of beauty. Nevertheless, the general climate of seventeenth-century rationalism, even of the critical type, helped along this sort of antihistorical thinking by its search for universal principles on the mathematical model. Even Leibniz, for example, who was the most historical-minded of the rationalist philosophers, thought of history as the working-out in time of principles of perfection established a priori in the universe.

---

[15] La Bruyère, *Caractères*, "Des ouvrages de l'esprit" (no. 10).

[16] Fréart de Chambray, *A Parallel of Architecture both Ancient and Modern*, John Evelyn (trans.), J. P. (*sic.*), London, 1680, Preface, p. 2. This work originally appeared in French in 1650.

[17] Boileau, *L'Art poétique*, Chant I; R. P. Le Bossu, *Traité du Poëme Epique*, Michel Le Petit, Paris, 1675, p. 2. The latter work first appeared in 1671.

It was the Ancients' contention that antiquity first apprehended the "point of perfection" in the arts, and understood it best. Temple, who was a distinguished diplomat and much interested in Europe overseas, included among the ancients of antiquity those of the East as well as the West, the Chinese, Indians, and even Peruvians. But usually the ancients referred to were the Greeks and Romans, especially the latter. The modern Ancients, it should be noted, were by no means uncritical of the ancient ancients, nor did they counsel slavish imitation of them. However, as Perrault said, the Ancients did bend the knee to ancients, and look to them for counsel and guidance, and for rules and models. Aristotle and Horace had laid down the rules for the poetic art, according to Le Bossu, and the poems of Homer and Vergil were "by the consent of all the centuries," the most finished models ever to appear in their particular genre of writing. The frontispiece to the 1683 edition of Boileau's *L'Art poétique* shows the Muse pointing to busts of this same duo as to masters supreme. "In our writings [as in our architecture]," La Bruyère summarized, "we can only reach perfection and, if possible, surpass the ancients, by imitating them."[18]

Some attempts were made, mostly halfhearted and superficial, to explain the superior excellence of the ancients. Sir William Temple perhaps came closest to providing a real historical analysis.[19] Climate and soil had a lot to do with it, he thought, as did the long reign of peace in certain ancient empires, unknown in Europe since the barbarian invasions, and the freedom of thought and inquiry permitted in the Greek and Roman republics. By comparison, modern Europeans had allowed themselves to be embroiled in endless disputes, both ecclesiastical and civil, often leading to war, which was the eternal enemy of the Muses. Likewise, greed and avarice, though characteristic of individual men in all ages, had become general since the discoveries overseas, to the detriment of poetic inspiration and ethics.

Temple was clearly a degenerationist though his analysis did not absolutely rule out the possibility of a limited "recovery." His figure of a recovered consumptive epitomizes his view of how modern European and ancient civilizations compared. Let us suppose a strong man becomes consumptive at the age of thirty, and continues in a state of

[18] La Bruyère, *Caractères* (no. 15). For many other examples, see René Bray, *La formation de la doctrine classique en France*, Nizat, Paris, 1951, Pt. II, Chap. 6.

[19] It has been argued, with some justification, that Temple had a better historical sense than many of his contemporaries and understood well the relativity of cultures in history and in the world. This historical sense is particularly conspicuous in his essay *Of Heroic Virtue*.

extreme infirmity until age fifty; but then recovers his health up to age sixty. "It might perhaps truly be said in that case, that he had grown more in strength that last ten years than any others of his life; but not that he was grown to more strength and vigour than he had at thirty years old."[20] That was Temple's view in brief: the moderns had made some notable achievements during the last one hundred and fifty years, but, to change the metaphor, could not produce the same quality of oak, fig, or plane tree because nature had never since managed to concoct the same ideal mixture of seed, sun, and soil. Incidentally, Temple was perfectly capable of arguing simultaneously the sameness of human nature "in all times and places," so that perhaps, after all, he too was only trying to say that the ancients, through happy circumstance, had approximated best, to date, the "point of perfection." However that may be, it is not in doubt that in his main essay on the subject Temple compared the moderns unfavorably with the ancients all along the line: not only in language, literature, and the arts but in ethics (he particularly admired the ethical emphasis in ancient Confucian wisdom) and the sciences. Temple neither kept up with the sciences, nor, as a philosophical skeptic, thought them especially worth pursuing. Hence, we are not too surprised to hear him say that "there is nothing new in astronomy [or in physic] to vie with the ancients," or that none of the modern scientific academies could outshine or eclipse the Academy of Plato or the Lyceum of Aristotle.[21] Despite his undisputed open-mindedness in certain cultural areas,[22] Temple always remained temperamentally an Ancient who, to quote the concluding lines of his essay, loved best "old wood to burn, old wine to drink, old friends to converse with, and old books to read."

Others among the Ancient party were more evenhanded than Temple, not insisting on ancient superiority in the sciences and stressing more than he the possible recovery of the consumptive, especially in the arts. Fréart de Chambray, for example, who yielded nothing to Temple in his admiration of the ancients, especially the Greeks, and especially in architecture, wanted chiefly "to reestablish all the arts in that primitive splendor from whence this unworthy neglect [in the "many ages of ignorance," that is, the Middle Ages] has precipitated

[20] Sir William Temple, *An Essay upon the Ancient and Modern Learning* (1690), in *Five Miscellaneous Essays,* S. H. Monk (ed.), University of Michigan Press, Ann Arbor, 1963, p. 56.

[21] Ibid.

[22] For instance, in his political and historical analysis, and in his appreciation of Chinese gardens and Gothic poetry.

them."[23] Not surprisingly, Fréart believed this could be done in architecture only by returning to the rules of Vitruvius. La Bruyère, as we have seen, went one step farther and urged vying with the ancients in approximating perfection of form and thought. But to do so, one had to "imitate" them, that is, to follow the rules they discovered, as, for example, Racine did in the drama.

The Modern "thesis," or philosophy of history, was strikingly different. Perrault states this thesis succinctly in the preface to his *Parallèle des anciens et modernes,* which was the book, consisting of five dialogues, in which he took his case to the public. He meant every word of his poem read to the French Academy the year before, in which he said, "In a word I am convinced that if the ancients are excellent, as one can hardly deny, the moderns nevertheless yield to them in nothing, and even surpass them in a great many things. This is emphatically what I think and what I mean to prove in my dialogues." In the first dialogue Perrault has the Abbé, who speaks for him, repeat that he "esteems," but does not "adore" the ancients, and that he hopes young people will be taught henceforth that it is possible, not merely "to equal" but sometimes "to surpass" them, by avoiding the false steps they took. As in the poem, so in the longer prose work Perrault aimed to open people's eyes to the glories of the century of Louis XIV "to which Heaven has sent a thousand lights which it refused to all of antiquity."[24]

Perrault's thesis, which he recognized was not original with him, rested on two simple assumptions. The first was that nature had not degenerated, that, to the contrary, the forces of nature had remained the same throughout the ages. In Fontenelle's famous figure, it all came down to whether the trees of bygone days were larger and more beautiful than those of today. Clearly, they were not; ergo, moderns had brains equal to those of the ancients. "Nature uses a certain paste which is always the same. . . . Certainly, it has not formed Plato, Demosthenes, and Homer from a clay finer nor better prepared than our philosophers, orators, and poets of today." Perrault made this same point pictorially in a book, published a few years later, on France's illustrious men of the seventeenth century. The frontispiece (Plate 11) shows the Sun King, on horseback and raised high on a dais, surrounded by a host of great marshals, engineers, doctors of theology,

---

[23] Fréart de Chambray, op. cit. (see note 15), pp. 3–4.

[24] Charles Perrault, *Parallèle des anciens et des modernes en ce qui regarde les arts et les sciences,* reprinted with introductions by H. R. Jauss and M. Imdahl, Eidos Verlag, München, 1964, pp. 92, 94, 126 (in 1st and 2nd dialogues).

PLATE 11. *Louis XIV Surrounded by Illustrious Men of His Times.* Frontispiece to *Les Hommes Illustres* by Charles Perrault (1696).

scholars, painters, statesmen, jurists, writers, and scientists. Obviously, "Nature" had once again been prodigal in showering the earth, and particularly France, with a richness of talent, thus raising the arts and sciences to a new pinnacle of perfection ("*à leur dernière perfection*").[25]

Another simile, much used throughout the seventeenth century, will illustrate the second assumption. This was the simile of youth and old age. In the simile, as used by Fontenelle and Perrault, old age stood not for degeneracy or even arrested consumption but for superior experience and knowledge. An old man knew more than a young man, and, by a like token, the last ages of history knew more than the first. It was not only a matter of superior knowledge but of improved methods of thinking. As Fontenelle put it, it was necessary that mankind go astray for a long time, as young men normally do, that it make mistakes and profit by those mistakes, in order that finally it might learn how to reason correctly. "What is basic to philosophy and effects everything else, I mean the method of reasoning, has been greatly perfected in this century," he declared.[26] An "age of virility," in which men reasoned better than ever before, better than Plato, Aristotle, or Pythagoras had succeeded ages of infancy and youth.

This thesis and these two assumptions drew on many streams of thought, but primarily on the scientific revolution. It is not perhaps sufficiently understood that the scientific revolution was, among other things, a judgment on history. It fixed in people's minds the idea of invariable and dependable laws of nature, thus making degeneration seem less likely. But above all, it demanded a critical and even scornful attitude toward the intellectual achievements of the past, of antiquity as well as of medieval scholasticism. Aristotle, Galen, and the rest, for so long unquestioned "idols" in their respective fields of knowledge, had to be overturned before the new science could bear fruit. And they were, in fact, shown either to have been wrong in many instances, or else not to have done anything the least bit useful for mankind. In his book, significantly titled *Plus Ultra: Or, the Progress and Advancement of Knowledge since the Days of Aristotle* (1668), Joseph Glanvill reviewed their achievements, in field after field, only to conclude that "the way" most of these ancient "philosophers" took

[25] Fontenelle, *Digression sur les anciens et les modernes*, in *Oeuvres diverses,* Gosse and Neaulme, La Haye, 1728, Vol. II, p. 125. Charles Perrault, *Les hommes illustres qui ont paru en France pendant ce siècle,* Antoine Dezallier, Paris, 1696, Preface.

[26] Fontenelle, op. cit. (see note 25), Vol. II, pp. 128–130.

was not like to bring much advantage to knowledge, or any of the uses of human life; being for the most part that of notion and dispute, which still runs round in a labyrinth of talk, but advanceth nothing. And the unfruitfulness of those methods of science, which in so many centuries never brought the world so much practical, beneficial knowledge, as would help toward the cure of a cut finger, is a palpable argument, that they were fundamental mistakes, and that the way was not right.[27]

This was palpably a Baconian judgment. But Descartes, too, was essentially antihistorical in his attitude, regarding the philosophy he was taught in school as so much rubbish and needing to be replaced by clear, distinct, and useful ideas. It was better, he thought, to leave old political practices and customs alone, if only because men had got used to them. Philosophy, however, was quite another matter. Even if one must never tear down all the houses in a city in order to make the streets more beautiful, it did sometimes become necessary for individual owners to rebuild their own houses when they were in danger of collapse. Philosophy, like such houses, was built on insecure foundations, and this insecurity had spread to the other branches of learning.[28] The deduction from all this, from both Baconian and Cartesian science, was that the present knew better than the past, that there was simply no comparison between past and present as to correct thinking, or as to solid knowledge in chemistry, anatomy, mathematics, astronomy, optics, geography, and botany (all on Glanvill's list, plus reference to improved scientific instruments). It was this antihistorical judgment of the scientific and philosophic community that, more than anything else, gave the Moderns the courage to proclaim both equality and inequality (that is, in the sense of superiority) with the ancients.

Historical Pyrrhonism, which was widespread by the late seventeenth century, lent indirect support to this stance. How much did one really know about the ancients? Were the "facts" reported by the ancient historians reliable? Did they not mix in a lot of poetry with their history, and did they not, even a Titus Livy, relate "prodigies" (*prodiges ridicules*) as fantastic as the miraculous events reported in the annals of medieval monks? Pierre Bayle, who would have liked to turn history into a science, thought that history, including the history of antiq-

[27] Joseph Glanvill, *Plus Ultra*, Introduction. Glanvill, who was an Anglican clergyman, also wrote his book to refute charges of materialism and atheism against the Royal Society, of which he was a member.

[28] See on this, the concluding section of Part I, and the opening paragraphs of Part II, of Descartes' *Discourse on Method*.

uity, was a tale of follies as well as of crimes—of the follies committed by credulous or biased historians.[29]

But could history ever be a science? Perhaps Bayle himself was not entirely sure, despite the canons he laid down for a "truthful" historian.[30] In any case, the philosophers felt quite sure that history ranked lower in the scale of knowledge than philosophy or science. History could never yield anything more than opinion or probability since it depended on "common observation" or "particular testimonies," both of which were notoriously unreliable. "I would not be thought here to lessen the credit and use of history," Locke says in his *Essay*. "But"— he was skeptical all the same. The truth forced him to say that historical evidence was subject to such a great variety of contrary observations, tempers, circumstances, and designs, "that it is impossible to reduce to precise rules the various degrees wherein men give their assent."[31] The Cartesian philosopher Nicolas Malebranche called history a "false science," or "a science of memory," which, even if the facts it reported were more or less correct, fostered in its devotees the wrong attitude of mind. The reading of history encouraged memorizing rather than thinking, respect and submissiveness to "oracles" rather than doubt and criticism. Malebranche was particularly hard on those historians who wrote uncritically about ancient authors such as Aristotle and Plato. Reason will not permit us to think of them as infallible. To the contrary, reason wishes

> that we adjudge them more ignorant than the new philosophers, since in the times we live in, the world is older by two thousand years, and has more experience than in the times of Aristotle and Plato. Modern philosophers can know all the truths the ancients have left, and find still others.[32]

[29] See especially Chapter five, "De l'autorité des historiens," in Bayle's *Pensées sur la comète.* On historical Pyrrhonism in general, see Hazard, *La crise de la conscience européenne,* Vol. I, Pt. I, Chap. 2.

[30] For Bayle's strictures on history writing, see especially his *Dictionnaire historique et critique,* article "Remond," Remarque D.

[31] Locke, *An Essay concerning Human Understanding,* Bk. IV, Chap. XVI, Sects. 9–11.

[32] Nicolas Malebranche, *De la recherche de la vérité* (1674), in *Oeuvres complètes,* J. Vrin, Paris, 1962, Vol. I, p. 294. Chapters IV and V are especially pertinent to Malebranche's views on history and historians. As a convinced Catholic, Malebranche, of course, distinguished between ancient philosophy and ancient theology. "En matière de Theologie on doit aimer l'antiquité (the reference is to the Church Fathers), parce qu'on doit aimer la vérité, & que le vérité se trouve dans l'antiquité" (idem).

Was this a theory of progress? Yes, it was, but only in a limited sense. It is important to remember, first of all, that the Moderns still lived partly in the nonrelativistic world of the Ancients. They shared their belief in absolutes, which men should try to imitate, not discard. Perrault's Abbé believes, as much as Boileau or La Bruyère, in an ideal beauty. The moderns, he is made to say at the outset, as though to set the whole tone of the book, could conceivably come closer to "the idea of perfection" than the ancients, and, in fact, had done so with the palace of Versailles, which surpassed both Tivoli and Frascati in beautiful works. Although he was well aware of a "relative and particular" kind of beauty, and of significant oscillations in taste in, for example, architecture and oratory, the Abbé never tired of calling attention to the other and superior kind of beauty, which he described as "universal and absolute," hence pleasing "in all times and places, and to all sorts of persons."[33] And there were other things that did not change in the historical spectrum of the Moderns. Human nature did not change, nor basically did physical nature. If the Moderns did not believe in degeneration, neither did they have any inkling of an evolving nature that was productive of novelties. The Moderns lived in the static, even if "new" world described by contemporary science.[34]

What, then, did or could change and advance in history? As we have seen, the Moderns did develop a progressive conception of knowledge. But what kind of knowledge developed, and what about the progress of behavior, or morals? Here there was a split in the Modern camp. William Wotton, in answer to Temple, and having read both Fontenelle and Perrault, distinguished sharply between the arts and sciences, now separated, practically for the first time, in these debates. There had been progress in science (the natural sciences) and metaphysics; in the latter, too, because it depended on knowledge of the laws of the mind, and on superior logic, which owed so much to Bacon and Descartes. The point, often made before, was simply that the sciences needed a great deal of time to develop to perfection. On the other hand, Wotton argued the superiority of the ancients in eloquence and poetry, not because of their superior genius, but because they came first in time, because these arts developed more quickly, and because of special circumstances. The Greeks excelled in oratory, for example,

---

[33] Charles Perrault, *Parallèle des anciens et des modernes* (see note 23), pp. 103, 135, 192 (in 1st and 2nd dialogues).

[34] See p. 59.

because their type of political structure "obliged great numbers of ingenious men to take pains about it."[35] And perhaps Swift, though defending his patron against Wotton, meant to make the same distinction in his simile of the spider and the bee. Swift's bee, in *The Battle of the Books,* very unlike Bacon's bee in the *Novum Organum,* stands for the ancients who excel in poetic inspiration and language (signified by the bee's wings and "voice"). His brash opponent, the spider, on the other hand, is a builder who shows great skill in science and mathematics.[36] The bee predictably complains that the spider does not build with proper materials.

Perrault likewise separated the arts and sciences, and discussed them separately in the five dialogues of the *Parallèle.* But Perrault, unlike Wotton, saw progress in all the arts and sciences since antiquity. He understood very well the difficulty of convincing "opinionated" people of progress in any of the arts save those whose secrets can be "calculated and measured." To do so was to go against the tide of current opinion, and Perrault himself appears to back down, or at least to equivocate, halfway through. Maybe the Ancients were right after all, that at least, in "the things of taste and imagination," the ancients were the true masters. Maybe, even if only for the sake of peace, no decision should be made in this area as between ancients and moderns. Despite this apparent hesitation, I do not think Perrault meant to exclude any of the arts, not even poetry and eloquence, from his general rule of progress. He had as much as said so in the poem on *Le Siècle de Louis le Grand.* Now he spelled it all out in detail, notably in the third dialogue on eloquence. To the President's strong demur on poetry and eloquence (the President is the champion of antiquity), the Abbé replies that these arts required as many centuries to perfect as physics and astronomy. The reason is because they depend on knowledge of the heart of man, which is a very deep subject, and one in which new discoveries are made every day. Just as anatomy had recently found in the heart, valves, conduits, and movements that were not known previously to exist, so in morals (*la Morale*) had been found recently "a thousand

---

[35] William Wotton, *Reflections upon Ancient and Modern Learning,* Chap. III. Wotton was a scholarly prodigy, expert in Celtic studies as well as Greek, Latin, and Hebrew. He was a Fellow of the Royal Society and held M. A. and B. D. degrees from Cambridge.

[36] Bacon's bee (*Novum Organum,* no. XCV) was a Modern, gathering materials in the new inductive way, in contrast to the spider who, like the scholastic philosophers, makes cobwebs "out of his own substance."

delicate sentiments," aversions, desires, and dislikes, which the ancients never knew anything about.[37] Such knowledge had made possible the richness of the modern drama, as well as of modern painting, which Perrault had discussed along similar lines in the previous dialogue. "Painting," said the Abbé, "is an art so vast that the duration of all the centuries has been necessary to discover all its secrets and mysteries."[38] For obvious reasons, then, ancient painting must be ranked below that of, for instance, Raphael, Titian, and especially Le Brun. Fontenelle's way of showing progress in the arts was somewhat different. He was one of those who, caught up in the scientific movement, preferred prose to poetry because it said things more concretely and precisely. Fontenelle did admire metaphysical poetry, which was useful, he thought, for presenting images of the order of the universe and for vivifying rational ideas. But this was not the kind of poetry the ancients, for example, Homer, wrote; the moderns were much better at it. Thus did Fontenelle argue in the *Refléxions sur la poésie* (1678). In the *Digression,* Fontenelle is more equivocal, choosing merely to separate the arts and sciences, to concede possible ancient superiority in the former, but to urge, his main point, modern superiority in the latter, which relied on "accurate reasoning," as developed recently by Descartes and others.

None of the Moderns said anything very definite about moral progress. This was clearly not their central "thesis," and some of them, conspicuously Fontenelle, did not believe in it at all. How they argued this point depended somewhat on how bound they were to Christianity. It has been noticed that the Moderns in France were recruited from the *"catholiques fervents"* of the Counter Reformation as well as from the *"esprits forts."*[39] Perrault was one of these Catholics, and perhaps that is why he makes his chief interlocutor in the *Parallèle* an Abbé. The Abbé, as a convinced Christian as well as a Modern, declares early his veneration for "the sacred books" as against "ancient profane authors." Perrault must have believed, then, in a progress in morals from ancient pagan to Christian times. But thereafter he drops the subject and devotes the rest of his big book to talking about what he was really interested in, that is, progress in the arts and sciences. No

---

[37] Perrault, *Parallèle des anciens et des modernes* (see note 23), pp. 186–187. See also pertinent remarks, pp. 98, 175, 445 (Prefaces to Vols. I and II, and conclusion at the end of the 5th dialogue).

[38] Ibid., p. 150.

[39] See Hubert Gillot, *La Querelle des anciens et des modernes en France* (Paris, 1914).

doubt, progress in knowledge, which included moral knowledge, might be supposed to lead eventually to some sort of progress in moral behavior. But Perrault does not say that anywhere, and Wotton, who makes the same point about the superiority of Christian "moral rules," confessed great fear "that in the arts of knavery and deceit, the present age may have refined upon the foregoing."[40] Fontenelle, who was an *esprit fort,* was skeptical even of the possibility of moral progress. His doctrine of the constancy of nature cut two ways. If it argued the equality of ancients and moderns in brain power, and hence a possible progress in knowledge, it also argued their equality in the commission of "follies." In the famous dialogue between Montaigne and Socrates in Fontenelle's *Dialogues des morts* (1683), Montaigne holds that the world has become ten times more foolish and corrupt than in ancient times. Not so, says Socrates, the ancients were pretty bad too. Things have not changed much in that respect. But, says Montaigne, "I should have thought the world was always in motion, that everything changed, and that centuries, like men, had their different characters"; that some ages were therefore more learned and civilized than others, some more virtuous, and others more wicked. Socrates agrees only with the first part of this asseveration.

> Men change their dress, but not the form of their bodies. Politeness, coarseness, knowledge or ignorance . . . ; all these are no more than the outside of mankind; and these indeed change. But the heart does not change, and the essence of man is in the heart. . . . Among the prodigious number of irrational men born in any span of a hundred years, Nature produces perhaps thirty or forty rational. . . . I leave you to judge if they are to be found anywhere or at any time in numbers sufficient to bring virtue and integrity into fashion. . . . Nature acts always with great regularity, but let us not judge how she acts.[41]

This view, based on an "Augustinian" view of human nature, was still quite common in the late seventeenth century.

On the whole, the Moderns were much more present- than future-minded. That is, they were mainly concerned to show how much and

---

[40] Wotton, *Reflections upon Ancient and Modern Learning,* Chap. II. But Wotton, like Perrault, was writing mainly about moral knowledge rather than moral behavior, and he actually believed that the ancients had laid down all the "rules" insofar as this could be done by "unassisted reason."

[41] Fontenelle, *Dialogues des morts,* in *Oeuvres diverses* (see note 25), Vol. I, p. 23.

what kind of progress had been made in and up to their own day. Unlike the millenarians (and unlike Tennyson!) they did not often dip into the future as far as eye could see. Fontenelle foresaw the progress of knowledge continuing since nature could be counted on always to produce the same quantity (not very many) of good minds to build on the good minds of the past. But Fontenelle's real advice to people was to live in the present. This counsel was chiefly directed at past-minded people such as Temple who preferred old books to read. Entirely too much time and effort was being spent on teaching the young to learn the classics of antiquity by rote, and to be overawed by them to the point of intellectual paralysis. But it was also a counsel against trying to read the future. In the *Dialogues des morts* Fontenelle expressly warns against "inquietude about the future." Joan, Queen of Naples, begs Anselm to give her at least one paltry prediction. He refuses and tells her astrology has always been a cheat. Alas, "people will never suffer themselves to be undeceived about the future. . . . They never concentrate simply upon being happy in the present moment. . . . As if the time still to come were differently made, than times past and present."[42] Perrault was similarly present-minded, as might be deduced from the title of his poem. He wanted primarily to glorify the age of Louis XIV. Anticipating Voltaire, he talks about happy ages of history (*"les regnes heureux des grands monarches"*), which come when great rulers like Louis XIV bring calm and peace, and make possible the leisure necessary to develop the arts and sciences to a high degree of perfection. The century we live in, Perrault says, has passed through phases of youth (up to the time of Cardinal Richelieu), adolescence (when the French Academy was founded), and virility (*"l'âge viril"*: how like Fontenelle this sounds), and even now might be going into old age, as perhaps could be inferred from certain contemporary changes in taste.[43] And there Perrault drops the subject, and lets us guess whether he construed old age as decline, or whether, like Fontenelle, he thought that, with respect at least to the sciences, there never would be an old age. This much at least was clear: the sun of the present was to be basked in and enjoyed, for the future was uncertain.

To recapitulate, the idea of degeneration still had some supporters at the end of the seventeenth century, chiefly among the Ancients. Nor had the idea of historical cycles been entirely given up, even by the

---

[42] Fontenelle, ibid., Vol. I, p. 48.
[43] Perrault, *Parallèle des anciens et des modernes* (see note 23), p. 114 (2nd dialogue).

Moderns. But a new idea of history was now definitely in the making, a view that put an entirely new light on what men collectively were able to achieve on earth—with or without the help of God. This was not yet a full-fledged idea of progress. It was really more a mood than an idea, historically optimistic, even to some extent melioristic.[44] The Moderns, brought up on Baconian and Cartesian ideas, caught the optimistic side of this mood in their "parallels" between ancient and modern knowledge, which exulted in present achievements. The millenarians, and Leibniz as well, caught, better than the Moderns, the melioristic side that anticipated a future that was superior even to the present, that included moral as well as intellectual progress. Attention has already been called to Leibniz's conception of an improving human nature and of the progress of "rational souls" toward "a moral world within the natural world," which Leibniz called the City of God.[45] Leibniz did not flatter himself that his age was prepared to accept his vision of an endlessly improving world. Within a hundred years, however, this futurism (though not necessarily Leibniz's particular kind of futurism) would have become almost a commonplace of European thought.

---

[44] See A. O. Lovejoy, *The Great Chain of Being,* Harper Torchbooks, New York, 1960, p. 261, for a useful distinction between optimism and meliorism.
[45] See p. 91.

PART III

The Eighteenth Century

Being and Becoming

The Proper Study of Mankind

Theism and Atheism

Systems of Nature

Liberty and Equality

The Philosophy of History

Being and Becoming

The note of becoming, already audible in seventeenth-century thought, grew more clamorous in the eighteenth century. Yet this note can be, and in the historiography of the period often has been, exaggerated out of all proportion. This exaggeration comes from focusing too narrowly on the Enlightenment, as though the Enlightenment constituted the only part of eighteenth-century thought worth mentioning; or else from overstating some features of Enlightenment thought itself —the assault on "systems," for instance, and the insistence on reform— at the expense of others. Before trying to assess the growth of becoming, it will be useful therefore to examine briefly the scope and nature of the Enlightenment,[1] as well as of certain other broad characterizations of eighteenth-century thought.

Was the eighteenth century an "age of enlightenment"? Immanuel Kant, as is well known, said it was, and so did the French *philosophes.* Kant also called it an "age of criticism," thus associating it, as many were later to do, especially after the French Revolution, with the destruction of time-honored principles. But in Kant's mind the constructive side was always uppermost, criticism being construed by him as a necessary first step toward enlightenment. By enlightenment Kant meant simply the free, public as well as private, use of reason, severely

---

[1] No attempt is made here to describe the Enlightenment, the literature of which is now vast, and the main features of which are too well known to repeat.

restricted hitherto by authority, and dogma. Kant was under no illusion that he yet lived in "an enlightened age," an age in which enlightened men were permitted everywhere to do their own thinking. Still, he believed great strides had been made in "the century of Frederick" (Frederick the Great of Prussia), who did not presume to censor men's thoughts, at least in matters of religion.[2] Denis Diderot, embattled coeditor of the most ambitious publishing venture of the century, the *Encyclopédie raisonné des sciences, des arts, et des métiers* (1751–1772), said much the same thing, but with more overt reference to change. For Diderot, the eighteenth century was "a philosophical age" in which thinking men, employing the laws of reason, found their rules, even in aesthetics, not in authoritative books of the past but in "nature." Like so many of the *philosophes,* Diderot was intoxicated with the "revolution" occurring in the minds of men, which he saw as sweeping all before it, and, in the end, making obsolete even the *Encyclopédie* itself.[3] The Enlightenment, then, as Ernst Troeltsch and many others were later to say, was the hinge on which the European nations turned from the Middle Ages to "modern" times, marking the passage from a supernaturalistic-mythical-authoritative to a naturalistic-scientific-individualistic type of thinking. On this interpretation the Enlightenment represented the major thrust of eighteenth-century thought. In passing, however, we may note, as modern scholarship has increasingly made clear, that the Enlightenment itself is something of a moving target, subtly different in different countries, and as between earlier and later phases; that it was at all times a complex movement, riven by frequent doubt, changes of mind, and internal divisions; and that it by no means exhausted all capital or seminal thinking in the eighteenth century. For instance, neoclassicism, though sometimes interwined with the Enlightenment, cannot be written off as a mere facet of Enlightenment thought. Nor can the German or French *Sturm und Drang,* nor romanticism, nor of course the *antiphilosophes,* who, while in retreat, still had the strength to counterattack and to persuade, as the French Revolution and its aftermath were to show.

Age of Reason and Age of Happiness (or the pursuit of happiness), also often used as broad labels, particularly the former, are open to the same objections. It is well to remember what the Scottish philosopher David Hume, alternately friend and foe of the Enlightenment,

---

[2] Immanuel Kant, "What is Enlightenment?" This famous essay was published in the *Berliner Monatschrift* in 1784, and has been translated a number of times.

[3] Denis Diderot, art. "Encyclopédie," *Encyclopédie ou Dictionnaire raisonné des sciences, des arts, et des métiers* (hereafter referred to as *Encyclopédie*).

said about reason and the passions in man's makeup—we return to this theme in the chapter on eighteenth-century anthropologies. "Reason," Hume said, "is, and ought to be the slave of the passions, and can never pretend to any other office than to serve and obey them."[4] The French *philosophes* also put limits on reason's cognitive power, differing considerably in this respect from the great rationalists of both the Middle Ages and the seventeenth century. As they saw it, reason, bound to sense experience, could not penetrate beyond the world of appearances. On the other hand, reason could read that world, the world of empirical nature, very well, deduce general laws therefrom, and thus hope to control better the course of human action. In the eighteenth century, rationalism became increasingly tied to empiricism, as Kant's summarizing (as well as innovating) *Critique of Pure Reason* (1781) makes clear.

"Age of happiness"? "Happiness," says a modern historian, was "the universal obsession of the age."[5] And, indeed, the literature of happiness was enormous, representing something new in the ethical outlook of countless people. Emphasizing the pursuit of "earthly happiness" as a conscious goal, and even "as a right supplanting the idea of duty," it signified a revolt against Christian asceticism and otherworldliness. But in the second half of the eighteenth century there was a revolt against happiness, or at least a stiffening of moral resolve, a rejection not only of rococo luxury but also of "philosophic" pleasure, a call for a return to simplicity, the homely virtues, and patriotic duty. This new morality not, to be sure, eclipsing the "old" is reflected in the Kantian revolution in ethics, with its categorical imperative to stern duty, by both Rousseau and Diderot, and in art by painters such as Jacques-Louis David and Jean-Baptiste Greuze. An attempt was made to institutionalize this morality in the Republic of Virtue during the French Revolution.

In a recent book, the art historian Kenneth Clark writes that Giambattista Piranesi "has a good claim to be reckoned the first great artist of romanticism."[6] Clark bases his claim on Piranesi's first series of etchings on imaginary prisons or *Carceri* in the 1740's, in which

---

[4] David Hume, *A Treatise of Human Nature*, Bk. II (*Of the Passions*), pt. III, Sect. III.

[5] Paul Hazard, *La Pensée européenne au XVIIIᵉ siècle* (Paris, 1946), Vol. I, Chap. II. The major book on this subject is by Robert Mauzi, *L'idée du bonheur dans la littérature et la pensée française au XVIIIᵉ siècle* (Paris, 1960).

[6] Kenneth Clark, *The Romantic Rebellion*, Harper & Row, New York, 1973, p. 46.

cyclopean architecture, fantastic staircases, and instruments of torture make their appearance. Piranesi also frequently infused the monuments of classical antiquity itself with dread and melancholy. Other historians, as Clark points out, have sought and found origins of romanticism at least as far back as the 1750's and 1760's. The point to be made here is not to settle on an exact date, which is in any case fruitless, but simply to remind ourselves that the eighteenth century was also an "age of romanticism." We defer dealing directly with this movement until we come to the nineteenth century, because it did not reach its apogee until then. But it is well to make the point now that romanticism also constituted a revolution in thought, as mighty in its way as the Enlightenment or the scientific revolution, and coloring deeply the thought of modern Europe and America.

Though very different, the "many eighteenth centuries" thus far reviewed had one thing in common. In one way or another they all connoted change from past standards, and in some instances an awareness of change as more than a passing phenomenon of human life and history. But, of course, there was continuity as well as change in eighteenth-century thinking, and this is what Carl Becker was trying to say in his controversial *Heavenly City of the Eighteenth Century Philosophers.* One does not have to agree with everything Becker said to take his main point, namely that the eighteenth century was "an age of faith as well as reason." Becker himself was concerned to show that the thought of the *philosophes* was, both in style and content, closer in certain respects to the Middle Ages than to the twentieth century. Mention is made of Becker here, however, not in order to make this particular point, which is somewhat dubious, but to emphasize (as in his way he himself emphasized without using the actual words) that there was still much "being" at the core of eighteenth-century thought, even in the thought of the most advanced philosophers and *philosophes;* that the "becoming," so immediately obvious, was still often referred to timeless standards, some of hoary vintage. Evidence in support of this thesis, of a becoming still mixed with being, is provided in the course of this and subsequent chapters. But lest it be given too much weight, it needs to be seen against the backdrop of important new developments in the classification and comparison of the arts and sciences, and of a rather profound reshuffling, of the perennial questions. To these subjects, interrelated and both involving change and becoming, we accordingly turn next.

In a youthful and perceptive essay, ostensibly about literature but in fact about learning in general, the future historian of the decline and fall of the Roman Empire commented on the fickleness of human taste in "studies." "All countries, all centuries," Edward Gibbon observed, "have seen some science the object of a preference often unjust, while other studies languish in a scorn as little reasonable." Thus, metaphysics and dialectic dominated thought following the death of Alexander the Great, politics and eloquence under the Roman Republic, and, successively, poetry, and grammar and jurisprudence under the early and later Empire. Coming down to his own day, Gibbon deplored the decline of letters ("Belles-Lettres," but including historical scholarship) which, as he thought, had set in with the famous dispute between the Ancients and Moderns. Physics and mathematics now sat on the throne. But perhaps, he added, "their fall [too] is not far off."[7] Currently, the French Encyclopedists, for whom Gibbon felt no affinity, had begun their mighty effort to report, reassess, and reorder the arts and sciences. And somewhat later Kant did likewise, and in the process ruminated on the changes that had recently occurred. Like Gibbon, Kant noted "the floating condition" of the sciences in his time, with some of them rising in public esteem as others fell off, whereas still others remained on a more or less even keel. These are only a few examples of the intense interest that was taken in the comparison of the arts and sciences all through the century. The opinions expressed, though varied and often conflicting, even as between the coeditors of the *Encyclopédie,* give us a key to what was happening centrally in eighteenth-century thought.

Certain trends stand out unmistakably. To begin with, the terminology itself was obviously in a state of considerable flux. "Philosophy" took on a new meaning in the *Encyclopédie;* "science" was defined more precisely; and finer distinctions were made among the different kinds of arts, namely liberal, mechanical, and "beaux." Attempts to unify the arts and sciences, or to keep them unified, were visibly breaking down. The *Encyclopédie* is again good evidence at this point. The editors, Diderot and Jean Le Rond d'Alembert, commenced their labors with high hopes of ordering and connecting all the parts of human knowledge. They soon gave up this "encyclopedic" enterprise, at least in the sense of laying out a system in the manner of the rationalist philosophers of the seventeenth century. Though they probably continued to assume a general order of the universe, they did not believe the human mind could know that order in anything like its entirety. In the preliminary discourse, D'Alembert speaks repeatedly of "the laby-

[7] Edward Gibbon, *Essaie sur l'étude de la littérature* (1761), Sect. II. Gibbon wrote this essay in French, which he had just previously learned while he was in Switzerland.

rinth" of nature, of "impenetrable mysteries," and therefore of "the limited quantity of certain knowledge." So, in the end, the editors of the *Encyclopédie* went about their work in a systematic spirit, but with no real hope of finding a complete system. They derived this distinction from the philosopher Condillac who in his *Traité des Systèmes* (1746) excoriated "the spirit of system," although not denying the possibility of having principles based on known phenomena. On this basis one could make cross references, as in a dictionary, generalize when the facts allowed, and even construct a tree of knowledge to gather the branches "under a single point of view." The Encyclopedists did, in fact, do the latter, following Sir Francis Bacon's scheme of subsuming everything under the three human faculties of memory, reason, and imagination. But they admitted frankly that this was only one way to do it; that what was known, or to be known, could be viewed from any number of vantage points. Said Diderot: "the real universe and the world of ideas have an infinite number of aspects by which they may be made comprehensible, and the number of possible 'systems of human knowledge' is as large as the number of these points of view." Likewise D'Alembert: "One can create as many different systems of human knowledge as there are world maps having different projections."[8] Both men had become rather extreme perspectivists, partly in consequence of their empiricism, which, especially in Diderot's case, emphasized discrete facts as the basis of all knowledge. In Diderot's case the difficulty of generalizing was compounded by his awareness that the facts were by no means yet all in and by his belief in nature's continual flux. Few philosophers of the eighteenth century were so radically perspectivist as these two, certainly not Condillac himself, nor the Wolffian rationalists in Germany, nor the English moralists, nor even the French materialists (save for Diderot). Christian Wolff, who dominated German philosophy for half a century, constructed an elaborate system of knowledge, noting differences, but also showing how all the parts hung together in a rigidly deductive sequence. But Wolff's system came relatively early[9] and looked back to the "universal science" that was so popular in the preceding century. The tide was definitely turning in the perspectivist direction indicated by the *Encyclopédie,* as can also be

[8] Diderot, op. cit. (see note 3); D'Alembert, *Encyclopédie,* Discours préliminaire, Pt. I. For the quotations in the text, here and elsewhere, I have used the English translation in the appropriate volumes of the Library of Liberal Arts, *Preliminary Discourse* and *Encyclopedia.*

[9] Wolff's *Preliminary Discourse on Philosophy in General,* which features division of the sciences, was written in 1728.

gauged by the distance between Wolff and Kant on this score. Kant, though he took all knowledge for his province, had more trouble than Wolff in binding the parts together. In fact, the "critical philosophy" of Kant found unity only in the human reason, which, though it is its nature to assume and seek unity, cannot actually cognize it in nature. Kant lived and thought in a borderland between subjectivity and objectivity.

As previously noted, the arts and sciences were also classified and ranked in new ways in the eighteenth century. Only vestiges of "theological dominance," as D'Alembert called it, remained. In the *Encyclopédie*'s tree of knowledge, theology, both natural and sacred, still appeared as a science, but in subordination to history and philosophy (these two corresponding, respectively, to the human faculties of memory and reason). Differing from Bacon in this instance, D'Alembert explained that "to separate Theology from Philosophy, would be to cut the offshoot from the trunk to which it is united by its very nature."[10] At least among the more radical *philosophes,* the tables had been completely turned. Theology, once queen of the sciences, had now become a mere subject, or else was dismissed as hardly worthy of notice. Generally speaking, theological premises continued to exercise a certain influence in some realms of thought, as, for example, in natural philosophy and ethics. Nevertheless, it seems clear that the process of secularization, well under way in the seventeenth century, was accelerating, and that more and more of the sciences were becoming autonomous, or very nearly so.

Philosophy was something else again. It both advanced and declined in prestige, depending on what kind of philosophy one was talking about. Kant noted a growing indifference to metaphysics. On the other hand, the Encyclopedists, as we have seen, hailed the century as a golden age of philosophy. "Philosophy," said D'Alembert, "constitutes the dominant taste of our century."[11] These views were not contradictory. Metaphysics certainly did suffer a setback, especially innatism (or innate ideas), to which both Kant and the French empiricists objected, as being out of touch with sense experience, and therefore "illusory." Though he was opposed to these "dogmatists," Kant nevertheless deplored the antimetaphysical trend, and tried to turn it around by rehabilitating metaphysics on a new critical basis. This was the essence of his "Copernican revolution" in philosophy. But philosophy,

[10] D'Alembert, Discours préliminaire, Pt. I (see note 8).
[11] D'Alembert, ibid., Pt. II.

as understood and praised by the Encyclopedists, usually connoted something quite different. In its most general signification, as, for example, in the encyclopedic tree, it simply meant the sum of knowledge that proceeded from human reason, which included metaphysics and theology, but also the whole "science of man" and "science of nature." Whenever it expressed their personal preference, it stood for empiricism as opposed to innatism. But it also had utilitarian and activist overtones, following Bacon's conception of knowledge,[12] which was greatly admired. Used in this sense, it reflected the down-to-earth and reformist concerns of many eighteenth-century, particularly French, intellectuals. D'Alembert praised Bacon's conception of philosophy as "the science of useful things," contributing to man's happiness. The true philosopher, said another contributor to the *Encyclopédie*, "cultivates not only the mind; his attention and his preoccupations extend further": to social intercourse, and the betterment of civil society, which he regards "as a divinity on earth."[13] Philosophy, in this new popular sense, embraced the active as well as the contemplative life.

Philosophy also frequently included natural philosophy, of course, and natural philosophy, as Kant observed, remained "in the most flourishing condition." The foundation of new scientific academies in other parts of Europe, the extraordinary glorification, first of Newton, and later of the Comte de Buffon, the excitement aroused by new hypotheses in "natural history," the revolution in chemistry, the amateur botanizing and biologizing: all testify not merely to natural philosophy's holding its own but to its having become, in Condorcet's phrase, "common"; that is, not limited to the few, but à la mode, to a degree unimagined even in the late seventeenth century. Several qualifications are to be noted, however. The first is that mathematics, as the most abstract of the sciences, lost some of its glitter, as Gibbon predicted it might. Yet this "revolution in the sciences," as Diderot called it, or decline of mathematics, can be exaggerated. Both Diderot and Buffon attacked mathematicians for reasoning without reference to the facts of nature, and indeed, as we shall see, were beginning, along with others, not to think of nature as primarily a mathematical machine. Kant, going against tradition in German philosophy since Leibniz and Wolff, put no faith in the mathematical ideal of certainty and tried to disentangle metaphysics from mathematics. On the other hand, D'Alembert, who was a mathematician, praised geometry as a creative and imaginative way of

---

[12] On Bacon's conception of knowledge, see pp. 31–32, 47–48.
[13] *Encyclopédie*, art. "Philosophe," probably by the grammarian Dumarsais.

thinking. More important, the *esprit géométrique* continued, to some extent, to serve as a model in the social sciences. With his new term "social mathematics" (*mathématique sociale*) the Marquis de Condorcet, also a mathematician and permanent secretary of the *Académie des Sciences,* tried to strike a balance between mathematics and the observation of social facts. Even such schemes as his, however, intended no subordination of politics, economics, and law to natural philosophy, and this is a second qualification to be noted. In the *Encyclopédie* the social sciences appear under the rubric of philosophy and ethics rather than the "science of nature." Here the editors again broke with Bacon. "We do not know why the celebrated author who serves as our guide . . . has placed nature before man in his system."[14] Thus, the empire of science, that is, natural science, dealing, as Bacon would say, with the corporeal world, was wide in the eighteenth century, but not so wide as to swallow up moral and political philosophy. It was intended, by some at least, that the latter should stand clear, not only of theology but also, though in lesser degree, of natural philosophy.

Nor did science lord it over art. The *Encyclopédie* distinguished between art and science, but not to the former's detriment. Both the mechanical and fine arts, though described as having practice and action as object, rather than speculative study, attained a new dignity. The editors, reviewing the historic division between the liberal and mechanical arts, concluded that the latter had been demeaned unduly. Here again, as in the popular definition of philosophy, the criterion was usefulness to society. The *Encyclopédie* included eleven volumes of *planches* or plates depicting the techniques of the trades and crafts of contemporary Europe—a sort of review of technology—on the eve of the Industrial Revolution (Plates 12 and 13). Following Bacon here, Diderot envisaged a society in which the mechanical arts, allied with science, would give power over nature for man's benefit. His was also a society that put a premium on work, of the hands as well as the mind. "Let us teach them [artisans; Diderot was himself the son of an artisan] to think better of themselves." There was an implied leveling principle in this statement, and D'Alembert likewise insisted on more equality of reputation between manual and mental workers. "Society ought not to degrade the hands by which it is served."[15] The fine arts, on the other hand, had pleasure for their principal object, were said to imitate

---

[14] D'Alembert, Discours préliminaire, Pt. I.
[15] Ibid. See also Diderot's famous article, published separately, on "Art" in the *Encyclopédie.*

"la belle Nature," and were made to depend on imagination rather than reason. No slight was intended, however, for the fine arts achieved a new independent status in the eighteenth century, not bound as before to the other arts.[16] There was also a trend to separate aesthetics from ethics, as Kant did when he identified a third faculty of the human mind, namely, the faculty of judgment, distinct from both cognition and volition.[17]

In the encyclopedic plan, history too was accorded a special place, issuing from "memory," just as the fine arts, as well as poetry and the drama, originated in "imagination." There was considerable difference of opinion, however, as to its reliability as knowledge. Early in the century Giambattista Vico, finally breaking free of Cartesian influence, claimed that his "new science" of history had far greater certainty than the sciences of nature. Only God could know the world of nature since he had made it. By a like token, man had made history and could therefore know it.

> Whoever reflects on this cannot but marvel that the philosophers should have bent all their energies to the study of the world of nature . . . ; and that they should have neglected the study of the world of nations or civil world, which, since men had made it, men could hope to know.[18]

But Vico was not much read in the eighteenth century, and in any case, few, even among historians, shared his conviction. Neither Voltaire nor D'Alembert, for example, thought that history could ever command the certainty of mathematics, or of physical objects revealed to the senses. All the same, history became a much talked about subject, "philosophy of history" (a new term) was born with Voltaire, and men began to think and write about history in new ways. Among other things, it was now thoroughly secularized, though not as much by Vico as by some others.

[16] P. O. Kristeller points out that separate articles on the Beaux Arts and on aesthetics now began to appear with some frequency in dictionaries and encyclopedias. See "The Modern System of the Arts," *Journal of the History of Ideas,* Vol. XII (1951), no. 4, and Vol. XIII (1952), no. I, Sect. VII.

[17] Kant thus went against the tradition of Lord Shaftesbury who coupled the sense of beauty with the moral sense. Others, Hume and Diderot, for example, also continued, though not on Shaftesbury's terms, to connect aesthetics and ethics.

[18] Giambattista Vico, *The New Science (Scienza nuova,* 1725), trans. by T. G. Bergin and M. H. Fisch, Cornell University Press, Ithaca, New York, Bk. I, Sect. III, Principles. no. 331.

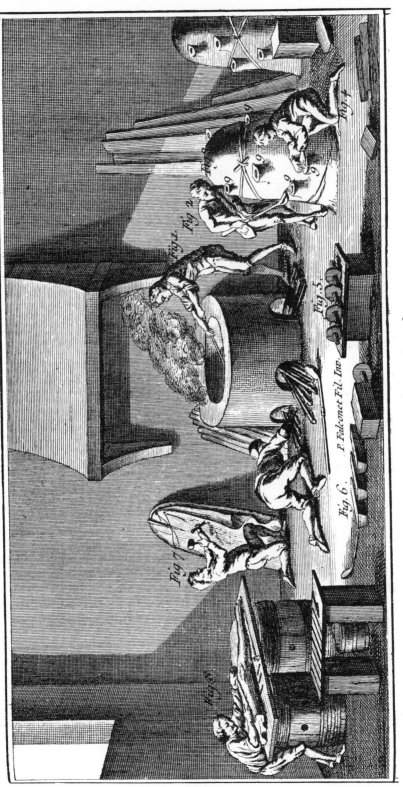

PLATE 12. *Casting Sculpture in Lead.* From the illustrative plates for the *Encyclopédie* edited by Diderot and d'Alembert.

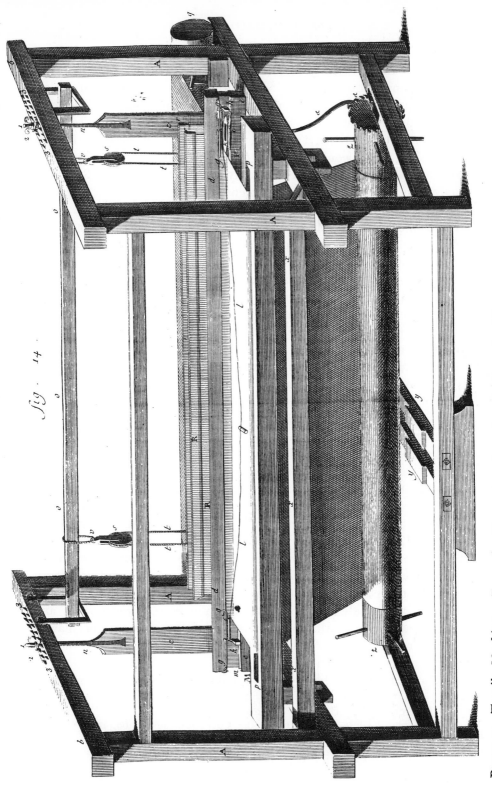

PLATE 13. *Textile Machinery.* From the illustrative plates for the *Encyclopédie* edited by Diderot and d'Alembert.

The perennial questions, or rather the relative importance attached to each of them, could not remain unaffected by these oscillations and comparisons among the arts and sciences. The question of nature, although hardly receding in importance, was not now quite so thought-provoking or disturbing as it was in the days of the Copernican and Newtonian revolutions. Theology, as we have seen, declined further in prestige. Yet it would be wrong to say that religious, including some theological, questions had become only of peripheral interest. Religious indifference is not a mark of eighteenth-century thought, though anti-religious animus is. Men engaged in endless debate, either to explain religion, or to explain it away. But precisely because the supernatural now seemed more dubious or remote, and the natural seemed more familiar and predictable, the question of man, and the related questions of human society and human history, became paramount, as in no previous century since the *quattrocento* in Italy. Typically, the editors of the *Encyclopédie* put man at the center of their enterprise. They started out by asking themselves if the various branches of knowledge could be gathered together "under a single point," and did not see how they could. Then they thought some more, and concluded, as in his way Vico also concluded, that whereas the plan of the universe must forever remain mysterious, man and the things men did were knowable. Diderot had another thought: suppose man were banished from the face of the earth; there would then be nobody to contemplate nature, and darkness and silence would resume their sway. "It is only the presence of men that makes the existence of other beings significant." And that is how —at least as Diderot explained it—they hit on the idea of organizing the *Encyclopédie* around man's principal faculties. "For man is the unique starting point, and the end to which everything must be related."[19] A caveat, however: this new anthropocentrism—different in certain respects from medieval and even Renaissance anthropocentrism[20] —did not mean that the *philosophes* and philosophers of the eighteenth century necessarily thought man a paragon, or perfectible. Diderot himself was acutely aware of the limits on man's cognitive powers, and many found him less than rational or moral. But man, whether flawed or not, man's nature, politics, and historical fate, did now become the center of intellectual inquiry.

Thus far we have been speaking mainly of change. But amidst all

[19] Diderot, art. "Encyclopédie," *Encyclopédie.*

[20] Different because, subsequent to the Copernican revolution, man was not thought to be at the physical center of the universe, nor was everything else created (necessarily) for man's benefit.

this change, were there no fixities—universally valid standards, norms, principles—by which to guide and judge this change? Indeed there were, though their presence is often overlooked or understated, and some of them dated back to the seventeenth century and beyond. In the résumé of his *Essay on Customs* (definitive edition, 1769), Voltaire spoke of "a small number of invariable principles," which give to history a certain unity. Sprinkled through the same work one encounters phrases like these: "Nature being everywhere the same"; "man, in general, has always been what he is"; "God has given us a principle of universal reason," and the like. Voltaire was thinking here primarily of the sameness of human nature throughout the ages, which was still a common assumption in the eighteenth century. But he thought pretty much the same way about morals and aesthetics, and about physical nature too, since he was a Newtonian. All this has to be understood, to be sure, in the context of what Voltaire called "the empire of custom," which he represented as vaster than that of "nature," lending great variety to the spectacle of the universe, just as nature gave it unity.[21] Thus, there was certainly tension in Voltaire's thought between, on the one hand, "invariable principles" that he found in nature, and, on the other hand, a relativism impressed upon him by observation of the changing human scene. The former, however, is the point I especially wish to make here. Voltaire, despite changing his mind often in a long lifetime, still lived partly in a static world of eternal laws, of perfect models, to be aspired to rather than surpassed, of timeless reason. And so did most of his contemporaries, the English deists, for example, the Physiocrats, even a man like Montesquieu, who was more aware even than Voltaire of the relativity of human customs. This awareness of an "empire of nature" did not mean these men were all conservatives wanting to keep things as they were, or to turn the clock back. It simply meant that, whatever their social and political persuasion, they thought things out, more often than not, in terms of what they understood to be changeless verities. One might call this the rationalistic, as opposed to the empiricist, strain in eighteenth-century thinking. But to call it thus would be slightly misleading, since Voltaire himself preferred Locke to Descartes, whereas others, more radical philosophically than he, for example, David Hume, discovered principles of regularity in the phenomena they observed. These principles often turned out to be identical with those that others called "invariable"—for example, in Hume's case, the sameness of human nature the world over. The

---

[21] Voltaire, *Essai sur les moeurs,* Chap. CXCVII.

truth is that they all, regardless of their philosophical persuasion, more or less fluctuated between the two poles of "nature" and "custom," and that is why one may speak of a mixed being and becoming in their thought.

The history of aesthetics illustrates this mixture admirably. It has been said that in the eighteenth century "the concept of general beauty [was] being discarded in favor of an individual standard," and that the term "taste," now used frequently, reflected this "basic shift."[22] Yet in the fine arts at least, neoclassical theory and style, emphasizing permanence and general truths, not merely persisted, but experienced a great revival, starting roughly at midcentury, extending into the revolutionary epoch, and influencing persons of all shades of political or philosophical opinion. Increasing awareness of variety of taste is not in question. "The great variety of Taste, as well as of opinion, which prevails in the world, is too obvious not to have fallen under every one's observation" is the way Hume commenced his essay "Of the Standard of Taste" (1757). It was common, even among confirmed neoclassicists such as Voltaire, to point out how differences in men's sense organs, education, or national experience, created divergent tastes, both individual and national. How could it have been otherwise in a century of empirical philosophy and of increasing travel and discovery? But the remarkable thing is not so much the observation of variety as the determination of so many to hang on to some sort of timeless beauty or consensus regarding beauty.

Neoclassical aesthetics expresses this timelessness best, of course. Treatises or discourses by Voltaire (1731–1733), Batteux (1746), Buffon (1753), Winckelmann (1755, 1764), Anton Raphael Mengs (1762), and Sir Joshua Reynolds (1769–1790), to mention only some of the best known, harped on the idea of a general or ideal beauty inherent in nature (*la belle Nature*), of a universal standard of "perfection" to be sought in all works of art, or even of an internal model of good and bad taste in the individual's own mind. The painter, Reynolds told the prize winners and members of the Royal Academy in London, should strive to cut through the variety of particular appearance to the timeless generality of nature's "central form." He

> must divest himself of all prejudices in favour of his age or country; he must disregard all local and temporary ornaments, and look only on those general habits which are every where and of every age; he

[22] René Wellek, *A History of Modern Criticism. The Later Eighteenth Century,* Yale University Press, New Haven, 1955, p. 24.

calls upon posterity to be his spectators, and says with Zeuxis, *in aeternitatem pingo.*[23]

Voltaire, too, believed in an "eternal" or perfect artistic form and taste. The taste of a nation could be corrupted, he said, in his article by that title for the *Encyclopédie*. Such a misfortune usually happened after a century, such as that of Louis XIV, "in which perfection was reached." Buffon is an especially interesting case in this connection. As a biologist he eagerly embraced change, preaching geological evolution, and even rejecting for a brief spell the idea of fixed species. But as an aesthetician and member of the French Academy, Buffon lined up with the neoclassicists, subjecting literary style to fixed rules and laws, universal and changeless.

Others such as Hume and Diderot spoke a more ambiguous language, yet in the end also came round to universal standards of aesthetics. Hume, opposing the neoclassicists, rudely dismissed all eternal and immutable ideas of taste "fixed by reasonings *a priori*." "Their foundation [he is talking about rules of composition] is the same with that of all the practical sciences, experience"—and experience, differing enormously among individuals, made for great variety of taste. Hume seems here to be advocating an aesthetic subjectivism, moving beauty back from the object itself to the individual mind and its perceptions. Yet he could not hold, he said, with another "species of philosophy" which cut off all hope of ever attaining any standard of taste. Hume went in search of a universal standard of taste and found it, not to be sure in *la belle Nature,* but in human nature, that is, in human approbation or blame, in models and principles "established by the uniform consent and experience of nations and ages."[24] It was not the same, Hume believed, with moral and aesthetic principles, as with speculative opinions. Whereas the latter were "in continual flux and revolution," the former achieved a certain stability, owing to the sameness of human nature.

Diderot's profile on taste is at least superficially like Hume's. Diderot too came to find uniformity in the midst of diversity, and eventually traced the former back to the subject from the object. But he differed

---

[23] Sir Joshua Reynolds, *Discourses on Art,* Huntington Library, San Marino, California, 1959, pp. 48–49. This was the third of fifteen discourses, delivered to the students of the Royal Academy on December 14, 1770, on the occasion of the distribution of prizes.

[24] Hume, "Of the Standard of Taste," *Essays Moral, Political, and Literary,* T. H. Green (ed.), Longmans, Green, London, 1898, Vol. I, pp. 274, 269.

from Hume in moving closer to neoclassicism. Even in an early article, written for the *Encyclopédie,* Diderot found a "real" as well as "relative beauty." Relative or perceived beauty meant diversity in men's judgments, which was caused by, among other things, prejudices, differences in values, and personal and environmental differences. But despite this diversity, Diderot wrote, "there is no reason at all to think that real beauty, which consists in the perception of relations, is a creation of fantasy." The facade of the Louvre, because of the wonderful arrangement of its parts, would be beautiful regardless of whether there were men to see it. But some years later Diderot put this "real beauty" back into the artist's mind. In the *Salon* of 1767 he spoke of an "ideal model of beauty, which exists nowhere except in the heads of artists like Agasias, Raphael, Poussin, etc." Diderot is not always very clear, but as Wellek suggests, he does seem here to be following Lord Shaftesbury, whose work he knew and admired, and for whom the sense of beauty was an innate sense, if not an innate idea. If so, this was sheer neo-Platonism, just as the earlier article on beauty also sounds somewhat Platonic—bizarrely mixed, of course, with Diderot's empiricism and, therefore, with a sense of the relativity of artistic judgment and taste.

In an early chapter of the *Decline and Fall* Gibbon turned aside from his main purpose to speak briefly of "the balance of power," intellectual and cultural, of the nations of Europe. Though by his time they had attained, in his opinion, "almost the same level of politeness and cultivation," the balance fluctuated, and would continue to fluctuate. Gibbon then went on to assert Europe's supremacy over the rest of the world. Fluctuations in Europe, he wrote, "cannot essentially injure our general state of happiness, the system of arts, and laws, and manners, which so advantageously distinguish, above the rest of mankind, the Europeans and their colonies."[25] The points Gibbon made deserve further comment, in conclusion.

By the middle of the eighteenth century there was no intellectual balance of power in Europe, as Gibbon knew perfectly well. France had long since become the preponderant power of the "European republic," providing the new *lingua franca,* as well as institutions and ideas to kindle new movements in both the worlds of thought and action. The reasons for this French hegemony are clear. In addition to being the most powerful, populous, and literate country in Europe, France was a nation in ferment, discontented with her *Ancien Régime,* and therefore

[25] Gibbon, *The Decline and Fall of the Roman Empire,* Chap. XXVIII.

thinking hard about how to change it for the better. Much of the impetus for French intellectual life, however, especially in the beginning, and especially in "philosophy" and politics, came from across the English Channel. Here we have Voltaire to comment, in his *Letters concerning the English Nation* (1733), as, it will be recalled, he commented in another work on the intellectual attainments of all the countries of Europe during the century of Louis XIV.[26] Knowing England well from his residence there during an early exile, Voltaire compared her favorably with Rome, and with France too in certain respects. Above all (for Voltaire, that is), England was a model of freedom, religious as well as political. England's science was superior to French science, as witness Bacon, father of experimental philosophy, Locke, who exorcized innate ideas, and the incomparable Newton who created a new universe. Voltaire also praised the English for honoring learning above all other nations and for encouraging the arts, not so much through institutions, in which the French excelled, as by the prestige they enjoyed among the people. "The portrait of the prime minister hangs above the fireplace in his office; but I have seen that of Mr. Pope [the poet, Alexander Pope] in twenty houses."[27]

Of the other European countries Germany clearly marked the greatest change since the seventeenth century. Italy and the United Provinces, though not ceasing to make important contributions, moved further toward the periphery of European intellectual life. Both Naples and Leiden continued to be distinguished universities. The Italians in particular did interesting, and sometimes seminal, work in fields as varied as bacteriology (Spallanzani), electro-chemistry (Volta), political economy and legal reform (Genovesi, Galliani, Beccaria), and philosophy of history (Vico), not to speak of the fine arts in which there were important changes of taste. Still, it scarcely seems credible to speak of an "Italian Renaissance in the Eighteenth Century," save possibly in a rather narrow political sense.[28] One can, however, justly speak of a German revival, which laid the foundations for Germany's intellectual leadership in the next century. Eighteenth-century Germany, of course, lacked a great national culture, and the culture she

[26] See pp. 41–44.
[27] Voltaire, *Lettres philosophiques* (as the *Letters concerning the English Nation* came to be called in the French edition), especially Chaps. VIII, XII–XV, XX and XXIII.
[28] See the essay by Alessandro P. d'Entrèves in *Art and Ideas in Eighteenth-Century Italy,* Italian Institute of London, Rome, 1960. The author is concerned principally with showing the preparation in the Italy of that century for the *Risorgimento* of the next century.

had was still derivative, in large degree, especially from France and England. But there were now important new stirrings, as Mme. de Staël was later to point out in her book on Germany. "Intellectual Germany is almost unknown to France," she reported in 1810; "very few French men of letters have troubled themselves about her." But they ought to do so, for Germany, more than any other country of Europe, might now be considered "the fatherland of thought," of study and meditation.[29] Mme. de Staël was thinking chiefly of the new romantic movement in which many Germans distinguished themselves. But she also wrote at length of the new German philosophy, the Idealism of Kant and others. Had she seen fit to draw up a full list of Germany's attainments she might also have mentioned Germany's "free" (that is, comparatively free of ecclesiastical dominance) universities, among them the new universities of Halle and Göttingen; Germany's own unique kind of *Aufklärung,* by no means a carbon copy of the French Enlightenment; the establishment at Berlin by Frederick the Great of a new Académie des Sciences et Belles-Lettres (1744), which soon rivaled in prestige older academies in Paris and London, but which contemplated a union of all parts of knowledge, including speculative philosophy; the *Sturm und Drang* of Goethe and Schiller at Weimar, more individualistic, but less political- and practical-minded than the French Enlightenment; and the Counter Enlightenment, as it is sometimes called, of Jacobi, Hamann, and Herder, which fed into romanticism.

Gibbon, it will be recalled, spoke not only of intellectual life inside Europe but of Europe's collective intellectual superiority to the rest of the world. In this latter opinion, however, he was not especially representative, or up-to-date. An avalanche of information about the world overseas, plus the spirit of reform, caused many of Gibbon's contemporaries to view Europe in a quite different light, as one of many civilizations, with many things to learn as well as teach. Voltaire, for example, wrote a new kind of universal history, very different from Bossuet's, in which chapters on the history of Western Christendom alternated with chapters on China, India, America, and so on. In particular, Voltaire set China up as a model for Europe and Europeans in morals, religion, government, and general deportment, if not in science. The Physiocrats likewise lauded China as an example of a great and perdurable agricultural society, protected, as was not the case in France, by a wise government. Not everybody felt about China as Voltaire and

[29] Mme. de Staël, *De l'Allemagne* (1810/1813), "Observations Générales."

the Physiocrat Dr. Quesnay did. But obviously many people had developed doubts about Europe's achievements to date, and consequently sought "Paradise beyond the horizon."[30] Gibbon notwithstanding, European narcissism was not generally characteristic of eighteenth-century thought.

[30] See on this subject, Henri Baudet, *Paradise on Earth. Some Thoughts on European Images of Non-European Man,* Yale University Press, New Haven, 1965, Chap. II.

The Proper Study
of Mankind

Know then thyself, presume not God to scan; The Proper study of Mankind is Man.

Alexander Pope's famous couplet, dating from the early 1730's, turned out to be prophetic. The question of man did, indeed, become "proper" in eighteenth-century thought—not only for "Augustan humanists" like Alexander Pope but also for the *philosophes* of both France and Germany, and for philosophers of the stature of Hume and Kant. To put it another way, anthropology, that is, the study of man, or of mankind, became the new queen of the sciences, displacing natural philosophy, which had been so all-absorbing in the seventeenth century, as well as theology, the old queen of Christian culture. Hume made this study the motif of his *A Treatise of Human Nature,* written only a few years after Pope's *An Essay on Man.* Human nature, Hume asserted, was "the capital or center" of the sciences; no question of importance could be decided without reference to it; the science of man constituted "the only solid foundation for the other sciences."[1] Even mathematics, natural philosophy, and natural religion depended on it,

[1] David Hume, *A Treatise of Human Nature* (1739), Introduction.

not to speak of logic, morals, criticism (sentiments), and politics. Kant agreed, although he stated the proposition in a different way. Kant reduced the field of philosophy to the following questions: What can I know? What ought I to do? What may I hope? What is man? But in reality, Kant said, "all these might be reckoned under anthropology, since the first three questions (answered, respectively, by metaphysics, morals, and religion) refer to the last."[2] Diderot similarly, as we have seen, put man at the center of the great *Encyclopédie.* How best to organize an encyclopedia encompassing all present knowledge? On what plan? Should one commence with the mind of God, and then "descend" to his creatures? But to proceed in that way would bind men of science too closely to the prevailing theology of a small corner of the world. Should one perhaps start with nature? But the book of nature was still far from complete, and in any case nature would be but "a vast solitude" without man to observe it. The conclusion appeared ineluctable: only the presence of man made the existence of other beings significant. "Why should we not [then] make him the center of all that is?" Man was obviously "the unique starting point" and "the end to which everything was related," without whom "the rest of nature" signified nothing. So the editors of the *Encyclopédie* decided to adopt Sir Francis Bacon's plan, seeking in man's faculties—memory, reason, and imagination—the main divisions for their great work.[3] The same decision, to put man at the center of thought, was made by many others, as is attested by the almost endless number of books on the subject in the eighteenth century.

Hume sought to explain this new anthropocentrism historically, as a sort of natural progression of the sciences, which history recorded as having happened more than once. The natural sciences developed first, to be followed about a hundred years later by "moral subjects." This had happened, for example, in ancient Greece in the interval between Thales and Socrates, and again in the nearly equal space of time between Lord Bacon and some later philosophers such as Locke and Shaftesbury, who put anthropology "on a new footing." Hume's observation is correct as far as it goes. There were, indeed, "philosophers" in his own day who aspired to apply the experimental method, developed earlier by Newtonian science, to the science of man, and to the other collateral sciences that Hume mentions. Others, however, studied man for precisely the opposite reason, because they distrusted

---

[2] Immanuel Kant, *Introduction to Logic* (published 1800), T. K. Abbott (trans.), Philosophical Library, New York, 1963, p. 15.
[3] Diderot, art. "Encyclopédie," *Encyclopédie.* See also pp. 47–48.

science, did not think there could be a "science of man," and consequently went out of their way to defend human nature against any suggestion of scientific reductionism. Pope himself was one of these. But the chief reason for the new anthropocentrism was an increasingly secular culture, intent on "happiness," and skeptical, following Locke, of metaphysical knowledge.

But what to think of man? Pope proposed "a general map" in his *Essay*, blocking out the greater parts, if not the particulars, which could be filled in later. "The science of human nature," he wrote, "is, like all other sciences, reduced to a few clear points."[4] But the points made by Pope, though representative of a certain group, usually called Augustan humanists, by no means commanded general assent, nor did any other single design. There was a running debate all through the century over certain key, and interlocking, questions. Was man *born* good, bad, or neutral? Was his nature fixed for all time, or was it changeable, and therefore conceivably improvable and even perfectible? If the latter, how was change effected?—from the inside or outside? The answer to this last question depended, of course, on whether the mind was thought to be active or passive, and on the will, whether man was thought to have free will or, on the contrary, to be entirely conditioned by experience and environment. How rational was man, and to what extent was he driven by passions and self-interest? Were all men equal, as to nature, or did one have to distinguish between an elite, specially endowed, and the general run of mankind, "the people"?

None of these questions was exactly new, but they were put now with a new urgency and in new ways, as men reflected on recent science, including Lockean sensationalism, and on the social problems of their age. The answers to these questions were, as always, mixed, and sometimes ambiguous or paradoxical. Yet the overall reputation of human nature did change, and change for the better. The old view of man's wretchedness died hard, as we shall see. But a new view did finally take shape, not so much of man's greatness, as of his capability to do the things that needed to be done to make the world better for the human race. Contemporaries took note of this change of view. The Marquis of Vauvenargues, himself by no means an optimist, wrote in 1746 that although diatribes against human nature were still the fashion (as in the days of La Rochefoucauld), there were signs pointing the other way. Perhaps, the Marquis thought, since nothing is permanent, man

---

[4] Alexander Pope, *An Essay on Man,* The Design.

was "on the point of rising again, and having his virtues restored to him."[5] Writing at the end of the century, Kant could look back and observe that this had indeed happened. There were people who still talked about "the radical evil in human nature." But recently a "more modern" belief had gained a following, chiefly among philosophers and educators, namely that the world was steadily getting better, and "that the predisposition to such a movement [was] discoverable in human nature." Kant himself did not entirely share this belief, which he attributed to Rousseau, but he perceived the possibility of taking a "middle ground" between these extremes, and holding that man as a species was "neither good nor bad," or else "partly good, partly bad."[6] Kant thus staked out three and possibly four major positions, all of which found spokesmen in eighteenth-century thought.

Pessimism about human nature persisted, to a perhaps surprising degree, in both old and new guises. Was Voltaire flogging a dead horse when he attacked the doctrine of original sin? He certainly did not think so, for he returned to the subject again and again, first in the letter on Pascal, tacked onto the *Lettres philosophiques,* and later in a succession of articles in the *Philosophical Dictionary.* Voltaire felt obliged to defend the human race against the "sublime misanthrope" (Pascal), to point out that no such doctrine was to be found in the Bible, that it was rather the brainchild of "a debauched and repentant African," namely St. Augustine. "People cry to us that human nature is essentially perverse, that man is born evil."[7] The "people" Voltaire had in mind were mainly the Jansenists who, despite living under the papal ban, continued to hammer away, in sermons, journals, and books, at man's inherent corruption, and to accuse their opponents, the Jesuits, of Pelagianism. *Manon Lescaut* (1731), the Abbé Prévost's immensely popular novel about a man destroyed by illicit passion, contains more than a hint of this Jansenist doctrine, which taught that God alone could restore man to moral health.[8] Meanwhile, in England the doctrine of original sin was revived in the evangelical movement. Al-

[5] Vauvenargues, *Réflexions et Maximes,* No. 219. Vauvenargues, befriended by Voltaire, was a moralist and writer of maxims in the tradition of La Rochefoucauld and La Bruyère.

[6] Kant, *Religion within the Limits of Reason Alone,* Theodore Greene and Hoyt Hudson (eds.), Harper Torchbooks, New York, 1960, pp. 15–16.

[7] Voltaire, *Lettres philosophiques,* no. 25 (not completed until 1742); *Dictionnaire philosophique,* arts. "Homme," "Méchant," "Péché originel."

[8] Ironically, Prévost was trained as a Jesuit, and might therefore have been expected to be more "Pelagian."

though disagreeing on predestination, John Wesley and George Whitefield agreed on man's fallen condition and his liability to eternal death without God's intervention.

It was not of Jansenists or Methodists, however, or of original sin, that David Hume was thinking when he criticized "those who have depreciated our species."[9] Very likely, he was thinking, above all, of Bernard de Mandeville, whose *The Fable of the Bees* (1714; enlarged edition 1723), many read, and usually denounced. But many others could have fitted Hume's description almost equally well. Dr. Samuel Johnson, for example, or Edward Gibbon among his English contemporaries, or, across the Channel, some of the French materialists, and even Rousseau himself in certain moods. As Lovejoy says, it is "a radical historical error" to hold, as Carl Becker did, that "the Philosophers" of the eighteenth century generally praised man to the skies, especially for his ability to follow reason and common sense."[10] On the contrary, it was still quite common in Hume's day, and not merely among a handful of "Augustinian" Christians, to describe human nature in the most unflattering terms; to picture man as moved, not by reason, but by the passions, called by Pope "Modes of Self-Love"; and as characterized by egoism and hedonism, by self-interest and self-esteem, and above all, by pride, which became the cardinal vice in some of the new secular moralities.

Not only "conservatives" talked this way. It is not especially surprising that Vauvenargues, a protégé of Voltaire, but more the follower of the French aphorists of the past century, should have had serious reservations about man's "greatness." He sounds very much like La Rochefoucauld when he avers, in his own book of maxims, that men are superior to savages only in being "a little less ignorant," that man's ruling traits are self-seeking and vanity, particularly in the present age of scientific advance. "Reason misleads us more often than nature." "Everything in the universe proceeds by violence. . . . This is the most general, absolute, unalterable, and ancient law of nature."[11] The Augustan humanists in England, also reflecting an older tradition, a blend of Augustinian and Renaissance wisdom, talked the same

---

[9] See Hume's essay "Of the Dignity or Meanness of Human Nature."

[10] Arthur O. Lovejoy, *Reflections on Human Nature,* Johns Hopkins University Press, Baltimore, 1961, p. 53.

[11] Vauvenargues, op. cit. (see note 5), nos. 123, 187, 356, 501, 502, 528. Vauvenargues also echoed Pascal, as in the following sort of statement, repeated several times: "The head does not understand the aims of the heart." (no. 124).

language. Jonathan Swift, whom we have already observed lampooning the "moderns," warned against probing too deeply into man's brain, heart, and spleen lest the scalpel expose all sorts of "flaws and imperfections of nature." Projecting this view onto a broader historical canvas, Edward Gibbon observed "the inevitable mixture of error and corruption," which attended the history of the Christian Church "among a weak and degenerate race of beings."[12]

Dr. Mandeville was also a conservative, not looking for reform of either human nature or society. But Mandeville created a scandal by stating his views in the most brutally frank and objectionable way, thus inviting attack by some of the most illustrious men of his age. He was even dragged into the law courts. Unlike Swift, who wanted to keep man's "anatomy" covered up, Mandeville, who was a physician, deliberately chose, as he put it, to lay back the smooth white skin so that men might examine "the little pipes" underneath, which is to say, "the nature of man abstract from art and education."[13] Mostly, Mandeville was attacked for appearing to defend vice, which, according to the famous paradox of *The Fable of the Bees,* brought about public benefits. But for our purposes here the more important point is Mandeville's realistic anthropology. Starting from Hobbist premises he attacked both rationalist and "benevolent" views of human nature, championed, respectively, by the Latitudinarians (and in general, by Stoics), and by Lord Shaftesbury. Man was neither rational, in the sense of being able to control his passions by reason, or virtuous—sociable by nature. "All untaught animals," Mandeville wrote, "are only solicitous of pleasing themselves; and naturally follow the bent of their own inclinations, without considering the good or harm that from their being pleased will accrue to others."[14] Hence, the only way to get man, "an extraordinary selfish and headstrong as well as cunning animal," to behave decently toward his kind, and thus make society possible, was to manipulate his passions, balancing his pride and ambition with other passions such as the desire for approbation, associating

---

[12] Swift, *A Tale of a Tub* (1704), Sect. IX, "A Digression concerning the original, the use, and improvement of madness in a commonwealth"; Gibbon, *Decline and Fall of the Roman Empire,* Chap. XV. On Swift on the "moderns", see p. 133.

[13] Bernard de Mandeville, *The Fable of the Bees,* Phillip Harth (ed.), Penguin Books, Bungay, Suffolk, England, 1970, p. 53 (Preface).

[14] Ibid., p. 81 ("An Enquiry into the Origin of Moral Virtue"). For his attack on Shaftesbury, see the essay entitled "A Search into the Nature of Society."

selfishness with shame, persuading him that it was in his own best interest to cooperate with others, and so on. Mandeville's altogether cynical view of human nature was reminiscent of that secular Augustinianism we took note of in the seventeenth century.[15] And, indeed, Mandeville refers several times to "fallen man" who, however, could, by his very vices, make a nation prosperous and great.

Mandeville had no disciples. But many people, by no means all conservatives, echoed his views or shared his overall estimate, at least in part. Disillusion may be too strong a word,[16] but there was certainly a disposition in some quarters not to expect too much of human nature. This was owing in part to the new cosmology, which made man seem less central in the total scheme of things, and more submerged in nature; in part also, to the current vogue of Lockean psychology, which put strict limits on the range of human knowledge. This disillusion, if such it may be called, is detectable, not only in Mandeville but in people as far apart in other respects as a "cosmic Tory" like Pope, the political reformers who devised constitutional checks and balances to curb man's fractiousness, and Rousseau. Pope's *An Essay on Man,* a textbook for many, did not go to Mandevillian lengths, but did, all the same, put man down as "reasoning but to err," and as animated, above all, by pride, yet "with too much weakness for the Stoic's pride." Hume himself could also on occasion describe man as guided, especially in religion, "not by reason . . . but by the adulation and fears of the most vulgar superstition."[17] Nor did Rousseau, as is sometimes said, glorify human nature in the raw, but, to the contrary, saw concealed in "the natural man" the seed of an *amour-propre* that would one day corrupt him almost beyond redress. This was not all that Rousseau said about man in the *Discourse on the Origin of Inequality among Men* (1755), but he did say it. To pride, he wrote, to our insatiable ambition and desire for reputation and advancement, we owe "a great many bad things, and a very few good ones," our virtues and our science, but also our vices.[18] There is obviously something left over in Rousseau of

---

[15] See pp. 83–84.

[16] Both Lovejoy (op. cit.; see note 10) and Lester Crocker speak of a new "disillusionment with mankind" in eighteenth-century thought. I owe much to both Lovejoy and Crocker in this and in subsequent paragraphs, but I think they exaggerate.

[17] Hume, *The Natural History of Religion,* Sect. VI, #6, "Origin of Theism from Polytheism."

[18] Rousseau, *The Social Contract and Discourses,* Everyman's Library, J. M. Dent, London, 1947, p. 217.

the Calvinistic doctrine of original sin Rousseau was reared on in Geneva, and of Hobbism too, though Rousseau dissociated himself from both Hobbes and Mandeville in the *Discourse*.

Thus, the Mandevillian or semi-Mandevillian image of man loomed rather large in eighteenth-century thought. Another image, however, rose to disturb men even more as the century progressed. This was the machine-man, projected by the materialists and determinists. Many saw some truth in it, but fought it in its extreme form because it appeared to degrade man utterly, to deprive him of all creativity and freedom, and hence to endanger ethics. This was not, of course, how Dr. La Mettrie, the chief proponent of the idea, saw it. Like Dr. Mandeville, Dr. La Mettrie fancied himself a realist, but, more importantly, he was a scientist genuinely interested in the possible connection between physiology and psychology, and in telling the truth as he saw it. "Let us then conclude boldly," he wrote in *L'Homme machine* (1748), his big book, "that man is a machine, and that there is in the whole universe only a single substance differently modified." La Mettrie was combatting Cartesian dualism, of course, denying that there was any sort of immaterial soul, making mind or soul dependent on body, on, for instance, food, disease, age, and climate. "The diverse states of the soul are always correlative with those of the body,"[19] which La Mettrie described as functioning automatically, by the force of irritability after first responding to stimuli. "From animals to man, the transition is not violent," he went on to say. That is, La Mettrie extended Descartes' idea of animal automatism to man, and found the difference between man and animal one of degree, not of kind. He also banished free will in the most brutal language:

> When I do good or evil; when I am virtuous in the morning, vicious in the evening, it is my blood that is the cause of it. . . . Nevertheless, I persist in believing I have made a choice; I congratulate myself on my liberty. . . . What fools we are! Fools all the more unhappy, for that we reproach ourselves ceaselessly for having done what it was not in our power to do![20]

[19] Julien Offray de La Mettrie, *L'Homme machine*, Aram Vartanian (ed.), Princeton University Press, Princeton, 1960, pp. 158, 197.

[20] La Mettrie, *Anti-Sénèque, ou Discours sur le bonheur*, in *Oeuvres philosophiques*, Berlin, 1775, Vol. II, p. 122. In this work, also published in 1748, La Mettrie developed the moral implications implicit in *L'Homme machine*.

The machine-man idea, inspired partly by current physiological theory, was very much in the air at that time, but was also very much resisted by Christians in general, by Wolffian rationalists, and by some of the *philosophes,* including even Diderot who strenuously objected to the complete mechanizing of human nature.[21]

The strength of the opposition to both Mandeville and La Mettrie is a reminder that the "depreciators of the species" by no means had it all their own way, even during the first half of the century. There were also the optimists and semioptimists who, as Kant observed, became more vocal as time went on, and who in hindsight appear to represent best the main new thrust in eighteenth-century thinking about man. In addition to the images thus far considered, the eighteenth century produced at least four other images, which, for the sake of analysis, we may call moral man, rational man, economic man, and perfectible man. Between these and the other images there was, of course, considerable overlapping. But all four images of man were quite optimistic, even if in different ways. All enjoyed a considerable vogue, though at somewhat different times and for different reasons. Although stemming partially from earlier notions, all, moreover, represented substantially fresh thinking on the subject.

Moral man was the creation of Lord Shaftesbury against whom, it will be recalled, Mandeville and the Augustan humanists directed their criticism. Shaftesbury, seeking to refute Hobbes, and much influenced by the Cambridge Platonists and also by Aristotle, discovered a moral sense in man, which enabled man to distinguish between good and evil and to seek social rather than merely private ends. Nature, of course, also compelled man to seek his own good, but self-love, as properly understood, harmonized perfectly with benevolence. Only contrary habit and education, inculcating as it were "a second nature," could uproot man's "original and pure nature."[22] This was Shaftesbury's answer to the doctrine of original sin, as well as to Hobbist egoism. Man was not innately evil but innately good, though he needed experience to develop from his moral sense a mature set of moral values.

Shaftesbury's optimism inspired a whole line of British moral philosophers from Francis Hutcheson to Hume and Adam Smith. Voltaire

[21] Diderot's barbs, however, were reserved mainly for Helvétius rather than La Mettrie. For his views, see especially his *Réfutation de l'homme d'Helvétius* (1773–1774), in which he refused to reduce the mind to sense impressions.

[22] Anthony Ashley, Earl of Shaftesbury, *Characteristics of Men, Manners, Opinions, Times* (1711). See especially the treatise entitled *An Inquiry concerning Virtue and Merit,* Pt. III, Sect. I.

also possibly owed something to Shaftesbury in his refutation of Pascal,[23] as did Diderot who translated Shaftesbury's *Inquiry concerning Virtue* into French. But it is arguable that the idea of moral man reached its peak later in the century when revulsion set in, above all in France, against the pleasure-seeking *Ancien Régime.* In art the latter was mirrored in the rococo, with its voluptuousness and freedom from any sort of social responsibility. Of François Boucher, named *Premier Peintre du Roi* in 1756 and master of the artificial and erotic, Diderot said: "This man has everything except truth." Against Boucher (Plate 14), Diderot the moralist pitted Jean-Baptiste Greuze of whom Diderot wrote in his *Salon* (art criticism) of 1765 that Greuze was the first "to conceive the notion of endowing art with moral content." Diderot was thinking of such homely (and to him, true-to-life) pictures as *The Ungrateful Son* and *Filial Piety.* This moral trend in painting reached its climax in Jacques-Louis David, who emphasized the stern Roman virtues, heroism and patriotism, as in his epoch-making "Oath of the Horatii" of 1785 (Plate 15). At about the same time Rousseau was appealing to "conscience," and Kant to man's sense of duty. None of these thinkers was so unqualifiedly optimistic about human nature as Shaftesbury. But they *were* saying in one way or another that man was born, if not good, at least with some instinct or faculty that made possible a virtuous and socially dedicated life. "Virtue!" said Rousseau, concluding his prize-winning essay (*Discourse on the Sciences and Arts,* 1749), "Are not your principles graven on every heart? Need we do more, to learn your laws, than examine ourselves and listen to the voice of conscience?" Of course, there was self-love too, but Rousseau learned to distinguish between *amour soi* (concern for self-preservation and approbation), with which "the original man" was endowed, and *amour-propre* (selfishness) into which man could all too easily degenerate in civil society. Kant too, though no soft optimist, thought man essentially a moral being who felt himself categorically bound and free if not always willing to obey the moral law. Moral man was the norm, the ideal to which it was possible to aspire.

Both Rousseau and Kant made morality ultimately dependent on reason. We turn next, therefore, to the image of rational man, somewhat tarnished, as previously noted,[24] by comparison with the lofty views of the seventeenth-century rationalists. Most eighteenth-century

[23] Voltaire admired Shaftesbury, and believed, at least at the time he wrote the *Lettres philosophiques,* in an innate feeling of benevolence. Later in life Voltaire appears to have mostly rejected this moral optimism.

[24] See p. 89f.

PLATE 14. *Autumn*, by François Boucher.

Musée du Louvre, Paris. (Cliché des Musées Nationaux.)

PLATE 15. *Oath of the Horatii*, by Jacques-Louis David.

thinkers did recognize definite limits to man's cognitive powers, did call attention to his passionate nature, did also fear "the people," that is, the lower classes, as ferocious and irrational, and as probably beyond hope of enlightenment. "The people," said Voltaire, "is between man and beast"; "the *canaille* will always be a hundred to one."[25] But to say that reason could not have transcendent knowledge did not rule out knowledge of the laws of nature, or the ability to apply that knowledge to the benefit of the human race. Likewise, to say that the passions were powerful was not necessarily to denigrate either them or reason, or to exclude the latter from playing a key role in moral life. This is the other side of the coin, which needs re-emphasizing just now in view of contrary emphases in recent historiography.

The English deists went far in their defense of rational man. Having taken up the cudgels against revelation, they naturally wanted to stress reason in religion, which meant asserting the sufficiency of the human understanding, both to apprehend religious truth and to direct the moral life. "We live under no necessary fate of sinning," said John Toland. "There is no defect in our understandings but those of our own creation." According to Matthew Tindal, God made man to be happy, and man "being a rational agent" was happiest when he ruled his life by "the rules of right reason."[26] Reason was man's great weapon in the battle for enlightenment against religious authority and superstition. Kant similarly called for freedom from authority, especially religious, in order that men might think for themselves and thus hasten enlightenment. There was "no lack of reason" among men, only lack of courage—and freedom—to use it. This was, in fact, a general assumption of the eighteenth-century Enlightenment, enshrined in the great *Encyclopédie* itself. "Philosophy," its editor asserted, was currently making giant strides, overturning authority and tradition, and teaching men how to observe "the laws of reason."[27]

To stress man's reason was not, however, necessarily to deplore or deny the passions. There was, in fact, a powerful movement in early eighteenth-century thought to rehabilitate the passions, in opposition to Christian asceticism. Diderot participated in this movement. It made him angry, he said, to hear people continually inveighing against the passions, considering only their bad side. To do so was the height

---

[25] See on the irrationality of *"le peuple,"* the recent study by Harry Payne, *The Philosophes and the People,* Yale University Press, New Haven, 1976.

[26] John Toland, *Christianity not Mysterious,* London, 1696, p. 59; Matthew Tindal, *Christianity as Old as Creation,* London, 1730, p. 114.

[27] Diderot, art. "Encyclopédie," *Encyclopédie.*

of folly, for great passions alone could raise men to great deeds, make possible "sublimity" both in men's actions and in art. Diderot, however, intended no insult to reason, the reverse in fact. Reason was needed to harmonize the passions, and thus to make individuals happy and society workable; and also, of course, to produce "philosophy."[28]

Rousseau was more suspicious of the passions, if not of feeling. He emphasized the need for a strong bridle to control the passions lest they become dominant. Conscience was such a bridle, but conscience needed reason to guide it. In *Emile* (1762), the tutor impressed upon his pupil that the mark of a virtuous man was to be able to control his passions, "for then he follows his reason, his conscience." The latter two went hand in hand in Rousseau's thought. Conscience, endemic to man, provided the right instincts. Reason, developed later, provided rules for moral conduct, laws to restrain the passions in social and political life. Rousseau, despite his reputation for emotionalism, believed strongly in rational controls—hence, in the possibility of rational as well as moral man. Kant did likewise. In Kant's view, as in Rousseau's, man had a dual nature, noumenal as well as phenomenal. Belonging to the phenomenal or sensible order subjected man to all the ordinary mechanisms of nature. But by virtue of belonging also to a noumenal or intelligible order, man was free to follow reason: by means of "practical reason," to recognize the moral law, and to move the will to obey it. Kant was far from saying that men always did act rationally. What he said was that they could do so if they wished. "Morality," Kant wrote, "serves as a law for us because we are rational beings. . . . Freedom also is a property of all rational beings."[29]

The optimists considered thus far all believed in some sort of fixed human nature. Man was born with a moral sense, or conscience, or sufficient reason. As the century proceeded, however, the emphasis shifted more and more to man's "perfectibility," a term very much in vogue from Rousseau's time on. The doctrine of perfectibility, meaning possible change for the better, is usually associated with the triumph of Lockean sensationalism, which did indeed tip the balance in favor

---

[28] Diderot, *Pensées philosophiques* (1746), Sects. 1–5. There were, of course, many other stances on reason and the passions in eighteenth-century thought. Hume, for example, differing sharply from both Diderot and the deists, demolished rationalistic ethics. Reason could not motivate the will, or even oppose (though it might guide) the passions. The latter alone could make man desire an object or end. On the other hand, Hume did not think badly of the passions, and scolded those who insisted too much on man's egoism. But few shared, at least completely, Hume's antiintellectualism in the realm of ethics.

[29] Kant, *Foundations for a Metaphysic of Morals* (1785), Sect. III.

of nurture over nature. Intellectual and moral development might as easily come, however, from realizing man's nature, that is, his inner potentialities thwarted at present by defects in the society he inhabits. As we shall see, Rousseau also believed in man's malleability and perfectibility, nearly as much as the extreme environmentalists, but he argued from very different premises.

Of the close tie between sensationalism and the eighteenth-century image of perfectible man, there can be no question whatever. Consider the following two works, written within several years of one another during the French Revolution, both by social reformers. "The Characters of Men Originate in their External Circumstances" is the title of a key chapter in William Godwin's *Enquiry concerning Political Justice* (1793). "What is born into the world is an unfinished sketch, without character. . . . In fine, it is impression that makes the man, and, compared with the empire of impression, the mere differences of animal structure are inexpressibly unimportant and powerless."[30] These assertions, denying not only innate ideas but even the barest of an original constitution, including even instincts and mind as ordinarily understood, enabled Godwin to assert a basic human equality, and hence the omnipotence of education for shaping mind and character. Condorcet's *Progress of the Human Mind* (1795) started and ended the same way. "Man is born with the faculty of receiving sensations. . . . This faculty is developed in him by the action of external objects, etc." Thus, what man was depended entirely on experience, or on change from without, on the impressing upon him of certain habits and knowledge. This being so, perfectibility was possible, indeed probable, by means of education over the centuries. "Is it not probable that education, by improving these qualities [intelligence and moral sensibility], has an effect on, modifies, perfects, human organization itself?"[31] Condorcet meant that improvements, gained by experience, might then be transmitted by inheritance from parents to their offspring.

This image of perfectible man, reaching its apogee in the heady atmosphere of the Revolution, descended, as we have said, from Locke. In Godwin's case, Locke was filtered through David Hartley's associa-

[30] William Godwin, *Enquiry concerning Political Justice*, 2nd ed., G. G. & J. Robinson, London, 1796, Vol. I, pp. 38, 41 (from Bk. I, Chap. IV). ". . . the characters of men are determined in all their most essential circumstances by education" (ibid., p. 46).

[31] Marie Jean Antoine Nicolas de Caritat, Marquis de Condorcet, *Esquisse d'un tableau historique des progrès de l'esprit humain,* 3rd ed., Paris, 1797, p. 389. Condorcet uses the term *perfectibilité* rather sparingly, *perfectionnement* more often.

tionist psychology, and Godwin also read Helvétius and Rousseau. Condorcet was a friend of Helvétius, who in turn profited greatly from the philosopher Condillac's embellishments on Locke. Locke, however, was clearly the seminal thinker, his famous *tabula rasa* the vivifying metaphor.

Locke himself was not a complete environmentalist. He not only recognized "various tempers, different inclinations" in children but also wanted education to suit each man's station in life as well as his capacity to learn. Nevertheless, Locke did think of the mind (at least of gentlemen) as like white paper or wax, "to be moulded and fashioned as one pleases." Nine of every ten men were good or evil, useful or not, "by their education."[32] The only "natural tendency" men had at birth was the impulse to pursue pleasure and to avoid pain. As John Passmore points out, Locke turned his back on both Augustinianism, which insisted on original sin, and the moral optimism of the Cambridge Platonists.[33] But Locke put in the place of the moral optimism a new environmental optimism, stressing education.

Locke's followers of the next generation in England and France carried his environmentalist doctrine farther. Again, in two well-known books of the same vintage—David Hartley's *Observations on Man* (1749) and Condillac's *Traité des sensations* (1754)—we can watch the human mind become purely passive, as, of course, it never was completely for Locke. Hartley, influenced by Newton as well as by Locke and the Rev. Mr. Gay, tried to make of psychology a science with general laws. Hartley related psychology to physiology by the law of association, which was comparable, in his view, to the law of gravitation in astronomy. Impressions made by external objects "beget" sensations, which in turn "beget" vibrations leading to the brain and produce pleasure or pain. The vibrations leave behind them simple ideas, which then become complex ideas by means of association. Thus, in Hartley's system the mind is a complete blank acted upon by outside forces and functioning mechanically; Lockean "reflection" has completely disappeared as a source of ideas. From this "law," however, condemned by some as deterministic and materialistic, Hartley drew the most opti-

---

[32] John Locke, *Some Thoughts concerning Education* (1693), Sect. 1, 216. Cf. *An Essay concerning Human Understanding,* Bk. II, Chap. I, Sect. 2; and Bk. II, Chap. XI, Sect. 17. In the latter section the mind is also compared to an empty or dark closet, in opposition to the advocates of innate ideas. See further on Locke's anthropology, pp. 92–93.

[33] John Passmore, *The Perfectibility of Man,* Duckworth, London, 1970, pp. 159–160. I owe much to Passmore's discussion of the whole subject.

mistic conclusions. Assuming a passive mind, one could imprint upon it the highest moral and religious ideas, drawn from the stock of human experience. Association, moreover, led inevitably to the derivation of higher from lower ideas, with the consequence that "the moral sense" was "guaranteed necessarily and mechanically."[34] Condillac came to somewhat similar conclusions about the mind, but without sharing Hartley's exuberance. Indeed, it is hard to imagine the Abbé de Condillac, who was apparently a dry stick, being particularly enthusiastic about anything. He did, however, invent (or perhaps more accurately, borrow)[35] a famous image—the statue man—which shows how far Condillac was prepared to go along the road of sensationalism. Let us imagine a lifeless statue, he said in his latest work, the *Traité des sensations,* to which we shall give, one by one, the five senses. By this device Condillac tried to demonstrate that all knowledge, and the mental faculties themselves, derived from sensations, especially from the "master-sense, touch," which alone of all the senses could tell man that the outside world of space and objects existed. Thus, all Condillac left man with in the end was a sensory organization, which could also register pleasure and pain, but without much of a mind, at least an autonomous mind able to reason and reflect. Man, then, was essentially what he acquired, or rather what came to him from the outside, or else was put into him. Condillac did not say that environment made the man—or that man was perfectible—but others who quoted him did say so, above all Claude Adrien Helvétius.

It is no wonder that Helvétius aroused opposition, even among his philosophic friends. He was the most extreme of the environmentalists, preaching a radical equality. All men are born equal, that is to say, without a specific "temperament" or "interior organization," save for *"amour de soi."* Hence, education and laws—or "circumstances"— make the man, even the genius. "Quintilian, Locke, and I say: The inequality of minds is the effect of a known cause, and this cause is the difference of education." In other places in *De l'Homme* (1772), Helvétius appears to contradict himself, as when he says, almost in Hobbesian vein, that "the natural man" (*l'homme de la nature*) is cruel and bloodthirsty, and lives in a state of war. But his purpose in the chapter where this statement occurs is to refute Rousseau (and Shaftes-

---

[34] David Hartley, *Observations on Man*, Pt. I, Conclusion (Vol. I, p. 504 in the 1791 ed.). This statement is made, significantly in the midst of some concluding remarks on "the mechanism of the human mind."

[35] The idea of the statue man was in the air at the time, and was used by others too, conspicuously Diderot.

bury) whom Helvétius thought of as championing the reverse position, namely that man was born good. "No individual is born good," he had said in the previous chapter; "no individual is born wicked. . . . Goodness or wickedness—is the product of their good or bad laws."[36] Change the laws, devise a more perfect education, and man could learn to fuse his *amour de soi* with the public interest, and thus build a better society. The Baron d'Holbach, concurring in this view, made the connection between environmentalism and perfectibility even more explicit. "It is evident," he said, "that nature has made man susceptible to experience and consequently more and more perfectible."[37] Holbach, however, probably did not share with Helvétius the latter's belief in equality, or the potential perfectibility of *all* men, for Holbach, like Voltaire and others, had his reservations about *"le peuple."*

Nor certainly did Rousseau, between whom and Helvétius there was a running battle, or Diderot, who wrote a refutation of Helvétius. The so-called *idéologues,* the spiritual descendants of Condillac and Helvétius (one of them, Cabanis, was Mme. de Helvétius' adopted son), also modified Helvétius' doctrine considerably, making the mind less passive, and even Godwin broke with him over the question of the state control of education. Yet all these people believed in some degree of perfectibility, although arguing from different premises (except in the case of Godwin). "Man is not born blank," said Diderot. Hence, education could not do all, as Helvétius said, but merely a great deal. By the time he wrote the *Réfutation de l'homme d'Helvétius* (1773–1775), Diderot had come to believe, though perhaps somewhat ambiguously, in some sort of inherent moral quality of the individual, and especially in variations of brain structure as between individuals, which separated geniuses from ordinary people and explained different reactions to the same environment. Still, "circumstances," that is, legislation and education, could modify character and with exceptions, raise or lower the level of enlightenment. One would expect the editor of the *Encyclopédie* to believe at least that much. Rousseau similarly denied man's blankness, yet had faith in his perfectibility, much more so than the Encyclopedists. To deny man's blankness was not, for Rousseau any more than for Diderot, to deny the importance of social conditioning. But as Rousseau came to view him, man was no mere passive

[36] Claude Adrien Helvétius, *Oeuvres complètes,* London, 1777, Vol. III, pp. 62, 267–268, 275.
[37] Baron d'Holbach, *Essai sur les préjugés* (1770), quoted in Henry Vyverberg, *Historical Pessimism in the French Enlightenment,* Harvard University Press, Cambridge, 1958, p. 214.

recipient of ideas, but could impose his will (following his judgment, based on conscience and reason) to better his character. In the end, in *Emile* for example, Rousseau's book on education, it was the will that was emphasized. Thus, society made the man, but man also made the society. "Artificial man," corrupted by civilization, had, indeed, turned into a mere product of society that forced everybody to be alike. But it was not too late for man to rediscover his "natural" self,[38] and even to achieve a still higher existence. He could do this by creating a new kind of government or state, which would bring out the best in him, submerging his individual will in the "general will." In the *Social Contract,* Rousseau finally joined his anthropology to politics.

One final image remains to be considered, if only because it became famous through Adam Smith. This is the image since known as economic man. It too was an optimistic image, not so much, however, because of its estimate of human nature per se, as of its assumption of a pre-established harmony in nature as a whole. Man might be motivated primarily by egoism or self-interest—both the French Physiocrats and Smith assumed this to be the case—but this very self-interest worked automatically to produce an identity of interests, or the general good.

But did Adam Smith the political economist contradict Adam Smith the moral philosopher? It would seem not, though Smith became increasingly absorbed in the principles of political economy as the years went on, and might be expected, therefore, to focus more on some features of human nature than on others. In *The Theory of Moral Sentiments* (1759), written while Smith was professor of moral philosophy at Glasgow, his focus was on private ethics, and he found in man, somewhat in the manner of Shaftesbury and Hutcheson, a considerable degree of "fellow-feeling," of "sympathy" for others, though no innate moral sense. Smith expressed contempt for moral systems like Mandeville's, which derived all human sentiments from refinements of self-love. Compare these findings with the famous statements, quoted *ad nauseam* from *The Wealth of Nations* (1776): "It is not from the benevolence of the butcher, the brewer, or the baker that we expect our dinner. . . . We address ourselves not to their humanity, but to their self-love, etc." Smith had not changed his mind. He had changed his

---

[38] Rousseau's natural self, or natural man, is not, however, to be confused with "the noble savage," as Dr. Johnson and others chose to believe. Rousseau's natural man was really an ideal or a possibility. He possessed certain natural or original virtues, to be sure, but had to acquire others, needed for living in a "civil state." On the whole, though opinions were mixed, "enlightened" Europeans of the eighteenth century did not take an exalted view of savages.

interests. Now he was concerned, no longer with the private world of ethics, but with the public, the economic, world, where he observed individuals intent on their own gain, and hardly ever "intending" the good of others. But the remarkable thing was that nature (or Providence) had so contrived things that despite intentions to the contrary, individuals "necessarily" labored for the public interest, that is, by increasing society's annual revenue to its utmost capacity. This was the doctrine of natural or pre-established harmony, preached also by the French Physiocrats who, however, emphasized more the individual's natural rights, or freedom, vis-à-vis property, which similarly worked to the general advantage. The harmony obviously did not depend on human contrivance or reason. The general wealth derived from the division of labor, Smith wrote, "is not originally the effect of any human wisdom which foresees and intends that general opulence. . . . It is the necessary . . . consequence of a certain propensity in human nature which has in view no such extensive utility."[39] Intending only his own gain, the individual was "led by *an invisible hand*" to promote ends that were more general and beneficial. Others, of course, emphasized more an *artificial* harmony, which did depend on "human wisdom," the wisdom of the statesman, and this idea takes us back to Mandeville and Pope where we began. Smith, much as he might deplore Mandeville's cynicism, nevertheless shared with the latter the notion of a *natural* harmony: "private vice" (Mandeville) or "self-interest" (Smith) turned into "public benefit" automatically. Pope, on the other hand (though Pope is by no means unambiguous), preached an artificial harmony or "counterpoise." For Pope, as for Mandeville and Smith, "Each individual seeks a sev'ral goal" and "Heav'n's great view is One, and that the Whole," but creating that whole was the work, at least in part, of wise legislators and patriots.[40] This was a view in which, as Lovejoy has shown, Montesquieu, the chief framers of the American constitution, and even Helvétius acquiesced, and we return to it in a later chapter. In other words, though human nature in general might not be especially admirable, it yet might contribute, or rather be made to contribute, to a beneficial social result.

Of the anthropologies considered in this chapter, all, it should be noted, were essentially static, except for the conception of perfectible

---

[39] Adam Smith, *The Wealth of Nations,* Bk. I, Chap. II.

[40] Alexander Pope, *An Essay on Man,* see especially Epistle II, lines 237–238; Epistle III, lines 283–294. In this last passage Pope accords more to "reason" than in some other passages where reason errs, or plays "the card," that is, compass, to the passions' "gale." Of course, he is talking about a small, specially gifted, elite.

man. Emile Durkheim, the nineteenth-century sociologist, would appear to be right, then, in his observation that the *philosophes* assumed human nature was always and everywhere the same, that, in other words, humanity was not "a product of history." This assumption, he wrote, was "the immovable rock on which they based their political systems as also their moral speculations."[41] Most eighteenth-century thinkers, whether optimistic or pessimistic about man, conservative or reformist, had, indeed, not grasped the idea of an "historical" human nature, changing according to time and place (though many did, as we have seen, talk about the different *moeurs* or customs of nations). The whole thrust of classicism, still powerful in the eighteenth century, was to emphasize the uniformity, not the singularity or changeableness of human nature, and thus to rule out historical relativism. But even the empiricists, who thought men malleable, assumed some sort of universal structure of mental faculties and motivations on which the conditioners could go to work. We are not surprised to hear Dr. Samuel Johnson, a classicist and conservative, distinguish between the passions and customs of men, the latter only being "changeable," but the former "uniform," discoverable, as he said, "by the same symptoms, in minds distant a thousand years from one another."[42] It is perhaps more surprising to hear Holbach, a religious and political reformer, speak in very much the same vein. Holbach wanted nothing less than a "universal morality" based on the nature of man, and here is how he began his book on the subject:

> In order to be universal Morality must be conformable to the nature of man in general, that is, founded on his essence, on the properties and qualities that one finds constantly in the beings of his species and by which he is distinguished from other animals. From which one sees that Morality presupposes the science of human nature.

> Man is a sensible, intelligent, reasonable, sociable being, who in all the instants of his duration seeks without interruption to preserve himself and to render his existence agreeable. . . . Behold the qualities and properties which constitute human nature, and which are to be found constantly in all the individuals of our species.

[41] Emile Durkheim, *L'Evolution pédagogique en France,* Felix Alcan, Paris, 1938, Vol. II, pp. 190–191.
[42] For Dr. Johnson on the uniformity of human nature, see Paul Fussell, *The Rhetorical World of Augustan Humanism,* Oxford University Press, Oxford, 1965, Chap. 3.

There is no need to know more to discover the conduct which every man must observe in order to attain the end which he proposes to himself.[43]

Dr. Johnson and Holbach, disagreeing on nearly everything else, were nevertheless agreed on some sort of "original" human nature, or as Pope called it, "man in the abstract," which did not change. This was still a widely held assumption in the eighteenth century.

Yet there were intimations of a different notion, to become powerful in "the nineteenth century," as John Stuart Mill called it, in comparison with "the eighteenth century."[44] Empiricism, after all, did encourage people to think that man could change and be changed, through different kinds of experience. Condorcet, also an environmentalist, contemplated the possibility of change in man's bodily and mental constitution, through the inheritance of acquired characteristics. Rousseau and Lessing also believed that men might surpass their "original" state, more, however, by making use of inborn predilections and grow in moral consciousness through education of one sort or another. Finally, a genuinely historical way of thinking about man was to come through strongly in Johann Gottfried von Herder and others, as we see when we take up the reactions against "the eighteenth century," chiefly in the Romantic Movement.

[43] Baron d'Holbach, *La Morale universelle ou les devoirs de l'homme fondés sur sa nature,* Amsterdam, 1776, pp. 1, 4–5.

[44] Mill was always comparing "the eighteenth" and "the nineteenth" centuries. By the former he meant mainly the Enlightenment, which he associated with "universal principles of human nature." Whereas in "the nineteenth century," Mill thought man had learned to think of human nature as changing with the times.

Theism and Atheism

The question of man, as we have said, became central in eighteenth-century thought. The question of God or of religion, however, continued to be, in David Hume's words, "interesting" and even "of the utmost importance," not only because it was thought to illuminate human nature but on its own account. This was not only true for the Christian apologists, French Jesuits and Jansenists, both suffering grievous setbacks in the eighteenth century, a handful of orthodox Anglican bishops, and on the more enthusiastic side, German Pietists and English Methodists. Freethinkers and unbelievers, "pagans," also worried the subject almost to death, debating endlessly the origins of religion, the existence of God, miracles, priestcraft, and the social and moral utility of religious belief. It has been said, with some truth, that around the middle of the century the *philosophes* became preoccupied increasingly with other, more earthy problems involving political and social reform. But Hume's rhythm was different, as was Rousseau's and Immanuel Kant's. Hume only began to write systematically about religion after 1751, twelve years after his *Treatise of Human Nature* first appeared. Rousseau likewise did his most striking pieces on religion in his middle age, following his break with the Encyclopedists, and Kant wrote his principal theological work, *Religion within the Limits of Reason alone* (1793), after reaching the age of seventy. Mention of these names suggests other prominent thinkers of the eighteenth century, philosophers, psychologists, scientists, and historians, for whom religion was by no means a dead issue. Some, like David Hartley, founder of associationist psychology, were genuinely religious men.

Nevertheless, it could not be said that the eighteenth century was a religious century in the same degree as was the seventeenth century. The eighteenth century, as is well known, marked a crisis of major proportions that threatened, especially in France, to overturn ancient altars and destroy religious faith altogether. This crisis, predicted by Bishop Bossuet,[1] is usually associated with the Enlightenment. But in fact it spread far beyond intellectual circles to envelop educated people in general. The crisis might be thought of as coming in several waves. First, there was the assault on revealed religion in the name of a "Religion of Nature and Reason," as Matthew Tindal called it. The titles of successive books written by English deists on the threshold, and during the first half, of the century chart the course of this first wave: *Christianity not Mysterious* (1696) by John Toland who tried to out-Locke Locke's *The Reasonableness of Christianity,* published the preceding year; Thomas Woolston's *Discourses on the Miracles* (1727–1730), explaining miracles as hoaxes perpetrated by fraudulent priests and calling for a return to a "primogenial" religion of nature and freedom; Tindal's *Christianity as Old as Creation* (1730), which likewise discovered an Ur-religion engraved on the hearts of every man, preceding any of the ecclesiastical establishments of the world; and William Wollaston's *Religion of Nature* (first published in 1722, but reaching a seventh edition in 1750).[2] Although the object of these and similar works was to purge religion of all mystery and superstition, there was also concern to preserve a hard core of theistic belief. This first wave was soon followed, however, by a second, led by the skeptics and atheists, which menaced natural as well as revealed religion, deism as well as orthodox Christianity. Both waves were set in motion by historical (including intellectual) forces originating much earlier,[3] but only now achieving maximum power. The crisis produced by these forces might be said to have culminated in the numerous cults of Reason, Nature, and the Supreme Being established in Paris and throughout France at the height of the Revolution. The architect Jacques-Germain Soufflot's famous neoclassical church of St. Geneviève,

[1] See p. 66.
[2] Wollaston, an Anglican clergyman, was the most conservative of this group of deists. Nevertheless, he scandalized many of his confreres by constructing his theory of religion on reason rather than revelation, and on nature—the presumed universal order of nature.
[3] See pp. 66–67.

begun during the reign of Louis XIV, was turned into the Pantheon or burial place for the Nation's great men, and the drive to de-Christianize a whole nation had begun. Some notion of the rites celebrating these cults may be gathered from contemporary paintings now housed in the Museum of the City of Paris (known as the Musée Carnavalet), such as, the rendering of the *Festival of the Supreme Being* on the Champ de Mars on June 8, 1794, by Pierre Antoine de Machy (Plate 16). This particular cult, promoted by Robespierre, was, however, deistic rather than atheistic. De Machy also did a Festival of Unity, showing the burning of the emblems of monarchy, and a remarkable *Demolition of Saint-Jean en Grève* (a church of the thirteenth century; Plate 17), the last emblematic of the deliberate destruction of Christian monuments. No wonder romantics of the postrevolutionary epoch, Thomas Carlyle among them, called the eighteenth century one of the great Ages of Unbelief of history.

Yet even the cults[4] scarcely indicate the extent of the crisis. Max Weber speaks of the "disenchantment" (*Entzauberung*) of the modern world, of the stripping away of man's illusions, of a "world robbed of gods." This was what really happened in the eighteenth century, not only for some few freethinkers and skeptics but for many people who still called themselves Christians. A great many people, not including the masses, of course, especially the rural masses, lost their sense of the miraculous, the sacred and the transcendental, with the predictable result that Christian revelation receded in importance and even began to seem outmoded or fraudulent. But the reason why people were questioning their religious beliefs was not because they had become world-weary (which was partly what Weber meant) but, on the contrary, because they had learned to love the world more, to seek "happiness" in it, and not to fear, at least not in the same degree, the precariousness of life to which an earlier and more otherworldly religion spoke. This increasing feeling of at-homeness in the world was the result of improved economic and political prospects, which promised more security and prosperity to more men than had previously been thought possible. The more worldly mood is already apparent in Toland's early book. Though professing to be a Christian, Toland wanted a down-to-earth religion, concealing no mysteries and stressing morals. His master Locke to the contrary, Toland was convinced that there was nothing

---

[4] The cults turned out to be short-lived, not outlasting the Revolution, though some, conspicuously the *culte décadaire*, dedicated to the *Patrie*, flourished as late as the Directory.

"above reason" in the Gospels, that reason, or man's ordinary faculties and ideas, could "penetrate the veil," that no doctrine could properly be called a mystery. "Everything is toned down," a French priest complained nearly a century later; "everything is given an air of reasonableness. . . . [People] are wary of anything that savors even remotely of the miraculous or the unexpected."[5] Clearly, as Groethuysen remarks, the crisis, which was more advanced in France than elsewhere, extended to "doctrine" as well as to "belief," which is to say, that it involved a contraction or watering down of the faith, even among professing Christians.

This dual crisis, of both doctrine and belief, is best revealed in the great debates, which raged all through the century, over the existence and nature of God. How to prove the existence of God? Old proofs no longer sufficed or gave way to new proofs, which were, in turn, deemed inadequate by many. Proof was now decidedly a puzzlement, to a far greater degree than had been the case in the age of Descartes or Spinoza. And even if one found one or more of the proofs reasonably convincing, what then of God's nature? Was he the God of Christian revelation? Could one really say very much at all about him?

Most, though not all, of the major proofs and disproofs of the existence of God are listed toward the end of Immanuel Kant's *Critique of Pure Reason.* Kant mentions ontological, cosmological, and physico-theological proofs. Kant himself, as is well known, demolished all of these "rational" proofs, and in later works he supplied a new sort of moral proof. Since in the *Critique* he was only asking how far the speculative or practical reason could take one along this theological road, Kant did not list other less exclusively rationalist proofs, such as Rousseau's appeal to interior feeling, or the summoning of historical evidence that might be thought to substantiate the Christian miracles, or possibly even show that religion was "natural" to man. All through this battle of the proofs, as it may be called, one can sense a diminution of confidence, first in revelation, but then also progressively in rational, scientific, and historical arguments. Among those engaged in the battle, a fair number ended up as skeptics or atheists and nearly everybody confessed to skepticism in some degree.

Supernatural revelation faded out early as a primary proof, except,

---

[5] John Toland, *Christianity not Mysterious: or, a Treatise shewing that there is nothing in the Gospel contrary to Reason, Nor above it,* London, 1696, especially Sect. III; Jean-Baptiste Massillon, Sermon for the Feast of the Incarnation, 1786, quoted in Bernhard Groethuysen, *Die Entsthehung der Bürgerlichen Welt- und Lebensanschauung in Frankreich,* Max Niemeyer, Halle, 1927, Vol. I, p. 20.

PLATE 16. *Festival of the Supreme Being*, by Pierre Antoine de Machy.

Musée Carnavalet, Paris. (Photo: Lauros-Giraudon.)

PLATE 17. *Demolition of Saint-Jean en Grève,* by Pierre Antoine de Machy.

of course, among conservative religious groups like the Jansenists in France and the Pietists in Germany. Disbelief in revelation was the distinguishing mark of the deists. But the foremost Christian apologists of the day sounded as though they, too, could do very well without revelation, save as a not too important supplement to "natural religion." In the words of Samuel Clarke, a leading English theologian and follower of Locke and Newton, revelation was needed to make the principles of natural religion "more clear and plain" in a "sceptical and profane age." These principles, Clarke declared in his famous Boyle lectures on *The Being and Attributes of God* (1704–1705), were "in general deducible, even demonstrably, by a chain of clear and undeniable reasoning." Yet in the present corrupt state of the world, as in early Christian times, they "could not be certainly known but by revelation."[6]

Reason, then, overshadowed revelation in the early eighteenth-century debates. This was the golden age of rational or natural theology, when confidence abounded in reason's speculative power, not merely to prove God's existence but also to reveal much about his nature. At first, it was common to stress, and usually to mix, ontological and cosmological proofs. For example, both Clarke and Christian Wolff, the German philosopher, did so. The physico-theological proof, however, assumed greater importance as time went on, for understandable reasons. This proof, starting as it did from nature and nature's laws, seemed more scientific to people who, like Voltaire, inhabited Newton's cosmos.

Clarke, called by Voltaire "a reasoning engine," particularly delighted in the mathematical method to demonstrate God's existence, omnipotence, wisdom, and beneficence. Clarke's twelve propositions, presented as axioms, boiled down essentially to the cosmological proof, to reasoning a posteriori from contingent to necessary and unchangeable being. Presently existing objects must owe their being to some external cause, which is self-existent, and which exists necessarily. Wolff, who later became Kant's primary target, stressed as well, indeed almost seemed to prefer, the ontological proof, which he developed at length in two textbooks on natural theology. This proof, derived from Descartes, represented the extreme of abstract reasoning, divorced from any mixture of empiricism. As we have seen,[7] it proceeded a priori from essence to existence, from the idea the thinker has of a perfect being, to existence as an attribute of perfection. Wolff's arguments carried great

---

[6] Samuel Clarke, *A Demonstration of the Being and Attributes of God* (1705), Vol. II, Introduction.

[7] See p. 71.

weight in Germany because of his prestige as chancellor of the University of Halle and leader of the German Enlightenment.

Voltaire, taking off from Locke and Newton rather than Descartes, preferred the physico-theological proof, otherwise known as the argument from design. This proof not only caught on, but stayed on, as a force down into the nineteenth century. Bishop Berkeley, though he reacted sharply against scientific materialism, offered a variant of it in his philosophy of immaterialism.[8] David Hume, though he personally disagreed with it, featured it in the *Dialogues concerning Natural Religion* as the most formidable and popular proof of his day. This proof was ultimately enshrined by William Paley in his famous *Evidences of Christianity* (1794), which Charles Darwin read as a student at Cambridge. Voltaire used it as a stick to beat atheists. For Voltaire, as for Paley, though Voltaire was no Christian, the watch, signifying the order in the universe, argued the existence of the watchmaker, and the ends for which things appeared to be made, for example, the eye for seeing, argued the existence of a designer. "I say to you: Continue to regard all superstition with horror; but adore with me the design which manifests itself in all nature, and consequently the author of this design, the primordial and final cause of everything."[9] Voltaire was clearly a "final-causer" in the manner of Newton, employing both teleological and analogical arguments, and both astronomical and anatomical analogies. Voltaire believed he was being very scientific, the reverse of metaphysical, in his proof of God's existence.[10]

The battle of the proofs shifted ground about at midcentury as the tide in European thought ran more strongly toward empiricism. Empiricism demanded hard facts for any conclusions, barred the mind from exceeding sense experience. Could the available evidence, scientific or historical, support belief in God's existence? Hume epitomizes the growing skepticism. He brought a powerful mind to bear on "two

[8] Berkeley, disputing the atheists, argued that God normally chose to convince man's reason "by works of nature," that is, by their great harmony and order, "rather than to astonish us into a belief of His Being by anomalous and surprising events." See *A Treatise concerning the Principles of Human Knowledge* (1710), Pt. I, no. 63.

[9] Voltaire, *Dictionnaire philosophique* (1764), art. "Dieu, Dieux." Despite increasing disgust with metaphysics, Voltaire here stands by the argument he had developed at great length earlier in the *Traité de métaphysique* (1734).

[10] Of course, Voltaire recognized "difficulties" concerning God's existence, even in the early *Traité de métaphysique*. Responding to the "materialists," he took his stand essentially on probability. From the argument that eyes were obviously made to see, Voltaire could conclude only that "il est probable qu'un être intelligent et supérieur a préparé et façonné la matière avec habileté." (Chap. 2).

questions in particular" (as stated in *The Natural History of Religion,*
1751): one, concerning the foundation of religion in reason, and the
other, its origin in human nature. Hume's answers to both questions
were skeptical in the extreme. In the *Dialogues concerning Natural
Religion,* written after *The Natural History,* Hume dismembered all
the aforementioned rational proofs. He has one of his interlocutors,
Cleanthes, refute another's "metaphysical reasoning," that is, making
use of the ontological and cosmological proofs. "The argument a priori
has seldom been found very convincing, except to people of a metaphysical head who have accustomed themselves to abstract [and mathe-
matical] reasoning."[11] But the design argument, which Cleanthes defends, does not stand up to the empirical test either. Does the world, of
which we have only an imperfect knowledge, really exhibit the order
Cleanthes says it does? Can we infer from the world we perceive a
cause, that is, God, "so remote from the sphere of our observation"? In
any case, need the cause be a mind like man's? Could it not be some
sort of act of generation within nature itself? Or if it is a mind, then
must there not be a cause of the mind itself, and so on *ad infinitum?*
Philo, "careless skeptic," and probably Hume's mouthpiece, shows how
empirically weak the analogy is between a watch or machine and nature
as a whole, and between a watchmaker and the presumed Author of
nature.[12] Proof of deity obviously fell far short of "perfect evidence."

But what about a possible foundation for religion in human nature?
Could it be true, as some deists said, that religion was not only an idea
of reason but an innate idea, "written," in the words of Matthew Tindal,
"in the hearts of every one of us from the first creation."[13] Hume answered this question, the second raised in *The Natural History,* by
delving into history, and here he definitely broke new ground. He concluded, on the basis of travelers' and historians' reports, that religious
belief, though widely diffused over the human race, was neither universal nor uniform. Hence, it could not have sprung from "an original
instinct or primary impression of nature." How then did it arise?
Hume fell back on psychological explanation. Some few may have

---

[11] Actually, a third interlocutor, "Philo," says this, but he and "Cleanthes" are in
agreement on this point.

[12] Hume, *Dialogues concerning Natural Religion,* especially Pt. II (for Philo's
attack on Cleanthes), and Pt. IX (for Cleanthes' and Philo's attack on Demea).
The *Dialogues* were written between 1751 and 1761, revised later, and published
posthumously.

[13] Matthew Tindal, *Christianity as Old as the Creation* (London, 1730),
Chap. VI.

reasoned things out, but the majority were swayed by their passions, by the hopes and fears of everyday life, dread of the unknown, thirst for revenge, fear of survival, and the like. Speaking of the migration from polytheism, which he believed to be the original form of religious faith, to monotheism, Hume was of the opinion that men "are guided to [the latter] notion, not by reason, of which they are in a great measure incapable, but by the adulation and fears of the most vulgar superstition."[14] Fear predominated in Hume's theory of religious origins.

Though he was a skeptic distrustful of both reason and revelation, Hume was no atheist. But there were atheists, an increasing number of them, who not only refused to accept any sort of proof but categorically denied the existence of God. Hume met some of them at the Baron d'Holbach's table in Paris—fifteen out of eighteen present on one occasion were atheists, according to Diderot's report. Diderot, a few years before, distinguished between three classes of atheists, "the true atheists"; skeptical atheists, "a fairly large number," who were not quite so sure of their ground; and the braggarts.[15] Holbach, called "the personal enemy of God," was the best known and most feared among "the true atheists" of his time. He popularized all the Humean ideas, but added something new to the discussion. At the heart of Holbach's atheism lay a concept of nature, or matter, which is discussed more fully in the next chapter. Clarke and the theologians, he wrote, "base the existence of their god on the necessity of a force which has the power to commence movement."[16] But suppose matter had always existed, and that motion was inherent in matter. In that case, nature sufficed, and God was not needed to account for the phenomena of the universe, the great cosmic machine, or even mind itself. Thus, whereas for Voltaire, Newtonian science appeared to support, indeed require, belief in a first mover, it did just the opposite for Holbach. Diderot himself offers an interesting variation on the atheist argument. He was initially a deist who, however, based his deism, not on mechanistic physics, but on patterns, purposefulness, and order that he perceived in the biological world. By the time he wrote the *Letter on the Blind* (1749) Diderot had, however, given up this biological finalism and come to believe, like Holbach, in the self-creativity of matter. A blind man deprived of sight could hardly be expected to see, or to accept, the order and perfection of

[14] Hume, *The Natural History of Religion*, Sect. VI.
[15] Diderot, *Pensées philosophiques* (1746), No. XXII.
[16] Holbach, *Système de la Nature* (1770), Vol. II, Chap. II. Holbach also blasted other proofs, by Descartes, Malebranche, Newton, and the deists.

nature. Nature's variety, the disorder as well as the order, the monstrosities as well as the wonders, could be explained naturalistically, without reference to divinity.

Immanuel Kant reveals, better than any of the skeptics and atheists, the real dilemma of eighteenth-century thought about God's existence. Kant tested all the arguments, and, for a time, defended some of them, particularly the physico-theological proof that seemed closest to Newtonian science. But in the end Kant pronounced them all "impossible." On the theory of knowledge he worked out, God became "speculatively unknowable." Thus, neither philosophy nor science any longer led to God, as they had done in the days of Descartes, Newton, and Christian Wolff. Speculative reason could not demonstrate God's existence, and nature did not reveal him ineluctably. No wonder Kant was called the "All-Destroyer"—the destroyer of natural theology.

Kant, however, tried to save something from the wreckage. He still thought the idea of God could be useful, both to science and morals. It could abet science by holding up to it, as a goal, the possible interconnectedness of things. More important, the idea of God could stretch man to achieve the highest moral stature possible. But to save God Kant had to work out a new proof, different from any of the old rational and scientific proofs. He deduced God, as well as freedom and immortality, from man's moral nature. "Morality," he wrote, "leads ineluctably to religion."[17] Kant accepted as a fact, possibly because of early Pietist teaching in his student days at the University of Königsberg, man's moral experience, his innate sense of difference between right and wrong, and his obligation to obey the moral law. But for man not merely to feel obliged, but to want to be, and to become, virtuous in the fullest sense, he must be assured of the moral nature of the universe, which, in turn, required belief in God's existence. In Kant's new moral proof, God clearly never became more than a postulate of "practical reason," actually an "object of faith." Kant might, therefore, be said to have restored religion to faith, more than to reason, and to have subordinated it to morality.

Before leaving the battle of the proofs, brief mention should be made of one other figure who, in fact, preceded Kant somewhat in time. This was Rousseau, who evoked more the spirit of the romantic movement still to come. Rousseau was primarily concerned to bring the affective

[17] Kant, *Religion within the Limits of Reason Alone,* Preface to first edition. For Kant's moral proof, see especially the *Critique of Practical Reason* (1788), Pt. I, Bk. II, Chap. II, Sect. V.

side of human nature back into religion. His Savoyard Vicar, beating the path back from Enlightenment skepticism, does not disdain rational proofs. But he does say that reason—the speculative reason of the philosophers—is not nearly enough to produce religious conviction. "I affirm them [rational deductions about God's attributes] without understanding them, and at bottom that is no affirmation at all. In vain do I say, God is thus, I feel it, I experience it." Hence, the Vicar turns to interior feeling to find God. Emile is advised to consult his heart in matters of religion and conduct, "for feeling precedes knowledge." "To exist is to feel; our feeling is undoubtedly earlier than our intelligence, and we had feelings before we had ideas."[18]

As remarked previously, the crisis in eighteenth-century religious belief extended to ideas about God's essence as well as to his existence. To understand how the lines were drawn in this second battle, however, it is necessary to clarify the use of certain words. Kant calls attention to a growing distinction between the terms *deism* and *theism*. "The deist," he says, "believes in a God, the theist in a living God."[19] The deist, that is, was one who could say little or nothing about God save that he existed, and was the cause of the world; whereas the theist thought reason capable of saying much more, namely that God was "Author of the world" (not merely the abstract first cause), the principle and source of all natural and moral order—thus, in some sense, a personal God. Clarke, however, further distinguished between several sorts of deists. There were deists who believed in a Supreme Being who created the world, but did not govern it. Others believed in a general Providence, still others that God had moral attributes, which, however, did not argue rewards and punishments in a future life. Finally, there were those who had "just and right notions of God, and of all the divine attributes in every respect," but without accepting any sort of supernatural revelation. It was the latter, "the only true deists," as he called them, that Clarke wanted to attract back into the Christian fold.[20] Obviously, the meaning of these terms was not only confusing but confused in the eighteenth century—Voltaire's article on "Theism" in the *Philosophical Dictionary* was originally published under the title "Deism"! Nevertheless, Kant was right: there was a tendency, as time went on, to assign fixed and different meanings to them, and thus to

[18] Rousseau, *Emile* (1762), "The Creed of a Savoyard Priest."
[19] Kant, *Critique of Pure Reason*, Div. II, Chap. III, Sect. 7.
[20] For Clarke on the deists, see *The Being and Attributes of God*, Vol. II, Introduction.

distinguish more sharply between Christian, deist, and theist. Despite what is sometimes said, the trend, at least among rationalist believers, was toward a deism[21] that reduced God's attributes to a minimum, to the point of dechristianization and even depersonalization. A few examples illustrate this trend.

The divine attributes listed by Clarke in his Boyle lectures[22] may be taken as a convenient point of departure. God was, for Clarke, among other things, the one and only unchangeable and independent being existing from eternity, distinct from the world or any material thing, yet also omnipresent, intelligent, endowed with liberty, infinitely powerful and wise, and good and just as became the supreme governor and judge of the world. To this list of attributes, which could be known by reason alone, Clarke tacked on others that were revealed fully only in the Christian Scriptures, such as the begetting of the Logos or Son of God and his divine commission on earth, the latter being attested to by authentic miracles. Though largely a product of natural theology, Clarke's God was still identifiable as the Christian God, and therefore very much a personal God, interested in men's fate, interfering and providing. Christian Wolff likewise identified God with the God of Christianity, after first describing him as *ens a se,* that is, independent being, unlike nature or the human soul, and as *ens perfectissimum,* having all realities in the highest possible degree, and freely creating the world.

The deists' idea of God was quite different. They preached a return to the simple religion of nature, which, as they thought, preceded, and was superior to, all the positive and revealed religions of the world. This Ur-religion, common to all men, inculcated belief in a universal God, who played no favorites among the peoples of the earth, not even excepting the Christians and Jews; who ruled constitutionally, without overturning the laws of nature by miracles; and who, himself rational and good, promulgated the moral law, but gave men the strength to observe it without special divine interposition. The deists were palpably

[21] It is true that after midcentury the issues over which the English deists fought, for example, reason versus revelation, excited less controversy, and that more emotional types of religious expression began to find favor. One is reminded, however, of Sir Leslie Stephen's remark that "deism was not dead, but sleeping," and that it was prominently on display during the epoch of the French Revolution. Certainly it was prominent in many of the revolutionary cults.

[22] Clarke, it should be noted, distinguished between the essence or substance, and the attributes, of God. Man could know nothing about the former, but much about the latter.

more interested in morals than in theology.[23] But they still believed that right conduct depended on right belief. Therefore, they preserved a minimal theology, paring the list of divine attributes down to those few which could, in their opinion, put an end to the fanaticism, hatred, and immorality engendered by the gods of revelation. Voltaire sums up the deist credo thus:

> United in this principle [i.e. of divine Providence] with the rest of the universe he [the theist] embraces none of the sects which all contradict each other. His religion is the most ancient and the most widespread: for the simple adoration of a God has preceded all the systems of the world. He speaks a language which all peoples understand. . . . He has brothers from Peking to Cayenne, and he counts all the sages among his brothers. He believes that religion consists neither in the opinions of an unintelligible metaphysics, nor in vain appearances, but in worship and justice. To do good, that is his cult; to submit to God, that is his doctrine.[24]

But already in Voltaire we can see the disintegration of deist belief, or, to put it another way, the metamorphosis of theist belief into a more spare type of deism. By the time he made this statement Voltaire had long since developed serious doubts about divine Providence, and was beginning to question God's freedom in creating the world. This was in fact the substance of the debate between Voltaire and Rousseau in 1756. Voltaire's optimism had been shaken by the Lisbon earthquake of 1755, which had caused untold damage and suffering. This, and other great disasters of history, raised the question of evil. Doubtless, everything was arranged, ordered, by Providence; but if so, it was not for man's benefit. There *was* evil in the world, and there was no use denying the fact. Yes, Rousseau replied, but the evil was man's doing, not God's. Voltaire retreated into ignorance. No philosopher had ever explained satisfactorily the origin of either moral or physical evil. Perhaps God was not free, that is, sufficiently powerful, to create a different kind of world, and hence to make men happy. Perhaps God was above good and evil, in which case there might be a general, but

---

[23] Deist principles, says Tindal in *Christianity as Old as Creation* (London, 1730, p. 331; Chap. XIV), "contain nothing to divert them [that is, deists] from entirely attending to all the Duties of Morality, in which the whole of their religion consists; and which leaves them no room for those endless Quarrels and fatal Divisions, which Zeal for other Things, has occasion'd among their Fellow-Creatures."

[24] Voltaire, *Dictionnaire philosophique*, art. "Théiste."

not a particular, Providence. Said the philosopher to the nun in the *Philosophical Dictionary*: "I believe in a general Providence, from which has emanated the law which rules everything. . . . But I do not believe that a particular Providence changes the economy of the world for your sparrow or your cat."[25] The philosopher of Ferney continued to the last to believe in "the supreme Artisan" of the heavens and earth, but abandoned belief in God's omnipotence, or beneficence toward men—save as the ultimate source of reason and the moral instinct in man. Voltaire's God was still a personal God, but only just barely.

In Hume this trend toward a minimal theology was carried to its ultimate conclusion. Few in his time, deists or theists, could perhaps go quite so far. Certainly Kant, his philosophical follower, did not. For a skeptic, Kant could muster a surprising array of divine attributes. He did so, of course, not on the ground of the speculative reason but of morals. The moral principle in man demanded a moral God, omnipotent, omniscient, and just, who makes the Summum Bonum possible and the pursuit of it infinitely desirable.[26] By contrast, Hume was willing to say almost nothing about God, save that he probably existed (by the a posteriori evidence of at least a certain amount of order observable in the world). But was one entitled to go farther and call the deity a mind or intelligence? "Philo," at least, in the *Dialogues,* concluded that disputes about the divine nature were "merely verbal," and dismissed all analogies between God and human minds. Above all, Hume refused to connect God in any way with moral life, to attribute to him attributes such as Providence, justice, or love. Hume fitted perfectly Kant's definition of a deist, that is, a man who believed in a God, but not a living or personal God. The pendulum had swung a long way from Clarke's "true deists," who agreed with the Christians in everything except supernatural revelation.

No account of the religious crisis of the eighteenth century would be complete without mention of two closely connected movements in thought, namely, "critical deism," as Sir Leslie Stephen called it, and secularization, the latter as manifested chiefly in the effort to secularize ethics. So much has been written about the former that there is need here only to define it, and give a few examples. Narrowly conceived, critical deism refers to the attack on external evidences, that is, on the credibility of the facts of Christian history as reported in the

---

[25] Ibid., art. "Providence."
[26] For Kant on God's attributes, see especially the *Critique of Practical Reason,* Pt. I, Bk. II, Chap. II, Sect. VII.

Bible. More broadly, it signifies the attack on organized religion in general, and on Christianity and the Christian Church in particular. It was the destructive side of the deistic (also atheistic) movement. Growing up side by side with "constructive deism," critical deism waxed as the latter waned, and became, as Stephen says, "ferocious and menacing" during the revolutionary epoch. Stephen was thinking primarily of English deism, but, in fact, critical deism flourished chiefly in France where, increasingly since the Revocation of the Edict of Nantes by Louis XIV, it was associated with a bigoted and fitfully persecuting church and a corrupt clergy. Voltaire epitomizes the spirit of critical deism and it was institutionalized during the Revolution with the promulgation of the new non-Christian calendar in 1793 and the establishment of the cults designed to displace Christianity. "Ecrasez l'infâme," Voltaire exclaimed. Why crush Christianity? Because it originated in imposture and fear; because it encouraged "sick men's dreams" (Hume's phrase), superstition and fanaticism, leading to wars and massacres; because it preached a false, cruel, and immoral God, revealed in the Bible, chiefly the Old Testament; because it blocked intellectual progress and subjected men to the rule of priests and tyrants. Because also, said Holbach, who was not any kind of deist, it was not even "useful." In the notions men had formed of God, especially the Christian God, was to be found the real source of all the prejudices and evils from which men suffered.

It followed, according to Holbach, that morality should be divorced from theology. Morality "ha[s] nothing in common with imaginary systems made to rest on a force distinct from nature."[27] Was atheism compatible with morality? Most assuredly it was, Holbach argued, in this respect following the tradition of Pierre Bayle. Voltaire, however, demurred. This was still a subject of great debate in eighteenth-century thought: whether men would be virtuous, whether they could be counted upon to perform their social duties, without belief in God and divine sanctions. The deists, Voltaire included, did not think they could, but often did distinguish between "two religions": one for the uneducated masses, whom they feared, a "civil religion" (to use Rousseau's phrase) inculcating a "just and vengeful God"; the other for the enlightened, who did not need such crude beliefs to perform the duties of citizenship. The tide, however, was already beginning to turn toward a more undilutedly secular ethics. This is made clear in Hume's

---

[27] Holbach, *La Morale universelle, ou les devoirs de l'homme fondés sur la nature* (1776), Preface.

Dialogues where Cleanthes and Philo lock horns over precisely this issue. Cleanthes, representing more or less the deist position, argues that even a corrupt religion is better than no religion at all, that the doctrine of a future state is "so strong and necessary a security to morals" that we ought never to abandon it. Philo objects that a corrupt religion is never "favorable to morality," not even among the vulgar, and that a steady attention to eternal salvation begets a narrow selfishness and downgrades the benevolent affections. Philo never actually says so, but it is pretty clear he thinks morality would do better on its own.[28] This was Hume's own position. Revolting against the Calvinism on which he was brought up, Hume wanted to exclude religion from the supervision of conduct and to establish a science of morals that was free of religious motives and sanctions. This was also the desire of the French radicals, conspicuously Holbach and Diderot, who were more candid than Hume in this respect, and who rejected the "two religions" idea out of hand. Holbach, who wrote a textbook on the subject, wanted a "morality of nature" as opposed to a religious morality, based purely on motives of pleasure and pain and social needs, and guided by experience. Originally a deist, Diderot moved to an almost identical view that, however, never completely satisfied him because it seemed too deterministic. The Earl of Shaftesbury at the beginning and Kant at the end of the century represent an intermediate point of view. Neither exactly secularized morals. Both believed in a moral God and in some sort of relationship between morals and religion. At the same time neither Shaftesbury nor Kant allowed religion to supply the motive for a moral action through divine commandments or sanctions. Shaftesbury found the motive in man's "natural moral sense," which, however, could not be complete without piety toward God. Kant did much the same thing, as we have seen.[29] That is, he started with moral man, who could perceive his duty perfectly well without God, but who, as it turned out, needed God in order to combine virtue with happiness. Kant always insisted on morality's independence, even though morality did "lead ineluctably to religion," just as in "the strife of the faculties" in the German university he insisted on philosophy's independence of theology.

A book by Gotthold Ephraim Lessing, invoking certain Leibnizian ideas, calls to mind one further question. Had eighteenth-century thinkers begun to contemplate a possible "education of the human race"?

---

[28] Hume, *Dialogues concerning Natural Religion*, Pt. XII.
[29] See p. 192.

That is, had they begun to think in terms of the historical development of religious ideas and beliefs? To some extent they had, and this will become more apparent when, in a later section, we discuss the rise of historicism in the romantic movement. On the whole, however, they had not. Not only the orthodox but those who broke with orthodoxy, the deists, "neologists," and atheists, continued to think of "the true religion," or of morality (in the case of the atheists) in largely absolutist and static terms. The deists wanted to substitute a natural religion "as old as creation," unchanged and unchanging, for revealed religion. In Tindal's words, "Our religion must always be the same. If God is unchangeable, our duty to him must be so too."[30] Holbach, though he conceded the relativity of human customs, said very much the same thing about morality. He believed in a "universal morality," the same for all men, save in outward form. In men who are susceptible of reason, Holbach wrote, "Nature does not vary, it is a question only of observing it well, in order to deduce from it the invariable moral rules which they ought to follow."[31] Nor did Kant, or for that matter Wolff, think at all historically about religion or morals. For Kant the source of religious faith was to be found in the moral consciousness, or in man's noumenal sense, which did not change. Hume most certainly did think about religion historically, but like so many of his contemporaries who explored religion's origins, he thought of it as pursuing a cyclical course in history, and as sinking, more often than not, into sheer idolatry.[32]

A sense of genuine historical development is what makes Lessing's *Education of the Human Race* (1780) such a landmark. Lessing not only saw, much more clearly than Hume, religion's historical dimension, but saw it as a development upward of man's religious consciousness. This was, indeed, the way Lessing solved the problem of reason and revelation. It was not necessary to take sides in the contemporary debate on the subject, he thought. Religion should be viewed as a progressive revelation, better understood and illuminated by reason in the course of time. "What education is for the individual, revelation is for the whole human race." That is, religious truth was revealed to men in

[30] Matthew Tindal, *Christianity as Old as Creation* (see note 13), Chap. II.
[31] Holbach, *La Morale universelle* (see note 27), Preface.
[32] On this point, see Hume's remarkable chapter (Sect. VII) in *The Natural History of Religion* on "Flux and Reflux of Polytheism and Theism." See also Frank Manuel, *The Eighteenth Century Confronts the Gods,* Harvard University Press, Cambridge, 1959, for the "Euhemerist-historical" interpretation of religious myths as the historical apotheosis of a king, hero, or genius, and of religions as essentially political institutions founded by princes.

stages, and in proportion as they themselves, so to speak, grew up. There were three main stages in the religious education of the human race. In the first stage, of childhood, the ancient Jews rose to the conception of a unitary God, but for themselves only, and appealing to the senses through punishments and rewards, but without belief in a future life. "But each primer is only for a certain age." Men eventually outgrew the Old Testament primer, and the human race was now ready for "the second great step of education," of boyhood, or of Christianity, which preached a universal God and inner purity as preparation for personal immortality. Mankind is destined, however, to grow still further into manhood, and to apprehend rationally what was once only revealed, and to develop still higher conceptions of God and moral conduct. It should be noted, in conclusion, that Lessing's theory was a providential and teleological theory. As such, it could probably only have come out of the German Enlightenment, which was never so antireligious, or anti-Christian, as the French. For Lessing, the whole historical process was God-directed from beginning to end, though man was led by the hand eventually to reason for himself. "Just as in education [of the individual], since not everything can be brought to pass at once, the order of the development of the powers of man is not a matter of indifference; so God, in his revelation, felt constrained to maintain a certain system, a certain moderation."[33] Thus, in the end it is necessary to conclude that Lessing, too, was an absolutist. There was a divine plan for education, "a new, eternal gospel" toward which the human race was pointed. Lessing's innovation, which foreshadowed Hegelianism, was to think of this eternal gospel as unfolding temporally, and in terms of an expanding human consciousness.

[33] Gotthold Ephraim Lessing, *The Education of the Human Race* (*Die Erziehung des Menschengeschlechts*, 1780), J. D. Haney (ed.), Columbia University Press, New York, 1908, p. 34, and Sect. 5.

Systems of Nature

The question of nature, as previously stated, did not generate quite the same intellectual excitement in the eighteenth century as it had in the previous century, but that could hardly have been expected in the aftermath of such giants as Galileo and Newton. Interest in all aspects of nature, however, remained high, and, indeed, the word *nature* became a shibboleth for the eighteenth century, offering to many a new authority, as well as new standards of excellence, principles, and laws. Nature was even addressed as a goddess, as in the Baron d'Holbach's famous apostrophe: "O Nature! sovereign of all beings! etc." But in this chapter we speak only of nonhuman nature. "Who are you, Nature?" Voltaire's Philosopher asked.

> For fifty years I have been seeking you, and I have not found you yet. Are you always active? Are you always passive? Did your elements arrange themselves, as water deposits itself on sand, oil on water, air on oil? Have you a mind which directs all your operations . . . ?[1]

Nature's answer was enigmatic. Her world was arranged according to mathematical laws, but she knew nothing, she said, nor could man know anything about first principles. For a skeptic, however, Voltaire had formed a remarkably clear picture of what nature was, if not why

---

[1] Voltaire, *Dictionnaire philosophique*, art. "Nature."

it was. That picture might even be called a system, though Voltaire would have objected. However, many natural philosophers did, in fact, construct systems of nature, and some actually called them that, in an age that was not supposed to believe in systems. Of these systems, two especially stand out as general types. Let us call them the static and the dynamic or transformist. The former, symbolized by the erection of Newton's tomb in Westminster Abbey (completed in 1731; Plate 18), was clearly regnant up to the publication of the first three volumes of Count Buffon's immensely popular *Natural History* in 1749. Thereafter, the flow of ideas ran toward the second system, which might be symbolized by the many contemporary busts of Buffon, including the one commissioned for the French crown and placed in the Louvre. It is well to remember, however, that transformist ideas encountered stiff resistance even among scientists, including Buffon himself, in the matter of biological species. Nevertheless, the flow was real enough, and to account for it, it will be necessary to interpose a third idea to do with nature. This idea, which is too loose to be called a system, was discussed by both Buffon and Diderot around midcentury. This idea, which we may name, after Diderot, the experimental idea, consisted essentially in trusting to experience rather than to mathematics, deeming the latter to be too confining to read the riddle of nature.

"*Nothing new under the sun:* no new production; no species whatever that existed not from the beginning."[2] Thus did the Abbé Pluche describe nature in one of his many books of popular science. This "truth," as he called it, of a static nature, was widely assumed during his lifetime. It was the product ultimately of a mixture of Platonic and Christian ideas, especially the biblical story of creation, according to which God made the world complete in six days in all its forms and parts. But in the 1730's when Pluche first burst into print, support for this way of looking at things came not only from churchmen but also from deists, not only from religion but also from science itself. Newtonian physics, Linnaean biology, and preformationist doctrine all lent this view of nature new credence, as possibly also did the relatively stable political conditions prevailing in Europe up to 1740 or 1750.[3] Of the many spokesmen for a static system of nature, we may single out for further comment three men who were, in other respects, com-

---

[2] Abbé Pluche, *The History of the Heavens,* J. Wren, London, 1752, Vol. II, p. 202. The original French edition of the *Histoire du ciel,* which I was unable to consult, appeared in 1739.

[3] The political parallel is suggested by Norman Hampson in *The Enlightenment,* Penguin Books, Baltimore, 1968, pp. 87–88.

PLATE 18. *Newton's Tomb,* by William Kent and Michael Rysbrack. Westminster Abbey, London.

By courtesy of the Dean and Chapter of Westminster.

pletely different: Pluche himself, Voltaire, and Carolus Linnaeus, the great Swedish biologist, all of whom wrote important books about nature (on different levels) during the 1730's.

Noel-Antoine, the Abbé Pluche was the great scientific popularizer of his time. His *The Spectacle of Nature* (1732), written for the edification of the young, ran quickly through eighteen editions and was translated into all the major European languages, thus rivaling in popularity Buffon's *magnum opus* at a later date. Pluche wrote as a pious Catholic, yet as one who refused to subscribe to the papal bull *Unigenitus* banning the Jansenists, and who was in constant touch with the savants and literary men of Paris. Though he frequently drew on the arguments of William Derham's *Physico-Theology* (1713), also a widely read work on nature and natural theology, Pluche was abreast of the latest science, citing the publications of the French Academy of Sciences and England's Royal Society, and works by, among others, Newton, Malpighi, Swammerdam, Leeuwenhoek, and especially René Antoine Ferchault de Réaumur, whom he consulted, not only on insects, which were Réaumur's specialty, but on the plan for his whole work. Pluche's message was providential, anthropocentric, and optimistic. In the *Spectacle,* he laid out before his readers' eyes, in nine volumes, the wonderful works of Providence, beginning with the very small, and rising by degrees in the chain of being to the solar and planetary systems. Everything in the universe was created with design, and for man's benefit, by a wise Creator. Pluche obviously shared the cosmic optimism so popular in Augustan England, of physico-theology, and of Leibniz and Alexander Pope. "Whatever is, is right," because God was good and wanted to communicate his goodness to creation in a multitude of ways. No fallen nature, the nature of the Abbé Pluche, but the best of all possible worlds. Everything was created, moreover, once and for all. The static nature of Pluche's nature becomes more explicit in his *The History of the Heavens* (1739), which has already been quoted. Although God created a wonderful variety of organized bodies, at the same time "he limited their number. Nor shall any action or concurrence imaginable add a new genus of plant or animal to those of which he has created the *germina,* and determined the form." Likewise, God created a number of different elements, thus varying the scene of the universe. "But he prevents the destruction of that universe by the very immutability of the nature and number of these elements." Pluche also went out of his way to emphasize that motion never produced anything of itself, but was "a mere effect of the constant, though most free will of the Creator." At the beginning of time, God once and for all regulated the constant and simple laws of motion. Thereafter, he entered into his rest, "having produced what was necessary for the duration of the world."[4]

Voltaire twitted the good Abbé for his simplistic notions about nature, especially his anthropocentrism. "Monsieur the prior (the Abbé's mouthpiece in *The Spectacle of Nature*) had a little too much *amour-propre* in flattering himself that everything had been made for him."[5] But Voltaire took this position, or rather insisted on it, only gradually. Earlier, in the 1730's when Voltaire introduced Newtonianism to France, his view of nature was not so very unlike that of Pluche, though Voltaire wrote as a deist rather than a Christian. In the *Elements of the Philosophy of Newton* (1738), Voltaire was concerned to defend final causes against the Cartesians. Descartes, because he taught that the world was still in the process of development, tempted one to say: "Give me matter and motion, and I will make the world." But clearly this was all wrong. As Newton taught, there could not be an effect without a cause; hence, an immaterial first cause or supreme being must have created everything, the whole world machine, both matter and motion, and the laws by which they were guided. Thus, Voltaire's nature, like that of Pluche and natural theology in general, was essentially passive, receiving its original impress, and continuing support, from a superior power. Voltaire was also quite optimistic at this earlier date. He did not exactly say the world was made for man. But he did say that "what is bad in relation to you, is good in the general arrangement," that "there is more good than evil in the world," and that there were more tranquil times in history than there were great crimes and disasters.[6]

Voltaire never abandoned this general position. He did, however, shift his emphasis in the 1750's, and again after 1765. Brooding on the misfortunes of human life, Voltaire turned against the cosmic optimism of Leibniz and Shaftesbury, and of popularizers like Pope and Pluche. In the face of physical disasters such as the great Lisbon earthquake of 1755, the axiom "Tout est bien" seemed strange indeed. Doubtless, everything was ordered by Providence; but it was all too clear that for a long time it had not been ordered "for our present well-being." Voltaire now contemplated a nature that was indifferent to man, whose empire was destruction, for which man could have no feeling of kinship. He forswore Plato and Epicurus for Bayle, "great enough to do

---

[4] Abbé Pluche, op. cit. (see note 2), pp. 27, 192, 203.
[5] Voltaire, *Le philosophe ignorant* (1766), Première question.
[6] Voltaire, *Eléments de philosophie de Newton*, Chap. I, "De Dieu."

without systems," who taught men to doubt.[7] Yet Voltaire did not doubt the immutable laws and forms of nature, or nature's God. As we shall see, Voltaire, in fact, later soft-pedaled his ridicule of the providentialists, in order to defend his system against the materialists.

Meanwhile, another system, soon to rival Newton's in fame, and complementing it on the biological side, had come to the public's attention. This was the *Systema Naturae* (1735) of Linnaeus, who was an original scientist, ambitious to describe and classify the vast biological world revealed by the voyages of discovery and the microscope. To bring order out of chaos he invented, as is well known, the binomial system of nomenclature for plants and animals. What is perhaps not so well known is that Linnaeus was a pious man, who saw in nature the plan of God, "great Creator and Conservator of all." "The earth," he wrote, "is like a mirror in which Heaven shows itself, as a man reflects himself in still-standing water."[8] Linnaeus found there, and named, fixed species, existing, as he thought, in the divine mind before creation, and not modifiable by addition or subtraction. As he grew older, it is true, Linnaeus developed some doubts, and actually withdrew from later editions of his work assertions that no new species could appear. But by that time the Linnaean order, now acclaimed all over Europe, stood for the immutability of species. Preformation doctrine militated in the same direction. This was the theory, worked out by Malpighi and Swammerdam in the previous century, that the female ovum contained in embryo all the parts that would unfold afterward in the animal body. Thus, Réaumur, though like Linnaeus he also wavered somewhat, believed that the organs of the butterfly already existed in the caterpillar. The effect of this doctrine, as it became popular in the early eighteenth century, was, like the effect of both Linnaean and Newtonian doctrine, to put limits to nature's creativity, to attribute to God the entire power to make the "germs" from which bodies were produced. Thus, science and religion together contributed to uphold, and even to strengthen, the static system of nature.

Opposition to this system was not long in coming, however. The opposition, and concomitant groping toward an alternative and dynamic system, resulted from a number of factors: the desire to free science from religious premises; the thought of Leibniz; the discovery of fos-

---

[7] For this middle phase in Voltaire's thinking about nature, see especially *Le Poème sur le désastre de Lisbon* (1756), and, of course, *Candide* (1759).

[8] From Linnaeus' *Philosophia botanica* (1751), quoted in Norah Burlie, *The Prince of Botanists*, Witherby Ltd., London, 1953, p. 90.

sils, which made it seem likely that some species had undergone change, or else disappeared; successful experiments with cross-breeding, which impressed even Linnaeus; new developments in geological and biological thought; the debate over scientific method that disturbed deep-seated assumptions about the nature of nature; and possibly even a change in the political climate, particularly in Europe.

Diderot, though he was not a scientist, caught the winds of change remarkably well in a little book of thoughts written at midcentury. He had been reading Leibniz, knew his Bacon, and was excited by the new biology. Like Pascal's *Thoughts,* Diderot's own *Thoughts on the Interpretation of nature* (1751, enlarged version 1754) succeeded one another just as they occurred to him, and were not wholly consistent. Diderot's primary purpose appears to have been to establish the superiority of what he called experimental over rational philosophy, the latter signifying to him a mixture of bad metaphysics and worse mathematics. Why had science made so little progress up to then? It was because "the abstract sciences" had occupied the best minds for too long a time, and with too meager results. Diderot, though at the time already associated with the mathematician D'Alembert in their joint venture of the *Encyclopédie,* turned his back on mathematics and made the prediction—it is one of the greatest, and most erroneous, predictions of the eighteenth century—that before a hundred years had passed, one would not be able to count three great geometricians in Europe. Observable facts culled from experience constituted the true richness of philosophy. Rational philosophy, however, either blinded itself to the facts, or else ran ahead of them to make premature pronouncements. Experimental philosophy was more patient, researching the facts ceaselessly, during entire centuries; never knowing what would, or would not, come of its labors, but confident that in the end it would discover something real in nature. In a word, the experimentalists declared war on systems, thus opening nature up to new and less rigidly mathematical interpretations. It is interesting to observe, incidentally, that contemporary taste in gardens likewise marked a partial turning away from mathematical models, especially in England. The new, so-called "English garden," to be seen, for example, at Stourhead, new home of the Hoare banking family, presented nature in a more "natural" guise, less geometrized than the French formal garden, as conceived by Le Nôtre and his imitators. However, the motivation for this change of taste was perhaps as much political as it was aesthetic. The new freedom in landscape was thought of, by

Shaftesbury and others, as more fit for a free people like the English, than the French garden, which now began to be associated with auto- cratic rule.

Yet Diderot was already hard at work thinking up a system of his own, and not hesitating to use the word itself on occasion in a non- pejorative way. Is this a paradox? It depends, of course, on the mean- ing that Diderot and his contemporaries attached to the word. Hostility to systems in general is supposed to be a hallmark of eighteenth-century philosophy, and in a sense it was. Did not Condillac write a book against systems, and did not Voltaire, citing Newton, join in the chorus of disapprobation which, as we have seen, also included the Encyclo- pedists? But few went so far as Hume, who limited the power of the human mind to appearances, and raised doubts about the logicality and permanence of the laws of nature. There were obviously good as well as bad systems. Even Condillac admitted that. A metaphysical system, such as the Cartesian, which ignored experience, was bad. So was a closed system, which did not admit new facts, or a system, so Voltaire would have said, that pretended to knowledge of first principles (not, however, to be confused with final causes in which Voltaire believed; one could know that God created the universe, but only describe gravitation externally, not penetrate its essence). But there were also good systems. In fact, despite what D'Alembert says in the preliminary discourse to the *Encyclopédie*,[9] the initial wave of revulsion against sys- tems had begun to abate somewhat just about the time Diderot was writing his *Thoughts*. Significantly, the word *system* appeared in the titles of important books about nature, by the scientist Pierre de Maupertuis (1751), and a bit later, by Holbach (1770). Diderot him- self, after scoring one kind of system, that is, "rationalist philosophy," proceeded to project another kind that he could approve. Partly, this was an ideal, a single principle, assumed to exist, which would eventu- ally clarify and unite all known phenomena, as well as phenomena still to be discovered, "to form a system." Nature, Diderot said, was like a woman who likes to disguise herself, and who, shedding her disguises one by one, holds out hope, to those who follow her assiduously, "of knowing one day her whole person."[10] Diderot also favored bold hy- potheses, suggested perhaps by some facts, but running ahead of the facts, and fired by the imagination. A literary man, Diderot recognized

[9] D'Alembert: "Le goût des systèmes, plus propre à flater l'imagination qu'à éclairer la raison, est aujourd'hui presque absolument banni des bons ouvrages."
[10] Diderot, *Pensées sur l'interprétation de la nature*, nos. XLIV, XII.

the important role that was played by imaginative genius in science as well as poetry. It was upon such hypotheses that he and Buffon, and, indeed, the whole Holbachian circle, constructed a new dynamic system of nature, essentially at variance with the static system defended by Voltaire and others. Obviously, Diderot did not wholly follow his own advice about an exclusively "experimental philosophy."[11]

The new currents in geological and biological thinking also did much to inspire a dynamic view. Count Buffon, superintendent of the Jardin du Roi, was a key figure in this change in thought. A professed enemy of systems, he nevertheless sought to embrace "Nature in general" in his encyclopedic *Natural History,* which, as noted, began coming out in 1749. Though not an atheist, Buffon tried to relate this history, extending from the origin of the solar system to the appearance of man on earth, without reference to final causes. There must be no mixing of physics with theology, he said, no recourse to causes outside nature. This stance inevitably got Buffon into trouble with the theological faculty at Paris, which forced him to recant his views on the origin of the earth as contrary to Scripture. But in the *Epochs of Nature,* the most famous part of his work, which did not appear until the end of his life, Buffon was back at the old stand, explaining how the earth had first formed from the shock of a comet colliding with the sun, how this original molten mass progressively cooled, permitting the consolidation of rocks and mountains, and how in turn water covered the entire earth, land masses formed, and finally life made its appearance. Buffon's six epochs were obviously a naturalistic counterpart of the six days of creation described in Scripture. But the important thing to note here is that from his geological speculations emerged not only a new view of the age of the earth—Buffon calculated that the "history" he described had required 74,832 years (in private, he said millions of years)—but a new emphasis on the mutability of nature. The introduction to the *Epochs* is worth quoting in this connection.

> Though it appears at first sight that Nature's works do not change . . . , on closer observation it will be seen that it undergoes successive alterations, that it lends itself to new combinations, mutations both of matter and form. . . . We cannot doubt that it is very different today from what it was in the beginning. . . . These are the divers changes that we call its epochs. Nature is found in different states.

[11] For Diderot's distinction between rational and experimental philosophy, see ibid., no. XXIII.

Yet, as John Greene has observed,[12] Buffon stopped short of a full-fledged uniformitarian view of geologic change, insisting that the original mountain structure of the earth had remained fundamentally intact to the present day. Everything, moreover, happened according to plans prescribed by God. His "First View of Nature," inserted at the head of the twelfth volume of the 1764 edition of the *Natural History,* has a teleological ring about it. Nature, Buffon affirmed, was God's creature, receiving its power "from the divine power, the part which manifests itself," and having movement and life as its goals.

The vitalist trend in biology increased the presumption in favor of a dynamic nature. Two experiments in particular made a deep impression, Abraham Trembley's discovery in 1744 of the freshwater polyp's regenerative powers after being dismembered, and Father Needham's study in 1748 of animalcules, which appeared to prove the spontaneous generation of life. Needham, it should be noted, worked with Buffon, who had already propounded his theory of organic particles. These putative particles, or molecules, were organized into animate bodies, he believed, by a force that was inherent in nature itself (he called it a *moule intérieur,* or internal mold). At about the same time Maupertuis, president of the Berlin Academy of Sciences, hypothecated the appearance, from time to time, purely by accident or "error," of varieties in established biological types, which could be perpetuated by inheritance, and thus create new species. Then, slightly later, came Albrecht von Haller's discovery of continued muscular irritability after the death of the body.

The effect of all this speculation about the generative process was to suggest a new conception of matter, self-organizing and active. Could it be, Buffon mused, that there were two kinds of matter, one living, and one dead or brute? How did the former originate? Was "the living and animated" a physical property of matter itself? Maupertuis, repudiating Cartesian dualism, likewise attributed to matter some degree of intelligence, which could account for spontaneous generation and the emergence of new types. Though neither Buffon nor Maupertuis was a materialist, their hypotheses certainly provided fuel for the materialists. But there was another powerful reason for the wave of materialist thought in France, the antireligious animus. People such as Holbach and Diderot were looking for some way to eliminate God entirely from the system of nature, even as first cause, and contem-

---

[12] John Greene, *The Death of Adam,* Iowa State University Press, Ames, 1959, p. 75.

porary scientific thought showed them how to do it. They could give to matter properties that were formerly possessed only by the Creator. This is exactly what Holbach did in his *System of Nature,* which, in effect, substituted nature for God. Holbach's whole argument hinged on his conception of matter. Nature consisted only of matter and movement. But matter was not dead, as "the physicists" thought, but in continual movement. Whence came this movement? Well, said Holbach, "if by nature we understand a mass of dead matter, devoid of all properties, purely passive, we shall doubtless be forced to look outside nature for the principle of its movements." But, in truth, nature was a whole, moving "in virtue of its essence," hence capable by its own power of producing all the phenomena observable in the world.[13] Diderot, as early as the *Letter on the Blind* (1749), similarly spoke of "matter in fermentation," which caused the world to take shape. His spokesman, the blind professor Saunderson, derided any sort of finalist view of nature. The imperfections of the world, monsters, blindness, and the like, argued against divine design, or a single act of creation. The alternative was to think of nature, or rather matter, as ceaselessly moving, and as producing, by trial and error, the imperfect world we perceive. So Saunderson-Diderot, like Holbach, shook off tradition, and separated physics from theology.

Diderot had been converted to materialism, but not yet to transformism. He still thought of nature as producing static, though not always perfect, types. But in *The Dream of D'Alembert* (1769), the supreme statement of his materialism, Diderot put into the mouths of his interlocutors some distinctly transformist ideas. Diderot's thinking had itself been transformed in the ten years' interval from his meditating further on the implications of the new biology. Transformism may be defined as a developmental, as well as dynamic, idea of nature, and therefore as anticipating evolutionary theory. Neither Holbach nor Diderot stated it with perfect clarity. Mostly, they raised questions. "Everything changes in the universe; nature includes no constant form," said Holbach. But one was permitted also to ask whether, if nature produced man (the materialist hypothesis), it could not also produce new species, and cause old ones to disappear; and whether the human species had not arrived at its present state "by different passages or successive developments."[14] "Who knows," Diderot asked, "how many species of animals have preceded us, or will follow? Everything changes,

[13] Holbach, *Système de la nature,* Georg Olms, Hildisheim, 1966, Vol. I, pp. 25, 29 (Chap. II, "Du mouvement et de son origine").

[14] Ibid., Vol. I, pp. 98, 105 (Chap. VI, "De l'homme").

only the whole remains. The world is continually beginning and end-ing."[15] Concerning the mechanics of evolution, if it was evolution they were talking about, Holbach only said that all changes came about from a recombination of atoms, Diderot that they were traceable to an internal dynamism, or teleology. Paying little or no attention to the possible selective action of a changing environment, Diderot spoke of "an inherent disposition" in the undifferentiated germ cell to produce differentiated organs, of organs creating needs (but also of needs creating organs, whatever that meant), of *"un principe vital,"* which not only maintained but brought about changes in the life process.[16] The language was vague, but clearly the French materialists were groping for words to express a transformist view of nature. Nor were the materialists the only ones to do so. One remembers what Goethe had to say in his autobiography about Holbach's *System of Nature,* how it repelled him in its "melancholy, atheistical twilight." Yet Goethe too had transformist ideas, as had Maupertuis, as we have seen, Buffon at times, Caspar Friedrich Wolff, and Erasmus Darwin. All put forward notions about variations within species, or possible new species, caused by chance, scientific breeding, volition, or even environment (which, however, for Buffon only had a degenerative effect), and proceeding over long spans of time. Transformism was now in the air.

But resistance developed, and there were people who played with the idea only to reject it. One can understand Voltaire's resistance since he did not essentially alter his earlier premises. From 1765, when he apparently first realized the full implications of the new "philosophy," down to his death thirteen years later, Voltaire attacked materialism in print almost as often as *l'infâme.* He refused to consider, even as a hypothesis, that motion was inherent in matter. Motion, on his belief in intelligent design, had to be something added to matter at the creation. Voltaire was also quick to ridicule those recent scientific "discoveries," which he thought gave comfort to materialism and undermined his static view of nature. Maupertuis, Buffon, Trembley, and especially Needham, the Irish Jesuit who "travelled in Europe in secular habit" and deceived even "good scientists," felt the acid of his

---

[15] Diderot, "D'Alembert's Dream," in *Rameau's Nephew and Other Works,* Jacques Barzun (trans.), Library of Liberal Arts, Bobbs-Merrill, Indianapolis, 1964, p. 117.

[16] Lester Crocker has pointed out the similarity of Diderot's *principe vital* to Henri Bergson's *élan vital.* See "Diderot and Eighteenth Century French Trans-formism," *Forerunners of Darwin,* Bentley Glass (ed.), Johns Hopkins University Press, Baltimore, 1959, p. 141.

wit. Only disreputable motives, "the love of novelty, the craze of systems, and above all, conceit" would have persuaded men to destroy the "germs" from which, as every sensible person knew, organisms developed.[17] In these views, Voltaire received unexpected support from the younger scientific community, an important segment of which was currently defending ontogenesis against the new-fangled epigenesis. The Abbé Spallanzani, a brilliant physiologist, repeated Needham's experiments and came to very different conclusions, thereby dealing spontaneous generation a severe blow. None other than Haller himself, and his friend the Swiss naturalist Charles Bonnet, similarly condemned Needham, and upheld preformationism. Bonnet's philosophy is particularly interesting because he used the word *evolution,* though in an old rather than a new sense. For Bonnet, evolution meant the process of ontogenesis, by which individual organisms developed from germs bearing God's imprint from the Creation. Variations occurred, of course, but always in consequence of differences between the primordial germs, and always within species. "I at first assumed, as a fundamental principle," Bonnet said in his *Contemplation of Nature* (1764), "that nothing was generated; that everything was originally preformed." Several years earlier he had written that nature was admirable in the conservation of both individuals and species. "No changes, no alteration, perfect identity. Species maintain themselves victoriously over the elements, over time, over death, and the term of their duration is unknown."[18] Though Bonnet and his friends were experimental scientists, they had their metaphysical reasons for refusing to accept the idea of a "living matter," having the power of creation and adaptation. As both Christians and mechanists, they began with the assumption that nature had the power to function only as a machine created by God.

Had Voltaire only known it, the great Buffon himself ultimately rejected transformism. That is, Buffon's philosophy of change did not encompass biological species, or, more deeply, the larger order of nature. Buffon actually contemplated two orders of nature.[19] First, there

---

[17] Voltaire, *Des singularités de la nature* (1768), Chaps. XII ("Des germes") and XIII ("De la prétendue race d'anguilles formées de farine").

[18] Quoted by Bentley Glass, op. cit. (see note 16), pp. 164, 167.

[19] Jacques Roger (*Les sciences de la vie dans la pensée française du XVIIIe siècle,* Armand Colin, Paris, 1963, pp. 575–577) makes a nice distinction between Buffon the biologist and Buffon the naturalist. The former, predominant in the "Vues de la nature" of 1764–1765, meditated on nature "au sens large." The latter perceived nature more in little, the many varieties of living forms, the influence of environment, the heredity of acquired characters.

was the temporal order, described in the *Epochs,* "living," ceaselessly active, in continual flux. But this order had to be seen against the backdrop of an eternal order of things, created and guaranteed by God. This second order, as we may call it, Buffon delineated with great conviction and vividness in his famous two "Views of Nature." This was the order of universal laws, of interior molds, and species that never changed.

> Minister of God's irrevocable orders, depository of his immutable decrees, Nature never separates herself from the laws which have been prescribed for her; she alters not at all the plans which have been made for her, and in all her works she presents the seal of the Eternal: this divine imprint, unalterable prototype of existences, is the model on which she operates, model all of whose traits are expressed in ineffaceable characters, and pronounced forever.[20]

Buffon had come to think of biological species as belonging to this model of immutability. Individuals changed, but species did not change. "Time itself," he wrote in the "Second View," "is relative only to individuals, to beings whose existence is fugitive." Species, on the other hand, were "perpetual beings, as ancient as Nature herself."[21] Buffon had considered and stated the hypothesis of evolution, only to reject it. The infertility of the products of cross-breeding, and the "missing links," or the absence of gradations between species, convinced him of its implausibility. Buffon's enormous prestige, thrown into the scales against evolution, did much to stem the transformist tide in the late eighteenth century.

Immanuel Kant, for one, was much impressed by Buffon's arguments. Early in his career, Kant, combining mechanical and teleological explanations as was his wont, boldly projected a theory of cosmic evolution. In his *Universal Natural History and Theory of the Heavens* (1755), Kant represented nature (matter) as organizing itself, by mechanical laws, from an original chaos into the well-ordered stellar systems of the present, and as continuing to develop *ad infinitum.* It did so, however, according to the principle of plenitude, laid down by the First Cause, which decreed a universe striving for ever greater variety and fullness. But Kant never extended this principle to the organic world. He certainly did not think the idea of organic evolution

---

[20] Buffon, "Première Vue," *Oeuvres philosophiques,* Presses universitaires de France, Paris, 1954, p. 31.
[21] Buffon, "Seconde Vue," ibid., p. 35.

absurd, and at one point even spoke of it as "a daring adventure of reason." The most that Kant seems to have been willing to concede, however, was that there were variations within species, as, for example, in the descent of yellow, black, and brown races from a probable original white stock. Kant's orthodoxy in this area of thought is surprising. The father of the critical philosophy reasoned here in terms of certain well-worn presuppositions: the sterility of hybrids, mostly on Buffon's say-so, and also Buffon's definition of species as distinct entities; a version of preformationism, according to which all species characters were assumed to be latent in "nature's original models," or special "germs"; and in general, the habit of thinking teleologically about nature. This last aspect of his thinking he took over from Leibniz. It comes through most clearly in the *Critique of Judgment* (1790) where, having first warned against excluding mechanical causation, Kant nevertheless concluded that it was "absolutely impossible . . . to derive from Nature itself grounds of explanation for purposive combinations," for example, living beings.[22] This was to reinforce his conviction (not, of course, his certain knowledge) that nature pursued ends determined from the beginning. Thus, though Kant claimed that experience disproved transformism, or showed no example of it, he was, in a sense, predisposed to believe in the fixity of species, if not planets. In an earlier work Kant declared that it must be presumed, as a general principle of science, "that throughout organic nature, amid all changes of individual creatures, the species maintain themselves unaltered—according to the formula of the schools, *quaelibit natura est conservatrix sui.*"[23]

Ernst Cassirer says that in the eighteenth century a new conception of nature was "in the making," which "no longer [sought] to derive and explain becoming from being, but being from becoming."[24] This is exactly right. It was "in the making"—but not yet dominant, as it

[22] Kant, *Critique of Judgment*, Pt. III, Sect. 78.

[23] Kant, "Bestimmung des Begriffs einer Menschenrace" ("Conception of Race," 1785), quoted by A. Lovejoy, "Kant and Evolution," in *Forerunners of Darwin* (see note 16), p. 184. The French philosopher Jean-Baptiste-René Robinet likewise drew back from affirming a concept of organic evolution, after postulating a dynamic nature, and variations in nature from an original prototype or "germ." Since he did not think of species themselves as developing, Robinet ended up, like Kant, by holding to the fixity of species. See Robinet's *De la nature* (1761), which created a considerable stir in Paris, and which did have an influence on Diderot's transformist thinking.

[24] Ernst Cassirer, *The Philosophy of the Enlightenment,* Princeton University Press, Princeton, 1951, p. 80.

was to become in the next century. The last decade of the eighteenth century marked the publication of some remarkable transformist works: in England, Erasmus Darwin's *Zoonomia* (1794) and James Hutton's *Theory of the Earth* (1795); and in France, Pierre Laplace's *Treatise on Celestial Mechanics* (1799), which advanced the nebular hypothesis (anticipated by Kant) of the solar system, and Lamarck's first discourse on evolution in 1800 (not actually published until the following year, under a different title); not to mention Goethe's treatises on plants and animals, which were vaguely evolutionary. But only a few years before, the great Linnaeus, symbol of nature's fixity, had been given a royal funeral, and both Buffon and Kant had declared themselves against biological transformism. It is also well to remember that the evolutionary ideas of Erasmus Darwin and Lamarck soon fell on evil days in England in the wake of the political reaction against the French Revolution.

Mention should be made, in conclusion, of a way of looking at nature, an attitude rather than a system, which was inherited from the preceding century. This was the Baconian idea of nature as useful to man, as a field for human exploitation. Buffon was a more vehement spokesman for this idea than even Diderot. For Diderot, though he was much interested in technology—witness the eleven volumes of plates of machines and industrial processes in the *Encyclopédie,* was always somewhat skeptical of man's ability to comprehend nature as a whole, and put limits even to what utilitarian science could achieve. Buffon was more optimistic in this respect than Diderot. Man had now entered the seventh and last epoch of the earth's history, "when the power of man seconded that of Nature." "Seconded," he said, but he really meant "exceeded." Always, Buffon's comparison, reminiscent of things said by Thomas Henry Huxley a hundred years later, was between brute and cultivated nature. Brute nature, nature left to itself, turned into a jungle, or became "hideous and dying." But how beautiful by comparison was "this cultivated Nature," which bore the imprint of man's power.

> The state in which we see nature today is as much our work as its; we have known how to temper and modify it, bend it to our needs and desires; we have founded, cultivated, fructified the earth: the aspect under which it presents itself is, then, very different from that of times anterior to the invention of the arts.[25]

[25] Buffon, *Epoques de la nature,* in *Oeuvres philosophiques* (see note 20), p. 118; see also p. 34.

Conceivably, man could lose his empire again, as during the barbarian invasions. But if man was vigilant, he could remain master of the earth, as God intended. Buffon, too, was a Baconian—and neoclassical in his taste for a gardenlike nature, well shaped and pruned, molded by the hand of man.

Liberty and Equality

Interest in political and social questions quickened enormously during the eighteenth century. Partly this was because politics and political economy were widely thought to be branches of the science of man, which was the rage of the age." 'Tis evident," Hume summarized, "that all the sciences have a relation, greater or less, to human nature." This relationship, he thought, was particularly true of politics, which considered men in their social state, and as dependent on each other. However, in speaking of politics as a science, or of reducing it to a science,[1] Hume suggested another reason for the growing interest in the subject, namely the scientific revolution. We have seen how in the seventeenth century some thinkers, inspired by the new science, dreamed of applying the scientific method to social studies. This endeavor continued into the eighteenth century. There were skeptics, of course, and plenty of disagreement as to what kind of science it constituted. Some, like Turgot, distinguished sharply between physics and the moral sciences, attributing to the former recurrent laws but to the latter patterns that changed with the progress of knowledge. Hume vacillated, now linking politics to natural philosophy, now to moral philosophy, in which the unexpected had to be conjured with. Still others, like

---

[1] This was the subject of a separate essay by Hume. He spoke of the dependence of political science on the science of man in, among other places, the introduction to *A Treatise of Human Nature*.

Condorcet, leaned toward the mathematical side, seeking precise rules of political behavior, but basing them on social facts or "truths of detail." Science beckoned to all these men, if in varying degrees. Science held out the prospect of greater prediction and control in society, as well as in nature, of an improved political machinery for the protection of man's freedom and happiness.[2]

The barometer of political concern also naturally rose in proportion as actual political problems multiplied and demanded solution. This was especially so after midcentury in France where the absolute monarchy threatened to break down, and, in any case, ran counter to powerful individual and class interests. In a general way, France repeated England's experience of the seventeenth century. From being largely apolitical, or political only in a theoretical way, French intellectuals became more and more *engagés,* not content merely to talk, but wanting to act, and agitating for specific reforms. After 1789 all countries joined in political debate. Englishmen, for example, relatively quiescent in political theory since the time of Locke, produced in a few years a number of major works to defend, or denounce, the French Revolution.

Furthermore, despite important borrowings from the past, the eighteenth century marked new departures in political thinking. Out of France, though not without English and American help, came the modern liberal creed, which involved discussion of political means as well as ends. In rebuttal came "classic," but essentially new, arguments for conservatism. Out of eighteenth-century political thought, whether liberal or conservative, came new touchstones for testing political and social institutions.

Jeremy Bentham identifies two of these touchstones, one very ancient and the other freshly minted, and alludes to a third, in his *Anarchical Fallacies,* or thoughts on the French Declaration of the Rights of Man of 1789. When he penned this attack in the early 1790's, Bentham was still technically a Tory, though already a legal reformer of some note. Yet the gist of his criticism was not so much substantive as methodological. Bentham denounced the revolutionaries' appeal to natural law, and opposed to it the touchstone of utility. Imprescriptible rights, supposedly imprinted on the minds of every man, and protected by social or political contract, were metaphysical nonsense. Moreover, these rights chained the legislator down to a code for all time, thus

---

[2] Peter Gay calls the second volume of his work on the Enlightenment "The Science of Freedom."

subjecting the living to the dead. Moral and political questions should be discussed, not by an appeal to "their goddess, Nature," which was a figment, but by reference to utility. Utility simply meant concern for the general welfare, or the happiness of individuals and communities, and obviously could be arrived at only experimentally and on the basis of facts culled from experience. In the course of time, but certainly not in advance, it might be possible to deduce some general propositions in politics as in physics.

Of the two chief touchstones juxtaposed by Bentham (a third, divine right, he passed over with hardly so much as a glance), the palm was already passing to utility, as opposed to natural law. Yet this trend can be exaggerated. Bentham himself testifies that natural law arguments, which he set out to unmask, still met with "general reception." Doubtless, Bentham was thinking primarily of the French and their Revolution, but he might also have mentioned Tom Paine's immensely popular *The Rights of Man* (1791–1792), written to refute Edmund Burke, and Condorcet's slightly earlier pamphlet on the American Revolution. Both of these works stated unequivocally, as did the Declaration of the Rights of Man itself, the familiar doctrine of natural rights. Condorcet, in other respects very much the empiricist, found these rights discoverable by reason, prior to positive law, and applicable to all peoples. "The study of laws instituted by different peoples and in different centuries," he wrote elsewhere, "is useful only to give to reason the support of observation and experience."[3] It seems clear that by this time political philosophy in general had, indeed, begun to employ more empirical arguments, but that natural law thinking persisted at the popular level and supplied many of the slogans for political action. It also still had sufficient standing to elicit spirited rejoinders by thinkers of the stature of Bentham and Burke.

Throughout the eighteenth century as a whole, natural law showed remarkable durability, more than it is given credit for in recent historiography. Many of the major universities of Protestant Europe had long since established chairs of natural law. New translations of the seventeenth-century masters, chiefly Grotius and Pufendorf, manuals and commentaries by Christian Wolff, Burlamaqui of Geneva, and others transmitted the teachings of natural law to intellectual France, where it became axiomatic to speak, as D'Alembert did in the *Encyclopédie,* of a natural law that was "anterior to all particular con-

[3] Condorcet, *Essai sur la constitution et les fonctions des assemblées provinciales* (1788), quoted by Henri Sée, *Les Idées politiques en France au XVIIIᵉ siècle,* Hachette, Paris, 1920, pp. 210–211.

ventions," and as "the first law of peoples."[4] Thus, appeals to nature continued to be made, even by many of those who, on the whole, favored utility in political argument. Natural law, however, now had more than one meaning. It could mean, as it had done traditionally, an unchangeable rule of justice for all men, existing prior to human laws or conventions, and discoverable by reason. On the other hand, natural law could mean an empirical generalization from the facts of human nature and history. Most political thinkers, even of the new breed, combined or confused these two meanings. Both meanings, however, served to fix universal legal norms, which could not be changed at the will of the sovereign.

Voltaire frequently referred to natural laws and natural rights. Engraved in men's hearts, they obviously belonged to his empire of nature as distinguished from the empire of custom, in which laws, like everything else, varied enormously. Montesquieu enlarged this latter empire, observing differences everywhere. His "spirit of the laws" (*esprit des lois*), it should be noted, did not signify legal uniformity, but rather heterogeneity among nations. "Spirit" was what gave each nation its special character, and was influenced, he said, by all sorts of physical and social causes. Yet in the famous first chapter of his masterpiece, Montesquieu spoke pure natural law language, even if he did not call it by that name.

> Laws, in their most general signification, are the necessary relations arising from the nature of things. . . . Before laws were made, there were relations of possible justice. To say that there is nothing just or unjust but what is commanded or forbidden by positive laws, is the same as saying that before the describing of a circle all the radii were not equal.[5]

Montesquieu, like many other political thinkers of the eighteenth century, was clearly at one and the same time a believer in the natural

---

[4] The *Encyclopédie* included several articles on natural law, one by Diderot that is frankly skeptical, and that is discussed later (see page 223), the other by the lawyer Boucher d'Argis, which summarizes the meanings attached to it in the eighteenth century, and the chief authorities such as Cicero, Grotius, Pufendorf, Barbeyrac, and Burlamaqui; it also refers the reader to Montesquieu's *The Spirit of the Laws*. Engraved in men's hearts by God, and established by reason, natural law is described therein as "perpetual and unchanging." In this respect, it is said to differ from the positive law, which "is subject to change by right of the same authority that established it" (see the article, "Droit de la Nature").

[5] I have used Thomas Nugent's eighteenth-century translation here. *Sur l'esprit des lois* was first published in 1748.

law tradition, and a political relativist. Probably what he meant to say was that there were natural laws, "fixed and invariable," of society as well as physics, but that they were, and must be, applied differently in different parts of the world. The Physiocrats present a more clear-cut case. Utilitarian in their conception of human nature, they nonetheless postulated natural laws of economics prior to, and not to be suspended by, governments. "Neither men nor their governments *make* them [that is, rules of justice, liberty and property] and cannot *make* them," said Dupont de Nemours, summarizing the views of Dr. Quesnay. "They recognize them as conforming to the supreme reason which governs the universe."[6]

Rousseau modified natural law theory to suit his own purposes. Nevertheless, he was profoundly influenced by it. A superficial reading of the *Discourse on the Origin of Inequality* and *The Social Contract* (1762) might persuade one otherwise. In the earlier work, Rousseau has harsh words for the natural law philosophers, both ancient and modern, and appears to banish natural laws and natural rights from his state of nature. In *The Social Contract,* the doctrine of sovereignty, or the general will, might seem to rule out inalienable rights. But such was not Rousseau's intention. He was trying to make the point that men became conscious of moral notions only in society, not that such notions, for instance of justice and injustice, did not exist antecedently, or were only rules of utility, as Hume said. "The eternal laws of nature and order exist," Rousseau wrote in *Emile,* which appeared in the same year. "They take precedence over positive law for the wise man; they are written in the depths of his heart by conscience and reason; to be free he must obey them."[7] Earlier in the same section Rousseau had criticized Montesquieu for concerning himself only with the positive laws of nations, and not with general principles. But to judge wisely in matters of government, it was necessary, he thought, to combine the two. One "must know what ought to be in order to judge what is," Rousseau said, and presumably this knowledge of the "ought" could come only from consulting natural law. Admittedly, Rousseau sounds like Hobbes sometimes, as when he says in *The Social Contract* that the sovereign, once it is created by social contract, "is sole judge of

---

[6] Dupont de Nemours, *Maximes du Docteur Quesnay,* partially reprinted in *Les Ecrivains politiques du XVIIIᵉ siècle,* A. Bayet and F. Albert (editors), Armand Colin, Paris, 1935, p. 332.

[7] Rousseau, *Emile,* Bk. V, toward the end. See on Rousseau and natural law the illuminating discussion by Robert Derathé, *Jean-Jacques Rousseau et la science politique de son temps,* Presses universitaires de France, Paris, 1950, Chap. III.

what is important" in the matter of powers, goods, and liberty. This statement, however, comes midway in a chapter on "the limits of the sovereign power," and Rousseau has already exempted from the sovereign's control (or rather included in his conception of what sovereignty really is, that is, the general will in which all participate) "the natural rights they [citizens] should enjoy as men." Of course, the law did not exist simply to protect natural rights, as it did for Locke, but was a positive means to moral growth. All the same, Rousseau went along pretty far with the natural rights "school," even while modifying, sometimes profoundly, its conceptions of contract, law, and the state. Clearly, natural law was still widely invoked in political debate, perhaps more at the popular level by the time of the French Revolution, but still to some extent also by major political thinkers like Rousseau.

Utility, however, now rivaled nature as a political touchstone. The new importance it had taken on reflected the growing empiricism, which was suspicious of anything that smacked of apriorism. Bentham's arguments, advanced in *Anarchical Fallacies* and elsewhere, go back a long way to Helvétius on the French side, and to Hume on the English side. But perhaps one can observe the transition to a new way of thinking about politics best in a thinker like Diderot, who, at first, talked traditional natural law language but soon found it inadequate to express his political notions. In an early article on "Droit naturel" (*Encyclopédie,* 1755), Diderot gave up the contract idea (for societies, though not governments), preferring to base legislation on human needs and desires, which he thought were pretty much the same the world over. The "general will" (*sic*), not natural law, he thought, could best determine where in a society "the general and common interest" left off, and the rights of "particular wills" began. Others developed this position farther. Helvétius does not even mention natural law in his chief works. The art of legislation consisted, for him, in simply calculating the greatest happiness of the greatest number, happiness being equated with what a nation thought was in its best self-interest. Hume, though less crudely utilitarian (or rationalistic) in his anthropology, explicitly rejected the philosophy of natural law. In place of eternal laws of nature, social contracts, and natural rights, Hume put "felt" utility. Laws were merely conventions rooted in experience and habit. Though utilitarianism obviously opened the door to political relativism, it is worth noting again that no eighteenth-century utilitarian quite carried relativism to its logical conclusion. All sought the universal in political life, and to some extent found it, though now, of course, it had to be based on observed facts, such as, preeminently, a common human nature, that is, more or less the same human needs, pleasures and pains, everywhere.

Turning now from the method to the substance of political thought, the first thing to note is that there was no necessary correlation between the two. The method (or the touchstones) tell us much about how men thought, but not what they thought substantively about political and social arrangements. A utilitarian, for example, could be a liberal, conservative, or revolutionary, just as a believer in "nature" could subscribe to an autocratic or democratic version of the social contract. A second thing to note is the wide variety of expressed political ends and means, exhibited not only as between different countries but in the same country at different times and in different circumstances. English political thought, for example, was more complacent than the French, and the German less liberal than either the English or French. Moreover, the French themselves grew steadily more radical in response to specific political developments under the monarchy and going into the Revolution. But amidst the welter of ideas and panaceas two stand out in the sense of being à la mode. The first was a modernized absolutism, exhibited chiefly but by no means exclusively in Germany, the second a modernized liberalism, chiefly on display in France. A third idea, a modernized conservatism, collected a considerable following during, and in reaction to, the French Revolution; this is discussed in a later section and different context.[8]

The new absolutism, sometimes called enlightened despotism, contrasts sharply with the divine right theory at certain points. Significantly, the key analogy had changed. The king, formerly represented as a species of divine being, and as ruling his kingdom absolutely, in the same manner that God exercized his sway over the whole creation, was now said to be "the mainspring" of the machine of state. Frederick the Great of Prussia, as is well known, also called himself "first servant of the state" (le premier domestique), and "citizen," making himself useful to his fellow citizens. This manner of speaking meant that the king derived his power, not from God, as Bishop Bossuet had said, but from the consent of the people, and on condition that he provide for their happiness and well-being.[9] Nothing was said by Frederick, however, about the people's right to resist, should he fail to carry out his obligations, nor about sharing his power with others. Thus, although

---

[8] See p. 288f.

[9] See Frederick the Great's *La Réfutation du Prince de Machiavel* (1740), Chap. 1, and *Testament politique* (1752), Introduction, Conclusion, and the section on the education of a prince.

Frederick subscribed to the social contract, he did not do so on Lockean terms. "Enlightened" absolutism was palpably a reflection of the rise of the bureaucratic state in early modern Europe and of the new scientific rationalism. Among the chief advocates of this absolutism were German civil servants, administrators, and professors, who talked incessantly about efficiency, central planning, and organization. Said one of them:

> A properly constituted state must be exactly analogous to a machine, in which all the wheels and gears are precisely adjusted to one another; and the ruler must be the foreman, the mainspring or the soul . . . which sets everything in motion.[10]

Thus, the chief justification for absolutism was its superior efficiency. As Frederick himself said, Newton would never have been able to "arrange" his system of attraction if he had had to work in concert with other philosophers such as Leibniz and Descartes. Just so, the prince must "make" his system, and execute it himself.

It may be remarked in passing that the idea of "enlightened government" was by no means confined to the proponents of absolutism. Some constitutionalists, as well as cameralists, also thought of the state as a mechanism, to be manipulated to produce more security, freedom, and equality. This way of thinking is evident, for example, in Helvétius' conception of the "legislator," who calculates men's pleasures and pains in order to promote the general interest. In his famous pamphlet in support of the Third Estate at the commencement of the French Revolution, the Abbé Siéyès, another constitutionalist, made express mention of "the social mechanism," which, he said, could not be understood except by analyzing it into its parts, "as if it were an ordinary machine," and then putting it back together again.[11] It was one of Edmund Burke's most telling criticisms of French revolutionaries in general, that, like Siéyès, they conceived politics in abstract, and essentially unhistorical, terms, as though one could dismantle and reassemble the state like a machine, and so make it more efficient.

Increasing efficiency, however, was not the hallmark of the "liberal-

---

[10] J. H. G. von Justi, quoted by Geraint Parry, "Enlightened Government and Its Critics in Eighteenth-Century Germany," *The Historical Journal*, Vol. VI, no. 2 (1963), p. 182. Justi was professor of cameralist studies at Vienna and Göttingen, and served for a time in the Prussian mining administration.

[11] Abbé Siéyès, *Qu'est-ce que le Tiers État?* (1789), reprinted in Jacques Godechot (ed.), *La pensée révolutionnaire en France et en Europe 1780–1799*, Armand Colin, Paris, 1964, p. 80.

ism" that developed, chiefly in France, in opposition to absolutism. Liberalism, it should be remarked, was a nineteenth-, not an eighteenth-century word, as were two other words, radicalism and individualism, of which we make use in the ensuing discussion. Liberalism, however, existed before there was a word for it, as discussed in an earlier chapter.[12] But how to define it? For liberalism was no static thing, but accumulated new meanings as the century progressed. It has been customary to restrict its meaning, by, for example, distinguishing between liberals and radicals, or else by identifying liberalism exclusively with middle-class political and economic demands, or, as Basil Willey does, with a particular belief, held, for example, by such a one as Adam Smith, that society would be better off if nature was left to itself, with a minimum of human, that is, governmental interference. Although all these meanings have some merit, they tend to obscure the broadness of the liberal movement, which centered in reform of the established order, and emphasized liberty of the individual and equality. Looking at liberalism in this way, it is possible to descry a more or less continuous movement, by no means limited to a single class, becoming ever more radical, which, though checked in the mid-1790's, supplied the basic ideas for the liberalism of the next century. There are difficulties in this interpretation, of course. Among those who might conceivably be called liberals, there were differences of opinion on nearly every conceivable question: as to the best form of government; as to whether reform should come from above or below; as to whether reform could be accomplished within the established structure of society, or only by transforming that structure pretty completely; as to how to balance liberty and equality, the individual and community, and so on. It may be noted, however, that the differences of opinion had more to do with means than with ends. On at least some fundamental ends, there was agreement, whereas there was almost total disagreement on means. We might think of liberalism, then, as a genus consisting of many species, political, economic, and social.

Was the Baron de Montesquieu a liberal? Some have seen him, not without cause, as a conservative, even a reactionary. He advocated no radical reform of French institutions. Like his older contemporary, the Comte de Boulainvilliers, Montesquieu, in fact, wanted to restore the historic French constitution, and with it the powers and privileges of the nobility, of the robe as well as the sword (he himself was a *parlementaire*). Yet Montesquieu was also a social critic, the most cele-

[12] See p. 107.

brated of his time, and as such, was very much concerned about liberty, and about how to acquire it and preserve it.

To perceive the liberal side of Montesquieu's thought, one should first go to *The Persian Letters* (1721) before proceeding to his masterpiece, *Sur l'esprit des lois* (1748). In *The Persian Letters,* a book really about Europe and France, Montesquieu did two things more or less simultaneously. He compared European and Asiatic institutions, to the detriment of the latter, while, however, showing how the former had itself fallen into decay. "Europe," Montesquieu has one Persian visitor write to the other, "is not like Asia." In Europe "mild government" prevails, which accords better with reason than the despotic governments of Asia. In Europe there existed states, including republics, based on "the fundamental principle" of liberty, and limiting the power of the rulers in a thousand different ways. But alas, France in particular had grown corrupt, abandoning the old laws, and losing many of the liberties established by her first kings in general assemblies.[13]

But what was liberty? Unfortunately, Montesquieu was not very good at definitions, but he did try to define it in the *Esprit*. First of all, he distinguished between liberty of the subject and liberty of the constitution. The first obviously referred to civil liberties, above all, security of the individual person, religious liberty, freedom of thought, legal justice, and the like. Though the safeguarding of these liberties was perhaps Montesquieu's primary concern, he did not think of them as natural rights in the Lockean sense. They were liberties guaranteed by and in society, and fixed precisely by law. "Liberty is a right of doing whatever the law permits."[14] Farther along Montesquieu says, somewhat enigmatically, that "the subject may be free and not the constitution." What I take him to mean by this statement is that the subject could not be free, not at least in the long run, unless the constitution was also free. The constitution was the means of preventing despotism and securing individual freedom. This conviction accounts for the infinite pains Montesquieu took to describe the proper machinery of government. He offered two ways of ensuring "constitutional" liberty in France. The first, as already noted, was to put the ancient constitution back to rights. This constitution—Montesquieu had been reading Tacitus' *Germania*—originated, he believed, in the German forests, among the tribes that invaded the Roman Empire, including the Franks. Montesquieu waxed rhapsodic about this early

[13] See especially Letters LXXX and CXXXI.

[14] Montesquieu, *Sur l'esprit des lois,* Bk. XI, Chap. 3. On individual liberties in general, see Bk. XII.

"Gothic government." Once the serfs were freed, there followed, he wrote:

> so perfect a harmony between the civil liberty of the people, the privileges of the nobility and clergy, and the prince's prerogative, that I really think there was never in the world a government so well tempered, as that of each part of Europe, so long as it lasted. Surprising, that the corruption of a conquering nation should have given birth to the best species of constitution that could possibly be imaged by man![15]

But there was another species of constitution that Montesquieu had observed with his own eyes only very recently, and that he admired equally. This was the English constitution, characterized, as he appears to have thought, by the separation of powers, executive, legislative, and judicial.[16] The two constitutions, the "Gothic" and the English, however, really came to the same thing in Montesquieu's mind, and, in fact, he connected them by saying, again on the authority of Tacitus, that the English borrowed their system from the Germans. He obviously wanted a "moderate" government in which the head, a monarch in France, was limited by traditional intermediary powers, and by "fundamental laws." To prevent the abuse of power, to safeguard liberty, it was necessary that "power should be a check to power."[17]

The French *philosophes,* while praising Montesquieu for reminding men "they were free," were quite critical of him, and with them the liberal movement veered farther to the left. Montesquieu was too respectful of "Gothic" institutions to suit them, too concerned to show that reform should be gradual, and should accommodate itself to the special "spirit," including the traditional social order, of a people. Impatient of the past, the *philosophes* thought they could make over the political present, according to the principle of utility, or general happiness. Helvétius, who typifies this antihistorical attitude, denounced "the stupid veneration of peoples for the laws and ancient usages." From Locke he claimed to have learned that laws were good for one

[15] Ibid., Bk. XI, Chap. 8. Thomas Nugent's translation.
[16] Franz Neumann thinks Montesquieu knew perfectly well that the separation of powers was not actually working in England, but that he heard it discussed there, and was himself actually "the father of the doctrine," which the American colonists and others latched onto later. See *The Spirit of the Laws,* Hafner Publishing Co., New York, 1949, p. lvi.
[17] Ibid., Bk. XI, Chap. 4. "Of the Constitution of England" is the subject of Chap. 6.

century only, after which time they should be declared null unless re-examined and confirmed by the nation. Helvétius therefore recommended that "the Legislator" (*le Législateur*) be empowered to make all the changes in laws, customs, and religion which the times and circumstances demanded. In this way he could "dry up the source of an infinity of evils, and without doubt assure the repose of peoples, while extending the duration of empires."[18]

What, more precisely, should the wise Legislator (a term also used by Rousseau) devise at this critical juncture of history? First of all, some change in the form of government seemed called for. There were those who defended monarchical absolutism, at least for France, as the best way to bring about desired reforms. Voltaire was one of these, as were also the economic reformers known as Physiocrats. Voltaire championed "the cause of the king" against the *parlements,* which he considered supportive of privilege and religious intolerance. But disillusionment with the *thèse royale* (or enlightened absolutism, as we previously called it) set in with Louis XVI's dismissal of the liberal minister Turgot in 1776. Voltaire himself despaired of reform from the top at the end of his life. The alternative, however, was not necessarily the *thèse nobilière* on Montesquieu's model, or the English constitution. "The government of all," as Helvétius called it, began to seem more attractive, especially after the American Revolution. "Let noone be astonished," he wrote, "if this form of government [that is, one in which power is shared by all classes of citizens] has always been adjudged the best."[19] Rousseau, of course, had already praised popular sovereignty in *The Social Contract,* and his disciple Condorcet included the right to help make the laws, "either directly or through representatives," among the rights of man. Up to 1789, however, most *philosophes* obviously did not want full democracy, or else considered it a utopia, ideal for a people of gods, but "not for men," as Rousseau said. The sort of participatory democracy Rousseau had in mind could be realized only in very small states—perhaps not even Corsica, for which he made suggestions for a constitution, could qualify—where there was simplicity of manners and no flagrant inequality of rank and fortunes. The Abbé Siéyès more nearly caught the mood of the later *philosophes* when he identified the political nation with the Third Estate. The Third Estate, predominately bourgeois, stood for "the general interest," as opposed to "the particular interest" of the caste of nobles. "Le Tiers"

[18] Helvétius, *De l'esprit* (1758), Discours II, Chap. XVII.

[19] Helvétius, *De l'homme,* Sect. IV, Chap. XI. He compares the government "of all" with that of a single person, and of several persons.

had in it "everything necessary to form a complete nation," and demanded representation at least equal to that of the first two estates.[20] Condorcet himself initially championed this *thèse bourgeoise,* as we might call it, but during the Revolution broadened it out to include "the people." The people, he thought, had saved the Revolution, and must therefore be included, along with the Third Estate, in the electoral process. He now advocated, as did others, a unicameral legislature elected by universal and equal suffrage. Condorcet would also have laicized the state, that is, separated church from state, which neither Voltaire nor Rousseau advocated, nor certainly Montesquieu, at least not in *Sur l'esprit des lois,* where Christianity appears as the form of religion best suited to moderate government. Thus was the ground laid, in the ideas and constitutional experiments of the revolutionaries, for the democratic liberalism of the nineteenth century.

The wise Legislator, it was thought, in addition to liberalizing the form of government, would, above all, protect and extend the rights of individuals. This was, of course, the core of liberal doctrine: to widen the domain of individual freedom. Montesquieu probably did not think of the individual as standing out, or apart from, an historic class or corporation, or from society in general. With most of the *philosophes,* however, as with Locke, the individual preceded society, and must be free, within limits, to order his life as seemed best to him. In the Abbé Siéyès' conceptualization, which was a blend of Lockean and Rousseauean ideas, "individual wills" (*volontés individuelles*) were the starting point of all political societies. Though forming for convenience' sake "a common will," they delivered over to governments only that portion of power necessary to maintain good order. The basic "right to will" remained with them as their inalienable right. By the time of Siéyès and Condorcet, any typical list of individual rights had come to include the right of property, that is, economic freedom, as well as civil liberties, and sometimes also, as previously noted, participation in the governing process in some form or degree.

The new economic freedom, articulated best by the Physiocrats, reflected current fears for the French economy, hobbled by an outmoded feudalism, inequitable and burdensome taxation, and a host of regulations dictated by the "mercantilist fallacy," as Adam Smith called it. If agriculture, the only real source of wealth, was to become truly productive, the "régime prohibitiv" would have to reverse itself, and

---

[20] This thesis was argued in the popular pamphlet *Qu'est-ce que le Tiers Etat?* of 1789, referred to in note 11.

free capital for investment, remove barriers to free trade, and allow the individual more scope to use his property as he saw fit (*laissez-faire*). The Physiocrats appealed to natural law doctrine in support of economic freedom. The Natural Order (*Ordre Naturel*), expressive of God's will, must not be contravened by the Positive Order, or "artificial" laws of men. The former prescribed eternal laws of economic well-being, and made these laws depend for their working on "the greatest possible liberty" of the individual. This liberty, construed as a natural right, was not abrogated when men entered into a society. In fact, just the reverse was true, as Dupont de Nemours makes clear in his succinct statement of Physiocratic ideas:

> The sovereign authority is not instituted in order *to make laws;* for the laws are all made by the hand of the one who created rights and duties. The social laws, established by the Supreme Being, prescribe uniquely the conservation of *the right of property,* and of the *liberty* which is inseparable from it. The ordinances of sovereigns, which are called *positive laws,* must be only *declaratory acts of these essential laws of the social order.*[21]

The economic self-interest of individuals, however, did not clash with the general interest, but was, on the contrary, identical with it, at least as a general rule. Behind the doctrine of the Physiocrats, and of Adam Smith too, was the assumption of a natural harmony between self-interest and the general interest, and of an equilibrium between economic supply and demand, provided the Natural Order was adhered to. In the words of Condorcet, also an economic liberal, there existed, in spite of apparent chaos, a "general law of the moral world which causes the efforts of everyone in his own behalf to serve the interests of all; and which, despite the apparent conflict, the common interest demands that everyone should understand his own interest and be permitted to pursue it without opposition."[22] Physiocratic influence, at high tide in the 1760's, apparently began to wane soon after 1770. This decline of influence is perhaps enough to explode the *thèse bourgeoise,* which has been maintained in connection with them. Had their notions

[21] Dupont de Nemours, *De l'origine et des progrès d'une science nouvelle* (1768), Sect. VIII. Dupont was the great popularizer of the ideas of Dr. Quesnay, founder of the Physiocratic "school." See also his *Maximes du Docteur Quesnay,* and *Physiocratie.*

[22] Condorcet, *Esquisse d'un tableau historique des progrès de l'esprit humain, 9th Epoch;* quoted by Jacob S. Schapiro, *Condorcet and the Rise of Liberalism,* Harcourt Brace Jovanovich, Inc., New York, 1934, p. 162.

actually been implemented, by Turgot or others, bourgeois agricultural entrepreneurs would indeed have profited greatly. On the other hand, bourgeois manufacturers, and bankers, marked down as "sterile," would not have profited, and hence objected strenuously to Physiocracy, insofar as they understood it. Yet the notion of economic freedom did catch on generally, as witness the twenty-seventh article of the Declaration of the Rights of Man, which maintained the "sacred" right to property. The Physiocrats, it should be noted, championed economic, but not necessarily political, liberalism. Turgot, who never aligned himself formally with their "school," criticized them for their advocacy of "legal despotism," which, it was thought, could best promote the natural laws of the social order.

But what of equality, in addition to liberty? Should the wise Legislator strive to make men equal as well as free? Montesquieu assumed a hierarchical society, while affirming the equality of all vis-à-vis civil liberties. Likewise, most of the *philosophes* believed in some sort of society of ranks, based, however, not on feudal privilege but on property and enlightenment, which in turn rested on inborn degrees of talent. With few exceptions the *philosophes* feared "le peuple," characterized by Voltaire as a class apart, "between man and beast," doing manual work for others. The "imbecile" people, swayed by passion and superstition, might at any moment become the instrument of demagogues wishing to throw society into turmoil. "Let us cease then," said Holbach, "to suppose a pretended equality which one believes to have originally existed between men. They were always unequal." Nature made them so, and society supported nature. Holbach, who wanted to level down the parasitic classes, especially priests, and make them go to work nevertheless felt good about this basic inequality between governing classes and those who were governed. It established a necessary "chain of services" at different levels, without which a society could not subsist.[23]

The idea of equality, however, steadily gained ground. The older *philosophes*, increasingly concerned about the misery of the lower classes, began to discuss ways of improving their economic lot, providing some sort of public instruction, and opening careers to talent. Younger men like Condorcet went much farther, projecting a future society of near equals. "Our hopes, as to the future condition of the human species," Condorcet wrote during the French Revolution, "may

[23] For Holbach on inequality, see *La politique naturelle* (1773), Vol. I, 1st Discourse, section X ("Origine de l'inégalité entre les hommes"); 4th Discourse, section XI ("De l'inégalité entre les Citoyens"). On "le peuple," see also p. 172.

be reduced to three points: the destruction of inequality between different nations; the progress of equality in one and the same nation; and lastly, the real improvement of man."[24] It was the essence of "the social art" to realize these hopes, through the equalization of education and fortunes, as well as by giving the people the franchise. Although Condorcet continued to talk Physiocratic language, his emphasis was now, much more than before, on equality. Or perhaps it would be more accurate to say that he, like many others, now saw an indissoluble link between liberty and equality. In his last work, Condorcet noted how "disproportion" in education and wealth in ancient republics had led to the destruction of liberty by tyrants. These kinds of inequality must therefore continually diminish, without becoming absolutely extinct, "since they have natural and necessary causes."

The two great philosophers of equality, whom everybody quoted, were Helvétius and Rousseau. Helvétius, a figure of controversy among the *philosophes,* as we have seen, proclaimed the omnipotence of environment in the formation of character and fortune. Inequalities of wealth, status, and even understanding were the result of "chance," that is, of social arrangements and habit, not of heredity. Therefore, if the environment were changed, by means of good laws and education (the wise Legislator), equality would result. Actually, Helvétius was not nearly so revolutionary or optimistic as these words imply. "There is no society in which all the members can be equally rich and powerful," he wrote.[25] But men might become more or less equally happy if the present disproportion of riches were reduced, and all received some sort of property stake in the community, and if they were taught the dignity of labor and the pleasure of being usefully employed in the stations into which they were born. Rousseau, too, was an environmentalist, though less so than Helvétius, and not more optimistic. What was the origin of inequality among men? To the consideration of this question, proposed by the Academy of Dijon for its prize contest of 1751, Rousseau devoted his second Discourse. Men were originally equal (though not as to physique or mental endowment), but fell from that estate with the introduction of private property, which enables some men to lord it over others. Was it possible ever to make men equal again? Yes, it was, because what society had taken away, society could restore, and even make better. This was the theme of *The Social Contract.* Rousseau postulated a society of equals—equal

[24] Condorcet, op. cit. (see note 20), 10th Epoch.
[25] Helvétius, *De l'homme,* Sect. VIII, Chap. I. See this whole section for his ideas on equality.

morally and politically through individual and full participation in the decisions they must obey, and by participation, equally identified with the community. Rousseau, however, did not really believe that such a perfectly egalitarian society could ever exist in reality, except possibly in very small states. It was an ideal to be approximated as nearly as possible. By equality, at least in the real world, Rousseau understood, not that power and riches should be absolutely identical for all men,

> but that power shall never be great enough for violence, and shall always be exercised by virtue of rank and law [Rousseau permitted differences of rank, awarded for service to the community]; and that, in respect of riches, no citizen shall ever be wealthy enough to buy another, and none poor enough to be forced to sell himself.[26]

The socialists, as might be expected, carried equality farther, exalting it even above liberty, or representing it as the key to liberty. But the socialists, conspicuously the Abbés Morellet and Mably, were essentially moralists, and they were not numerous. Their views paralleled Rousseau's to some degree. Evil came, not from nature but from environment. Nature made men both social and equal. Men fell from this natural state with the growth of larger communities and private property. The latter, particularly, opened up a Pandora's box of evils, including pride, avarice, luxury, and despotism. The moralist speaks in the following lines:

> The more I reflect on it, the more I am convinced that the inequality of fortunes and conditions, so to speak decomposes man and alters the natural sentiments of his heart; because superfluous needs give him desires useless for his true happiness. . . . I believe that equality, by maintaining the modesty of our needs, conserves in our soul a peace which opposes the birth and progress of our passions. . . . Equality must produce all the goods because it unites men, elevates their soul, and induces mutual sentiments of benevolence and friendship.[27]

Morellet, however, was more optimistic than Mably. Morellet mapped out a thoroughgoing program of reform by a wise Legislator, which

---

[26] Rousseau, *The Social Contract,* Bk. II, Chap. XI (translation of quotation in the text by G. D. H. Cole, Everyman's Library edition, London, J. M. Dent, 1947, p. 42).

[27] Gabriel Bonnot de Mably, *De la législation ou Principes des lois* (1776), in *Les Ecrivains politiques du XVIIIᵉ siècle* (see note 5), pp. 304–305.

would restore man's primitive equality and make him better again. Morellet called this a "Model of legislation conformable to the intentions of Nature."[28] Mably, perhaps because he was more experienced in actual statecraft, did not think habit was so easily changed. A return to man's primitive condition seemed to him impossible in a country like France, depraved by centuries of wrong habit. "No human force to-day," he warned, "would be able to attempt the re-establishment of equality without causing greater disorders than those one would wish to avoid."[29] The best that could be hoped for was a "republican monarchy," or mixed government, in which the king would be more limited than Montesquieu would have liked, by subordinating the executive to the legislature. "Gracchus" Babeuf was one of the very few French socialists who combined a program with a strategy of action. In his Conspiracy of Equals of 1796, Babeuf worked out a plan for seizing power, and afterward for using the triumphant dictatorship to establish a communist society. Though the conspiracy failed, Babeuf provided a model for revolutionary socialists in the nineteenth century.

With Rousseau and the socialists, community took on a new importance. It is not true that the *philosophes* had no sense of community. Nevertheless, they put the individual and his liberty first, and society and the state existed to preserve them. "Society is useful only because it furnishes to its members the means of working freely for their happiness. . . . Liberty is therefore a debt [owed by government], and not a favor."[30] For Holbach, author of this statement, and his fellow liberals, liberty was the antidote to the despotism they all hated and fought. This individualism was enshrined, though in somewhat muddled fashion, in the Declaration of the Rights of Man, and carried to the extreme by such as William Godwin, "arch-priest of anarchism." Godwin, who was read in the *philosophes* and descended from English dissenters, put society down as "nothing more than an aggregate of individuals." Government, he declared in *An Enquiry concerning Political Justice* (1793), was "an evil, an usurpation upon the private

[28] See Morellet's *Code de la nature*, Part IV, published in the same year as Rousseau's *Discourse on Inequality* (1755).

[29] Quoted by Cecil Driver, "Morellet and Mably," *The Social and Political Ideas of Some Great French Thinkers of the Age of Reason*, F. J. C. Hearnshaw (ed.), Barnes & Noble, Inc., New York, 1967, p. 244. Mably, brother of the philosopher Condillac, served as private secretary of the Cardinal de Tencin, then minister of foreign affairs, but later broke with him, and abandoned politics and diplomacy.

[30] Holbach, *Système social* (1773), Pt. II, Chap. III ("De la liberté"). Holbach is obsessed throughout this work with "false politics," that is, despotism and tyranny.

judgment and individual conscience of mankind,"[31] and Godwin looked forward to a time when men could dispense with government altogether, and live freely, at first in small parish units, but ultimately in a completely free state in which each man would be arbiter of his own destiny. Godwin based his utopia on a much more optimistic conception of human nature than most French and English liberals were willing to accept.

Gradually, however, a more positive attitude toward community developed as men began to see the need for more equality as well as liberty, and for fraternity too, in order to correct the abuses, not merely of a despotic but of an individualistic and indulgent society. In this as in so many other areas Rousseau showed the way. Rousseau by no means wanted to swallow up individuality. He wanted the individual to participate directly in government, to help make the laws, and to be free to criticize them and propose their repeal. Yet he does seem to have felt—perhaps because of the puritanical streak in him, reinforced by reading Plato—that individualism had gone too far and needed to be disciplined. Certainly in *The Social Contract* there is much emphasis on duties as well as rights, and on the cultivation of the social sentiments. The passage from the state of nature to the civil state produced, Rousseau said, a remarkable change in man, substituting for "natural liberty," bounded by the strength of the individual, "civil liberty" limited by the general will, and a new moral liberty curbing his appetites. In *The Social Contract,* and in the advices he gave for the governments of Corsica and Poland, Rousseau also preached a new religion of patriotism. In contrast to Christianity, which was hostile to the social spirit, a new "civil religion" should be instituted to inculcate loyalty to the state and the duties of citizenship. Though Rousseau wanted perpetual peace and universal toleration among nations, he pointed toward the age of nationalism that commenced with the French Revolution. Rousseau's "rediscovery of community" also prefigured the new organic conceptions of society and the state, which surfaced later in reaction to the liberal (and early revolutionary) emphasis on the primacy of liberty and individual rights.

---

[31] William Godwin, *An Enquiry concerning Political Justice,* G. G. J. & J. Robinson, London, 1793, pp. 90, 380. Actually, Godwin was not entirely consistent in his anarchism, for he sometimes appears to countenance "good" government.

The Philosophy of
History

The term philosophy of history was coined by Voltaire who, however, defined it rather narrowly in his work by that title of 1765. To
read history *en philosophe* meant to discover, in the records of the past,
"useful truths," which could be applied to the present, especially in the
struggle against *l'infâme,* superstition, intolerance, and fanaticism. By
casting doubt on Old Testament history, for instance, the philosophic
historian could weaken the foundations of revealed Christianity and
the Catholic Church. Philosophy of history, however, signified much
more than polemics in the eighteenth century. It signified more to
Voltaire himself, as he had already made clear in other historical works.
A broader definition, shared by Voltaire and others, would have included some degree of historical Pyrrhonism; broadening the scope and
subject matter of history; history as "the science of causes and effects"
(Gibbon), and history as a source of wisdom for statesmen and philosophers. Above all, it came eventually to mean a drastic reinterpreta-
tion of the historical process; finding in history, in the words of the
Marquis de Chastellux, "a principle of perfectibility, a cause of melioration."[1]

---

[1] François Jean, Marquis de Chastellux, *De la félicité publique* (1772), 3rd Sect.
Chap. III. Chastellux, who served under Rochambeau in the American Revolution,
also wrote books about America.

"History," Gibbon reported in his autobiography, "is the most popular species of writing." He was right, at least for the second half of the century. People began to read history avidly as never before, and philosophers no longer thought it beneath their notice. Well over half of David Hume's published works were historical or pertained to history. Likewise, the French philosopher Condillac wrote lengthy historical tomes to instruct his pupil, the son of the Duke of Parma, and even Immanuel Kant, hardly a historical thinker, dashed off several thoughtful essays on the subject. Others, not so undilutedly philosophers, such as Montesquieu, Vico and Voltaire, Gibbon, of course, and William Robertson, the Encyclopedists, and many art critics pondered history deeply, and a few penned masterpieces. How truly historical-minded all or any of these eighteenth-century thinkers, including the historians, were, is open to question and is discussed later.[2] What is not questionable is that in their hands history attained a new and independent status, and a new dignity and popularity. Why this interest in history, and the philosophy of history, in a century that used to be called antihistorical? In the first place, history was thought to be useful, not merely in the old way, as a teacher of morals, but now also as a guide to truth, as religious authority and metaphysical certainty weakened. History widened men's experience, on which empirical philosophy had taught so many of them to rely, above everything else. "Abandoning theory for experience," Chastellux "interrogated" history to discover the facts—in particular, to discover what had gone wrong in the past, to trace errors back to their source, and thus to learn how to turn history around.[3] Actually, Chastellux, and most of the others, took to history certain presuppositions, imbibed from current philosophy, which they wanted "the facts" to substantiate. But in the process, they did succeed in setting the historical record straight in some instances, and, above all, in teaching men to look at the course of history through new glasses. History allied itself more with philosophy than with erudition in the eighteenth century—hence the appropriateness of Voltaire's new term—and that alliance helps to account for the excitement generated by history among philosophically minded men.

But before turning to the big panorama they beheld, let us examine briefly some of the other ingredients of "philosophy of history" as it was then understood. First, historical Pyrrhonism, about which Voltaire also wrote a book, appearing only four years after *La philosophie de*

---

[2] I leave out of consideration in this chapter the preromantics, Herder, Burke, and the like, who are discussed in connection with the Romantic Movement.

[3] Chastellux, op. cit. (see note 1), Introduction.

l'histoire. Historical Pyrrhonism, of course, went back to the seventeenth century, especially to Pierre Bayle, who was widely read and admired in the eighteenth century. It meant skepticism, both of the ability of human reason to discover historical truth, and of the reliability of the sources of historical information. Bayle[4] had made it his life work to show how the facts of history had been distorted, particularly by religious partisans. He thought it possible to establish some historical facts with precision, but not to write connected histories. Giambattista Vico, who knew Bayle's work but was not impressed by it, came to precisely the opposite conclusion. Not only was a science of history possible (*La Scienza Nuova,* his masterpiece of 1725, referred to history or "the world of civil society"), but knowledge of history was more certain even than knowledge of physical nature. A professor of rhetoric, partial to human studies and deeply read in the natural law theorists and Hobbes, Vico formulated his theory of knowledge accordingly. "The rule and criterion of truth is to have made it," he was saying as early as 1710, in opposition to Descartes. Since nature was made by God, only God could really know it. History, on the other hand, or the world of nations, was made by man; therefore, man could come to know it, and it had a reality superior to that of mathematics.

Most of the philosophical historians of the eighteenth century took a position midway between these two extremes. The following statement by Voltaire epitomizes the most general stance. "I want neither an exaggerated pyrrhonism, nor a ridiculous credulity."[5] From Bayle principally, and Fontenelle, the philosophical historians learned a healthy skepticism with regard to historical sources, and developed a critical method of research, which, to be sure, they did not always follow. But they did write histories. The key word was probability. "Historical truths are only probabilities," said Voltaire. The wise man, said Hume, proportioned his belief to the evidence, but the evidence often "exceeds not what we call probability."[6] Obviously history could never achieve the same level of certainty as mathematics. Voltaire said as much. Yet the human mind was capable of constructing a "science" of history based on probable truth. Experience, though by no means infallible, could be a reasonably safe guide "in reasoning concerning matters of fact." Hume was skeptical, but not so skeptical that he could not write a six-volume *History of England,* or not think history "in-

---

[4] On Bayle, see also, pp. 130–131.

[5] Voltaire, *Le pyrrhonisme de l'histoire* (1769), Chap. I.

[6] Hume, *An Enquiry concerning Human Understanding,* Sect. X, Of Miracles; Voltaire, *Dictionnaire philosophique,* art. "Vérité."

structive," permitting men to extend their experience to all past ages, and thus to acquaint them more broadly with human affairs.

Philosophy of history, then, meant more than mere skepticism. Gibbon called it a science of causes and effects, putting himself in opposition to the Pyrrhonists. The Pyrrhonists, jumping to conclusions, delivered history up to chance. To the contrary, Gibbon argued,

> History is for the philosophic mind what gambling was for the Marquis de Dangeau. He saw in it a system, relations, a succession, where others discerned only the caprices of fortune.[7]

Gibbon learned this lesson from Montesquieu, as did many others. Voltaire, it is true, attributed much in history to chance, but by chance (*le hasard*), he meant no interruption of the chain of causes and effects, but only unforeseen (and sometimes quite trivial) events, or a combination of events over which individual men had no control. Even Gibbon came to believe in a sort of "lottery of life," which determined the fate, for the most part adversely, of most people in history.

Actually, there was much difference of opinion, and much confusion, about causes. Montesquieu, however, provided several other leads, on which most philosophical historians could agree. Among other things, he dispensed with theological causes. Not all did so, most conspicuously Vico, who as a devout Catholic and reader of *The City of God,* featured divine providence in his new science. It has been said that Vico, who was also a student of Lucretius and Epicurus, secularized the idea of providence, or merely paid lip service to it. The truth is, probably, that Vico compromised, insisting, as previously stated, that men made history, yet also allowing for a general providence. For clearly, many things happened in history that man did not intend. Were these effects not traceable ultimately to "a mind often diverse, at times quite contrary, and always superior to the particular ends that men had proposed to themselves"?[8] As late as 1750, Turgot, while still in holy orders, orated at the Sorbonne on the role of "holy religion" in history. But praising Christianity for its civilizing mission had itself gone out of fashion by that time, and was, in any case, hardly the same thing as seeing God's hand in everything. The tendency, exemplified by Turgot himself in other discourses, was now clearly to reject final for natural

---

[7] Edward Gibbon, *Essai sur l'étude de la littérature,* Sect. XLVIII.

[8] Giambattista Vico, *The New Science,* Rev. trans. of 3rd ed. by T. Bergin and M. Fisch, Cornell University Press, Ithaca, 1968, p. 425 (section 1108).

causes, to a degree not conceivable in the days of Bossuet and Bayle.[9]

Among natural causes, Montesquieu distinguished between moral and physical. The chief physical cause was climate, whereas moral causes could be personal or impersonal. For Montesquieu, they were overwhelmingly impersonal—he lists, all in a jumble, such things as religion, laws, and customs, all of which, together with climate, determined what he called the "general spirit of nations." Along with these and other causes, Voltaire could also emphasize, in the intervals when he believed in free will, the roll of great men in history, a Louis XIV or Oliver Cromwell. Human nature, whether regarded as fixed or malleable, set the bounds of possibility, constituted, in fact, the basic "moral" cause. It explained the crimes and follies, if not all the misfortunes, of history. Blame not man's calamities on the distant heavens, said Volney in *The Ruins* (1791), for they have their source "in man himself, he carried it with him in the inward recesses of his own heart."[10] However, human nature also explained how man was able to bring order out of chaos, and better his condition. Kant thought that man could set a moral goal, or Idea, for himself in history, and then realize it through his actions. As we shall see, teleology, whether idealistic like Kant's, or tied to laws of nature and therefore more deterministic, like Volney's, figured prominently in eighteenth-century discussions of historical cause and effect.

Philosophy of history signified, in the third place, a new kind of universal history, not confined to the history of a single nation or civilization, or, as to subject matter, not confined exclusively to military and dynastic events. It is instructive to compare Turgot's plan for a universal history with Bossuet's *Discourse.* Turgot thought the latter too narrow and proposed, according to Dupont de Nemours, "to rewrite the book" on a broader plan. This plan, had Turgot ever followed through with it, would have encompassed, among other things,

> The early beginnings of mankind; the formation and intermingling of nations; the origin of governments and their revolutions; the progress of languages, of natural philosophy, of morals, of manners, of the arts and sciences; the revolutions which have brought

[9] This statement is more true of French than of English thinkers. English millenarians, referred to later, still featured the role of Providence. See, for example, Joseph Priestley's historical lectures on "Divine Providence in the Conduct of Human Affairs."

[10] Comte de Volney, *Les Ruines ou méditations sur les révolutions des empires,* Chap. 3. Volney, born in 1757, was elected to the National Assembly in 1789, imprisoned during the Terror, and afterward traveled in America.

about the succession of empire to empire, of nation to nation, and of religion to religion, etc.[11]

It was just such a plan that Voltaire tried to execute in his massive *Essay on Customs* (final text, 1769). Prior to that, Voltaire had written *Le Siècle de Louis XIV*, which, though primarily about France and Europe, put in, as we have seen, new material on social history and the arts and sciences.[12] The Scottish trio, William Robertson, Lord Monboddo, and Hume, Gibbon, and many others all, in one way or another (Hume, for example, chiefly through the history of religion), afforded glimpses of a vast arena of history, much more than national, or even European or Christian, in scope. Why, Voltaire asked, should we neglect to know the mind of those nations to which European merchants have traveled from early times? Why indeed? Thus, the *Essay on Customs* commenced with chapters on China, India, and Islam, prefaced by an introduction on the remote origins of the races of mankind. Bossuet drove Voltaire back into ancient history, since the Bishop of Meaux's "pretended Histoire universelle" not only dealt with a handful of four or five peoples but also related events particularly to "the little Jewish nation, either ignored or justly scorned by the rest of the earth."[13] Voltaire was actually more Europe-oriented than he let on, for, after all, the bulk of the *Essay* dealt with European history from Charlemagne to Louis XV, and with lands conquered by Europeans. All the same, the non-European world had now definitely come within the ken of European historians, and comparisons could be and were made, by no means always to the advantage of Christian Europe. The reasons for this new *étrangisme,* and for the new universal history in general, are fairly obvious. The reasons originated both outside and inside Europe, from increased contact with the outside world through overseas discoveries and trade, as well as from the dissatisfaction felt by many, chiefly Frenchmen, with the way things were going inside Europe itself. The superior wisdom of Chinese or Islamic civilization, or the comparative innocence of savages, could be conjured up to expose European superstition and vice, and call for reform.[14]

[11] Turgot, "On Universal History," in Ronald Mack (ed.), *Turgot on Progress, Sociology, and Economics,* Cambridge University Press, Cambridge, 1973, p. 64.

[12] See note, p. 42.

[13] Voltaire, op. cit. (see note 5), Chap. II.

[14] On the subject of European images of non-European man in the eighteenth century, see the suggestive pages in Paul Hazard, *La crise de la conscience européenne,* Chap. I; Henri Baudet, *Paradise on Earth,* Chap. II; and Hugh Honour, *The New Golden Land. European Images of America,* New York, 1975, Chaps. 4 and 5.

Finally, and above all, philosophy of history connoted pattern or meaning, interpreting history overall in a new, apocalyptic, and progressive way. Since, however, the idea of progress caught on slowly, and was by no means universally accepted, something needs to be said first about rival and older interpretations. Degeneration theory still had some life left in it, even if providentialism did not. As might be expected, this theory appealed to conservatives of one kind or another, classical purists, champions of an older political and social order now superseded, and *antiphilosophes,* all of whom had some reason for denigrating the present. Count Boulainvilliers thought that France had degenerated sadly from the good old days of the Franks when the nobility counted for something. States were, in general, like individuals who born free fell into servitude through the accidents of life. The French nobility, confronted by a tyrannical monarchy, almost certainly faced a still bleaker future. Boulainvilliers wanted to restore their "original" rights, but he spoke as though the trend he was describing constituted a "destiny," experienced by all peoples.[15] Similarly, classicists bemoaned the falling away from artistic and literary standards set, not only by the Ancients but by Moderns of the Age of Louis XIV. This decay was said to have been caused not only by a frivolous society but also by the intrusion of philosophy into the arts, and by the expansion, and hence vulgarization, of the reading and viewing public. Some even suggested a drying up of talent, thus harking back to the old idea of the degeneration of nature. To some extent, as we shall see, the *philosophes* shared this view of a decline of the arts. Talk by moral primitivists of a great fall from an earlier and harmonious social state was also fairly common. Men as different as Simon Linguet, conservative and *antiphilosophe,* and Mably, radical reformer, attributed the fall to the institution of private property and pronounced it irrevocable.

Mostly, however, eighteenth-century theories of degeneration combined with a cyclical idea of history, which was not so ineluctably pessimistic. That is, as Vico would have said, whereas the normal *corso,* which the nations of the world ran, ended in decline and fall, it was followed by *ricorso,* or a recurrence, of the cycle, thus enabling humanity to rise again like the phoenix from its ashes. Vico is sometimes represented as an exception among eighteenth-century philosophers of history, and in some ways he was an exception, as, for example, in his search for a "new science," which suggests more the sort of conceptuali-

---

[15] "Et dans le fond il est évident que les Etats ont leur destinée aussi inévitable que celle des Particuliers" (Boulainvilliers, *Histoire de l'ancien gouvernement de la France,* The Hague, 1727, Vol. II, p. 270).

zation that was popular in the preceding century. In his philosophy of historical cycles, however, Vico was unique only in his extreme schematization. Belief in the "flux and reflux" of history, of nations, governments, religions, and the arts abounded in the eighteenth century, counting among its adherents many of the major thinkers, not only Vico but Condillac, Montesquieu, Hume, Grimm, Raynal, and prominent art critics such as the Abbé Dubos and Winckelmann, not to speak of many lesser figures.[16] None of these men was without hope for the civilization he lived in, not even Montesquieu. Doubtless, this long-range view came partly from reading ancient history, particularly the history of Rome, which fascinated all of them. But the present, too, inspired misgivings, though more among the French than the English. For some, the flux and reflux of history appeared to be built into nature itself, on the analogy of the cycle of living organisms, including man. Human nature, though unchanging, was obviously unstable, capable both of creating civilizations and destroying them.

Of the figures mentioned, several deserve further notice: Vico, not because he had any great influence in the eighteenth century, but because he was an innovator; Montesquieu, to show that "the President" of the *philosophes* did not believe in the idea of progress; and Hume, simply as a Briton and major philosopher. All three had an organic view of the cyclical process; that is, could see how the different elements of a culture intertwined and stood or fell together. Vico was the most schematic. All nations, he thought, ran through three political stages, the age of the gods or theocracy, of heroes or aristocracy, and of men or equality (recognized in both republics and monarchies), in the last phases of which decay set in. This cycle or *corso* had occurred twice already in history, once in the ancient world, and again in the Christian era. The cycle would presumably be repeated again, since human nature remained fixed, though each time on a higher level, so that it was more like a spiral than a circle. Vico's originality lay in the fact that he recognized the close correspondence between the stages of the political cycle and changes in men's ideas of the world and nature, customs, laws, language, religion, and even types of human character.

Montesquieu was not only less schematic but less optimistic than Vico. He had the same notion of an organic culture, but each nation was unique, had its own "general spirit" (*esprit*), and therefore observed its own rhythm of progress and decay. That all, or almost all,

[16] For French believers in "the world in flux," see Henry Vyverberg, *Historical Pessimism in the French Enlightenment*, Harvard University Press, Cambridge, Mass., 1958, especially Chap. 17.

nations did in fact describe a circle, however, Montesquieu had no doubt. Even England, whose constitution he admired so much, must eventually lose its liberty and perish, just as Rome, Sparta, and Carthage had done.[17] Although Montesquieu hinted at the possibility of reflux as well as flux, he said nothing about a spiral carrying mankind upward, despite setbacks. Hume, unlike the Frenchman Montesquieu, was reasonably well satisfied with the progress, political and otherwise, made by his own country, and in his own day. Nevertheless, he too saw flux and reflux for the long term. In religion, men, Hume said, had "a natural tendency to rise from idolatry to theism, and to sink again from theism into idolatry." This he attributed to the feeble apprehensions of the vulgar, reason and more refined ideas being always confined to the few. The same circular movement occurred in the arts and sciences. But there the cause is less clear. All Hume was willing to say was that it was "conformable to experience," that once having risen to perfection, they would "naturally, or rather necessarily decline." Of course, Hume also believed that the arts and sciences went hand in hand with political liberty, or the lack of it.[18]

How widespread was belief in linear progress, in comparison to belief in cycles, which contemplated both progress and decay? By midcentury the idea of progress had incontestably begun to catch on. "I know you are one of those," Hume wrote to Turgot in 1768, "who entertain the hope, that human Society is capable of perpetual Progress toward Perfection, that the Encrease of Knowledge will still prove favourable to good Government, and that since the Discovery of Printing we need no longer Dread the usual returns of Barbarism and Ignorance."[19] (Hume himself was skeptical, and said so). Turgot was indeed "one of those," having delivered a stirring address on the subject eighteen years earlier, and having written a few other pieces too, all unpublished until much later, but circulating at the time in manuscript. But Turgot was by no means the only one, or even the first, to "entertain the hope." It is well to remember that the Abbé de Saint-Pierre

[17] "As all human beings have an end, the state we are speaking of will lose its liberty, will perish" (Montesquieu, *Sur l'esprit des lois,* Bk. XI, Chap. VI; see also *Pensées et fragments inédits de Montesquieu,* G. Gounouilhon, Bordeaux, 1899, Vol. I, pp. 114, 278; Vol. II, p. 210).

[18] For Hume's ideas on flux and reflux, see *The Natural History of Religion,* Sect. VIII, and the essay "Of the Rise and Progress of the Arts and Sciences," especially the 4th maxim.

[19] Hume to Turgot, June 16, 1768, *The Letters of David Hume,* J. Y. T. Greig (ed.), Clarendon Press, Oxford, 1932, Vol. II, p. 180. Hume's sentence has been slightly abbreviated.

had been talking about perfectibility, the progress of universal reason and perpetual peace, years before Turgot; that the English had long since developed their own theory of millenarianism under religious auspices; that Joseph Priestley gave lectures on progress at an English dissenters' academy in the 1760's; and that Lessing was soon to publish his essay on the progressive education of the human race. Thus, around the time of Hume's letter to Turgot, progress was being much written and talked about, and even to some extent simply assumed. Gibbon, for example, assumed it, despite his melancholy subject and his misgivings about human nature. Having told his tale of decline and fall, Gibbon could nevertheless comfort himself with the thought, which he did not try to prove, that mankind was progressing, and that very likely no people would ever again "relapse into their original barbarism."[20] But the heyday of belief in the idea came, as might be expected, just before and during the first years of the French Revolution when current events seemed to portend, at least for reformers, "a change," as Priestley put it, "from darkness to light." Then, within a few years of each other, appeared such works, all of them apocalyptic in character, as Restif de la Bretonne's play about *The Year 2000* (1790), Volney's *The Ruins* (1791), Anacharsis Cloots' *Universal Republic* (1792), Condorcet's *Progress of the Human Mind* (1793), and works of a similar nature by Priestley and Godwin in England.

"A change from darkness to light": this was, in essence, what the idea of progress proclaimed, and it was a new idea. This idea said that mankind had at last reached the decisive turning point in its history, when its forward impetus, always interrupted, aborted, or reversed in the past, had become irreversible. It was the opposite of primitivism, locating the golden age in the future rather than the past. It was as much prophecy as philosophy of history. Though formulated usually as a hope or possibility, the idea of progress often came close to being a teleology. All this, implied or stated in Priestley's phrase, and in Hume's letter, and Gibbon's "General Observations," is epitomized in Condorcet's famous last words,[21] often quoted: "We are approaching one of the grand revolutions of the human race"; mankind's progress, though it may be more or less rapid, "can never be retrograde."

The idea of progress is clear enough—or as some might say, simple

---

[20] Gibbon, *Decline and Fall of the Roman Empire,* General Observations, appended to Chap. XXXVIII.

[21] "Last words" in the sense that they constituted the central message of his *Esquisse d'un tableau historique des progrès de l'esprit humain,* written shortly before his death in 1794.

enough—as a general principle. However, certain questions arising in connection with it require further analysis. In what, precisely, was progress supposed to consist? Was progress observable throughout history, or was it confined, at least in large part, to recent and future history? How did the progressivists account for progress, and what were the assumptions, metaphysical and psychological, that made possible their own advocacy of it?

Turgot's youthful address, or discourse, mentioned previously, is a good place to begin in order to answer these questions. Entitled "Philosophical Review of the Successive Advances of the Human Mind," and delivered at the Sorbonne in 1750 (actually it was the second of two discourses that he delivered in that year; the other dealt with the advantages that Christianity had procured for the human race), Turgot's address defined progress in the broadest possible way. There was progress on nearly all fronts, in morals as well as in science and technology, and in politics and general happiness, though not necessarily at the same speed or simultaneously. Turgot was less sure of progress in the fine arts. It was this universality of conception that chiefly distinguished Turgot from the Moderns of the seventeenth century. Nobody disputed that there had been progress in scientific knowledge. As in the seventeenth century, the chief points made by Turgot and others were better methods of thinking and the accumulation of facts, which, among other things, made possible an improved technology. Turgot emphasized, above all, precision in speaking and thinking. Progress depended on the development of exact languages capable of communicating ideas clearly and without prejudice. It depended on learning to understand phenomena before seeking causes; by means of logic, to analyze sensations properly, so as not to be deceived; and by means of mathematics, to deduce general axioms from more particular truths. Turgot, like D'Alembert, was very partial to mathematics. Mathematics demonstrated man's ability to think abstractly, as well as concretely. Doubtless, all sciences had their origin in the senses. "But mathematics," Turgot said, "has this advantage, that it is an application of the senses which is not susceptible to error."[22] Science, in short, had liberated the human mind for good and all, and created a permanent, new sort of intellectual class, able to think clearly, critically, and sanely, and, thanks to the invention of the compass and printing press, to communicate across international borders.

The innovation, then, lay not in proclaiming the progress of science,

---

[22] Turgot, "On Universal History" (see note 11), p. 96.

but in recognizing a concomitant progress of morals and happiness. The former, in fact, translated itself into the latter. On this point, Turgot's disciple Condorcet was more insistent even than he, for Turgot, erstwhile priest, thought that Christianity, as well as Stoic philosophy, had much to do with the improvement of morals. "Truth, happiness, and virtue": these three, said Condorcet, nature had connected by an unbroken chain. Condorcet, a democrat, looked forward to the day when, through education, the scientific spirit and scientific truth became the property, not merely of an elite, but of the masses. When that happened, the latter must inevitably become more civilized, tolerant, politically more responsible, and peace-loving—in a word, more virtuous, and therefore happier. Chastellux measured progress exclusively by the greatest happiness principle, and saw the closest connection between happiness and the discovery of scientific "doctrines" to guide man's actions. The Germans Lessing and Kant made a special point of moral progress, but disentangled it from the hedonistic principle. The goal of history, for Lessing, would come when the human race had learned, at long last, to love virtue for its own sake, without the incentives, previously supplied by revelation, of future rewards and punishments. For Kant, not happiness, but the achievement of the highest culture and morality, constituted "Nature's secret plan" for man. "It seems not to have concerned Nature that he should live well [that is, happily], but only that he should work himself upward so as to make himself, through his own actions, worthy of life and well-being."[23] Rousseau, of course, was also greatly concerned about the progress of morality, but perhaps did not believe in it much, except for individuals and small communities. But he deserves mention here because he swam against the tide of opinion, growing ever stronger, which linked moral progress with science. Although Rousseau later disowned the extreme views set forth in his first discourse on the progress of the arts and sciences, he never got over his suspicion that science, or the abuse of science, was a corrupting influence. Rousseau associated science with overweening pride, with overemphasis on the analytic intelligence, and with materialism and the creation of artificial needs.

Turgot, as previously indicated, largely exempted the fine arts from his saga of progress. This he did for several reasons, partly because, like the old Moderns, he tended to give the palm to the ancients in such matters, but partly also because he valued them less than the sciences.

[23] Immanuel Kant, "Idea for a Universal History from a Cosmopolitan Point of View" (1784), Third Thesis.

The aim of the fine arts, according to Turgot, was merely to please, and they employed mainly the passions and imagination, which, unless kept within strict limits, could prove inimical to science. Though in general more sympathetic to artistic endeavor, Turgot's philosophical contemporaries similarly saw no linear progress in the fine arts, and, in fact, many thought they lived in a time of artistic and literary decline. This they attributed to the rise of "the philosophic spirit" of which, in other respects, they approved heartily, but which, as D'Alembert said, introduced "frigid and didactic discussions into things of sentiment." "Thus, we have at the same time more principles for good judgment, a larger fund of enlightenment, more good judges, and fewer good works." This state of affairs, of alternating periods of creativity and imitation in the arts, had occurred more than once in history. The centuries of Demetrius of Phalerum, and of Lucan and Seneca, had followed, respectively, those of Demosthenes, and Cicero and Vergil, "and our century that of Louis XIV."[24]

The next question to be considered is how the progressivists compared past, present, and future, and especially what they thought about the past vis-à-vis progress. In most, though not all, areas, as suggested, they compared the past unfavorably with the present, and conceived of progress as a leap taken quite suddenly by mankind in modern times. Some, however, including Turgot, were beginning to think of progress more in a developmental way, as proceeding incrementally from lower to higher stages, and as more or less continuous throughout history. But despite some difference in conception, all believed that progress had accelerated rapidly in the last few centuries and that it was probably now irreversible.

The past did not come in for unmitigated condemnation, of course, even by believers in the leap. To some extent, these believers shared with others the conception of some relatively happy ages in the past. Yet I do not find among them that unreserved admiration of antiquity that is so often found among eighteenth-century intellectuals. Chastellux found both the Greeks and Romans sadly wanting in wisdom, common humanity, and even political sagacity. Likewise, Condorcet who, while praising some things, Greek mathematics, for example (which, however, he did not think very original), and Roman jurisprudence, condemned both for resting their cultures on slavery. Of Greek philosophers, Condorcet also said that "instead of discovering

---

[24] For D'Alembert's ideas about rise and decline in the arts, see the Preliminary Discourse to the *Encyclopédie*.

truths, they forged systems; they neglected the observation of facts in order to abandon themselves to their imagination."[25] This was the voice of Bacon, and the point was made often in the eighteenth as well as in the seventeenth century. But, as might be expected, the progressivists vented their spleen most particularly on the Middle Ages, "A disastrous age" Condorcet called it, marked by the decline of learning, bad taste in art, oppression, misery, and above all superstition and priestcraft. Similarly, Chastellux could say of the medieval past that "not only had the peoples not known true happiness, but they had not taken the road which could lead them to it." The big change came at the Renaissance, with the invention of printing and the scientific revolution, especially as the latter was extended to politics and morals. Thereafter, mankind was on the right road, and nothing could turn him from it. But to accelerate their progress, Chastellux concluded, men needed "more to forget than to learn, to allow to be obliterated, as much as possible, all old ideas, and to hasten to raise the edifice of reason on the ruins of opinion."[26] Men had to shake off, and even to forget, the past in order to ensure a better future.

Turgot, as we have said, had a more developmental conception of progress, and was therefore more respectful of past ages, including the Middle Ages. Compare Turgot's view of the Middle Ages with that of Chastellux or Condorcet. They were barbarous times, no doubt of it. Yet there was progress in the midst of the barbarism, in technology especially, but also in logic and mathematics. The progress made by the sciences in such times, Turgot said, would become apparent at a later date, "like those rivers which after disappearing from our view for some time in a subterranean passage, reappear further on swollen by all the waters which have seeped through the earth."[27] Every age, in other words, made its contribution, though some obviously more than others, for Turgot too believed in acceleration since the Renaissance. He also believed that unless arrested or prematurely destroyed, all societies went through essentially the same stages of development:

[25] Condorcet, op. cit. (see note 21), 4th Epoque.

[26] Chastellux, op. cit. (see note 1), 3rd section, chap. III, and "Vues ulteriéures sur la Felicité publique." Few went so far as Sebastian Mercier, a follower of Rousseau, who in his utopia describes a burning of history books, preserving a few, but abridging or destroying others by Tacitus (because he painted humanity in somber colors, and "il faut n'avoir pas une mauvaise idée de la nature humaine"), most of Voltaire (for the same reason), Bossuet, and others. See L'An deux mille quatre cent quarante (1772), Chap. XXVIII, "La Bibliotèque du Roi."

[27] Turgot, "A Philosophic Review of the Successive Advances of the Human Mind," in op. cit. (see note 11), p. 56.

on the intellectual level, successive modes of religious, metaphysical, and mechanistic explanations of phenomena, an anticipation of the law of the three intellectual stages, made famous by the positivists of the nineteenth century; and on the social level, the "three stages" of hunters, shepherds, and husbandmen, the last making possible more sophisticated societies based on towns and trade, and generating a leisure class. Lessing and Rousseau, and Vico, as already noted, were others in the eighteenth century who traced the intellectual or social history of peoples through successive stages of development, though in Rousseau's account progress to the third or patriarchal stage was unhappily followed by decline, brought on by the institution of private property and all its attendant evils. One noteworthy thing about the progressivists in general, whether of Turgot's or Condorcet's persuasion, is that although they professed to write universal history, and in a sense did so, they nevertheless put Europe at the center of history, and saw Europeans as the leaders of world revolution. In this Europocentrism the progressivists differed from Voltaire, as a result, at least in the case of a Condorcet, of the stir caused by the American and French Revolutions. They pictured the revolution as commencing in Europe among an elite of thinking men, then spreading to the European masses, and finally spreading abroad to the less advanced and even savage peoples of the earth. Europeans, said Condorcet, having put behind them the worst features of colonialism, would carry, first to America and then to Asia and Africa "the principles and the example of the liberty, enlightenment, and reason of Europe."[28]

Why was that? It was because the Europeans had been the first to see the light, the light of science, which in turn made enlightenment in general possible. Ideas—or genius, as Turgot personalized it, great thinkers like Descartes, Locke, and Newton—moved history. Yet progress did not depend on reason alone, especially in the earlier stages of history, as Turgot insisted when he said:

> Thus the passions have led to the multiplication of ideas, the extension of knowledge, and the perfection of the mind, in the absence of that reason whose day had not yet come and which would have been less powerful if its reign had arrived earlier.[29]

---

[28] Condorcet, op. cit. (see note 21), 10th Epoque. It is interesting to compare Turgot and Voltaire on China. Whereas Voltaire compared Europe unfavorably with China in certain respects, especially religion, Turgot put China down as an arrested civilization.

[29] Turgot, "On Universal History," in op. cit. (see note 11), p. 70.

But Turgot meant to say much more than that the passions, man's restless curiosity, ambition, even "fits of rage," played a role, together with reason, in driving humanity forward. As Turgot said just before the passage quoted, ambitious men, the founders of nations, themselves "contributed to the designs of Providence, to the progress of enlightenment, and thus to the increase in the happiness of the human race, *with which they were not concerned at all.*" Evidently, the providential idea was by no means dead, only secularized and harnessed now to the idea of progress on earth. History had an overall beneficent design or goal, achievable in spite of, but essentially by working through, individual men or groups of men, who did not seek it in the least. Turgot was by no means alone in this belief. One is reminded of Adam Smith's invisible hand, Priestley's Providence, Kant's "Nature's plan," and, indeed, to look ahead a bit, of Hegel's "cunning of reason." Kant, for example, seeking for a clue to the idiocy of things human, thought it possible "to have a history with a definite natural plan for creatures who have no plan of their own."[30] Thus, though man made history, he also worked unconsciously to further "Nature's purpose," which included the establishment, eventually, of perfectly constituted states and perpetual peace among nations.

Behind this analysis of the causes of progress lay a boundless optimism about nature—an optimism no longer shared by Voltaire after the Lisbon earthquake—rather than human nature. True, as Lockeans, the progressivists put much emphasis on man's ability to learn by experience, and to behave more rationally when exposed to the right kind of environment. Condorcet based his whole argument for progress on sensationist psychology. The human race as a whole followed the same learning process as the individual, receiving sensations from the outside world, combining, refining, and meditating on them, and thus building up the body of scientific knowledge. The utilitarian progressivists (Condorcet himself was one) also believed that man had an instinct for happiness that could not be frustrated as he learned by experience what constituted true happiness. "By the law of sensibility," said Volney, "man has the same invincible tendency to make himself happy, as the flame has to ascend, the stone to gravitate, or the water to gain its level."[31] Yet human nature remained a constant, compounded not merely of reason and instinct but of the most unruly passions, as history showed. Condorcet was almost alone in suggesting the possi-

---

[30] Kant, op. cit. (see note 23), Introduction.
[31] Volney, op. cit. (see note 10), Chap. XIII.

bility of the melioration, transmittable by inheritance, of man's natural faculties. Therefore, the greater hope, at least for many, lay in a "nature" that, so to speak, bent human nature to its larger purpose. Cosmic optimism was still a powerful belief at the end as well as the beginning of the century, affecting now even the interpretation of history and appearing to turn even evil to good purpose.

Another question, reserved for the last, may now be raised. The answer is implicit in the materials thus far discussed, but we need to make it explicit because of its bearing on the balance struck between being and becoming in eighteenth-century thought. How genuinely historical-minded were these philosophers of history of the eighteenth century? How alert to the uniqueness or individuality of peoples and epochs, how far committed to a developmental view of history? The question itself is somewhat anachronistic, and the answer is, in any case, complex and variable, even in the thought of the same individual. But it is possible to make at least this generalization: the sense of change in history was more acute by far than the sense of individuality.

At the beginning of his second Sorbonne discourse, Turgot makes an important distinction between the order of nature and the order of history. "The phenomena of nature," he said, "governed as they are by constant laws, are confined within a circle of revolutions which are always the same." But history "affords from age to age an ever-changing spectacle. Reason, the passions, and liberty ceaselessly give rise to new events."[32] Turgot was not merely uttering the banality that times change. He was saying that unlike nature (he seems not to have been aware of recent transformist notions of nature), history breaks up old patterns, is nonrepetitive and innovative. This was essentially a new idea, developmental in conception rather than merely dynamic. Turgot was not the only advocate of this idea. Vico made a similar distinction between history and Cartesian science, perceiving, at least within each historical cycle, an evolution of language and modes of perception. And the progressivists coming after Turgot, though not grasping the developmental idea completely, nevertheless saw change on a grand scale, predicting the coming of a new epoch, different and superior to any that had preceded it.

Yet even Turgot did not go the whole way with his idea. As we have seen, the history of the fine arts represented for him an important exception. Whereas time constantly produced new discoveries in the

---

[32] Turgot, "A Philosophic Review," in op. cit. (see note 11). Turgot repeated this comparison in the introduction to his essay "On Universal History."

sciences, literature and art had "a fixed limit" imposed on them by nature "which they cannot surpass." "The great men of the Augustan age reached it, and are still our models." Turgot still clung to the notion of perfection, though less so than Voltaire, Lessing, and some others. Turgot also speaks of human nature remaining the same throughout history, "like the water of the sea during storms, and always proceeding towards its perfection."[33] That is, there were certain broad uniformities that did not change, conspicuously human nature. Likewise, Hume, though acutely aware of variety and change in history, kept coming back to the uniformities. He voiced one of the commonest assumptions of his age when he said:

> It is universally acknowledged that there is a great uniformity among the actions of men, in all nations and ages, and that human nature remains still the same. . . . Would you know the sentiments, inclinations, and course of life of the Greeks and Romans? Study well the temper and actions of the French and English. . . . Mankind are so much the same, in all times and places, that history informs us of nothing new or strange in this particular.[34]

The purpose of history, for Hume, was in fact to discover, amidst all varieties of circumstances, "the regular springs of human action and behaviour."

Not that the empiricist Hume missed the individual, the idiosyncratic element in the life of nations. He thought England, for instance, had gone its separate way and achieved, through its Protestant Succession, a happy and unique balance of order and liberty. Both Montesquieu and Voltaire identified a "spirit" that was peculiar to each country or age. Gibbon comes very close to the spirit of historicism, which insists on individuality, when he speaks of the study of ancient literature as "this practice of becoming, in turn, Greek, Roman, disciple of Zeno or of Epicurus."[35] In other words, the historian must try to see the Greeks and Romans through their own eyes, as peoples, in certain respects profoundly unlike ourselves. Gibbon counsels getting inside that "empire of custom," which Voltaire wrote so much about. Yet eighteenth-century philosophers of history, including these and others, tended, on the whole, still to look for the universal, the typical; for the

---

[33] Turgot, ibid., p. 52; "On Universal History," p. 64.
[34] Hume, *An Inquiry concerning Human Understanding,* Chap. VIII, Pt. I, Of Liberty and Necessity.
[35] Gibbon, op. cit. (see note 7), Section XLVII.

general laws binding on all peoples, for the stages through which all had to go. Vico, though better able than most to empathize with particular peoples in history, called for "an ideal eternal history traversed in time by the histories of all nations." Let us reflect, he wrote toward the end of his great work, on the comparisons between ancient and modern nations.

> There will then be fully unfolded before us, not the particular history in time of the laws and deeds of the Romans or the Greeks, but (by virtue of the identity of the intelligible *substance* in the diversity of their *modes* of development) the ideal history of the eternal laws which are instanced by the deeds of all nations.[36]

For the Germans, this universal history meant evolving toward an ideal, which implied a norm for the human race as a whole. For many others, there was also, of course, a good deal of looking down on past epochs from the vantage point of eighteenth-century norms, which prevented Voltaire, for example, from entering into the spirit of the ancient Jews, or a Robertson or Condorcet from appreciating the Middle Ages. Robertson thought of the Middle Ages as a time of infancy or early youth, not deserving even to be remembered, except insofar as it prepared the way for modern and more mature times. So we are still a long way from Johann Gottfried von Herder and historicism. Philosophy of history broke new ground in the eighteenth century but, like eighteenth-century political thought, by no means dispensed entirely with the categories of Natural Law philosophy.[37]

---

[36] Vico, op. cit. (see note 8), pp. 414–415 (Sect. 1096). Vico uses the term "ideal eternal history" repeatedly (see pp. 97, 104).

[37] The sense of historical particularity, however, grew faster among the Germans, as Ernst Cassirer pointed out, and as a recent book by Peter Hans Reill (*The German Enlightenment and the Rise of Historicism,* University of California Press, Berkeley, 1975) demonstrates in detail. That is, if Kant and Lessing, for example, talked about history in universal terms, other Germans, who are not so well known, developed a keener "appreciation of the unique," as Reill calls it. Further reference to German historicism in the eighteenth century is made in connection with the discussion of Herder in the next section.

PART IV

The Nineteenth Century

Becoming over Being

The Romantic World

The New Enlightenment

The Evolutionary World

Fin-de-Siècle

Becoming over Being

If ever the century concept breaks down, it is in the nineteenth century. Despite the *Weltschmerz* experienced by a not inconsiderable number of people of all ages and classes in the years immediately following the French Revolution, the nineteenth century started out with high hopes in some quarters for a new "organic" epoch. "The philosophy of the eighteenth century," said the Comte de Saint-Simon in his sketch for a New Encyclopedia, "has been critical and revolutionary; that of the nineteenth will be inventive and constructive."[1] According to the Saint-Simonian philosophy of history, observed by John Stuart Mill to be à la mode in Europe in the early decades, history showed an alternativity of "organic" and "critical" epochs, but with progress running through them all. An organic epoch was one in which men were united by a firm belief in some positive creed. A critical epoch, on the other hand, was characterized by the spirit of analysis rather than synthesis, by spiritual chaos and class conflict. The nineteenth century was destined to be the third great organic epoch of history (the first two being those of "religious" Greece and Rome, and the Christian Middle Ages), following the long critical epoch from the Reformation to the French Revolution. Though differing on what the new integrating principle would be, many of Saint-Simon's younger contemporaries.

[1] Saint-Simon, *Esquisse d'une nouvelle encyclopédie,* quoted in Frank E. Manuel, *The Prophets of Paris,* Harper Torchbooks, New York, 1965, p. 118.

Positivists, Hegelians, Philosophical Radicals, and Utopian Socialists agreed enthusiastically with this optimistic prognosis.

As things turned out, however, no prognosis could have been less accurate. Far from developing any sort of new organicism, the nineteenth century became, in fact, the most "critical," that is, disunited, century to date in European history. It is questionable how much intellectuals were aware of this state of affairs prior to midcentury. Many believed that they lived in a time of crisis. But perhaps the more normal attitude was that of the young Mill, who thought of himself as living in "an age of transition." "Mankind have outgrown old institutions and old doctrines," he wrote in 1831, "and have not yet acquired new ones."[2] After about 1850, however, there was an increasing awareness that the crisis was not only continuing but had deepened. Matthew Arnold was one of those who observed this to be the case. Before taking up his pen to prescribe a cure, Arnold brooded deeply, in poems and private correspondence, on the "strange disease of modern life," which he diagnosed as "multitudinousness" and "anarchy."

Arnold was a good observer, although he understood the symptoms better than the causes. He perceived that there was no center to modern thought, no consensus, no general standards acceptable to nation or class. Arnold also perceived the spread of this multitudinousness into the individual mind itself, diverting it with a myriad of impressions, preventing it from ever achieving a view of the whole. In *Empedocles on Etna* (1852), the human soul is compared to a mirror hung by the gods on a cord in space, and tossed by every gust.

> *Hither and thither spins*
> *The wind-borne, mirroring soul,*
> *A thousand glimpses wins,*
> *And never sees a whole;*
> *Looks once, and drives elsewhere,*
> *And leaves its last employ.*
> (lines 82–86)

It would be too much to expect Arnold, or anyone else at that time, to have perceived that Europe as a whole, and not merely England, was undergoing a vast particularizing process. This process, begun much earlier, reached its climax in the nineteenth century. The "Commonwealth of Europe," as Edmund Burke called it, now broke up into

[2] John Stuart Mill, *The Spirit of the Age*, University of Chicago Press, Chicago, 1942, p. 6.

fervidly self-conscious national units. The nations themselves, failing to achieve the unity desired by superpatriots, fragmented into hostile social groups; or else, as Arnold complained, drifted into anarchic individualism, "every man for himself," especially in the very liberal society of England. Despite the efforts of the synthesizers, already somewhat anachronistic, the compartments of knowledge similarly tended to go their separate ways, and no one "science" was strong enough to hold them together. Theology, though it was becoming modernized, had long since lost its power to do so. Philosophy (metaphysics), in spite of bursts of real vigor as in the Idealist Movement, steadily yielded territory to the new sciences. In the nineteenth century, psychology, for example, once known as "mental philosophy," became autonomous, and aspired to be a science in its own right in the systems of Gustav Fechner and Wilhelm Wundt. Science (natural science) came closest to establishing a hegemony as its prestige increased, as a result of the Positivist Movement, and of exciting new generalizations coming out of geology, biology, and even physics. But scientism, if not science per se, ran into serious trouble with the romantics early on, and even more so later on among neoidealists and "spiritualist" philosophers, and, indeed, among men of letters in general. Perhaps even more important for the trend toward multitudinousness, science itself was breaking up into the sciences. Political and historical thought also ceased, to a large extent, to speak a universal or general language, and became steadily more partisan. History, which was a special case, gained greatly in importance and prestige, as we shall see. But history, to use the philosopher Wilhelm Windelband's famous classification, was less a "nomothetic" than an "idiographic" science. That is, history now concerned itself more with the individual, the particular, and the unrepeatable, than with general laws. This growing fragmentation of knowledge represented the *reductio ad absurdum* of that modernity that had started out by seeking invariable laws, but ended by producing its own gravediggers. "It is of the essence of the modern spirit," said the historian Ernst Troeltsch, "that it brought forth out of itself the most varied and antithetical streams of thought."[3] The anarchy, moreover, now began to spread for the first time from the uncommon to the common mind. This anarchy can be exaggerated, especially by contrast with what was still to come. But it *was* one of the principal and most significant developments in nineteenth-century thought.

---

[3] Ernst Troeltsch, "Das Wesen des Modernen Geistes," in *Gesammelte Schriften,* J. C. B. Mohr, Tübingen, Vol. IV, p. 331.

Arnold only half understood the reasons for this growing anarchy. But he was on the right track when he attributed it to living in an "epoch of expansion," for it was, indeed, partly the result of the enormous expansion of knowledge in all fields, which threatened to overwhelm even the best minds. Arnold speaks of the "hopeless tangle," which each day brings to choke the soul, of suffering from "congestion of the brain," by which he meant that the increasing complexity of knowledge inevitably contributed to the general perplexity. He was also right in pointing to the centrifugal effect that liberalism had, especially in England, in setting up the individual as the final court of appeal. Arnold does not mention directly, in this connection, either the French or the Industrial Revolution. But he did connect science with "anarchy," in the sense that, on the whole, science, as he understood it, promoted specialization, whereas the humanities, now more and more on the defensive in a scientific age, preserved the symmetry of knowledge.[4] Nineteenth-century Europeans in general were aware, far more than their predecessors, of the stepped-up pace of modern living, and how this contributed to the general confusion. Arnold himself referred to the "sick hurry" of his times which he coupled with "divided aims." "The most salient characteristic of life in this latter portion of the 19th century is its SPEED," another Englishman observed in 1875, and speed, though exciting, aborted leisure, which alone permitted men to reflect on the value and purpose of what they saw and did.[5]

In view of this unprecedented multitudinousness, it is preferable not to treat the nineteenth century as a whole, but to break it up into a number of styles or worlds of thought. No number, of course, has any particular significance and this study of the century can be done in several ways. But with the structure of this book in mind, one can identify four such worlds[6] which characterized this century. These may

---

[4] For Arnold's opinions on the "two cultures," see his essay "Literature and Science" (1882).

[5] W. R. Greg, "Life at High Pressure," quoted in Walter E. Houghton, *The Victorian Frame of Mind 1830–1870*, Yale University Press, 1957, p. 7.

[6] There is also something to be said for breaking the century into more or less equal halves, with some such date as 1848 or 1859 marking the dividing line between the halves. Georges Sorel, for example, saw a great change of ideas after the former date. After 1848, which saw the dashing of men's hopes in France, Germany, and elsewhere, a time of iron and materialism set in, as compared with the earlier period, which had continued, in the manner of the eighteenth century, to believe in the future happiness of the human race, and to construct utopias. Other historians see a broad change in the European intellectual climate, especially after Darwin. A. V. Dicey, in *Law and Opinion in England in the Nineteenth Century* (1905) proposed a tripartite division, commencing with a period of Old Toryism, proceed-

be called the Romantic World, the world of the New Enlightenment, the Evolutionary World, and the *Fin-de-Siècle.* The last, though a contemporary term, is the least satisfactory, but that is because it was the most chaotic of the four worlds, and consequently the most baffling to the historian. These worlds, it hardly needs to be said, were neither sealed off from one another nor were they wholly stable. On the contrary, there was considerable cross-fertilization, as well as some progression from one world to the other. Nevertheless, each world, if not organic in the Saint-Simonian sense, did have a measure of unity that was not displayed by the century as a whole. Within each world, that is, there was a discernible consensus, some agreement on general principles, some fairly distinctive answers to the perennial questions. As already noted, this consensus was least marked at the century's end.

In the first of these worlds, the Romantic World, which reached its zenith between 1780 and 1830, all the questions were re-examined in the light of reason (a reason, however, very different from Locke's or Kant's "understanding") and imagination, with results that were radically different from those arrived at by the rational-empirical thought of the eighteenth century. Once again, religion, though not necessarily the old-time religion, and metaphysics, resumed their sway. Nature was both humanized and spiritualized in a new conception of "Natural Supernaturalism." The romantics, thirsting for the Infinite, also enlarged man's cognitive faculties, and gave free rein to the emotional and irrational side of human nature. But their greatest impact on nineteenth-century ideas came as the result of a strongly developed historical sense, which emphasized the differences, rather than the similarities, between peoples, and their several destinies. This conviction was codified in nineteenth-century theories of cultural and political nationalism, with frequently deplorable results.

I have adopted the term New Enlightenment for the second of these nineteenth-century worlds, because this world seems to me to have been a continuation, in spirit if not always in doctrine, of the eighteenth-century Enlightenment. Chronologically, it ran more or less in tandem with the Romantic World until about midcentury. Although not uninfluenced by the latter, the spirit and aims of the New Enlightenment were quite different. One should think of it as a congeries of movements in ideas, by no means identical, indeed sometimes clashing, yet sharing

---

ing through a middle period of individualism, and ending in a period of collectivism, which was also marked, however, by a new emphasis on the instinctual side of human nature, and by the broad use of the historical method in studying ideas and institutions.

some common attitudes and assumptions. Among its chief inhabitants were the Benthamites and Millites in England, the French Positivists, the Young Hegelians in Germany, and the so-called Realists in art and literature, the last to be found in nearly every country. The New Enlightenment was the most optimistic of the nineteenth-century worlds. In this world, scientism reached its apogee, that is, science viewed as the hope of mankind for ordering the world and providing a brighter future. The view of nature provided by the New Enlightenment, though not necessarily materialistic, ruled out metaphysics and religion. The question of religion, however, remained very much alive. The assault on traditional religion continued, conspicuously among the Young Hegelians of the first generation, who called for a movement "from religion to philosophy" and, indeed, also to anthropology. The New Enlightenment, in general, sponsored the birth of a new "religion," which apotheosized man and his exploits in history. Its anthropology was, if anything, more optimistic than that of the Old Enlightenment, and on it was built a variety of liberal and socialist doctrines of social organization. Historicism, so conspicuous in the Romantic World, also pervaded the New Enlightenment. Mostly, however, its philosophy of history centered in a doctrine of progress, viewed not so much as an aspiration, but rather as a general "law," encompassing improved methods of thinking as well as knowledge, social justice as well as reason.

Darwinism, or Evolutionism, though in some ways a world peculiarly its own, might also be regarded as a second phase of the New Enlightenment.[7] But for all its promise of "evolution," this third world was, on the whole, more somber than the second. Its somberness traces in large part to the chilling picture of nature presented in *The Origin of Species*. With Darwin the question of nature became central again, not merely for scientists but for the general educated (and even to some extent, uneducated) public. His picture of nature, especially its mindless mechanism, inevitably reacted back on, and exacerbated the debate between science and theology. Thus, the period after 1859 became the heyday of agnosticism and "honest doubt," though by no means all of the latter is attributable to Darwin. Darwinism also stimulated fresh thinking, not all of it flattering to the human race or very pleasant, about the nature of man and the behavior of social groups, including

---

[7] The philosopher Alfred Fouillée, in his review of philosophy in the nineteenth century, pictured it this way. See his *Le mouvement idéaliste et la réaction contre la science positive,* Germer Baillière et Cie, Paris, 1896, pp. xiii–xiv.

nations. Above all, it drove home to men the eternal flux of things, and "the war of nature" as well as nature's creativity.

Darwinism helped to mold the *Fin-de-Siècle*. This fourth world, however, is the least easy to characterize because it was the least unified. Nevertheless, it is not difficult to discern in it some new trends. Strong doubts were expressed, not only about God—Nietzsche and others now pronounced the death of God—but about nature, too, as the positivists described it. A "reaction against positivism" had set in, which in some quarters amounted to a disillusionment with science in general. In this increasingly skeptical climate a new culture of the Self, of subjectivism, and of experience for the sake of experience, was able to thrive. Furthermore, a new crop of psychologists and social thinkers detected more clearly than before the strong irrational streak in human nature, and the role played by unreason and "myth" in history and political life. These trends should not be exaggerated, for they by no means swamped the major assumptions of the Enlightenment, either old or new. But taken all together, these trends do give some indication of the kind of thinking that lay ahead in the more anxious century to come.

These four worlds, clashing with one another in so many ways, testify vividly to the multitudinousness of nineteenth-century thought. In the midst of the general cacaphony, however, a major theme can be heard gradually to assert itself. This was the theme of becoming, always somewhat muted, as we have seen, in the previous two centuries, but now sounding distinctly louder and even insistent, and quite drowning out being. The nineteenth century, because it tipped the balance in the former's favor, may therefore be called the first real Century of Becoming.[8] Ernest Renan may have been the first to take note of this important development. "The great progress of criticism," he wrote in the preface to his doctoral dissertation of 1852, "has been to substitute the category of *becoming* (*devenir*) for the category of *being* (*être*)."[9] "Formerly," Renan went on to say, "everything was considered as being. One spoke of philosophy, law, politics, art, and poetry in an absolute manner. Now, however, everything is considered as in the process of becoming (*en voie de se faire*)."

[8] I first called the nineteenth century the "Century of Becoming" in the third edition of my *Main Currents of Western Thought*, Knopf, New York, 1970. That edition also adopted the structure of four worlds of thought for the century, though for the fourth, the term "Toward the Twentieth Century" (much inferior, as I now think) was used, rather than *Fin-de-Siècle*.

[9] Ernest Renan, *Averroes et l'Averroisme*, A. Durand, Paris, 1852, p. ii. Also quoted p. 20.

The rise of historicism, or the historical spirit, in the nineteenth century fully supports this statement. The French historian Augustin Thierry predicted, as a young man, that "history would put its stamp on the nineteenth century, as philosophy had done in the eighteenth."[10] Renan's gloss on this famous forecast is interesting and worth quoting. "Yes," he said, "history is, in a sense, the peculiar and original creation of our time." Every century favored a particular mode of thought to convey its deepest convictions. The present century did not encourage great poetry or art, or new systems of philosophy, because these genres "presuppose a faith and a simplicity which we no longer have." This, however, was precisely the reason for "our superiority in history."

> The great events which marked the end of the end of the last century and the beginning of this one, the number and variety of events which followed, and our reflection upon them, our concern to understand the vicissitudes and the laws of human revolutions: all that forms an excellent condition for the comprehension of the past.[11]

Renan was right, at least in his main contention. Thinking about the world in historical terms was an original creation of the nineteenth century. By history was meant, however, not simply "comprehension of the past," or even finding the origins of the present in the past, but a sense of incessant movement in human life, of continual change and development. In a word, history was the science of becoming. And as such, it did, indeed, come to be, now for the first time, the queen of the sciences, or the idiom in terms of which nearly everything was explained: God himself who was now thought to "develop," along with man; nature, especially after Sir Charles Lyell and Darwin; and even society, which was now understood more as an open-ended evolution, or as conditioned by a changing environment. This "revolution" in thinking, as Friedrich Meinecke later called it, ran parallel to, and no doubt partly reflected, the new dynamic world ushered in by the French and Industrial revolutions. Renan himself, as can be gathered from the foregoing quotation, partially explained it this way.

Two further observations may be made about nineteenth-century thought as a whole. The first is that this was the European Century

[10] Augustin Thierry, *Dix Ans d'Etudes Historiques,* "Preface," Garnier Frères, Paris, 1866, p. 18.

[11] Ernest Renan, "M. Augustin Thierry," *Essais de Morale et de Critique,* Michel Lévy Frères, Paris, 1860, pp. 104–106.

par excellence. Soon after World War I Paul Valéry raised the question of whether Europe, in view of its suicidal "domestic" politics, could hold its world preeminence for long? Could it possibly remain what it seemed, "the elect portion of the terrestrial globe, the pearl of the sphere, the brain of a vast body"?[12] This question would be raised many times thereafter, especially after World War II, when a spate of books appeared bemoaning "the end of European history" ("end" in the sense of superiority and dominance, intellectual as well as political and economic, over the rest of the world). But in the nineteenth century, Europe and Europeans were never prouder of their achievements. History was customarily written as though Europe (or some portion thereof, some one or more nations, since this was the heyday of European nationalism) were, indeed, the center of the universe where all new and creative ideas originated. It was also widely assumed that the "primitive" mind represented a much lower stage of development than that of "cultured" Europe. All this was in rather sharp contrast to the eighteenth century when, despite the idea of progress, Europeans were likely to locate their paradise in some other portion of the globe, in the exotic East or in primitive America. The new self-esteem, to be sure, began to wear thin toward the end, as Europeans discovered serious cracks in their own culture. Throughout most of the nineteenth century, however, Europeans proudly carried the "White Man's Burden."

The second observation is that within Europe itself there was a significant shift in the balance of intellectual power. Auguste Comte, at the conclusion of his lectures on the Positive philosophy, spoke of the European West, and of what he expected each of five main constituent nations to contribute to the "impending philosophical regeneration." What Comte missed, though he paid lip service to her "natural aptitude for systematic generalization," was Germany's rise as a foremost power. England and France had dominated Enlightenment culture. In the nineteenth century, however, Germany rose to equality with these two nations, and even surpassed them in some fields of knowledge. She excelled in the "natural," as well as the "cultural," sciences. It is tempting to relate this intellectual upsurge to extraordinary political events, to Germany's achievement of national unification and eventually European hegemony. In truth, however, the growth of German influence in European thought had begun much earlier with the *Sturm und Drang* of Goethe, Schiller, and Herder, the Romantic Movement (so important in Germany), and the Idealist philosophy of

[12] Paul Valéry, *Collected Works,* Pantheon Books, New York, Vol. X, p. 31.

Immanuel Kant and his successors. Still known primarily as a nation of philosophers in Hegel's day, the Germans went on to be leaders in all the other fields of thought, notably in historical scholarship, and the history and psychology of religion, but also in the more precise "nomothetic" sciences, including physics and the new experimental psychology. In the nineteenth century, intellectual currents radiated out from Germany to the other countries as they had not done since the Protestant Reformation.

"Wonderful Century!" That was what the scientist Alfred Russel Wallace called the nineteenth century as he looked back over it toward the end of his life. Wonderful, certainly, but increasingly unsettling too, thanks partly to the very idea of evolution that he and Darwin had sponsored simultaneously; thanks to having to get used to living in a world of perpetual evolution, or "becoming"; thanks to the growing multitude of ideas that Arnold noted, and the mounting "criticism," not only of the old culture of Europe but also the new, which ever since the days of Newton, had seemed to so many to be the chief hope of the world. The nineteenth century, wonderful though it might be, was indeed a Century of Becoming.

The Romantic World

The roots of the Romantic World lay deep in the eighteenth and even the seventeenth century. The Romantic World is commonly represented as a counter-movement to the Enlightenment, just as the Enlightenment is said to have countered the supernatural Christian system. Although there is truth in this view, it should be understood that the Romantic Movement would not have been the same without the Enlightenment, that in part it actually grew out of the Enlightenment, and that in any case it did not constitute a simple return to the world the Enlightenment had left behind.

In truth, the Romantic Movement was as much a revolution as a counter-revolution. It may, indeed, be thought of as the first great protest against the "modern world," that is, the rational-scientific civilization, which had begun to form in the seventeenth century, and which assumed major proportions in the eighteenth century. But it protested in the name of a new modernity. Some of the romantics thought of themselves as "modern" in the sense of Christian, and anti-classical in artistic taste. But they were modern in still another sense. We might say that they were more modern than they knew, especially in their exploration of the night-side of life, of dreams and the unconscious, and in providing the theoretical basis for modern nationalism. In these, among other areas, the romantics obviously set in motion waves of thought that were not to have their full impact until the twentieth century.

There is a special difficulty, however, in trying to define romanticism. This is not only because of the "plurality of romanticisms" to which Arthur Lovejoy called attention. Lovejoy could discover no "one fundamental 'Romantic' idea" in the welter of national movements that others had loosely identified as romantic.[1] Lovejoy also noted a cleavage between "Germany and the West," which became a common topic of discussion during World War I, and continued to be such on through World War II. This cleavage was traced back to the Romantic Movement, which Ernst Troeltsch and others claimed to be peculiarly German, or, at any rate, radically different in Germany than in other countries. Pluralism, however, and a certain amount of nominalism too, is common to all intellectual movements, and one fails to see how it applies more to romanticism than to, say, the Renaissance or Reformation. Mainly, the difficulty in defining romanticism stems rather from the nature of the movement itself. The romantics, of whatever country, had a penchant for the mysterious and put a premium on individual feeling and expression. They also throve on paradoxes. Consequently, it is not always easy to know what the romantics were talking about. What exactly did Friedrich Schleiermacher mean, for instance, by "expansive soaring in the Whole and the Inexhaustible"? Or the philosopher, Friedrich Wilhelm von Schelling, by "real-idealism"? The difficulty is compounded by the word romanticism itself, which was uncommonly vague save among the Germans, not universally acceptable even to the romantics themselves, and variously understood. Moreover, it had little or no institutional organization, no central publishing venture such as the eighteenth-century *Encyclopédie*, no central doctrine, not even so loose an authority as the Bible constituted during the Protestant Reformation.

Yet there can be no real doubt that there was a Romantic Movement and, what is more, that it effected a real transvaluation of Western values. Even Lovejoy came round to this view. In a passage worth quoting from a later work, Lovejoy stated unequivocally that romanticism, "more than any other *one* thing has distinguished, both for better and worse, the prevailing assumptions of the mind of the nineteenth and of our own century from those of the preceding period in the intellectual history of the West."[2] As we shall see, romanticism by no

[1] Arthur O. Lovejoy, "On the Discrimination of Romanticisms" (1924), *Essays in the History of Ideas*, G. P. Putnam's Sons, New York, 1960.

[2] Arthur O. Lovejoy, *The Great Chain of Being*, Harper & Row, New York, 1960, p. 294. It is only fair to point out, however, that Lovejoy was still unhappy about the term *romanticism* even at this later date.

means displaced, or drove out, the Enlightenment; although it did pose a serious threat to it. Briefly, romanticism may be defined then, first of all, as a European-wide movement, possibly affecting Germany most deeply, but by no means exclusively, since it became a major influence nearly everywhere in Europe. German romanticism, to be sure, was rooted in its own *Sturm und Drang* movement of the eighteenth century, and in German pietism, which went back further still, and it owed a special debt to such individual German thinkers as Leibniz, J. G. Hamann, the "Wizard of the North," Goethe (for all that he called romanticism a "sickness"), and Immanuel Kant. Yet romanticism also borrowed freely from foreigners, especially Rousseau, whom everybody read, just as they borrowed from it. There was, in fact, a fairly free flow of ideas among English, French, and German romantics. Romanticism was, moreover, much more than an artistic and literary movement. After a time, it became a philosophical movement, and the romantics also developed ideas about politics and history. Recent political events, of course, in particular the French Revolution and Germany's War of Liberation, stirred up thinking about all these subjects.

What, essentially, was romanticism?[3] It is easier to say what it was not, or what European romantics were opposed to. John Stuart Mill, no romantic himself, but a sympathetic and informed observer, put his finger unerringly on what the romantics disliked. Romanticism, he said in an essay on Armand Carrel (1837), represented a reaction "against the narrownesses of the eighteenth century." Although Mill was speaking here primarily of literature, it is clear from what follows, and from other essays, conspicuously the famous one on Coleridge, that Mill thought of romanticism as a revolt against narrowness on many fronts, in philosophy and science, and in historical and political thought, as well as in poetry and the drama. "Fractional," "partial," "insignificant," "poor," were among the adjectives Thomas Carlyle employed in an essay on Diderot (1833); he denounced "Diderot's habitual world" as "a half-world, distorted into looking like a whole." The reference in both cases was, of course, to the European Enlightenment, which by then had become a stereotype, and partly also a caricature. The romantics thought that world too narrow, because of its addiction, as they believed, to geometric thinking and the allied doctrine of neoclassicism, or else to Lockean empiricism. The geometric spirit, though metaphysically bold, tried to subject all life to reason, and thus to mech-

---

[3] I have covered some, though not all, of this same ground in my article, "Romanticism, ca. 1780–ca. 1830," *Dictionary of the History of Ideas*, Scribner's, New York, 1973, Vol. III.

anize and demean it. Neoclassicism, similarly ambitious in seeking out nature's ideal patterns, imposed universal and iron rules on art and the artist. Empiricism offended for the opposite reason, because it was too skeptical, because it severely limited human knowledge to the sense world of appearances. Newton became an arch-symbol of this narrowness. Opinions about Newton varied, of course, even among the romantics (one thinks of Saint-Simon, who preached a cult of Newton), but William Blake's depiction of Newton struck a common chord. Blake did not see in Newton the great imaginative genius celebrated by Alexander Pope. On the contrary, Blake demoted Newton to the material world, making him look downward, as though trying to fathom the world by means of a pair of compasses, that is, by measurement and "reason" alone (Plate 19).

In opposition to Newton's world, suffused in light, the romantics offered their own nighttime world. The night, in contrast to day or light, signified that which "dost uplift the heavy wings of soul," and carry it beyond the space-time world into infinite regions. "How paltry and childish seems now the Light to me!" said the German poet-philosopher Novalis (Friedrich von Hardenberg). Novalis preferred, to the flashing stars seen in the sky, "the infinite eyes which the Night has opened to me."[4] This was one of the most positive marks, or predispositions, of the romantic mind: its yearning for the Infinite, which was manifested in a great variety of ways, both secular and religious. Goethe, though he had affinities, not always admitted, for certain features of romanticism, once said: "The highest happiness of man as a thinking man is to have probed what is knowable and quietly to revere what is unknowable."[5] This was a "classical" rather than a romantic maxim, putting limits, as Kant had done, on what the human mind could know and aspire to. Yet Goethe too, through Faust, also reached for the Infinite in his own special way, as did other romantics, whose metaphysical sense was not so highly developed as Novalis'. Caspar David Friedrich's painting, *Moonrise on the Sea* (1820–1826; Plate 20), is a fine visual rendition of this romantic *Sehnsucht*. Three people, seated on a rock, look out to sea and to the ships in full sail, as though yearning for spiritual comfort. Other marked predispositions, which were more or less universal among the romantics, were a strong sense of the irrational, even of its primacy, in human life, and an emphasis on particularity or individuality, as opposed to generality,

[4] Novalis, *Hymnen an die Nacht* (1799?), No. 1.
[5] Goethe, *Maxims and Reflections* (posthumous), Hermann Weigand (ed.), Pantheon, New York, 1949, p. 94.

PLATE 19. *Newton*, by William Blake.

Nationalgalerie, Berlin (West). (Photo: Jörg P. Anders.)

PLATE 20. *Moonrise on the Sea*, by Caspar David Friedrich.

whether in art, history, or anthropology. The latter, however, did not prevent the romantics from wanting to put the world together again if they could, to join subject and object, the ideal and the real, spirit and matter, after a century, as they believed, of putting asunder. Individuals, they felt, merely particularized a greater Whole, Spirit, or Universe. This penchant for synthesis, as opposed to analysis, reflected the romantic concern, particularly in the generation of the French Revolution, for a world that seemed shattered almost beyond recall. Paradoxically, however, the romantics also felt strongly that art consisted more of freedom than order, less of fixed rules and laws than of spontaneous creation. The romantics were keenly aware of living in a world of creativity and becoming. Some of these predispositions are on parade in a painting by John Martin, entitled *The Bard,* first exhibited in London in 1817 (Plate 21). The painter, taking his subject from an ode by Thomas Gray on Edward I's conquest of Wales and the king's order to put all the Welsh bards to death, reflects to a remarkable degree the romantic's feeling for aspects of experience that eluded "classical" rules or rational analysis: his sense of the mysterious and the Infinite, as shown in the bard's communion with things unseen on the mountaintop; his preference for a wild and untamed nature; and his evocation of the past, particularly the medieval past, as suggested by the castle in the background. These predispositions, born out of opposition between night and light, provide the key—William Wordsworth would say "the prelude"—to romantic ideas about "Man, Nature, and Society." Without this key, the ideas—that is, romantic answers to the perennial questions; the sort of questions Wordsworth himself set out to explore in his philosophical poem, *The Excursion*— must often seem hopelessly in conflict.

Natural Supernaturalism

It has often been said that romantic thought centered in a new idea of nature. It is difficult, if not impossible, however, to separate romantic ideas of nature and God. Thomas Carlyle makes this clear in his Journal (February 1, 1833) where he wrote:

> That the Supernatural differs not from the Natural is a great Truth, which the last century (especially in France) has been engaged in demonstrating. The Philosophers went far wrong, however, in this, that instead of raising the natural to the supernatural,

PLATE 21. *The Bard,* by John Martin.

Center for British Art, Yale University. (From the collection of Mr. and Mrs. Paul Mellon.)

they strove to sink the supernatural to the natural. The gist of my whole way of thought is to do not the latter but the *former*.

Following Carlyle, who here expresses a fairly common romantic notion, it makes sense to consider the two ideas together.

Romanticism touched off a religious revival. This revival took many forms, not least of which was a new nature mysticism. All the forms were inspired, however, as Carlyle intimates, by a deep sense of metaphysical loss, occasioned by the Enlightenment and its revolutionary aftermath. It was widely believed that the world had lost its metaphysical and religious bearings in the eighteenth century, and that men needed to recover them if there were ever again to be heroes and great works of art. In "the Unbelieving Century" God had become nonexistent or peripheral and bound by his own rational laws. Carlyle vividly describes this feeling of loss in his chapter on "The Everlasting No" in *Sartor Resartus* (1833–1834), that great source book for romantic views on God and religion. Carlyle's spokesman, Professor Teufelsdröckh, tells of the spiritual crisis he went through (obviously owing to the corrosive effect of Enlightenment skepticism): how, as "the spirit of Inquiry" took possession of him, he had moved from doubt to disbelief, and consequently was shut out from hope. At best, he thought, there might be "an absentee God," sitting idle since the first Sabbath, and looking at the Universe from the outside in.

But how to recover a living faith? Some romantics never succeeded in doing so, and their failure was doubtless a source of melancholy. Many, on the other hand, went over or back to Roman Catholicism, though they discovered new and romantic reasons for doing so. Others remained Protestant, though they, too, gave their religion a romantic look. Still others, however, and they were not few, renounced "church clothes" altogether, and invented new gods and new mythologies. One of these was William Blake, who, in his epic poem "Jerusalem," served up an exceedingly bizarre mixture of Christian and private mythology. Such perhaps also was Novalis who, though certainly a Christian, preferred to shroud his religion in mystery and fable. "The great mystery has been revealed to all, yet remains eternally unfathomable," says Sophia (Wisdom) in "Klingsor's Fairy Tale."[6] But such, above all, were the natural supernaturalists, those like Carlyle himself, who discovered a new sort of god at work in the world and in nature. Indeed,

---

[6] "Klingsor's Fairy Tale" (1799) was inserted into Novalis' novel *Heinrich von Ofterdingen* as chapter ix.

this god, immanent rather than transcendent, appears in some shape or form in nearly all the varieties of romantic religious experience.

The Vicomte de Chateaubriand, author of *The Genius of Christianity* (1802), called "the Bible of Romanticism," is a good example of the new type of Roman Catholic apologist.[7] In order to resurrect a cult supposed to be in its grave, Chateaubriand proposed, not rational proofs of the existence of God, or a restatement of doctrine, but a direct appeal to the human heart. "The Christian religion," he said, "is itself a species of passion, which has its transports, its ardors, its sighs, its joys, its tears, its love of society and solitude."[8] Chateaubriand showed how poetic Christianity was, how mysterious, how aesthetically satisfying (especially in its churches, which, in contrast to Greek temples, however elegant, excited feelings of awe and infinitude), and how impressive also was its historic achievement. Far from being hostile to civilization, as Gibbon had said (though not consistently), Christianity contributed to it a superior morality, a great art and literature, and every sort of improvement, ranging from agriculture to the most abstract sciences. Were he to rewrite his book, Chateaubriand said later in his *Memoirs,* he would show further how Christianity had laid the basis for true social cohesion, equality, and justice. This was an appeal calculated to win the hearts even of young men, in a time of mental and moral shipwreck (as Chateaubriand represented it).

At almost exactly the same time a young chaplain in Berlin, educated by Moravian Pietists, was trying to revive Protestantism, by appealing, however, more to individual experience than to social usefulness. All the chief notes of romantic Protestantism[9] appear in Friedrich Schleiermacher's "theology of feeling," notably in the early *Addresses on Religion to its Cultural Despisers,* which he wrote in 1799, at the insistence of his romantic friends in the Prussian capital. Schleiermacher

---

[7] Roman Catholicism experienced a considerable revival following the French Revolution. There were a number of spectacular conversions, such as those of Tieck and Friedrich Schlegel, and a number of artists. H. A. Korff says these conversions took on "an epidemic character" (*Geist der Goethezeit,* Koehler Amelang, Leipzig, 1953, Vol. IV, Bk. III, Chap. 1). But more important, many others, such as Chateaubriand himself, came back into the Catholic fold after a brief flirtation with unbelief.

[8] Chateaubriand, *Génie du Christianisme,* Pt. II, Chap. VIII.

[9] Protestantism probably profited less from romanticism than Catholicism. Some Protestants like Novalis actually thought that the Reformation was a mistake, leading to the unbelief of the Age of Reason. Nevertheless, under "romantic" Protestantism one might also include Pietism in Germany and Evangelicalism in England, as well as some aspects of the Oxford Movement, led by John Keble and John Henry Newman. Newman, of course, later converted to Roman Catholicism.

advocated turning away from French culture, which had become indifferent to religion, as well as from deism and rational theology in
general. After wrestling with Kant since his university days, Schleiermacher rejected the latter's "religion within the limits of reason alone,"
which made God and immortality depend on man's moral consciousness. Religion was not the same thing as morality, or philosophy. Like
so many of his contemporaries, Schleiermacher thirsted for the Infinite,
which was something quite different from trying to reconcile religion
with reason, or to reduce it to ethics. "True religion," he said in his
famous definition, "is sense and taste for the Infinite."[10] But where was
the Infinite to be found?—In man's inmost soul, in "feeling," he said.
Despite his resistance to Kant, Schleiermacher had learned from the
critical philosopher to distrust rational proofs of God's existence, hence
to move religion back to a precognitive state. Feeling, however, was
individual, even though it was also a faculty of the human soul and
corresponded in some way, not made very clear, to an objective reality.
Schleiermacher distrusted the generalizing and universalizing of Enlightenment religion. For a long time, he said, he had been content with
the discovery of a "universal reason." But later Schleiermacher saw
that man must rise to "the still higher level of individuality." "I was
not satisfied to view humanity in rough unshapen masses, inwardly
altogether alike."[11] Thus, Schleiermacher individualized, as well as
psychologized and emotionalized religion. Each individual was a unique
embodiment of the All, and experienced the All in his own unique way.
If Schleiermacher's God was not pantheistic, he was certainly immanent, to be found in the world, more particularly in man's soul. As
head, later on, of the theological faculty at the new university of Berlin,
Schleiermacher was able to influence Protestant theology profoundly
in this new and "romantic" direction.

The romantics also characteristically found God in Nature, not all
of them, of course, not Alfred de Vigny or Blake, or Lord Byron, but
certainly an impressive number. These "natural supernaturalists," revolting against the Newtonian machine, sought to make nature a place
in which man could once again live and feel close to God, and thus

---

[10] Friedrich Schleiermacher, *Reden über die Religion,* Second Speech on "The
Nature of Religion."

[11] Schleiermacher, *Monologen* (1800), 2nd Soliloquy (see *Soliloquies,* H. L.
Friess [ed.], Open Court, Chicago, 1926, pp. 30–31). Schleiermacher's individualism comes across best in this, his spiritual autobiography, which was written
a few months after the *Addresses,* and which became a popular classic.

solve the problem of dualism that had plagued thinking men since the time of Descartes. The impetus to this new way of thinking about nature came from, among others, Rousseau, whom the contemplation of nature sent into mystical ecstasies (as in *Les Rêveries du Promeneur Solitaire,* 1776–1778); Goethe, who is his morphological studies was always trying to discover the original and inner principle of things, the eternal in the finite; "holy Spinoza," revived in Germany in the late eighteenth century, who appeared to teach an immanent God, identical in some fashion with the universe. This new nature mysticism blossomed in Schelling's *Naturphilosophie,* much admired by Samuel Taylor Coleridge as well as the Germans; in Wordsworth's nature poetry; and in landscape painters such as John Constable in England and David Caspar Friedrich in Germany. The latter called Nature "Christ's Bible," and saw in it symbols of the divine presence. A painting such as *Man and Woman Contemplating the Moon* (1819; Plate 22) shows the religious awe that Friedrich intended to convey through landscape painting. Here he evoked, in characteristic romantic fashion, the twilight as the borderline between the phenomenal and transcendental worlds. For the two human figures, nature is practically coterminous with the next world, or else leads into it in the distance.

The natural supernaturalists radicalized the idea of God, as well as nature. First of all, they divinized nature and brought God down from heaven to dwell in

> *. . . the light of setting suns,*
> *And the round ocean and the living air,*
> *And the blue sky, and in the mind of man.*[12]

Wordsworth also thought of God as "transcendent power," having "infinitude," and thus escaped complete pantheism. Nevertheless, with God and nature thus communing, man too could commune with "every form of creature," and, indeed, in great moments, as when Wordsworth crossed the Alps, commune with God himself. The philosopher Schelling, combatting Fichte's conception of nature as an obstacle to be overcome by the ego, similarly strove to synthesize God, man, and nature by representing nature as "visible Spirit," culminating in man himself, and Spirit as "invisible Nature."

More radical even than Schelling's doctrine of identity, however, was

---

[12] Wordsworth, *Tintern Abbey* (1798), lines 97–99.

Nationalgalerie, Berlin (West). (Photo: Jörg P. Anders.)

PLATE 22. *Man and Woman Contemplating the Moon,* by Caspar David Friedrich.

the new conception of nature as an organism, alive, growing, creative, *becoming*. In *The Prelude* (written 1799 to 1805), Wordsworth tells how as a student at Cambridge he fell in love with Newton's laws, and conceived of a God "superior and incapable of change." The romantic imagination changed all that. Not finding the concepts of mechanical science congenial, romanticism turned increasingly to biological analogies, describing nature as *naturans,* that is, animated by a living principle, as opposed to a *natura naturata,* that is, a finished and dead product. Johann Gottfried von Herder was a key figure in this turn to "biological" thinking. In his *God, Some Conversations* (1787), which was a widely read book, Herder pumped life into Spinoza's abstract philosophical system, depicting nature as pulsing with God's activity, and straining to realize all its potentialities. "The more we learn about matter," he wrote, the more forces we discover in it, so that "the empty conception of a dead extension completely disappears." "All is change, all is process, haste, and migration," the work of an immanent God who is the Life-force in creation.[13] Herder was fumbling for a conception that later crystallized in Schelling's *Naturphilosophie*. This was the conception of the Absolute as becoming, and the concomitant idea of a creative evolution. Schelling's God, or Absolute, realizes itself, its potentialities and purposes, in the temporal process, in nature and art. Thus, nature is a creative power, bursting to achieve ever new and higher forms, and to become self-conscious through man himself.[14] This view, largely though not entirely the creation of romantic philosophy and literature, explains the spiritual distress caused later on by Darwinism. Who could reconcile a nature "red in tooth and claw" with Mrs. Browning's "Earth's crammed with heaven"? Yet despite strong vitalistic and teleological overtones, *Naturphilosophie* also helped to create a climate that was favorable to the idea of evolution.

It is important to note that the romantics were not necessarily anti-scientific. They all disliked a certain kind of science, mechanical science, the product of the mere "understanding," and they were split down the middle as to whether mechanical inventions enhanced or degraded human life. But not a few romantics, Schelling, for example, who became secretary of the Academy of Sciences at Munich, and the French

[13] Johann Gottfried von Herder, *Gott: einige Gespräche,* 2nd and 5th Conversations (see *God, Some Conversations,* Frederick H. Burkhardt [ed.], Bobbs-Merrill, Indianapolis, pp. 105, 185).

[14] Schelling developed his *Naturphilosophie* in a series of books, beginning with *Ideas toward a Philosophy of Nature* in 1797.

philosopher Maine de Biran, who admired the physicist Ampère, eagerly followed the latest developments in science. Some romantics contributed more positively to the advancement of science by their own bold speculations, especially in the life sciences and psychology. One thinks of the painter-physician Dr. Carl Gustav Carus, who explored the "soul" in seminal books about the unconscious; of the brilliant young physicist J. W. Ritter, a convinced Galvanist and advocate of an "artistic physics" (he wrote a book on *Physics as Art,* 1806), seeking to link man to nature, and art to science; of Ritter's student Gotthilf-Heinrich von Schubert, who translated Erasmus Darwin and investigated the symbolic language of dreams or, as he so graphically put it, "the night-side of science"; and of Coleridge, who hobnobbed with scientists, lectured at the Royal Institution, and wrote a book on the *Theory of Life* (c. 1817). Although Coleridge like the young Wordsworth, admired Newton's "sublime discoveries," he objected to his metaphysics. Coleridge wanted a "more comprehensive theory of life," as the full title of his book indicates, which would encompass mechanistic science, but at the same time remove it from its "philosophic throne." The body could not be explained simply as a hydraulic machine, or could chemical affinities, electricity, heat, and the like be explained simply by mechanics. Coleridge, in fact, turned the Newtonian metaphor upside down, and explained, in the manner of *Naturphilosophie,* inorganic as well as organic nature by means of the emergent attributes of life.

Much as the romantics exalted art and the artist, they showed little disposition to think in terms of "two cultures," to pit art against science, unless it was mechanical science. In this respect, Shelley was more characteristic than Keats. Keats feared lest "cold philosophy" (Newtonian optics) clip the wings of angels and "conquer all mysteries by rule and line." Shelley, on the other hand, thought "Science, and her sister Poesy" could, together, enlighten the cities of the free.[15] In fact, there was a marked tendency to romanticize science, as Balzac did in his novel *The Quest of the Absolute.* Novalis, himself an amateur scientist as well as a great poet, thought of science as a gateway to the Infinite. Some of Victor Hugo's poems also merit reading on this point. Hugo became a sort of poet laureate of science, glorifying it as a great adventure into the unknown and penetrating the mystery of nature.

[15] John Keats, *Lamia* (1820), lines 229–238; Percy Bysshe Shelley, *The Revolt of Islam,* Canto V, LI, 5.

Romantic Man

Man, as understood by the romantics, was not the measure, as in "classical" thought. They commonly saw man in the context of great cosmic forces that enveloped him in a whole or infinity greater than himself. "Man," said Dr. Carus in his *Nine Letters on Landscape Painting* (1831), "when he contemplates the magnificent unity of a natural landscape, is made conscious of his own insignificance and, feeling that everything is a part of God, he loses himself in the Infinite and renounces his individual existence."[16] This emphasis on a greater whole by no means contradicts an equally strong emphasis on individuality, already noted in Schleiermacher, or on human creativity. It does, however, make clear the essentially metaphysical nature of romantic man. In romantic anthropology, man is not merely "bent toward the earth," as Victor Hugo so graphically put it, but "thrown toward heaven, his fatherland."[17]

This explains why the romantics undertook their own Copernican revolution in epistemology. Man had to be endowed with knowing faculties that were commensurate with his metaphysical needs and ambitions. Lockean epistemology was obviously inadequate to the task, since it made knowledge dependent, very largely, on sense impressions. Even Kant, though he made the mind more active with his famous categories, limited knowledge to appearances in the phenomenal world. Hence, Coleridge, very much anti-Locke, though grateful to "the sage of Koenigsberg" (and perhaps not perfectly understanding him), posited a special faculty of the mind, which he surprisingly called "Reason," to distinguish it from the "Understanding." This famous distinction, expressed by nearly all the romantics in one form or another, was already familiar in Germany, thanks to the philosopher F. H. Jacobi, and to Kant himself. The "Understanding" (*Verstand*), to be sure, could only know appearances. In Schopenhauer's metaphor, it resembled a man who goes round and round a castle sketching the facade, but never finding an entrance. "Reason" (*Vernunft;* Jacobi called it *Glaube,* or faith), however, could penetrate the walls, that is,

[16] Quoted in Marcel Brion, *Art of the Romantic Era*, Frederick Praeger, New York, 1966, p. 110. Although dedicated to Goethe, this volume owed much to *Naturphilosophie*, as well as to Carus' mentor Caspar David Friedrich.

[17] Hugo, *La Préface de Cromwell* (1827), Maurice Sourian (ed.), Société française d'Imprimerie, Paris, n.d., pp. 222–223.

get behind appearances to the thing-in-itself, or, in Coleridge's words, take as its field "invisible realities or spiritual objects." It was "the organ of the super-sensuous." Coleridge, in this respect typical of the general romantic endeavor, transformed the mind from a mirror (or *tabula rasa*) into a lamp which could throw its beam over "A new Earth and new Heaven,/ Undreamt of by the sensual and the proud."[18]

Coleridge, overflowing with metaphors, also compared the mind to a plant, which assimilates the outer elements, but which by its respiration makes its own contribution to the environment. In other words, the mind was also wonderfully creative, capable not only of penetrating the mysteries but of rendering and vivifying them in works of original genius. By means of Imagination, sister to Reason, and described by Coleridge as an "esemplastic" or shaping power, man could bring new worlds to life, by creation and invention. This was supremely true of the artist, who, indeed, became the ideal man of the Romantic World, displacing the *philosophe*. For Shelley, for instance, the poet was more than human, a visionary participating in the eternal, lifting the veil from "the hidden beauty of the world." Similarly, for Schelling, who developed a full-blown philosophy of art, the artist, alone of men, directly intuited the Absolute, and hence presented in his work "an infinity which no finite understanding can fully unfold."[19]

This romantic doctrine of the genius cannot be fully understood, however, without reference to the unconscious. Indeed, romantic anthropology, in general, assumed the existence of an "irrational," or unconscious, mind. If the romantics did not invent the unconscious, they were the first to talk about it freely and at length. The unconscious was used to explain not only the creative process but also the "night side" of human life, the world of dreams, monsters, and apparitions. It was more a metaphysical than a scientific concept. The artist was commonly pictured as an unconsciously growing plant, or as a vessel through whom the Eternal acted and expressed itself. Some, like the artist-poet William Blake, believed in poetic automatism. "I have written this Poem," Blake said of his *Milton,* "from immediate Dictation . . . without Premeditation and even against my Will." Of course,

---

[18] Coleridge, *The Friend* (1809–1810), *Complete Works,* Harper & Brothers, New York, 1884, Vol. II, pp. 144–145; *Dejection: An Ode* (1802), lines 69–70. See also Wordsworth, *The Prelude,* Bk. XIV, Conclusion, lines 70–77: "a mind/ That feeds upon infinity."

[19] On the artist as visionary, see Shelley's *Defense of Poetry* (1831) and Schelling's *System des transzendentalen Idealismus* (1800).

the unconscious expressed itself preeminently in dreams. Here the contrast between romantic and Enlightenment thought is striking. The latter attempted to reduce the dream to a natural phenomenon, originating in sense experience and explicable by mechanical laws. The state of wakefulness was the superior state; in dreams the "soul" lost touch with the real world. Romantic psychologists like Dr. Carus and von Schubert, the latter the author of a seminal book on the *Symbolism of Dreams* (1814), stood this proposition on its head. In dreams, man speaks a superior language, which enables him to look backward and forward, without the usual temporal restraints, hence to be prophetic. In dreams the soul, precisely because it is withdrawn from sense impressions, has contact with divine reality, thus enabling the "hidden poet" in man to emerge. The opening lines of Novalis' novel *Heinrich von Ofterdingen* (1799) make clear the new romantic view. Heinrich and his father are talking about dreams. "Dreams are froth," says the father, who is a skeptic. "The times when heavenly visions were seen in dreams have long passed by." Heinrich objects. Maybe dreams are not sent directly from heaven, but should we not think of them, nonetheless, as "heavenly gifts," which rend the mysterious curtain that hides our inward natures from view, release the chained fancy, and guide us "in our pilgrimage to the holy tomb."

As stated earlier, the unconscious cut two ways. It could lead man to a superior world, but it could also let loose the demonic in him. The romantics were acutely aware of an anxious and troubled human nature, of forces hidden in man that could tear him and his world apart. Von Schubert himself gave lectures on the "night side" of science, warning of the evil as well as good manifestations of the unconscious. Heinrich von Kleist, influenced by von Schubert's theories, peopled his dramas of the same period (1806–1808) with figures like Panthesilea, the Amazon queen, who was swept away by elemental passions, or Kätchen von Heilbronn, in whom love was represented as a primitive, unconscious force. And Coleridge, though he extolled man's Reason and godlike Imagination, nevertheless, in his greatest poem, made his hero commit an essentially irrational (unconscious) crime, the killing of the albatross, for which he must suffer until he became conscious of what he had done. Of the visual artists, Francisco Goya, after the onset of deafness in 1792, best illustrates this nightmarish quality. In the *Caprichos* and *Proverbios,* and in the fantastic paintings he put on the walls of his country house (called the *Quinta del Sordo,* or deaf man's house) apparitions, frightful in appearance, rise out of the depths of the unconscious. Reason has forsaken man altogether in, for instance, the well-known engraving entitled *The Dream of Reason Produces Monsters* (Plate 23).

Arthur Schopenhauer was the philosopher of this night side of romantic anthropology. Schelling, too, detected dark impulses, largely unconscious, in the soul, but was optimistic about man's freedom to overcome and transmute them. Schopenhauer, however, did not believe in freedom, or at least did so only to a limited degree. In *The World as Will and Idea* (1818), Schopenhauer identified the thing-in-itself (that is, reality) as "the will to live," and this will was blind, planless. groundless, riding herd on man, involving him in endless striving, hence suffering and strife. "Eternal becoming, endless flux, characterises the revelation of the inner nature of will." Only by denying his own nature, that is, will, by stilling desire altogether, or turning to aesthetic contemplation, can man achieve any sort of peace. Schopenhauer's will is reminiscent of the Freudian id. Moreover, Schopenhauer keeps saying that men are not what they pretend to be; "they are only masks." Tear off the mask, look into the unconscious (though Schopenhauer does not actually use the word), and what does one see? A boundless egoism and malice, causing misery to self and other selves, caused by the overriding will to live. Schopenhauer wrote in a later essay on human nature:

> It is a fact, then, that in the heart of every man there lies a wild beast which only waits for an opportunity to storm and rage, in its desire to inflict pain on others, or, if they stand in his way, to kill them. . . . In trying to tame and to some extent hold it in check, the intelligence, its appointed keeper, has always enough to do. People may, if they please, call it the radical evil in human nature. . . . I say, however, that it is the will to live, which, more and more embittered by the constant sufferings of existence, seeks to alleviate its own torment by causing torment in others.[20]

There was no consistency in the romantic image of man. But there was a common denominator. What all the romantics were trying to say, though in different ways, was that man was much more than a thinking machine, that human nature could not be accounted for exclusively, or even primarily, in terms of sense and "understanding." In other words, romanticism projected a wider view of man than the En-

---

[20] Arthur Schopenhauer, *Parerga* (1851), essay on "Human Nature," in Richard Taylor (ed.), *The Will to Live,* Doubleday (Anchor), Garden City, pp. 282–283, 286. See also *The World as Will and Idea,* Random House (Modern Library), New York, 1928, pp. 133–134.

PLATE 23. *The Dream of Reason Produces Monsters*, by Francisco Goya.

lightenment. But the romantic view of man was not necessarily more optimistic. At its deepest, it perceived man's tragic dilemma, the inner discord stirred up in his soul by the presence there of both godlike and tigerish qualities. Romantic awareness of "The Tyger" (William Blake) in man increased rather than diminished as time went on. Doubtless, this awareness was owing partly to the course taken by outward political events, in which man's destructiveness was becoming only too apparent. In any case, many of the romantics began to talk more of man's need for social and historic ties, which could curb his individualistic "will to live." Thus, as we shall see, historic man came to be an important adjunct to romantic anthropology.

The Social Organism

Romantic ideas about social and political organization can be understood only in the light of this anthropology, as well as the general history of the period. Romanticism has been accused of nearly every political sin in the book, of revolution as well as reaction, of proto-fascism and antinomianism, even of *Weltpflucht,* or lack of concern for social problems. And it is true that over several generations romanticism ran nearly the whole gamut of contemporary political creeds, from conservatism to liberalism and socialism and even anarchism. However, as this statement implies, most romantics did take sides in the political conflicts of the times. It is simply not true that they shied away from politics, or refused to think about it, though not many romantics actually held public office. Indeed, out of the Romantic World came a number of strikingly new and influential ideas concerning the organization of societies.

Of these ideas, one stands out above all the others, namely the social organism. This was not, of course, a new idea. Nevertheless, it now made new sense and was given a new twist. Its contemporary appeal is easy to understand. It reflected the fear of chaos in an age of revolution, the dismay felt by many, not merely the aristocracy, at the toppling of institutions and the dissolving of ancient ties. Yet it also antedated the French Revolution in, for instance, the reflections of Rousseau and Burke (not so opposed to each other in political mood as the latter liked to think) and Herder. Thus, the social organism represented a revulsion not only against the excesses in Paris during the Revolution but also against the entire Enlightenment way of thinking about social problems.

Coleridge hits the keynote in one of his "lay sermons" on politics, *The Statesman's Manual* (1816), in which, among other things, he summarized his views on the causes of the Revolution and France's subsequent "chastisement." He attributed the debacle largely to false ideas, not least of which was

> the general conceit that states and governments might be and ought to be constructed as machines, every movement of which might be foreseen and taken into previous calculations; the consequent multitude of plans and constitutions, of planners and constitution-makers, and the remorseless arrogance with which the authors and proselytes of every new proposal were ready to realize it, be the cost what it might in the established rights, or even in the lives, of men. . . .

To this "machine" conceit Coleridge opposed "the right idea of the State," which he described as a "moral unit" or "organic whole."[21] That is, Coleridge thought of the state—or society—as more like an organism than a machine. The English Constitution, for instance, was not *made* as a machine is made; it *grew* as an organism grows over a period of time. The state further resembled an organism in consisting, not of atomic individuals, each pursuing his own selfish interest, but of organs—the historic organs of king, church, and proprietage—each contributing in different ways to the life of the whole.

This organic theory was neither original with Coleridge nor was it confined to England. It became, indeed, a quite common view among the romantics of all countries, many of whom, like Coleridge, started out as enthusiasts of revolution, and were subsequently disillusioned. Coleridge himself inherited the idea from Edmund Burke, who, years before, had castigated the revolutionaries for treating politics as though it were a "geometrical demonstration," without reference to human nature or history. Burke's influence became pervasive in Germany as well as in England, but the Germans did not need Burke to tell them that the times called for a new emphasis on *Gemeinschaft*. The German romantics attacked a political science based on the abstract model of geometry, and substituted for it a sort of political biology, which stressed "natural" growth as opposed to conscious planning, and community feeling as opposed to mere individual rights. Schleiermacher

---

[21] Coleridge, *The Statesman's Manual*, W. G. T. Shedd (ed.), *Complete Works*, Harper & Brothers, New York, 1884, Vol. I, p. 440; *On the Constitution of the Church and State* (1830), ibid., Vol. VI, p. 95.

sounds like Burke when, in a paper read before the Royal Academy of the Sciences in Berlin in 1814, he denounced contemporary political "engineers" for treating states always as "objects upon which man has to exercise his ingenuity," and never as "historical formations of nature." "Never has a state, even the most imperfect one, been made."[22]

For most romantics, especially after the Revolution, the nation or nation-state constituted the highest form of social organism. Thus, the latter was not necessarily a reactionary concept. Romanticism, in fact, contributed more to the rise of nationalism, soon to become one of the great modern myths, than either the Jacobins or Napoleon. This romantic nationalism, it should be understood, did not negate romantic individualism. It is true that the spectacle of the Revolution, and its aftermath of French imperialism, engendered a stronger feeling of identity between the individual and the state, particularly in Germany. Nevertheless, the romantics were careful, even at the height of Germany's War of Liberation, to preserve the dignity of the individual, especially the genius. The new thought was that the individual could best develop his potentialities in the corporate community and with the help of the state, which was now represented as a cultural leader.

The more important point, however, is that romantic thought depicted the nation itself as a great individual, different from, though not necessarily antagonistic to, other nations. That is, romantic individualism expressed itself politically chiefly in the idea of the nation. This idea is another instance of the romantic revolt against the generalizing and universalizing tendencies in eighteenth-century thought. In his *Addresses to the German Nation* (1808), the philosopher Fichte, who had moved from an earlier rationalism to a romantic view of society, speaks of the "individuality of nations."

> Spiritual nature was able to represent the essence of mankind only as highly manifold gradations of individuals, and of individuality, in general, of nations. Only in so far as each one of these nations, left to itself, develops and takes shape in accordance with its own peculiarities, and in so far as each individual in each of these nations also develops and takes shape in accordance with this common peculiarity as well as with his own individual peculiarity, is the phenomenon of divinity reflected in the way it should be. . . .[23]

[22] Schleiermacher, in H. S. Reiss (ed.), *The Political Thought of the German Romantics, 1793–1815*, Basil Blackwell, Oxford, 1955, p. 175.

[23] Johann Gottlieb Fichte, *Reden an die Deutsche Nation*, 13th Address, in ibid., p. 108.

Herder had developed this idea years before when as a young man he took a sea voyage from Riga to France, observing en route the peculiarities of each country as it passed before his eyes and beginning to form in his mind the idea of a *Volk* and *Volksgeist.*

The national idea, however, underwent considerable change in the hands of successive romantic thinkers. A largely cultural idea at first, it took on a more political cast, particularly in Germany, under the impact of French imperialism. Herder's nationalism, for instance, was purely cultural and humanitarian, whereas Fichte's, hammered out in the shadow of France's humiliation of Prussia, was political as well as cultural. Herder's chief contribution to nationalism was the idea of the *Volk,* which in turn was based on his idea of nature. As will be recalled, what impressed Herder about nature was not its mechanical regularity but its richness and variety. "Nature," he wrote, "has distributed its gifts differently according to climate and culture. . . . Let us rejoice that Time, the great mother of all things, throws now these and now other gifts from her horn of plenty and slowly builds up mankind in all its different component parts."[24] This variety, he thought, extended to the history of peoples. In the course of history, each *Volk* came to have a unique character, or soul (*Geist*), exhibited preeminently in its religion, language, and literature. The *Volk* was not formed by a contract, or by man's will; it grew, as an organism grows and ultimately becomes a living whole greater than its individual parts. Though Herder championed the cultural rights of all peoples, including the Jews and Slavs, he addressed himself primarily to Germans. He reminded the Germans of their great literary heritage, setting the example by his collection of *Volkslieder,* urging freedom from imitation of classical and French models. Herder emphasized the youth of German culture, and the great future that lay before it. In a word, he called upon the Germans to become conscious of themselves as a unique and creative people, who had a significant contribution to make to civilization. Jacob Grimm, best known with his brother as a collector of fairy tales, carried this idea further with his work on the origins of the German language and Germany mythology. Two eminent jurists, K. F. Eichhorn and F. K. von Savigny, extended it to the law. The latter, appointed professor of Roman Law at Berlin in 1810, and in close contact with leading romantics, contended that laws should be grounded, not on abstract metaphysical principles as in the Natural

[24] Quoted in Hans Kohn, *The Idea of Nationalism,* Macmillan, New York, 1944, p. 434.

Law, but on the collective consciousness of a nation. *Volksrecht* (national or popular law) should reflect the *Volksgeist,* or national genius.[25]

With Fichte the idea of the *Volk* entered the political stage, though in somewhat ambiguous fashion. Fichte never really ceased to be a cosmopolitan or to believe in individual freedom—the latter in order that ego might get on with man's principal business, which was to seek truth, or, in his more activistic language, create the objective world. But under the pressure of political events, especially after the humiliation of Prussia at Jena and in the Treaty of Tilsit, Fichte began to shift his emphasis. The *Addresses,* delivered at Berlin in a war-charged atmosphere, focused on nation and state, which were more than aggregates of individuals, and through which individuals achieved their freedom. In particular, Fichte emphasized the German nation as the spiritual embodiment of the Eternal and the role of Germany in world history, succeeding the French. Fichte put Germany "in the center of the civilized world like the sun in the center of the universe," represented Germany as the great philosophical nation, and preached her civilizing mission. The chief instrument in accomplishing this mission was the state, though Fichte hardly foresaw the united German state of the future. In an earlier work, *The Closed Commercial State* (1800), Fichte had advocated the control of national economic life by the state. He now extended this control to other fields, notably education, and called upon Germans to sacrifice their individual interests to the larger interest of the state. Other German romantics, such as Adam Müller, a disciple of Burke, carried this organicism to the extreme of swallowing up the individual in society and equating society with state and nation. But no one surpassed the rationalist philosopher Fichte in his fiery advocacy of German nationalism.

The organicism thus far described, even Fichte's, misses one important note in romantic social thought, its messianism. Organicism could be and usually was a dynamic idea, suggesting the sort of development that a plant undergoes. Nevertheless, it inevitably emphasized continuity with the past as the source of present habits, achievement, and loyalties. A nation, said Burke, is "an idea of continuity, which extends in time as well as in numbers and space." But romanticism could also

[25] See Savigny's introductory article of 1815 for the new *Zeitschrift für geschichtliche Rechtswissenschaft,* where he contrasts the "historical" school of law with the "revolutionary" school of natural law (reprinted, in part, and translated, in my *Main Currents of Western Thought,* 3rd ed., Alfred A. Knopf, New York, 1970, pp. 480–482).

lend itself to a rapturous futurism, throwing reason to the winds and conjuring up all sorts of utopias, democratic and socialist, as well as nationalist. These utopias might or might not be conceived on the organic model. They could be anarchist, that is, very individualistic, though not in the atomistic sense. Actually, they were mostly dreams and prophecies, never very concrete, of a Great Society unlike any that had been seen before.

The messianic turn in romantic thought came chiefly in France after 1830, and with the "second generation" in England, where an earlier and sometimes melancholic mood gave way to apocalyptic expectations roused by the French and Industrial revolutions. Names that come to mind in this connection are the Saint-Simonians and Fourierists, Victor Hugo and Percy Bysshe Shelley, the French historian Jules Michelet, and the Italian patriot Giuseppe Mazzini. It is not easy to characterize schemes and dreams as different as Fourier's phalansteries, Michelet's Age of the People, and Mazzini's Third Rome. Suffice it to say that they were all full of passion for social justice and freedom, and with compassion for "les misérables," the downtrodden in a new age of industrial exploitation. All refused to be bound by "classical" limits as to ends, and all exhibited a carelessness bordering on contempt concerning means. Shelley, according to his wife, "believed that mankind had only to will that there should be no evil, and there would be none."[26] The point was that man's basic instincts were good and had only to be set free to deliver mankind from servitude and hate. "Emancipation by love" is the central message of Michelet's *Le Peuple* (1846). This famous work is an epitome of messianic romanticism. Michelet, following Herder, whom Michelet's friend Edgar Quinet had translated into French, prophesied the advent of a Great Society comprised of nations, each contributing in its unique way to the march of humanity. Thus, Michelet espoused the principle of nationality, but, unlike Fichte, found its chief locus among "the People," whom Michelet also called "the Barbarians," but not in a pejorative sense. The People were, on the contrary, those who, unlike the upper classes, thought instinctively and acted accordingly. Embedded in Michelet's book is an attack on "Machinism" (*Machinisme*) that would have done Carlyle credit.

Machines (whether manufacturing or administrative) have furnished man, among numerous advantages, with one unfortunate

---

[26] Mary Shelley, quoted in C. M. Bowra, *The Romantic Imagination*, Harvard University Press, Cambridge, 1949, p. 123.

faculty, that of combining forces without combining hearts, of co-operating without loving, of acting and living together without knowing each other—the moral power of association has lost all that mechanical concentration has gained.[27]

It was this moral power that Michelet wanted to recover for his beloved France, and through France, for the world. In an industrial society the chief disease was "coldness," "paralysis of the heart," which produced want of sociability. To Michelet the People alone had the vitality, the instinctual sap, the capacity to love, which were needed to make society great again. In his own peculiar way Michelet also wanted organicism. But his was a new kind of organic society based on democracy, with strong ties to the national past, yet with an equally strong faith in "the young country of the future."

Historicism

These social and political ideas provide a natural bridge to romantic ideas about history. It is obvious from the foregoing that most romantics, even those who, like Michelet, looked to the future, had a strongly developed historical sense. In his essay on Coleridge (1839), John Stuart Mill calls attention to "the brilliant light which has been thrown upon history during the last half century" by the romantic "school" (he calls it the "Germano-Coleridgian" school). In spite of being brought up as a Utilitarian, Mill greatly admired, and was lavish in his praise of, those "great writers and thinkers" from Herder to Michelet, who had compensated for "the disrespect in which history was held by the *philosophes*" and had given history "an interest like romance."[28] Though he did not use the word, Mill was clearly thinking about "historicism," which Friedrich Meinecke has called "one of the greatest revolutions in western thought." Historicism did not originate with the Romantic Movement, but the latter provided the favorable climate that it needed to grow and spread. It became, in fact, still another facet of the romantic revolt against the generalizing tendencies of the Enlightenment.

The word "historicism" (a translation of the German *Historismus*)

---

[27] Jules Michelet, *Le Peuple*, Pt. I, Chap. VIII, "Machinisme administratif, industriel, philosophique, littéraire."

[28] J. S. Mill, *On Bentham and Coleridge*, Harper Torchbook, New York, 1962, pp. 130–131.

is of late nineteenth-century, not romantic, vintage, and since its appearance it has acquired a number of quite different and even contradictory meanings. Correctly used, however, it means real empathy for the past, along with the twin ideas of temporal individuality and development. In the late eighteenth and early nineteenth centuries these conceptions seemed new by comparison with certain Enlightenment ideas about history.

The romantic empathy for history is implied, of course, in the organic conception of society. It went much deeper than a mere interest in history, or even a conviction that history had something to teach. It really amounted to a piety. The romantics, living in times of rapid change, saw the folly of cutting loose completely from the past, of trusting to naked reason rather than history. They learned to revere their ancestors rather than to deplore them, to see in the historic nation a society with which they could identify even while it continued to grow. Edmund Burke had this piety, and his bias was on the side of "continuity," "old prejudices," "prescription," all favorite words. No greater tribute to history has ever been made than in the following apostrophe in Burke's *Reflections on the Revolution in France* (1790):

> We know that we [modern Englishmen] have made no discoveries; and we think that no discoveries are to be made, in morality; nor many in the great principles of government, nor in the ideas of liberty, which were understood long before we were born. . . . Instead of casting away all our old prejudices, we cherish them, etc.[29]

Yet not even Burke quite catches the "historic passion" (as the French historian Augustin Thierry called it) that motivated the romantics: their ability not merely to revere history but to feel their way back into past ages, to understand each on its own terms, and to appreciate "local color" (again Thierry), that is, the unique spirit of each.

Herder conceptualized this new historicism[30] in two seminal essays. In the first, written in 1774, he compared history to a tree, which throws out many branches and is forever renewing itself. He was especially concerned just then to puncture the pride of the Enlighten-

---

[29] Edmund Burke, *Reflections on the Revolution in France,* Pt. VI, Sect. i.

[30] It is not maintained here that Herder was the first to do this, or that other Germans, contemporary with Herder, had no "appreciation of the unique" in history. Reference has already been made (see p. 255, note 37) to Reill's study of the subject.

ment, which preened itself on its own accomplishments and handed down lofty judgments of praise or blame on past ages. The butt of his criticism was a minor Swiss writer named Isaak Iselin whose *History of Mankind*, published ten years earlier, had celebrated man's progress from savagery to the civilization of the Age of Reason. In opposition to this doctrine of progress, Herder proclaimed an historical relativism. In opposition to the generalizing tendencies of "the philosophers," he upheld the individuality of cultures and peoples. "Each nation, also each epoch," Herder said, "has the center of its happiness in itself, just as each sphere has its center of gravity." That being so, there can be no universal standards of judgment. If you truly wish to understand another country or century, you must plunge deeply into it, and "feel it all inside yourself."[31] Thus, Herder rehabilitated all ages and peoples, the Egyptians and Phoenicians, as well as the Greeks and Romans, also the Middle Ages, which he refused to treat with condescension. The only age that Herder had nothing good to say for was his own, which he thought overrefined, too rational and mechanized in its thinking to be vital. When he wrote this early piece Herder had not yet freed himself completely from Rousseau's historical pessimism.

Of all the past ages of history, the Middle Ages had the greatest appeal for the romantics. Other ages also came in for praise, including ancient Greece, which the poet Hölderlin, for instance, romanticized as a country still in touch with holy nature. But only the Middle Ages, stretched to include the Christian martyrs of the reign of Diocletian at one end and Shakespeare and Milton at the other, could inspire a cultural movement of the magnitude of the Gothic Revival. This movement embraced nearly every field of thought: religious thought (Christian apologetics of Chateaubriand, and the Oxford Movement in England); historiography (impressive studies of the Norman Conquest, the Dukes of Burgundy, the Crusades, and the like by "romantic" historians such as the Thierry brothers, de Barante, and Michaud); the novel (notably novels by Sir Walter Scott, Hugo, and Chateaubriand, which everybody read, including the historians); art and architecture (including the Houses of Parliament, designed by Sir Charles Barry after the fire of 1834, and many neo-Gothic churches by Welby Pugin); and landscape. The change in taste from "classical" to medieval landscape can be seen to perfection at Stourhead, England, home of the

---

[31] Johann Gottfried von Herder, *Yet Another Philosophy of History*, in F. M. Barnard (ed.), *Herder on Social and Political Culture*, Cambridge University Press, Cambridge, 1969, p. 182.

Hoare family, and referred to earlier (see page 207) in connection with the development of the English garden in the eighteenth century. A Pantheon, after the manner of Claude Lorrain, but also in the Palladian tradition, was put up in the gardens in the middle of the eighteenth century to satisfy the classical tastes of Henry Hoare II and his architect. A generation later, a small Gothic cottage was built nearby, with Gothic seat and porch added in 1806, so that the two, obviously the product of very different tastes, can be seen side by side by the visitor today (as shown in Plate 24). The Gothic Revival also inspired the restoration of medieval buildings, such as Cologne cathedral, and collections of medieval paintings and historical documents. The *Monumenta Germaniae Historica,* pet project of the newly founded (1819) Society for the Early Study of German History, is an example of the latter. Not all romantics, to be sure, discovered the same things in the Middle Ages. It was not so much Christianity that caught Herder's eye as the Germanic Middle Ages, a youth movement spearheaded by the Goths, Angles, Franks, and others, which brought new vitality and energy to a civilization grown feeble. Not unexpectedly, Herder described the Middle Ages in Germany as an age "uniquely itself." Novalis is more typical in his idealization of the Middle Ages as a great Age of Faith, characterized by unity, mystery, and "the sacred sense," which evaporated in the Age of Reason that succeeded it. The Middle Ages were also frequently represented as the golden age of chivalry, now threatened by a ruthless industrialism, as well as a period of craftsmanship and good taste.

Herder's second essay, the longer but unfinished *Ideas for a Philosophy of History* (1784–1791), brings out more the concept of development, as the first essay had struck the new note of individuality ("virtues peculiar to a nation or century") and relativism. In this essay Herder talked about "the education of mankind" and its striving toward *Humanität*. By *Humanität* (Humanity) Herder meant man's essentially "human essence," his noble constitution for reason and freedom, his finer senses and impulses, including his sympathy for others, which Herder said "is not ready made, but potentially realizable." Herder had finally got Rousseau out of his system. He now compared history to a chain, each link of which is necessary to "God's epic through all centuries, continents, and generations." This was not, however, a doctrine of progress, at least not in the Enlightenment sense. There was enough of Rousseau still left in Herder for him to be skeptical about progress toward some future perfect state. *Humanität* was a value or guiding principle, approximated by each culture in its own peculiar way,

PLATE 24. *Pantheon and Gothic Cottage. Stourhead, England.*

and perhaps never fully realizable by any culture on earth. Still, Herder was now thinking more in terms of a goal, and of progress toward that goal. Herder had come to realize more fully the developmental aspect of history, how history changes shape "like an eternal Proteus," how each people carries on its back what had gone before, and yet tries to improve on it, to approximate *Humanität* more nearly, each, to be sure, in its own peculiar way. Already in the first essay Herder had exclaimed, "This indeed is genuine progress, continuous development. . . . Becoming on a grand scale!"[32] This historicism bore fruit in later writers, as has been said, and conspicuously in Hegel, who despite real and important differences from Herder, nevertheless enshrined it as a doctrine. In the chapter on "The Principle of Development" in the *Lectures on the Philosophy of History,* Hegel contrasted history with nature. Nature could only repeat itself endlessly (Hegel obviously did not have a romantic conception of nature). History, on the other hand, was never static and was characterized by change, by perpetual novelty, and by progress toward perfectibility, the nature of which, however, was still "undetermined." In Hegel, Spirit also embodied itself historically in the particular, that is, in the *Volksgeist.*

Herder, though he continued to denigrate the present, his own age (as Hegel did not), ended up with an essentially optimistic view of history. So did most of the romantics, though the degree of optimism depended somewhat on the individual and the generation. In France, for example, among the *émigrés,* and also following Waterloo, there was understandably a good deal of *Weltschmerz.* In his confessions, Alfred de Musset speaks of "la maladie du siècle," whose vogue he attributed to the times in which young Frenchmen lived, between two worlds, between a past forever destroyed and a future but dimly guessed. But this mood wore off as Michelet and Mazzini and others surveyed the dizzy prospects that the future held for France, Italy, and indeed for all mankind. In Germany, too, in the generation following Herder, the idea of "development" was in the air, as Novalis and Friedrich Schlegel and even Schelling demonstrate. Novalis, believing that the world had taken a turn for the worse since the Middle Ages, nevertheless anticipated the coming of a new golden age, of a new "Europe," which would climb still greater spiritual heights than the old "Christendom." "Pro-

[32] For the quotations in this paragraph, see ibid., pp. 187–188, 215–216, and especially 266–267 where (in Bk. IV, Chap. iv and vi of the *Ideas*) Herder discusses *Humanität.*

gressive, ever augmenting evolutions are the stuff of history," he said.[33]
And Schlegel, at first preferring "classical" to "modern" (romantic)
poetry, in the end saw in the latter signs of a new and more interesting
literary history. He came to like its willingness to break old rules in
order to create new forms, its eternal restlessness or spirit of "becoming,"
yet also its transcendentalism, which augured a finer sense of the Infinite
(*Unendlichkeit*).

Romantic historicism commonly explained history by the operation
of "spiritual," as opposed to material forces. "It is the spiritual always
that determines the material," Carlyle said, and for Carlyle, as for many
romantics, Spirit worked through heroes, and thus shaped the course of
history. "The History of the world is but the Biography of great men"
who, Carlyle kept saying in his popular lectures *On Heroes and Hero-
Worship* (1840), "are sent into the world."[34] Nevertheless, Carlyle's
hero was no puppet like Hegel's "World-Historical Individual," who
was always more the object than the subject of history, used by "the
cunning of reason" to do its will. Carlyle's hero stands out as a creative
individual, inspired from above but not determined, whose thoughts
and actions make or break history. Carlyle reacted even more strongly
against determinism from below. "Man is heaven-born," he insisted,
"not the thrall of Circumstances, of Necessity, but the victorious sub-
duer thereof."[35] The romantics would have none of the current environmentalism, popularized by the Enlightenment, which tended to denigrate heroes as the products of "circumstance" or social conditions.

In retrospect, romanticism shapes up as an even more important
movement than has been supposed. Despite the evanescence of some of
its ideas, romanticism put its permanent stamp on the modern world.
Its modernity consisted above all in its awareness of becoming. The
romantics were conscious, far more so than the *philosophes,* of living
in a world of endless change. "Truth," said Carlyle, quoting Schiller,
"immer wird, nie ist; never is, always is a-being." But for Carlyle, as
for most romantics, this was, for the most part, an intoxicating rather
than a terrifying prospect. In change, Carlyle goes on to say, "there is
nothing terrible, nothing supernatural; on the contrary, it lies in the

---

[33] Novalis, *Die Christenheit oder Europa* (1799), in Charles E. Passage (ed.),
Hymns to the Night and Other Selected Writings, Bobbs-Merrill, Indianapolis,
1960, p. 48.

[34] Thomas Carlyle, *On Heroes and Hero-Worship,* "The Hero as Divinity," "The
Hero as Man of Letters."

[35] Carlyle, "Boswell's Life of Johnson" (1832), *Critical and Miscellaneous
Essays,* Dana Estes, Boston, n.d., Vol. II, pp. 427–428.

very essence of our lot and life in this world."[36] Change was not yet terrifying, because becoming could still be connected up, though not necessarily in traditional ways, with being. Or perhaps it would be more accurate to say that being was now identified with becoming, which is to say that truth was thought to unfold only in a world perpetually in process. This was not yet the world of Jean-Paul Sartre, or even of Nietzsche or Max Weber.

[36] Carlyle, "Characteristics" (1831), ibid., p. 379.

The New Enlightenment

"The French *philosophes* of the eighteenth century were the example we sought to imitate, and we hope to accomplish no less results." This sentence from John Stuart Mill's *Autobiography*[1]—Mill is speaking of the young Philosophical Radicals of the 1820's—may serve to introduce a world of ideas that although roughly contemporaneous with the Romantic World, nevertheless clashed rather sharply with it. I have called this world the New Enlightenment because of its similarity, in mood and general intent, if not always in doctrine, to the Old Enlightenment of the eighteenth century. Its chief proponents were the English Utilitarians and Radicals to whom Mill refers, the French Positivists, the Young Hegelians of Germany, and assorted "realists," scientists, liberals, and socialists everywhere in Europe. Despite some cross fertilization, these groups obviously constituted no sort of family. Nevertheless, they had something in common; in different ways and degrees they all carried the spirit of "enlightenment" into the midnineteenth century.

The New Enlightenment was, to be sure, no mere copy of the original. Its leaders frequently criticized, as well as praised, the older movement. The original Enlightenment was a bit too "metaphysical" and dogmatic for the modern positivist's taste. In view of the French Revolution, which it was widely believed to have caused, the Old En-

---

[1] J. S. Mill, *Autobiography* (1873), Chap. IV, "Youthful Propagandism."

lightenment seemed too negative,[2] too critical and analytic, to bring about the social harmony everybody wanted. Having as its setting the agricultural and commercial world of the Physiocrats and Adam Smith, the old Enlightenment largely ignored the problems created by the Industrial Revolution. Significantly, Auguste Comte dated modern history from the commencement of the "industrial movement," to which he devoted a whole section of his famous lecture course on the Positive Philosophy. Like his mentor, the Comte de Saint-Simon, Comte was keenly aware that industrialism had already begun to change the face of the world, intellectually as well as politically and socially, and that it called for new panaceas unknown to the *philosophes.* The latter also came under attack for ignoring certain ideas that were recently popularized by the romantics. Inimical though they might be to romantic "philosophy" in general, New Enlightenment intellectuals, in fact, borrowed rather freely from the romantic stock of ideas, more than they always realized. A certain amount of romantic historicism rubbed off on some of them, as also did romantic nationalism, and "the cultivation of the feelings." Mill himself advocated the last as a means of tempering the hard-boiled utilitarianism on which he was brought up. In the *Autobiography* Mill tells how he weathered an early mental crisis by reading the romantic poets. They, especially Wordsworth and Coleridge, brought home to Mill a side of life that had never before been revealed to a mind made "irretrievably analytic." The romantic poets taught Mill to cultivate his feelings, and not merely to subject them to "the dissolving force of analysis."

> I never turned recreant to intellectual culture, or ceased to consider the power and practice of analysis as an essential condition both of individual and of social improvement. But I thought that it had consequences which required to be corrected, by joining other kinds of cultivation with it. The maintenance of a due balance among the faculties, now seemed to me of primary importance. The cultivation of the feelings became one of the cardinal points in my ethical and philosophical creed.[3]

This is an important statement, for it shows where Mill's loyalty ultimately lay. Despite the attraction the romantic poets had for him, Mill did not think they were very good philosophers. For the really serious things, for a logic of thinking and a philosophy of man and

[2] See p. 270.
[3] J. S. Mill, *Autobiography,* Chap. V, "A Crisis in My Mental History."

society, Mill clearly preferred the "intellectual culture" of the Enlightenment. Mill speaks of the Enlightenment again in connection with his father's death. "As Brutus was called the last of the Romans, so was he [James Mill] the last of the eighteenth century: he continued its tone of thought and sentiment into the nineteenth (though not unmodified nor unimproved) . . ."[4] John Mill thought of himself in much the same way, as a sort of up-to-date *philosophe* who stood in the main line of the Enlightenment, modifying and improving upon it as the new age demanded. In any case, he and his circle certainly owed more to the Old Enlightenment than to any other intellectual movement. The line of descent from Old to New Enlightenment is perfectly clear in the case of the Utilitarians and Positivists. The Founding Fathers, Saint-Simon (1760–1825) and Jeremy Bentham (1748–1832) were suckled on eighteenth-century "philosophy," the former particularly on D'Alembert and the Idéologues, the latter on Hartley and Hume, Adam Smith and Helvétius. On the other hand, the Young Hegelians go back more immediately to Hegel, who stimulated their minds, even while they were outgrowing him or standing him on his head. Nevertheless, some of them, conspicuously Arnold Ruge, but later on also Friedrich Engels, acknowledged their debt to the *philosophes* for clearing the way for modern democracy or socialism, as the case might be.

In brief, the New Enlightenment, taken as a whole, exhibits many of the same general traits as the Old Enlightenment: the same aversion from the supernatural and from metaphysics; the same emphasis on science and "free thought" (in the sense of criticism of the religious tradition); the same preoccupation with social problems and social activism; the same optimism about human nature and history. The New Enlightenment, like the Old, was at its core realistic rather than romantic, despite borrowings from the Romantic Movement. The word *Realism,* in fact, graced a particularly important new movement in art and literature that ran parallel to Positivism in France, beginning in the 1850's.

On the other hand, the New Enlightenment, possibly because it came after the French Revolution and confronted the Industrial Revolution, had a much more profound sense of change. Not all, certainly, but many of the spokesmen of the New Enlightenment thought in terms of a continually developing reality: of a developing god or "spirit," as in the case of the Young Hegelians of the first generation; of a developing social order; even of a developing nature. Mill's world, to be

[4] Ibid., Chap. VI, "My Father's Death."

sure, was not yet the world of evolution. Significantly, Mill himself paid scant attention to Darwin, though Mill lived until 1873. This was still a world of Statics as well as Dynamics, as Comte would say. Yet within Mill's lifetime, and within Comte's as well, Jean Baptiste Lamarck, Sir Charles Lyell, and Robert Chambers published ground-breaking works on cosmic and organic evolution. These events do not argue universal acceptance of the evolutionary idea, particularly of organic evolution. They do argue, however, that the idea of evolution was gaining ground. On this as well as other evidence, it seems clear that the historical sense, as it may be called, the sense of development and change, was now permeating thinking in nearly every sphere. This was not yet open-ended becoming, since most thinkers still had more or less fixed goals or ends in view. A sense of change, however, may lead, and historically it did lead, to a more radical sense of becoming.

The Cult of Science

"Science, d'où prévoyance; prévoyance, d'où action." This maxim, stated in the second "lesson" of Comte's *Positive Philosophy* (1830–1842) might serve as the motto of the New Enlightenment, particularly in France and England, but increasingly, as time went on, in Germany too. According to Comte's maxim, action depends on science, and science is fundamentally concerned with prevision or prediction.

Science is Comte's key word, and indeed the popularity of science was just then approaching high tide in the Western intellectual community. In her autobiography, Beatrice (Mrs. Sidney) Webb speaks of the "cult of science," which inspired the mid-Victorian world of her youth. It seemed to her

> that two outstanding tenets, some would say, two idols of the mind, were united in this mid-Victorian trend of thought and feeling. There was the current belief in the scientific method . . . by means of which alone all mundane problems were to be solved. And added to this belief in science was the consciousness of a new motive; the transference of the emotion of self-sacrificing service from God to man.[5]

The chief evidence for this cult is the rapid growth of "scientism" from the 1820's into the 1870's and 1880's, and indeed beyond. Scientism

[5] Beatrice Webb, *My Apprenticeship*, Longmans, Green & Co., London, 1926, p. 130.

means, not merely the growth of science itself, but the attempt, in marked contrast to the romantic disposition, to answer all questions scientifically, to turn everything possible into a science, including in some respects even the humanities, and to apply the principles of science to the world of action. Thus, Comte aimed to create a new science of society, or "social physics." Similarly, there was to be a new "religion of science" (Ernest Renan), a "scientific socialism" (Marx), a "science of human nature" (John Mill), and the like. Emile Zola, in an essay entitled "The Experimental Novel" (1870), even proposed "a literature governed by science," along lines laid down by the great physiologist Claude Bernard. We novelists, Zola wrote, "are continuing, by our observations and experiments, the work of the physiologist, who has continued that of the physicist and the chemist."[6] Strictly speaking, there was nothing new in all this. The New Enlightenment was only pushing farther a tendency that was already well marked in the Old. The impetus to do so came partly from revolutionary France, which seized on science as a means of coping with social change and war. It had encouraged science study in the schools and established new institutions for scientific research and applied science, such as the famous *Ecole polytechnique,* founded in 1794 to train engineers and technologists. The *Ecole* was the breeding ground for a whole generation of science zealots, including Comte himself. However, the deeper reason for the mounting scientism was the continuing triumph of science itself, its ability to push back the frontiers of knowledge and reduce the world to general laws, as, for example, Uniformitarianism in geology and the Conservation of Energy in physics.

The word *science,* though still a somewhat protean term, had begun to narrow down to its present-day meaning. That is, science now referred, more often than not, to the kind of knowledge associated with the natural sciences, especially physics. Science in this sense was now widely assumed to provide the only truly reliable knowledge. The "moral sciences," as theology, politics, psychology, history, and the like were still widely known, could carry credibility only insofar as they succeeded in assimilating, or at least approximating, the method and aims of the physical sciences.

In proportion as this notion grew a rift very naturally developed between science and philosophy. This happened sooner or later even in Germany, the home of philosophic Idealism. The great German scien-

---

[6] Emile Zola, *The Experimental Novel and Other Essays,* Cassell Publishing Co., London, 1893, p. 17.

tist Hermann von Helmholtz describes the "schism," as he called it, in a lecture delivered at Heidelberg in 1862. "It has been made of late a reproach against natural science [*Naturwissenschaft*] that it has struck out a path of its own, and has separated itself more and more widely from the other sciences." Helmholtz blamed the rift on the excesses of the Hegelian philosophy, which scandalized the experimental scientists.

> The philosophers accused the scientific men of narrowness; the scientific men retorted that the philosophers were crazy. And so it came about that men of science began to lay some stress on the banishment of all philosophic influences from their work; while some of them, including men of the greatest acuteness, went so far as to condemn philosophy altogether, not merely as useless, but as mischievous dreaming.[7]

The champions of science condemned philosophy on several counts, for its metaphysical pretensions and for its faulty reasoning. In his lectures on positivism, Comte states the first point unequivocally. Philosophy (actually metaphysics), he charged, was both outmoded and unproductive. Henceforth, knowledge must be limited to "laws" rather than "causes," that is final causes and essences. According to Comte's famous Law of the Three Intellectual Stages, Theology and Metaphysics, which characterized the thinking of former ages, had now been superseded by Positivism.

> In the final, the positive state, the mind has given over the vain search after Absolute notions, the origin and destination of the universe, and the causes of phenomena, and applies itself to the study of their laws—that is, their invariable relations of succession and resemblance.[8]

If this conception required giving up one kind of knowledge, it put within man's reach another, which promised to increase his power over nature. In the words of the great physiologist Claude Bernard, "science, in humbling our pride, proportionately increases our power." Knowledge of the essence of phenomena like electricity, fire, or life was not necessary to understand their immediate or determining cause, or to control them. With some variation this was the line taken by "posi-

[7] Hermann von Helmholtz, *Popular Lectures on Scientific Studies*, Longmans, Green & Co., London, 1873, pp. 5, 7–8.
[8] Auguste Comte, *Cours de Philosophie Positive*, Première Leçon.

tivists"[9] throughout the century. Neither Bernard nor John Mill, both of whom wrote important books about science, was as hostile to philosophy as Comte. Bernard, for example, thought that philosophers might inspire science, by holding up to it goals presently beyond its ken. Nevertheless, the main thrust of the New Enlightenment was clearly to bring knowledge down out of the Hegelian and romantic clouds, and to keep it within observational bounds. In Germany the Hegelian philosophy itself underwent a similar transformation, as Ludwig Feuerbach and others attacked it for being too abstract, too far removed from the real world. Actually, the Young Hegelians did not so much exile the word *philosophy* as transform its meaning. Ultimately, as will be seen, philosophy became, in Moses Hess's phrase, a "philosophy of activity," that is, social action, as opposed to a "philosophy of spirit."[10]

This trend in thinking, which was hostile to metaphysics, spread even into the art world in the new theory of painting known as Realism. Realism, like positivism, emphasized the concrete. The artist Gustave Courbet (or perhaps it was Champfleury, the chief theorist of Courbet's circle) defined painting as "an essentially *concrete* art [which] can only consist of the representation of *real* and *existing* objects. . . . An *abstract* object, invisible and nonexistent, is not part of painting's domain."[11] In other words, Courbet took the world as he saw it. As opposed to the romantics[12] or classicists, Courbet chose for his canvases strictly contemporary subjects with which he was personally familiar—a burial in his home town of Ornans, *Stone Breakers* along the road, his studio in Paris, peasants returning from the fair (Plate 25), and the like—and never mythological or supernatural subjects, or even historical tableaux. His friend the socialist Pierre-Joseph Proudhon was sharp enough to see the parallel between Realism and Positivism. "Courbet," Proudhon observed in his book on art, "is an expression of the times. His work coincides with the *Positive Phi-*

[9] A distinction should be made between Positivists and positivists in the nineteenth century. The former I should like to have refer to the followers of Comte. The latter is a broader term, signifying those who believed in the scientific conception of knowledge. Thus, both Claude Bernard and John Mill were positivists in this latter sense, but hardly Comtists.

[10] See p. 324.

[11] Gustave Courbet, Letter to a Group of Students (1861), in Elizabeth Holt, *From the Classicists to the Impressionists*, Doubleday & Co., Garden City, New York, 1966, p. 352.

[12] Significantly, Caspar David Friedrich's style of painting, emphasizing misty and mysterious landscapes, had already begun to give way in Germany, after about 1830, to a more naturalistic style.

Musées de Besançon, France.

PLATE 25. *Peasants of Flagey Returning from the Fair,* by Gustave Courbet.

losophy of Auguste Comte."[13] Realism, of course, also spread to the novel, which depicted increasingly the world of contemporary manners and social problems, as in the novels of Balzac, Dickens, Mrs. Gaskell, and others. Anthony Trollope, himself a realist, regretted that no method of photography had yet been invented that could put the characters of men "into grammatical language with an unerring precision of truthful description."[14]

"Science," as mentioned, also accused "philosophy" of faulty reasoning. The latter indeed was singled out as the root of all men's troubles. All the major books on scientific method attacked "apriorism," which signified a method of thinking in advance of observation or without verification by either experience or experiment. In John Mill's *System of Logic* (1843), for example, apriorism heads the list of "fallacies" or types of bad reasoning, and Descartes, Coleridge, and "the modern German metaphysical philosophy" are mentioned as among its chief practitioners. Mill described the *Logic* as "a textbook of the opposite doctrine—that which derives all knowledge from experience," and claimed that it had begun to make headway against the *"à priori* view of human knowledge" (also called the "Germano-Coleridgean doctrine") in the universities and in free-thinking circles. Similarly, for Bernard, whose *Introduction to the Study of Experimental Medicine* (1865) has been called the *Discourse on Method* of the nineteenth century, apriorism conjured up the old ghost of scholasticism, which he was at great pains to compare unfavorably with "experimental reasoning." The former not only began but ended with an idea spun a priori out of man's mind, or else borrowed "from some irrational source, such as revelation, tradition, a conventional or an arbitrary authority." It proudly imagined, moreover, that the idea in question, actually nothing but a figment of the mind, accurately represented reality.

> The more modest experimenter, on the other hand, states an idea as a question . . . which, moment by moment, he confronts with reality by means of experiment. He advances, thus, from partial to more general truths, but without ever daring to assert that he has grasped the absolute truth.[15]

[13] Pierre-Joseph Proudhon, *Du Principe de l'Art et sa Destination Sociale,* Garnier Frères, Paris, 1865, p. 287.

[14] Quoted in Wilbur Cross, *The Development of the English Novel,* Macmillan, New York, 1899, p. 223.

[15] Claude Bernard, *An Introduction to the Study of Experimental Medicine,* Macmillan Publishing Co., New York, 1927, pp. 27, 49.

The fact that it foreswore metaphysics does not mean, however, that the New Enlightenment had formed no ideas or models of nature. Scientific doubt might be fundamental to the creed of the New Enlightenment, but there were obviously limits to doubt. "One must doubt but by no means be skeptical," said Bernard. He meant that it was impossible for a scientist to get on with his work without making certain assumptions about nature. Such assumptions constituted, in truth, "an a priori certainty" Bernard once admitted in an unguarded moment.[16] The most basic and widely held of these assumptions were naturalism and determinism. Materialism was not nearly so basic, but it was growing at midcentury, especially in Germany. With or without materialism, however, New Enlightenment nature was very different from romantic nature.

Naturalism might be thought of as the obverse of Carlyle's natural supernaturalism.[17] At least that is how Ernest Renan thought of it in his book on *The Future of Science* (1848), written immediately after he left the seminary of St. Sulpice where he was training for the priesthood. Supernaturalism, Renan argued, was a superstition that the human intellect, now raised to the level of science, had left behind. In the phenomenal world there "is but one sole order of government which is nature." Having renounced the Christianity of his youth, Renan "restored to nature that which [he] had formerly looked upon as superior to nature."[18] A mature scientist like Bernard, more cautious than the youthful Renan, did not say that there was nothing but nature. Positivism was essentially agnostic. But Bernard was unwilling to admit, as the proximate causes of phenomena, anything remotely resembling occult causes, vital forces, essences, or God—in a word, anything indeterminate. In fact, he made it his lifework to remove all such "causes" from the life sciences, including medicine.

"Science rejects the indeterminate." Determinism was the chief dogma of midcentury science, the chief attribute of nature, as it was understood in the world of the New Enlightenment. "We must believe in science, that is, in determinism," says Bernard again. "The absolute principle of experimental science is conscious and necessary determinism in the conditions of phenomena."[19] Bernard, however, and others too, went out of their way to dissociate determinism from fatalism or

---

[16] Ibid., pp. 52–54.

[17] See p. 274.

[18] Ernest Renan, *The Future of Science,* Roberts Brothers, Boston, 1891, pp. 40–41.

[19] Bernard, op. cit. (see note 15), pp. 55, 35, 53.

necessity. As we shall see, determinism did not necessarily rule out free will. It is important to understand this in view of the "revolt against positivism" later in the century, when determinism came under fire. All that determinism usually implied was the reign of law in nature, as opposed to chance; effects following regularly from determinate conditions; hence nature's predictability given sufficient knowledge of the conditions. Nevertheless, this constituted a mighty faith, not only for science but more generally, for it meant that even if God was no longer in his heaven, or was unknowable, at least men could be sure of living in an ordered and predictable world.

Paradoxically, materialism took deeper root in "idealistic" Germany than elsewhere. Science, of course, need not be materialistic even when it is deterministic. Certain recent theories, however, lent themselves rather easily to a materialistic view of nature. One was John Dalton's revival of the atomic theory in the first decade of the century. More important were the laws of the conservation of matter and energy. The former, as stated by Antoine Lavoisier, appeared to establish the immortality of "matter" by showing its persistence through chemical change. The latter, generalized by Helmholtz in an epoch-making essay in 1847, did the same for "energy" or "force," seemingly demonstrating that energy was never created, nor could it ever be destroyed, despite all the transformations it underwent, as, for example, from work to heat. The total amount of energy available for use in the universe remained constant. This "law" also told against vitalism, since animals, like machines, were shown to depend, not on an internal vital force but on physical energy (food, air) supplied from the outside, in order to move and work.

Kraft und Stoff (Matter and Energy) was, in fact, the title of a popular book published in Germany in 1855. The author was Ludwig Büchner, a doctor of medicine and younger brother of the romantic poet Georg Büchner. The zoologist Karl Vogt and the physiologist Jacob Moleschott were others who championed materialism in the 1850's. According to the contemporary historian of the movement, Friedrich Lange, "the whole character of the time began to incline toward Materialism" from about 1830. Taken up at first by certain "epigoni" of Idealism, as, for instance, Feuerbach who, however, was certainly not a complete materialist, materialism soon made converts among the scientists. As we shall see, materialism spread further with the advent of Darwinism. Lange's *History of Materialism,* published in 1873, is witness to the still rising tide of the movement at that date, even though Lange himself was an Idealist.

Several of the chapter titles in Büchner's book, which ran to sixteen editions in Germany alone between 1855 and 1889, reveal the main drift of this midcentury materialism: "Immortality of Matter," "Immortality of Force," "Immutability of the Laws of Nature," "Free Will." Much of the argument was taken up with demonstrating the age-old materialist proposition that mind is a product of matter, or the physical composition of the brain. However, there was also special reference to the laws of the conservation of matter and energy which, for Büchner, argued that nature and "matter" were coextensive, that matter and energy could not have been created but were immortal, and that there was no such thing in nature as a vital force, spirit, or soul. The book also reveals the close connection in Büchner's mind between materialism and necessitarianism, or lack of free will. Büchner hoped that the new science would "put an end to the reign of philosophical transcendentalism, which rejects experience."

This materialism should not be exaggerated. It was always just a little bit tainted, even among its foremost German advocates. Büchner, for instance, occasionally talks a bit like a pantheist, and Moleschott was sometimes willing to admit that "matter" behaved suspiciously like what had traditionally been called "spirit." Mechanism, embodying the idea of determinism, was clearly more central to the New Enlightenment picture of nature than materialism.

The mechanical model of nature, thus, still held firm. In passing, however, it should be noted that another model, the genetical model, was fast gaining ground, among laymen as well as scientists. Nature was being historicized in successive works by James Hutton (1785, 1795) and Sir Charles Lyell (1830) on geology, Georges Cuvier on paleontology (1813–1815), and Robert Chambers on evolution (1844). Not everybody accepted this new "historical" geology and biology. Chambers' *Vestiges of Creation,* the work of a scientific amateur, drew the fire of scientists, including the young Thomas Henry Huxley. Nevertheless, by midcentury, the idea of evolution was very much in the air, as witness the wide sale of Chambers' book. As stated earlier, the world of the New Enlightenment was not radically evolutionary, at least with respect to ideas of nature. It too, however, helped prepare the way for Darwin.

It is possible to identify a number of contemporary attitudes toward, as distinguished from models of, nature. One in particular stands out as increasingly important, namely the Promethean attitude. There were those who in the Malthusian tradition still thought of nature as niggardly, scarcely able to yield enough food to meet the needs of a growing population. It was hard to hold this attitude, however, in the light of the conservation of energy theory. Nature could also be thought of as a vast storehouse of energy, never depleted, or else as offering "myriad horns of plenty." The latter phrase is from Tennyson's ode for the opening of the International Exhibition of 1862, which, among other things, put on display the latest machines, "harvest-tool and husbandry, Loom, and wheel, and engin'ry." It is true that the Victorians, especially men of letters, were ambivalent toward the machine. Nevertheless, there was increasing excitement in an industrial age about machines and the men who invented and put them to work. The machine had become a major symbol of "the dominion of man over inanimate nature." This was still a period of history when technology could be thought of as benign, as serving man's best interests, as subduing nature for the benefit of the human race. Samuel Smiles, chiefly renowned for his best-selling *Self-Help* (1859), typified this Promethean attitude in a stream of popular biographies of inventors, engineers, and promoters.

The Religion of Humanity

"Religion can never disappear from the world; it can only be transformed." If Saint-Simon did not say this (he is reported to have said it on his deathbed), he ought to have said it, for it epitomizes not only his own personal attitude but also that of the New Enlightenment in general, toward religion. The New Enlightenment pressed the attack on revealed Christianity. Thanks to the unsettling experience of the French Revolution, however, the New Enlightenment was less concerned to "crush," than to "transform," religion.[20] It valued religion for, among other things, its social utility. This explains the many attempts following Saint-Simon's *New Christianity* of 1825 to devise a religion, which would be, at one and the same time, scientifically credible, psychologically satisfying, and socially useful. Out of this climate came a new Religion of Humanity, which is usually associated with Auguste Comte, but which, in fact, spread far beyond Positivist ranks to include such very different groups as the Philosophical Radicals and the Young Hegelians, as well as a number of distinguished

[20] True, the Young Hegelians talked about passing from the age of religion to a new age of philosophy. Yet their "philosophy" never denied the existence of "spirit," or the "divine," at least as manifested in man. And David Friedrich Strauss actually used the term "religion of humanity" (*Humanitätsreligion*).

literary figures like George Eliot.[21] This "religion" also flourished, though in a more restricted version, among the new breed of liberal nationalists. To a Christian, or even a deist, the Religion of Humanity must have seemed like no religion at all, since it jettisoned God. It rested ultimately on "anthropology," or faith in man.

The dismantling of Christianity continued. In a positivistic climate Christianity was thought to deal with the unobservable, and therefore to be unscientific. It was also ethically suspect, too preoccupied, it was said, with self-love (with the individual and his personal salvation), too little concerned with social feeling, or altruism. Significantly, however, the new Higher Criticism represented Christianity not as imposture, but as myth, not as pathology, but as psychological projection or "alienation." "My faith was destroyed by historical criticism, not by scholasticism or logic."[22] This asseveration by Renan in his memoirs— he was recalling his experience as a seminarian in Paris, and his subsequent defection from the Roman Church in 1845—strikes the important new note in nineteenth-century Biblical and religious criticism. It was more profoundly historical than the "rationalistic" criticism of the Old Enlightenment. In large part the work of Germans, the Higher Criticism made heavy drafts on romantic historicism, and, in particular, on Herder and Hegel, as well as on science. David Friedrich Strauss, called the "Modern Iscariot," interpreted the life of Jesus mythically. Myth was a social product, the reflection in folklore of the ideas of a people living at a particular time and place in history. The Gospels, for example, recorded the *Volksgeist* of the early Christians, above all their passionate belief, inherited from the Jews, of the coming of the Messiah. Though not true for all time, this myth contained truth for its own time. Thus, Strauss represented Christianity as time-bound, already superseded, its particular myth no longer applicable, yet as an important stage in the progress of "spirit." Ludwig Feuerbach, similarly inspired by Hegel, took a more psychological tack, though his major book on *The Essence of Christianity* (1841) also viewed religions

[21] The Religion of Humanity should be seen in the context of the total religious history of the times. Organized Christianity continued to play a powerful social role on into the 1860's and 1870's, and to claim the allegiance of perhaps a majority of the middle and upper classes of Europe. On the other hand, working-class adherence to traditional Christianity, especially in the English towns, was either nonexistent, or declining rapidly. The Religion of Humanity, then, was still merely the most important of the new secular "religions" appealing to intellectuals. However, it gained ground steadily in proportion as society became secularized.

[22] Ernest Renan, *Souvenirs d'enfance et de jeunesse* (1883), Chap. IV, Le Seminaire d'Issy.

historically. "Theology is anthropology." By this famous dictum Feuerbach meant to say that religion, properly understood, originated in self-projection, or in human nature objectified. Through the ages man had created the gods in his own image, out of his own needs and changing ideals. Or, to put it in a more Hegelian way, religion represented the alienation of man from himself. But whereas in Hegel, alienation (*Entfremdung*) sometimes had a positive connotation—as when he argued that Spirit needed the experience of self-estrangement in the temporal process to achieve full consciousness—it was always thought of negatively by his disciples. "To enrich God," Feuerbach wrote, "man must become poor; that God may be all, man must be nothing."[23] Hence, the sooner man realized that Christianity was illusion or myth, was the result of self-alienation, the better it would be for man and the sooner he could develop a higher religion, or philosophy.

This higher religion was the Religion of Humanity. In Comte's version of it collective humanity became the new god. He called it the Great Being, who, however, was not at all like the "incomprehensible Being" of Christianity (or of deism), "whose existence admits of no demonstration, or comparison with anything real." The Great Being was neither supernatural nor absolute. "Its nature is relative; and, as such, is eminently capable of growth." Its growth, however, depended on the actions of men, in whom social feeling had displaced self-love. Hence, in Comte's church, which, to be sure, hardly anybody joined, there were to be saints' days in honor of the men (artists, rulers, scientists, and the like) who throughout history had dedicated their lives to the service of their fellow men. The aim of all should be, not only to worship but actually to become incorporate with, "this mighty Being," i.e. Humanity at its unselfish best, and thus to ensure happiness and progress on earth.[24]

The Young Hegelians came to similar conclusions, but by a different route. Though Hegel himself never quite worked through to a pure Religion of Humanity, he laid the basis for it. Seeking, like the romantics, to overcome dualism, he subjected God to the temporal process, and thus merged divine with human reason. God, depersonalized by Hegel as the Absolute or immanent Spirit, undergoes development, or rather becomes conscious of itself, of reality as a whole, only progres-

---

[23] Ludwig Feuerbach, *The Essence of Christianity* (*Das Wesen des Christentums*, 1841), Chap. I, Sect. 2. Strauss's *Life of Jesus* first appeared in 1835–1836.

[24] Auguste Comte, *A General View of Positivism*, J. H. Bridges (trans.), Reeves & Turner, London, 1880, pp. 245–247.

sively, in history and by means of human thought. Traditional theism, Hegel believed, had grown up in response to the devaluation of man and his social life in the ancient world. Man, despairing of his earthly state, created a transcendent God, static and wholly other, to whom he stood in the relation of slave to master. But now, having outgrown the wretched conditions of the ancient world, man could see himself for what he really is, a facet of the Absolute, and thus overcome the sharp distinction between God and man. Hegel's God was clearly a new God of Becoming, as well as Being. The Absolute, defined as the concrete universal whole, retains its nature and identity through all temporal change, but becomes conscious of itself only through the developing consciousness of humanity. Ernest Renan approximated Hegel's conception when he said, in his *Philosophical Dialogues,* that God (the ideal) will be realized through man's search for knowledge. "You think then, like Hegel, that God *is* not, but that he *will be?*" asks one of the interlocutors. "Not precisely," was the reply. "The ideal exists, it is eternal; but it has not yet been materially realized; it will be someday."[25]

Hegel's followers took the step that Hegel himself was never willing to take. They fully humanized God, as Comte was currently doing in France. With Strauss and Feuerbach, God finally became man. In traditional Christianity God, of course, became man uniquely in Christ. But among the Young Hegelians God, so to speak, incarnated himself in the whole human race. The real Christ was humanity, which had harbored "spirit" within itself all along, but which had objectified, squandered it in the gods of successive religions, up to and including Christianity. Even Hegel, according to Feuerbach, differentiated between God and man: the Hegelian Absolute, after all, used human thought to become conscious of itself. But now mankind, hitherto alienated from itself, sees that "the two are not different." There is not a shred of transcendence left in the new christology. The historical progress of religion (said Feuerbach)

> consists in this: that what by an earlier religion was regarded as objective, is now regarded as subjective; that is, what was formerly contemplated and worshipped as God is now perceived to be something *human.*[26]

[25] Ernest Renan, *Dialogues et fragments philosophiques,* Calmann-Lévy, Paris, n.d. (1871?), p. 78.
[26] Ludwig Feuerbach, *The Essence of Christianity,* George Eliot (trans.), Harper & Brothers, New York, 1957, p. 13.

Thus, the Young Hegelians created a new humanistic religion (they often, though not invariably, preferred to call it a philosophy) based on "spirit" which, however, was now located within man himself.

The Religion of Humanity, whether of French or of German hue, obviously rested on a belief in the greatness of man, or, at any rate, in man's ability to make his own providence. And, indeed, the estimate of human nature ran very high in the whole world of the New Enlightenment, higher even than in the Old. Of course, there was much disagreement about the exact qualities of greatness, also increasing tension, even within the same schools of thought, between universalist and relativist conceptions. Speaking generally, however, the New Enlightenment very nearly deified man in the sense that it ascribed to him, to the species if not to the individual, many of the properties and powers that were formerly invested only in God. Feuerbach makes this abundantly clear at the outset of his *magnum opus*. The first chapter of *The Essence of Christianity* is entitled "The Essential Nature of Man." In that chapter Feuerbach first distinguishes between man and the brute. This distinction is important, because later on in the century the distinction would be erased or blurred. Man is distinguished from the brute by "consciousness," which meant the ability of man not merely to act by instinct but to think consciously of others as well as oneself, to think about the species as a whole, to have as an object of thought "his [man's] own—not finite and limited, but infinite nature." The constituents of this infinite nature are Reason, Will, and Affection, which Feuerbach called the "divine trinity in man." These constituents, also called "essences," gave man "power." In Feuerbach, midnineteenth-century narcissism found complete expression:

> Consciousness is the characteristic mark of a perfect nature; it exists only in a self-sufficing, complete being. Even human vanity attests this truth. A man looks in the glass; he has complacency in his appearance. This complacency is a necessary, involuntary consequence of the completeness, the beauty of his form. A beautiful form is satisfied in itself; it has necessarily joy in itself—in self-contemplation. This complacency becomes vanity only when a man piques himself on his form as being his individual form, not when he admires it as a specimen of human beauty in general. It is fitting that he should admire it thus: he can conceive no form more beautiful, more sublime than the human.[27]

[27] Ibid., pp. 6–7.

Before pursuing further Feuerbach's trinity of constituents, still fairly normative, it should be noted that he assumed an "essential," that is, a universal, human nature. So too, to a degree, did Karl Marx, and so, above all, did Jeremy Bentham. Bentham, though he wrote an essay on the subject, actually took little or no account of the differences wrought by time and place on either human nature or legislation. More in the manner of the Old Enlightenment, Bentham deduced a whole political philosophy, as also did James Mill, from what he believed to be universal and unchangeable laws of human nature. "Nature has placed mankind under the governance of two sovereign masters, *pain* and *pleasure,* etc." But already this universalism was beginning to give way to a more dynamic anthropology, even within Utilitarianism itself. Mill, the son, if not the father, had learned from the romantics and Comte to think historically. Hence, although he continued to talk about universal laws, Mill was increasingly impressed by the "extraordinary pliability of human nature,"[28] and the probable further development of human capabilities, depending on time and place. This same tension is also observable among the Young Hegelians, who, despite their essentialism, a hangover from Idealism, certainly believed in man's developing consciousness. Like Feuerbach (and like Bentham whom, in other respects, he castigated as an "arch philistine") Marx postulated a "human nature in general," from which man had become alienated, and to which Marx very much wanted him to return. Coupled with it, however, was "human nature as modified in each historical epoch."[29] The former represented man's essential humanness, man as a truly social being. The latter, however, varied according to social and economic conditions, and could be thoroughly egoistic and self-seeking, as, for instance, under capitalism. In Marx's view, of course, the movement in history toward communism heralded the end of egoistic man, of alienation, and the discovery and recovery of man's essential nature.

Shades of romanticism, Affection (or love), one of Feuerbach's trinity, appeared on nearly everybody's list of basic human constituents. In Benthamism, to be sure, it is a conspicuously unromantic self-love that makes the world go round, but it is at least an enlightened egoism, which either automatically promotes, or else can be cunningly used

[28] J. S. Mill, *Autobiography,* Chap. V, "One Stage Onward." Mill says he borrowed this phrase from the jurist John Austin.

[29] Marx uses these terms in *Capital.* See on all this, Erich Fromm, *Marx's Concept of Man,* Frederick Ungar Publishing Co., New York, 1961, Chap. 4.

to promote, "the greatest happiness of the greatest number." Nevertheless, it was again John Mill who shifted the emphasis in utilitarian anthropology from egoism to altruism. His heart softened by reading the romantics, Mill widened the conception of the individual's happiness to include sympathy for others. Thus, he came to think sympathy "natural," though admittedly weaker than self-love at that particular stage in history. The point made by Mill was that egoism, fostered by modern institutions, could be gradually educated out of mankind, including "the uncultivated herd" and their employers. "The hindrance," he wrote, "is not in the essential constitution of human nature."[30] Mill could have learned this lesson, and perhaps did learn it in part, from Auguste Comte, who was just then preaching his new religion based on feeling or altruism, the latter a word actually coined by him. The Religion of Humanity would sing of "the marvellous advance of man from brutish appetite to pure unselfish sympathy."[31] Even the Young Hegelians, despite their highly intellectual and even frequently arrogant tone, wallowed in love of humanity. The mark of unalienated man, according to Feuerbach, was to be able to love humanity, an "affection" which was palpably impossible so long as one loved God. Moses Hess, socialist follower of Feuerbach, made the further point that to achieve this "real nature of man" also depended on throwing over the capitalistic system, which was rooted in egoism. It is true that Marx attacked Hess and Feuerbach for this sort of classless ethic. Yet Marx also argued, against Max Stirner, that "ego" was also an abstraction, the product of a certain type of social system, and Marx urged, especially in the early philosophical essays, the dis-alienation of man from his fellow men, and his restoration to his true "essence," or "species-being." Marx's class ethic came, in the end, to a classless ethic based on Affection.

The second constituent in Feuerbach's trinity, namely Will, excited more controversy. It is not hard to see why. Men of a scientific cast of mind naturally wanted a science of human nature. To have one, however, meant accepting determinism by men who also believed in their power over events. The Hegelians, predisposed as they were to believe in the power of mind to liberate itself, did not feel this tension acutely. Others, however, did, especially those more in the thick of positivistic science, such as John Mill, who worried about the problem

[30] J. S. Mill, *Autobiography*, Chap. VII, "General View of the Remainder of my Life." Mill is here commenting on the possibilities of socialism.
[31] Comte, *A General View of Positivism* (see note 24), p. 251.

endlessly. Mill marshaled all the arguments pro and con, and in the end reached a mediating position, which was fairly typical. Initially, he tells us, the doctrine of Philosophical Necessity, preached currently by the Owenites, but implied as well by associationist psychology, weighed on him like an incubus. Mill's father, the author of several books on the latter subject, stressed mental passivity, and boasted that by his discovery of its laws, he would make "the human mind as plain as the road from Charing Cross to St. Paul's." The son, the future champion of liberty, revolted against this extreme environmentalism (and mechanism).

> I felt as if I was scientifically proved to be the helpless slave of antecedent circumstances; as if my character and that of all others had been formed for us by agencies beyond our control, and was wholly out of our own power.

Yet as an apostle of science, as the proponent, along with Comte and others, of a new social science, Mill could not go along completely with the opposite theory of free will. So he struck a compromise with his own "doctrine of circumstances." Necessity, he thought, was a misleading term, easily confused with Fatalism. Properly understood, it meant simply the doctrine of cause and effect applied to human action, thereby envisaging in the latter a reasonable degree of regularity, and making some prediction possible. The trouble was that the term implied "irresistibleness," "a feeling of uncontrollableness," which Mill could not accept either. His solution was almost a conundrum: "I saw that though our character is formed by circumstances, our own desires can do much to shape these circumstances; . . . that our will, by influencing some of the circumstances, can modify our future habits or capabilities of willing."[32] The whole argument of the great essay *On Liberty* presupposes this sort of free choice to mold human character, and therefore to influence events. It contains the famous line that compares human nature, not to "a machine to be built after a model," but to a tree that grows "according to the tendency of the inward forces which make it a living thing."[33] The Victorians wanted both science and humanism though some came down harder on the side of either de-

---

[32] See on all this, including the quotations, Mill's *Autobiography,* Chap. V, "One Stage Onward," and *System of Logic,* Bk. VI, Chap. II, "Of Liberty and Necessity."
[33] J. S. Mill, *On Liberty,* Chap. III, "Of Individuality."

terminism or free will.[34] It is interesting to hear what Claude Bernard said on the subject. As we have seen, Bernard established determinism as "the first principle of science." Yet he too distinguished between determinism and fatalism, and made room for human free will. Bernard was speaking, in his *Study of Experimental Medicine,* of course, of a biological rather than an environmental necessity. All the same, he detected in human beings a "vital force" (*"la force vitale";* he also called it *"le pouvoir législatif"*), which "is above matter and disposes it," and gives to it its form.[35]

Of Feuerbach's three constituents, however, the New Enlightenment, like the Old, clearly prized Reason most. Reason, whether deductive, inductive, "inverse deductive" or historical (John Mill), critical or metaphysical, represented man's chief hope of progress. On this point there was the widest possible agreement. By and large, the New Enlightenment discounted Irrational Man. Reason was the firm rider of the horses, of Affection and Will. This belief in Rational Man reached a high point, oddly, among the Benthamites. The whole point about Benthamite hedonism is that it could be rationally calculated—by means of the famous moral arithmetic—for both the individual's and society's good. Both Bentham and James Mill, moreover, broadened rationalism's base to include the many as well as the few. According to John Mill:

> So complete was my father's reliance on the influence of reason over the minds of mankind, whenever it is allowed to reach them, that he felt as if all would be gained if the whole population were taught to read, if all sorts of opinions were allowed to be addressed to them by word and in writing, and if by means of the suffrage they could nominate a legislature to give effect to the opinions they adopted.[36]

Later, John Mill came to have serious doubts about the rationality of the many and hence of parliamentary majorities and public opinion. Nevertheless, he was never in fundamental disagreement with his father's major premise, at least in the long run. With the qualifications

[34] Charles Bray of Coventry, for instance, free thinker and phrenologist, was an extreme necessitarian. He and George Eliot disagreed on the subject. Samuel Smiles, on the other hand, belongs at the extreme other end of the pole. "It is *will,*—force of purpose," he argued in *Self-Help* (1859), "—that enables a man to do or be whatever he sets his mind on being or doing."

[35] Claude Bernard, *Principes de médecine expérimentale,* quoted in D. G. Charlton, *Positivist Thought in France during the Second Empire,* Clarendon Press, Oxford, 1959, p. 81.

[36] J. S. Mill, *Autobiography,* Chap. IV, "Westminster Review."

already noted, Mill never, despite his youthful cultivation of the feelings, "turned recreant to intellectual culture," or, it might be added, ceased to believe in the power of reason to improve individuals and societies. In view of this faith, exhibited also, though in different ways, by the Positivists and Hegelians, it is no wonder the historian W. E. H. Lecky could write a book celebrating *The Rise and Influence of the Spirit of Rationalism in Europe* (1866). Reason could discover laws of nature and society even if, as Mill insisted, some of them could be only "empirical laws." Reason could also set proper goals and persuade men, by debate and by evidence, to pursue them.

Significantly, there is no mention in this literature of anything comparable to original sin. Of course, there was much evil and suffering in the world, poverty, disease, injustice, and alienation. But the point was that there was nothing *in* human nature itself to prevent their melioration or removal. Hence, at the very time that Sören Kierkegaard, an eccentric in his own times, was agonizing over man's permanently sinful state, Strauss was attributing "sin" to man's finitude (fortunately temporary), Feuerbach to love of God (!) which detracted from love of man, Marx to an outmoded economic system, Mill to ignorance and consequent wrong choice, Herbert Spencer to "the non-adaptation of constitution to conditions," and so on. Even Christian theology itself to some extent reflected this optimism, as, for example, in the immensely influential Ritschlianism of the latter part of the century. Albrecht Ritschl,[37] ironically a Lutheran, rejected the doctrine of original sin, substituting for it a "kingdom of sin," which, however, originated, not in the child in whom he found an indefinite impulse toward good but in habit, imitation, and the wrong use of free will. Evil is remediable: this was the message of the New Enlightenment. "No one whose opinion deserves a moment's notice," Mill said in *Utilitarianism* (1863), "can doubt that most of the great positive evils of the world are in themselves removable . . . conquerable by human care and effort." Strauss described the human race in more metaphysical terms as "the Sinless One." Impurity might continue to cling to the individual, but it progressively disappeared in the race as finite spirit became "mindful of its infinite."[38]

---

[37] Ritschl (1822–1888) was successively professor of theology at Bonn and Göttingen. The core of his teaching on man is to be found in the third volume of his *Rechtfertigung und Versöhnung* (1874).

[38] J. S. Mill, *Utilitarianism*, Chap. II; Strauss, *Life of Jesus* (1835–1836), quoted in Hugh Ross Mackintosh, *Types of Modern Theology*, Nisbet & Co., London, 1937, p. 119.

On Liberty

The Religion of Humanity partly explains why the social question achieved such prominence in New Enlightenment thinking. Society, as Max Stirner shrewdly observed, was "a new spook, a new supreme being," taking the place of all the old spooks, or gods, in whom men no longer believed. Among Stirner's intellectual peers in Germany, Feuerbach, for instance, called for a "religion of politics," adapted to the needs of the present age and involving a program for social improvement. This, indeed, was the main thrust of the Young Hegelian movement, not merely to turn religion into philosophy, but to put a new interpretation on philosophy itself, to equate philosophy with politics and social reform. "Not being but action is first and last," Moses Hess wrote in opposition to Hegel, in an essay entitled "Philosophie der Tat" (Philosophy of Action). "Now is the time for the philosophy of spirit to become a philosophy of [social] activity."[39] Simultaneously, in France, Comte gave top priority in his system to *sociology,* and Benthamism, too, was essentially a social philosophy, concerned not at all with religion or metaphysics but rather with legal and political rearrangements.

Despite Stirner's slap at new spooks, New Enlightenment social thought is notable for its attempt to be scientific, to construct, in fact, a "social science" complete with laws and with predictive value. But what kind of science it should be was debatable, and was debated. Should it be deductive or inductive? What account, if any, should it take of history? Benthamite science was deductive, inferring, in the manner of Euclid, principles of legislation from supposedly universal laws of human nature. The result was a particularly static, even if reformist, conception of society, its aim being to enable legislators "to make laws for one country as for another." John Mill balked at this conception. The method he worked out, and elaborated in the *Logic,* was at once more empirical and historical. First of all, as we have seen, Mill thought Benthamite psychology much too simplistic. He also distinguished between "empirical" and truly "causal" laws. Because of the greater complexity of human affairs, only the former, or "approximate generalizations," were possible for social phenomena. But most im-

[39] Quoted in Sidney Hook, *From Hegel to Marx,* Reynal & Hitchcock, New York, 1936, p. 194. Hess's words are, of course, reminiscent of Marx's famous assertion in the *Theses on Feuerbach* that "philosophers have only *interpreted* the world; the point is, however, to *change* it."

portantly, Mill had learned, especially from Comte, but also from Coleridge and Michelet, to think historically. Comte's science of society included a Law of Dynamics, as well as a Law of Statics, which is to say, in Mill's words, that it had "a subject-matter whose properties are changeable." Mill contrasted the science of society with the repetitiveness of the solar system, in which there was observable "the perpetual recurrence of the same series in an unvarying order." Social science was more like the principle of movement in mechanics, or of life in biology. "Not only the qualities of individuals vary, but those of the majority are not the same in one age as in another."[40] On the whole, the trend was clearly toward a more historical and developmental view of society. This was perhaps especially the case in Germany, the home of *Historismus* and the Historical School of Law. Marx, for instance, was a devotee of the historical method, and worked out a highly sophisticated idea of social development.

The actual content of social thought might be thought of as commencing with the problem of reconstruction. At least that was how a good many contemporaries thought of it, for a considerable time after 1815. According to what principle should society be reconstructed: natural rights, utility, history, the labor theory of property (this last becoming increasingly important as socialist theories multiplied), and so on? How much, and what kinds, of liberty should there be? Which was more real, the individual, church or state, nation or humanity, or possibly even a particular social class?

Individualism flourished chiefly, though not exclusively, among the English liberals. Its most extreme statement actually came from the Young Hegelian group. Max Stirner's *Die Einzige und sein Eigenthum* (1845), an anarchist classic, was perhaps the ineluctible final conclusion of a generation of iconoclastic thought. Discarding as abstractions all ideals, Feuerbach's Humanism as well as Hegel's Absolute, Stirner proclaimed a cult of ego. The individual man should stop alienating himself once and for all, and take his stand on the only reality, namely, his own unique ego (*Die Einzige*), thus freeing himself from all authority, including "Society." John Mill, more representative in a bourgeois age, did not go so far. Nevertheless, he yielded to nobody in his defense of individual liberty. Mill grew up in an atmosphere of atomistic individualism. According to Bentham, who wished to clear the decks of all obstacles to a new and progressive industrial England,

[40] J. S. Mill, *System of Logic*, Bk. VI, Chap. X, "On the Inverse Deductive, or Historical Method."

the individual alone was real, the state was "a fictitious body." "The interest of the community then is, what?—the sum of the interests of the several members who compose it." It is true that Bentham left room for considerable tinkering by legislators, in order to obtain an "artificial identity" of individual interests in the community. However, as Halévy points out, this aspect of Benthamism was more or less nullified in the reigning "Manchester philosophy," which restored Adam Smith's "natural identity" of interests, hence complete *laissez-faire*.[41] To Matthew Arnold this seemed, later on, like "anarchy." It also worried John Mill, who saw the need, much more clearly than Bentham, for rectifying, "artificially" if necessary, the injustices of an industrial society. Nevertheless, Mill never recanted individualism. On the contrary, he firmed up his defense of it, in proportion as he developed serious doubts about egalitarian democracy. The latter, he came to think, threatened a new tyranny, potentially worse, in its threat to impose on mankind a new "yoke of uniformity," than any of the old tyrannies. *On Liberty* (1859) was written when Mill was in this mood, to reassert "the sovereignty of the individual." All progress in society depended on the advance and application of truth; new truths were discovered by individuals; hence, society should not only permit but also encourage human nature "to expand itself in innumerable and conflicting directions"; any attempt to curb this free development, by public opinion or otherwise, was obviously sheer lunacy; so ran Mill's argument. Mill defended individualism on grounds of utility, rather than natural right. In his view, liberty, the liberty of the individual, had greater social utility than either justice or equality.

Matthew Arnold, critical of English individualism in *Culture and Anarchy* (1869), referred his readers to "the notion, so familiar on the Continent and to antiquity, of *the State*." And indeed this notion, the notion of a collective whole that was greater than the sum of its individual parts, was stronger on the continent than in England. It was at the heart of Mill's quarrel with Comte. Not that Mill had no conception of an "interest wider than that of individuals" (Arnold again). But he thought that Comte, whom Mill greatly admired in other respects, threatened to establish a spiritual and temporal despotism as great as that of Ignatius Loyola. However that may be, Comte's "posi-

[41] Elie Halévy, *The Growth of Philosophic Radicalism*, Beacon Press, Boston, 1960, p. 514. The quotation from Bentham is from *An Introduction to the Principles of Morals and Legislation* (1780).

tive politics" allowed precious little freedom for the individual. Comte, fearful of revolution, sought to establish, as in the Middle Ages, a dual power, replacing priests by scientists and kings by industrialists and bankers. Against scientific "laws" and their proper administration, there obviously could or should be no dissent. Even French liberals and republicans emphasized authority more than their English counterparts. The philosopher Jules Simon, though no friend of authoritarian government, nevertheless typically put authority on a par with liberty. "The theory of liberty," he wrote, "is only half of social science." A book on "association" would be the necessary complement, and corrective, to a book on liberty.[42] Simon himself wrote such a book, *La Liberté,* which appeared in the same year as Mill's essay, and may be compared with it. Many Frenchmen also took the side of the state against the church and tried to forge "la société laïque." Though a lay society, severely limiting ecclesiastical control over education, was not necessarily an authoritarian society—it could conceivably be a republic or democracy —it did tend in practice to strengthen the hands of the state.

But it was in Germany that the idea of the state flourished in its greatest purity. Strictly speaking, the German idea, deriving from Idealist and romantic subsoil, does not belong in the New Enlightenment thought world. Nevertheless, some mention of this idea should be made here, especially in view of its future importance for Europe as a whole. The great historian Leopold von Ranke may be singled out for special attention in this connection. Ranke, though this aspect of his thought has been distorted, had at least some affinities with the New Enlightenment in his search for a science of history, in his preference for a historical as compared with a philosophical approach to reality, and in his concretism. For Ranke the state, for example, is real only when it assumes a concrete, that is, individual, historical existence. Yet he also had a metaphysics of politics. As Ranke says in his "Dialogue on Politics," written in 1836 for the *Historisch-politische Zeitschrift,* the state is a "spiritual force," in a sense preceding and absorbing the individual, and having a great moral and civilizing purpose. Instead of mere passing conglomerations created by contracts,

---

[42] Jules Simon, *La Liberté,* Hachette, Paris, 1859, Vol. I, Préface. Simon, like his master, the philosopher and great harmonizer Victor Cousin, tried to mediate between philosophy and religion, authority and liberty. A republican, he strongly opposed the Second Empire. The statesman-historian François Guizot is another example of a French liberal, who, while supporting individual rights balanced them with "Public Reason."

Ranke perceived in states "spiritual substances, original creations of the human mind—I might say, thoughts of God."[43]

Ranke's idea of the state cannot be properly understood, however, without reference to the idea of the nation that underlay it. As a believer in the national idea, Ranke becomes much more representative of general European social thought. Both Bentham, for all his universalism, and John Mill believed in the national idea, though in combination, of course, with liberal institutions. Mill thought that it was, in general, necessary "that the boundaries of governments should coincide in the main with those of nationalities."[44] This was exactly Giuseppe Mazzini's thought. Though as a liberal Mazzini protected the individual at one pole and made room for humanity at the other, he saw nationality as mankind's most fruitful form of "association," a term he borrowed from Saint-Simon. "Your country is the sign of the mission God has given you to fulfil towards Humanity." Shades of Herder, except that Mazzini, condemnatory of the new cosmopolitanism spawned by the Congress of Vienna, extended what was a cultural idea in Herder to include the *political* self-determination of nations. There are traces of Herder's *Humanität* in Ranke's thought too, but for the most part Ranke had moved away from Herder to a position halfway between the cultural and political nation. If Ranke did not actually identify the nation with the state, he came close to doing so. The cultural nation came first in time and was the product, not of conscious planning, but of mysterious forces. Now, however, at the present stage of history it sought a political form, though for Ranke this did not mean a unified Germany. Keenly aware, as a historian, of particularity, he was content to let the national idea express itself politically in the existing German states. Ranke is a good example of the European at midcentury, who had ceased very largely to think in terms of "general laws of politics," and who, instead, stressed the uniqueness of and the differences between, "the great powers." Ranke was keenly aware, for example, of the differences between French and German culture, and of the German's need to repel French ideas in order to fulfil his own destiny. Nationality, moreover, was not something that one shed at will. Said Ranke, again in the Dialogue:

> Germany is alive in us, we represent it, willy-nilly, in every country
> to which we go, in each climate. We are rooted in it from the be-

[43] Leopold von Ranke, *Politisches Gespräch*, translated as "A Dialogue on Politics" in Theodore H. Von Laue, *Leopold Ranke*, Princeton University Press, Princeton, 1950. See pp. 168–169.

[44] J. S. Mill, *Representative Government* (1861), Chap. XVI, "Of Nationality."

ginning, and we can never emancipate ourselves from it. This mysterious something, that animates the lowliest as well as the greatest, this spiritual atmosphere in which we breathe, precedes every constitution.[45]

This sort of national sentiment, already strong in the Romantic World, was fast becoming the primary social "idea" of Europe, for liberals as well as for conservatives. In the words of a Frenchman, writing for the *Revue des Deux Mondes* in 1868, the national idea inflamed the hearts of his contemporaries as religious ideas had done in the sixteenth century, "and like the latter, it will change the face of the world."[46]

By comparison, class, as an organizing principle, was not nearly so powerful, though it too was growing. In the first place, socialism itself was not well established as a movement in any European country by midcentury, and in the second place, socialist thought itself was not yet, by and large, committed to the class idea or to class struggle. Of course, there was sharp criticism of the capitalist order, of bourgeois individualism, and of the bourgeois conception of property. Socialism, assuming the social nature of man, called for a second revolution, greater than the first, which would collectivize or equalize property in one form or another, and thus establish social, and not merely political, justice for all. In the words of Proudhon (who was actually an anarchist, rather than a socialist), private property constituted theft. Employing a revised version of the old labor theory of value, Proudhon argued that land, precisely because it was not produced by labor, should revert to the community. In modern industry, on the other hand, everything was produced by the labor of all; hence industry, too, belonged to the whole body of laborers. Yet Proudhon was a moderate in action, hoping for cooperation between capital and labor to usher in the new order. It was still widely believed in those days, even by socialists, that it was possible for social groups to work together against a common enemy, in this case the old "feudal" order, and to achieve common objectives. Socialists, too, were optimistic about human nature, still somewhat under the spell of eighteenth-century "philosophy," which had stressed persuasion and voluntary action, still also perhaps not very knowledgeable about the real needs of the modern industrial worker. The "True Socialist" Moses Hess, for example, taught a classless ethic whose values would express the needs, not of one class only, but of the whole

---

[45] Leopold von Ranke, op. cit. (see note 43), pp. 165–166.
[46] Emile de Laveleye, quoted in Georges Weill, *L'Europe du XIXe siècle et l'idée de Nationalité*, Albin Michel, Paris, 1938, p. 1.

community. Like some of the other radical Hegelians, Hess put humanity first, and by so doing, believed he could counter the egoism inherent
in the capitalist system. Perhaps this mildness partly explains why John
Mill came to look rather benignly on socialism. If it could come
gradually, in proportion as human nature improved, and if it did not
squelch individualism, he was for it—in the distant future.

Marx's thought was the big exception to these generalizations, reflecting a militant turn in the radical movement during the 1840's.
Marx, despite his early "idealistic" utterances, injected a more realistic
note into discussions of human nature. The bourgeoisie was not potentially full of love for humanity, and it was naïve to think that it
could be persuaded ever to disgorge its surplus capital. Hence, the
proletariat had no alternative to organizing itself, as a class pitted
against the ruling class, and to achieving its just ends, by violence if
necessary. Marx literally saw class almost everywhere, at the seat of
political power, in the labor process, in all of history. The state was
not above class, as some seemed to think. The state was, in reality, an
instrument of class rule, upholding a class interest. Labor was, as
Proudhon said, the cooperative effort of a class, rather than of isolated
individuals. History revealed preeminently a struggle between classes
for the mastery of the earth, and it was the historic mission of the
proletariat to win. Marx felt it was his personal mission to exalt this
class, just as Ranke exalted the nation, and Mill the individual. Of
these three, only the last two, and particularly the last, claimed preeminence in New Enlightenment thought.

The Earthly Paradise

Conceptions of history are implicit in what has already been said
about scientism and the nature of man and society. With regard to
the question of history in particular, there was the same search for
"laws," the same tension between determinism and freedom, the same
general optimism. A few additional points, however, need to be made.

One is ethnocentrism. The New Enlightenment was more Europe-
oriented than the Old Enlightenment. This narrowing of range of
vision was reflected in the historiography, in the increasing preoccupation with national history, but also in general assumptions about the
superiority of Western, that is, European, culture to the rest of the
world. It is true that some universal history was still being written.
However, what Ranke, for instance, generally meant by universal his-

tory was the history of the great European powers (*Die Grossen Mächte*) and their relations with one another; or else, how great states, by developing their own unique personalities, concretized metaphysical forces. Thomas Henry Buckle, who similarly aspired to write universal history, actually limited himself to the *History of Civilization in England* (1856f.), and to general comments on some of the other Western countries. Moreover, Buckle compared the civilizations of Asia and Africa unfavorably with that of Europe, where alone, he contended, the human mind had learned to triumph over nature and go forward. This sort of adverse comparison was fairly common. In Sir Henry Maine's phrase, there were "stationary" and "progressive" societies. The former, arrested at an early stage, included China and India. The latter, said to be "the exception," usually boiled down to Europe. Early in *Ancient Law* (1861) Maine wrote:

> It is only with the progressive societies that we are concerned, and nothing is more remarkable than their fewness. In spite of overwhelming evidence, it is most difficult for a citizen of western Europe to bring thoroughly home to himself the truth that the civilisation which surrounds him is a rare exception in the history of the world. . . . It is indisputable that much the greatest part of mankind has never shown a particle of desire that its civil institutions should be improved since the moment when external completeness was first given to them by their embodiment in some permanent record. . . . Except in a small section of the world, there has been nothing like the gradual amelioration of the legal system. There has been material civilisation, but, instead of the civilisation expanding the law, the law has limited the civilisation.[47]

All the historians referred to thus far, and many others as well, aspired to write scientific history. This meant exorcizing once and for all the ghosts of metaphysics, as well as going beyond the mere chronicling of events to discover regularities and general laws. The antimetaphysical note is conspicuous in *The German Ideology* (1846), where Marx denounced Hegelian philosophy, Young as well as Old, as unhistorical. But Buckle perhaps articulated best the assumptions of this new kind of history. Though not much is known about Buckle himself, his book enjoyed a considerable vogue. John Mill was much im-

[47] Sir Henry Maine, *Ancient Law*, Chap. II. See also James Mill's *History of British India* (1817), Bk. II, "Of the Hindus," in which expressions like "the more skilful governments of Europe," "the less instructed and less civilized inhabitants of Asia," and "rude nations," abound.

pressed by it, and even Dostoevski read it. Like Claude Bernard with physiology, and at just about the same time, Buckle assumed a "universality," a "uniformity," that is, a determinism in the events of history. Also like Bernard, however, Buckle distinguished between determinism and fatalism. Historical events were neither the result of chance nor of supernatural interference. Down-to-earth causes, recognizable in the mass, if not always in the individual, determined the actions of men—Buckle called this the doctrine of Necessary Connexion. But these causes were mental as well as physical. If man was modified by "nature," that is, climate, food, soil, biology, so, on the other hand, was nature modified by man, especially by man's mind "developing itself according to the conditions of its organization." Historians should ascertain whether mind or nature had most influenced human actions, and in which parts of the world. Buckle adduced statistics of murder, suicide, marriage, and the like to demonstrate the regularity of these actions, and hence the possibility of prediction.[48] John Mill disagreed with Buckle only in his insistence that historical laws could be only empirical laws. There were too many variables in history as well as insufficient information, particularly about advanced societies, to permit the sort of scientific prediction that Buckle thought possible.

Actually, the only "law" the scientific historians at midcentury could agree on was the law of progress. But this was very nearly a universal conviction of the age. "If there is some idea that belongs peculiarly to our century," a French philosophy professor wrote in 1851, "it is, so it seems to me, the idea of Progress, conceived as a general law of history and the future of humanity."[49] In John Mill's words, history exhibited, not merely Progressiveness or progressive change, but Progress, change for the better. Mill preferred Comte to Vico, the idea of history as "a trajectory or progress, in lieu of an orbit or cycle."[50] Belief in historical relativism, also widespread by this time, had by no means banished teleology. History was thought to be moving toward an earthly paradise where men would be happy and well adjusted, at least in the Western portion of the world.

Different individuals and groups naturally disagreed, sometimes sharply, about the nature and dynamics of the trajectory, even about the course it described. Some, for instance, believed in the inevitability

[48] Thomas Henry Buckle, *History of Civilization in England,* Chaps. I–IV.
[49] A. Javary, *De l'idée de Progrès,* Librairie Philosophique de Ladrange, Paris, 1851, p. 1.
[50] J. S. Mill, *System of Logic,* Bk. VI, Chap. X, Sect. 3.

of progress, others only in its probability. Some stressed the role of mind, others physical or material forces, in bringing progress about. For some, the goal was greater knowledge, for others, it was the greatest happiness of the greatest number, greater freedom (for nation or individual), or equality, a higher morality, or some mixture of these.

The Hegelians emphasized expansion of consciousness. "Progress toward consciousness," said Renan in a good Hegelian statement, "is the most general law of the world." The early epochs of the history of the universe had known no consciousness. Consciousness had arisen only in historic times, driven by science, which, though it destroyed the supernatural paradise, made possible the establishment of paradise on earth, "when all will have participated in light, perfection, beauty, and thereby in happiness."[51] Renan came to believe that history might even surpass its human goal and produce types higher than man himself. As is well known, Marx objected to this sort of "German Ideology" as conceived in cloudland. "Consciousness," he said, "does not determine life, but life determines consciousness."[52] By "life" Marx meant the economic relationships in which men find themselves. Men act in accordance with these relationships, whether they are conscious of them or not. Not ideas, then, nor reason, but the class struggle, created by current modes of economic production and exchange, is the "real" agent of social change. Marx, keenly aware of the new economic realities in Europe, brought the Hegelian philosophy of history down from heaven to earth. Nevertheless, he shared with the "idealist" Hegelians their belief in a historical destiny. The dialectic of history worked inexorably for progress, for the liberation of the working classes and the classless society.[53]

The English rationalists, though not unmindful of economic and other environmental causes, ranked mind or intellect as "the main

[51] Ernest Renan, *Dialogues et fragments philosophiques,* p. 181. See also *The Future of Science, passim.*

[52] Marx, *The German Ideology,* in Lloyd Easton (ed.), *Writings of the Young Marx on Philosophy and Society,* Doubleday, Anchor Books, Garden City, New York, 1967, p. 415.

[53] It hardly seems necessary to note that Marx's philosophy of history was not a simple determinism. Did not Marx say that "men make their own history," and did he not also make room for the role of great personalities, including intellectuals like Newton, in history? His point was that men were conditioned by circumstances, chiefly economic and social, not of their own immediate choosing, which disposed them to think and behave, in the mass, in certain ways. Friedrich Engels expressly repudiated "the naturalistic conception of history," whereby men were prevented from reacting upon, and changing, nature, and creating new conditions of existence.

determining cause" of progress. "The intellectual changes are the most conspicuous agents in history," said Mill. He had been mulling over Comte and Buckle. He accepted Comte's "law" of the Three Stages precisely because it underlined the importance of intellect in history, the progression from theological and metaphysical to positivist thinking, which now also ensured social progress.[54] Buckle, too, though he included physical causes, nevertheless put his main stress on mind, which, once in motion, could not be stopped in its advance over physical environment, as well as over obscurantism. By mind, Buckle meant chiefly scientific, inductive reasoning. Moral truths once discovered did not change, but intellectual truths did, owing to the skeptical spirit of science, which provided the lever for upsetting old methods of inquiry, as in modern Europe, and which led to the decline of religious persecution and war. The young historian Lecky came to roughly similar, but somewhat more guarded, conclusions, only a few years later. In his *History of the Rise and Influence of the Spirit of Rationalism in Europe* (1866), Lecky celebrated the triumph of rationalism, defined as a mode of thought, generated in an entire society, which triumphed over religious obscurantism, drove out magic and witchcraft, eliminated persecution, and, by terminating belief in the miraculous, made possible the rise of modern science. At the same time, Lecky deplored the decline of the spirit of self-sacrifice in an increasingly materialistic civilization, which, he said, had given the age "a mercenary, venal, and unheroic character."[55] Among the rationalists, Mill had perhaps the most balanced conception of intellectual progress. He understood as well as Marx that men were placed in "circumstances," economic and social as well as political, and that their outlooks and actions were formed thereby. But "effects" could react back on "causes"; that is, human beings could, in their turn, "mould and shape the circumstances." What chiefly made this possible was man's ability to think and speculate. Intellectual activity produced new knowledge, which, in turn, made possible material, moral, and political advancement. As stated previously, this conviction explains Mill's insistence on liberty. Upon the liberty to think freely depended the progress of civilization. It followed, for Mill and other "liberals," that progress could not be inevitable, as

---

[54] J. S. Mill, *System of Logic*, Bk. VI, Chaps. X–XI.

[55] W. E. H. Lecky, *History of the Rise and Influence of the Spirit of Rationalism in Europe*, D. Appleton & Co., New York, 1866, *passim*, and Vol. II, p. 354. Lecky was only twenty-six when he wrote this book. See also his *History of European Morals* (1869) in which, however, he evinced a more highly developed relativistic sense.

it was for Buckle and Herbert Spencer (actually both *laissez-faire* liberals), Marx, and even Ranke.[56]

Jules Castagnary, friend of Courbet and member of the new Realist circle in France, said that whereas art had once glorified gods and heroes, now it should devote itself to the apotheosis of man. He pictured man, now fully conscious of himself as saying:

> Beside the divine garden from which I have been expelled, I will erect a new Eden. . . . At its entrance I will set up Progress. . . . and I will give a flaming sword into his hand and he will say to God, 'Thou shalt not enter here.' And thus it was that men began to build up the human community.[57]

This was the real faith of the New Enlightenment, shared, in one form or another, by men of all parties. Ultimately, it rested on faith in nature and man. Even the classical economists, usually represented as pessimists, shared this faith in man to a degree. David Ricardo, the economic theorist, and David Ricardo, member of Parliament, spoke two different languages. The economic theorist believed, neither in a natural harmony of interests nor in the power of the state, that is, man, to effect an artificial harmony. Hence, an iron law of wages doomed the majority of mankind to life at starvation level. But when Ricardo orated in Parliament as a member of a party, he could speak optimistically of an identity of individual interests, of prices becoming "natural and just," if only certain legislative steps were taken, of England's attaining a pitch of prosperity and happiness, which the human imagination could scarcely conceive.[58]

The historical optimism can leave one gasping. Ranke was not afraid of the growing power of the European states. Why should he be? In a famous essay of 1833 he assumes an ethical order in the universe that automatically guarantees, and restores if necessary, harmony among "the Great Powers." Herbert Spencer included in his first book, *Social Statics* (1850), a chapter on "the evanescence of evil." Comte lectured on the gradual melioration of human nature in accordance with the Lamarckian theory of acquired characteristics, which he thought guaranteed a more perfect social state. Winwood Reade, Victorian traveler and

[56] Along with Mill, some French liberals, like Michelet and Edgar Quinet, who believed in free will, questioned the inevitability of progress.

[57] Jules Castagnary, *Philosophie du Salon de 1857,* quoted in Werner Hofmann, *The Earthly Paradise: Art in the Nineteenth Century,* George Braziller, New York, 1961, p. 363.

[58] See on Ricardo, Elie Halévy, op. cit. (see note 41), pp. 340–342.

amateur historian, uses Castagnary's same figure of speech in describing man's historical destiny:

> The beautiful legend will yet come true; Ormuzd will vanquish Ahriman. . . . Earth, which is now a purgatory, will be made a paradise, not by idle prayers and supplications, but by the efforts of man himself, and by means of mental achievements analogous to those which have raised him to his present state. Those inventions and discoveries which have made him, by the grace of God, king of the animals, lord of the elements, and sovereign of steam and electricity, were all of them founded on experiment and observation. . . . When we have ascertained, by means of Science, the method of nature's operations, we shall be able to take her place and to perform them for ourselves. When we understand the laws [of nature], we shall be able to predict the future. . . .[59]

This statement, a fascinating mélange of romanticism and scientism, epitomizes the New Enlightenment faith in progress. In large part, it supplanted, and was compensation and consolation for, the loss of the old religious faith. It would sustain Western man very well until the day when historical as well as religious *malaise* set in, as it was to do in the twentieth century.

---

[59] Winwood Reade, *The Martyrdom of Man,* Trübner & Co., London, 1872, pp. 512–515. One also encounters the paradisiacal reference in the Young Hegelians. Thus Strauss: "So this earth is no longer a vale of tears. . . . The riches of divine life are to be realized right here and now, etc." (*Die christliche Glaubenslehre,* quoted in William J. Brazill, *The Young Hegelians,* Yale University Press, New Haven, 1970, p. 118).

The Evolutionary World

John Mill, as remarked earlier, never really grasped the significance of Charles Darwin. The great champion of liberty praised Mr. Darwin for opening a new "path of inquiry, full of promise, the results of which none can foresee." But rather in the manner of Francis Bacon on Copernicus, Mill dismissed *The Origin of Species* as just another "hypothesis," not yet proved.[1] Within a generation the hypothesis had become a dogma. Evolution and natural selection were household words. The retiring sage of Down, buried in Westminster Abbey only a few feet from the great Sir Isaac, had put his stamp on an age as surely as the more forceful sage of Woolsthorpe.

This Darwinian World, which we now enter, exhibits many of the same features as the world of Mill: the same scientism, the same overarching naturalism, and to a degree the same optimism. We might, in fact, think of it as simply a further extension, a second installment, of the New Enlightenment, save for one thing—the idea of evolution. But this idea made all the difference. "The second half of our century," a French philosopher wrote in 1896, "is evolutionist." "A dynamic positivism [has] displaced the older static positivism."[2] The change in outlook was not merely quantitative but qualitative.

[1] J. S. Mill, *System of Logic,* Bk. III, Chap. XIV, Sect. 5, note (added in the fifth edition, 1862).

[2] Alfred Fouillée, *Le Mouvement idéaliste et la réaction contre la science positive,* Germer Baillière & Cie., Paris, 1896, p. xiii.

This statement requires some qualification. It should be noted, first of all, that Darwinian evolution did not catch on equally in all countries. France resisted it more than England or Germany. In France, the Cuvierist tradition and reigning positivism combined to make scientists wary, for a time, of any sort of evolutionary theory. Even scientists inclined toward evolution did not give much credence to natural selection. For these and other reasons Darwin was not elected to the *Académie des sciences* until 1878, and even then by a less than conclusive vote, and only as a correspondent to the botanical section. Nevertheless, evolution made rapid headway among scientists and anthropologists after 1880, even though the French preferred to call it "transformism," and tended, nationalistically, to give more credit to Lamarck than to Darwin. One French scientist, still an antievolutionist, observed disappointedly in 1894 that all sorts of journals and publications were saying that transformism presently reigned as "master in science," and had "the assent of all somewhat well informed minds and those of all savants truly worthy of the name."[3] This statement parallels similar statements by Huxley for England, and Ernst Haeckel for Germany, at just about the same time.

It should also be noted that the idea of evolution, whether Darwinian or otherwise, was by no means new. If "the development hypothesis" was not as old as the hills, it was at least as old as Buffon and Herder, Schelling and Hegel, as we have seen. Herbert Spencer wrote an essay about it in 1852, in which he compared "statical" and "dynamical" ways of thinking and defended evolution against believers in special creations. It is also well to remind ourselves that personal awareness of living in a world of ceaseless change, ever on the increase in the nineteenth century, did not depend on evolutionary doctrine. Years before Darwin, and independently of Spencer, Matthew Arnold worried about time, as when, for instance, in "The Scholar-Gypsy" (1853), he compared the "sick hurry" of modern life with the stabilities of an older England.

> *For what wears out the life of mortal men?*
> *'Tis that from change to change their being rolls;*
> *'Tis that repeated shocks, again, again,*
> *Exhaust the energy of strongest souls*
> *And numb the elastic powers.*

[3] Armand de Quatrefages, quoted by Robert E. Stebbins in his chapter on France in *The Comparative Reception of Darwinism*, Thomas F. Glick (ed.), University of Texas Press, Austin, 1972, p. 132.

But Darwin drove the point home. After 1859 the idea of evolution not merely infiltrated but dominated European thought. It was next to impossible to consider any of the perennial questions without reference to evolution. It projected a radically new picture of nature as "cosmic process," but without design. Evolution opened up new fronts in the warfare between science and theology. It enveloped man himself, hitherto largely exempted, in the evolutionary process, thus calling attention to man's lowly, that is, animal origin. It standardized dynamic views of society and culture, and simultaneously created a bias in favor of "warfare" as the law of social as well as organic life. Largely as a result of the Darwinian Revolution, everything under the sun (and including the sun, according to the theory of stellar evolution) seemed to be in perpetual flux. This notion was a source of considerable unease for many people, as can be imagined. But in the Darwinian World, optimism prevailed over pessimism because of the emphasis in Darwinian theory itself on creativity, on nature's ability at whatever level to produce new and superior forms.

Herbert Spencer, who might be thought of as the philosopher of evolution, makes this clear. In his *First Principles* (1862), which introduced his ambitious "Synthetic Philosophy" in ten volumes, Spencer sketched "a Universe everywhere in motion." There is more tension in this book than in *Social Statics* in which, it will be remembered, Spencer delineated a law of progress. Now he contemplated an alternation of Evolution and Dissolution, even the eventual disintegration of the universe, owing to the persistence of motion and "force," which never allows anything to remain in a state of rest once it has achieved integration. Spencer's emphasis, however, was on the evolution. The dissolution, partly speculative in any case, had to do with "some period beyond the utmost stretch of imagination." For the present, and for the forseeable future, the "law of evolution" was in the ascendant, encompassing everything from the solar system to man (though, of course, dissolution claimed each individual man in death), and the societies that man built. Spencer defined evolution as the movement or "change" from the homogeneous to the heterogeneous (for example, in the human body, an increasing structural and functional differentiation), from the indefinite to the definite, from incoherence to coherence.[4] Spencerian evolution was still a doctrine of progress, as is borne out by

---

[4] See especially the six chapters in *First Principles* on the law and interpretation of Evolution (XIII–XVIII).

subsequent volumes on biology, sociology, and ethics. Darwin had corroborated Spencer's belief that evolution was, on the whole, constructive.

The Cosmic Process

In one of his last and most important lectures, Thomas Henry Huxley, called by Darwin his "General Agent," described nature as "the cosmic process." *Cosmic* meant that, in strict parlance, nature included all existence, even the world of man and morals. However, in later utterances, Huxley really meant that part of nature not touched by man, the "cosmic" as opposed to the "horticultural process." *Process* referred, of course, to nature's Heraclitean and evolutionary aspect. "Thus the most obvious attribute of the cosmos is its impermanence. It assumes the aspect not so much of a permanent entity as of a changeful process, in which naught endures save the flow of energy and the rational order which pervades it." Huxley also spoke of nature's "infinite variety," of the "internecine struggle for existence of living things," and of the suffering that was no accidental accompaniment, "but an essential constituent of the cosmic process."[5]

This was substantially Darwin's view of nature, and it had been over a century in the making. This view would obviously have been impossible without the geological revolution which preceded it, and probably also, though perhaps to a lesser extent, the biological revolution, which included such famous "forerunners" as Buffon, Lamarck, and Darwin's own grandfather, Erasmus Darwin. By Darwin's time, all or almost all of the constituent elements of the new view were already in the air, widely debated in educated circles, though not necessarily accepted, even by scientists. Darwin fused these elements into one system and supplied impressive supporting evidence. But he did more. He appears not to have been widely read at first in the history of evolutionary thought. He therefore relied a great deal on his own observations, particularly on those made in South America and the Galápagos Islands during the voyage of the *Beagle* (1831–1836). He returned to England convinced of the infinite plasticity or "divergence" of nature. Like Newton, Darwin eventually came up with a plausible explanation of how the system worked. If he was not the first to hit on

---

[5] T. H. Huxley, "Evolution and Ethics" (1893), and "Evolution and Ethics. Prologomena" (1894).

natural selection, he was the first to make it central and to think of it as an essentially progressive mechanism, combining with biological variations in individuals to produce new species. There is no doubt either that Darwin shook up his contemporaries, or that within a matter of years his theories overthrew older and religiously based views of nature.

Darwinian nature did not overthrow but, on the contrary, reinforced, and even exaggerated, those models of nature previously noted in the New Enlightenment view.[6] It marked the triumph of naturalism, as contemporaries were now beginning to call it. A hostile witness defined naturalism as a complete world-view which "separates Nature from God, subordinates Spirit to Matter, and sets up unchangeable law as witness."[7] Darwin did not pretend to a world-view, but he did banish "design" from nature. He was "driven" in the end, he tells us in his autobiography, to give up William Paley's arguments,[8] which had once seemed to Darwin so conclusive while a student at Cambridge. The beautiful hinge of a bivalve shell was so obviously *not* made by an intelligent being, "like the hinge of a door by man." Nor, for that matter, was the human eye nearly so perfect as Paley had thought it was. Hence, to argue back from the watch to the watchmaker (God) no longer convinced Darwin. "There seems to be no more design in the variability of organic beings and in the action of natural selection, than in the course which the wind blows."[9] George Bernard Shaw later argued that the Darwinian formula for evolution delivered the universe over to chance. But this was certainly not its intention. Like the positivists, the Darwinians, in one sense at least, ruled out chance as well as design. "Everything in nature is the result of fixed laws," Darwin said.[10]

But what of Materialism, of which the Darwinians were simultaneously accused? Certain lectures by Huxley, or the physicist John Tyndall, or a book like Ernst Haeckel's *Riddle of the Universe* (1899),

---

[6] See p. 311f.

[7] James Ward, *Naturalism and Agnosticism*, Adam & Charles Black, London, 1899, Vol. I, pp. 185–186.

[8] Bishop William Paley's *Evidences of Christianity* (1794) and *Natural Theology* (1802) were classics on the argument from design in nature.

[9] Charles Darwin, *Autobiography*, Nora Barlow (ed.), Collins, London, 1958, p. 87.

[10] Ibid. See also T. H. Huxley in "Evolution and Ethics. Prologomena": "As the expression of a fixed order, every stage of which is the effect of causes operating according to definite rules, the conception of evolution no less excludes that of chance."

might give the impression that materialism had at long last captured the scientific community. But this impression would be only partially right. Haeckel, a biologist, called Darwin's bulldog in Germany, came closest to being a genuine philosophical materialist. Haeckel preached "a wonderful unity" of organic and inorganic nature. According to his "monistic" philosophy, which he claimed to have learned from Darwin, as well as from the laws of the conservation of energy and matter, everything in the cosmos derived from "matter" in an ascending evolutionary series: life from nonliving carbon compounds by spontaneous generation, psychic activity from further material changes in the protoplasm, and so on. Haeckel's "matter," it is worth noting, was endowed with elementary consciousness. Huxley was a more typical figure. He, too, could, on occasion, talk a materialistic language, as in the famous lecture "On the Physical Basis of Life" (1868), in which he said he saw no distinction between simple protoplasm and water, except in the arrangement of the molecules. Thought itself was the result of molecular changes. The progress of science, Huxley affirmed, had always meant "the extension of the province of what we call matter and causation, and the concomitant gradual banishment from all regions of human thought of what we call spirit and spontaneity." But Huxley denied being a materialist. In the same lecture, he went on to express his fundamental skepticism of the terms people insisted on using. What do we know about "matter" or "spirit," or for that matter, "necessity"? They are "but names for the imaginary substrata of groups of natural phaenomena." Huxley donned his materialistic mantle only when he wanted to take the offensive against real or imagined opponents like the clergy. Scientists of the Darwinian persuasion were more like Huxley than Haeckel.[11] Like the positivists, they were mostly nominalists and agnostics rather than materialists.

The novel features of Darwinian nature were, as already hinted, the time factor and the element of struggle. Friedrich Engels, who was a close student of science and its bearings on society, commented on both of these features in his notes on the "Dialectics of Nature" (written 1873–1882). Up to about the nineteenth century, he said, science's picture of nature remained, time-wise, quite "conservative."

[11] John Tyndall, professor of natural philosophy at the Royal Institution, belongs somewhere between the two. Widely known for his Belfast Address of 1874, he openly professed "scientific materialism." However, this appears to have meant, very largely, the correlation of mental and physical processes in the brain. Somewhat like Haeckel, Tyndall contended that "matter," far from being dead, contained within itself the potentiality of life and mental activity.

Nature was not at all regarded as something that developed historically, that had a history in time; only extension in space was taken into account; . . . natural history was valid for all periods, like the elliptical orbits of the planets.[12]

This conception of time, or of timelessness, changed with the work of, successively, scientists like Laplace, Lamarck, Lyell, and finally Darwin. Nineteenth-century science, culminating in Darwin, historicized nature and provided it with a new time dimension. The geologists, though Engels ignored them, did the most to effect this "time revolution." To account for slow descent with modification in the organic world, Darwin obviously needed much more time than the traditional Christian chronology allowed. The geologists, conspicuously Sir Charles Lyell, whose *Principles of Geology* (1830) Darwin took with him to read on the *Beagle,* gave Darwin millions, rather than thousands, of years with the new doctrine of "uniformitarianism." Uniformitarianism explained geologic change, not by sudden "catastrophes" (followed by special creations), but by wholly natural causes observably at work in the present and therefore presumably uniform throughout time. But these causes, erosion, for example, obviously operated very slowly. Thus, Lyell not only provided a vastly extended time-scale but called attention to the change that was going on every day in the universe, incessantly, irresistibly, and irreversibly. As Engles summarized: with the new conception of nature, completed by Darwin, "all rigidity was dissolved, all fixity dissipated, all particularity that had been regarded as eternal became transient."[13]

Farther along in the "Dialectics," Engels also noted "the struggle for life," which in Darwinian theory had replaced former theories of natural harmony. Engels himself cautioned against seeing too much struggle, even in nature.[14] But he correctly identified this struggle as a mark of nature that Darwin himself featured, and that everybody was now talking about. Engels observed shrewdly that the Darwinian theory represented the transference, from society to nature, of "the bourgeois economic theory of competition," as well as the Malthusian theory of population. It is well known that Darwin did, in fact, read, and was

[12] Friedrich Engels, *Dialectics of Nature,* Clemens Dutt (ed.), International Publishers, New York, 1960, pp. 185–186.

[13] Ibid., p. 13.

[14] Engels' main point, however, was that there is no perfect analogy between nature and society. There is plenty of struggle in society, but struggle among men is not simply for existence but for better opportunities of enjoyment and development.

much impressed by, Malthus' famous *Essay on the Principles of Population* (1789) on his return to England in 1836. Darwin's frequent references in *The Origin of Species* to "the war of nature," "the great battle of life," and the like owed much to Malthus' theory that population outran food supply, the former increasing geometrically and the latter only arithmetically, thus causing a great struggle for existence. It should only be remarked—a point that escaped Engels—that unlike Malthus, Darwin did not think of the struggle as restrictive, but rather as creative of new species. This grim picture of nature, inevitably involving "great destruction" even if, as Darwin said, "the happy survive and multiply," explains why even Huxley had ambiguous feelings about the cosmic process. He could not view with equanimity the suffering inflicted on the deer by the wolf, however much he might admire the latter's fitness. Nature, Huxley thought, at least in the sense of the animal world, "is on about the same level as a gladiator's show."[15]

Thus, the new picture of nature was not altogether pleasing, even to those who accepted it. It seemed to put a new gulf between God and nature, or between nature and man.

> *Are God and Nature then at strife,*
> *That Nature lends such evil dreams?*

Nine years before the publication of *The Origin of Species,* Tennyson, who had read Lyell, Chambers, and Laplace, was worrying about this dualism. England's poet laureate, in fact, encapsulated all the intelligent layman's perplexities in confronting the new nature: the ethical aspects of this "Nature, red in tooth and claw," which appeared to be so careless of life, both of individual and species, and hence to belie the God of love; not knowing whether there was any "design," hence whether life was futile; the phenomenon of change itself, which swept away all the landmarks.

> *There rolls the deep where grew the tree.*
> *O earth, what changes hast thou seen!*
>
> . . . .
>
> *The hills are shadows, and they flow*
> *From form to form, and nothing stands;*
> *They melt like mist, the solid lands,*
> *Like clouds they shape themselves and go.*[16]

[15] T. H. Huxley, "The Struggle for Existence in Human Society" (1888).
[16] Alfred, Lord Tennyson, *In Memoriam* (1850), stanza CXXII. See also the famous stanzas LIV-LV on "Nature, red in tooth and claw."

Tennyson had found a new reason (in these stanzas Lyellian geology) to add to Matthew Arnold's concern about mutability. This new nature could not be a home for Tennyson. Yet he tried to understand it and to think that out of it good, perhaps "a higher race," might one day come.

Change did not in the least bother the scientist Huxley. He gloried in it, welcomed the ceaseless modifications eventuating in higher types. Yet in the end he, too, developed misgivings, as mentioned; felt it necessary to point out the difference between "the State of Nature" and "the State of Art." Nature, Huxley had come to believe, was "neither moral nor immoral, but non-moral." Therefore, man could develop a worthy civilization only by cultivating his own garden and surrounding it by a wall to keep nature out. Let the gardener once withdraw his watchful supervision and "the antagonistic influences of the general cosmic process" (the reference was chiefly to the struggle for existence aspect of nature) would invade the garden, and trample it down.[17] In a sense, then, man and nature were enemies, though man, Prometheus-like, could, if vigilant, commandeer any part of nature he chose for his own purposes.

Despite such misgivings, visibly growing, as we shall see later on, science was still very much on the upswing in the Darwinian World. Who doubted that science had "as yet done nothing but good," at least in its practical applications? Who could deny that, as an article in the new scientific journal *Nature* put it, the scientific movement was "sweeping along with it all classes and all opinions," that it represented "a new habit of thought," in the light of which all problems were being reconsidered?[18] In such a climate it is hardly surprising that, in the Comtean tradition, Huxley, Francis Galton (Darwin's cousin), and others should urge a new "scientific priesthood" to replace clergymen as the leaders of culture, or that they should press for a new and more scientific sort of education. Huxley, an immensely vigorous man, epitomizes this new type of cultural advocate. He lectured on science all over England, to all kinds of audiences, demanding a larger role for science in education. He debated with none other than Matthew Arnold, who was a school inspector, on the subject. Arnold, in his famous essay on "Literature and Science" (1882), asked the crucial question: were the sudies, long presumed to be the best "for all of us," still the best? or were other studies, mainly scientific, better for the

[17] T. H. Huxley, "Evolution and Ethics. Prologomena."
[18] The references, called to my attention by Frank Turner, are to Charles Kingsley, *Health and Education* (1872) and "Professor Tyndall and the Scientific Movement," *Nature* (1887). *Nature* commenced publication in 1869.

new age? No doubt Arnold and Huxley talked across each other a good deal, but in the main Arnold championed the traditional education, "mainly literary," whereas Huxley urged an education demanding "most favoured nation" status for the sciences. We are concerned here mainly with Huxley's arguments. He kept hammering away at the following points: that the traditional education in the classics did not equip an individual—or a nation—to compete successfully in the great struggle for existence; that (changing the metaphor), in the chess game of the modern world, a player could not make the proper moves unless he knew the rules of the game, which "are what we call the laws of Nature"; that scientific education was "an absolute essential condition of industrial progress"; that training in the scientific method also had ethical significance, because it inculcated a proper respect for evidence. Huxley, no friend of religious orthodoxy, thought the men of science far superior to the men of religion in intellectual veracity. Changing his metaphor once more, Huxley said he expected much more from Cinderella, that is, science, than from her ugly sisters, Theology and Philosophy, or from the Levites, the monopolists of "liberal" education. Cinderella because she "lights the fire, sweeps the house, and provides the dinner" was looked down on as a low and material creature. But in truth she, and she alone, saw the order that pervaded the world, watched the great drama of evolution unroll before her eyes, learned "to give up pretending to believe that for which there is no evidence, and repeating unintelligible propositions about things beyond the possibilities of knowledge."[19] The Darwinian World was at one with the New Enlightenment in these beliefs.

Man's Place in Nature

Toward the end of his life Huxley tended to separate nature and man in his speech, even to pit the one against the other. But all along, of course, he assumed "man's place in nature," which was, indeed, the subject of one of his most important books. Huxley assumed that man,

[19] T. H. Huxley, "Science and Morals" (1886). The Cinderella metaphor concluding this essay did not include reference to the Levites or to classical scholars. For Huxley's views on education, see especially "A Liberal Education; and Where to Find It" (1868), "Scientific Education: Notes of an After-Dinner Speech" (1869), and "Science and Culture" (1880). Needless to say, Huxley did not advocate an exclusively scientific education. He wished to expand liberal education to include science, modern history and literature, and the like.

too, was part of the cosmic process, that he had evolved from the primeval slime, or, more strictly, was descended from brutes. Even man's higher faculties of feeling and intellect originated in lower forms. "No absolute structural line of demarcation," he said, could be drawn between animals and ourselves. Drawings showing the similarity between the skeletons of manlike apes and man himself were included in his book of essays on *Man's Place in Nature* (1863) in order to illustrate this point (Plate 26). This was to wrest man out of his old religious setting, to deny him any sort of special creation, or special status, to explain him by wholly natural forces already at work. Darwin made substantially the same assumptions in his *Descent of Man,* published eight years later, in 1871.

This was the question—Huxley called it "the question of questions" —that disturbed his contemporaries most, that is, whether evolution applied to man, whether, so to speak, man was by nature more like ape or angel. The Darwinian answer, as it may be called, did not disturb Huxley in the least, nor did it disturb Darwin. To say that man was descended *from* brutes was not to say that he was *of* them. The glory of man was his present state, not the lowly stock from which he sprang. In an age when mountain climbing was the rage, Huxley called man "that great Alps and Andes of the living world."

> He alone possesses the marvelous endowment of intelligible and rational speech, whereby . . . he has slowly accumulated and organized the experience which is almost wholly lost with the cessation of every individual life in other animals; so that now he stands raised upon it as on a mountain top, far above the level of his humble fellows. . . .[20]

That was why, in Huxley's opinion, man had to (and could) combat the cosmic process: because he had risen above it, and developed an ethical sense and a capacious brain. Huxley, therefore, had hope "in his [man's] attainment of a nobler Future."

This view, even in Huxley's sugarcoated version, raised a storm, and no wonder. To many Christians it seemed blasphemous, not merely contradicting the Bible, but negating everything they had been taught about the nature and destiny of man. To idealists, not necessarily Christian, it seemed incredible that such a finely tuned instrument as man's intellect, able to think in abstractions and to generalize, could derive

[20] T. H. Huxley, "On the Relations of Man to the Lower Animals," *Man's Place in Nature* (1863), concluding paragraph.

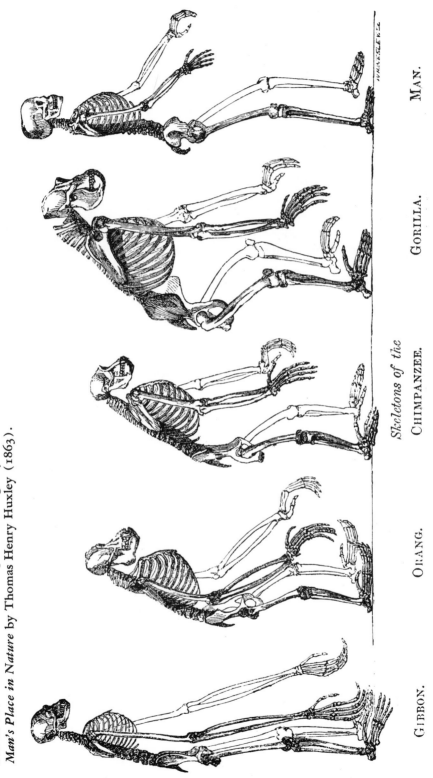

PLATE 26. *Man and Man-like Apes.* Drawings by Waterhouse Hawkins from *Man's Place in Nature* by Thomas Henry Huxley (1863).

Skeletons of the

GIBBON.   ORANG.   CHIMPANZEE.   GORILLA.   MAN.

from the animal world of instinct. Max Müller, the great German philologist (and an anti-Darwinist), said that "power of articulate speech" depended on precisely these qualities of intellect. As for the scientists, many of them, too, found it hard to give up long cherished assumptions, or to be convinced without a further show of evidence, of the "missing link," as it was popularly known (lack of intermediate fossil forms), or of natural selection.

Lyell and Alfred Russel Wallace, the latter the co-discoverer with Darwin of evolution by natural selection, are examples of scientists who agonized over the new anthropology. Despite what is sometimes said of him, Lyell never completely endorsed Darwin's theory. He conceded man's remote origins in the past, thus upsetting the Mosaic chronology, and after much vacillating, admitted the "probability" of natural selection. But he could never persuade himself that natural selection, or any other purely "secondary" natural cause, really explained the phenomenon of man. Man, Lyell persisted in thinking, inhabited a "Distinct Kingdom," that is, man was distinguished from the beasts by an "improvable reason" and by moral and religious faculties. "To man alone is given this belief" [in God and the world beyond], Lyell wrote in the last chapter of *The Antiquity of Man* (1863), "so consonant to his reason, and so congenial to the religious sentiments implanted by nature in his soul, a doctrine which tends to raise him morally and intellectually in the scale of being." But how, save by a "leap," could this qualitative change have come about? And how could there have been such a leap without the connivance of a higher law of development, attributable to "the Deity himself"? The great geologist had concluded that man must have been elevated to his proud estate by a cause outside the usual course of nature. Man was the one great exception to his own "uniformitarian" law of nature. Wallace, though arguing from less conventionally religious premises, came to similar conclusions. In a series of articles, which, incidentally, greatly disturbed Darwin, Wallace made two points: first, that the human brain marked a spectacular advance over any organ that nature had previously been able to produce; and second, that man's intellectual powers, as well as his aesthetic and moral gifts, could not be accounted for by natural selection. Thus, there seemed to him to be "evidence of a power which has guided the action of [the laws of organic development] in definite directions and for special ends."[21] Wallace, it should be added, had a bright view of

[21] Alfred Russel Wallace, article in the *Quarterly Review,* 1869, quoted in Alvar Ellegard, *Darwin and the General Reader,* Göteborg University, Göteborg, 1958, p. 308.

man's future. By acquiring a brain, *homo sapiens* gained the ability henceforth to control his own evolution.

Lyell understood better than most what was at stake in this debate. It was nothing less than the dignity of man. What alarms philosophers and theologians most, Lyell wrote, in one of his journals, is "fear lest the dignity of Man in relation to the Universe should be lowered by establishing a nearer link of union between him and the inferior animals."[22] Let man cease to be *sui generis,* as upheld by classical and Christian tradition, and he would become, like the animals, " a creature of the moment," incapable of high thoughts and aspirations, "ephemeral and insignificant" in his own eyes. But Lyell and Wallace fought a rear-guard action. As the fossil evidence kept piling up, most people were won over (though not always cheerfully like Huxley) to Darwin's picture of man as "descended from barbarians," as the fortuitous product of a brutal struggle for existence, as still bearing within his frame "the indelible stamp of his lowly origin." A "distasteful" and disillusioning picture indeed, or so it seemed to many of Darwin's and Huxley's contemporaries. Thanks in large part to Darwin, Western thinking about human nature underwent a profound sea-change. Henceforth, it was man's irrational nature that would be most talked about—his instincts, his aggressiveness, his kinship to the animal world. Darwinian man foreshadowed the irrational man of Sigmund Freud and the twentieth century.

But the Darwinians talked about men as well as man. They shaded "man" back into the animal world. But at the human level they talked about the differences between men. Thus, they "shattered the supposition of the essential unity of mankind."[23] On the whole, they were inclined to trace these differences to biological, rather than environmental, determinants. The New Enlightenment, like the Old Enlightenment, especially in England and France, still emphasized "circumstances," climate, political and economic systems, education, and the like. The emphasis now shifted from nurture to nature, and hence more toward fatalism, a bogey word in Enlightenment thinking.

The stimulus for this kind of thinking came only partly from Darwinism. As we have seen, romanticism and historicism accented the particular rather than the universal aspects of human nature and human

[22] Sir Charles Lyell, *Scientific Journals,* Leonard Wilson (ed.), Yale University Press, New Haven, 1970, p. 336. This particular remark is dated December 8, 1859.

[23] J. W. Burrow, *Evolution and Society,* Cambridge University Press, Cambridge, 1966, p. 130.

civilization, and in Darwin's own time nationalism and imperialism did likewise. However, Darwin, too, stimulated particularity in thinking, by his emphasis on variation and species. Evolution itself could not occur without initial slight variations among the individuals of an animal species. Similarly impressed by the diversity of human "species" or races, Darwin tried to account for it by sexual selection.

Basic human inequality, as it may be called, was discerned in three main areas in the Darwinian world: between the races of men, between nations, and between individuals. Race-thinking, of course, had been going on for a long time before Darwin. The most influential book on the subject in the nineteenth century, Count Gobineau's *Essay on the Inequality of Races,* had appeared in 1853, to be followed in 1859 by a book on the Aryan myth, Adolphe Pictet's *Indo-European Origins.* So it was not uncommon, by Darwin's time, to distinguish between races on the basis of color, shape of skull, or buttocks, or to relate mental and moral behavior to physical structure. The Darwinians, however, also believed in superior and inferior races, thus contributing to the current ethnocentric bias. Both Darwin and Wallace combined the currently fashionable monogenist and polygenist theories in their thinking. They thought that the various races of man might have descended from a common stock. But after a certain point—identified by Wallace as the time when men became capable of taking thought—different strains or varieties developed and went their separate ways. In line with Herbert Spencer's thought on the subject, Darwin and Wallace saw an ensuing mental and moral competition between races, with victory going to the best endowed in the struggle for life, and the emergence, ultimately, of a higher breed of men. In the most recent stage of history, "best endowed" obviously meant *Homo Europaeus,* just then carving out empires all over the world. Wallace wrote in 1864:

> The intellectual and moral, as well as the physical qualities of the European are superior; the same power and capacities which have made him rise in a few centuries from the condition of the wandering savage with a scanty and stationary population to his present state of culture and advancement . . . enable him when in contact with the savage man, to conquer in the struggle for existence, and to increase at his expense. . . .[24]

[24] Alfred Russel Wallace, "The Origin of Human Races and the Antiquity of Man Deduced from the Theory of 'Natural Selection'," *Journal of the Anthropological Society of London* (1864), quoted in John C. Greene, *The Death of Adam,* Iowa State University Press, Ames, Iowa, 1959, p. 318.

The inequality of nationalities, seen from the anthropological side, constituted only a variation of this race thinking. For example, it had become quite common then to identify *Homo Europaeus* with the Aryan, or the supposedly brainier and more vigorous section of the white race, and even to find its supreme modern representative in the Germans, French, or some other national group. This sort of thinking was endemic to the new "integral nationalism," which is discussed later in greater detail.[25]

More directly related to Darwin was the type of thinking opened up by the geneticists and eugenicists. This thinking accentuated differences between individuals, rather than groups. Darwin himself took a rather environmentalist line in his thinking about individual variations. According to his theory of pangenesis, elaborated in a book in 1868, Darwin concluded that changes in the germ cells originated in "gemmules," or material particles thrown off by the body, which could then be inherited. The German geneticist August Weismann exploded this theory, essentially a Lamarckian theory, of the inheritance of acquired characteristics. He distinguished sharply between germ cells, and somatic or body cells, contending that the former were not affected by changes impressed on the latter. This theory was strengthened enormously by Gregor Mendel's findings on heredity, actually made in the 1860's, but not disclosed until 1900. Contemporary with Weismann, the anthropologist Francis Galton, who was Darwin's cousin, used statistics to study the influence of heredity through several generations. Galton's findings, recorded in *Hereditary Genius* (1869), claimed to show not only that there were profound differences in intellect but that these differences were normally inherited, regardless of environment. Galton became convinced, he says in his memoirs, "that heredity was a far more powerful agent in human development than nurture." It was this conviction, corroborated as he thought by Weismann's research, that led Galton to propose a new science of eugenics. Eugenics, or the selective breeding of men was perhaps the sole means—Darwin himself agreed, though he thought the proposal utopian—of improving the human race, of checking the birthrate of "the Unfit," and furthering that of "the Fit by early marriages and healthful rearing of their children."[26] Eugenics notwithstanding, the overall effect of this sort of biological

---

[25] See p. 365.
[26] Francis Galton, *Memories of My Life*, Methuen & Co., London, 1908, pp. 323, 266.

thinking was to put a patina of fate on the behavior of individuals and groups. Or at least environment was now thought to be strictly auxiliary to biological qualities, which resided in the germ plasm, or "stirp," as Galton called it. Naturally, Herbert Spencer and assorted social reformers, who assumed the power of "nurture," resisted this trend.

Agnosticism

Given these views on nature and human nature, Darwinism's impact on religion is more or less predictable. It could only aggravate the religious crisis that was then overtaking Europe. To be sure, Darwinism was not the only solvent of religious belief in the late nineteenth century. In parts of Europe it was not even the most important solvent. But overall, and in the long run, Darwinism contributed powerfully, not only to the continuing "warfare between science and theology" but to the demise of religion as it was traditionally understood and to the rise of a new secular Europe. Ours is a time, Lord Acton wrote to Mary Gladstone in 1887, when "unbelief in the shape of doubt is yielding to unbelief in the shape of certain conviction."[27] Much of the unbelief found expression in the new "agnosticism," a word coined by Huxley to oppose the "gnostics" of church history, who professed to know all about first and last things. Yet agnosticism is really too neutral a word to catch the "certain conviction," which many people were now developing about a world without design, soul, or God, whose death was now being discussed openly.

It needs to be said that evolution *per se* could be, and sometimes was, interpreted in religion's favor. Much depended on which elements of Darwinism one chose to see, or call attention to. Liberal theologians, stressing the progressive, rather than mechanistic, features of Darwinism, were able to work out a new natural theology, which pictured God as supplying the original impetus and the goal for the evolutionary process. Thus, Frederick Temple, the future Archbishop of Canterbury, saw only an "apparent conflict" between religion and science. The doctrine of evolution destroyed none of the great verities. It left the argument from design "stronger than it was before," though it could not be understood any longer exactly in Paley's terms. It left man in

[27] Quoted in Gertrude Himmelfarb, *Lord Acton*, University of Chicago Press, Chicago, 1952, p. 164.

possession of a "spiritual faculty," in which his dignity chiefly consisted and it left intact the Moral Law, proclaimed by God himself through man's spiritual faculty.[28]

An attempt has been made recently to picture Darwin himself as this sort of natural theologian, and indeed to see the evolutionary debate in general, at least in England, as taking place within a theistic frame of reference.[29] But this was surely not the case. It is true that Darwin, a cautious man, only very slowly gave up the religious views on which he was reared, that he was still a theist when he wrote *The Origin of Species,* and that, to the end, his "theology" remained in something of a muddle. Nevertheless, Darwin's progression from Christian to theist to agnostic was steady and unmistakable, as his *Autobiography,* written late in life, makes clear. This progression is, in fact, a fairly accurate profile of what happened religiously to many educated people in the late nineteenth century. First came disbelief in Christianity as a divine revelation, prompted by reflections on the credibility of the Bible and modern Biblical criticism. Next, Darwin ceased to believe in the argument from design in nature. He had found an alternative explanation for how nature worked, in natural selection. The "argument from the existence of suffering" also seemed to him to tell strongly against the existence of an intelligent first cause. He still found it hard to believe that the universe was the result of blind chance, but concluded that the human mind, developed from the mind of the lower animals, simply could not solve such riddles. So, on his own testimony, he became, and remained, "an Agnostic."[30]

Agnosticism, not some new form of theism, was on the rise after 1859. It so exactly suited the mood and the need of the times that an appropriate word had to be found for it. Years later Huxley explained how he came to coin the word "agnostic." He was surrounded, he tells us, more particularly in the new Metaphysical Society, by colleagues

[28] Frederick Temple, *The Relations between Religion and Science* (1884). See especially Lectures IV and VI. The book is based on the Bampton Lectures, delivered by Temple, then Bishop of Exeter, at Oxford in 1884. Andrew D. White employed much the same tactic in his famous *History of the Warfare of Science and Theology in Christendom* (1896). There was, indeed, warfare between science and dogmatic theology, which presented a medieval and outworn picture of the world, but not between science and religion. Evolution contradicted theology, but not religion, according to White.

[29] Robert M. Young, "The Impact of Darwin on Conventional Thought," *The Victorian Crisis of Faith,* Anthony Symondson (ed.), Society for Promoting Christian Knowledge, London, 1970.

[30] Charles Darwin, *Autobiography,* Nora Barlow (ed.), Collins, London, 1958. See especially the long section on "Religious Belief."

who were "-ists" of one sort of another, that is, atheists, theists, materialists, idealists, and so on. He soon concluded he was none of these, yet wanted a tail like the other foxes. So he hit on "agnostic," as antithetic to "gnostic," and, to his great delight, "the term took." Huxley explained what the term meant to him. It was "not a creed, but a method," the essence of which lay in following one's reason in matters of the intellect, and not pretending to conclusions that could not be demonstrated.[31] It was simply the scientific spirit, which refused to go beyond the facts. But, despite its profession of neutrality, agnosticism carried with it an antireligious bias, at least as Huxley used it. He suffered all his life from the *odium theologicum,* as did all the Darwinians. Hence, though Huxley objected theoretically to materialism as well as to "spiritualism," it was the latter, that is, religious orthodoxy, that he particularly wished to demolish.

This agnosticism, hardly a new idea even if the word was new, had its roots in Enlightenment rationalism, especially in the empirical view of knowledge sponsored by Comte, Mill, and Spencer, and in the new historical criticism of the Bible. But Huxley, who liked military metaphors, was certainly right when he said that in the course of the past fifty years, science had brought to the front "an inexhaustible supply of heavy artillery of a new pattern, warranted to drive solid bolts of facts through the thickest skulls."[32] Huxley was thinking of science in general, of the scientific method, and of the "facts" science had recently unearthed in "natural" as well as civil and scriptural history, facts having to do with the physical changes that the heavens and the earth had undergone, the origin of man, the races of men, and the like. Late nineteenth-century agnosticism would indeed be unthinkable without the new geology and biology (not to speak of the law of the conservation of energy in physics),[33] as well as the Higher Criticism.

Evolution might be said to have completed the revolution in thinking, which commenced with the Higher Criticism. This was a revolution in the way one thought about the history of the world. The Higher Criticism, originating in German *Wissenschaft,* but now entering an "epoch of popularization," rewrote scriptural history according to a new

[31] T. H. Huxley, "Agnosticism," *The Nineteenth Century,* Vol. XXV (February, 1889).

[32] Quoted in *The Essence of T. H. Huxley,* Cyril Bibby (ed.), Macmillan, London, 1967, p. 110.

[33] Many agnostics, Spencer and George Romanes for example, cited the conservation of energy as a telling argument against any sort of design in the universe. What happened could be accounted for perfectly well by the persistence of force and the indestructibility of matter.

script, which questioned the authenticity or reliability of key texts, for example, the Pentateuch and Fourth Gospel, and the alleged historical events they reported. But far more important, it taught people to think of religions as historical phenomena, appropriate to a particular time and place, but as outgrowing their original context, as ever changing both in form and content, their "mythology" perhaps at last becoming outmoded. Mrs. Humphry Ward, the author of a popular novel bearing on the subject, called this "the new Reformation." As she wrote in *The Nineteenth Century,* quoting Adolf Harnack, the historian of Christian doctrine:

> We have grown more realistic, more elastic, *the historical temper has developed,* we have acquired the power of transplanting ourselves into other times. . . . Then we have realised that all history is one, that religion and church history is a mere section of the whole history of a period, and cannot be understood except in relation to that whole.[34]

The "historical temper" did not, as it happened, make Mrs. Ward (or Harnack) an agnostic. She remained, as did her clergyman-hero in *Robert Elsmere* (1888), a theist of sorts. But it is easy to see how the historical temper could, and did, promote an agnostic attitude in many others, such as Huxley, who was always referring to it.

Now seen in one light, Darwinian science merely projected this historical picture onto a larger screen. It presented an evolutionary-historical panorama of the entire universe, including prehistory as well as history, and inorganic as well as organic nature. In this universe of perpetual motion, everything was forever changing into something else, and the changes could be accounted for on naturalistic assumptions. Darwinism encouraged men to see everything, not only the animal kingdom, as developing from simple origins in a probable order of evolution and according to the principle of natural selection. Thus, it stimulated, among other things, an evolutionary view of religion and an evolutionary ethics, which, though less spectacular than the famous debate about design and special creation, probably had a more damaging effect on religious belief in the long run.

For the new breed of evolutionary anthropologists, conspicuously E. B. Tylor and Sir James Frazer, traced the origins of religion back to primitive practices and beliefs, such as ancestor worship, totemism, and

[38] Mary A. (Mrs. Humphry) Ward, "The New Reformation," *The Nineteenth Century,* Vol. XXV (March, 1889), p. 473. Italics mine.

animism, and found "survivals" of savage superstition still existing in Christian rites, such as the slain God in the Eucharist. Frazer, author of *The Golden Bough* (first two volumes, 1890), was convinced that religion had become largely outmoded. Religion, according to Frazer, had originated, like magic, as an attempt to explain and control nature. But just as magic had been superseded by religion, so now the latter was being superseded by science, "the golden key" that would unlock the treasury of nature. As an evolutionist, Frazer thought of religion, not as a system of absolutes, but as a temporal phenomenon corresponding to the state of knowledge (or ignorance) at a particular time in history. He felt the same way about morals. "The old view that the principles of right and wrong are immutable and eternal is no longer tenable," he wrote. "The moral world is as little exempt as the physical world from the law of ceaseless change, of perpetual flux."[35]

Archbishop Temple always thought that the Moral Law at least stood firm and was "incapable of being evolved." But evolutionary ethics undercut this position also. On Darwin's model, ethical values were shown to be both relative and progressive, and to have been produced as an aid in the struggle for existence. It is true, as Huxley's career indicates, that Darwinian science could be used in the service of widely divergent ethical theories. At the end of his life, Huxley had reversed his field and was saying that man could evolve a high ethical code only by combatting the cosmic process, which demanded ruthless self-assertion and the treading down of all competitors. In other words, Huxley advocated an "evolution of ethics," rather than an "ethics of evolution." But others, like the aging Spencer, but also W. K. Clifford, the brilliant young mathematician and philosopher; Sir Leslie Stephen, popularizer of Huxley's agnosticism; and the German Monists, tried to work out a "science of ethics," based largely on Darwinian principles.

Clifford was one of those young men who, while still in college, were swept off their feet by a "wave of Darwinian enthusiasm," and who found in natural selection "the master-key of the universe."[36] Applying this key to ethics, he discovered the origins of right and wrong, of "conscience," not in religion, but in tribal development. The moral conceptions of mankind had a social rather than an individual origin. Clifford agreed with Darwin (he had been reading the second and

---

[35] Sir James Frazer, *The Gorgon's Head and Other Literary Pieces,* Macmillan, London, 1927, p. 283.

[36] So Sir Frederick Pollock wrote in the Introduction to *Lectures and Essays by the Late William Kingdon Clifford,* Leslie Stephen (ed.), Macmillan, London, 1901, Vol. I, p. 42.

third chapters of *The Descent of Man*) that man's moral conceptions had been evolved because they were "useful to the tribe or community in the struggle for existence against other tribes, and against the environment as a whole. The function of conscience is the preservation of the tribe as a tribe."[37] Hence, those tribes succeeded best in which the conception of a "Tribal Self" became predominant over more immediate, or mere individual, desires. Clifford was also concerned to show the superiority of evolutionary ethics to religious ethics. Whereas the latter sapped the foundations of patriotism and intellectual honesty, the former emphasized "the social instinct," which is the spring of virtuous action. Perhaps Clifford was not as much of a relativist as he was thought to be at the time. He (and the others too) seemed to be thinking more in terms of stages of ethical belief and practice, leading ultimately to a higher morality recognized by all. It is a fact, however, that many of Clifford's contemporaries feared the relativistic implications of evolutionary ethics and feared that the Moral Law might ultimately fall once people realized that moralities varied from tribe to tribe, depending on conditions. Had not Darwin himself said, in *The Descent of Man,* that if men

> were reared under precisely the same conditions as hive-bees, there can hardly be a doubt that our unmarried females would, like the worker-bees, think it a sacred duty to kill their brothers, and mothers would strive to kill their fertile daughters; and no one would think of interfering.[38]

In conclusion, it should be remarked that the tone of the agnostics varied somewhat. There was some sense of loss, of course, of sadness at the inability to believe any longer in the "cradle-faith," and of loneliness in being flung upon a sea of intellectual and emotional uncertainty. This was true even of Clifford who, however, was more of an atheist than an agnostic, since he lamented the death of "the Great Companion." But, on the whole, the agnostics took their disbelief in stride, and some even exulted. According to George Bernard Shaw, Darwin's friends, himself included at that time, "were intellectually intoxicated with the idea that the world could make itself without design"; it seemed "a glorious enlightenment and emancipation" from

---

[37] W. K. Clifford, "Right and Wrong: The Scientific Ground of their Distinction," ibid., Vol. II, p. 150. See also essays entitled "On the Scientific Basis of Morals," and "The Influence upon Morality of a Decline in Religious Belief."
[38] Darwin, *The Descent of Man,* Pt. I, Chap. IV.

a moribund theology.[39] A less exuberant, but perhaps more normal reaction, was that of Sir Leslie Stephen, an acknowledged agnostic. It was true, he said in an essay on Cardinal Newman, that there was no longer an infallible guide or definitive system of universal truth, as in the days when Christianity flourished. Nevertheless, by reason and science, said Stephen, "we can attain enough truth to secure the welfare and progress of the race and a continual approximation towards a fuller and more definite body of definitive truth."[40]

Social Darwinism

Moving into the sphere of social and historical thought, it becomes particularly important to distinguish between Darwin and Darwinism. Darwin, often compared to Newton, was nevertheless not at all like Newton in one important respect. A rather retiring, vacillating, and even timid man, Darwin did not presume to lay down the law about the universe outside his special province. Not that he had no ideas about religion, history, or even politics. For the most part, however, he kept relatively quiet about them, committing them either to unpublished notes or to personal letters to friends and acquaintances.

Others, however, did what Darwin would not do, and openly applied the new biological ideas to their respective disciplines, particularly in the social sciences. A glance at the volume published by the Cambridge University Press to celebrate the jubilee of *The Origin of Species* is very illuminating in this respect. Roughly a quarter of the articles were on the social sciences, which by that time had come under strong Darwinian influence. Furthermore, during the fifty-year span, a great many books and articles were written, by amateurs as well as specialists, on such subjects as "Social Evolution," "Darwinism and Politics," "The Struggle for Existence in Human Society," and "A Biological View of our Foreign Policy."

But the subject is complicated. As Shaw said, apropos of this Social Darwinism, the author of the *Origin* "had the luck to please everybody who had an axe to grind," both socialists and capitalists, humanitarians (kinship with the animals!), as well as militarists. Darwinism, however, did not merely confirm prejudices that were already formed. It

---

[39] G. B. Shaw, *Back to Methusaleh*, Preface, "How We Rushed Down a Steep Place."

[40] Leslie Stephen, *An Agnostic's Apology and Other Essays*, G. P. Putnam's Sons, New York, 1893, pp. 240–241.

was a powerful influence in its own right, above all, in furthering an evolutionary view of society. It also appeared to lend scientific support to two ideas, which were on the rise in the late nineteenth century, the social organism, and struggle as the chief instrument of social progress, particularly in international affairs.

A French sociologist, writing for the Cambridge jubilee volume, observed that Darwinism was calculated "to further the application of the philosophy of Becoming to the study of human institutions."[41] This was the most important contribution of Darwinism to social thinking, and it greatly accelerated the trend, begun much earlier, toward thinking of society in genetical, rather than primarily in mechanical or "a priorist," terms. It assimilated society, as well as man, to nature, now understood as cosmic process. Darwinism, Professor Bouglé went on to say, enlarged "the sense of universal evolution," of institutions and cultures undergoing constant metamorphosis, in the same way as biological species. In this connection, Bouglé called attention to the work of Edward Burnett Tylor, called the Father of Anthropology, whose key book on *Primitive Culture* appeared in the same year as *The Descent of Man*. To be sure, Tylor did not need Darwin to teach him his evolutionary sociology. Tylor appears, in fact, to have learned much of it from Auguste Comte, whom he mentions, the new uniformitarian geology, and other sources. But Tylor learned from Darwin, too, and, in any event, illustrated admirably, perhaps better than anybody else except Spencer, the degree to which, by 1871, sociology was impregnated by the evolutionary idea. In the opening pages of *Primitive Culture*, Tylor subscribed to the notion, still repulsive to many people, as he observes, that the history of societies was "part and parcel of the history of nature"; that it, too, was subject, like the motion of waves and the growth of plants and animals, to definite laws. Tylor then goes on to describe the "law" of successive stages of culture, each of which "grows or is developed out of the stage before it." Owing to widely acting similar causes, societies tended to follow similar lines of development, to pass through successive stages of savagery, barbarism, and civilization, though in truth, some never did go all the way, and "survivals" were to be found even in civilized societies. Herbert Spencer, protagonist of *laissez-faire,* and Sidney Webb, the socialist, were others who saw society evolving in successive phases. The latter summarized a widely held view when he wrote in 1889:

[41] C. Bouglé, "Darwinism and Sociology," in *Darwin and Modern Science*, A. C. Steward (ed.), Cambridge University Press, Cambridge, 1910, p. 466. Bouglé was professor of sociology in the University of Toulouse.

Owing mainly to the efforts of Comte, Darwin, and Herbert Spencer, we can no longer think of the ideal society as an unchanging State. The social ideal from being static has become dynamic. The necessity of the constant growth and development of the social organism has become axiomatic. No philosopher now looks for anything but the gradual evolution of the new order from the old. . . .[42]

Some social Darwinians went out of their way to disentangle evolution from progress, to point out that changes were not necessarily changes for the better. A few developed real doubts, as, for example, Huxley, who on occasion could be quite morose about social progress. "The theory of evolution encourages no millennial anticipations," he said in the Romanes lecture of 1893. "Ethical nature may count upon having to reckon with a tenacious and powerful enemy [the cosmic process] as long as the world lasts." In the main, however, evolutionists were also progressivists, and took the progressivist side in the debate with the degenerationists, which raged from the 1860's on. Degenerationists, such as Archbishop Whately and the Duke of Argyll, concerned with upholding the Christian theory of creation, stressed the decline of the savage from a previously higher moral state. Evolutionists, Darwin and Tylor included, argued to the contrary, either that present-day savages were more highly developed than their ancestors, or else represented remains, or survivals, of an earlier and lower state of the human race. "Notwithstanding the continual interference of degeneration," Tylor wrote, "the main tendency of culture from primeval up to modern times has been *from savagery towards civilization*," and there was no question in his mind that Europe and America ranked highest in civilization in the contemporary world.[43] This is what Darwin believed, and to some extent even Huxley. For Huxley, though certainly no perfectibilian, did perceive considerable moral as well as intellectual progress in history, and saw "no limit" to what "intelligence and will, guided by sound principles of investigation, and organized in common effort" might achieve in the future. Much might be done, he thought, even "to change the nature of man himself" for the better.[44] Huxley obviously vacillated in his belief in man's progress, even in the same lecture.

[42] Sidney Webb, "Historic," *Fabian Essays in Socialism,* George Allen & Unwin, London, 1931, p. 29.
[43] See the first two chapters of *Primitive Culture* for Tylor's denunciation of the degenerationists, his doctrine of progress, and his ethnocentrism.
[44] T. H. Huxley, "Evolution and Ethics."

Sidney Webb, it will be recalled, wrote of the development of the "social organism." This was the second social idea that Darwinism helped to promote: politics on the analogy of a biological organism, society conceived not merely as evolving, but as able to function successfully only as a genuine whole, as "something more than an aggregate of so many individual units." The social organism idea usually emphasized the state, (it did not do so, however, in Spencer's thought) or collective society, not necessarily as primordial, or superior to, the individual, but as clearly important to individual development, and necessary to the survival of the group. It sometimes carried with it a conviction of human and social inequality. But it was by no means the monopoly of political conservatives, such as the new "integral nationalists" of Germany and France. It was also taken up by socialists, particularly of the evolutionary type, and by the new breed of liberals, headed in England by the Oxford philosopher Thomas Hill Green. It caught on as widely as it did because the times called for a more centrally organized society, whether to sponsor social legislation or to render more effective nationalist aims.

Darwinism was not the only, or the chief, source for the social organism idea, as is evident from a reading of, for example, Heinrich von Treitschke's lectures on *Politics* or Green's books on ethics and political obligation, both of which speak the language of neo-idealism. Yet Webb was not wrong in also coupling the idea with Darwinism, for Darwinism could scarcely help focusing attention on species as wholes, and on the reasons for their survival or extinction. Clifford was one of those who carried this species-thinking over into the field of social thought. His essays were full of organic and Darwinian imagery. The "tribe" (read "species") can exist, Clifford wrote, only by creating in the minds of its members a "Tribal Self," according to which the group's interests take precedence over the "self-regarding" virtues so extolled by the Benthamites. "Society is an organism," Clifford went on to say in another essay, and some portion of human nature is what it is "for the sake of the whole-society." The function of "conscience," our word for that portion, "is the preservation of society in the struggle for existence."[45] Clifford agreed with Darwin's premise (and Green's) that man is a social animal, and built his organicist social philosophy upon it.

Some of the Darwinians also professed belief in the collateral idea of social inequality. As we have seen, Francis Galton, among others,

---

[45] Clifford developed the idea of the Tribal Self in his essay "On the Scientific Basis of Morals." See also "Right and Wrong" for references to Darwin and the social organism.

stressed the biological (hereditary) differences between individuals, and advocated eugenics as a means of improving society. Others, particularly on the continent, used the idea of natural selection to uphold some sort of aristocratic doctrine.[46] Though himself a staunch democrat, Huxley thought that egalitarianism was nonsense, and went out of his way to refute it, partly in Darwinian terms. Toward the close of his life, Huxley was talking the same organicist language as Clifford, emphasizing the life of "the social body" as a whole, and, along with it, strong government and "inequality," which, among other things, meant distrust of the common man in politics. Oddly, he made Rousseau the butt of his attack in an article "On the Natural Inequality of Men" (1890). "The revived Rousseauism of our day," Huxley wrote, "is working sad mischief," teaching people that all men were born free and equal in a hypothetical state of nature.

> Men are certainly not born free and equal in natural qualities; . . . and as they develop, year by year, the differences in the political potentialities with which they really are born, become more and more obviously converted into actual differences—the inequality of political faculty shows itself to be a necessary consequence of the inequality of natural faculty.[47]

Huxley used this asseveration to denounce as hopelessly utopian the scheme for land nationalization currently advocated by Henry George.

Finally, Darwinism, for obvious reasons, gave a strong fillip to the idea, already growing in an age of *Realpolitik* and imperialism, that "warfare" was the law of the social universe. Of course, *laissez-faire* liberals had been saying something like that for a long time, and there is considerable irony in the fact that Darwin's idea of a struggle for existence was partially influenced by liberal doctrine (through Malthusianism), and then reappeared later in liberal doctrine as Darwin's idea. But in liberal doctrine, as for that matter also in early socialist thought, struggle by no means ruled out harmony. Struggle was the means to harmony in the thought of Herbert Spencer. Struggle among individuals

[46] For instance, Vacher de Lapouge who, in *Les Selections sociales* (1896), argued that "social selection" worked against "natural selection," and thus leveled society down unnaturally.

[47] T. H. Huxley, "On the Natural Inequality of Man," *The Nineteenth Century*, Vol. XXVII (January, 1890), p. 10. Generally, in politics Huxley tried to steer a middle course between what he called Anarchism or extreme Individualism (he had read Stirner) and Regimentation. He was a democrat in the sense that he thought democracy best supported freedom of thought and conscience.

and nations was necessary for social evolution. But Spencer predicted that eventually struggle would lose its social utility, as societies evolved from a "militant" to an "industrial" phase, in which there would be peace and cooperation. This was not the new Darwinian thought at all, though Spencer lived very much in the Darwinian world,[48] and was a chief exemplar of the idea of social evolution. But in the new perspective, struggle, construed more aggressively now as "warfare" on the authority of *The Origin of Species,* became the iron law of the universe, promoting progress but not necessarily harmony. It seemed both more scientific and more universal, applying to relations between nations, as well as to individuals within nations.

Prince Kropotkin, himself a scientist, protested against this interpretation of Darwinism. In *Mutual Aid,* written to refute Huxley's thesis in "The Struggle for Existence in Human Society" (1888), Kropotkin said that when he first examined the relations between Darwinism and sociology, he found that he could agree with none of the books or articles dealing with the subject. He had come to believe in a "law of Mutual Aid" in nature, which for the progressive evolution of the species was more important than the "law of Mutual Struggle." Perhaps Kropotkin partly misunderstood Huxley, for what Huxley was trying to say was that "ethical man" must oppose "the natural man" if the human race was ever to achieve a civilized state. That is, a limit must be put on the struggle for existence and "the state of mutual peace" must be substituted for "that of mutual war." Yet it is also true that Huxley was not very sanguine about this happy state ever coming to pass. "The effort of ethical man to work towards a moral end by no means abolished, perhaps has hardly modified, the deep-seated organic impulses which impel the natural man to follow his non-moral course." Huxley also found that as far as the present was concerned, the law of natural selection was still very much at work, among nations as well as among individuals. "In spite of ourselves, we are in reality engaged

---

[48] Spencer, however, was an evolutionist before Darwin, and had his own idea of evolution, which was not primarily Darwinian, though he was on good terms with Darwin and accepted natural selection. In order to formulate a general law of evolution, Spencer drew more on ideas supplied by continental biologists, especially Lamarck and Karl Ernst von Baer. Lamarck's idea of use-inheritance preserved for Spencer the possibility of social progress from one generation to the next. From German physiologists he learned that evolution, social as well as biological, represented advance from the simple to the complex, through differentiation. On Spencer's evolutionism, see J. D. Y. Peel, *Herbert Spencer,* Basic Books, New York, 1971, Chap. 6.

in an internecine struggle for existence with our presumably no less peaceful and well-meaning neighbours," that is, French, Germans, and so on. Good Malthusian that he always was, Huxley traced natural selection back to population and the competition for food and the raw materials of the earth. He spoke of an "eternal competition of man against man, and of nation against nation."[49]

Others, less ambiguous than Huxley, carried this "law" to extremes. Among them was Marx, who found in Darwinism a basis for the class struggle in history. There were also others who, as the historian Meinecke said, converted the idea of the nation into chauvinistic nationalism. Not all these "integral nationalists" rested their arguments on Darwinism. To my knowledge, Maurice Barrès and Charles Maurras among the French, and the German Treitschke did not so much as mention Darwin, nor did they need to do so, since they could draw on native sources, French history, monarchism, or "idealism," as the case might be, for their nationalism. Some national and racial theorists, however, found Darwinism very much to their purpose, as, for example, Félix Le Dantec who described a law of *"combat universel"* in his book on *Les Luttes entre Sociétés humaines* (1893); the Austrian sociologist Ludwig Gumplowicz, who similarly thought that a perpetual struggle of races was "the law of history"; Vacher de Lapouge, who presented his ideas of "social selection" and racial conflict not only in books but in the pages of the *Revue d'anthropologie;* Houston Stewart Chamberlain, Richard Wagner's son-in-law, who while developing his Pan-Teuton ideas, claimed to have completed Darwin's system; and the English scientist Karl Pearson, who, in an address delivered to the Literary and Philosophical Society of Newcastle in 1900, outlined ideas similar to those of Huxley in his essay, but with rather more optimism. England, Pearson told his audience in the context of the Boer War, was engaged in a struggle for existence among the nations of the world and must keep fit or become more fit economically and militarily and in every other way, if she were to survive. Darwin had taught Pearson that nations, like other types of life, were organisms subject to the laws of evolution, and as such, were perforce engaged "in continual struggle," not only to survive but to progress. Struggle, he pronounced, "is the source of human progress throughout world history." "This dependence of progress on the survival of the fitter race, terribly black as it may seem, gives the struggle for existence its re-

---

[49] All these quotations come from "The Struggle for Existence in Human Society."

deeming features; it is the fiery crucible out of which comes the finer metal."[50] No wonder Shaw said years later, apropos of World War I, that social Darwinism "had produced a European catastrophe." Darwin himself was not directly responsible for it nor did Shaw say he was. Some of his disciples, however, out-Darwined Darwin to fan the flames of international rivalry and war.

[50] Karl Pearson, *National Life from the Standpoint of Science,* Adam & Charles Black, London, 1901, pp. 34, 41.

Fin-de-Siècle

Not surprisingly, the phrase *Fin-de-Siècle* was on everyone's lips as the year 1900 approached. Mostly, though its meaning was never very precise, it had reference to the "decadence" of the 1880's and 1890's, and to certain new philosophical and artistic fads, identified by Max Nordau in his book entitled *Degeneration* (among others, Nordau came down hard on Nietzsche and the Symbolists, as well as the Decadents).[1] But since it had wider connotations, the phrase may be used to designate a new world of thought that was beginning to take shape toward the end of the century.

It is important to understand that this world did not supersede the two previous worlds we have just discussed or dominate thought toward and immediately after 1900. The Enlightenment mode, as we may call it, especially as reinterpreted and reinforced by Darwinism, continued to represent the mainstream well into the twentieth century. The placing of a bust of Auguste Comte on the Place de la Sorbonne in Paris in 1902 is symbolic of this continuity (Plate 27). Four years earlier the Sorbonne had celebrated Comte's centenary, and was currently remodeling itself along positivistic lines. Thus, despite the "Revolt against Positivism," positivism was still very nearly at flood tide

---

[1] Nordau was an Austrian doctor of medicine and journalist who lived in Paris. *Degeneration* (*Entartung*), published in 1892, was one of several books by Nordau on the ills of European civilization. It lists some of the ways the term *"Fin-de-Siècle"* was used at the time.

PLATE 27. *Bust of Auguste Comte,* by Jean-Antoine Injalbert, and *Place de la Sorbonne,* Paris.

(*Photo: French Embassy Press and Information Division, New York.*)

as an organized movement and was capable of renewing itself, though along more radical lines, in the "logical positivism" of Bertrand Russell and Ludwig Wittgenstein to come. The main body of social scientists and social reformers, as well as a substantial number of humanists, similarly expressed confidence in science or in reason to achieve progress.[2] Speaking at the International Freethinkers Conference in Rome in 1904, Ernst Haeckel, the German Monist and a socialist, spoke of "the wonderful height of culture, which man achieved in the nineteenth century, the astonishing progress of natural science and its practical application in technology, industry, medicine, etc.," which he said had raised hopes for "a mighty, further elevation of culture in the twentieth century."[3] L. T. Hobhouse, holder of the first chair in sociology at London University, said much the same thing in his *Mind in Evolution* (1901). Hobhouse looked forward to a *"regnum hominis,"* based on the mastery of external nature, made possible by science, and by man himself. In other words, the human mind had reached a new stage of evolution, which put the future under the control of reason. It was this kind of thinking that prompted Sir Norman Angell, on the eve of Sarajevo, to predict the end of war among civilized nations. Angell, like Hobhouse, subscribed to a "Law of Acceleration" of human rationality. War was now an "illusion" because, contrary to what the militarists said, human nature *had* changed; man had become more rational and civilized in the last one hundred years than in the preceding two thousand.[4] These were not voices left over, like Tylor's "survivals," from an earlier and now outdated stage of culture. They spoke for the majority, for an *Anschauung* that was still vigorous even in innermost intellectual circles.

This *Anschauung,* however, was in serious dispute by the end of the nineteenth century. As indicated, a new world of thought had risen to challenge its most basic assumptions. This world, as yet not sharply defined nor fully conscious of itself, is not easy to describe. *Fin-de-Siècle* only imperfectly describes it, for strictly speaking this world represented not so much an end as a beginning. That is, it contained within it the seeds of a new kind of modernity that was very different from scientific-rationalistic modernity, which would grow to maturity as the twentieth

---

[2] On the continuing belief in progress, see W. Warren Wagar, *Good Tidings,* Indiana University Press, Bloomington, 1972, Part Two.

[3] Ernst Haeckel, "Der Monistenbund: Thesen zur Organisation des Monismus," *Das freie Wort,* Vol. IV, p. 489.

[4] *The Great Illusion,* a famous book, appeared in 1910. Angell was an economist and journalist.

century unfolded. It was an end only in the sense of bringing to a head, and exposing to public gaze, certain trends in thinking that had been forming for decades. It was a world in revolt, not only against positivism but against the whole pattern of bourgeois values and conventions and bourgeois rationalism and conventionality in general. But it was above all a disoriented world (or one trying to stave off disorientation). In Nietzsche's metaphor, Europeans had cast themselves adrift, burning their bridges behind them and putting out to sea in ships. Before them stretched the open sea, mysterious, infinite, and dangerous. If homesickness for solid land should overtake them they were in serious difficulty, for there was no longer such land. Nietzsche, to be sure, was speaking only of a minority of "free spirits." He knew perfectly well that "most people in old Europe" still needed, and still clung to, the supports of religion, metaphysics, or science. Nobody, however, could expect to live for long in comfortable certainty. "Perhaps never before [in history] did such an open sea exist."[5] This *unprecedented openness,* observed by Nietzsche, was the culmination of a century of critical thought and corrosive doubt, but also, as we shall see, of the Heraclitean aspect of Darwinism. Disorientation, more radical than in any previous epoch, was its inevitable accompaniment: a feeling of not quite knowing where certainty lay, or even if there was a certainty, other than change itself, and of not knowing what the future might bring.

This disorientation could be either an invitation to new "experience" or cause for despair. Nietzsche himself exulted in the new openness despite its hazards, as did Henri Bergson who based his Philosophy of Change on it. All the Life-philosophers, as well as the "spiritualists" and idealists of the *Fin-de-Siècle,* were, in fact, quite optimistic, though scarcely untroubled. In their own peculiar way, even the Decadents reacted positively to a world in which change and flux appeared to be the only certainty. At least, one could, like Marius the Epicurean, "count upon the present," and fill it to the brim with vivid sensations.[6] Yet the decades of the 1880's and 1890's were also full of footloose, restless, and pessimistic people. The scions of an older generation, the Renans and Burckhardts, were perhaps not so much disoriented as disillusioned, some by knowledge itself, which, they had come to believe, might be incompatible with happiness, and others by the quality of the civilization they saw developing around them. "Les jeunes gens," the subject of essays and novels by leading figures of the French literary

---

[5] Friedrich Nietzsche, *The Gay Science* (1882), Sects. 124, 343, 347, 377.
[6] The reference is to Walter Pater's novel *Marius the Epicurean* (1885). See especially Chap. IX on "The New Cyrenaicism."

world such as Paul Bourget and Maurice Barrès, simply felt lost and could think of nothing better, at the moment, than to cultivate the self. Barrès called them *"Les Déracinés"* (the Uprooted). Of course, there were special reasons why Frenchmen of that particular generation should be pessimistic. They knew the worst, humiliation as well as horror, following the defeat of their country by Prussia in 1871, and the ensuing class warfare and bloodbath of the Paris Commune. But there were deeper reasons for the contemporary *malaise,* which was by no means restricted to Frenchmen. Frederic Myers, just then straining to find reasons for personal immortality in a godless world, called attention to "the underlying *Welt-Schmerz* (in 'our civilised societies'), the decline of any real belief in the dignity, the meaning, the endlessness of life"—this in the midst of a world pledged, as he recognized, to the pursuit of sanity, health, intelligence, and morality.[7] Thus, whereas some denizens of the *Fin-de-Siècle* exulted, others despaired or became world-weary. Some of the latter, it should be noted, eventually found a road back to belief and purpose, chiefly (in France at least) through Roman Catholicism or nationalism.

Translated into ideas, this disorientation, whether evoking a positive or negative mood, inevitably fashioned new answers to the perennial questions. Bergson, among others, postulated a new sort of indeterminate nature that was very different from "positivist" nature. Human nature simultaneously began to look less rational, knowledge more subjective and elusive, and history less predictable and understandable. The overall trend in thinking was toward a more chancy universe, subject to change without end or ends. It was a trend only, but it was a trend with a future. To repeat, the *Fin-de-Siècle* represented neither a unified nor a dominant mode of thought. It remained enclosed within the larger world, still potent, of Enlightenment expectation.

The Revolt Against Positivism

The new ideas about nature are best considered in connection with the revolt against positivism. This revolt, which began at least as early as the 1860's and culminated in the 1890's, occurred on a very broad front. By the time the French philosopher Alfred Fouillée wrote a book about it in 1896, the revolt against positivism numbered among

---

[7] Frederic W. H. Myers, *Human Personality and Its Survival of Bodily Death* (1903), Longmans, Green, & Co., London, 1915, Vol. II, p. 279. Myers (1843–1901), poet and essayist, was a founder of the Society for Psychical Research.

its adherents some of the best intellects of Europe, scientists as well as philosophers, social thinkers as well as creative writers and artists. Paul Bourget made it the subject of a celebrated novel, *The Disciple* (1889).

What was the revolt about? It was essentially a reaction against the cult of science and the world picture projected by science, which, it was believed, denigrated life and mind. One is reminded of an earlier revolt, and the late nineteenth-century reaction did, indeed, have at times a neo-romantic look, as for instance in Bergson's doctrine of intuition. It was not, however, so much a revolt against science *per se* as against scientism. More specifically, it centered on science's putative claim to take all knowledge for its province, and on the idea of determinism, or "the tightening grasp of law," which, it was thought, impeded freedom.

"The extension of science to everything which hitherto had been excluded from its domain," Fouillée observed, "was the nub of the positivist movement."[8] It was inevitable that sooner or later this imperialism should be challenged. James Ward, the English psychologist, challenged it in the famous Gifford Lectures. "But where is science to end?" Ward expostulated. Like Descartes, he compared science to the town. Townlike "in its compactness and formality, in the preeminence of number and measurement, systematic connexion, and constructive plan," science had steadily encroached on other realms of knowledge, in the same way that the town had extended its sway over the country.[9] But now a reverse process had set in, seeking to reclaim some of the lost territory. Ward himself, refusing to subordinate his own discipline to either mechanics or physiology, proclaimed a new subjectivist psychology. Similarly, Ward's countryman the idealist philosopher T. H. Green resisted the temptation, very strong in the Darwinian world, to treat ethics as a branch of biology. Impressive attempts were also made to give history autonomy, and to seek new and less "positivistic" guidelines in social thought. Comte, Mill, and Buckle, said Wilhelm Dilthey, mutilated historical reality "in order to adapt to the ideas and methods of the natural sciences." History differed from science, both as to subject matter and method. Like all "human studies," history was concerned with man and the human mind, rather than physical reality, with the individual as such and not merely the type, and with values, from which science was understandably free. Hence, apprehending his-

[8] Alfred Fouillée, *Le mouvement idéaliste et la réaction contre la science positive*, Germer Baillière & Cie., Paris, 1896, pp. x–xi.

[9] James Ward, *Naturalism and Agnosticism*, A. & C. Black, London, 1899, Vol. I, p. 5. The Gifford Lectures were delivered in 1896–1898.

tory depended, not so much on perception and abstraction, as on "understanding" (*Verstehen*), that is, on the ability to relive, to enter sympathetically into, the experience of other men, human beings like ourselves. This distinction between the two cultures was made many times in the late nineteenth century, especially by the neo-idealists. Benedetto Croce thought that history was an art, focusing on knowledge of the individual. In a similar vein, the philosopher Wilhelm Windelband, in a famous address of 1894, labeled history an "ideographic" study, dealing with the individual, whereas science was "nomothetic," in search of general laws. Despite important differences between them, all these works[10] aimed to confine science within its so-called legitimate field.

But exactly what was that field? The antipositivists, not content to stay on the defensive, carried the fight into science's innermost citadel, the knowledge of nature itself. And here, as it happened, they received unexpected support from some of the scientists. Science was currently re-examining its foundations, partly as the result of new empirical findings, partly also because of the "back to Kant" movement in philosophy. Starting from the Kantian limitation of knowledge to phenomena, a group of philosopher-scientists, most of whom were German, moved to purge science of all metaphysical vestiges, to limit it to sensible experience and ultimately to question whether it could ever be wholly free of subjectivism. This line of thinking, pursued by Ernst Mach, J. B. Stallo, and others, did not at all question the scientific enterprise. It did, however, dispute science's ability to reveal the actual workings of nature and the reality of some of its working concepts, such as matter, energy, and mechanical causation. It limited science, to a far greater extent than an earlier positivism, to a more or less instrumentalist function, featuring practical results rather than the exact representation of reality.

Meanwhile, philosophy was coming to similar conclusions. Philosophy, in fact, now took its revenge on science. Charles Renouvier, leader of the neo-critical school in France, attacked the presumption of the positivists, not only to cultural superiority (as representatives, so Comte had claimed, of the latest and highest stage of civilization) but also to absolute knowledge that was uncolored by the consciousness or

---

[10] They were all published within a few years of each other: Dilthey's *Introduction to the Human Studies* (*Einleitung in die Geistenwissenschaften*, 1883), Croce's *History subsumed under the Concept of Art* (*La Storia ridotta sotto il concetto generale dell'Arte*, 1893), and Windelband's *History and Science* (*Geschichte und Naturwissenschaft*, 1894).

"freedom" of the knower. Henri Bergson, the last of a long line of "spiritualist" philosophers going all the way back to Felix Ravaisson and Lachelier in the 1860's and 1870's, pressed this argument further. The scientific intellect, he said, was faultily constructed for acquiring absolute knowledge. It had been produced in the course of evolution as an appendage to the faculty of acting, as a chief aid to the vertebrates, up through man, to adapt themselves to the environment and to manipulate it. Its purpose, in short, was "to think matter," not to comprehend life. "What is the essential object of science? It is to enlarge our influence over things. . . . It is always practical utility that science has in view."[11] That being so, not intellect but "intuition" alone could give man a true knowledge of nature and life. Intuition, which Bergson defined as instinct become conscious of itself, entered right into its object, whereas intellect could only walk around it and take snapshots of selected "states" and "instants." "We must break with scientific habits," Bergson concluded, if we are ever to form a clear idea of nature as it really is.[12] Other contemporary "philosophers" like Samuel Butler and Nietzsche, who were more skeptical than Bergson, downgraded scientific truth without compensating for it by any sort of intuitive truth. Butler, who protested the domination of culture by scientists as well as priests, compared science to religion. Neither yielded, or could yield, truth. They were merely conventions, theories on which men could act, varying, therefore, with personal perspective and with the times and new needs. Nietzsche also, though he certainly admired it more than Butler, came to think that science was illusion. It has begun to dawn on a few people, he wrote in *Beyond Good and Evil,* "that physics, too, is only an interpretation of the world and an arrangement of it (to suit ourselves, if I may say so!)—and not an explanation of it."[13] Science, no less than religion, metaphysics, and art, rested on fictions (such as causation and the atom). It could produce power, but not truth.

Behind this debate over science's domain stood the real target of the antipositivists' attack. This was science's idea of nature, which was presumed to be mechanistic. "We reject radical mechanism," said

---

[11] Henri Bergson, *Creative Evolution,* Arthur Mitchell (trans.), Random House (Modern Library), New York, 1944, p. 358.

[12] Bergson, it should be added, intended no denial of science, but only, like some of the romantics, a denial of mechanistic science as a complete explanation of nature.

[13] Nietzsche, *Beyond Good and Evil* (1886), no. 14. (Translation by Arthur C. Danto, *Nietzsche as Philosopher,* Macmillan, New York, 1968, p. 87.)

Bergson. For Bergson and the other antipositivists, mechanism conjured up a particularly revolting set of images: "the tightening grasp of law," in T. H. Huxley's phrase, the reduction of life to physical categories, thus excluding freedom and value and leading in the end to moral irresponsibility, as Bourget tried to show in *The Disciple*.[14] But for Bergson, mechanistic explanation erred, above all, in affirming a static nature, which took no account of "time." That is, it regarded future and past as calculable functions of the present. In the astronomer Pierre Laplace's classic formulation, cited by James Ward as well as by Bergson, nothing could be without a cause to produce it. Hence, if for a given instant an intelligence should be acquainted with all the causes, it could include in one formula all the movements of all the bodies, large and small, in the universe; "nothing would be uncertain for it, and the future, like the past, would be present to its eyes." Bergson objected to "finalism," that is, teleology, as well as mechanism, for the same reason. In either case, "all is given"; the forces by which nature is animated are all fixed and prearranged.[15]

Bergson rejected the mechanical theory in favor of a "creative" nature that was characterized by time rather than space. Time was the chief new dimension. Both ancient and modern science degraded time, the former by comparing it unfavorably with timeless and motionless essence, the latter by restricting it to abstract clock time, which, because it was uniform like space, could not produce anything new. Bergson, to the contrary, thought of time as synonymous with novelty. "Time is invention or it is nothing at all. But of time-invention [modern] physics can take no account, restricted as it is to the cinematographical method,"[16] that is, taking snapshots of a still reality.

Bergson's universe was obviously inspired by Darwinism, but it was Darwin's creative aspect, not its mechanism, that caught and held the philosopher's attention. In *Creative Evolution* (1907), Bergson's masterpiece, evolution is explained by a vital impetus (*élan vital*),

---

[14] In *Le Disciple* Paul Bourget confronted the problem of science versus morality. Adrien Sixte, "an intellectual hermit," and a positivist educated in the doctrines of Hippolyte Taine, the positivist philosopher Maximilien Littré, and Darwin, devotes his life to the dissection of human emotion and behavior. His books, bearing titles such as *Psychologie de Dieu, Anatomie de la volonté,* and *Théorie des passions,* reduce religion and psychology to physical laws and teach a "Mohammedan fatalism." In the actions of his young disciple, Robert Greslou, accused of seduction and murder, Sixte's dehumanized teaching is shown to have the worst possible moral consequences.

[15] Henri Bergson, op. cit. (see note 11), pp. 43–45.

[16] Ibid., p. 371.

which is the mysterious source and force of life, pushing life to ever higher and more complex forms. Bergson thought of the *élan vital* as an explosive force, comparable to a shell suddenly bursting into fragments, which, themselves becoming shells, burst in their turn, "and so on for a time incommensurably long." Thus, philosophy, going beyond science, sees nature as it really is, as "a simple flux, a continuity of flowing, *a becoming.*"[17] With Bergson, being had at last been identified with becoming, which, however, he accounted for by a nonmechanistic principle.

Creative Evolution, made famous by Bergson's lectures and books, picked up a considerable following, chiefly among the young. It was, however, only one of many vitalistic philosophies of nature (life philosophies), which abounded in the *Fin-de-Siècle.* Despite some difference of opinion about teleology, all the "spiritualist" philosophers of France emphasized nature's essential contingency, spontaneity, and creativity. Jean Marie Guyau, for instance, who was Fouillée's stepson and collaborator, actually anticipated Bergson's *élan vital* with his own "expansion of life" philosophy, which admitted no *prévision,* only *nouveauté* in the universe. No wonder Nietzsche found in Guyau, whose books he read and annotated, a kindred soul. Years before Bergson, Samuel Butler similarly tried to work out a theory of evolution based on life or "cunning," as opposed to "luck." Preferring Lamarck (or what he understood to be Lamarck's views) to Darwin,[18] Butler hitched evolutionary change to the volitional activity of a life force. Organisms, instead of merely reacting automatically to changes in the environment, *willed* to reshape their bodies, and thus to improve themselves. In the course of geologic time, this desire became "unconscious memory" and was passed on through heredity. It was essentially this Butlerian philosophy that Shaw began to expound in *Man and Superman* (1903). Following Butler, but also going beyond him, Shaw (or Don Juan in the play) thought of Life as a raw force making innumerable experiments in organizing itself, as initially evolving bodily organs such as the eye, but as now evolving further "a mind's eye that shall see, not the physical world, but the purpose of Life,"[19]

[17] Ibid., p. 401.

[18] The whole subject of Lamarckism needs further investigation. A student of mine, Clark Dougan, is presently doing a study of "The Evolutionary Alternative," that is, of Lamarck and Lamarckism in late nineteenth-century French and English thought. Spencer was a Lamarckian (see p. 392, note 48), as also were, after a fashion, Freud and Engels, Bergson and Shaw, though all for rather different reasons.

[19] G. B. Shaw, *Man and Superman,* Act III, Don Juan in Hell.

and thus produce higher and higher individuals. Shaw's "vitality with a direction" was obviously more teleological than Bergson's or even Butler's version of evolution. Nevertheless, the resemblance between the life philosophies of the three is striking. All three thought dualistically, of life or will as acting creatively on matter and bending it to its purposes. Meanwhile, vitalism was making something of a comeback within science itself. Discredited earlier, it now found new champions in biologists such as Hans Driesch and Jacob Johann Uexküll. Driesch, for example, experimenting on sea urchins and discovering the marvelous restorative qualities of injured cells, concluded that organisms were fundamentally different from machines and hence could not be explained by mechanistic causality. There must be at work, in the life and formation of the organism, some sort of nonmechanical agency, which Driesch called successively a "soul,"[20] "psychoid," and "entelechy." He, too, thought in dualistic terms. The entelechy, itself nonspatial, "acted so to speak into space"; itself supersensible (though not outside nature), it used physico-chemical forces to achieve the life of the organism as a whole, and as an individual.

Thus, the Revolt against Positivism struck a blow against determinism and reductionism in nature. Perhaps it was partially based on a misunderstanding. Science, at least in theory, eschewed metaphysics. Moreover, as previously noted, a new breed of scientist-philosopher tended to think of mechanism, no longer as truth but simply as a tool of thought. This latter trend received added support with the appearance of Hans Vaihinger's *The Philosophy of 'As-If'* (published in 1911, but submitted as a dissertation in 1877) which asserted, among other things, that most scientific concepts were fictions, consciously adopted by scientists "as if" they were true in order to further scientific research. Of course, there were many others who, like the physiologist Jacques Loeb, continued to think of mechanism as truth, and, indeed, carried this view to extremes. Loeb, who was born in the same year as Bergson (1859), founded a science of animal tropisms and looked forward to the time when life itself, and psychic phenomena such as "free will," would be explained physicochemically. It was against this sort of extreme statement of the mechanistic thesis, articulated in books such as Loeb's *The Mechanistic Conception of Life* (1912), that the antipositivists rebelled. The novelist Thomas Hardy is an example of a man who found the "positivistic" view (for him this meant Darwinian evolution, understood mechanistically) repellent but true. Like the

---

[20] See Driesch's *Die Seele als elementarer Naturfaktor* (1903).

poet James Thomson in *City of Dreadful Night,* Hardy found "alone Necessity supreme" in an impersonal and meaningless universe. "The more we know of the laws and nature of the Universe," he wrote to a friend in 1902, "the more ghastly [and senseless] a business one perceives it all to be,"[21] but, unfortunately, there was nothing to be done about it. Butler, on the other hand, was one of those who found the new view repellent but untrue. It is hard to say what Butler ultimately believed, or whether he thought it possible to resolve any philosophical inquiry. But, Darwinism to the contrary, and even though it might involve contradiction, Butler clearly wanted to keep the door open to "free-will, cunning, spontaneity, individuality" in the universe. Otherwise, man as well as nature would be delivered up to "necessity, luck, fate," and surely this could not be true.[22] It was this accent on freedom and free will that made Bergson's lectures at the Collège de France so popular and uplifting. In the words of Raïssa Maritain, who as a student heard him lecture, "Bergson dissipated the anti-metaphysical prejudices of a pseudo-scientific positivism and recalled the mind to its real function, to its essential liberty."[23]

Irrational Man

Actually, however, the major new emphasis was on human irrationality rather than freedom, though in some instances, in the case of Bergson, for example, the two went together. The evidence is quite conclusive on this point. The *Fin-de-Siècle* was a time of general unmasking, of trying to get behind man's rational facade, or, as some preferred to say, of exploring the unconscious self, which might or might not lead to more freedom. This exploration was undertaken simultaneously by scores of philosophers, psychologists, and artists, and the results, by no means all flattering to human dignity, left rational man rocking on his pedestal.

This revolt against reason, as it may be called, ran parallel to the

[21] Quoted in William R. Rutland, *Thomas Hardy,* Russell & Russell, New York, 1962, p. 64.

[22] Butler was always arguing with himself about free will and necessity. See, for example, the section in *The Note-Books,* Jonathan Cape, London, 1926, pp. 322–326.

[23] Raïssa Maritain, *Souvenirs,* quoted in Phyllis Stock, "Students versus The University in Pre-World War Paris," *French Historical Studies,* Vol. VII, No. 1 (Spring, 1971), p. 98. Raïssa Maritain was the Catholic philosopher Jacques Maritain's wife.

revolt against positivism, which, indeed, partly explains the new philosophic emphasis on "intuition," as well as the opening up of a whole new subjective world by the symbolists and expressionists. August Strindberg, who epitomizes these new artistic trends, wrote in his autobiography that though as a young man he had become conversant with the natural sciences and thought himself a Darwinian, since then he had "come to recognize the deficiencies of a scientific method that recognizes the machine-like structure of the universe without admitting the existence of a machinist."[24] Henceforth, Strindberg, like so many of his artist contemporaries, began to ransack the unconscious and to write "dream plays," which could presumably tell so much more about life and human nature than the naturalistic drama, in which he, like Henrik Ibsen, had hitherto excelled. But this sort of neo-romanticism does not explain other manifestations of the revolt. In a penetrating brief essay on "Freud in his Historical Setting," Carl Jung links Freud and Nietzsche together as coming at the end of the Victorian era, which had a tendency "to see everything in a rosy light and yet to describe everything *sub rosa*." It was Freud's and Nietzsche's function to unmask this bourgeois hypocrisy and expose "the possible dark side of the human psyche."[25] Though in this particular essay Jung chose to emphasize Freud's destructive function, there is truth in what he says. Darwinism was another influence in the same direction, as Freud himself recognized later in his life. By calling attention to animal origins, Darwinism, as noted in the last section, stimulated study of the primitive and instinctual in man. To some extent, contemporary political events did the same thing. Social theorists as well as politicians could scarcely fail to take note of, and to conjure with, man's irrational behavior in the mass, in an age of increased social unrest and international conflict.

Obviously, however, the irrational meant different things to different people, and could inspire either optimism or pessimism. Bergson, often paired off against Descartes in French philosophy, was one of those who rejoiced in its promise. Intuition was the way to truth and could liberate and integrate the human personality. In his early work, Berg-

[24] August Strindberg, *Inferno, Alone and Other Writings,* Evert Sprinchorn (ed.), Doubleday Anchor Books, Garden City, N.Y., 1968, p. 143. Strindberg is recalling (in *Inferno,* 1897) "the great event of the Paris season" of 1895, when the literary critic Ferdinand Brunetière announced, in a famous essay, the bankruptcy of science. By that time Strindberg had acquired a considerable reputation as an amateur chemist.

[25] See C. G. Jung, *The Spirit in Man, Art, and Literature,* Pantheon Books, New York, 1966, pp. 35, 38–39.

son posited the existence of two selves, the surface or everyday self revealed by rational analysis, and the self of depth, or the unconscious self. The latter could be reached only by deep introspection, "which leads us to grasp our inner states as living things, constantly becoming, as states not amenable to measure." When this happens, which is all too seldom, we become free, capable of deciding and acting with the whole self, with the self that is not fashioned by society or reason. Bergson spoke of "the darkness of the night in which the intellect leaves us," which he compared with the light thrown by intuition on "the place we occupy in the whole of nature, on our origin and perhaps also on our destiny."[26] Bergson's nearest kin in this optimistic line of thinking were the "spiritualist" philosophers, who similarly thought intuition superior to intellect as a guide to certain kinds of knowledge and action. There is not only similarity but also some filiation, at this point with the thought of earlier romantics such as Maine de Biran.

Nietzsche's irrationalism was less purely optimistic and less concerned with knowledge than action. In his ruthless laying bare of human motives Nietzsche resembled Dostoevski. That man does not behave the way the Benthamites said he did, always in pursuit of pleasure or his own advantage; that far from behaving rationally at all times, he often chooses chaos and destruction; that he lies about himself and to himself: all these things had been said in Dostoevski's *Notes from the Underground* (1864) and were said again by Nietzsche. "The largest part of conscious thinking," Nietzsche wrote, "must be considered an instinctual activity, even in the case of philosophical thinking."[27] Behind logic stood value judgments, which, in turn, masked "the basic desires of man" for power, salvation, or revenge. But in Nietzsche's anthropology, cynicism about man as he is (or what "reason" tells him he is) was compensated for by optimism about man as he could be, if only he exercised fully the will to power. The will to power was basic to all men and all cultures. But in the present sad state of latter-day Christian culture it was applicable only to the few, not certainly to "the herd," who were content as always to conform to the will of others and to live in mediocrity. Thus, the will to power was an essentially aristocratic conception. Nietzsche defined it variously as the instinct of freedom, of self-overcoming, or of aspiring to a higher state of being. It was not identical with the "free will" discussed endlessly by bourgeois philosophers and by Christians. It was a more basic will, underlying and using

[26] Henri Bergson, *Time and Free Will* (*Essai sur les données immédiates de la conscience,* 1889, Conclusion). See also *Creative Evolution* (see note 11), p. 292.
[27] Nietzsche, *Beyond Good and Evil,* no. 3.

both reason and passion to achieve its ends. What ends? The point is that for Nietzsche there were no fixed ends, nor was there any fixed human nature. Historicism entered into his thinking on the matter. All philosophers, he wrote, share the common error of thinking of

> 'man' as an eternal verity, as something abiding in the whirlpool, as a sure measure of things. Everything that the philosopher says about man, however, is at bottom no more than a testimony about the man of a very limited period. Lack of a historical sense is the original error of all philosophers.[28]

In the end, however, Nietzsche's conception was more existentialist than historicist. He was not only saying that human nature changed with the times. More deeply, he was saying that man had the power to make himself and the world over. Zarathustra calls man "a bridge and not an end," an "arrow of longing" for the further shore. Even more than Bergson, Nietzsche stands out as the philosopher of becoming. "Your will and your valuations you have placed on the river of becoming," Zarathustra told his companions,[29] and the river would never cease to flow and change into something different.

Sigmund Freud, also a great unmasker, leaned more toward the pessimistic end of the spectrum. He was not, of course, a philosopher, but a scientist, who, moreover, started out in the mechanist camp and tried to reduce psychology to neurophysiology. He soon discovered, however, that physiological psychology could not take him into the mysterious reaches of the mind he wanted to investigate. Freud was soon to say categorically, in a very different vein, that the unconscious, not in the least measurable or even directly observable, was "the true psychic reality." In *The Interpretation of Dreams* (1900), his first big independent work, Freud proposed "a return from the over-estimation," by philosophers and psychologists alike, "of the property of consciousness" in the course of psychic events. "We are probably much too inclined to overestimate the conscious character even of intellectual and artistic production," he wrote. In fact, consciousness, that is, rationality as traditionally understood, functioned only as "a sense-organ for the perception of psychic qualities."[30] Anybody who took the trouble to

[28] Nietzsche, *Human, All-Too-Human* (1878), no. 2 (Walter Kaufmann's translation).

[29] Nietzsche, *Thus Spake Zarathustra* (1883–1884), speech "On Self-Overcoming."

[30] See the concluding section of *The Interpretation of Dreams,* entitled "The Conscious and Unconscious Reality."

analyze dreams, or observe the psychic life of a neurotic, could see that the most complicated operations of thought went on at a deeper level, both by day and night, often without arousing consciousness at all. For Freud this was a somewhat pessimistic conclusion, because it was tied to his newly worked out theory of repression, which implied mental conflict and the individual's refusal to recognize reality.

Throughout these early years Freud's reputation did not stand particularly high among his peers, no doubt because, as he said, he "disturbed the world's sleep" with his theories of sex repression and neurosis. The isolation Freud felt should not, however, blind us to the fact that the contemporary mental climate also gave him some much needed support. Indeed, without that support much of his work might not have been possible. As Lancelot Whyte says, the general conception of unconscious mental processes had become "fashionable," and even "a European commonplace," by the decade of the 1870's. Freud himself, though convinced that he had discovered a great new world, paid tribute to some of those who had helped him, such as Josef Breuer and Jean Charcot, and, what is more, came to recognize the parallel between certain psychoanalytical investigations and "the insights intuitively won by the philosophers."[31] All this is pretty well known and need not be elaborated on here: the new models of the mind, such as Max Dessoir's double ego and Pierre Janet's dual personality, each positing a layer of mind that escapes the control of "reason"; the new sexual pathology of Freud's contemporary and compatriot Baron Richard von Krafft-Ebing; and the speculations of certain philosophers, notably Eduard von Hartmann, whose *Philosophy of the Unconscious* (1869) ran to many editions and won for its author a considerable notoriety. Hartmann's unconscious, however, was really more of a throwback to earlier romantic metaphysical notions, particularly to Schelling's idea of an unconscious idea behind nature, which advances toward consciousness.

Equally significant, but not so well known, are the parallels in the literary and art worlds. One thinks in this connection of Arthur Schnitzler, like Freud a Viennese and with a medical background, and of Barrès and Marcel Proust, all of them explorers, albeit men of letters, of the hidden depths of the psyche. It was Proust who said, in the overture to his masterpiece *Remembrance of Things Past* (composed before the Great War and having obvious affinities with late

---

[31] Among the philosophers, he singled out Schopenhauer and Nietzsche whom however, he says he consulted only later, after he had formulated his own theory of repression. Still later he chose Empedocles as his favorite philosopher.

nineteenth-century Symbolism) that the individual's past lay hidden "beyond the reach of intellect," and could be recalled only by involuntary memory, set in motion by chance sensations. Proust also said that the world of sleep and dreams was the great reservoir of experience and that in it one not only recaptured past years and forgotten feelings but returned "to the most elemental kingdoms of nature (for it is said that we often see animals in a dream, but one forgets that in it we are ourselves animals, deprived of that reason which projects on things the clear light of certainty). . . ."[32] Proust talked Bergson's language and was much influenced by him, but he was also much more pessimistic about human nature. Many of the themes introduced by Proust and other symbolists would soon become prominent in literature: the profound difference between the "appearance" men present to each other and the "reality" or truth about them, hence the difficulty and even impossibility of ever getting to know or to love anybody, and the multiple and ever changing facets of the human personality.

This dark side of irrational man was made visual in *Fin-de-Siècle* painting, by, for example, Odilon Redon, symbolist painter of dreams and apparitions reminiscent of Goya, and especially by the new breed of expressionists, who, turning away from the outer world of objects, sought to depict inner states, man's "origins," as Redon would say, man stripped down to his most basic emotions. A lithograph of 1885 by Redon entitled *The Swamp Flower. A Sad and Human Face* (Plate 28) and paintings by respectively, James Ensor of Ostend (*Masks Confronting Death,* 1888; Plate 29) and Edvard Munch (*The Scream,* 1893; Plate 30) give some idea of the disconcerting material that frequently appears in works by these artists. In *The Scream,* the human figure is made to merge with the landscape, and one can almost hear the shriek of total anxiety, which the painter thought was endemic to human nature. Like his friend Strindberg, with whom he migrated to Paris in 1889, Munch sensed the fearfulness, loneliness, and wild passions that were located in the depths of the psyche.

As previously mentioned, there was also increasing awareness of the irrational behavior of crowds, as well as of individuals. A cluster of important works on social psychology appeared almost simultaneously with Freud's early studies: Gabriel Tarde's *Laws of Imitation* (1890), Scipio Sighele's *La coppia criminale* (1893), Gustave Le Bon's *The Crowd* (1895), and, a little later, *An Introduction to Social Psychology* (1908) by William McDougall, the Oxford psychologist, who later

[32] Marcel Proust, *A l'Ombre des jeunes filles en fleur,* Part III.

PLATE 28. *The Swamp Flower, a Sad and Human Face,* by Odilon Redon (1885).

Plate II from Hommage à Goya. *Lithograph, printed in black.* $10\frac{13}{16}'' \times 8''$. *Collection, The Museum of Modern Art, New York. Abby Aldrich Rockefeller Purchase Fund. (Photo: Geoffrey Clements.)*

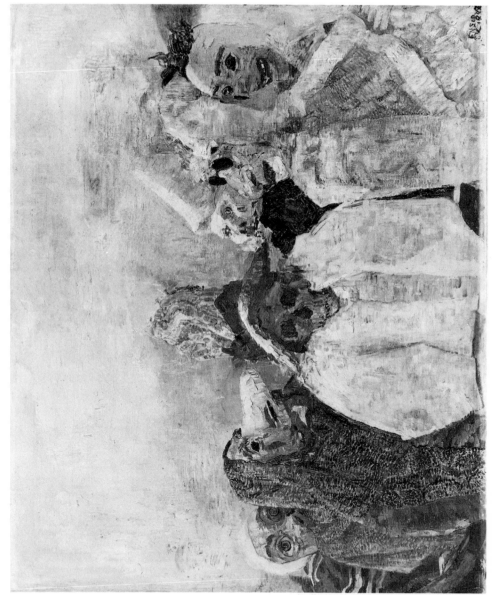

Oil on canvas, 32″ x 39½″. Collection, The Museum of Modern Art, New York. Mrs. Simon Guggenheim Fund.

PLATE 29. *Masks Confronting Death (Masques devant la mort)*, by James Ensor (1888).

PLATE 30. *The Scream,* by Edvard Munch (1893).

taught at Harvard. All of these works save the last drew on current theories of pathological susceptibility and hypnotism, and all were openly in conflict with the rationalistic assumptions of Benthamite psychology. "The substitution of the unconscious action of crowds for the conscious activity of individuals is one of the principal characteristics of the present age," Le Bon wrote. He compared the individual merging with a crowd to a "hypnotised subject" whose rational faculties had been destroyed and who, in consequence, was induced to commit acts that were contrary to his own best interests and those of civilization. In a crowd even a cultivated man became a barbarian, acting by instinct and exhibiting all the spontaneity, violence, and ferocity of "primitive beings."[33] McDougall would certainly not have assented to this pessimistic conclusion—he, in fact, thought rather well of the "group mind," a concept he fancied and of its possibly beneficent effects on individual behavior—nor would Georges Sorel (of whom more in the next section), who understood very well the central importance of irrational myths in mass movements. But all would have agreed with Le Bon's general principle, namely that the part played by reason in collective human action was minor, compared to that of instinct and the unconscious. Graham Wallas, who helped to plan the new London School of Economics and Political Science, applied this insight to politics. In his pioneering *Human Nature in Politics* (1908), Wallas called for a new political science that was based on the realities of human nature, as revealed by Darwin and the new crowd psychologists, rather than on the concepts of Bentham or even of Lord Bryce. It was wrong and dangerous to assume that men always acted from rational motives and could therefore conceivably create an intelligent, disinterested democracy. The truth was that men were still partly animals and formed their political opinions, at least in the present stage of evolution, largely by instinct or by "unconscious or half-conscious inference fixed by habit."

It remains to show how this growing psychologism,[34] along with historicism and skepticism in general, affected the theory of knowledge.

---

[33] Gustave Le Bon, *The Crowd* (*La psychologie des foules*), Macmillan, New York, 1930, pp. 5, 9–10, 33–36. Le Bon was a physician and political conservative as well as a social psychologist. No doubt growing apprehension of mass movements and revolutions, from 1789 through the early days of the French Third Republic, had much to do with the sort of observation to be found in his, and similar contemporary, works.

[34] Psychologism was also the name for a contemporary school of philosophy, opposed to idealism, which posits an objective reality, and to "logicism," which similarly taught that there were "laws" in reality, as well as merely in the mind.

Attention was called earlier to the critique of scientific reason among the antipositivists. It is not sufficiently realized that this critique extended to rational cognition in general, and that it was pressed by rationalists as well as by irrationalists. It is still too early to speak of epistemological despair (except perhaps in the case of Nietzsche, and Nietzsche did not despair, except about epistemology). There is no question, however, that epistemology was becoming a major problem again, even for rationalist philosophers. How and to what extent could the intellect rise above subjective and cultural perspectives, and attain universally valid truths? Unless this problem could be resolved satisfactorily, a real crisis in knowledge was in prospect.

Again, it was the Germans, some of whom have already been mentioned, who met the epistemological problem head on. In general, they compromised, continuing to believe in the possibility of rational and objective cognition, yet obviously bothered by relativist implications. The neo-Kantians, including Heinrich Rickert of Baden, were the most confident in this respect; Dilthey, and, a bit later, Ernst Troeltsch, and especially Max Weber, less so. Rickert has been called "the father of historical relativism." Nevertheless, he seems to have clung to a belief in "unconditionally and universally valid values," and to a belief in the power of the human mind to discover what they were. Dilthey was not so sure. The scholar could indeed study, know, and classify the value systems of different ages of history; but he had no way of testing their validity, unless it was by comparing what they had in common. In other words, cognition was limited, by man's position in history as well as by his individuality, which always sees things in a unique way. Dilthey saw the need for "universally valid cognition," but did not think that man could probably achieve it. What impressed him, above all else, was the flux of things: "the finitude of every historical phenomenon, whether it be a religion, an ideal, or a philosophic system, hence the relativity of every sort of human conception about the connectedness of things." Where were the means for overcoming this "anarchy of convictions"?[35] The young Edmund Husserl, later to become famous as the founder of philosophical phenomenology, tried to refute this "skeptical relativism" in lectures delivered at Göttingen in 1896. He singled out for special attack the psychologism of Christoph Sigwart, Wilhelm Wundt, pioneer of the new laboratory psychology "without a soul" at Leipzig, B. Erdmann, and others, which reduced

---

[35] From a speech by Dilthey to students and friends on the occasion of his seventieth birthday (1903). Quoted in George G. Iggers, *The German Conception of History*, Wesleyan University Press, Middletown, Conn., 1968, pp. 143–144.

logic and truth to psychology, that is, to changing "mental constitutions" and groups of facts. Husserl, who had himself started out as a psychologistic philosopher, thought that this was nonsense, but his lectures testify to the spread of relativistic ideas among contemporary philosophers.

An artistic parallel to philosophical relativism may be found in late impressionistic painting. Claude Monet exhibits this new perspectivism or relativism in art in his famous studies, begun in the 1890's, of haystacks, water lilies, the Thames River, and especially Rouen Cathedral, whose facade he painted many times in different lights and at different times of the day (Plates 31 and 32). Despite his continuing naturalism, Monet now perceived, much more clearly than before, that nature presented many modes of appearance and was always changing. "Nature," he wrote from his new home at Giverny in 1894, "is changing so rapidly at the moment, it is agonizing. With that, I dare not touch the cathedrals." He was also accused, as well as praised, by contemporaries for having destroyed the illusion of distance, and merging, in Seitz's words, "subject, sensation, and pictorial object." That is, Monet was now painting sensations as well as appearances. One has only to look at still later works of Monet, done when he was half-blind, to see the direction in which he was going. In, for instance, the sequence of Japanese footbridge canvases, of sometimes wild and hallucinated landscapes, Monet had obviously gone over "from impressionism to an art in which nature was re-formed according to distorted vision and anguish."[36] The tide of relativism had risen in the *Fin-de-Siècle,* and would rise still higher in the twentieth century.

The Illusions of Progress

The title and substance of a book by Georges Sorel point to a major change that had also come over historical and social thinking in the late nineteenth century. In *The Illusions of Progress* (1908), actually a loose collection of articles written originally for a socialist journal, Sorel denounced the idea of progress, not merely as bourgeois dogma but as "illusion," as philosophically false, as conveying a completely false view of the historical process. To keep the right perspective on Sorel's polemic, it is well to recall again that belief in progress continued strong all through the period in question. In the very same year that

[36] See on Monet, and for the quotations, William C. Seitz, *Claude Monet,* Museum of Modern Art, New York, 1960, pp. 31–32, 50.

PLATE 31. *Rouen Cathedral, Early Morning*, by Claude Monet.

Courtesy, Museum of Fine Arts, Boston. Tompkins Collection.

PLATE 32. *Rouen Cathedral, Sunset,* by Claude Monet.

Courtesy, Museum of Fine Arts, Boston. Julia Cheney Edwards Collection; bequest of Hannah Marcy Edwards in memory of her mother.

Sorel's book appeared, a former prime minister of England was telling a Cambridge audience that, despite perils, he could detect, thus far, "no symptoms either of pause or of regression in the onward movement which for more than a thousand years [had] been characteristic of Western civilization."[37] Balfour's optimism, reserved for "communities of the European type," was based, predictably, on the modern alliance between pure science and industry. But, as Sorel's and many other books testify, the air was, by then, rife with doubt. There was, first of all, much doubt that was not easily dismissed, about the quality of modern life and civilization. Sorel, for one, was always talking about "decadence" and trying to find the remedy for it. Second, there was the more deep-seated doubt that history observed any law whatsoever, or followed any prescribed course. At this point the new historical outlook can be seen to parallel some of the new ideas about nature and man. According to Sorel, a disciple of Bergson and Nietzsche, history was free, not determined; was the result, to a degree unsuspected by scientific historians, of human willing, whether conscious or unconscious. This was not necessarily a pessimistic view. It did, however, make the historical world seem less dependable, less amenable to rational calculation and control, and less predictable. On Sorel's assumption, history could go either way depending on what men chose to do, or not to do: toward greater progress, or even grandeur (though only for brief spells), or toward inertia or decadence.

Sorel and many of his contemporaries thought that they lived in a time of decadence. "It was a sad epoch," Maurice Barrès wrote in his *Cahiers*, "in which we accepted being representatives of decadence."[38] Barrès was thinking primarily of France, of course, and of his own generation, which had grown up in the wake of the disaster of 1871. But the idea of decadence, understood as a state of mind into which modern Europe had drifted, was by no means the property of a single country (even though, as Nietzsche observed, Schopenhauerian pessimism *was* stronger in France than elsewhere), or to a particular generation, class, party, or literary movement. If cultural despair, as it is also sometimes called, was conspicuous among conservatives, as well as self-styled literary epigoni such as Huysmans, Oscar Wilde, and the like, it

[37] Arthur James Balfour, *Decadence* (Henry Sidgwick Memorial Lecture), Cambridge University Press, Cambridge, England, 1908, p. 59. Balfour, prime minister of England from 1902 to 1905, was also known for his philosophical writings.

[38] Maurice Barrès, *Mes Cahiers*, Librairie Plon, Paris, 1935, Vol. IX, p. 27. The entry is dated 1911, but Barrès was referring back to the period of his youth when Paul Verlaine was widely read and discussed.

also entered profoundly into the thought of socialists such as Sorel, anarchist sympathizers such as Paul Claudel (at the time he wrote his play on *La Ville,* 1890), Voltaireans such as Anatole France (also a socialist), social scientists such as Emile Durkheim and Le Bon (to be sure, also a political conservative), philosophers such as Renouvier and Nietzsche, and even German "mandarins" or members of the academic establishment. All of these thought that civilization, French, German, or European, was in a parlous state, if not actually sick, and that progress in the bourgeois sense was a not unmixed blessing, or else a figment.

Decadence was attributed variously to bourgeois corruption, a declining sense of community and loss of spiritual values, the growth of state power and mass culture, and even the growth of knowledge. Oddly, not too much was said about irrational man in this connection, though one does begin to hear more now about evil in history. The historian Jacob Burckhardt, perhaps because he was brought up in a Christian minister's household, saw clearly the fallen side of human nature and believed it to be a permanent barrier to progress. "Evil on earth," he declared in a lecture of 1871, "is assuredly a part of the great economy of world history." But his analysis of "the present crisis" was, in the main, political and cultural. Comparing nineteenth-century Europe with the declining years of Greece and Rome, Burckhardt observed with mounting trepidation the irresistible march of the Leviathan state (deploring Prussianism, he turned down Ranke's chair at the University of Berlin), and industrialism. Both spelled death to the higher culture of Europe, the former because it threatened individual liberty and individualism, the latter because it spawned philistinism and a radicalism that not only loosened the bonds of discipline but made people think everything was possible ("insane optimism"). The heart of the great historian's argument, developed at length in his lectures and letters between 1868 and his death in 1889,[39] was that the social basis that had made European "culture" possible was fast disappearing. Some of the points made by Burckhardt are somewhat reminiscent of Nietzsche, who, indeed, much admired the older man, and was his academic colleague at Basel for a time. Nietzsche, too, attacked the materialism of the age, the state (which, like Burckhardt, he thought was antagonistic to culture), and egalitarian democracy. But Nietzsche's main point was somewhat different. He equated decadence, a word he

---

[39] See especially his lectures at the University of Basel entitled *Introduction to the Study of History,* and the many letters to his friend Von Preen. The quotation in the text is from the lecture *On Fortune and Misfortune in History.*

used often, essentially with a "general decrease in vitality," which stemmed from a certain kind of "virtue," the "old ladies' morality" of Christianity and the bourgeoisie, emphasizing pity, neighbor-love, and self-solicitude, and lacking self-assurance. Mainly for this reason, modern Europe seemed to Nietzsche a "weak age," not to be compared in vitality, or in its ability to produce a higher culture, with the Renaissance, "the last *great* age" of history.[40]

The two great French moralists Sorel and Emile Durkheim made rather different diagnoses. Of the two, Sorel more nearly approximated Nietzsche's ideas and may even have been influenced by him in his emphasis on the heroic virtues. As befitted an anarcho-socialist, however, Sorel's critique centered more exclusively on the bourgeoisie. The bourgeoisie, "conquérante" in 1848 (for Sorel, the great dividing line of nineteenth-century history), soon became "fainéante," corrupt, excessively individualistic, overintellectualized, living by illusions such as parliamentary democracy and the idea of progress. Sorel saw parallels between this bourgeois decadence and "the ruin of the ancient world" (the title of one of his books; he also wrote a book on the trial of Socrates). Antiquity had been undermined by intellectuals such as Socrates who deflated the civic and imperial myths that were its strength. Like Greece and Rome in decline, bourgeois Europe—in particular, France under the Third Republic—lacked great social myths, which enable men to defy fate and take heroic action. In the end, Sorel managed to sound more like Bergson than Nietzsche.

At first glance, Durkheim seems at completely opposite poles from Sorel. No Bergsonian, far from it, Durkheim was one of France's first academic sociologists, first at the University of Bordeaux and later at the Sorbonne, where, however, since there was still a prejudice against sociology, he was named professor of ethics and the philosophy of education. He was a social scientist in the positivist tradition, and politically a democrat, anxious to shore up the Third Republic, rather than to destroy it. Yet his diagnosis, though admittedly arrived at by a different method, bore a striking resemblance to Sorel's in certain respects. Societies, Durkheim observed, had always had collective myths to live by, and that was precisely what Europeans in the late nineteenth century no longer had or were in the process of losing. That was why there were so many more suicides, why modern societies were sick, if not actually decadent. "Our illness is not, then, as has often been believed,

---

[40] See especially *Twilight of the Idols* (1888), no. 37, "Whether we have become more moral."

of an intellectual sort," he wrote in his doctoral thesis; "it has more profound causes." As a social scientist, Durkheim understood the supreme importance for society of common beliefs and bonds, such as had been traditionally embodied in religion, the family, and local and vocational loyalties. In a time of rapid economic and social change, Europe suffered from *anomie*,[41] which is to say from a general collapse of the "collective conscience" (*conscience collective*). According to Durkheim, *anomie* was the inevitable result of the division of labor, which stimulated mobility and specialization, and thus not only separated people from each other but made them critical of traditional norms. In "anomic" (normless) or "egoistic," as opposed to "altruistic," societies, the individual is without discipline and finds no direction or meaning to life.

In his conception of *anomie*, Durkheim put his finger on the factor that seemed, to many, to explain the contemporary decadence better than anything else. That was the spiritual crisis, or the decline of old beliefs, which had left a religious and metaphysical vacuum. The literature of the *Fin-de-Siècle* was full of such phrases as "the critical attrition of revered traditions"; "the spirit of negation" among contemporary youth, caused, Paul Bourget said, by a collapse of belief and morals; "the underlying *Welt-Schmerz*," related by Frederic Myers, it will be recalled, to the decline of belief in the meaning of life, and the like. "Never, perhaps, did man's spiritual satisfaction bear a smaller proportion to his needs." Myers saw a close parallel in the Alexandrian decadence and Byzantine despair, which, he said, "found utterance in many an epigram which might have been written to-day."[42] Byzantinism or its equivalent, it may be noted in passing, was a major theme in contemporary literature and art.

The theme of disillusionment was prominent in all the literature dealing with the spiritual crisis and decadence. Thomas Hardy aptly characterized the age as one of the "disillusive centuries" of history (in *The Return of the Native*, 1877). The aging Renan and his disciple Anatole France worried this theme endlessly. Renan, for years a firm believer in the progress of science, grew progressively disillusioned, not, to be sure, with science itself (which he thought prevented man from being duped), but with the fruits of science. Could it be, he pondered

---

[41] Durkheim developed his theory of *anomie* at length in *Le suicide* (1897). See also his thesis, *De la division du travail social* (1893).

[42] Frederic W. H. Myers, op. cit. (see note 7), Vol. II, pp. 279–280. See also, on pessimism and the spiritual crisis, Bourget's *Essais de psychologie contemporaine* (1883–1886).

in a new preface written for an old book, "that the real abasement of the morality of humanity will date from the day it has seen the reality of things."[43] Could man live without illusions? But already this was an academic question for Renan. "We live by the shadow of a shadow," he had written in the *Philosophical Dialogues,* "by what will they live after us?" Pursuing this theme, Anatole France, becoming one of his nation's most popular writers, questioned whether too much knowledge was compatible with life itself, or with happiness. "Ignorance," he wrote in one of the skeptical essays that made up *Le Jardin d'Epicure* (1895):

> is the condition necessary, I do not say for happiness, but for existence itself. If we knew all, we could not endure life for an hour. The feelings which make it either sweet, or at least tolerable, are born of a lie and are nourished on illusions.[44]

But in the nineteenth century, Europeans had eaten of the tree of science, and now saw more clearly than in any previous time the way things were: man, kindred to animals, lost on a grain of sand in an immense and indifferent universe, his sense of his own identity and infinity suppressed, feeling, now that he had lost his innocence, "the tragic absurdity of living." Hardy said similar things more somberly (France was cynical and ironic, rather than somber). Hardy wrote often, especially in the novels, of man's having to face up to things as they really are, of his growing disillusionment as he learned the truth, thanks to the Higher Criticism and Darwinism, about God and nature. For Hardy, more so than for Anatole France, the fatal flaw was in the universe, not in human nature. Man's tragedy was that he lived in the wrong kind of universe, a universe in which "nothing was made for man," to whose ceaseless flux he found it impossible to adjust, in which no "fixed star" shone to light his way toward goal or haven. "The time seems near," he wrote, again in *The Return of the Native,* "if it has not actually arrived, when the chastened sublimity of a moor, a sea, or a mountain will be all of nature that is absolutely in keeping with the moods of the more thinking among mankind." Hardly the stuff of which to build higher cultures, this brooding melancholy, this new outburst of Schopenhauerian pessimism.[45]

---

[43] The book was *L'Avenir de science,* which was written in 1848, but not published until 1890 when Renan wrote the preface.

[44] Anatole France, *Oeuvres complètes,* Calmann-Lévy, Paris, 1927, Vol. IX, p. 409.

[45] Like so many of his contemporaries, Hardy had read Schopenhauer, though perhaps not before writing *The Return of the Native.* Shaw spoke of a cult of

Baudelaire wrote in 1855 that Europeans lived in an arrogant century, "which thinks itself above the misadventures of Greece and Rome." Nobody believed that any longer, at least not in the *Fin-de-Siècle* ambience. All the same, extreme pessimists such as Hardy were always in the minority, even in that world. The majority were still reasonably hopeful that Europe might yet, in Max Nordau's medical phrase, recover from the present derangement of its nervous system.

Admittedly, this was not Burckhardt's view—he thought he lived over an abyss—nor was it Hardy's (for who could cure the universe, in which man had to live out his days?), nor was it that of many of the neo-romantics. Arthur Rimbaud, for example, carrying out the resolution announced in his famous poem *Une Saison en Enfer* (1873), forsook the "hell" of Europe for Africa and the East, in search of a more primitive and vigorous civilization. Villiers de L'Isle-Adam, like his hero in *Axel* (1890), went inside to escape from the external world, now so universally unpleasing to the poetic imagination. As has often been pointed out, the neo-romantics of the late nineteenth century were apolitical and asocial by comparison with the old romantics. Feeling isolated in a world given over to materialism, they simply withdrew from it.

Others, however, more numerous, as has been said, prescribed cures for the sick patient. These cures naturally differed according to the social position or persuasion of the prescriber, and also according to his metaphysical hopes. But they were all in fundamental agreement that what Europeans needed above all else in their deranged state was something to live for and by, whether it was religion, nation, class, a new "lay morality," or the will to power.

Frederic Myers was one of those who was hopeful of some sort of religious revival, though not in the ordinary sense. He had had his "gradual disillusion" with the faith of his youth, and had seen how it affected society at large, causing, as he said, an Alexandrine decadence. But just as Christianity had rescued the ancient world from the doldrums, so there might again be a fresh incursion of the spiritual world to save modern Europe. Myers, like so many eminent men of his

---

Schopenhauer. Few, including Hardy, followed Schopenhauer to the letter. But he did become a symbol, as A. Baillot says (*L'Influence de la philosophie de Schopenhauer en France, 1860–1900,* Librairie Philosophique, J. Vrin, Paris, 1927, p. 10) "dans l'Europe troublée, du grand principe de resignation." In *Tess of the D'Urbervilles* (1891), Hardy says of his hero, Angel Clare, that he became wonderfully free from "the chronic melancholy which is taking hold of the civilized races with the decline of belief in a beneficent power," a theme to which he returned many times, in, for example, poems such as "A Plaint to Man" and "God's Funeral."

generation, had discovered spiritualism (he, in fact, helped to organize the new Society for Psychical Research in 1882), and hoped that this might be the means of gaining valid (scientifically verifiable) knowledge of the unseen world and of reassuring people about the afterlife. In this way Europe might regain its youth. What the age needed was not an abandonment, but an increase, of effort. The time was ripe, he wrote, "for a study of unseen things as strenuous and sincere as that which Science has made familiar for the problems of earth."[46]

The panaceas of Barrès and Sorel were more representative and may stand as examples of efforts made by the political right and left to cure the decadence. Barrès' intellectual profile, which was very typical, shows an initial disillusionment with traditional religious beliefs, followed by the formation of a "culte du moi" (the title of his celebrated trilogy of novels, 1888–1891, and signifying the centrality of the self, or "moi," as the only certainty on which to build a life), and then, discovering the inadequacy of self alone, by a belief in "national egotism." In the end, Barrès found certainty in his Lorraine subconscious, symbolized by the young maiden Bérénice, who is a figure of spontaneity and wholeness in Le Jardin de Bérénice. Henceforth, Barrès preached a philosophy of "national energy" (L'Energie Nationale), featuring a new cult of the land and the dead, which included a revived Catholicism as the embodiment of French culture. The roles of the individual and national egos had been reversed, the latter absorbing the former and giving direction to it, though never intentionally stifling it. Barrès became one of the chief advocates of the new "integral nationalism" that was then sweeping Europe.

For Sorel, combatting bourgeois decadence depended on creating class rather than national myths. Educated at the École Polytechnique, and for twenty-five years a practicing engineer in the employ of the French government, Sorel nevertheless thought in very unengineerlike terms, more like a social visionary than a social planner, more like Barrès than Marx. Taking his cue from Bergson, and to a lesser extent from von Hartmann, Sorel made myth (as distinguished from utopia) the moving force of history and the means of overthrowing the bourgeois order. In this respect he differed markedly from the other French Marxists, whether orthodox like Jules Guesde, or revisionist like Jean Jaurès. Myth, not an intellectual product like utopia, was a set of images capable of moving masses of men to revolutionary action. It

---

[46] Frederic W. H. Myers, op. cit. (see note 7), Vol. II, p. 280.

was not a spatial concept that was resolvable into stages, a model to be taken to pieces, a blueprint of the future. Myths "are not descriptions of things but expressions of wills," the big dreams of peoples and groups. Examples of great myths in history were early Christianity, the Reformation, and modern nationalism. The particular myth that Sorel was pushing at the time he wrote *Reflections on Violence* (1908) was the myth of the general strike, which was to be the means of stirring the working class out of its moral lethargy, of uniting it and giving it a worthy goal to achieve, of restoring heroism to a jaded and frivolous society. But despite his belief (at the time) in moral regeneration, Sorel always saw history within a more or less Vico-like framework. When great myths took hold, men could and did strive for a better world. But decadence was the more "natural" state, and when men wearied of the struggle, as they always did sooner or later, regression inevitably set in. Thus, Sorel was less Bergsonian than he appears at first glance. For though believing in a free and open-ended history, he was a pessimist about "natural nature" (as opposed to the "artificial nature" created by man), which he found chaotic and ever threatening to man's noblest enterprises.

To turn from Barrès and Sorel to Durkheim is to turn from the new irrational world of the *Fin-de-Siècle* back to the sober world of reason and science. Durkheim more properly belongs in the former world only in the sense that he saw the decadence and sought ways to cure it. He visualized no restoration of the collective conscience by which earlier societies had been ruled, no return to religion, not even the Religion of Humanity of Comte, and no reversal of the division of labor that characterized modern industrial society. But to offset *anomie,* which was the cause of social sickness, it was necessary to forge a new moral solidarity. To do this, Durkheim advocated a new lay ethic and a new type of institution. The ethic, to be taught in the schools, would emphasize the dualism of human nature (the subject of a famous paper by Durkheim): on the one hand, man's individuality and the dignity of the human person; but on the other, the social side of his nature and the degree to which society affects him, even in the way he thinks and hence the debt he owes to it. The institution that Durkheim advocated was the industrial syndicate, which, uniting management, labor, and consumer in a new social unit, would act as an antidote to the class warfare that threatened to destroy modern society. Thus might the Third Republic become whole again, though like Sorel, Durkheim recognized no permanently healthy state in society. "What exists in reality," he wrote, in opposition to Comte's law of progress, "are particular societies . . . which are born and die, progress and regress, each in its own manner, pursuing divergent goals."[47]

These prescriptions for recovery, based on a belief in the freedom of history as of nature, help to explain the partial evaporation of the pessimistic mood during the "Edwardian" period. Progress, however, had now been unmasked, and it was apparent to an increasing number that there was nothing automatic or certain about it.

[47] From "La sociologie" (1915), in *Emile Durkheim, 1858–1917*, Kurt Wolff (ed.), Ohio State University Press, Columbus, 1960, p. 378. Durkheim's essay on "Le dualisme de la nature humaine et ses conditions sociales" (1914) is reprinted in the same volume.

PART V

The Twentieth Century

The Triumph of Becoming

Problematic Man

Eclipse of God

The Mysterious Universe

The Open Society and Its Enemies

The Decline of the West

The Triumph of Becoming

The first half of the twentieth century, especially after 1914, marked a revolution in European thinking almost beyond compare. To a considerable extent, the extent of this revolution was understood at the time it was taking place, but it is easier to comprehend its scope now than it was then. There had been intellectual revolutions before, several of great magnitude: the scientific revolution, with which this book commenced, and the Christian revolution, which transformed the ancient world. But never before had there been a revolution quite so thoroughgoing, in the sense that it destroyed, in a comparatively short period of time, nearly all the "idols" that had been so painstakingly constructed, not merely by the Middle Ages but by "modern" times as well. It was a time when one kind of modernity gave way, at last, to another. The "old" modernity, initially sponsored by the Moderns of the seventeenth century, and productive of the Enlightenments, both old and new, effected profound changes in world-outlook, but left important bastions of being virtually intact. The "new" modernity, however, dispensed with being, leaving men without landmarks, casting them adrift on an endless sea of becoming.

The artist-critic Wyndham Lewis called this the triumph of the "Time-mind." Time-mind sees everything *sub specie temporis,* as perpetually restless, moving, and changing. Space-mind, its opposite, produces a world of solid objects and absolutes that exist eternally. Time-mind, however, focuses on the dynamic aspect of reality, forcing people into a "trance of action," hurrying them along, as the Futurists wanted them to do, at ever greater speeds, but without fixed goals, since reality was, on this view, a becoming, a history, an unending dialectical process. "Time-doctrine" was, in Lewis' view, mainly the outcome of science, with its instruments of research, "the inevitable child of positivist thought." He found it manifested in contemporary philosophy (he refers to the "einsteinian, bergsonian, or alexandrian world of Time"[1]), literature, and art. He also found it, not unexpectedly, among philosophic historians such as Oswald Spengler, who coined the phrase "World-as-history," that is, as wholly dynamic and never static. Lewis personally deplored this new "Time-cult," while recognizing its ubiquitousness. He would have agreed with his countryman, the philosopher Cyril Joad, that it involved the refusal of the modern world to recognize any sort of timeless area or order "outside the process of evolutionary change."[2] By this standard the new modernity spelled nihilism as well as temporality; living in a world become, in the words of the Spanish philosopher Ortega y Gasset, "scandalously provisional," not merely changing, but without standards or roots. The twentieth century, as Ortega viewed it in *The Revolt of the Masses* (1930), was the first period in history that recognized nothing in the past as a standard. It had broken even with "modern culture," or at least refused to recognize it as definitive, as the nineteenth century had done. The existential part of Ortega's mind rejoiced at the opportunity this situation gave European man to improvise and create. But another part was fearful, lest the "revolt" leave European man demoralized, possessed of fabulous power, but not knowing what to do with it, palsied by a sense of loss and insecurity. Who knew where this strange new world might gravitate? Ortega knew a revolution when he saw one.

The revolution, or crisis, as contemporaries more often called it, had been coming for a long time, as previous sections in this book have shown. It might be likened to a tidal wave, generated by underground earthquakes over a period of time, which at last had a cumulative

---

[1] Wyndham Lewis, *Time and Western Man*, Beacon Press, Boston, 1957, p. 437. "Alexandrian" refers here to the English philosopher, Samuel Alexander, and to Alexander's *Space, Time, and Deity* (see p. 472). Lewis' book was first published in 1927.

[2] C. E. M. Joad, *Decadence*, Faber and Faber, London, 1948, p. 243.

effect. By the end of the nineteenth century, becoming was already a major category of thinking, in both a decadent and "creative" sense, and Nietzsche was not alone in sensing the advent of a new sort of age, characterized by a transvaluation of values, and a new, and dangerous, openness of thought and culture. Still, there is a sense in which 1914 opened up a real gap, not only between generations but also in the way many older men, born in the nineteenth century, began thereafter to think about things. The year 1914 is, of course, purely symbolic, since it was not really until 1916 that the full horror of World War I began to penetrate, even among the participants. It was in 1916 that young Mark Gertler painted *The Merry-go-Round* (Plate 33), one of the more powerful antiwar depictions, which D. H. Lawrence called "the best modern picture I have ever seen . . . horrible and terrifying."[3] This picture could hardly have been done before the battle of the Somme and before the opposing armies had settled down to the apparently endless deadlock of trench warfare. It showed men and women as robots in uniform driven round and round, without meaning or purpose, by the machine of war. For Max Ernst, who was prominent in most of the new art movements of his time, the year 1933 would be more meaningful, since, though he fought in World War I, he initially turned away from it in disgust, to experiment and confront his own psychic problems in his art. But by 1933, and actually to some extent before that, Ernst had begun to take serious notice of the collapsing world around him. Thereafter, appeared in rapid succession such terrifying studies as his *Barbarians* and ruined cities series, and especially *Europe After the Rain*, the first version of which (1933) depicted a distorted and wasted continent as viewed from above. The version of 1940–1942, reproduced here (Plate 34) is a ground-level view of the same civilization, returned to its primitive state. These are partly prophetic pictures, but some of his other pictures commented more directly on actual events, for instance, the ironic *Angels of Hearth and Home*, which Ernst painted after the defeat of the Republicans in Spain.

But however the decisive date may differ for any particular individual, there is no denying that the Great War, as the Europeans have always called World War I, did shake the foundations of European life and thought. It is, indeed, inconceivable that such a holocaust, which took most Europeans by surprise, should not have done so. The history of the war's impact on intellectuals, and on thought and thought

---

[3] With regard to the war, Gertler called himself a "Passivist," and had connections with the pacifist group at Garsington, presided over by Lady Ottoline Morrell. His painting was unsalable in 1916.

patterns, has yet to be written and would not be easy to write. It deeply affected both psychiatrists and theologians. Freud wrote of the disillusionment caused by the war and of the changed attitude toward death, which it imposed on everybody, including himself. The war, in short, stripped off the last illusions Freud might still have had about rational man; it revealed, all too clearly, man's "primitive" nature.[4] An erstwhile colleague of Freud observed, a few years later, "the revolution in our conscious outlook, brought about by the catastrophic results of the World War." Carl Jung, who had also lived through it, believed that the war had shattered man's faith in his worth and in the rational organization of the world, and had thrown him back on himself.[5] Still another psychiatrist saw standards and ideals, which had become second nature to him, vanish in the aftermath of the war. "Like most European observers of these eventful years I saw that a cultural epoch was in process of dissolution." What Franz Alexander saw being eroded were precisely the presuppositions of the "old" modernity: belief in science, human rationality, and the gradual improvement of the human race.[6] Theologians were affected as deeply. The war caused many of them, Karl Barth, for example, to alter drastically the "modernist" views of God and man, which they had learned in seminary.

Out of, though not completely because of, the Great War also came some impressive works of literature, as well as new art movements, Dadaism and surrealism, among others. James Joyce's *Ulysses* was begun during the war. T. S. Eliot's *The Wasteland,*[7] and Thomas Mann's *The Magic Mountain,* which dealt with disease and death, followed soon after and showed the influence of the war. It is perhaps not so well remembered that George Bernard Shaw completed *Heartbreak*

[4] See Freud's essay "Thoughts for the Times on War and Death" (1915). Richard Hughes, in his novel *The Fox in the Attic* (1961; proposed as the first of a series of novels on "the Human Predicament") deals interestingly with the difference the war made in attitudes. Freud also made a big difference, Hughes believes. But he also describes the war itself as a "deep emotional upheaval," which was as disturbing as it was because "Western man" had been taught to believe in "emergent Reason" and in war as something that man had outgrown.

[5] Carl Jung, *Modern Man in Search of a Soul,* W. S. Dell (trans.), Harcourt, Brace, New York, 1933, pp. 234–235.

[6] Franz Alexander, *Our Age of Unreason,* J. B. Lippincott, Philadelphia, 1942, p. 7. Born and bred in Budapest, Alexander was lecturer at the Institute for Psychoanalysis in Berlin from 1921 to 1930.

[7] Paul Fussell points out that in its postwar context *The Wasteland* (1922) appears to have been much more of a war book, or "memory of the war" than had been thought. It was not completely that, of course. On Eliot and the war, see *The Great War and Modern Memory,* Oxford University Press, New York, pp. 325–326.

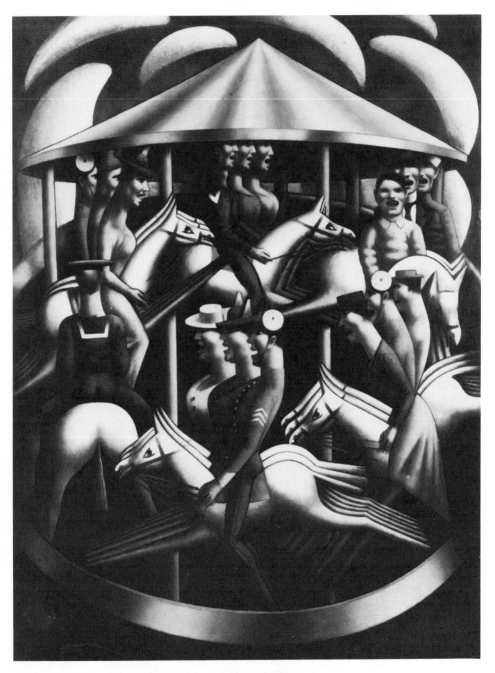

PLATE 33. *The Merry-go-round,* by Mark Gertler.

PLATE 34. *Europe After the Rain, II*, by Max Ernst.

Courtesy Wadsworth Atheneum, Hartford. Ella Gallup Sumner and Mary Catlin Sumner Collection.

House during the war and commented gloomily on the war at length in the preface. It would not be accurate to say that Shaw changed his mind during or because of the war, for another and more famous of his plays, *Back to Methusaleh,* published in 1921, returned to the theme of creative evolution. Still, the war certainly made Shaw less sanguine about man and man's prospects, as even some statements in *Back to Methusaleh* testify. Actually, he observes in the preface that the war did not disturb the preconceived ideas of most people, whether "in khaki or out of it." But as for himself, Shaw now saw nature taking its revenge on the cultured, leisured, and neglectful society of prewar Europe, and he raised the specter of Armageddon.

> Nature gave us a very long credit; and we abused it to the utmost. But when she struck at last she struck with a vengeance. For four years she smote our firstborn and heaped on us plagues of which Egypt never dreamed.[8]

It should also not be forgotten that Spengler completed *The Decline of the West* during the war, or that because of the war, the German historian Friedrich Meinecke began to develop doubts about reason and the use of state power in history.

Ernst Jünger, the German soldier-writer-philosopher, and author of possibly the most popular of all the war journals, best exemplifies the direct and revolutionary impact that war—*the* war—could have on a man's life and thought. Like the Englishman Siegfried Sassoon, another famous war memoirist, Jünger never got the war out of his system, but thought and wrote about it all his life. "The War is not only our father, but our son," he wrote. "We have created it, and it has created us."[9] However, unlike Sassoon, and so many others, who were embittered by the experience, Jünger reacted to it positively. It was a dreadful experience, of course, but full of ecstasy, too, requiring endurance and self-sacrifice and heightening man's sense of community. War was, as it were, the existential moment when man came to grips with reality, which was fraught with death, violence, and pain. Jünger saw the years 1914–1918 very clearly as a watershed between two cultures, marking a break with the brilliant, but soft and overintel-

---

[8] George Bernard Shaw, *Heartbreak House,* Preface, in *Collected Works,* William H. Wise, New York, 1930, Vol. XV, p. 8.
[9] Ernst Jünger, *Der Kampf als Inneres Erlebnis* (1922), in *Werke,* Ernst Klett, Stuttgart, 1960, Vol. V, p. 14. In this book Jünger tried to describe "trench mentality."

lectualized, culture of Wilhelminian Germany, and ushering in a new generation, with a new ideology. Though never a Nazi, he talked a lot about "a race, newly formed in the hard school of war," and having imprinted on it the characters of materialism and brutality. The new ideology of this new race of men is a bit fuzzy, but it is at least clear that it involved the replacement of the individualist-happiness-security syndrome of the old European bourgeoisie by a new "worker"-technician-engineer mentality. Jünger's "worker," not to be confused with socialist or lower classes, is a man completely adjusted to a world of machines, "total mobilization," and violence, the last now proved to be the only way to resolve conflicts. For, indeed, Jünger, a child of war, saw war as a permanent fact of human life. His was a world in which we might say there was pattern—he talked much of forms and types and "uniformness" (*Eindeutigkeit,* as opposed to individuality)—but no meaning,[10] and no progress. It was a world dominated by technology and war.

How should we think of this revolution in thought, which people as different as Jünger, Ortega, and Wyndham Lewis sensed and tried to describe, in the years following the Great War? It is not easy to be very precise, because, for one thing, we are too close to it, and because, for another, it presumably has not yet run its full course. The tendency is to focus too much on the negative and sensational features of the intellectual landscape, and not enough on the experimental and vital. We do this, not only because "the wasteland" did in fact loom large in the gaze of contemporaries but because we ourselves naturally associate the new ideas with the events, the horrendous events of 1914, 1916, 1933, 1939, and so on. Perhaps we can obtain a better focused picture by considering the revolution in the following ways: (1) as a "normal" revolution, which, though bringing important changes of outlook, can still be described as movement from one set of beliefs and models to another; (2) in the light of shattering new answers to the perennial questions; and (3) above all, in its connection with the definitive passage from being to becoming, as a state of mind by which to survey the whole world. Consideration of this last feature, which amounted to a new *Weltanschauung,* will return us to the discussion with which we started this chapter.

Nobody needs to be told that there was a revolution in physics in the early twentieth century or a psychoanalytical movement, called by

---

[10] J. P. Stern puts it this way in *Ernst Jünger,* Yale University Press, New Haven, 1953, p. 47. For Jünger's new ideology, see especially his *Die totale Mobilmachung* (1930) and *Der Arbeiter* (1932).

Thomas Mann "a world movement," which affected, not merely the sciences, but "every domain of the intellect," including literature, art, and religion. "Indeed," said Mann, "it would be too much to say that I came to psychoanalysis. It came to me."[11] Nobody needs to be told about the new movements in literature and art, which defied the past, experimented with new techniques and structures, and were expressive of new ideas. More people probably need to be told about new movements in philosophy, particularly philosophy of science, logical positivism, and existentialism, which registered changed attitudes toward epistemology, language, and metaphysics; and about new theologies, including the "crisis theology" of Barth and others. Described in this way, the revolution sounds reasonably normal, comparable to other revolutions like that of science in the seventeenth century or even the Romantic Movement.

But there is a sense in which the revolution was not normal. This becomes clear as we see how the perennial questions were answered. Man became problematic and not merely good, bad, or indifferent as in past debates. The universe became mysterious, hard to fathom or decipher, and nature became remote. For the first time, theological questions began to seem, not merely controversial, but meaningless, to a significant number of people, including some theologians. Social scientists wrestled with a new value-free political and social science, while shocking new social myths threw the whole world into turmoil. History became problematic, too, as evidenced by the "crisis of historicism," which threw into doubt, in the words of Ernst Troeltsch, "all firm norms and ideals of human existence." Even allowing for exaggeration—for, of course, these trends in thinking were not wholly discontinuous with past trends nor all-conquering in the present—all this adds up to a strange, new world of thought, barely recognizable in terms of past landmarks. John Galsworthy, popular author of *The Forsyte Saga,* sensed something of what this turnover of ideas portended when he wrote, in the preface to *The Modern Comedy,* and apropos of England and Englishmen at the time of the General Strike of 1926: "Everything being now relative, there is no longer absolute dependence to be placed on God, Free Trade, Marriage, Consols, Coal, or Caste." The third generation of Forsytes, the generation that grew up during the Great War, had decided that everything required revaluation, was determined to live "now or never," and knew that it had to live with

---

[11] Thomas Mann, "Freud and the Future" (1936), in *Essays of Three Decades,* H. T. Lowe-Porter (trans.), Alfred A. Knopf, New York, 1947, p. 414.

uncertainty. That was a pretty fair description of how many young people "above the property line" viewed the world in the 1920's. To grasp the real radicality of the new mentality, however, one has to enter the world of the psychoanalysts, surrealists, and existentialists, and, to the extent that it is possible, to penetrate the rarefied atmosphere of the scientific laboratories.

It is, of course, not possible to briefly summarize or synthesize the many and complex sides of this mentality. Some of its characteristics will emerge more clearly in the chapters to follow. Because of their all-pervasiveness, however, several of these characteristics merit advance comment. Cyril Joad, author of many guides to modern thought, described two such characteristics under the composite phrase, "dropping of the object." Leaving out, or dropping of, the object meant, on the one hand, subjectivism, or, as I shall call it, going inward; and, on the other hand, disbelief in any sort of transcendence. Going inward—to find the self, or oneself, or the Self (in the case of Carl Jung), or the marvelous; or simply to express dissatisfaction with the external world dominated by science and reason—became a habit with many people, especially as the psychoanalytical movement caught on. Another painting by Max Ernst, significantly titled *The Interior of Sight* (1929; Plate 35), expresses very well this interiorizing of thought. Ernst himself, it should be noted, always claimed to be "an intellectual artist," who maintained an objectivity toward, and conscious control over, his subjects. Nevertheless, he frequently turned to the world of dreams and the unconscious for his subjects, as in the picture mentioned. Though the latter probably meant many things to Ernst (he painted it at least three times), it is not hard to see in it the inward-turned eye, which probes the unconscious and finds there metaphorical images of both pleasure and horror (represented by the bird and snake), and their taming (by the oval and circle). André Breton, a medical student who became interested in psychiatry, tried to elevate this interiorizing, or "surrealism," into a philosophy. Influenced by Freud, but also by the symbolist and German romantic traditions, Breton declared war on "the realistic attitude, inspired by positivism," from St. Thomas Aquinas to Anatole France (!). He wanted a new kind of philosophy, revealed in sleep and by the unconscious, which in the end might yield "a kind of absolute reality, a *surreality*." In art this would be expressed by means of automatic writing or drawing. In the first manifesto of the movement, surrealism was defined as "Psychic automatism in its pure state. . . . Dictated by thought, in the absence of any control exercised by reason,

PLATE 35. *The Interior of Sight* (*Das Ei*), by Max Ernst.

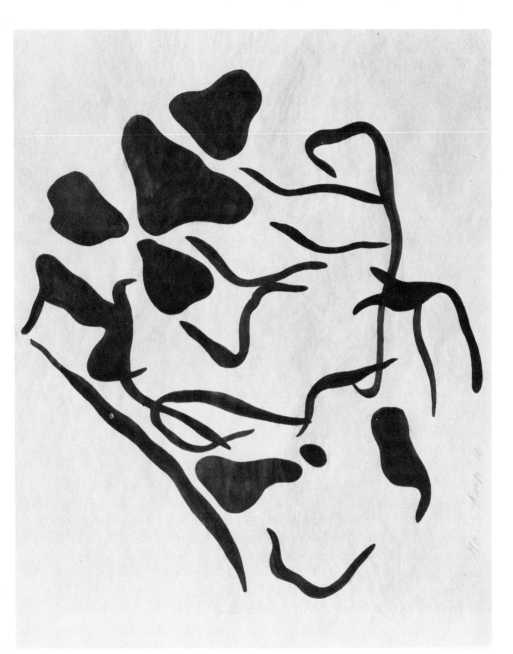

PLATE 36. *Automatic Drawing,* by Jean Arp (1916).

Brush and ink on gray paper. 16¾″ x 21¼″. Collection, The Museum of Modern Art, New York.

exempt from any aesthetic or moral concern."[12] Jean (or Hans) Arp had been doing this sort of automatic drawing as early as 1916, in his Dadaist period (Plate 36). Joad, who was a philosophical realist, might have approved Breton's pursuit of "the miraculous," and affirmation of a "surreality," though he would have been horrified by Breton's irrationalism. But, in general, Joad complained about the psychologizing of art, as of every form of modern thought, which, as he saw it, meant the nonknowability of "objects" other than mental states.

Neither psychologism nor skepticism, however, fully describes the new mentality. More than anything else, it was conscious of loss, loss of belief in transcendence. Three words, ubiquitous in "existential" literature, and coming increasingly into general use, testify to this sense of loss. The three words were the famous three a's, as we may call them, the Absurd, anxiety, and alienation. The Absurd, already prominent in André Malraux's early work, signified the kind of universe men supposedly lived in; devoid of meaning, at least for man; lacking being, or essence; in any case, irrational and incomprehensible. In an exchange of fictitious letters between two young friends, Malraux has the Chinese friend, traveling in Europe, observe that "in the depths of European man, where it dominates the great moments of his life, there resides an essential absurdity." Ling's European friend, traveling in China, agrees. For the modern European, there is no longer anything permanent in life; values have disappeared; he is left at last face to face with the Absurd.[13] Anxiety and alienation were the feelings caused by the Absurd. Anxiety, in Paul Tillich's definition, "is the state in which a being is aware of its possible nonbeing." "Today," he wrote at midcentury, "it has become almost a truism to call our time an 'age of anxiety'." Tillich rightly observed that literature and art had made anxiety a principal theme, and that educated people in general had become acutely conscious of it in themselves. He attributed its dominion to the contemporary sense of the meaninglessness of life (the Absurd), which in turn stemmed from the disintegration of accustomed structures of meaning, power, and belief.[14] For one of Jean-Paul Sartre's fictional characters, the Absurd was the key to his nausea, to his feeling of being *de trop* in the universe, that is, alienated. The meaning of this third

[12] André Breton, *Manifestoes of Surrealism,* University of Michigan Press, Ann Arbor, 1969, pp. 6, 14, and 26.

[13] André Malraux, *La Tentation de l'Occident* (1926), Ling to A. D., no. 7; A. D. to Ling, no. 8.

[14] Paul Tillich, *The Courage to Be,* Yale University Press, New Haven, 1952, p. 35, and *passim.*

"a" had obviously undergone considerable change, at least in literature, since the days of the Young Hegelians. Where they had thought of alienation as reification, that is as the projection of man's essence into unreal or unworthy objects, it now meant estrangement and homelessness in an alien universe. Thus, to the old "earth alienation" of the nineteenth century was added a new "cosmic alienation,"[15] which was usually thought of as a fate from which there was no escape. Alienation from self, from other men, or from work was presumably remediable in a more just and knowledgeable society. Cosmic alienation, on the other hand, was a permanent state, which, though it gave man freedom (freedom from any sort of necessity or causal being), doomed him to live like a stranger in an indifferent universe.

These words signified, not merely the toppling, but the abandonment, of absolutes. *This* was what was new, above everything else: not iconoclasm *per se,* which is characteristic of every revolution of the mind, but the realization, widespread in the twentieth century as never before, that icons were always changing and would continue to change. This was what Wyndham Lewis called the "Time-mind" and we have called becoming, or the sense of becoming, throughout this book. As we shall see, it is observable in the new importance attached to time in explaining the physical universe; in a new "process theology" basing itself on science, and in the historicizing of theology in general; in the shattering, at last, of the idea of a fixed human nature; and in the growth of a historicized and relativized social science. This intellectual world only faintly resembles the world of Hegel and Darwin; or, we might say, it was that world carried to the extreme—"by new modes of locomotion, and owing to the Great War," Galsworthy would say, though there were other reasons as well. In any case, it constituted an authentic revolution, marking, we might summarize, the triumph of the Heraclitean idea of continuous change. Joad thought that this was a sign of decadence. It was not always interpreted that way by contemporaries, however, nor need it be. In criticism of Spengler's idea of culture without issue, the philosopher-historian R. W. Collingwood remarked in 1927 that there was "no static entity called a culture, there is only a perpetual development. . . . And this conception of 'turning into', the conception of becoming, is the fundamental idea of all history."[16] He might have added that it was not until the twentieth century

---

[15] The terms are F. H. Heinemann's. See his *Existentialism and the Modern Predicament* (1953). On alienation, see also pp. 315–316.

[16] R. W. Collingwood, "Oswald Spengler and the Theory of Historical Cycles," *Antiquity,* Vol. I (1927), pp. 323–324.

that "the conception of becoming" was fully understood, with all its implications, as the key to the universe.

We should take note, in conclusion, of the significant shift in the European intellectual balance of power between 1918 and 1950. The chief point to be made, of course, is the decline of Germany, and secondarily, of Vienna. "Weimar culture," in which there has been a resurgence of interest since 1960, has been called "the first truly modern culture."[17] Certainly it was wonderfully experimental, inventive, and exciting in literature, art and architecture, and the drama. Impressive work was also done by academics, both in the universities and in new institutes such as the Deutsche Hochschule für Politik in Berlin. German "mandarins" figured prominently in all the major postwar intellectual movements, in philosophy, psychology and psychoanalysis, sociology, and in the natural sciences. Likewise, Vienna remained an important intellectual center for a time. Postwar Vienna was the home not only of the psychoanalytical movement (though Berlin was now becoming more important) but also of the famous Vienna Circle of logical positivists, and an important school of economic theory.

The advent of the Nazis changed all that, though not exactly overnight, for there were cracks, more noticeable now than then, in the Weimar facade. Weimar also nourished some potent irrational movements, especially among the young, hungering for roots and leadership. The mandarins contributed to their own downfall by their escapism and by their less than enthusiastic support for the democratic republic. The Nazis, however, delivered the *coup de grâce* to German intellectual life by corrupting the schools, stifling freedom of speech, and driving thousands of distinguished scholars and scientists into exile. Not only individuals but institutes had to migrate or else were closed down. Goebbels took over the Berlin School of Politics. The Warburg Institute of Hamburg, outstanding in the history of art, moved to London. The irony is that Germany, now once again on the rise politically, took a correspondingly deep plunge intellectually. Germany's reign as the foremost intellectual power of Europe came to an abrupt end, more conspicuously in the humanities than in the sciences. But Germany lost many scientists too, perhaps most importantly, of the younger generation who were so important for the future.

[17] Walter Laqueur, *Weimar. A Cultural History,* G. P. Putnam's Sons, New York, 1974, Preface. See also on Weimar, Peter Gay, *Weimar Culture,* and Fritz Ringer, *The Decline of the German Mandarins.*

Problematic Man

Thomas Henry Huxley, it will be remembered, had called the question of man "the question of questions." This question had been central to European thought, more or less continuously since the eighteenth century. It remained at the center of twentieth-century thought, but now with an important difference. In the words of the German philosopher Max Scheler, "man [had become] more of a problem to himself now than ever before in all recorded history."[1] E. M. Forster, the English novelist, said just the opposite. "Man," he wrote in an essay on English prose, "is beginning to understand himself better and to explore his own contradictions."[2] He attributed this better understanding to the "psychological movement," including Freud, which Forster thought had brought new subtlety and depth to the portrayal of human nature, and thus greatly enriched the art of fiction. The difference between these two views is perhaps more apparent than real. However, Scheler's view that man had become more problematic represents more truly the

---

[1] Max Scheler, *Man's Place in Nature* (*Die Stellung des Menschen im Kosmos*, 1928), Hans Meyerhoff (ed.), Beacon Press, Boston, 1966, p. 3. Martin Heidegger said very much the same thing in 1929: "Keiner Zeit ist der Mensch so fragwürdig geworden wie der unsrigen" (*Kant und das Problem der Metaphysik*, F. Cohen, Bonn, 1929, p. 200). See also Ernst Cassirer, *An Essay on Man*, Chap. I. Scheler was named professor of philosophy at the University of Cologne in 1919.

[2] E. M. Forster, *Two Cheers for Democracy*, Harcourt, Brace, New York, 1951, pp. 274–275.

new trend, and especially the new mood, in twentieth-century thought about man.

Of the continuing centrality of the question itself, there is no doubt whatever. The literature dealing with "man" between 1914 and mid-century is enormous by any standards. Philosophical anthropology, defined as the study or science of man to distinguish it from cultural anthropology, blossomed as an intellectual discipline after World War I, and produced important studies by Scheler himself, Ernst Cassirer, and others. Dubbing the twentieth century the "psychological era" of history, Otto Rank, one of the early Freudian group, called attention to the simultaneous vogue of psychology, and especially the new science of psychoanalysis. Famous lecture series addressed themselves to the problem of man, such as Scheler's lectures at Cologne in the 1920's, Martin Buber's inaugural course of lectures at Hebrew University, Jerusalem, in 1938 (*What is Man?*), and the Gifford Lectures of Reinhold Niebuhr in 1939. Above all, one thinks of the almost endless procession of volumes on "the nature and destiny of man," "the human condition," "the stature of man," "modern man in search of a soul," and the like, and of the many new images of man evoked by contemporary artists.

But why should man have become so problematic? Cassirer suggests one reason. There was no longer any "central power," theology, metaphysics, science, or whatever that was capable of providing a frame of reference to which differences of viewpoint, inevitable in any case, might be referred. Nor was there any generally accepted principle, even within special fields of knowledge, such as psychology. Huxley suggested another reason. Answers to the question of questions changed with each new accession to knowledge, thus confusing the issue. In his own time the new accession was Darwinism. In the twentieth century one such accession was the psychoanalytical movement. Problematic man, however, traces more to the new human *condition* than to anarchy of thought about human *nature*. Only a few general observations about this condition need be made here since more will be said about it in the chapters to follow. In his Jerusalem lectures, Martin Buber listed several of the most important reasons why the "anthropological problem" became insistent in the twentieth century. One was cosmic, and another was sociological. In times when man loses his traditional image of the universe, as had happened recently, he feels insecure and homeless, "and hence problematic to himself." The problem is compounded when, with the decay of old organic forms of community, man simultaneously loses his "sociological security" and is thrown back on his solitude. The psychiatrist Franz Alexander expressed it this way: periods of economic expansion and prosperity, when social organization is relatively successful, are "periods of extraverted scientific interest"; but in periods like the present (post–1914), of relatively acute pain and social distress, the intellect focuses "upon the center of the trouble, man himself."[3] Buber also did not fail to point out the new paradox of "man's lagging behind his works," of his greatly increased power through technology, yet at the same time his powerlessness and destructiveness in dealing with the enormous political and economic problems he faced.

Of course, older types or images of man persisted along with the new, and not all the new images were equally problematic. Under the circumstances, however, it is hardly surprising that the "classical" image, already under pressure since Darwinian days, should have come further unraveled; or that new images, such as Freudian man and existential man, should lack the clarity and self-confidence of the older image in its glory days. This problematic strain in man's new conception of himself can be illustrated best by pursuing certain themes, which crop up repeatedly in the literature bearing on the subject. These are the themes, not necessarily always to be found together, of epistemological despair, relativism (with respect to human nature), and self-depreciation. None of those themes went uncontested, as we shall see.

Epistemological despair means despair of ever finding out who "man" is. The litterateurs expressed it overtly, though it was implied, to say the least, in the crisis of knowledge perceived by certain contemporary philosophers, chiefly the logical positivists and philosophers of science.[4] Man is unnameable in Samuel Beckett's novel by that title: man, the self, himself, whom Beckett goes in search of and cannot find, just as he had previously searched for Godot (God?). "Where now? Who now? When now?"—the book begins with the spatial and temporal questions man asks in order to identify himself. "I, of whom I know nothing," he concludes; ". . . there is no name for me, no pronoun for me, all the trouble comes from that, that, it's a kind of pronoun too, it isn't that either, I'm not that either."[5] Beckett had been ringing changes on this theme, in his novels and plays, ever since his youthful book on Marcel Proust. In fact, it all went back to Proust—and to

[3] Franz Alexander, *Our Age of Unreason*, J. B. Lippincott, Philadelphia, 1942, p. 25.

[4] See p. 388–389.

[5] Samuel Beckett, *Molloy, Malone Dies, and The Unnameable*, Grove Press, New York, 1959, p. 562. *The Unnameable* was published in 1953.

Bergson. Bergson had recognized the problem of multiple selves and the difficulty of putting them together to form a whole self. He was optimistic: by introspection it was possible, though never easy, to find the underlying self, which endures, even while changing, and which unites present with past states of mind in an organic whole. Proust was less optimistic. Save for rare privileged moments, people did not understand themselves or others, and this was because personalities were multiple, and forever changing, and putting up false fronts.

This epistemological despair obsessed and baffled a whole generation of European writers from Proust to Beckett. The result was a new form of literature in which, as Nathalie Sarraute explained in one of her critical essays, author, characters, and readers all lived together in a new "age of suspicion." Author and reader had become wary of solid forms, thanks largely to the profuse growth of the psychological world, which destroyed all "usual motives and accepted meanings," and in the end created total skepticism, even of the psychological itself. Consequently, "the character," so solid in the traditional novel, still relatively solid even in *The Remembrance of Things Past,* "lost that most precious of all possessions, his personality . . . and frequently, even his name."[6] Not only Beckett but many of the best known figures of contemporary European literature wrote despairingly (though sometimes also comically) of a vanishing self, an incoherent self, a decentralized self, of a self that possibly did not even exist. "It seems to me sometimes that I do not really exist, but that I merely imagine I exist. The thing that I have the greatest difficulty in believing in, is my own reality": thus Edouard muses in his secret journal in André Gide's novel *The Counterfeiters* (1925). Man looks into a mirror and sees reflected there a stranger—or else so many faces that he is utterly confused: "the stranger inseparable from myself" is how Moscarda puts it in Luigi Pirandello's novel *One, None, and a Hundred Thousand* (1933). The soul detective in Eugène Ionesco's play *Victims of Duty* (1952) arrives at a flat to inquire of the present occupants how the previous tenant spelled his name. He spelled it "Mallot," says the husband, though he admits to not having known him. How, then, do you know it was spelled with a "t" rather than a "d", the detective asks reasonably. "Why, yes, of course, you're right," answered Choubert. "How *do* I know? *How* do I know? . . . How do I *know?* . . . I don't know how I know." The detective himself, though proud of being "Aristo-

[6] Nathalie Sarraute, *The Age of Suspicion. Essays on the Novel*, George Braziller, New York, 1963, p. 55. Sarraute's essay "L'Ère du soupçon" first appeared in *Temps Modernes* in 1950.

telianly logical," is likewise baffled. He never finds what he is looking for, nor do Beckett's "detectives," Watt, Malone, and Molloy, or the soul detective in Sarraute's *The Unknown Man.* "Personality doesn't exist," says Ionesco's commentator on the modern theater. "The characters lose their form in the formlessness of becoming."[7]

Relativism, the next theme to be considered, is less skeptical. Relativism does not deny the existence of self (or at least of a derivative self) nor does it despair of finding and defining it. On the other hand, relativism posits the infinite plasticity of the human self, or personality, which it sees as the effect of historical and cultural conditioning. Thus, there is no fixed human nature. Man is in large part what others make him. The qualities that characterize man are relative to a certain kind of society, education, and environment. He is problematic in the sense that he is no one thing: his nature varies according to his nurture, which, in turn, varies according to the time, place, and culture. The impetus to this relativistic anthropology came mainly from three groups, the behaviorists and behavioral scientists, the cultural anthropologists, and the left wing of the Freudian movement. All three groups, in their several ways, stressed sociology, as much or more than biology; that is, they stressed the social, and therefore the changing and variable determinants of personality and behavior. By so doing, they shattered the age-old view of a fixed, or ideal, nature of man. The French sociologist Emile Durkheim had insisted years before in his critique of a "classical" education that there was no such thing as an "ideal nature of man," always and everywhere the same. Modern youth should be instructed in the reverse doctrine, inculcated by "the teachings of history" that "humanity, far from being invariable, is made, unmade, and remade ceaselessly; that far from being one, it is infinitely diverse, as well in time as in space."[8] This view was implicit in nineteenth-century historicism, as Durkheim well knew, but was now carried further by anthropologists and psychologists, who had the opportunity to observe vastly different personalities in different cultures.

Behaviorism, however, descended, not from historicism but from what Gordon Allport calls the Lockean tradition. More immediately, however, it was a revolt against introspectionist psychology and an attempt to extend to humans I. P. Pavlov's discovery of the conditioned reflex in animals. As its name indicates, behaviorism limited itself to

---

[7] Eugène Ionesco, *Victims of Duty,* in *Plays,* John Calder, London, 1962, Vol. II, pp. 274, 308.

[8] Emile Durkheim, *L'évolution pédagogique en France,* Felix Alcan, Paris, 1938, Vol. II, p. 194.

the observation of behavior, dispensing altogether with such "religious" concepts as consciousness, mental traits, and even instincts. It postulated an empty mind, or organism, which responded to external stimuli (known as the S-R model). Thus, the most important thing about the human personality was that it could be (and, in fact, was constantly being) "conditioned," that is, modified, molded, and changed by the environment, almost *ad infinitum*. Although behavioristic theory was developed chiefly by Americans and Russians, the general concept of conditioning attracted considerable attention in Europe beginning in the 1920's and soon found its way into European literature, as in Aldous Huxley's *Brave New World* (1932).

Anthropology's impact came slightly later, but carried the same relativistic message. Its position on "man" is brilliantly stated in André Malraux's wartime novel, whose central theme was the search for the basic nature of man. A group of intellectuals are assembled in the forests of Alsace-Lorraine, among them an ethnologist, named Möllberg. Möllberg puts the question to the company: the notion of man, does it mean anything? Underneath the beliefs, myths, and mental structures of men the world over, is it possible to isolate a fundamental idea, true for men in all places and running all through history? Möllberg himself gives a relativistic answer. "Fundamental man is a myth." Comparative studies of the civilizations of history reveal only irreducible differences.[9] Malraux himself did not accept this conclusion, but it was a fair statement of the position assumed by contemporary anthropology. What impressed the new generation of anthropologists was less "raw human nature" than human plasticity, observable in the myriad cultures of the earth. "Anthropology," Clyde Kluckhohn summarized, "holds up a great mirror to man and lets him look at himself in his infinite variety." Distinguishing between a "primary potential human nature" (man's presumably common genetic endowment), and a "secondary human nature," Ashley Montagu said it was the latter "that we know as *human nature,* and this human nature is not built in but is *bred* into us."[10]

The neo-Freudians, many of whom migrated to America during the

---

[9] André Malraux, *Les Noyers d'Altenburg* (published in 1948, but written during World War II). The conference of the intellectuals is reproduced in Malraux's *Anti-Memoirs* (1967).

[10] See Clyde Kluckhohn, *Mirror for Man,* McGraw-Hill, New York, 1949, p. 11 & *passim,* and M. F. Ashley Montagu, *Anthropology and Human Nature,* Porter Sargent, Boston, 1957, p. 37. This was also the point of view of ground-breaking studies by Ruth Benedict and Margaret Mead in the 1930's.

Nazi upheaval, accused Freud of ignoring this cultural relativism in his estimate of man. They themselves were not extreme relativists. There were basic human needs, if not a fixed human nature, as Freud had supposed. But the satisfaction of these needs, by no means exclusively biological, depended on the way society was organized. "Man's nature, his passions, and anxieties are a cultural product," Erich Fromm declared. The trend among the neo-Freudians was clearly away from Freud's biological orientation. Freud himself—both Karen Horney and Fromm point this out—was a cultural product. That is, all his famous assumptions—biologism, determinism, sexual conflict, human destructiveness—reflected either well-established philosophical convictions of the late nineteenth century, or else the competitive society he lived in. Human personality, then, varied from society to society, from, for instance, Middle Ages to Renaissance; in other words, it depended to a large extent on the process of learning and acculturation. "But," Fromm went on to say, "man is not only made by history, history is made by man." Fromm was obviously trying to find a middle ground between biological and sociological determinism. By leaving room for human creativity he thought he could show how to build a "sane society" that was more responsive to human needs than the capitalistic *Gesellschaft,* which had developed since the Renaissance.[11]

A relativistic view of man could be construed optimistically or pessimistically. On the whole, the theoreticians, particularly the Americans and those who left Europe for America, saw considerable hope in it, suggesting, as they thought, the possibility of manipulating, or molding, human nature for the better. On others, however, the relativistic view left a very different impression. Aldous Huxley, for example, was appalled by behaviorism's potential for making men into robots—who can ever forget the Central London Hatchery and Conditioning Center in *Brave New World?* And others did not fail to point out its resemblance to fascism. The Austrian writer Robert Musil deplored relativism because it left modern man without a solid view of himself. That is at least partly the message of his enigmatic and unfinished novel, *The Man Without Qualities* (1930–1942). Ulrich, Musil's antihero, is trying to find out who he is in a world lacking traditional landmarks. His father, who lived in an ordered world, had qualities. But the son, having to cope in a singularly disordered world (in the novel, it is the prewar Austro-Hungarian Empire), simply becomes a "man without

---

[11] For the neo-Freudian viewpoint, see Karen Horney, *The Neurotic Personality of our Times* (1937) and Erich Fromm, *Escape from Freedom* (1941), and *The Sane Society* (1955); also, the later works of Alfred Adler.

qualities," or, rather, one who passively takes on the qualities of his environment or of those around him. This passivity is vividly described in the chapter on architecture as a projection of the human personality. Arrived home from his travels, Ulrich conceives the ambition of re-modelling his château according to his own tastes. But since he suffers from the "incoherency that is characteristic of the present era," he finds he cannot choose from among the multitude of styles available to him, which range from Assyrian to Cubist. So he takes the next step "towards letting himself be shaped by the external circumstances of life itself"; he abandons the project to his tradespeople, confident that they would provide "all that was wanted in the way of tradition, prejudices and limitations."[12] Ulrich is David Riesman's "other-directed" man. Rela-tivism had deprived him of any sort of "inner" or "tradition-direction," and in consequence, he became problematic to himself and to others.

Musil's man without qualities is suggestive of the next and last theme to be considered in this chapter, that of self-depreciation. Here the point is not so much not knowing what man is as not liking or denigrating what one sees. Man, then, is problematic also in this final sense, that he thinks poorly of himself and of his prospects. Not merely his ambiguity and relativity but his insignificance in the scheme of things, his power-lessness, bestiality, and positive evil are remarked on. Man has qualities, but they are seldom admirable or heroic qualities. Twentieth-century literature is full of this kind of comment, which Malraux called "the death of Man," following hard on the heels of the "death of God." Others have called it the new realism. Never before, says one critic, had man "accepted so low an estimate of what he *is*."[13]

To understand this lowered estimate properly, it will be useful to recall once again the image it very largely replaced. This was the image of rational man, grown noticeably weaker since Darwin's time, as we have seen, yet still going strong at Oxford when Cyril Joad was a student there on the eve of World War I. In his autobiography, Joad writes of the "supreme self-confidence" of the undergraduates of his generation, of their optimism about reforming society, and of their

---

[12] Robert Musil, *The Man Without Qualities* (*Der Mann ohne Eigenschaften*), Eithne Wilkins (trans.), Secker and Warburg, London, 1953, Vol. I, pp. 16–17. Musil, an Austrian of the lower nobility, wrote his doctoral dissertation at Berlin on Ernst Mach who portrayed life as a dynamic process of becoming. It has been said correctly that *The Man Without Qualities* is not merely "the spiritual biography" of an empire (the declining Austro-Hungarian Empire) but of a whole age, "our own."

[13] Joseph Wood Krutch, *Human Nature and the Human Condition*, Random House, New York, 1959, p. 99.

belief in the power of reason. "I really believed that people could be persuaded by reason. . . . What was more, I believed that, once convinced of their truth (i.e. the truth of the propositions for which you were arguing), they would act accordingly." He also thought evil to be the result, not of human nature but of specific circumstances, "and if of specific circumstances, of removable circumstances"—a statement that sounds remarkably like John Mill, whom, indeed, he mentions. The young Joad, in short, had "the notion of human perfectibility." At the time of writing (1933), Joad himself still clung to this notion, though he was now alarmed at its decline since the Great War, thanks largely, he thought, to the psychologists, who were hard at work reducing man to animal or machine. But as time went on, Joad's own estimate of man also declined. During the 1930's, when human affairs were worsening, he became convinced of "the fact of human wickedness," and perhaps of its ineradicability. "Man's true enemy," he was already saying in 1939, "is within himself; it lies in the strength of his own uncontrolled passions and appetites."[14]

Joad's loss of faith reflects accurately, though somewhat tardily, reports on man coming in from contemporary psychological and religious thought, as well as literature and art. Gordon Allport believed that modern psychology had "trimmed down the image of man" to such an extent that democracy itself was in danger. Watsonian behaviorists would have vigorously denied this was so, but significantly Freud, and the main body of orthodox Freudians, would not. Freud, who became, in Thomas Mann's words, "a world movement" between the two world wars, thought of himself as a realist destroying man's illusions about himself. Copernicus had destroyed the cosmological illusion that man stood at the center of the universe. Darwin destroyed the biological illusion that man was a being essentially different from, and superior to, animals. Finally, psychoanalysis delivered the blow that "is probably the most wounding of all," namely that man was not even master in his own house, that the ego (reason) did not, as had been commonly assumed, direct the will and all the mind's working.

Of course, Freud was also a good "pre-Freudian rationalist," who believed in the possibility of a science of man and in healing. All the same, his anatomy of the mental personality was hardly flattering to man nor did he expect therapy to achieve happiness. His emphasis was

[14] C. E. M. Joad, *Under the Fifth Rib*, E. P. Dutton, New York, 1933, pp. 18–19, 23, and *passim; Guide to Modern Wickedness*, Faber & Faber, London, 1939, Introduction and Article on Evil, pp. 38–57.

on man's instinctual endowment. Though Freud changed his mind several times about the nature of the instincts, he always regarded them as basic and as in conflict. Ultimately, he came to see life in Empedoclean terms, as an eternal struggle between the instincts of Eros and Thanatos, love and death, the latter being manifested in man's destructiveness toward both himself and others. Freud was not sanguine about the power of reason to hold the aggressive and destructive instincts permanently in check, either in the individual psyche or in society. "Civilized society," he wrote, "is perpetually menaced with disintegration through the primary hostility of men towards one another. . . . The passions of interest are stronger than reasoned interests."[15] He could, it is true, talk rather optimistically at times of putting ego over id, and even of the possible future "primacy of the intellect." But more often Freud's language conveyed the opposite impression, of a "poor ego," weak from the dynamic point of view, embattled by id, superego, and reality itself, and frequently having to give way under its task. For Freud, as for Plato, reason was the rider of the horse. But Freud's rider, far from being in firm command, "all too often" takes orders from his more powerful mount and is forced to guide it the way it wants to go. The horse, of course, was the id, described by Freud as the great reservoir of instinctual energy, "a chaos, a cauldron of seething excitement"; in popular language, standing for "the untamed passions," primitive and irrational, demanding outlet. Who could doubt it? Man was more than half animal, and what is more, a sick animal who did not really want to get well. Mitigating this biological-psychological image somewhat is the role played in Freud's system by the analyst, who can help individuals understand their hidden self and thus gain a measure of honesty and insight. Freudian man could also build great civilizations, though he did so only in self-protection, and at the expense of happiness, that is, by sublimating and renouncing his most powerful instincts. All in all, the Freudian image was hardly a heroic or rational image. Freud was right in believing that he had delivered a great blow to man's narcissism, greater even than the blows administered by Copernicus and Darwin.

Self-depreciation was equally conspicuous in contemporary religious thought. Erich Fromm says that Freud taught a "secularized version of

---

[15] Freud, *Civilization and Its Discontents* (1930), Joan Riviere (trans.), Jonathan Cape, London, 1930, p. 86. For Freud's comparison with Copernicus and Darwin, see his essay "One of the Difficulties of Psychoanalysis" (1917), and for "the poor ego," *New Introductory Lectures on Psychoanalysis* (1937).

the concept of original sin." Freud, of course, did not think of it as sin, that is, in traditional moral terms. He did, however, recognize an evil inherent in man's nature, for example, man's incestuous and murderous impulses. This conviction of an "original sin" lay at the heart of the new theology, sometimes called neo-orthodoxy or Christian realism, which grew up during and after World War I and which ran parallel to the Freudian movement. Its leaders attacked liberal or modernist theology, chiefly for its "immanence-faith," as Emil Brunner called it. Immanence-faith,[16] descended from German Idealism and taught by Schleiermacher and Ritschl, among others, found God in existing things, establishing a continuity between God and nature and man. Thus, it puffed man up, teaching him to think of himself as Godlike, rational and potentially good, capable of saving himself. What Jesus first realized, said one "modernist" theologian, is true potentially of all men, "that the true man or higher self is divine and eternal, integral to the being of God, and that this divine manhood is gradually but surely manifesting on the physical plane."[17] Significantly, this same "modernist" was singing a different tune by 1916, with the emphasis now on sin and evil. Indeed, the war opened the eyes of many a theologian to the "realities" of human nature, as perhaps it helped to confirm and deepen Freud's views about the aggressive and death instincts. During the war, Karl Barth, who, like the Rev. Campbell, had been brought up on modernism, took to reading Luther, Calvin, and St. Paul all over again, as well as Sören Kierkegaard. Repudiating immanence-faith, Barth began to preach a radical discontinuity, or dualism, between God and man. God was transcendent, not immanent, "Wholly Other," above rational knowledge. Man, on the other hand, was mired in sin in consequence of the Fall, living under God's judgment. In his commentary on the *Epistle to the Romans* (1918) Barth wrote that the men who inhabit this world of death "are men of sin. Sin is that by which man as we know him is defined, for we know nothing of sinless men. Sin is power—sovereign power. By it men are controlled." And Emil Brunner wrote to the same effect: "Evil is lodged in the very centre of his [man's] will. . . . Something has happened [the commission of original sin] over which we have no longer any control;

---

[16] On immanentism or immanence-faith, see p. 444.

[17] R. J. Campbell, *The New Theology*, Macmillan, New York, 1907, p. 107; quoted in W. M. Horton, *Contemporary English Theology*, Harper & Brothers, New York, 1936, p. 34. On Campbell, minister at the City Temple, London, see further p. 444.

and the damage is beyond our ability to repair."[18] Barthian man was helpless and hopeless, as little able to save himself as was Freudian man. God alone could save man, by revelation and grace, just as in the Freudian system the psychiatrist played the role of healer, or at least father confessor.

The Roman Catholic philosopher Jacques Maritain rejected Barth's "annihilation of man before God," and, in general, the Pauline (or Augustinian) emphasis was stronger in contemporary Protestant than in Catholic thought. The neo-Thomists in particular were careful to preserve the Thomistic Analogy of Being, and thus not to put such a great gulf between man and God. Still, there was much emphasis in Catholic thought on the ubiquitousness of evil in the world, of the sin of "angelism" (Maritain: man's pride of intellect, causing all the diseases of modern life, secularism, bourgeois materialism, and Marxism), and of demoniacal forces working through man. Dom Aloïs Mager, dean of the Faculty of Theology at Salzburg, was thinking of Nazism when he wrote in 1946, that "in theological language we would say: the consequences of original sin are not in themselves demonic: they are human: but they are points of entry for demons."[19] This Satanism, as it is sometimes called, this emphasis on the satanic in, or else using, human nature, is even more conspicuous in Catholic literature than in Catholic philosophy or theology. The novels of Georges Bernanos (for example, *Sous le Soleil de Satan,* 1926), François Mauriac, and Graham Greene are filled with Satanism.

In fact, creative literature and art in general record best the new lowered estimate of man, not only the irrationality, sickness, or evil possibly endemic to his nature but his essentially unheroic stature. This is so well known that a few examples should suffice to demonstrate it. With respect to the portrayal of human evil, it would be strange indeed if in a time of major wars and concentration camps, writers and artists had not been obsessed with man's inhumanity to man. This is the theme of William Golding's *Lord of the Flies* (1954), as of Jean-Paul Sartre's late play *The Condemned of Altona* (1959). Golding,

---

[18] Karl Barth, *The Epistle to the Romans* (*Der Römerbrief*), Edwyn Hoskyns (trans.), Oxford University Press, Oxford, 1933, p. 167; Emil Brunner, *The Theology of Crisis,* Charles Scribner's Sons, New York, 1930, pp. 53–54. Brunner, for a time professor of theology at Zurich, was somewhat less radical about sin and natural theology than Barth. Barth, Swiss preacher and theologian, held chairs of theology in three German universities before being banished by the Nazis.

[19] *Satan,* Sheed & Ward, New York, 1952, p. 489. This volume consists of essays by continental European Catholics. Dom Aloïs Mager's essay is titled "Satan in Our Day."

trying to discover what man (or preman) is like when civilization is stripped away, conducts an experiment. Arranging a plane crash, he drops a group of English schoolboys on an uninhabited island and watches what happens to them. All but a few of the boys revert to savagery. They do not become noble savages, but cruel and irrational savages, who wreak their primal destructiveness on one another. The theme of Sartre's play is not liberty, so conspicuous in his existentialist works, but fatality: man condemned by his own nature to do evil. Sartre had been thinking about the criminality of the twentieth century. Who or what was ultimately responsible for it? The voice of the "hero" Franz von Gerlach, coming from a tape recorder played after his death, gives the answer: "The century might have been a good one had not man been watched from time immemorial by the cruel enemy who had sworn to destroy him, that hairless, evil, flesh-eating beast— man himself." Von Gerlach, the Nazi "butcher of Smolensk," had first struck at the beast he saw in the eyes of his neighbors, on the ground of self-defense. But he then discovered the beast still living in himself, and began to feel guilty and condemned. "Man is dead and I am his witness."[20]

The twentieth-century British painter Francis Bacon, ironically a collateral descendant of the great Elizabethan, made this his special subject. The expressionists had already revealed a primitive human nature that was often violent and uncontrolled. The surrealists of the 1920's had also conjured up disturbing images from the unconscious, while remaining, however, "officially" optimistic (as is apparent from André Breton's successive manifestos, which connected the movement with romanticism and communism and talked about "the liberation of man"). Bacon's nightmarish subjects—screaming figures enclosed in transparent boxes, studies of the Crucifixion, slaughterhouses, and embryology—followed this general line, but were decidedly not optimistic. His *Painting* of 1946, for example, depicting a monstrous butcher under an umbrella (Plate 37), communicates a feeling of terror. Here we are meant to see, surely, not merely the horrors of a particular war, but all the bestiality and evil and the terror of which man is capable at any time.

Man the victim, however, looms larger in twentieth-century literature and art than man the doer of evil. This is the image that projects best of all the new mood of self-depreciation: "a reduced and con-

---

[20] Sartre, *The Condemned of Altona* (*Les Séquestrés d'Altona*), end of Act V. See also Act II.

PLATE 37. *Painting,* by Francis Bacon (1946).

Oil and tempera on canvas. 6′ 5⅞″ x 52″. Collection, The Museum of Modern Art, New York.

tracted self," basically insignificant, ordinary, helpless in the face of circumstances; *de trop,* lacking either authenticity or stature; in a word, antihero. One thinks in this connection of James Joyce's Mr. Bloom, poor trusting little man; of Franz Kafka's "K"; of Sartre's Roquentin; and many others. "K", served with a warrant for an unnamed crime, tries to find justice, is unable to find it, and ends by being destroyed for his attempt. Again, in *The Metamorphosis* a man awakes one morning from uneasy dreams to find himself transformed into a gigantic insect. He crawls around the room, "a regular human bedroom, only rather too small," but never gets out, and his movements are more and more confined until his death. Whatever else he may be, Kafka's Gregor Samsa is a transparent image of modern man's ever diminishing stature. This was the kind of image Sartre was projecting in the 1930's. In *Nausea* (1937), Antoine Roquentin, Sartre's antihero, visits the Bouville museum, and there observes the portraits of the town's elite in the nineteenth century. "Without mental reservation," he jotted down in his notebook, "I admired the reign of man"—all those respectable citizens, who understood everything, their rights and duties, even what happened to them after death, hence carried themselves so confidently. But, of course, it was all an illusion, as he had explained previously to "the Self-Taught Man" with whom he conversed in the town café. Like the people in the paintings, the latter was a humanist who believed in man, if not God, in his courage and humanity, in humanity as a goal. Not so, says Roquentin. All man knows is that he exists, and that the world exists, and for no reason. "We were a heap of living creatures," he wrote, musing on the human condition, ". . . we hadn't the slightest reason to be there. . . . And I—soft, weak, obscene, disgusting, juggling with dismal thoughts—I, too, was In the Way." True, man was free. But the freedom, he felt, "was rather like death."[21] So much for "the reign of man": man was simply *de trop.*

In the art of the Swiss sculptor-painter Alberto Giacometti, it is not so much the feeling of man's gratuitousness as it is of human remoteness, loneliness, and fright that is uppermost. Here again, the artist's own verbal explanation of his aims does not necessarily agree with what we think we see in his work. Giacometti himself was an experimenter, who was much interested in problems of space and in how distant objects appeared to the human eye or in imagination or memory. But what are we to make of such works as *Woman with Her Throat Cut,* the

---

[21] Sartre, *Nausea* (*La Nausée*), Lloyd Alexander (trans.), New Directions, London, 1949, pp. 114–123, 151, 165, 172–173.

often reproduced *City Square* in which attenuated figures pass each other without communicating, and *Hands Holding the Void*. It is known that Giacometti formed a connection for a time with the surrealists and that he was a friend of Sartre. Whatever this may signify, many of Giacometti's works do certainly present the image of a frightened self, in perpetual fear of the void (1934–1935, Plate 38), and much reduced in size or mobility. Apropos of a group of tiny figurines done in 1945, Giacometti said that, as he had begun to work from memory again, "to my terror the sculptures became smaller and smaller. . . . Head and figures seemed to me to have a bit of truth only when small."[22] Man the victim stands out even more clearly in certain respects in representative works by two British artists. *Roman Actors* (1934, Plate 39) by Wyndham Lewis, who created a style of painting known as vorticism, depicts mechanized human figures, typical, as Lewis would have said, of a robot-driven civilization. This image of robot man obviously contrasts sharply with the Promethean image, which became so popular from the elder Bacon's time on, of man in control of nature. *Seated Woman with Arms Extended* (1953–1957, Plate 40) by the somewhat younger sculptor Kenneth Armitage, whose work came to public attention at about midcentury, represents an obviously helpless human figure, man as a sort of bug, but with inflexible limbs, unable to control his environment. This work has been compared to Kafka's helpless bug in *Metamorphosis*.

The themes developed in this chapter—epistemological despair, relativism, and self-depreciation—by no means encompass all that was said about man during this period. Existential and personality psychologists, as well as the neo-Freudians, fought to strengthen or transcend the ego in a counter move against biological determinism, or behavioristic conditioning. In the 1930's, and during the Resistance, many writers likewise began to emphasize "engagement" and "rebellion," and, like Malraux, to define man as "the sum of his acts, of what he has done and of what he can do." Malraux's odyssey in this respect is significant, if not quite typical. From having highlighted "the death of Man" in an early work (*La Tentation de l'occident*, 1926), he began later to talk about "the power and glory of being Man," of man's revolt against fate, in the world of art as well as action.

Existentialism stressed above all man's freedom to define himself. The philosophers of the movement, Martin Heidegger, Sartre, and

---

[22] Quoted in *Alberto Giacometti*, Introduction by Peter Selz, Museum of Modern Art, New York, 1965, p. 47.

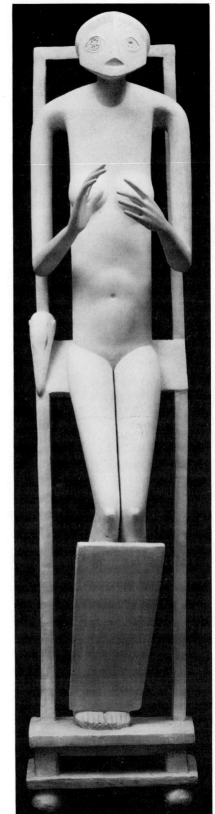

PLATE 38. *Hands Holding the Void,*
by Alberto Giacometti.

Yale University Art Gallery.

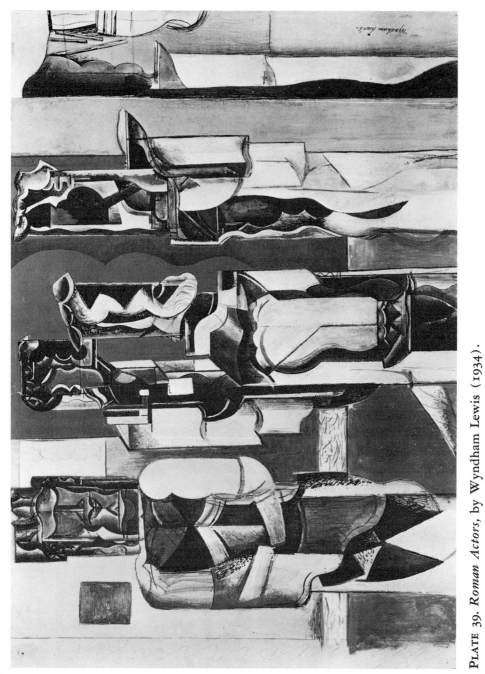

PLATE 39. *Roman Actors*, by Wyndham Lewis (1934).

Watercolor, gouache, and ink. 15⅛" x 22⅛". Collection, The Museum of Modern Art, New York. Francis E. Brennan Fund.

PLATE 40. *Seated Woman with Arms Extended,* by Kenneth Armitage.

Gabriel Marcel all commented on the loss of a sense of "being" in modern times. Yet man *is* being, or *Dasein.* However, being as understood by the existentialists was not a static but a dynamic concept. Man must not be thought of in terms of static substances, or as reducible to causal laws applicable to all of nature (positivism), or as subsumed under universal concepts (idealism). Thus, to think of *man as being* really meant to think of him as *potencia,* or becoming. To exist meant, literally, to stand out, to emerge, to choose, to transcend the forces operating upon one, not to be bound entirely by the past, but to point toward the future.

In the words of Ludwig Binswanger, one of the founders of the "school" of existential psychology, the *Umwelt,* or world of objects, of biological drives and natural laws, to which man must adjust, should not be allowed to dominate the *Eigenwelt,* man's own world, of self-awareness, mind, and "spirit." Man—always by man the existentialist meant the individual man, the self, rather than *das Man,* the mass lacking uniqueness and originality—could choose to make the *Eigenwelt* uppermost in his life; Binswanger called this "Dasein choosing." That was the trouble with Freud, as Binswanger saw it. Freud thought of *man as nature (Homo natura),* explicable in terms of mechanisms, drives, and laws. It was the alleged passivity of Freud's system to which Binswanger objected. To the idea of *Homo natura,* "a genuinely natural-science, biopsychological idea," as he called it, Binswanger opposed his own "anthropology." Freud saw in all human metamorphosis or change "always the same basic form of the instinct itself persisting as an indestructible, ever-present operational factor," which did not permit a concept of genuine change. Existence, however, as conceived by "anthropology," envisaged the possibility of "genuine metamorphosis." As Binswanger put it, Freud presented only a torso of the whole; his idea about the instinctual nature of man needed "enlarging." Interestingly, Binswanger related his existential psychology, not so much to Freud (from whom he admittedly learned much), as to Herder, Goethe, and Dilthey, who taught him that man could be learned only from his history. History, of course, signified, for Binswanger, not a determinism, but man's creativity, as expressed in science, art, ethics, and religion.[23]

[23] See especially two essays by Binswanger, "Freud's Conception of Man in the Light of Anthropology" (an address in commemoration of Freud's eightieth birthday, 1936), and "Freud and the Magna Charta of Clinical Psychiatry," both reprinted in *Being-in-the-World. Selected Papers of Ludwig Binswanger,* Jacob Needleman (trans.), Basic Books, New York, 1963. Freud corresponded with Binswanger, but called him a conservative, and his existential analysis "a reactionary movement back to 'spirit'."

"Man has no nature; what he has is history." Ortega y Gasset, similarly influenced by Dilthey, also used existential language to express his concept of man. Neither science nor idealism could discover man's nature, for man was more than body or spirit, both of which were static concepts. Man was not "a being already," but "an infinitely plastic entity," who, possessing freedom, himself determined what he was going to be. Ortega exulted in this human plasticity, which he said was revealed by history.[24] Albert Camus talked very much to the same effect, though he professed not to be an existentialist (he tended to identify existentialism with Sören Kierkegaard, whose "leap" into religious faith demanded, he believed, the abandonment of reason). "I am optimistic as to man," Camus could say after World War II. Like Malraux, Camus had developed a more positive view of man, possibly because of, or at least during, the Resistance. Camus denounced the Hegelian-Marxist dialectic of history, which he thought made man a puppet. Man was free, not simply carried along by an inevitable process. He could choose to defy the Absurd, and combat social injustice wherever he found it. Thus, there are heroes as well as antiheroes in Camus' works—the conqueror, the rebel, the good doctor who combatted the plague—as, indeed, the hint of a heroic quality in man is conspicuous in much of existentialist thought and literature.

Yet it was a bittersweet heroism. The heroes, when there were heroes, were absurdist heroes. They knew they lived in an absurd world. They knew that they were problematic and that the world was problematic. Everything in the world might be free, but there was despair in the freedom. Existentialist language referring to man was always somewhat ambiguous. "I am optimistic about man," Camus said. But just before that statement, he had said, comparing his position to the Christian position, that he was "pessimistic as to human destiny."[25] And Sartre, Camus' rival on occasion, in his wartime play *The Flies* had his hero Orestes say at the end—after he had acted heroically in defying Zeus and the tyrant Aegisthus, and restored freedom to the people of Argos—"I am doomed to have no other law than mine." "Human life," Sartre said, "begins on the far side of despair." Thus, not even existential man escaped being problematic. Emmanuel Mounier, one of the

---

[24] See Ortega's famous essay on "History as a System," reprinted in *Philosophy and History. Essays Presented to Ernst Cassirer*, R. Klibansky (ed.), Clarendon Press, Oxford, 1936.

[25] Albert Camus, "Fragments of a statement made at the Dominican Monastery of Latour-Maubourg in 1948," in *Resistance, Rebellion and Death*, Justin O'Brien (trans.), Alfred A. Knopf, New York, 1961, pp. 72–73.

leaders of the Personalist movement in France and editor of the new journal *Esprit,* spoke of "the dislocation of the classical concept of man" in the twentieth century, which he compared to the dislocation of Euclidean perspectives by the later geometries. There is no doubt that there was such a dislocation, or that, because of it, man became less clear about his nature and thought less well of himself. Writing in the 1930's, Mounier was understandably worried lest this "negation of man by man should carry its frenzy to the point of destruction of man by man."[26] It was quite common by then to talk of anguish, as Mounier did, as having replaced the happiness that had once been a new idea in Europe.

[26] Emmanuel Mounier, "The Crisis of the Twentieth Century," in *Be Not Afraid. Studies in Personalist Psychology,* Cynthia Rowland (trans.), Harper & Brothers, New York, 1954, pp. 146–148.

Eclipse of God

Dietrich Bonhoeffer's now famous theological letters, written in a Nazi prison, describe, with agonizing clarity, the salient features of Europe's religious landscape in the first half of the twentieth century: the all but total secularization of culture; the rise of new theologies to meet this situation; and the hint—alas, there was no time for anything more, since Bonhoeffer was executed when only thirty-nine years old —of a much more radical theology to come, of a "religionless Christianity," as he named it. Brought up in a secular family, which ridiculed theology, and persecuted by the German state (not, however, for his religious opinions but for his role in the Resistance), Bonhoeffer was better placed than most to appreciate the lengths to which secularism had gone. In a letter of June 8, 1944, to his friend Pastor Bethge, he wrote feelingly of the world's "great defection from God" in the twentieth century. The secular movement, which he thought began about the thirteenth century,

> has in our time reached a certain completion. Man has learned to cope with all questions of importance without recourse to God as a working hypothesis. In questions concerning science, art, and even ethics, this has become an understood thing which one scarcely dares to tilt at any more.[1]

[1] Dietrich Bonhoeffer, *Letters and Papers from Prison*, Eberhard Bethge (ed.), Macmillan, New York, 1966, pp. 194–195.

Bonhoeffer's library, bequeathed to Bethge, contained works by Ernst Troeltsch, Karl Barth, and Emil Brunner. He had certainly also read Rudolf Bultmann and Paul Tillich. These were the titans of the "old" liberal theology in Germany, and of the new theologies that had sprung up during and after World War I. Bonhoeffer, by the time he wrote his last letters, was critical of all forms of Christian apologetics. Barth, despite his important role as critic of modern civilization, was too conservative for him. Barth expected the modern world to swallow the Christian revelation whole, and to take it on the faith of Bible and Church. Bultmann's fault, on the other hand, was not that he went too far with his demythologizing of the New Testament but that he did not go far enough. Tillich bravely tried to interpret and shape the whole world in a religious sense, but "the world unseated him and went on by itself." Even the Confessing Church, set up to oppose the Nazified church in Germany, and of which Bonhoeffer was a leader for a time, had lapsed into a conservative restoration of historical Christian theology. Bonhoeffer's own message, though none too clear, seemed to point beyond these theologies to a new sort of radical Christianity, characterized by complete honesty, dispensing with all "religious jargon," including the term God itself, which had become meaningless for most people, yet keeping the suffering Christ, and thus speaking to modern man's condition. But it remains an open question as to whether Bonhoeffer's own religionless religion did not represent a bankruptcy of the whole theological undertaking, at least as that was traditionally understood.

Bonhoeffer was, of course, right about secularism's "having reached a certain completion" in the twentieth century. This is, by now, so generally understood that it scarcely seems necessary to say more about it, or to document it in any detail.[2] Nevertheless, certain points need to be emphasized, both in order to put this secularism into proper historical perspective and to explain how it affected the new theologies. First of all, it is important to distinguish between two kinds of secularism. The first kind, of which Bonhoeffer was really speaking, was called "genuine secularism" by Karl Heim. Genuine secularism, which Heim found more prevalent among the soldiers of World War II than World War I, validated Nietzsche's prophecy. It was "silent," having completely lost interest in religious questions, regarding such questions as meaningless and not even worth responding to, certainly not militantly,

---

[2] See the author's *Religion and the Rise of Scepticism*, Harcourt, Brace, New York, 1960, Chap. IV.

as the anticlericals and atheists of past centuries had been wont to do. "The discussion of these questions," Heim said, "is not a dialogue between the Church and the World. It is never more than a monologue of the Church with itself."[3] From the intellectual world, we might cite as an example of this new "secularist man" the atheist existentialist who *begins* his argument with the assumption that God is dead. Jean-Paul Sartre, for instance, accepting Nietzsche's madman's cry as a valid statement of fact, proceeded to build his philosophy on man's rather than God's existence. This humanistic existentialism, Sartre believed, gave man real dignity, for whereas it made him responsible for everything, it set him free to create all the essences there were, or ever could be, in the universe.

Sartre did, however, also find man's situation distressing, and his distress forms a bridge to another kind of secularism characterized, not by indifference to religious questions, but by anguish at man's inability to answer them positively, hence by his feeling of cosmic homelessness. This was a major theme of serious literature from Franz Kafka to Albert Camus: the plight of twentieth-century man, convinced of God's death, yet not exulting in it, as Nietzsche had done, but despairing; living without transcendent meaning, yet aware of the need for it. "We are the dispossessed," Arthur Koestler has one of his fictional characters say, ". . . the dispossessed of faith; the physically or spiritually homeless." His hero Julien Delattre, described as a poet who enjoyed a certain vogue in the 1930's, longs for a new home, but without much hope, for a new cosmic loyalty "with a doctrine acceptable to twentieth-century man."[4] *The Castle* (written by Kafka probably in 1922) is the perfect example of this second kind of secularism, with its antihero "K" trying to establish telephonic communication with the Lord up there on the cliff, but never succeeding. "K," or Kafka, finds God alternately remote, cruel by human standards, incommensurable with the human mind, and probably nonexistent. "K" dies without receiving official confirmation by the Castle bureaucrats of his appointment as land-surveyor in his village down below.

Why this drift toward secularism, whether "genuine" or despairing? As Bonhoeffer observed, twentieth-century secularism represents the

---

[3] Karl Heim, *Christian Faith and Natural Science*, Harper & Brothers, New York, 1953, p. 16. Heim, a well-known German philosopher and theologian in the aftermath of World War I, relied heavily on Helmut Thielicke's essay, "Der Mensch des Säkularismus," for his conception of secularism.

[4] Arthur Koestler, *The Age of Longing*, Macmillan, New York, 1951, pp. 28, 137.

culmination of a movement that extended back to the Middle Ages. But there were also particular reasons for the surge of secularism in the twentieth century. There were, of course, the special events, unparalleled by anything that had happened before. As an Oxford don put it bluntly in the "Honest to God debate" of the 1960's: "How can we think of God after the Somme, after Auschwitz."[5] Among the more important intellectual reasons, there was the patent failure of religion to encompass, or even to fit satisfactorily into, the scientific world-view. As we shall see, the demythologizing theologians recognized this failure as a special problem, and consequently went to great lengths to convince people that the validity of Christianity did not depend on the acceptance of an outmoded, Biblical cosmology. There was also the new science of psychoanalysis, which, at least as presented by Freud, appeared to explain religion away as an illusion, not deserving of a future. Man had palpably invented the gods, in order to allay his anxieties in the face of life's dangers. "The New Psychology," C. S. Lewis wrote in his autobiography, "was at that time [after World War I] sweeping through us all. We did not swallow it whole (few people then did) but we were all influenced. What we were most concerned about was 'Fantasy' or 'wishful thinking'."[6] Nor did the antimetaphysical climate, exemplified by both existentialism and the positivistic explosion, make things easy for a certain kind of religious thinking. It made theological metaphysics suspect, thus driving religion into the realm of faith, which, for the foregoing, as well as other reasons, "secularist man" could no longer accept.

But of all the reasons for an inflated secularism in the twentieth century, historicism was probably the most compelling. Almost everybody alludes to this, sooner or later, as a chief stumbling block to religious belief, as, for example, Sartre when he said, "God spoke to us and now is silent"—by which he meant that in the past man believed he heard God, but was incapable now of believing any such thing. Ernst Troeltsch, himself a theologian, but of the historical as opposed to the dogmatic school, spelled out "the problem of historicism" in the 1920's. History, Troeltsch said in an early work, "is no longer merely one way of looking at things, but the basis of all thought about values and norms." Unfortunately, however, the study of history had led, in his opinion, not to better understanding, but to the undermining, of

---

[5] Alasdair MacIntyre, in his essay "God and the Theologians" (1963), reprinted in *Against the Self-Images of the Age*, Schocken Books, New York, 1971.

[6] C. S. Lewis, *Surprised by Joy*, Harcourt, Brace, New York, 1955, p. 203.

"all firm norms and ideals of human existence."[7] History showed everything, law, morality, religion, and art, to be in ceaseless flux. Troeltsch may have convinced himself that he had overcome historicism with history. He believed that the study of history uncovered absolute truth, though refracted in myriad forms, none of them absolute, not even Christianity itself. All the same, Troeltsch understood very well, and made it his business to point out, the problem that historicism had created for Western culture. In consequence of historical criticism, he wrote, people everywhere—he was speaking of the postwar era—were impressed "with the relativity and transitoriness of all things, even of the loftiest ideals of civilisation."[8] How could religion, which depended on belief in absolute truth, survive in such a climate?

The new theologies, those mentioned by Bonhoeffer and others, rose in answer to this crisis, as some called it—the crisis of secularism, which threatened to engulf the world; but also the crisis of world events, to which, it was felt, older theologies could not possibly speak. Here we shall deal only with the best known of these new theologies: "neo-orthodoxy," as expounded by Barth and modified by Bultmann and Tillich; neo-Thomism, championed by, among others, Jacques Maritain; neo-mysticism (mentioned in passing only); and the "process" theology, or philosophy of religion, of Alfred North Whitehead and some others. The mere mention of the names of these men, all of them in the front rank of intellects, underlines the continuing vigor of religious thinking in a secular culture. This is a paradox. On the one hand, European culture was becoming secularized to the point of ignoring, or deploring, religious questions. On the other hand, theology experienced a renaissance, engaging in lively debate about how men should talk of God in the new age.

To understand neo-orthodoxy, it is necessary, first, to recall the principal emphasis of liberal Protestantism, which it sought to overcome. Liberalism, though by no means all of one piece, came to be known chiefly for its optimism about man and history. On the whole, it preferred not to make metaphysical statements about God. This was the heritage of Kant, who said man could not know God, knowledge being

---

[7] Ernst Troeltsch, quoted in Georg Iggers, *The German Conception of History,* Wesleyan University Press, Middletown, Connecticut, 1969, pp. 178, 189. Toeltsch's major book, *Der Historismus und seine Probleme,* was published in 1922.

[8] Troeltsch, *Christian Thought. Its History and Application,* University of London Press, London, 1923, p. 7. The title of this book is a misnomer. It consisted of lectures, written for delivery in England, on historicism and its "overcoming" (*Überwindung*).

limited to the phenomenal world. Avoiding "Greek" categories such as self-sufficiency, being, substance, and changelessness, liberal Protestantism pictured God as immanent in life and culture, and as known to men in experience (Schleiermacher); as not separate from nature and history, but as unfolding Absolute (Hegel), or even as finite and changing, struggling to achieve evolutionary development and historical progress (evolutionary theology); as guaranteeing, through Jesus, the fulfillment of man's moral personality, and the building of the Kingdom of God on earth (Albrecht Ritschl); or as revealing himself in the great value systems and religions of history (the historical school of Adolf Harnack and Troeltsch). Summing up the liberal message, the Rev. R. J. Campbell, minister at the City Temple, London, urged men to have done with thinking of God "as above and apart from His world instead of expressing Himself through his World." "When I say God, I mean the mysterious Power which is finding expression in the universe, and which is present in every tiniest atom of the wondrous whole. I find that this Power is the one reality I cannot get away from, for whatever else it may be, it is myself."[9]

This "new theology," as Campbell called it, collapsed with the coming of World War I. Campbell himself abandoned it, as did Barth and Tillich, though, as we shall see, it left its mark on all of them. Of the German-speaking trio (including Bultmann), who provided theological leadership in the next decades, perhaps only Barth was very "orthodox." Pointedly warning against Schleiermacher, the "father of modern theology," Barth identified himself with "the ancestral line" running back through Kierkegaard to Luther and Calvin, and so to St. Paul and Jeremiah. What was wrong with Schleiermacher? Schleiermacher, like liberal theology in general, had sought to overcome Luther's dualism, and thus to build a bridge between heaven and earth, across which man might reverently cross. Barth wanted to restore dualism, which was why his opponents dubbed his theology neo-orthodoxy. He himself called it a theology of crisis, or dialectical theology (in the Kierkegaardian, however, rather than the Hegelian sense, since God alone could provide syntheses for man's theses and antitheses). Barth's theology first appeared full-blown in his *Römerbrief* of 1918 (commentary on St. Paul's *Epistle to the Romans*), the book for which he was always best known, and which, though somewhat modified later, contained his central message. This message is said to have made Adolf Harnack,

---

[9] R. J. Campbell, *The New Theology*, Chapman & Hall, London, 1907, pp. 4, 18. For an excellent synopsis of liberal Protestant theology, see Langdon Gilkey's article, "Idea of God since 1800," *Dictionary of the History of Ideas*, Vol. II.

Barth's old teacher at the University of Marburg, shudder. The Kierke-gaardian note in it was unmistakable.[10] Barth, like Kierkegaard, put a great gulf between God and nature. God, insofar as it was possible to say anything at all about him—for in this early stage of his thinking Barth denied even the possibility of a natural theology—was transcend-ent, not immanent, "wholly other." Man knew about God only through revelation, only as God spoke to him in the Bible or acted upon him through Jesus Christ. Nature, on the other hand (no Thomistic analogy of being here), was sunk in sin, man having lost the divine image, and history likewise being alienated from God, and meaningless. Therefore, if a bridge were ever to span this abyss, it would have to be thrown down from "yonder," rather than "here," from "above" rather than "below"—even Barth's space metaphors derived from an earlier age, before the advent of modern science.[11] This was obviously a theology brought to a head, if not actually created, by the disillusionment of the Great War. It might be thought of as the religious analogue of Oswald Spengler's *Decline of the West,* which was published at very nearly the same time as the *Römerbrief.* No wonder Harnack, bright star of the religio-historical school, shuddered. According to Barth, God was righteous, man (and man's history) unrighteous. Only God's initiative could restore man to faith and sanity.

Though they shared some of Barth's views, neither Bultmann nor Tillich can be narrowly identified with the neo-orthodox movement. There were obviously other influences at work upon them, conspicu-ously existentialism. Both were much impressed by Martin Heidegger, who also taught at the University of Marburg during the 1920's.[12] Moreover, both Bultmann and Tillich though in different ways, tried to relate religion to secular culture, yet without falling back into liberal optimism. Bultmann, two years older than Barth, achieved fame much later, with the publication during World War II of his article entitled "New Testament and Mythology." All through this article, which set off a great debate in Protestant circles, Bultmann hammered away at the problem of communication. Why was Christianity becoming un-intelligible to the modern world? It was because its message was con-

---

[10] Kierkegaard's complete works were translated into German just before World War I (1909–1911), and, of course, had an added appeal in the postwar situation.

[11] To express his meaning, Barth also invented new terms such as "wholly Other" and "dialectical theology."

[12] Bultmann was made professor of New Testament and Early Christian History in 1921, Tillich professor of Theology in 1924, at Marburg.

cealed in the wrong guise. How could modern man, brought up on modern science, be expected to accept "the cosmology of a prescientific age"? How could modern man believe in a three-storied structure of the world (heaven, hell, and earth), in angels and the intervention of supernatural forces on the earth, in the Ascension as literally true, or in the Resurrection, which was surely intolerable as a "nature miracle." Bultmann's answer was clear. "If the truth of the New Testament proclamation is to be preserved, the only way is to demythologize it"[13] —faith must not be tied to an outmoded world-view. Thus far Bultmann stood with the liberals. But he thought that the liberals threw out, or at least seriously distorted, the *kerygma* (Gospel message), along with the mythology. He, therefore, distinguished sharply between the historically conditioned, mythological, world-view of Christianity and its eternal essence. The latter he explained in existential rather than historical terms, interpreting the New Testament as a description of man's encounter with God in the here and now. It told essentially of man's plight, of his living in despair in a world of impermanence and death, and of his deliverance by God through Christ. Bultmann took issue with the existentialist philosophers at one critical point. Man, "totally fallen," was not autonomous, as they said, could not achieve "authentic Being" merely by reflection and self-assertion. Only the transcendent God could deliver man from himself, through the saving work of Christ. "This is precisely the meaning of what was wrought in Christ. At the very point where man can do nothing, God steps in and acts—indeed he has acted already—on man's behalf."[14] Despite his emphasis on demythologization, Bultmann obviously remained neo-orthodox in important respects. Like Barth, who criticized his program, he believed in an alienation between God and man, which only God could overcome; in a God, moreover, about whom man could say little without "mythologizing the transcendent"; who was known to man only through his (God's) revelation.

Paul Tillich's theology (and philosophy of religion) is harder to characterize, as he belonged to no school, nor did he found a school.[15] In his own phrase, he stood "at the boundary" between liberalism and

---

[13] Rudolf Bultmann, "Neues Testament und Mythologie" (1941), in H. W. Bartsch (ed.), *Kerygma and Myth. A Theological Debate,* Harper & Row, New York, 1961, p. 10.

[14] Ibid., p. 31.

[15] Tillich was certainly influential, however, and much studied, especially after World War II, in the United States, as well as in Europe. He came to the United States in 1933, when Hitler rose to power, but returned to Europe frequently after the war.

orthodoxy, theology and philosophy, and religion and culture. As to the last, Tillich thought of himself as following in the footsteps of Schleiermacher, who in his day tried to win over religion's "cultural despisers." For Tillich, to do the latter entailed, not merely demythologizing an outmoded cosmology or employing words and concepts suited to the times, but a re-examination and appreciation of secular culture itself. He was against isolating religion from the rest of culture, as he thought both kerygmatic and liberal theology did, the one by reserving for it a special realm alongside other realms, the other by standing in judgment on it. Hence, he began very early to talk about a "theology of culture,"[16] which as a philosopher as well as theologian, he was peculiarly well fitted to do. "Religion," Tillich wrote, "is the substance of culture, culture is the expression of religion."[17] Philosophy, for example, was not to be thought of as a wholly autonomous enterprise, unrelated to religion. Philosophy asked existential questions, and theology answered them. This was Tillich's so-called method of correlation, which he also applied to art. A person impressed by the mosaics of Ravenna, or the paintings of the Sistine Chapel, or the older Rembrandt, would be hard to put to it to say whether his experience was religious or cultural.

> Perhaps it would be correct to say that his experience was cultural as to form, and religious as to substance. It is cultural because it is not attached to a specific ritual-activity; and religious, because it evokes questioning as to the Absolute or the limits of human existence. This is equally true of painting, of music and poetry, of philosophy and science.[18]

Actually, culture was ambivalent. On the one hand, it could, as in the cases mentioned, point beyond itself to an eternal meaning. On the other hand, if it lost all sense of meaning, it could lapse into triviality or demonism. To use his own terms, Tillich wanted a *theonomous* (secular-religious), as opposed to a *heteronomous* (authoritarian-religious) or *autonomous* (secular) culture.

Tillich's God, insofar as he thought it possible to talk of God, was both transcendent and immanent. In fact, he spoke of the immanence

---

[16] Tillich's first paper on the theology of culture appeared in 1919, and, as *Privatdozent* of theology at Berlin from 1919 to 1924, he lectured frequently on the relation of religion to philosophy, art, politics, and psychology.

[17] Tillich, *The Protestant Era,* University of Chicago Press, Chicago, 1948, p. xvii.

[18] Tillich, *The Interpretation of History,* "On the Boundary. An Autobiographical Sketch," Charles Scribner's Sons, New York, 1936, p. 49.

of the transcendent. Tillich was critical of Barth's supranaturalism, which put God "outside" the natural world. At the same time, he had too keen a sense of the ambiguity of the temporal order, of its tendency toward the demonic, to think of God in the Hegelian sense. There must be something, Tillich said, that "supports the times but is not subject to them." God could be said to be "the creative and abysmal ground of being," the source of meaning, erupting into everything finite, nature, history, and man. But God was also "being-in-itself, not *a* being,"[19] a symbol for the unconditioned transcendent, in no sense relative, or becoming.

Tillich, however, also spoke of transcending theism. By this he meant, not only that the name "God" had lost its potency in modern times, had even become banal, but that traditional theism was bad theology.

> The God of theological theism . . . is a being, not being-itself. As such he is bound to the subject-object structure of reality, he is an object for us as subjects. At the same time we are objects for him as a subject. And this is decisive for the necessity of transcending theological theism. For God as a subject makes me into an object which is nothing more than an object. He deprives me of my subjectivity because he is all-powerful and all-knowing. . . . God appears as the invincible tyrant, the being in contrast with whom all other beings are without freedom and subjectivity.[20]

So Tillich postulated a "God above God," who was ultimately beyond rational categories, who could be spoken of only in symbols, who was encountered in religious experience. Tillich's conceptualization, like Bultmann's, was existential. Man, "thrown" into existence, experienced himself as finite being. This caused anxiety, from which man could be delivered only in the experience of self-transcendence—or when, as we say symbolically, God reveals himself to man as Spirit. Tillich learned early, he tells us in one of several autobiographical sketches, that religion began in *experience* of the presence of the divine, or "the holy," from which he then advanced to the idea of God, "and not conversely."[21] In this emphasis on experience Tillich aligned himself

---

[19] For the terms and phrases used in this paragraph, see Tillich's *Systematic Theology*, the first volume of which was published in 1951.

[20] Tillich, *The Courage to Be*, Yale University Press, New Haven, 1952, pp. 184–185.

[21] Tillich, "Autobiographical Reflections," in *The Theology of Paul Tillich*, C. W. Kegley (ed.), Macmillan, New York, 1952, p. 6.

with Schleiermacher, the phenomenological theology of Rudolf Otto, and the mystics. With his formulations of a "theology of culture," and of a "God above God," Tillich reached out to his contemporaries, to whom the concepts of traditional theology had become meaningless.

Mysticism, to which Tillich referred frequently in his writings, calls for some further note in passing. Though not a major movement in religious thought, it was highly symptomatic. Dean Inge of St. Paul's, London, spoke of "a great revival of interest in the subject" as early as 1899. Inge's Bampton Lectures on Christian mysticism were followed by a stream of books of major importance by William James (1902), the Baron von Hügel (1908), Rudolf Otto (1917), and Evelyn Underhill, not to speak of Aldous Huxley who discovered mysticism early, then dropped it for the "noble savagery" of D. H. Lawrence, and finally returned to it as his personal philosophy, in his novel *Eyeless in Gaza* (1936) and especially *The Perennial Philosophy* (1945). In all these and other works, there is mention of "numinous experience," beyond conception or understanding, but available to man through some special faculty, or a priori category of mind, he is presumed to have. Tillich, who was not uncritical of mysticism, spoke of it as arising in times when there was criticism of traditional sacramental and ecclesiastical forms of religion. One could also say that the neo-mysticism of the twentieth century coincided with the growth of depth psychology, and the appreciation of the nonrational side of mental life; with the criticism of immanental theologies and the revival of the concept of the supernatural; with impatience with dogma, as opposed to firsthand experience. Rudolf Otto, in a book that ran into many editions,[22] and which influenced Tillich, contrasted the rationalism of traditional Christianity with a "profounder religion." The essence of the latter was to be found in the idea (or rather the experience) of "the Holy," which, Otto said, contained in it an element over and above the moral or rational. This was the "numinous," which cannot be expressed, but leads to a feeling of the transcendent as sole and entire reality. Tillich criticized Otto's mysticism as being too otherworldly. All the same, Tillich considered mysticism essential to all genuine religious experience. It was the vertical line, pointing to "the eternal meaning as such," without which the horizontal line, symbolizing the active or social element of religion, would be impotent.

Meanwhile, neo-Thomism, the chief new theological movement to

---

[22] Rudolf Otto, *Das Heilige* (*The Idea of the Holy*, 1917). In its way this book was as influential as Barth's *Römerbrief*, which came out the following year.

develop within the Roman Catholic Church, was upholding rationalism, as well as opposing, in its own way, secularism and modernism. Roman Catholicism was not without its modernists. Neo-Thomism, however, harked back to a traditional line of thought, to the metaphysics of St. Thomas Aquinas. The way had been prepared for it by the revival of scholasticism in the nineteenth century, and by the pronouncements of three popes, the last of whom, Pius XI, in the encyclical *Studiorum Ducem* (1923), confirmed the primacy of St. Thomas for Christian theology. Thomism, it was asserted, in contrast to Kantianism and Bergsonianism—and to Barthianism which, according to Jacques Maritain, "annihilated man before God"—upheld the power of the human intellect to know the essential nature of things; yet at the same time, in contrast to Cartesianism, subordinated it "to the object, to God, to being," thus restoring it to order and coherence. Significantly, neo-Thomism centered in a philosophy of being, which the Catholic historian of medieval thought Etienne Gilson found at the core of the Western tradition since the Greeks. Henri Bergson, still at the height of his popularity, constituted the chief enemy with his philosophy of duration (as well as his anti-intellectualism). All the early neo-Thomists learned from Bergson, yet eventually turned against him as the arch-apostle of Heraclitus. "What is new in Bergsonian philosophy is the pure becoming of Heraclitus," said Maritain in his first book. Bergson and his disciple Edouard Le Roy asserted that "everything in fact becomes, everything evolves; . . . that there are changes but not things which change, that movement does not imply a mobile, and that the real is pure becoming."[23] To overcome these "errors," it was crucially important to reassert, in the words of Father Garrigou-Lagrange, chief luminary of the Louvain school of theology, "the primacy of being over becoming," that is, to relate change to a permanent ground of existence. St. Thomas, following Aristotle, did this by interpreting change as actualized potentiality, as proceeding from a cause, which led the Christian back ultimately to pure essence, to free being, or God himself. "Being," Maritain concluded, "is the only thing that endures."

No wonder Maritain later attacked Pierre Teilhard de Chardin as well. Teilhard, a Jesuit and noted paleontologist, who was much influenced by Bergson, tried to work out an evolutionary theology. In his "new religion," as Teilhard sometimes called it, Christ became "the

---

[23] Jacques Maritain, *Bergsonian Philosophy and Thomism,* Mabelle Andison (trans.), Greenwood Press, New York, 1968, pp. 278, 280. This study first appeared in 1913.

evolutor" (*évoluteur*), guarantor of the ascent of matter from the primeval slime to life and consciousness, an ascent that would eventuate ultimately in a collective super-Humanity, or Whole Christ. Christ was both the motor and participant in this temporal process. There had to be divine initiative, or "grace," from the beginning of time, in order to draw matter toward consciousness and unity, to "point Omega" in history. But there was also a sense in which Christ or God was not yet perfected, or whose perfection could be enhanced in the course of evolution. The scholastics, then, had not said the last word when they described God as being-in-itself, for being acquired additional perfection as mankind developed a superconsciousness and was drawn into union with God. This divine-human unity was what Teilhard meant by the Whole Christ. Hegel-like, Teilhard wrote toward the end of his life that what infused Christianity with life was "not a sense of the contingence of the created, but rather a sense of the mutual completion of the world and of God."[24] The neo-Thomist's reaction to this "neo-Christianity" was predictable. Maritain dismissed it as just one more Christian gnosis; as, like Cartesianism, a product of "angelism" or the sin of the intellect; as "theology-fiction." Teilhardism represented "a purely evolutive conception where being is replaced by becoming and every essence or nature stably constituted in itself vanishes."[25]

Teilhardism, however, was by no means the only theology to emphasize becoming. In its broader aspects Teilhardism belonged, in fact, to a rather large family of religious thought, sometimes called "process theology" or finitism, which is to be sharply contrasted with the neo-Thomist philosophy of being, or for that matter, with neo-orthodoxy, or even biblical existentialism. Process theology took its inspiration in large part from modern science or from the philosophy of science. Teilhard himself was obviously steeped in evolutionism. The religious thought of Samuel Alexander and Alfred North Whitehead, however, derived, as much or more, from the side of modern mathematics and physics. Alexander's Gifford Lectures, delivered during World War I,[26] spoke the language of emergent evolution. But the stuff of which all existents were composed, he called Space-Time, a conception that was

[24] Teilhard de Chardin, *Contingence de l'univers et goût humain de survivre* (1953), quoted by Maritain in *The Peasant of the Garonne*, Holt, Rinehart, and Winston, New York, 1969, p. 264.

[25] Maritain, ibid., p. 122. Understandably, Teilhard was frequently in trouble with his ecclesiastical superiors who forbade the publication of his most speculative works.

[26] At the University of Glasgow, 1916–1918. Alexander, appropriately born in 1859, was at that time professor of philosophy at the University of Manchester.

reminiscent of Minkowski and Einstein,[27] as Alexander did not fail to point out. Out of Space-Time emerged successive levels of existence, matter, life, mind, and deity. God was any being which possessed deity, defined as the next level of perfection toward which the universe was striving. Or else God could be said to be "the whole universe engaged in process towards the emergence of this new quality."[28] In any case, God was "not a creator but a creature," forever in the making, immanent, evolving as the world evolved. Alexander, making use of new notions of matter and evolution, jettisoned the old static God of theism. In the midst of disaster (the reference was to the war), who could rest content with a God who did not share the vicissitudes of his creatures, yet who permitted suffering to exist. But the case would be different if deity was seen to be

> the outcome of the world's movement and in particular, to the extent of their value, of the efforts of human beings. It is not God then who allows the struggle, but the struggle which is to determine . . . what deity is to be.[29]

Whitehead, too, criticized the idea of a static and imperial God, detached from the world of nature or presiding over it. But for Whitehead, the scales were more evenly balanced between finitism and eternity. Like Alexander, he started with the experienced world, and found in that world, or in nature, among other things, creativity, actual entities in process, and "eternal objects." But none of these was fully explanatory or effective, without reference to God. Whitehead thought God must have a bipolar nature. He did not think of God as creating the world out of nothing, any more than Alexander did. But in his "primordial" or mental nature God was, in a sense, unchanging and even transcendental, giving pattern to creativity (not an entity in Whitehead's theological system), organizing the eternal ideas and providing the lure, or "object for desire," for each particular creative act. Whitehead's God showed the influence of both Plato and Aristotle, of whom he was a keen student. God, however, also had a "consequent" or physical nature, which Whitehead emphasized more and more as his work proceeded. It is, for example, much more conspicuous in *Process and Reality* (1929) than in his earlier *Religion in the Making*

[27] On Minkowski and Einstein, see pp. 456–457.
[28] S. Alexander, *Space, Time, and Deity*, Macmillan, London, 1920, Vol. II, p. 429. But see the whole of Book IV on Deity.
[29] Ibid., Vol. II, p. 400.

(1926). In his consequent nature, God prehends, or "feels," temporal occasions and shares in each new creative advance in the world. Thus, the world reacts back on him, his experience is enriched, and he can be said to be, like the world, finite and in process.

> Neither God, nor the World, reaches static completion. Both are in the grip of the ultimate metaphysical ground, the creative advance into novelty. Either of them, God and the World, is the instrument of novelty for the other.[30]

In such a conception, Whitehead was clearly more in the Bergsonian than the Platonic stream of thought, and was moved, too, by new notions of physical science, especially by quantum theory which, like evolution, suggested to him "a rhythm of process" throughout the universe. Toward the end of his life, Whitehead remarked on the disaster that Christian theology had been, with its attempt to banish novelty, to formularize truth for all time. It had been a mistake to conceive of God as creating the world from the outside, "at one go." An all-foreseeing Creator, who made the world as we find it now— who could believe in such a being?

> God is *in* the world, or nowhere, creating continually in and around us. . . . But this creation is a continuing process, and 'the process is itself the actuality'. . . . In so far as man partakes of this creative process does he partake of the divine. . . . His [man's] true destiny as co-creator in the universe is his dignity and his grandeur.[31]

Whitehead ended up talking like Alexander.

The finitists, though they had done with older theisms, kept God (redefined, of course) in their systems. Soon, however, there appeared a type of theology that debated, not how to talk of God, but whether it was possible to talk about God at all in a secular age.[32] Dietrich Bonhoeffer was the catalyst of this most radical theology. One can see more clearly now how others, less radical, prepared the way for this theology: Barth, by discouraging any sort of natural theology (which means

[30] Alfred North Whitehead, *Process and Reality,* Macmillan, New York, 1936, p. 529. See especially Pt. V, Chap. II, "God and the World."

[31] *Dialogues of Alfred North Whitehead* (as recorded by Lucien Price), Mentor, New York, 1954, pp. 296–297. For Whitehead's remarks on Christian theology, see ibid., pp. 143–145. For Whitehead's idea of nature, see pp. 473–474.

[32] I am indebted to Langdon Gilkey for this formulation (for reference, see note 9).

talking and speculating about God); Bultmann, by demythologizing the transcendent; and Tillich, by wrestling with problems of theological language. But Bonhoeffer was groping toward a substantially new idea. This was a secularized Christianity, completely divested of metaphysics and cut to the dimensions of the world of man. "You would be surprised and perhaps disturbed," he wrote to his friend Bethge in the spring of 1944, "if you knew how my ideas on theology are taking shape." To the end, Bonhoeffer continued, in part, to talk traditional God-language, to speak of "being in God's hands," of the revelation of God in Christ, even of the being and transcendence of God. But there does not seem to be much doubt that he was trying to formulate some kind of new "secular" theology that would not require such language. Bonhoeffer's argument, partly sketched at the beginning of this chapter, was as follows. Whether we like it or not, the world has become completely secularized. The time of "religion as such," when men could be told everything by words, theological or pious, was over. "Men as they are now simply cannot be religious any more." So what was man to do? Having "come of age," it was neither possible nor desirable, for mankind to reclaim "the land of childhood," as in the Middle Ages. As "mature" men, they must acknowledge the situation. "God," wrote Bonhoeffer paradoxically, "is teaching us that we must live as men who can get along very well without him."[33] We can live without God, the *deus ex machina* who has died, but not without Christ. Christ, entirely within human ken, as God was not, signified, for Bonhoeffer, simply "concern for others," "freedom from self, maintained to the point of death," or crucifixion. Bonhoeffer's preoccupation with the crucifixion is reminiscent of "the suffering God," so much discussed by English theologians during and after World War I.[34] This suffering God, weak and powerless in the world, was to be the starting-point for Bonhoeffer's new "worldly" theology.

A radical departure from other theologies, past and present, this was almost a nontheology. It reflected the invasion of theology itself by secularism, an acceptance of secular conviction, or lack of conviction, which not even Tillich, much less Barth or Maritain, would have tolerated. It reflected, too, the fading of metaphysical vision, so noticeable also in contemporary philosophy. Carried to the extreme by Bonhoeffer's followers, the self-styled "death-of-God theologians" of

[33] Bonhoeffer, op. cit. (see note 1), pp. 162, 219.
[34] By G. A. Studdert-Kennedy, Canon Streeter, and J. K. Mozley, among others. See W. M. Horton, *Contemporary English Theology*, Harper & Brothers, New York, 1936, pp. 47–58.

Europe and America,[35] it meant the restriction of theology to empirical statements about man and his world and the loss of any sort of transcendent Being in whom man's life could be anchored.[36] When Martin Buber spoke of "Eclipse of God" in the twentieth century, he was thinking of "the conceptual letting go of God," of the confinement of God to man's subjectivity by modern philosophers and psychologists. With Bonhoeffer and the death-of-God "school," theology itself began to contribute to this eclipse.

[35] The American theologian William Hamilton of the Colgate Rochester Divinity School invented this term in an article of 1965. But one might also include in the group mentioned the Bishop of Woolwich in England, John A. T. Robinson, whose *Honest to God* (1963), quoting Bonhoeffer freely, sold over a million copies; and Thomas Altizer and Paul Van Buren, the latter two also Americans.

[36] See in this connection, Nathan Scott, *The Broken Center,* Yale University Press, New Haven, 1966, pp. 172–173, and Chap. V, *passim.*

The Mysterious Universe

What is nature? The old question was answered in essentially novel ways in the wake of the "revolution" in physics in the first third of the twentieth century. Three epoch-making papers, dated 1900, 1905, and 1916, inaugurated a new era in scientific thinking. The first, presented in two installments to the Physical Society of Berlin by Max Planck, marked the birthday of quantum theory. The two others were, of course, Albert Einstein's famous papers on the special and general theories of relativity. Younger physicists, conspicuously Niels Bohr, Erwin Schrödinger, and Werner Heisenberg, contributed further, and importantly, to quantum theory in the 1920's. Institutionally speaking, this work was done, in the main, in Berlin, Copenhagen, and Göttingen. Throughout this period, the University of Göttingen was recognized as one of the great centers of mathematics in the world. Hermann Minkowski, Einstein's teacher, was professor there when he wrote his piece on the "four-dimensional world-view." Planck and Einstein, though of very different temperaments, became friends in Berlin, conversed on scientific matters at the Academy there, and played chamber music together. Bohr and Heisenberg collaborated at the former's institute in Copenhagen.

Did the work of these men constitute a revolution—another scientific revolution, comparable to the revolutions associated with Copernicus, Galileo, and Newton, or with Darwin? In the preceeding paragraph, I put the word revolution in quotation marks, pending further examination of the question, which it deserves, before going on to the new scientific concepts and the philosophizing about what the concepts meant. The answer, it seems to me, is reasonably clear. There was *not* a revolution, if by revolution is meant an abrupt change, without preparation, or previous work by others; complete obliteration of the old science by the new; or the wide acceptance, or even understanding, of the new concepts by the larger cultivated community. The hypotheses of the founding fathers, as they may be called, would be inconceivable without forerunners and without contemporaries working along similar lines. This is particularly true of Einstein, even though it is known that, as a young man, he did his thinking largely in isolation from the world of professional physicists. In his autobiographical notes, which he somewhat whimsically called his obituary, Einstein first of all remarked on the poor scientific instruction of his youth, which, he said, imposed dogmatic rigidity in matters of principle. "In the beginning (if there was such a thing) God created Newton's laws of motion together with the necessary masses and forces. This is all; everything beyond this follows from the development of appropriate mathematical methods by means of deduction."[1] But then he goes on to mention the electromagnetics of Michael Faraday and Clerk Maxwell as being decisive in the breakdown of Newtonian mechanics. In the case of Faraday, whose engraved portrait hung in Einstein's study, this was to go all the way back to the early nineteenth century. Curiously, Einstein ignored the famous Michelson-Morley experiment of 1887, which exploded the idea of a stationary ether through which the earth moved. Einstein also minimized Minkowski as a mathematician, but there is no doubt that he knew of, and put to use, the more markedly non-Euclidean geometries of the nineteenth century, particularly the "elliptic" or spherical geometry of Bernhard Riemann, which enabled Einstein and others to conceive of the so-called curvature of space, or space-time. H. A. Lorentz and Ernst Mach also come in for praise in Einstein's account, the former for replacing Newtonian action at a distance by the electromagnetic field, the latter for his "incorruptible skepticism and independence" toward the Newtonian absolutes. Mach's *Science of Mechanics* (1883), put in Einstein's hands in 1897, had characterized absolute space and motion as "pure mental constructs, that cannot be produced in experi-

---

[1] Einstein, "Autobiographical Notes," in *Albert Einstein: Philosopher-Scientist,* P. A. Schilpp (ed.), Library of Living Philosophers, Evanston, 1949, p. 19.

ence."[2] Rejecting the abstraction of isolated bodies rotating in an empty universe, Mach also talked much about relative motions. "For me only relative motions exist." A year before the publication of Einstein's first paper, another physicist, Henri Poincaré, actually discussed a principle of relativity, which, however was not explained or developed very fully. Thus, we have here the same story, as in the case of Newton or Darwin, of innovators standing on the shoulders of giants.

When it came, the break with the "classical" past was by no means complete. Classical physics[3] continued to be valid on the level of daily experience, in the middle zone between microcosm and macrocosm, and was still being taught in the schools. Nor did the innovators themselves, especially of the first generation, necessarily think of themselves as revolutionaries or fully abandon classical modes of thought. Pages could be written about the conservatism of Planck and Einstein, just as they have about Copernicus and Newton. Planck tells us how for years he tried to fit his quantum of action into classical theory. He eventually gave up the attempt, yet in other respects continued to live by classical habits of thought. Perhaps he was predisposed to do so, as a Prussian, and as a traditionalist toward family and state. At any rate, Planck was forever harping on absolutes in his scientific autobiography. It was his belief in the outside world as "something independent from man, something absolute," yet accessible to human reasoning, that decided him to devote himself to a scientific career in the first place. Conversion to quantum and relativity theory did not mean, for Planck, giving up this belief. On the contrary, he said, "our task is to find in all these factors and data, the absolute, the universally valid, the invariant, that is hidden in them."[4] The velocity of light was such an invariant, as also his own elementary quantum of action, and the least-action principle inherited from classical theory. Einstein, though much less tradition-minded, likewise clung stubbornly to certain traditional assumptions. Though perfectly prepared to throw over some Newtonian absolutes ("Newton, forgive me"), he retained some others, conspicuously the strict determinism of physical events. Himself an important

[2] Ernst Mach, *The Science of Mechanics,* in *The Changeless Order,* Arnold Koslow (ed.), George Braziller, New York, 1967, p. 143. Mach, the well-known Austrian physicist and philosopher, was named professor of physics at Prague, where his book was published.

[3] "Classical," as used here, refers, of course, to the physics of the seventeenth century, culminating in Newton.

[4] Max Planck, *Scientific Autobiography and Other Papers,* F. Gaynor (trans.), Greenwood Press, Westport, Conn., 1949, p. 47.

contributor to quantum theory, Einstein nevertheless rejected the Principle of Indeterminacy. "In our scientific expectation we have grown antipodes," he wrote to Max Born in 1944. "You believe in God playing the dice and I in perfect laws in the world of things existing as real objects."[5] Younger physicists, Born included, considered Einstein's "skepticism" in this matter—it might better be called his conservatism —a tragedy, both for him and themselves.

By comparison with the physicists, the general educated public was radically conservative in its scientific world-outlook. This public, as Alfred North Whitehead observed in 1934, never did accept, or perhaps bother to understand, the new scientific ideas, even as stated within a semitraditional framework by Planck and Einstein. In proportion as science grew more abstract and shadowy, "the common-sense notion still reign[ed] supreme in the work-a-day life of mankind. . . . It is supreme in literature and is assumed in all the humanistic sciences."[6] Assumed also, one might add, in the social sciences, which for a long time continued to be based on the model of classical determinism. Another quite different, but equally important, phenomenon, that was not mentioned by Whitehead, was a growing hostility toward science, in general, or at least toward scientism. This, as we shall see further, marked a return to an earlier attitude toward science that was much in evidence, though in different form, in the seventeenth century.

This is not to say that there was no revolution in the scientific community itself, or among philosophers who tried to interpret it. Provided the term is defined carefully, and within the limits suggested, there was, indeed, a scientific revolution. Again, Whitehead, who is a good witness, testifies to the fact. When he went up to Cambridge in the 1880's, he tells us, physics was supposed to be very nearly a closed subject. During the next decade, he reports, there were a few tremors, "but no one sensed what was coming." Only a few years later "the Newtonian physics were demolished, done for! Still speaking personally, it [the revolution in physics] had a profound effect on me." Looking back years later, Whitehead compared the effects of the new physics with those of the Industrial Revolution. The latter, though far-reaching, were "as nothing when compared to the scientific revolution which has been going on for the past fifty years."[7] Whitehead obviously had no doubts

---

[5] Quoted in Schilpp (see note 1), p. 176.
[6] Alfred North Whitehead, *Nature and Life,* University of Chicago Press, Chicago, 1934, p. 4.
[7] *Dialogues of Alfred North Whitehead* (recorded by Lucien Price), Mentor, New York, 1954, pp. 126, 277.

that there had been a "paradigm-switch" (in Kuhn's phrase), that is, a fundamental change in ways of conceiving the physical world.

To appreciate the extent of the switch it is necessary to recall briefly certain basic assumptions of classical science. In the Newtonian system bits of matter moved in absolute space and time. Of these two, which were independent of each other, space was by far the more important, since it alone was truly immutable, and since the locomotion of matter involved primarily change in spatial relationship. But change was also said to occur in time, which itself did not change but rather flowed uniformly. By conceiving of space and time in this way, as absolute containers independent of physical content, it became possible to identify material entities in different points of space and at different instants of time. Matter and motion, the other two cornerstones of classical physics, also had attributes of absoluteness, especially matter. For the basic units of matter, the atoms, did not change, though they moved in space and time. Atoms were rigid, that is, constant as to mass, volume, and shape, and the total quantity of matter (atoms) in the universe remained the same, though its distribution might change, as expressed by the laws of the conservation of matter and energy. The atoms were also impenetrable and inert, and therefore did not move, unless acted upon by outside forces, for example, by gravitation. Thus, motion, too, was an independent if hazier entity, not inherent in matter. It was continuous, as matter was not, and mathematically calculable. But motion brought about no sort of qualitative change, only the spatial displacement of atoms or their aggregates.

A prime feature of this system was its rigorous determinism, and hence, predictability. Pierre Laplace's famous fiction expresses admirably this deterministic feature, carried to its logical extreme. Let us imagine, he wrote in his *Essay on Probability* (1812), an intellect that at a given instant could know all the forces governing nature, as well as positions of all the entities that compose it, and that in addition was great enough to subject all these data to analysis. Such an intellect

> would be able to embrace in the same formula the movements of the largest bodies in the universe and those of the lightest atom: nothing would be uncertain for it, and the future, like the past, would present itself to its observation.[8]

---

[8] Pierre Laplace, *Essai philosophique sur les probabilités*, Courcier, Paris, 1816 (3rd ed.), pp. 3–4. For previous reference to Laplace, see p. 375.

Two things are immediately obvious about the Laplace universe. First, there was no uncertainty about it, at least not ideally or potentially, nor about man's perceptions of it. If one knew present causes, one could predict future effects and reconstruct the past. The whole history of the universe, past, present, and future, was fixed, a chain of irresistible (and equivalent) causes and effects. In truth, the universe might almost be said not to have a history, and this is the second point to be made about it. Clearly, time was accidental to it. There was change, of course, but change was not the same as time, and change, as previously noted, did not alter the basics of the universe or produce novelty. Differences in successive states boiled down to spatial distributions of matter and energy, and, given enough time, these states could conceivably be reversed and repeated. All in all, the system described by Newton and Laplace was more Parmenidean than Heraclitean, characterized more by being than becoming.[9]

Quantum and relativity physics changed this picture profoundly. They did not, however, substitute one picture for another, since the events they described were not picturable. One could not make a model of the new universe, of either the microcosm or macrocosm. The new physics, more abstract than the old, collapsed all four Newtonian absolutes, which now became abstractions in their own turn. After Einstein's paper on special relativity, it made no sense to speak of an absolute motionless space, or of absolute time. Einstein showed that space and time measurements varied with the motion of the observer; that, consequently, there was no such thing as an absolute simultaneity of events; that the time rate of moving clocks was slower than that of clocks at rest; that the length of rods at rest, or in motion, similarly differed, and so on. "There is no more common-place statement," Einstein summarized a few years later, "than that the world in which we live is a four-dimensional space-time continuum."[10] The latter phrase actually originated with Einstein's old mathematics teacher Minkowski, who in a famous lecture of 1908 at Cologne pointed up the significance of his pupil's special theory. "Henceforth," Minkowski declared, "space by itself, and time by itself, are doomed to fade away into mere shadows, and only a kind of union of the two will preserve an independent

---

[9] See on this Milič Čapek, *The Philosophical Impact of Contemporary Physics,* D. Van Nostrand, Princeton, 1961, pp. 59, 137.

[10] Einstein, *Relativity,* Robert Lawson (trans.), Henry Holt, New York, 1921, p. 65.

reality."[11] Henceforth, one should speak then, not of points in space or instants in time, but of events having dimensions of both space and time. It should be added that space, in the new conception, not only lost its static character (by being conjoined with time) but also its homogeneousness. Space-time—this point emerged more clearly in Einstein's second relativity paper—not only was not Euclidean but also exhibited a variety of structures or geometries. Thus, gravitation was explained, not as a mechanical force, but by the "curvature" of the field through which bodies passed.

If anything, the concept of matter was more thoroughly "bolshevized" than were the concepts of space and time. This, at any rate, was what Sir Arthur Eddington thought as, in the Gifford Lectures of 1927, he surveyed the wreckage of classical physics. Lord Rutherford, he said, not Einstein, was "the real villain of the piece." Eddington's specific reference was to Rutherford's work on the structure of the atom, but he was also thinking generally of the whole new conception of "the atom of action."

> When we compare the universe as it is now supposed to be with the universe as we had ordinarily preconceived it, the most arresting change is not the rearrangement of space and time by Einstein but the dissolution of all that we regard as most solid into tiny specks floating in void.[12]

It had become very difficult, if not impossible, to say exactly what matter was. Material particles had shed the qualities ascribed to the atoms of classical physics, shape, size, indestructibility, and so on. Heisenberg speaks of particles as having not substance but mathematical form, and as therefore not having "even the quality of being," but only "a possibility for being or a tendency for being."[13] Partly, this was because matter was now identified with energy. It was, therefore, not passive but active, a moving pattern of electrons. Some scientists, indeed, thought of the latter as waves rather than particles. The pattern, whether of waves or particles, had no self-contained existence but was continually changing, affected both by its own rhythmical motion and its environment, including time.

[11] H. Minkowski, "Space and Time," in *The Principle of Relativity*, W. Perrett (trans.), Methuen & Co., London, 1923, p. 75.

[12] A. S. Eddington, *The Nature of the Physical World*, Macmillan, New York, 1928, p. 1.

[13] Werner Heisenberg, *Physics and Philosophy*, Harper Torchbooks, New York, 1962, p. 60.

An element of uncertainty had entered into physics, especially micro-physical systems. The original quantum theory showed matter to be discontinuous: radiant energy was emitted in jerks, or discontinuous quanta, that were hard to predict. Heisenberg's Principle of Indeter-minacy (or Uncertainty, as it is sometimes called) of 1927 stated further the impossibility of determining, at one and the same time, the position and velocity of an electron. Sir James Jeans said that Heisenberg made it appear "that nature abhors accuracy and precision above all things."[14] Heisenberg did no such thing. He did, however, raise serious questions about Laplacean determinism and predictability. Whether the uncertainty about electron behavior was owing to lack of knowledge, or to the influence of the scientist's measuring instruments on objects, or existed in the nature of things, was debatable, of course. Clearly, however, there now existed a "crisis of determinacy," to which scientists and philosophers of science were obliged to respond.

What is nature? We return now to the original question. Whitehead said, correctly, that the scientific revolution put everything into a muddle, both epistemology and philosophical cosmology. But he would have been the first to admit that out of the muddle did come some new ideas of nature, based, at least in part, on data obtained from quantum and relativity physics. Materialism persisted in one form or another, as, for example, in Lenin's early philosophical work. But there is some truth to the contention, often made, that modern physics favored, or made to seem plausible, idealist views, such as those of Eddington and Jeans. Whitehead's own philosophy of organism, which was decidedly antimaterialistic, emphasized both ideality and process in nature. But before we take up some of the characteristic, new answers to the ques-tion of nature, it is important to note that there were those who said that the question was not a legitimate one in the first place (the posi-tivists), or who ignored the question (the existentialists), or who sought reality elsewhere than in nature (the cubists).

The logical or empirical positivists, centered at the universities of Cambridge and Vienna during and immediately following World War I, greatly reduced the scope of philosophy. To build a new philosophy that was suitable to the new science, which was their aim, required the elimination of metaphysics. The function of philosophy, as they con-ceived it, was critical, not speculative: to subject scientific knowledge to logical analysis, to clarify the language it used, to insist on a method of verification for all assertions and propositions—in other words, in

---

[14] Sir James Jeans, *The Mysterious Universe,* Macmillan, New York, 1930, p. 28.

the philosopher G. E. Moore's phrase, "to get everything exactly right." But metaphysics was neither exact nor capable of verification. "Metaphysical propositions," said Rudolf Carnap, leader of the Vienna group, "are neither true nor false, because they assert nothing, they contain neither knowledge nor error, they lie completely outside the field of knowledge. . . ."[15] Carnap was willing to concede their "expressive," if not "representative," functions, in the manner of poetry and music; but he was also suspicious of them as supportive of reactionary politics. However that may be, it is obvious that the question of nature, in its ontological aspects, would be thought meaningless in such a group. According to Ludwig Wittgenstein, philosophy was "not a theory but an activity." "Most propositions and questions, that have been written about philosophical matters are not false, but senseless."[16] Nature—the "truth" about it, its "essence" and "meaning"—was just such a senseless question.

Back of this skepticism lay, not only a century of positivistic skepticism about metaphysical "causes" (as distinguished from "laws" of nature) but also the recent findings of physics. Relativity especially, and later the Indeterminacy principle, created a greater awareness of the role played by the human mind—or the observer or operator—in making experiments on what had traditionally been thought of as the external and objective world. The latter could not be disentangled from the observer and his instruments, as had been previously thought. Within the scientific community itself there was considerable sympathy for this "operationalist" point of view, though scientists such as Einstein and Planck never carried it to the same lengths as the positivists. Einstein, for example, despite his assault on Newtonian absolutes, always believed in the existence of an external world, and, apparently more and more so as time went on, in the power of the human mind eventually to comprehend it, and to "grasp reality, as the ancients dreamed."[17] And so did Eddington. But Eddington also stated very early, and independently of the positivists, the difficulties involved in grasping "the nature of the physical world." He went pretty far in the direction of subjective idealism. The mind selected for study certain patterns of nature, rather than others. "The things which we might

[15] Rudolf Carnap, *The Logical Syntax of Knowledge,* quoted in Albert William Levi, *Philosophy and the Modern World,* Indiana University Press, Bloomington, 1959, p. 366.

[16] Ludwig Wittgenstein, *Tractatus Logico-Philosophicus,* Routledge & Kegan Paul, London, 1960, pp. 62, 77 (nos. 4.003 & 4.112).

[17] Einstein, Herbert Spencer Lecture, Oxford, 1933, quoted in Jeremy Bernstein, *Einstein,* Viking Press, New York, 1973, p. 127.

have built but did not, are there [in nature] just as much as those we did build." What is more, the mind put into nature certain values of its own. "The mind has by its selective power fitted the processes of Nature into a frame of law of a pattern largely of its own choosing." Finally, Eddington went on to say, "Our knowledge of the external world cannot be divorced from the nature of the appliances with which we have obtained the knowledge."[18] This, as we shall see, was not all Eddington had to say about nature. But he did say it.

The existentialists did not so much reject as ignore the question of nature. This was partly because, as Levi has pointed out, existentialism was an urban phenomenon, concentrating on man, not nature, as though man in anguish could be described without reference to the natural order.[19] But there was more to it than that. Conceivably, the existentialists might have found in the new physics support for their philosophy of freedom. But they do not seem to have looked at it that way. They were in revolt against positivistic science, as well as against idealism. True philosophy, seeking man's authentic "existence," had no more to do with the objective and impersonal, the deterministic and materialistic, with the "nature" studied by scientists, than with the Hegelian Absolute. The existentialists were obviously thinking of nature on the old Laplacean model, and, not surprisingly, it turned out to be nonhumanistic. In Karl Jaspers' words, "the abstract sciences lack the sentiment of a humanist culture."[20]

There is the further suggestion by Jaspers that the whole attitude toward science was changing in Western culture. He spoke of "increasing doubt concerning science in general," even while the sciences continued to achieve extraordinary results. The doubt was traceable, he thought, to among other things, science's failure to give man a comprehensive view of the world and to its degeneration into mere specialization, and hence meaninglessness. "Scientific superstition," he said ominously, "is very readily transformed into hostility to science."[21] There is a good deal of truth in these observations, made in 1932, and they are worth calling attention to in passing. The "superstition," by which Jaspers meant the rage of scientism, had reached its peak in

---

[18] A. S. Eddington, op. cit. (see note 12), pp. 241, 244, 154.

[19] See Albert William Levi's essay, "The Concept of Nature," in *The Origins of Modern Consciousness,* John Weiss (ed.), Wayne State University Press, Detroit, 1965.

[20] Karl Jaspers, *Man in the Modern Age,* Eden & Cedar Paul (trans.), Henry Holt, New York, 1933, p. 153.

[21] Ibid., p. 158.

nineteenth-century culture, as we have seen.[22] The "hostility" commenced when science—really, applied science, or technology—began to seem a threat to human values. As the philosopher R. G. Collingwood put it so well, voicing an increasingly common fear, the gigantic increase in man's power to control nature had not been accompanied by a corresponding

> increase, or anything like it, in his power to control human situations. . . . I seemed to see the reign of natural science, within no very long time, converting Europe into a wilderness of Yahoos.[23]

In his famous essay on "The Two Cultures," C. P. Snow pointed out that this fear or hostility was manifested chiefly by literary men who were not conversant with the latest science. The grandson of Thomas Henry Huxley, apostle of science, is an example of a twentieth-century man of letters who had a foot in both cultures. Always interested in science, and respectful of pure science and scientists, Aldous Huxley nevertheless began talking early about the idiocy of science, and the evil effects on man of scientific materialism.[24] By the end of World War II, he was saying that man's "every victory over Nature" constituted an important causative factor in the progressive centralization of power and oppression, and in the corresponding decline of liberty, during the twentieth century. The assault on science, as ushering in a new age of technological barbarism, of bureaucracy and statistics, or robots, had now set in. How different science and technology had looked to a younger H. G. Wells, whose hero in *The New Machiavelli* (1910) had learned from his father that "science was coming, a spirit of light and order, to the rescue of a world groaning and travailing in the muddle for the want of it."[25] How different, Huxley's satire notwithstanding, science still looked in the 1920's and early 1930's when many popular books were written about it, and even about the new physics, by Eddington, Jeans, J. W. N. Sullivan, and others. But by 1945, even Wells had lost this faith, always somewhat ambivalent in him, as can be seen in his last salute to the future: *Mind at the End of its Tether!* Of course, there was still much reverse sentiment, as expressed, for example, by Huxley's brother, the eminent biologist Julian

---

[22] See p. 305.

[23] R. G. Collingwood, *An Autobiography,* Oxford University Press, London, 1939, p. 91.

[24] In, for example, his novel *Antic Hay* (1923).

[25] H. G. Wells, *The New Machiavelli,* in *Works,* Charles Scribner's, New York, 1924–1927, Vol. XIV, p. 37.

Huxley, who wrote much about "evolutionary humanism" and of bridging the gap between Snow's two cultures. We discuss this theme further when we return to the philosophy of nature and the new physics.

The cubists were another group who might be said to have turned their back on nature. Parallels were drawn, somewhat farfetched, between cubism and the new physics, for example, by the young poet Guillaume Apollinaire, who lived among the early cubists and articulated their ideas. Apollinaire spoke of "the scientific cubism born of Picasso" and called attention to their preoccupation with geometry (no longer exclusively Euclidean), the science of space, "simultaneity," and the "fourth dimension." In Apollinaire, however, the last does not seem to refer to time, but rather to some sort of timeless space ("it represents," he said, "the immensity of space eternalizing itself in all directions at a determined moment");[26] and "scientific cubism" turns out not to have been very scientific, but to refer to the painter's withdrawing into himself for his conception of reality, rather than copying nature. It was this inward thrust that marked the cubists, above all else. They deliberately and consciously annihilated external nature, and went inward to find their own forms that looked like nothing in nature, as it was then generally understood: volumes, structures, solids, antiportraits, and so on. This was what Apollinaire called the *"surnaturel"* or *"surréal."* Cubism, he said, aimed "not at an art of imitation, but at an art of conception."[27] It did not have, and it did not seek, a representation, or idea, of nature. Georges Bracque's landscapes, for example his *View of La Roche-Guyon* of 1909 (Plate 41), shows how far a cubist master could go in abandoning an external for an inner structural conception.

As indicated previously, however, many others, particularly philosophers, did both raise and try to answer in new ways, the question of nature. They did this despite Eddington's injunction against "prying philosophers" rushing to conclusions before science had completed its "structural alterations." Whitehead, in *Science and the Modern World* (1925), spoke of "the patent dissolution of the comfortable scheme of scientific materialism," which had dominated the preceding three centuries. In truth, however, materialism persisted as a philosophy of nature, among Marxists, and, no doubt, also among many men of

[26] Guillaume Apollinaire, *Les peintres cubistes,* Hermann, Paris, 1965, p. 52. This work first appeared in 1913.
[27] Ibid., p. 56.

PLATE 41. *View of La Roche–Guyon,* by Georges Bracque.

Stedelijk Van Abbe Museum, Eindhoven, The Netherlands. (Photo: Martien Coppens.)

science,[28] though the latter would be hard to prove. Lenin took alarm, as early as 1908, at the "crisis in physics," and set out to scotch the creeping idealism that accompanied it, and which he thought played into the hands of political and social reaction. He did so in *Materialism and Empirio-Criticism,* his only foray into formal philosophy. This was, first of all, a polemic, written to bring down the "deviationists" within the Communist Party in Russia, Bogdanov and others, who evinced neo-Kantian tendencies. It was also, despite its heavy reliance on authorities, especially Friedrich Engels, a classic defense of the materialistic philosophy of nature in the twentieth century, and was so regarded by European Marxists for the next fifty years. Upon the position it expounded, especially its epistemology, depended, as Lenin and his communist followers thought, the whole fabric of Marxist social criticism. Lenin hammered repeatedly at the following points: that there is an objective, external world of nature, existing independently of the human mind, or consciousness; that this world is composed of matter, which exists eternally; that the mind, a function of organized matter, reflects this reality through the senses, which copy or photograph it. It has been said that this sort of materialism demanded a return to classical physics. Lenin, however, was very careful to distinguish between metaphysical and dialectical, or "old" and "new," materialism. The latter made room for advances in scientific knowledge, new ways of conceiving "matter," he would have said. "Dialectical materialism insists on the approximate, relative character of every scientific proposition concerning the structure of matter and its properties."[29] Hence, Lenin himself could go along with the new ideas about the electron, for example, as opposed to the old atom. Moreover, taking into account the early date at which he was writing, that is, before the outlines of the new physics had become fully visible, Lenin can hardly be blamed for continuing to believe in the ether, three-dimensional space, and the like. The thing he wanted to make certain of was that matter itself did not disappear, that is, nature's objective existence outside the mind and independent of man's perceptions, which was what distin-

---

[28] F. Sherwood Taylor, director of the Science Museum, South Kensington, London, was of the opinion that the majority of scientists, as of 1947, adopted materialism as a working hypothesis ("The Scientific World-Outlook," *Philosophy,* Vol. XXII, no. 83, November, 1947, p. 203).

[29] V. I. Lenin, *Materialism and Empirio-Criticism,* in *Collected Works,* International Publishers, New York, 1927, p. 221. From the chapter entitled "Matter has Disappeared."

guished dialectical materialism from "relativist agnosticism and idealism."[30] Ultimately, Lenin fell back on an absolutist position. Matter
was an absolute, and there was an absolute truth, which human beings
could and did approximate, despite historical and physiological conditioning. Time and space had "objective reality," and who could doubt
the existence of "objective law, causality, and necessity in nature"? Why
this insistence on an absolute, as well as on a relative truth? The intention was clearly to give support for the class struggle, which, as previously stated, was believed by Lenin to require a dialectical-materialist,
rather than an agnostic or idealist, concept of nature.

Lenin boasted that the majority of scientists, especially physicists,
espoused materialism, though not necessarily dialectical materialism.
Whitehead, as previously quoted, reported just the opposite. What this
means is that between 1908 and 1925 the tide had turned, among
those Europeans who thought it possible to philosophize about nature,
toward idealism, or a combination of idealism and positivism. By the
later date, the new physics appeared to many to open the door to, or
at least not to slam the door shut on, an idealist (Lenin would have
said "bourgeois") interpretation of nature. To be more specific, changing conceptions of matter, time, and determinism by the scientists inclined some philosophers to conceive nature, no longer as machine,
but as mind, organism, or else some sort of "neutral stuff" underlying
both mind and matter (such, for example, was Bertrand Russell's
view). This tilt toward idealism, and away from materialism or
mechanism, was the philosophical revolution that accompanied the
scientific revolution. It put a deep gulf between Soviet Russian and
Western European philosophies of nature.

Some idea of the philosophical revolution may be gathered from a
series of interviews that J. W. N. Sullivan, the mathematician and
popularizer of science, conducted with some English, French, and
German scientist-philosophers in 1934. Despite inevitable disagreement
among them about some things, notably determinism,[31] Sullivan found
remarkable unanimity on the mind-matter problem. To a man, they
opposed materialism. Prince Lucien de Broglie, sounding very much
like Russell, thought that there might be one substance out of which
both consciousness and matter are built. Others went further in an
idealist direction. Max Planck regarded consciousness "as fundamental,"

---

[30] Ibid., p. 222.

[31] As already noted, Einstein rejected the Principle of Indeterminacy. So also
did Planck and Schrödinger. "God does not play dice with the world," was Einstein's
famous rejoinder to Bohr on the subject.

and matter "as derivative from consciousness." Jeans expressed himself in almost identical words. His "inclination toward idealism" was the outcome, Jeans said, largely of modern scientific theories. He mentioned particularly the Principle of Indeterminacy, which seemed to make room for "mind" in the universe. But his argument, developed more fully elsewhere, rested mainly on the mathematical structure of nature, which, similarly, he could not explain apart from mind. "In general," Jeans concluded, "the universe seems to me to be nearer to a great thought than to a great machine. It may well be, it seems to me, that each individual consciousness ought to be compared to a brain-cell in a universal mind.."[32]

Eddington, also interviewed by Sullivan, stands out in this group, not so much for the lucidity, as for the typicality and comprehensiveness of his views of nature. He touched on all the big issues being debated at the time. He wrestled with the epistemological problem, as Jeans did not, and came to some rather skeptical conclusions, as we have seen.[33] Eddington spoke of "an inscrutable nature," whose mathematical structure the "pointer-readings" (readings on instruments) of physics could reveal, but not its essence or real qualities. He did not think it inconsistent, however, to go on from there to describe the "mind-stuff" of which the universe was composed, and to distinguish between metrical and nonmetrical aspects of reality. By the latter, Eddington simply meant to say that scientific experience was not the only kind of experience. Physics dealt, by choice, only with measurable quantities. But there was also the whole world of feelings, purpose, and values. The scheme of physics was obviously, especially as recently formulated, but "a partial aspect of something wider."[34] As to "mind-stuff," Eddington, like Jeans, was suitably impressed by the Principle of Indeterminacy, which he thought dethroned the materialist hypothesis. In fact, the more Eddington thought about it, the more mind, not matter, seemed to be at the center of things, both in the "physical" and "spiritual" worlds. His epistemology itself pushed him toward that conclusion, the only direct knowledge man possessed being knowledge of mental states. "I do not know," he said to a group of American Friends (Eddington was a Quaker, as well as a distinguished physicist and astronomer)

---

[32] J. W. N. Sullivan, *Contemporary Mind,* Humphrey Toulman, London, 1934, pp. 132–133, 152, 159, 164. See also Sir James Jeans, op. cit. (see note 14), p. 158.
[33] See pp. 464–465.
[34] A. S. Eddington, op. cit. (see note 12), pp. 331–332.

whether this view (materialism) is still held to any extent in scientific circles, but I think it may be said that it is entirely out of keeping with recent changes of thought as to the fundamental principles of physics. Its attractiveness belonged to a time when it was considered that the way to understand or explain a scientific phenomenon was to make a concrete mechanical model of it.[35]

Whitehead, whom Sullivan did not interview, also rejected the machine model, but, in his own concept of nature, emphasized life more than mind (though mentality, of course, was an ingredient of life), or what he called process. Whitehead's delineation of nature as process links him with all those, and they were now many, who upheld a dynamic as opposed to a static concept of nature. Among these were, conspicuously, the evolutionists, among them Bergson, discussed in an earlier section,[36] Samuel Alexander the philosopher, and the zoologist Lloyd Morgan; but also Eddington himself, who put in a chapter on "Becoming" in his *The Nature of the Physical World*. Eddington was convinced "that a dynamic character must be attributed to the external world."[37] Whitehead frequently referred to Bergson, praising him for his objection to "spatialisation" (that is, minimizing time) as a way of thinking about nature, and for introducing into philosophy organic conceptions of physiological science. "I am greatly indebted to Bergson," Whitehead wrote in the preface to his mature philosophical work *Process and Reality* (1929). He also found suggestive, and said so, Alexander's *Space, Time, and Deity* (1920), and Morgan's *Emergent Evolution* (1923). These three books were all delivered originally as Gifford Lectures, and all featured a dynamic nature. Alexander, taking over the word "emergent" from an earlier work by Morgan, saw nature as ceaseless change, involving the emergence of higher from lower orders of being, matter from space-time, life from matter, mind from life, and so on indefinitely. An "emergent," such as mind, as opposed to a mere "resultant" of something lower, signified the appearance of novelty, the qualitatively new. It was this, "the something more" in Morgan's phrase, which distinguished the doctrine of emergence from mechanistic doctrine. As an empiricist, Alexander did not say why nature exhibited process and emergence, above all else.

[35] A. S. Eddington, *Science and the Unseen World* (Swarthmore Lecture), George Allen & Unwin, London, 1929, p. 19.

[36] See pp. 375–376.

[37] A. S. Eddington, op. cit. (see note 12), p. 93. See Chapter V, *passim*.

He simply stated as fact, that nature exhibited a striving or nisus toward the realization of ever higher stages.[38]

Whitehead, of course, by no means simply recapitulated what these and other thinkers said. In fact, he disagreed with them all in important ways, while retaining a fundamental agreement as to process. But he described the latter in his own way. He was disposed toward a "philosophy of organism," not only or primarily by biological ideas, but by the recent findings of physics. From relativity theory Whitehead learned to think in terms of physical "fields" and "events," rather than isolated objects, hence of wholes or patterns, rather than parts. Quantum theory further suggested the rhythmic or periodic, as opposed to enduring, character of atomic entities, hence that the patterns were forever changing. Matter conceived as activity or energy, plus the new significance attached to time, convinced Whitehead, once and for all, that process was at the heart of nature. "It is nonsense to conceive of Nature as a static fact, even for an instant devoid of duration."[39]

> The actual world is a process, and the process is the becoming of actual entities. . . . How an actual entity *becomes* constitutes *what* that actual entity *is*. . . . Its 'being' is constituted by its 'becoming'. This is the 'principle of process'.[40]

Yet there was also permanence as well as process in Whitehead's system. The permanence came from his affinity with Plato. "All things flow," but by participation in "eternal objects," which remain and provide both the uniformities of nature and new potentialities. Basically, what Whitehead was trying to do was to fuse nature with life. Undoubtedly, he was also influenced in this direction by his sympathy with romantic poetry, or "the romantic reaction" against eighteenth-century mechanism, as he called it in a famous chapter in *Science and the Modern World.* "A dead Nature can give no reasons." "A dead Nature aims at nothing."[41] Life was what Whitehead found lacking in Cartesian-Newtonian science. It excluded from nature all the important things: reasons, aim, meaning. Science had abstracted from the world as a whole, in order to study, with great success, a particular

---

[38] For what Alexander had to say about nisus toward deity and God, see p. 452.

[39] Alfred North Whitehead, op. cit. (see note 6), p. 27.

[40] Whitehead, *Process and Reality,* Macmillan, New York, 1929, pp. 33–34. I have changed the text slightly, but not its meaning, for the purpose of quotation.

[41] Whitehead, op. cit. (see note 6), p. 9.

aspect of the world. It was now high time to restore life to nature, including values, all the things that Wordsworth had found in it, and more. Life signified individual enjoyment, "creative advance," and aim or novelty. All these things were involved in what Whitehead meant by process.

This was how Whitehead proposed to unite the two cultures. In effect, he was saying that the gap between science and humanism, originating in the seventeenth century and widening in Victorian times, was the fault of science. Science had, for too long, allowed itself to be identified with a singularly bleak and unhuman view of the external world. But now it was possible, thanks to a second scientific revolution, and despite (or because of) the increasing abstractness of science, to see nature in a different light, as organism rather than machine, as full of life in creative process, and capable of being enjoyed.

The debate resumed after World War II, owing to the fear generated by the machines in the aftermath of the war. Science, according to many, threatened to bring on a technological civilization, reducing men to robots. It was only a little later that Sir Charles Snow created a stir with his essay on the two cultures. F. R. Leavis, the Cambridge don, crossed swords with Snow[42] on behalf of literature, and Julian Huxley, Jacob Bronowski, and others leaped to the defense of science. "Science is human," said Bronowski, who reviewed all the contributions of science to civilization since the Renaissance. Evolution had taken a new turn, said Huxley, who coined a new term, "Evolutionary humanism." With the emergence of man, evolution was no longer biological, blind, and necessitarian (which was what had offended people), but psychosocial, with man in "the dominant evolutionary position," conscious of what he was doing.[43] The extent to which these arguments were convincing is another story. But in retrospect, the part played in the debate by the new physics seems clear enough— and paradoxical. The new physics, more abstract by far than Newtonian physics, made science seem, perhaps not less dangerous, but more humanistic. And it made nature seem to be, not only more "mysterious" (in Jeans' phrase), but to partake more of becoming than being.

---

[42] On the Snow-Leavis debate, see the article by Lionel Trilling, "Science, Literature and Culture," *Commentary*, Vol. XXXIII (January–June, 1962), pp. 461–477.

[43] See the essays by J. Bronowski and J. Huxley in *The Humanist Frame,* Julian Huxley (ed.), Harper & Brothers, New York, 1961.

The Open Society
and Its Enemies

Two quite different, and seemingly contradictory, statements are frequently made about political and social thought in the twentieth century. On the one hand, it is said that political philosophy is dead, or dying; on the other, that never has this philosophy been more vital, engrossing, and even original than in the years between 1914 and 1950. There is truth in both of these statements. The first refers primarily to academic political theory, reflecting, above all, the decline of liberal democracy. The second refers more, though not exclusively, to political debate in the marketplace, to partisan or ideological politics.

The argument of the first is as follows.[1] Political philosophy traditionally concerned itself with "first principles," including the ethics of political decision and behavior; with questions about the ends of government, whether government existed to serve individuals, or whatever; the best form of government, and so on. But in the twentieth century new horrendous events and new modes of thought conspired to make

[1] See, on "the death of political philosophy," Peter Laslett, Introduction to *Philosophy, Politics, and Society,* Basil Blackwell, Oxford, 1956; Alfred Cobban, "The Decline of Political Theory," *Political Science Quarterly,* Vol. LXVII (September, 1953); and especially, Arnold Brecht, *Political Theory. The Foundations of Twentieth-Century Political Thought,* Princeton University Press, 1959.

this kind of discourse difficult, if not obsolete. Doubtless, the spectacular growth of state power and of bureaucracy would have made discussion of rational and ethical controls over government seem a bit out-of-date. But even without such developments, traditional political philosophy would have found the going rough. New schools of sociology and philosophy both militated against it. The new value-free social science, expounded brilliantly by Max Weber, insisted on the rigid separation of "Is" and "Ought," thus reducing political thought to a discussion of means rather than ends, and the probable consequences of action. Weber believed very much in a science that could help men to find rational solutions to social problems. Science, however, could not discuss first principles. "An empirical science," he wrote in an early essay, "cannot tell anyone what he ought to do, but rather what he can do."[2] Values and value judgments belonged to the realm of faith, not knowledge, and, as Weber was quick to point out, faith was hard to come by in the "disenchanted" world of the twentieth century. The sociology of knowledge, developed by Karl Mannheim and others, likewise had a limiting effect on political theory, by historicizing it. Political knowledge, like every other form of cultural knowledge, was said to be socially determined, hence relative to, the social and economic conditions prevailing at a given time in history. This historicism appeared to rule out ethical judgments, made with reference to a reality outside a particular social structure. At the same time, the logical positivists criticized traditional political philosophy on linguistic and logical grounds, writing it off as "metaphysics." Political philosophers, said T. W. Weldon, "talked little about actual political institutions, but dealt with ghostly or abstract entities, the State, the Individual, Society, the General Will, the Common Good, and so on."[3] Political philosophy should re-examine its language, to see how much of it really made sense.

All this is not to say, however, that political thought was now moribund, or that there were no new departures in political and social thinking. Nothing could be farther from the truth. If traditional political philosophy languished, or had limits imposed upon it in academic circles, political ideologies flourished in the rough and tumble of everyday life, and even incited men to violence and war. At the center of the

[2] Max Weber, " 'Objectivity' in Social Science" (1904), in *Max Weber on the Methodology of the Social Sciences*, E. A. Shils (trans.), Free Press, New York, 1949, p. 54.

[3] T. W. Weldon, "Political Principles," in *Philosophy, Politics, and Society* (see note 1), p. 26.

stage was, of course, the three-cornered battle between liberalism, now put on the defensive, and communism and fascism. Of the three rivals, fascism was the newest, though, as we shall see, in Germany, it grew out of a "Volkish" type of thought having roots in the nineteenth century. But communism, too, and Marxism in general, underwent revision, nor was communism as monolithic as is sometimes supposed. Moreover, these were not the only new political doctrines. To mention only two others, an impressive attempt was made, by the Roman Catholic convert Jacques Maritain and by the Anglican convert T. S. Eliot, to revive the idea of a Christian society, with links, especially in Maritain's case, to historic liberalism. And out of World War II also came the idea of a United States of Europe, called by Jean Monnet "the great European revolution of our epoch."

A new type of political discourse accompanied new or revised political doctrines. Max Weber frequently remarked on the increasing rationalization of life and thought in modern Europe. Rationalization, as he defined it in his famous address on "Science as a Vocation" (1919), meant "that principally there are no mysterious incalculable forces that come into play (for example, in politics), but rather that one can, in principle, master all things by calculation."[4] Weber both feared and approved this trend, which he also called "intellectualization" and "bureaucratization." But, in fact, as Weber also sometimes recognized, the greatest danger in modern political discourse went the other way, that is, in the direction of irrational forces and irrationalism, which threatened to destroy the fabric of rationalized political and social life. Traditional political philosophy, especially liberalism, discussed political questions according to the rules prescribed by rational discourse, and with the expectation that reason could, and would, supply the correct answers. Not so, however, much of the new political thought of the twentieth century. As we have seen, irrationalism had been gaining in momentum and prestige since the late nineteenth century.[5] It was now applied to political thought, as before it had been applied, for the most part, to philosophy and psychology. This new political irrationalism was manifested at two levels, first, in the observation, by academic theorists, of nonlogical conduct in the social arena; and second, in direct appeals, as among the fascists, to intuition and myth as guides to social action, and in the disbarment of the critical

[4] Max Weber, "Science as a Vocation," in *From Max Weber*, H. H. Gerth (trans.), Oxford University Press, New York, 1946, p. 139.
[5] See p. 378 f.

reason for individuals or for the masses, as among the Bolsheviks. Both Bolsheviks and fascists also advocated violence as the only means likely to gain the ends prescribed by the elite.

Vilfredo Pareto, the noted Italian economist and sociologist, who also became a disillusioned liberal, mirrors the irrational turn taken by social thought at the academic level. There is irony in this, for Pareto, like Freud, with whom he has been compared, was himself a hard-headed rationalist, who claimed merely to be observing irrational behavior in others. Methodologically, he followed the old positivist line, refusing scientific status to intuition, or *Verstehen*. "We are here setting out to apply to the study of sociology the methods that have proved so useful in the other sciences," he wrote in his master work.[6] Pareto wanted a scientific sociology without metaphysics, and indeed without values, based on a "logico-experimental" method. His aim, like that of Comte, was to find "experimental uniformities" in social and political life. "From that point of view there is not the slightest difference between the laws of political economy or sociology and the laws of other sciences."[7] But Pareto's sociology revealed, above all, the limits of reason in social behavior. He wrote contemptuously of former social theorists, the *philosophes,* Mill, Spencer, Comte himself, who, as Pareto thought, had suppressed altogether, or else denigrated, the part played by nonlogical actions. "The worship of Reason," he wrote, "may stand on a par with any other religious cult, fetishism not excepted."[8] After studying the logical and rational aspects of social behavior, Pareto concluded that there was much still to be accounted for. There were the "residues," as he called them, which were manifestations of deep-seated (and, therefore, frequently "subconscious") instincts and sentiments, and which issued in the nonlogical actions that were observable in history. These residues, never delineated very clearly by Pareto, included the human drive to combine and manipulate, and to protect and defend existing combinations. Almost all social theories were, therefore, merely rationalizations or "derivations" from the residues, expressive of man's hunger for thinking. Though the derivations varied greatly in history, the residues did not. The ultimate determinants of social behavior were essentially changeless. Pareto, following Machiavelli, believed that the art of governing consisted, not

[6] Vilfredo Pareto, *The Mind and Society,* Arthur Livingston (ed.), Harcourt, Brace, New York, 1935, Vol. I, p. 5 (paragraph 5). This work, entitled originally *Trattato di sociologia generale,* was written and published during World War I.

[7] Ibid., Vol. I, p. 52 (paragraph 99).

[8] Ibid., Vol. I, p. 196 (paragraph 300).

in trying to destroy the residues, which was in any case impossible, but in utilizing them for the advantage of the ruling elite. The leaders of the Western democracies, deluded by a false doctrine of reason, intellectualism, and humanitarianism, did not understand this, and would, therefore, be displaced soon by regimes that were prepared to stifle dissent and use violence in their own defense. Because of this prediction, and because of the general emphasis on irrationalism in his late thought, Pareto has been represented as a foremost theorist of Italian fascism and of totalitarianism in general.

Whatever doubts there may be about Pareto's connection with fascism (and it was, in fact, ambiguous[9]), there can be no doubt about the connection between twentieth-century totalitarianism in general and political irrationalism. This connection is much more obvious in fascist than in communist theory. But it is to be found in the latter too, not so much in communist philosophy *per se,* which, as George Sabine has said, "was never overtly irrational,"[10] as in the myths that developed alongside the doctrine, and, above all, in the state of mind demanded of the communist masses. George Orwell, though hardly an impartial witness, called attention to this irrational side of twentieth-century totalitarianism, both communist and fascist, in essays and novels written over a period of fifteen years. "The very concept of objective truth is fading out of the world."[11] When Orwell made this statement in 1942, he was still thinking of fascism, against which he fought in the Spanish Civil War. But already in that war, he had begun to lump fascism and communism together, to think of them as merely different species of the same totalitarian genus. His famous novel *1984* (1949) is therefore probably a composite portrait, though by that time he saw Stalinism as the chief threat to the democratic socialism he himself professed. The novel *1984* portrayed a society in which a small elite, or Inner Party, determines what is to pass for truth, in which history is rewritten to conform with that truth, and in which the truth is communicated to "the dumb masses," or "proles," by means of Newspeak. Newspeak is not a rational language intended to develop discourse among rational men.

---

[9] Pareto accepted a senatorship under Mussolini's regime, yet remained sufficiently liberal to plead for economic freedom and freedom of thought, teaching, and publication.

[10] George Sabine, *A History of Political Theory,* Henry Holt, New York, 1950, p. 907.

[11] George Orwell, "Looking Back on the Spanish War," quoted in Raymond Williams, *George Orwell,* Viking, New York, 1971, p. 60.

The intention was to make speech, and especially speech on any subject not ideologically neutral, as nearly as possible independent of consciousness. For the purposes of everyday life it was no doubt necessary, or sometimes necessary, to reflect before speaking, but a Party member called upon to make a political or ethical judgment should be able to spray forth the correct opinions as automatically as a machine gun spraying forth bullets. . . . From the foregoing account it will be seen that in Newspeak the expression of unorthodox opinions, above a very low level, was well-nigh impossible.[12]

It was of this sort of calculated irrationalism that Isaiah Berlin was thinking when he observed "the great gap" that divided twentieth- from nineteenth-century political thinking.[13]

If Orwell's depiction of communism was approximately correct in this respect, it follows that communist theory itself underwent some rather drastic changes in the twentieth century. And this, in fact, happened in several ways. First it happened in Lenin's, and in Stalin's, revision of classical Marxism in a totalitarian direction, and also in the evocation, by the Hungarian Marxist Georg Lukács and others, of an earlier, humanistic Marx, to whom communists were urged to return, as to a purer model. The latter attempt met with a considerable response from Western European Marxists who were unable to accept completely either Soviet doctrine or practice. The attraction of communism, of whatever variety, for European intellectuals in general is another subject about which something needs to be said.

Lenin, of course, would have denied being a revisionist. Did he not speak out, early, against the revisionists, Eduard Bernstein and the rest, for betraying the revolution with their accommodations with democratic capitalism? Yet Lenin clearly did revise classical Marxism in his elitist conception of revolution, which he stated boldly in *What Is to Be Done?* (1901), and in his conception of the state, outlined in *The State and Revolution,* a work left unfinished by the onset of the Russian Revolution. In between these two works, Lenin wrote *Materialism and Empirio-Criticism,* referred to in the last chapter.[14] The curious thing is that Lenin's materialism, developed in this book, logically demanded determinism in social action. Mind reflected matter, as a mirror-image; just so did the "consciousness" of the masses, and

[12] Orwell, *1984,* Appendix, "The Principles of Newspeak."
[13] See Isaiah Berlin's article "Political Ideas in the Twentieth Century," reprinted in *Four Essays on Liberty,* Oxford University Press, London, 1969.
[14] See p. 469.

hence their "spontaneity" in action, reflect modes of economic production. Lenin, however, now emphasized voluntarism—the "conscious will" of an elite—to effect social revolution, especially, but not exclusively, in the economically immature countries of the world. No doubt Lenin did so, not as a philosopher pondering the problem of determinism and free will in the abstract, but in response to circumstances, that is, the recent history of trade unionism, both in Russia and Europe. The fact remains that he jettisoned the old spontaneity theory, which made revolution depend on the reflex action of the masses, and substituted for it a theory of willed change.

> We have said that there could not have been Social-Democratic consciousness among the workers. It would have to be brought to them from without. The history of all countries shows that the working class, exclusively by its own effort, is able to develop only trade union consciousness.[15]

In Lenin's theory, the emphasis had shifted from the proletariat, as in classical Marxism, to the vanguard of the most revolutionary class, to the organized Party. And this shift had important consequences. It required the stifling, for the present, of any sort of "freedom of criticism" (attacked by Lenin in the first chapter of *What Is to Be Done?*), the insistence on Party doctrine as "a solid block of steel," and the deferment, to the indefinite future, of even "primitive democracy." Lenin fully developed these ideas later in his theory of the state, which likewise compromised the older "classical" theory: not as to the ultimate objective, which called for the withering away of the state and the governance of society by mature and free workers, but as to what should happen in the interim: the establishment of a Party dictatorship, wielding complete power, requiring that the masses "unquestioningly obey the single will of the leaders of the labor process," and organizing society into a single office and factory, characterized by "factory discipline." "Until the 'higher' phase of communism arrives, the socialists demand the strictest control by society and by the state of the measure of labor and the measure of consumption."[16] From this "revised" theory of the state it was only a short step to Stalinist repression.

Contrasting rather sharply with this totalitarian trend in Marxism

---

[15] V. I. Lenin, *What is to be Done?*, Chap. II, "The Spontaneity of the Masses and the Consciousness of the Social-Democrats," in *Selected Works*, Foreign Languages Publishing House, Moscow, 1960, Vol. I, pp. 148–149.

[16] V. I. Lenin, *The State and Revolution*, in ibid., Vol. II, p. 380.

was the trend, much in evidence in Western Europe, to humanize Marxism. Denounced as heresy by the Bolsheviks, this trend grew to major proportions in the anti-Stalinist climate of the 1930's and 1940's, and especially following the publication in 1932 of the so-called economic-philosophic manuscripts of Marx's early period. It began, however, much earlier, with Georg Lukács' *History and Class Consciousness* (1923), which created a sensation. The odd thing is that Lukács, from the time he joined the Communist Party in Hungary in 1918, had no idea of opposing Lenin. In his preface he, indeed, praised Lenin as a great theoretician, as well as man of action. The essays which comprised the book, however, belied this praise. Lukács, who perhaps lacked a thorough knowledge of Lenin's thought at this time, differed sharply from Lenin on basic points. His purpose, Lukács said, was "an exposition of Marx's theory *as Marx understood it,*" even against Engels (he did not say "against Lenin," though what he said amounted to that). It is as if Lukács knew intuitively what was in the early manuscripts, that the young Marx had been obsessed with the problem of man's alienation in industrial society. In any case, Lukács' emphasis was on Marx as a moral philosopher, on Marxist idealism as opposed to materialism, humanism as opposed to scientism. By thus "Hegelianizing" Marx, Lukács appeared to be putting communism back on humanist foundations. Educated in successive idealisms, the latest being Hegel's, he denounced materialism as "an inverted Platonism." Yet, as the latter phrase indicates, Lukács had misgivings about idealism too. He liked Hegel's idealism best because, though it was contemplative like the rest, and viewed an objective order passively, it emphasized becoming. "Reality *is* not, it becomes," Lukács kept saying.[17] But Marx improved on Hegel's philosophic becoming by converting it into "praxis." Praxis meant the ability of the proletariat, in proportion as it grows more class conscious, to participate in, and transform, history. By so doing, it overcomes the duality of subject and object, which plagued even Hegelianism, and hence, man's alienation. Like Lenin (but more like Sorel and Rosa Luxemburg, from whom he learned much in his syndicalist days), Lukács stressed the role of consciousness in history. But it was the consciousness of the proletariat, as well as an elite. Nor was the end, the achievement of the classless society, a dead certainty for Lukács, since it depended, not on the inexorability of scientific laws, but on human reason and resolution.

[17] See especially Lukács' essay on "Reification and the Consciousness of the Proletariat," in *History and Class Consciousness.*

The reaction of Party regulars, intent just then on Bolshevizing all the national communist groups, to *History and Class Consciousness* can be imagined. Bucharin and Zinoviev, at the Fifth Congress of International Communism in 1924, denounced it as idealist and revisionist, and Lukács was pressured to recant. He, in fact, made a complete about-face, taking his stand on Lenin's *Materialism and Empirio-Criticism,* and professing to see in idealism the source of the Fascist counter-revolution. Nevertheless, "Lukácsism" grew in Western Europe, where it was seized on by Marxists who were looking for an alternative to Stalinism. Lukácsism, indeed, helps to explain the prestige of the Left, often remarked on, among European intellectuals. There were, of course, many reasons for its appeal, both emotional and rational: the sense of social guilt felt widely by the "mandarins" living in a do-nothing capitalist society (Sartre, not yet a Marxist, wrote about this guilt at length in his essay on literature in 1947); the "opium" theory of ex-communists such as Arthur Koestler, that is, communism as a substitute for religion in a world lacking, but longing for, a faith; the Myth of the Left, as Raymond Aron calls it, optimistic in a pessimistic world, promising revolution and emancipation; the "family" theory, fostered by Louis Aragon, the French poet-novelist, which represented membership in the Party as a close and comradely association; and, at the same time, communism as doctrine, closely reasoned, and therefore appealing also as science, to, for example, "normaliens" (distinguished scholars in the Ecole Normale Supérieure in Paris), and to the group led by the French philosopher Henri Lefebvre. But it was just this scientific side—communism as science, in the manner of Lenin—that threw a good many intellectuals off, especially when it was associated with Stalinist materialism and repression. To many, Lukácsism—or something like it, for there were others, Karl Korsch in Germany,[18] Antonio Graziadei in Italy, and even to some extent, Antonio Gramsci, leader of the Italian Communist Party, who wrote in somewhat the same vein and at roughly the same time—appealed precisely because it affirmed a humanist Marxism, which gave man something to do in history, and which emphasized his alienation and the cure for alienation, in an unjust society. To "committed" existentialists like Sartre, this message was doubly appealing. Even Lefebvre, a Party philosopher in the 1930's, and certainly no Hegelian, found in praxis, the fusion in man of thought and meaning-

---

[18] Karl Korsch's *Marxismus und Philosophie* appeared in the same year as Lukács' book, and was likewise condemned. *Pravda* linked Lukács and Korsch together as opponents of Marxist realism and materialism.

ful action, the core of Marxist teaching. Significantly, Lefebvre could not stomach Stalinism in the end and was expelled from the Party in 1958. Thus, in Western Europe there were two kinds of communist intellectuals who might be called the scientists and the humanists, or the Party regulars and the irregulars, for both of whom, as Sartre said, Marxism constituted "the philosophy of our time." Sartre himself was essentially one of the latter, flirting with the Party after World War II, yet warning against dehumanization and determinism.

Fascism, communism's great foe, appealed less to intellectuals, because of its more overt irrationalism, its more parochial appeal, and its "hostility to the humane," as Thomas Mann put it. Fascism, in fact, put in motion a great migration of its own intellectuals to other countries—the first great brain-drain of the twentieth century. All the same, fascism palpably enjoyed great success, if not among intellectuals generally, at least with other "classes," especially the middle classes, to such an extent that the period from 1918 to 1945 has been called the "era of Fascism." Ideologically speaking, fascism belonged to the species of will philosophy, which was peculiarly appropriate to countries like Italy and Germany, both of which were on the brink of economic and political disaster after World War I. By strength of will, not merely an individual but a whole nation could lift itself up by its bootstraps and achieve greatness. No wonder Sorel's "myth," Pareto's "residues," and Nietzsche's "philosophy of life," as well as the ready-made Hegelian philosophy of the state, were made to do double duty in explaining the fascist view of the world. Mussolini defined the nation as "a multitude unified by a single idea, which is *the will* to existence and to power,"[19] and the state as "the universal ethical will," the creator of right, and indeed of the nation itself. The National Socialists of Germany, of course, also frequently invoked "Volkish philosophy," which went back to the Romantic Movement, and which had been refined and developed in the late nineteenth century by such disappointed academics as Paul de Lagarde and Julius Langbehn, and, on a lower level and later still, by the poet and journalist Dietrich Eckhart, who had such an important influence on Adolf Hitler. Volkish philosophy went against will philosophy in its emphasis on biological and racist determinism. The two, however, were in agreement in their appeal to myth and intuition, as opposed to reason.

There is still much difference of opinion as to what kind of a society

[19] Benito Mussolini, "The Doctrine of Fascism," in *The Social and Political Doctrines of Contemporary Europe,* Michael Oakeshott (trans.), Cambridge University Press, 1942, p. 167.

the fascists wanted. Was fascism essentially a conservative movement, hostile to both democratic liberalism and socialism, wanting to restore a past antedating both? Or was it a revolutionary movement, disrespectful of the past, aiming to create a wholly new kind of state or nation? It was an odd mixture of both, judging by the "doctrine" developed by Mussolini, Hitler, and various court philosophers. By the time he wrote his article on doctrine for the *Italian Encyclopedia* in 1932, Mussolini, originally a socialist, and afterwards, for a time, very much the pragmatist, had moved visibly to the right. That was, in fact, how Mussolini characterized the twentieth century, as "a century of the Right," in contrast to the nineteenth century, which glorified liberalism and socialism. The Right meant, above all, collectivism—the opposite of individualism and political egalitarianism—and the conception of the State, defined by him as "an absolute before which individuals and groups are relative,"[20] and upon which all ethics and culture, and, indeed, the nation itself depended. At this stage Mussolini, prompted by the Hegelian philosopher Giovanni Gentile, put much emphasis on history and the value of tradition. "Outside history," he said, "man is nothing." "Fascism is an historical conception." Yet Mussolini also said, "One does not go backwards," and represented the fascist state as "not reactionary, but revolutionary," as "a new fact in history." He wanted no return to the world as it had been before 1789. Monarchical absolutism, theocracy, and feudal privileges were as much things of the past as liberalism and democracy. Mussolini could also speak the language of becoming: absolute monarchies as well as republics were to be judged, he said, not *sub specie aeternitatis,* but as political forms that had had their day and been surpassed. He rejected the idea of a political doctrine that "holds good for all times and all peoples." At least some of the time, Mussolini thought of history and life in Nietzschean (and perhaps also Bergsonian) terms, as "a continual change and coming to be," open-ended, without any set goal.[21] The future—there was obviously a strong dash of Futurism as well as historicism in his thinking—would be decided, though never for all time, by decision, struggle, and war.

German National Socialism exhibited this same conservative radicalism, or radical conservatism, but with an important difference. In Nazi "doctrine," hostility to modern industrial society was much more pronounced, and state was subordinated to nation, and nation to race.

[20] Ibid., pp. 175–176.
[21] Ibid., pp. 165–166, 172, 175, 177.

No one person, unless it was Hitler, who was no philosopher, spoke for the Nazis as a whole. In a book such as Alfred Rosenberg's *Myth of the Twentieth Century* (1930; enlarged edition 1938), however, one can find ideas that were undoubtedly in wide circulation, and which had at least some official sanction. Though Hitler did not think highly of Rosenberg's book, German libraries were required to stock it and it sold in the hundreds of thousands. According to Albert Speer, Hitler's chief architect and armaments minister, the public regarded this book "as the standard text for party ideology."[22] Strictly speaking, the doctrine in Rosenberg's book was not political philosophy at all, but a *Weltanschauung* (a word he used frequently), even a religion. But within the world-view was embedded a political, or at least a social, philosophy, which called for a truly radical transformation of German society. The world-view to which he gave credence, he called "myth," which is to say, not a logically developed philosophy, nor one to be understood by a study of cause and effect, but "an activity of soul" or "affirmation," made true by an exercise of will. However, Rosenberg undoubtedly also thought of this myth, which was a racial myth, as science as well, based on irrefutable evidence coming from biology and history. He referred many times, as did Hitler, to degeneration in history, which was said to have been caused by improper racial mixture, and which could be rectified only by a return to the "rule of nature" or to "blood law," which determined all the activities of man. This racial interpretation of history was, of course, not new, but was a throwback to the "scientific racism" of the late nineteenth century, especially to the ideas of Count Gobineau and Houston Stewart Chamberlain. In his book, Rosenberg paid special tribute to the latter's *Foundations of the Nineteenth Century* (1899), which used the term "race chaos" and distinguished between German "culture" of the spirit and the materialistic "civilization" of other peoples.

This, then, was the challenge Germans faced in the twentieth century: either sink back into race chaos, or will "a new life-Myth" based on Volk and race. "The Coming Reich" Rosenberg delineated—Moeller van den Bruck had called it "the Third Reich" in his famous book by that title of 1923, and the name had stuck—was the reverse of the modern industrial-urban society, riven by individualism, class struggle, and cosmopolitanism. Rosenberg's model, like that of many other high-ranking Nazis, was an earlier form of society, pre-Christian, largely agrarian (hence, the emphasis on *Lebensraum*, plenty of land

---

[22] Albert Speer, *Inside the Third Reich*, Macmillan, New York, 1970, p. 96.

for a large peasant population to till), narrowly and blatantly nationalistic and militaristic, guided by the principles of "Blood and Soil." There was no socialism about it, unless it was the "Prussian Socialism" of Oswald Spengler and some others, which called for the mobilization of all the country's resources, and all its groups and interests, for the aggrandizement of the nation. The Nazis, indeed, proclaimed a radical inequality among men, not only between races, Aryan and Jew, but within the master race itself. Hitler himself, as is well known, expressed contempt for the masses, whose understanding was small, and who would not know what to do with liberal freedom even if they had it. A society that was "true to nature," he said openly in *Mein Kampf,* had to be built on "the aristocratic principle," rejecting "the democratic [and socialistic] mass idea."[23] The Coming Reich, then, projected an organic society, the opposite of "the mechanical atomism of someone like Hobbes"[24]; of common racial origin, yet essentially aristocratic; a society faithful to "the Volk-soul," which would permeate everything, culture, the state, and the life of individuals and groups; a society uniquely itself, unlike any other, yet not static, for it must be capable of growth or "Becoming," by which Rosenberg meant moving toward a goal of perfection supplied from within, and not frozen by absolutes—liberalism, Marxism, and the like—imposed from without. In Rosenberg's murky metaphysical language, which he claimed Leibniz inspired with his doctrine of monads, "A mathematical schematicism which posited a logically-comprehensible *immutable* Being, would inhibit the perception of the *Becoming* of self-forming Being."[25] Ultimately, Rosenberg preached a "religion of the blood," tracing back, as he believed (following Paul de Lagarde's musings), to the Germanic Middle Ages, and based on honor rather than love. This religion, ultimately mystical and indefinable and thwarted by Christianity in history, must be revived if Germans were ever to achieve the Coming Reich. Rosenberg's language, like Nazi language in general, was apocalyptic, but apocalyptic in a primitivist rather than futuristic sense, that is, recalling, and advocating a return to, a primitive past, not pointing to a modernistic future.

Meanwhile, what of liberalism, the third member of the triad of competing political and social doctrines? In his autobiography, Arthur

---

[23] Adolf Hitler, *Mein Kampf,* Reynal & Hitchcock, New York, 1941, p. 661; see also pp. 56, 234.

[24] Alfred Rosenberg, *Der Mythus des 20. Jahrhunderts,* in *Race and Race History,* Robert Pois (ed.), Harper & Row, New York, 1970, p. 87.

[25] Ibid., pp. 87, 89.

Koestler spoke of a "Liberal Götterdämmerung," of the mass migration of the sons and daughters of the European bourgeoisie to the radical Right or Left during the years following World War I, and during and after the Great Depression. And, indeed, liberalism was much derided, not only by communists and fascists but by a wide variety of socialist, Christian, and "new" radical thinkers. Undoubtedly, liberalism suffered much from its identification with laissez-faire capitalism, which had fallen on evil days. Harold Laski, for example, philosopher of the English Labor Party, accused liberalism of failing to operate successfully in the economic and social spheres; T. S. Eliot, of materialism and vulgarity, with too much emphasis on the profit motive; Herbert Marcuse, of leading to fascism, as individualistic capitalism was displaced by monopoly capitalism. Yet liberalism had its defenders too, increasingly so as the struggle with totalitarianism intensified. Much of the defense of liberalism was, no doubt, halfhearted, in the manner of the novelist and critic E. M. Forster, who was willing to give two cheers, but not three, for democracy. He did not "believe in Belief," he said, but in an age of militant creeds, one had to make some profession of faith, and Forster did believe in the importance of the individual and freedom of criticism, both permitted in liberal democracies. Democracy "is less hateful than other contemporary forms of government, and to that extent it deserves our support."[26] There was nothing halfhearted, however, about the defense of old-style "negative" liberals such as Alain of France during the 1920's, or, more significantly, since Alain had no great following, the Austrian-born economists Ludwig von Mises and his follower Friedrich von Hayek. The latter's *The Road to Serfdom* (1944), which argued that state planning, not liberalism, led to totalitarianism, won respectful attention in the Western world. But the chief support for liberalism came from those prepared to accept, or actively advocate, at least some degree of "positive liberty" or state intervention: from, for instance, John Maynard Keynes, who in his widely read *General Theory of Employment, Interest, and Money* (1936), showed how, by government pump priming, a capitalist economy could get itself out of depressions; from the Catholic philosopher Jacques Maritain, who showed how democracy could be made compatible with Christianity; and from the Viennese philosopher, Karl Popper, who, though certainly opposed to large-scale state planning, proposed "piecemeal" social engineering in an "open society."

[26] E. M. Forster, *Two Cheers for Democracy*, Harcourt, Brace, New York, 1951, p. 69.

Like Thomas Mann, Jacques Maritain discovered the virtues of liberal democracy in midcareer. His politics, somewhat reactionary at first, changed after 1926, when Pope Pius XI condemned Charles Maurras and his *Action française,* and as French Catholics in general became more liberal-minded in the 1930's. But Maritain did not merely reflect, but helped to lead, this important change in outlook. He countered Maurras' "integral nationalism" (or fascism) with his own "integral humanism," or Christian-personalist democracy, as he sometimes called it. Maritain believed, with T. S. Eliot, that democracy ultimately depended on belief in religious or metaphysical principles, and not merely on the scientific method. Yet Maritain knew that there could be no return to the "sacral" era of the Middle Ages. To combat totalitarianism he, therefore, advocated a pluralistic democracy, by which he meant agreement, by men belonging to plural, and very different, philosophical and religious creeds, on certain "practical points of convergence" or conclusions.[27] The conclusions, not to be confused with the theoretical justifications for them, which must inevitably clash, were all the familiar rights and liberties assigned to individuals in liberal democracies. Maritain's "democratic secular faith," however, went beyond mere individualism. He, in fact, distinguished sharply between individualism and personalism. Individualism, having its roots in matter, sought its own selfish ends, whereas personalism, rooted in spirit, was committed to the common good, as well as to self. Maritain and other personalists of his time (for in this respect he was part of a personalist movement, largely though not exclusively Catholic)[28] obviously wanted to steer a course between bourgeois liberalism on the one hand, which they thought absolutized the individual, and totalitarianism, which dwarfed the individual, subordinating him completely to society. Thus, Maritain preached a "new democracy," which was both pluralistic and personalistic, not stopping short at political reform, but pressing also for social reform; wary of collectivism, yet open to "associative ownership of the means of production" by producers and consumers.

Karl Popper, one of the few authentic political philosophers of the

[27] On Maritain's idea of pluralist democracy, see especially *Man and the State* (1951). See also *Humanisme intégrale* (1936) and *Christianisme et Démocratie* (1943), the latter for his admonition that democracy must now go beyond political to social reform.

[28] The Personalist movement included the French philosophers Gabriel Marcel and Lavelle, and Emmanuel Mounier, editor of the new journal *Esprit.* Maritain developed his personalist ideas in *La personne et le bien commun* (1947).

period,[29] defended liberalism more from the standpoint of scientific method. In his autobiography, Popper described *The Open Society and its Enemies* (1943) as his "war effort," and, indeed, that massive and learned work reads somewhat like a war book, though it begins with Plato and scatters its shots among Marxists, fascists, and contemporary social scientists. Marxism came under attack for its "historicism" (somewhat eccentrically equated by Popper with historical determinism); fascism, for its surrender of the use of reason in social life to prophetic Leaders; and social science, especially the school of Karl Mannheim, for its utopianism or advocacy of a "holistic" social engineering. What these three very different groups had in common, Popper contended, was intellectual arrogance, based on a false conception of science, which betrayed them into thinking they had discovered laws of history, and hence could prophesy the course of historical events and make plans for whole societies. Science, however, could not be made to countenance such grandiose knowledge. All scientific knowledge is hypothetical and tentative, growing only through trial and error elimination. Popper saw the closest connection between this critical or rational attitude, generated by true science, and the maintenance of an "open" or free society. As he wrote in his autobiography:

> *The Poverty [of Historicism]* and *The Open Society* were my war effort. I thought that freedom might become a central problem again, especially under the influence of Marxism and the idea of large-scale "planning" (or "dirigism"); and so these books were meant as a defence of freedom against totalitarian and authoritarian ideas. . . . Both grew out of the theory of knowledge of *Logik der Forschung* and out of my conviction that our often unconscious views on the theory of knowledge and its central problems ("What can we know", "How certain is our knowledge?") are decisive for our attitude towards ourselves and towards politics.[30]

Popper's Open Society was distinguished from the closed societies of history by its insistence on "piecemeal," as opposed to Utopian, social engineering; by its recognition that there were no perfect societies on

---

[29] Popper was a broad-gauged philosopher, known for his work on the logic and philosophy of science, as well as philosophy of history and politics. He has been wrongly included in the Vienna Group of logical positivists.

[30] Karl Popper, "Intellectual Autobiography," in *The Philosophy of Karl Popper*, P. A. Schilpp (ed.), Open Court, LaSalle, Ill., 1974, Vol. I, p. 91. *The Poverty of Historicism*, Popper's diatribe against historical determinism, was completed in outline as early as 1935, but not expanded and published until 1944 and 1945. The *Logik der Forschung*, also mentioned in the quotation, was his important book on scientific method, published in 1934.

earth, and never would be, but that it was possible for the piecemeal engineer to search out, and combat by rational means, the greatest and most urgent evils of society; by its recognition that freedom was more important than equality, and that, indeed, the attempt to realize full equality endangered freedom; and by its conviction that democracy alone could provide the institutional framework for continuous reform without violence, for the use of reason in politics, and for freedom of thought and the progress of science.

Popper also struck a blow for objective truth in the social sciences, as opposed to the radical relativism he found in the "sociologism" of Mannheim and others. Both he and Mannheim came out of the same chaotic intellectual world of clashing ideologies and despair of truth. But they responded to it in different ways. Popper was not entirely fair to Mannheim. After all, Mannheim, a refugee from fascism as was Popper, did distinguish between democratic planning and dictatorship, and was himself a liberal after his own fashion, insisting upon freedom of thought and the free development of personality, even if in a planned society. He also sought to overcome the worst features of relativism, chiefly by dramatizing the role to be played in modern society by the intelligentsia, the only class, in Mannheim's opinion, capable of rising above class ideologies, of synthesizing them, and hence of obtaining a measure of control over them. It may be doubted, however, whether Mannheim ever escaped the snares of his own relativism or believed in any sort of "truth as such." As he saw it, all knowledge save natural science was "situationally conditioned," or socially relative: that was, indeed, the chief principle of the sociology of knowledge. He was more interested in the social origins of ideas than in their objective validity. Hence, he could write, in *Ideology and Utopia* (1929), his most important book, that

> A modern theory of knowledge (in contrast to the "liberal" theory of an objective, unbiased truth) . . . must start with the assumption that there are spheres of thought in which it is impossible to conceive of absolute truth existing independently of the values and position of the subject and unrelated to the social context.[31]

Mannheim went even farther than that. The very idea of truth, he wrote, "has not remained constant through all time but has been involved in the process of historical change."[32]

[31] Karl Mannheim, *Ideology and Utopia,* Harcourt, Brace, New York, 1936, p. 79.
[32] Ibid., p. 291.

Popper conceded that there was a "kernel of truth" in sociological relativism. But he thought that sociologism had gone much too far, that the radical relativism it inculcated led to despair of reason, and in any case broke down in the light of scientific method. Ultimately, Popper fell back on a compromise position, which he called "fallibilistic absolutism." This meant, first of all, that men might err, did err, and never attained certainty. "But this does not imply," he wrote, "that the quest for the truth is mistaken," or "that *truth* is 'relative'."[33] Scientific results were relative only insofar as they corresponded to a certain stage of scientific development, and were liable to be superseded as men learned more. Truth, for Popper, meant quite simply correspondence to the facts as ascertained by science, and it was always growing and must be allowed to grow. Clearly, both Popper and Mannheim believed in becoming, in scientific as in political and social thought. But Popper also held firm to a realm of being that was hard to reach but existent all the same. For Popper, this "truth as such," undermined by Mannheim and the relativists, guaranteed at least some stability in an unstable world.

No discussion of twentieth-century social thought would be complete without at least mention of the European Economic Community, which may eventually turn out to be the most important European idea for social reorganization of the century. This was the brainchild of Jean Monnet, cognac salesman, international businessman, member of joint ministries in two wars, deputy secretary-general of the League of Nations, and finally president of the High Authority of the European Coal and Steel Community, inaugurated in Luxembourg in 1952. Though no social philosopher, Monnet had a vision of a new society, of a European Europe, that was greater than any of its parts, beginning on the economic level. Europe, once the center of the civilized world, he explained, had squandered her resources and prestige in internecine wars, and as presently organized, no longer lived "in the rhythm of the times." What was to be done? The answer was clear: not simply to hold discussions among sovereign nations or pursue national grandeur as in the past, but to create new institutions with which the European nations would fuse a part of their sovereignty, and which would be capable of developing "the common European interest." The new reality, said Monnet

---

[33] Karl Popper, *The Open Society and Its Enemies,* Routledge & Kegan Paul, London, 1969, Vol. II, pp. 221, 375, 377. See especially the whole addendum, added in 1961, entitled "Facts, Standards, and Truth: A Further Criticism of Relativism."

respects the deep national realities, it excludes neither diversity of temperaments and habits, nor respect for traditions and the unique character of each country. But it eliminates the vestiges of another age, the mutual fear and the protection of small closed markets.[34]

Thus, Jean Monnet, too, pleaded for an open society, democratic and liberal, but on a new Europeanwide basis. To make this supranational Europe was to make peace, and to lay the foundations for a European cultural renaissance. Such, at any rate, was Monnet's hope, with the establishment of the European Economic Community.

[34] Jean Monnet, *Les États-Unis d'Europe ont commencé*, Robert Laffont, Paris, 1955, pp. 45–46.

The Decline of
the West

R. W. Collingwood, in his autobiography (1939), portrayed historical thought not only as having come of age methodologically in the twentieth century but as having attained a new preeminence, even a queenship, among the sciences. It seemed to him

> as nearly certain as anything in the future could be, that historical thought, whose constantly increasing importance had been one of the most striking features of the nineteenth century, would increase in importance far more rapidly during the twentieth; and that we might very well be standing on the threshold of an age in which history would be as important for the world as natural science had been between 1600 and 1900.[1]

If that was true, "the wise philosopher" would do well to concentrate more on the problems of history, and thus help lay "the foundations

---

[1] R. G. Collingwood, *An Autobiography*, Oxford University Press, London, 1939, pp. 87–88. There is some doubt about exactly when, or even if, Collingwood was converted completely to historicism. I shall not enter into this controversy, but instead refer the reader to works by T. M. Knox (see editor's preface to Collingwood's posthumously published *The Idea of History*, 1945), Alan Donegan (1962), and Louis Mink (1969).

of the future." Collingwood himself, acting on his own advice, went confidently ahead to work out a rapprochement between philosophy and history, and even, eventually, to historicize philosophy—in the same way that nature had been historicized since Darwin, theology since the Higher Criticism, and so on. Philosophy, he argued, should give up the illusion of dealing with eternal ideas and problems, and realize that "all metaphysical questions are historical questions," that is, that they boiled down to "absolute presuppositions,"[2] made at a certain time and in a certain context, and were subject to change over the centuries.

Collingwood's prophecy, made, as he tells us, at the end of World War I, had become a commonplace by the 1930's, when he began to write his autobiography. By then, the historicity of things, especially, he would say, men's thoughts, was widely assumed and discussed. But strangely, nowhere in Collingwood does one encounter the contemporary "crisis of historicism," as Ernst Troeltsch called it. There is much in Collingwood about history, and the study of history, but less than one might expect about the problem these had now begun to pose for men of letters and philosophers, as well as historians, especially but not only in Germany. The focus in this last chapter is principally on this crisis. The crisis—a much overworked word, yet indispensable for anyone talking about twentieth-century thought, including the philosophy of history—was partly provoked by World War I (actually by the two world wars), yet also, as we have seen,[3] preceded it. Partly it was an internal crisis, coming from within the study of history itself, especially when considered in juxtaposition to philosophy. But it was also, undoubtedly, the product of cataclysmic events. The crisis consisted in a preoccupation with the problem of historical knowledge, and a loss of faith in the meaning—and reason—of history. The point is not that these emphases were strictly new, but only that they reached crisis proportions in the twentieth century, especially after 1914.

Before considering this crisis in detail, it will be prudent to return briefly to Collingwood and to mention briefly Whitehead and Lenin. All three (some others would do equally well) demonstrate that older philosophies of history survived, and even to some extent flourished, though not without considerable modification, in twentieth-century

[2] R. G. Collingwood, *An Essay on Metaphysics*, Clarendon Press, Oxford, 1940, Chap. VI ("Metaphysics an Historical Science"). See also *An Autobiography*, Chaps. VI and VII.

[3] See p. 403.

soil. Collingwood is an example of an historicist—one of its leading theoreticians, in fact—who kept the faith, both with respect to historical knowledge and the lessons to be drawn from history. It was possible, he thought, to recover the past, or important segments of it, by rethinking the thoughts (though not the feelings; it was not possible to do that) of those who went before. "Presuppositions," then, were not absolutely tied to historical context, or to the thought of the knower, but had a certain objectivity, as well as truth, about them. Ergo, historical inquiry could be the royal road to self-knowledge and practical wisdom. History familiarized men with past ways of thinking about things, which could be revived as a guide to present actions. "We study history in order to see more clearly into the situation in which we are called to act."[4] Armed with this conviction, Collingwood could speak, in the postwar era, of a "science of human affairs," which would do for the human situation what natural science had already done for the world of nature, that is, get it under control. It may be added that, despite his skepticism about the "propositions" of metaphysicians (as compared with their "presuppositions"), Collingwood never gave up on metaphysics as the science of being. That is, he never completely historicized it. Being, the object of metaphysical thought, constituted the reality of which history, science, art, and religion were the appearances.

Collingwood also retained some vestiges of belief in "the old dogma" of historical progress. Fundamentally, however, he was skeptical of progress. Viewed, not merely as a possibility,[5] but as actual historical fact, it was largely an optical illusion, he thought, impossible of verification, and dependent on the perspective of the viewer, including that of the historian. Whitehead, on the other hand, had the strong faith of the Victorian liberal in "the slow drift of mankind towards civilization," which was moral and aesthetic, as well as intellectual. Whitehead, of course, was well aware of the problem of historical knowledge, of the impossibility of "mere knowledge," without taking into account the presuppositions or standards of the historian. But Whitehead did not dwell on it, as Collingwood did, or let it warp his overall view.

[4] Collingwood, op. cit. (see note 1), p. 114.
[5] Collingwood believed in the possibility of progress, created, as he put it, "by historical thinking," that is, by the retention in the mind of what had been achieved in the past, and improving upon it. In this way, "by way of continuity," Einstein had made an advance on Newton. See Collingwood, *The Idea of History*, Oxford University Press, New York, 1957, p. 333; also his essay, "A Philosophy of Progress," in Collingwood, *Essays in the Philosophy of History*, University of Texas Press, Austin, 1965.

Whitehead's philosophy of history, presented mainly in *Adventures of Ideas* (1933), might be said to be a blend of Mill, Lecky, and Platonic Idealism. He by no means ignored the presence of evil, discord, and mistakes in history, or the precariousness and limitations of civilization. Nevertheless, he saw, in the main, "reason" in history, the victory of persuasion over force, the power of great ideas, based on feeling, to modify epochs and meliorate the human condition. Discord was actually a plus, as it had been for Mill, in promoting adventures of ideas and in preventing the sort of "anesthesia" that brought all civilization to a halt. Whitehead believed in "process" in history, as in nature. "Thus each actual thing is only to be understood in terms of its becoming and perishing."[6] But he interpreted historical process, or becoming, optimistically, as a good Victorian liberal should.

As also, of course, did the Marxists whose optimistic, even if Manichean, philosophy of history appealed widely in an age of nihilism. Two points only need be made here about it, since in other respects it remained substantially the same doctrine worked out by Marx and Engels. The first point is, that, owing to changed circumstances, Lenin smuggled a new voluntarist element into the doctrine. Initially a strict determinist, he changed his mind when it became apparent that industrial workers did not develop spontaneously the class consciousness expected of them in their economic situation. Obviously, to carry forward the necessary goals of history—first, the revolution, and afterwards, the classless society—the masses everywhere, including those in backward countries and living under imperialist domination, had to be worked upon by an intellectual elite, which was conscious of the goals and which could articulate and organize them effectively. Thus, to the classical Marxist doctrine of necessary laws, economic processes, and "spontaneity" in history, Lenin tacked on the role of "consciousness," or willed change. This idea appears already full-blown in an early work, *What Is to Be Done?* (1901). Later, Lenin was to try to square these apparently irreconcilable ideas by means of the Lamarckian notion of acquired characteristics. This notion, which had the authority of Engels himself, made it plain that variations in intellect and leadership, evoked by the economic environment, could be inherited. In any event, the elitist-voluntarist idea became a permanent element in the Soviet canon—seized on by Stalin, who wanted to stress the power of

[6] Alfred North Whitehead, *Adventures of Ideas*, Macmillan, New York, 1933, p. 354. For other examples of continuing belief in progress, among social scientists as well, see W. Warren Wagar, *Good Tidings*, Indiana University Press, Bloomington, 1972.

Party, dictatorship, and the cult of personality in the shaping of history.

The second point to be made is that many of those who were attracted to communism in Western Europe saw the tragedy involved in the communist interpretation of history. Mostly, the European Marxists, such as the French writer Louis Aragon, preferred to see only the triumph of "reason" in history and the joy and promise involved in becoming identified and going along with it. On the other hand, Jean-Paul Sartre, definitely a sympathizer, though not a Party member, after World War II, saw the "anguish" of history and objected to the determinism, which cleared the path of history in advance of human choice. Albert Camus, leftist-oriented but not a communist, also objected to communist determinism (he called it "historical absolutism"), but in addition, and in opposition to Sartre, protested a "revolution" which he thought exacted too great a cost in human terms, sacrificing the innocent as well as the guilty, threatening the person and freedom of the other person, and justifying means by ends.

Liberals and Marxists, the latter more than the former, were not the only groups to preach an onward and upward progress in history. Attention may be called especially to the optimistic biologists, or evolutionists, who, taking the long view, not only cited progress already made but predicted a rosy future for mankind. A hasty reading of Teilhard de Chardin and Julian Huxley might persuade one that Europe's plight, and the world's plight, in the twentieth century had completely passed them by. But that certainly was not the case. Both recognized clearly enough the tragic dissension of the twentieth century, following the great expectations of the nineteenth. "Our feet still drag in the biological mud," said Huxley, even after thousands of years of human evolution.[7] But the chief point they wanted to make was that recent events constituted but "one tick of evolution's clock," and that with the advent of man, evolution had passed from a purely biological to a psychological state, and was at last becoming conscious of itself, and therefore capable of directing its future. Obviously, both Teilhard and Huxley, who pursued parallel roads of thought and esteemed each other, took a decidedly more optimistic view of human potentialities than those described in the chapter on "Problematic Man." They saw man, and human history, in a cosmic context. The world, they thought—one is reminded here of similar things said by Bergson, Lloyd Morgan, and Samuel Alexander—was one gigantic process of becoming,

---

[7] *The Humanist Frame,* Julian Huxley (ed.), Harper & Brothers, New York, 1961, p. 20.

achieving ever higher levels of existence and organization. There was nothing inevitable about this upward process, as the Marxists contended. Huxley, especially, was forever saying, as an "evolutionary humanist," that it depended, now and henceforth, on man's free choice and the intelligent use of his powers. Teilhard was perhaps more deterministic, since his "science" was closely interwoven with his theological finalism, despite his own assertions to the contrary. Teilhard, in *The Phenomenon of Man* (published posthumously, in 1955), and elsewhere,[8] looked forward to the time when history would have evolved toward a final state of "Point Omega," in which man would have surpassed himself. In this state of "ultra-hominisation," as he entitled the process, man would have gone beyond "individuality" to achieve "personality," whose special mark was to love, and unite with, others. Teilhard spoke of this tendency toward synthesis as the "within of things," and as "biologically necessary." Both he and Huxley saw the evolution of life and history as going contrary to the second law of thermodynamics, as, so to speak, gathering up and putting together, rather than multiplying, the fragments of the universe.

As stated previously, the novel thing in philosophy of history was not the optimism, whether old or new, but, on the contrary, the pessimism, or the skepticism, which first of all, questioned the validity of historical knowledge itself. Was an objective study of history possible, as had been assumed by the "positivistic" nineteenth century? Did history really constitute an objective world, consisting of past events to be discovered? Was the historian really a neutral observer, able to reconstruct and interpret the past, independently of his own ideas and prejudices and those of his times? These questions were debated furiously all through the 1920's and 1930's by historians, philosophers, and social scientists. Though centering in Germany, the debate raged throughout Europe, and spread to the United States. The prestigious journals of Germany, especially *Die Neue Rundschau* and the *Historische Zeitschrift,* were full of the debate, and key books by Troeltsch (1922), Karl Heussi (1932), and many others, discussed it, along with other "problems" of historicism. The Italian philosopher-historian Benedetto Croce had been puzzling over similar questions since the 1890's, when he asked whether history was art or science. And in England, Collingwood and the philosopher Michael Oakeshott did likewise, as did American historians as well known as Carl Becker and

---

[8] See especially, the essays collected in the volume entitled *L'Avenir de l'homme* (1959), translated as *The Future of Man,* 1964.

Charles Beard. In perspective, the debate over historical knowledge can be seen as part of the wider philosophical debate between neo-idealism and positivism, which commenced in the late nineteenth century and affected the philosophy of science. But it was also to some extent internally generated by the remorseless logic of historicism, which threatened to relativize the historian himself, as well as his ideas about history.

Conclusions about historical knowledge ranged from complete to moderate skepticism. Nearly all the disputants conceded, in Kantian fashion, that mind or consciousness played a role in constructing the historical world. But this could mean, as with Croce, merely that the facts of history—he did not dispute that at least some facts, though not all the facts, were ascertainable—had to be re-experienced and interpreted by the historian before they could live in the present. Troeltsch, acutely aware that every age had to understand anew, and from its own standpoint, the major movements of history ("Where then remains the reality and objectivity?")[9] continued to believe in the possibility of finding universal norms and values in history. His friend Max Weber, though skeptical of norms, thought that at least objective knowledge of the social world was attainable by means of a rational method. Others, however, particularly in Germany, carried epistemological skepticism to the extreme, and there is some evidence that, despite rebuff by academic historians, this radical historicism (or rejection of historicism) reached a fairly wide public.[10] This distressing state of affairs prompted a contributor to the respectable *Historische Zeitschrift* to conclude that "The age of historicism is over. . . . Faith in objective historical thought has disappeared."[11] In his important book on *Experience and its Modes* (1933), the Cambridge philosopher Oakeshott summed up, not perhaps the most extreme position on the subject, but one that was representative of contemporary opposition to an objective, or positivistic, theory of history. The chief objection to this theory, he thought, was that there could be no historical "course of events" independent of our experience of it.

---

[9] Ernst Troeltsch, "Die Krise des Historismus," *Die Neue Rundschau,* Vol. XXXIII (1922), Pt. I, p. 579.

[10] See Karl Heussi's remarks (*Die Krisis des Historismus,* J. C. B. Mohr, Tübingen, 1932, pp. 36–37). For instance, Theodor Lessing's book, *Geschichte als Sinngebung des Sinnlosen* (1921), ran to four editions, despite professional academic disdain.

[11] C. H. Becker, "Der Wandel im Geschichtlichen Bewusstsein," *Die Neue Rundschau,* Vol. XXXVIII (1927), Pt. I, p. 113. Becker was Prussian minister of culture at the time he wrote this article.

The distinction between history as it happened (the course of events) and history as it is thought, the distinction between history itself and merely experienced history must go; it is not merely false, it is meaningless. . . . History is experience, the historian's world of experience; it is a world of ideas, the historian's world of ideas.[12]

As Collingwood, who attacked him, was careful to point out, Oakeshott did not mean to say that history was *only* the historian's ideas, or that there were no historical facts. Oakeshott did say, however, that the historical world, taken by itself, was an abstraction from "the real world," and consequently could not give any sort of "unqualified reality."

Doubts about history's meaning paralleled these doubts about historical knowledge. By meaning is meant possible values to be discovered in history, whether national or universal; and history as directed toward a goal, or going in a desirable direction. For an increasing number of people, history, like man (or because of man) became problematic. This is understandable in the light of contemporary events. The Thirty Years' War of the twentieth century almost guaranteed new views of history, with doubts arising about its meaning, at least as traditionally construed. Almost certainly, however, there would have been a crisis of meaning, though less intense, even without the events. Ernst Troeltsch makes this clear in his famous article of 1922 on historicism, in which the crisis was traced, not to the Great War, which he scarcely mentions, but to the problem of value posed by historical relativism. Historicism, in its deepest sense, he said

> meant the historicizing of all our knowledge and perception of the spiritual world, as it developed in the course of the nineteenth century. We see here everything in the flux of becoming (im Flüsse des Werdens). . . . State, law, morality, religion, art are dissolved in this flux, and intelligible to us only as ingredients of historical developments. . . . Historicism shook all eternal truths.[13]

Troeltsch himself, as mentioned, managed somehow to find values in history, in spite of relativism. But for many others, relativism was the rock on which their hopes of meaning foundered.

Significantly, this re-exploration of historical meaning was by no means confined to professional historians or to professional philoso-

[12] Michael Oakeshott, *Experience and its Modes,* Cambridge University Press, Cambridge, 1933, p. 93. See also pp. 11, 147–148, 155.
[13] Troeltsch, "Die Krise" (see note 9), p. 573.

phers. Indeed, one might say that it became even more the endeavor of Everyman, of literary men and artists, existentialists, Christians, and psychoanalysts. Troeltsch mentions dilettantes and journalists in his article, singling out, in particular, Oswald Spengler, the high school teacher whose *Decline of the West* made such an impact after World War I, and H. G. Wells. Others who come readily to mind are Freud and Carl Jung, the poet William Butler Yeats, and the novelist and essayist Thomas Mann, Christian thinkers such as Nicolas Berdyaev and Paul Tillich, and André Malraux, Karl Jaspers, and Jean-Paul Sartre. All of these, and others too, speculated about history's meaning and came to some rather novel, and not infrequently, pessimistic conclusions. As Pierre-Henri Simon says, history became the special malaise of the twentieth century, as metaphysics and religion had been of the nineteenth.[14] This malaise may be discussed conveniently under several heads: antihistoricism; a new appreciation of the role played by unreason in history; the revival of cyclical theories of history; and, of supreme importance, the realization that perhaps Europe itself did not occupy the center of the historical universe, and was, in any case, in the throes of cultural decline, and that the decline had commenced centuries before. This last thought inevitably involved a certain amount of reperiodizing and rewriting of Western, and especially European, history in relation to the rest of the world.

Benedetto Croce, in an address of 1930, called attention to the decay of the historical sense, amounting at times to an outspoken "antihistoricism," in the Europe of his day. Croce was both shocked and alarmed. Those people who, like the futurists of his own country and the new breed of authoritarians, turned their back on the past, or else tried to arrest it in frozen molds, were "the atheists and unbelievers of today." They deprived man, he said, of "the last religious belief remaining to him," that is, history, which could join him to the All, to all those who labored in past and present for beauty and truth.[15] Antihistoricists were, indeed, to be found in abundance in the 1920's, not only in the groups mentioned by Croce but among the so-called political decisionists of Germany[16] and among the existentialists, who were much more present- and future-minded than they were past-minded,

---

[14] Pierre-Henri Simon, *L'Esprit et l'histoire,* Armand Colin, Paris, 1954, Chap. I.

[15] Benedetto Croce, "Antihistorismus," *Historische Zeitschrift,* Vol. 143 (1930), p. 466.

[16] Ernst Jünger, author of *In Stahlgewittern* (1919), is an example of a "political decisionist." The only values remaining for him, after the debacle of the war, were life and struggle. On Jünger, see pp. 408–409.

since they emphasized "life," personal decision, and struggle to define man's essence and his history. World War I, bringing in its wake disillusionment with past institutions and ideas, certainly helped this antihistoricism along. But its roots went deeper. This can be seen in the futurist movement, which started prior to 1914, and whose early leaders—the poet Filippo Tommaso Marinetti and a number of painters, including Umberto Boccioni—glorified war. Futurism, unlike most other manifestations of antihistoricism, was essentially an optimistic movement, exalting the modern world of the machine, the city, and science, of speed, motion, and change. It originated in Italy, the least modern of the European powers, and preoccupied, like no other country in Europe, with its past. The futurists revolted against this past-mindedness, this world of cemeteries, museums, and antiquaries. Much of what they had to say is contained in Marinetti's fiery manifesto of 1909, which launched the movement.

> Why should we look behind us, when we have to break in the mysterious portals of the Impossible? Time and Space died yesterday. Already we live in the absolute, since we have already created speed, eternal and ever-present.[17]

Down with Poussin and Ingres, said the painters in a later manifesto, down with all those who petrified their art with an obstinate attachment to the past. Down, even, with the cubists for continuing to paint "objects motionless, frozen, and all the static aspects of Nature."[18] The futurists painted, instead, feet moving, racing cars, and cities. In Boccioni's painting *The City Rises* (1910–1911; Plate 42), the viewer is not supposed to be detached but involved in the building, the tumult, and the dynamism of the modern city. Dynamism was their keynote, and insofar as futurism had any metaphysical base, it came from Nietzsche and Bergson, whom the futurists quoted freely. Boccioni spoke the latter's language when, in *Lacerba*, futurism's short-lived periodical, he described dynamism as "life itself in the form which life creates in its infinite, uninterrupted becoming"[19]—becoming as opposed to any sort of dead past, life as opposed to history.

Like the futurists, Sigmund Freud looked askance at the past, al-

---

[17] Marinetti, Manifesto of Futurism, February 20, 1909, in Joshua Taylor, *Futurism*, Museum of Modern Art, New York, 1961, p. 124.

[18] Technical Manifesto, April 11, 1910 (signed by Boccioni, Carrà, Russolo, Balla, and Severini), in ibid., p. 127.

[19] Quoted in Rosa Clough, *Futurism*, Greenwood Press, New York, 1961, p. 96.

PLATE 42. *The City Rises*, by Umberto Boccioni (1910).

Oil on Canvas. 6' 6½" x 9' 10½". Collection, The Museum of Modern Art, New York. Mrs. Simon Guggenheim Fund.

though the past was by no means dead for him. He was, in fact, obsessed by the past, especially by the primitive past, and recognized its power over the present. Thus, Freud found meaning in history, but it was not the meaning of the Christians or rationalists. Freud is an excellent example of those, a steadily increasing number in the twentieth century, who saw history as the reign of unreason. He did not always see it that way, of course. He sometimes talked, as the positivists had done, about evolution toward more reason through animistic, religious, and scientific phases of history. But normally, as in *Totem and Taboo* (1912), *Group Psychology* (1922), and in several war essays, it was the unreason that Freud stressed. This was perhaps natural in an "age of psychology," as Otto Rank called it. In any event, the psychoanalysts, most of whom had an interest in history, were among the chief exemplars of an "irrational" historicism. They were not the only exemplars, however, as is evident, for example, in the changing views of an academic historian such as Friedrich Meinecke. Meinecke, brought up in the Rankean tradition, never gave up completely on reason in history. But World War I gave him second thoughts about the behavior pattern of the state in history. "State reason" (*Staatsräson*), about which Meinecke wrote an important book in 1924, was not identical with unreason, of course, but it could, and often did, behave barbarously. He could no longer subscribe unqualifiedly to Ranke's confidence that the state had always protected Europe from the ill use of power and violence. "The historical world," he concluded, "seems to us more obscure and, with respect to its further progress, more dangerous and uncertain than it did to him and to the generations that believed in the triumph of reason in history."[20]

Freud, too, reflected much on war and came to conclusions that are not dissimilar about states and nations. But his argument, since he was a psychologist and not a historian, was rather different. There had always been wars, and probably always would be. Why was that? It was for the same reason that the communists were wrong about the abolition of private property as the cure for human ailments: because human nature was murderous at bottom (though there was love too, and some rationality). In a sense, then, it is misleading to say that, in Freud's thought, ontogeny repeats phylogeny. Though that is true, it is truer to say that, for Freud, collective events, or history, reflected

---

[20] Friedrich Meinecke, *Machiavellism* (*Die Idee der Staatsräson in der neueren Geschichte*), Douglas Scott (trans.), Yale University Press, New Haven, 1957, p. 424.

individual psychology.[21] Freud traced man's origins back to a primitive state of nature in which there was fratricidal conflict and murder of the father by the horde, followed by a feeling of guilt and the need to expiate it. Thereafter, despite the "progress" of civilization, human nature did not change much, especially in the mass. In other words, Freud thought history was, in large part, a projection of man's unreason, and that even civilization, admittedly a great achievement, was but a thin veneer, bought by a degree of renunciation and sublimation that was almost too great for man's instinctual constitution to bear. In time of war, human beings simply regressed to "the primal man in each of us." Carl Jung, on the other hand, saw more the effect of history on the individual, or of phylogeny on ontogeny. Nevertheless, Jung did not believe, any more than did Freud, in reason as the controlling factor in history. When man denied his emotional nature, as he frequently did in history, there were, according to Jung, severe disturbances in the psyche, and group neurosis.

As may be surmised from the foregoing, Freud had a cyclical conception of history. Conflicts of a sexual-aggressive nature in the primitive past, thought to have been overlaid and forgotten, proved to be merely latent, thus making for an "oscillating rhythm," or eternal recurrence in history. This was another symptom of the crisis of historicism: the revival of cyclical, as opposed to linear-progressive, theories of history. Oswald Spengler and Arnold Toynbee are only the best known among those who developed such theories. Many literary celebrities did likewise, for example, Yeats, Thomas Mann, James Joyce, and Camus.[22] Not all were equally gloomy, or resigned to "destiny," as we shall see. All, however, point to a decline of historical optimism, stressing, at the very least, possible repeatables, reversibles, and recurrences in history, as well as the fragility of civilizations. The popularity of Spengler's work testifies to the wide currency of such ideas in the aftermath of World War I, and again, after a temporary eclipse of his reputation in the 1930's, during and after World War II. Ridiculed by the scholarly world as arrogant and unscientific, *The Decline of the West* nevertheless aroused wide interest and gained supporters as well

[21] Freud said this plainly enough, in his autobiography dated 1925. "I perceived," he wrote, "ever more clearly that the events of human history . . . are no more than a reflection of the dynamic conflicts between the ego, the id, and the super-ego, which psychoanalysis studies in the individual—are the very same processes repeated upon a wider stage" (*An Autobiographical Study*, James Strachey [trans.], Hogarth Press, London, 1946, p. 134).

[22] See, for instance, Camus on the future return of the plague bacillus (*La Peste*, 1947, last paragraph), after it has been driven from the city.

as detractors, even among scholars. Spengler claimed not to be pessimistic, yet rejected out of hand the straight-line progression of ancient-medieval-modern history, which had become so prevalent. Dismissing the latter as the "trivial optimism of the Darwinian age," he substituted for it his theory of cycles, suggested to him possibly by Nietzsche's "eternal recurrence," but more generally available in classical studies, in which he was well versed, and in the general climate of prewar Europe. According to Spengler, all the great cultures of world history had a unique soul or destiny, yet all went through analogous phases of life and death, in the manner of biological organisms or the seasons of the year. History had no meaning, because all cultures eventually died without issue, and were, moreover, entirely relative to one another as to values. Toynbee, likewise steeped in classical scholarship, and impressed by Spengler, revised this script somewhat. He too observed cycles of genesis, growth, and breakdown, in the twenty-six civilizations of world history, but he made them less rigid and combined them with, as he called it, a Jewish Zoroastrian view of history as the progressive execution of a divine plan. "It looks as if the movement of civilizations," he wrote, "may be cyclic and recurrent, while the movement of religion may be on a single continuous upward line."[23] Thus, for Toynbee, there were absolutes, and consequently, overall meaning in history.

All the same, Toynbee, especially in the first volumes of *A Study of History,* published before World War II, had much to say about civilizations in distress, and, in particular, the distress of Europe, which had now entered its "time of troubles." The decline of Europe or of the West: how many Europeans, not only world historians such as Spengler and Toynbee, nor only Germans, harped on this theme before, between, and after the two world wars. "We are now taking part in the beginnings of the barbarization of Europe" (Nicolas Berdyaev, 1933); "Europe is in the waning moon" (Yeats, 1936); "Realities of our time: The Decline of Europe" (Cyril Connolly, 1946); "I happen to believe that Europe is doomed, a chapter in history which is drawing to a finish" (the author's chief spokesman, in a novel by Arthur Koestler, 1951) are typical statements by people who thought of themselves as epigoni, witnessing the end of an era, or perhaps a whole civilization.[24] The vaunted progress in European history had been interrupted or reversed, since the Renaissance as some said, since the Enlightenment as

[23] Arnold Toynbee, *Civilization on Trial,* Oxford University Press, New York, 1948, pp. 235–236.
[24] See on this whole subject, my article "Twentieth-Century Version of the Apocalypse," *Journal of World History,* Vol. I, no. 3 (1954).

others said, or later still. Disenchantment, dehumanization (caused by hypertrophy of "the Machine"), loss of soul, mass culture and similar words were uttered *ad nauseam* to describe Europe's present plight. This talk about decline and decadence, widespread by the 1920's and 1930's, expresses, perhaps better than anything else, the historical malaise that had overtaken twentieth-century Europeans.

Spengler expressed this epigonic mood in two important concepts, neither of which was entirely original with him. The first was his replacement of what he called the "Ptolemaic" by the "Copernican" viewpoint in history. This meant seeing Europe, not at the center of the historical universe, around which all the other cultures orbited, but as one of eight distinct cultures, none of which was supreme, and some, at different times in history, surpassing Europe in soaring power. To write history in the Ptolemaic way, he said, had "become natural from long habit," as indeed it had.[25] Spengler proposed to set the record straight, not according to Europe any sort of privileged position vis-à-vis the other great cultures of world history. Another phrase, "From Culture to Civilization," expressed Spengler's second concept. The Faustian culture of Europe, still at its peak in the eighteenth century, had already passed into its last phase of winter, or "civilization." Culture signified creativity, spontaneity, and spirituality. Civilization, on the other hand, spelled world-weariness, the oversophisticated intellect, and soullessness. The symbol of civilization was the megalopolis, or world-city, characterized by outward rather than inward direction, dedicated to the cult of bigness, in the grip of machine organization, peopled by masses without roots.

Max Weber, older than Spengler and a much greater thinker, had similar misgivings about modern European history. Like Spengler, Weber compared the cultures of the world and found that of Europe unique, exhibiting, as no other, "rationalization." Unlike Spengler, Weber very much believed in thinking and acting rationally, which alone could give man truth and freedom. Rationalization, however, had had other less desirable side effects, namely "disenchantment" (*Entzauberung*) and bureaucratization. Disenchantment (again, by no means an altogether bad thing in Weber's mind) robbed man of his gods, leading to an anarchy of values and consequent disillusionment and unhappiness. Bureaucratization, though also having advantages, meant the discharge of public business by calculation, hence without

---

[25] Spengler's discussion of Ptolemaic and Copernican history is to be found in the introduction, Sixth section, of *The Decline of the West*.

regard for persons, nullifying genuine community. Weber was clearly ambivalent about rationalization. It had freed modern Europeans by delivering them from illusions and giving them rational control over their undertakings. At the same time, it had imprisoned them in an "iron cage" of mechanization and specialization, in which they lived under the curse of *Epigonentum,* and from which it was difficult to escape.

Others developed these themes further and more pessimistically, in the following decades. Christians emphasized the disenchantment, or spiritual disorders, as did some psychoanalysts. The point usually made was quite simple, namely, as Albert Schweitzer said, that a civilization (or Spenglerian Culture) depended on world-view. "The present collapse of civilization" in Europe traced, then, not primarily to failure of institutions, not even to the Great War, which was only a symptom, but to the abandonment of religious and ethical beliefs since the Enlightenment. Carl Jung made the same point without, however, sharing Schweitzer's partiality for the Enlightenment and rational thinking. European civilization and Europeans were in trouble because of the death, beginning with the critical attack in the Enlightenment, of the God-archetype and its traditional religious symbols. The void thus created brought crashing down the whole European structure of values. For on Jung's theory, a society could function well only if the individuals comprising it were provided with symbols (and therefore meanings) in which they had faith. Only then could psychic energy be turned outward to produce creative social arrangements and institutions.

The existentialist philosopher Karl Jaspers, though far from oblivious of spiritual decline, emphasized more the effects of "apparatus," that is, Weber's bureaucratization, plus the world of technique. Apparatus, created by man for his own comfort and use, in the end came to have dominion over him and to reduce the individual to a category or function. Not only machines but "the masses" had turned the tables on their masters in modern times. This latter was the motif of Ortega y Gasset's book *The Revolt of the Masses* (1930). By "masses" Ortega did not mean especially workers or any social class, but technicians and specialists of all sorts, men who were highly trained but lacked "integral culture," principles, or a sense of historic duties. Present-day Europe, the product of the liberal and Industrial revolutions of the nineteenth century, was the first period in history that recognized nothing in the past as a standard. Possessing more knowledge and power than any previous world, "the world today goes the same way as the worst of worlds that have been; it simply drifts."[26] Machines and masses, as well as "disenchantment," figured prominently in many a contemporary analysis of the "decline of the West."

Prognosis of the future varied according to where one stood in the great debate, now revived, between determinism or destiny, and freedom. Spengler was a determinist. Up to now, he said, everybody had been at liberty to hope what he pleased about the future. But now that the facts were in, it was incumbent upon everyone to inform himself of what can and will happen, "with the unalterable necessity of destiny." For Europeans,

> whom a Destiny has placed in this Culture and at this moment of its development . . . our direction, willed and obligatory at once, is set for us within narrow limits. . . . We have not the freedom to reach to this or to that, but the freedom to do the necessary or to do nothing. And a task that historic necessity has set *will* be accomplished with the individual or against him.[27]

Though he disclaimed being a pessimist, Spengler maintained, not only that Europe was already well advanced into its "civilization" stage but that, like other cultures such as the Egyptian and Greek, it must eventually die, and die without issue. It became quite common to talk about history in this way, as determined, in whole or in part, by impersonal forces, and as portending, at best, a doubtful future. Even Christians preached a determinism of sorts, which saw the world as being given over increasingly to sin and Satan, and a future without hope, unless God interfered miraculously to negate time and its evil effects.[28]

Against destiny, humanists and existentialists rose to defend freedom in history. "*Pace* Spengler," Toynbee wrote, "there seems to be no reason why a succession of stimulating challenges [in history] should not be met by a succession of victorious responses ad infinitum."[29] Europe was not doomed, as Spengler believed, but was still free to experi-

---

[26] Ortega y Gasset, *The Revolt of the Masses*, W. W. Norton, New York, 1932, pp. 47–48.

[27] Oswald Spengler, *The Decline of the West*, Knopf, New York, 1932, Vol. II, p. 507; see also Vol. I, p. 39.

[28] So, for example, argued Christian "apocalyptists" at the Oxford Conference of 1937. See H. G. Wood et al., *The Kingdom of God and History* (1938), which reports views expressed at the conference. See also essays by European Roman Catholics, in *Satan* (1952), to much the same effect, emphasizing the impossibility of gaining victory over "the devil" in this life or in history.

[29] Toynbee, op. cit. (see note 23), p. 12.

ment and to extricate herself from an admittedly parlous situation. But Toynbee is somewhat suspect as a champion of freedom, because of his later view of the world as "a province of the Kingdom of God." That is, as already mentioned, he came to think of history, not merely as man's response to successive challenges but also as a field of purposeful action, dictated by a power that was greater than human, and revealed in world history in the rise of universal churches from the ashes of dead civilizations. André Malraux defended freedom less ambiguously. In his philosophy of history, developed in *The Psychology of Art* (1947–1950), and particularly in the revision of it entitled *The Voices of Silence* (1951), freedom confronts destiny. There *is* destiny, destiny in Spengler's sense—for Malraux too was obsessed by Spengler —of fatalism, determinism, and irrationalism. But for Malraux, destiny (*destin*) was always more a feeling that came over man periodically, than an objective "law" of history. "The *consciousness* we have of destiny, as profound as that of the Orient . . . is the Apparition of the Twentieth Century."[30] Destiny overcame the European world with the death of the absolute, and of absolute values (associated in his mind with the rise of the bourgeoisie, the first caste ever without values). Henceforth, civilization had no transcendence, no noble goals, but only facts, to guide it, and man had, increasingly, the feeling that he was not in command of his life, but was dominated *by* something, he knew not what. Man, however, was free to subdue destiny, as history showed time and again, mainly through his art. Hence, man the creator might yet again, like the Greeks, like the Middle Ages, give to "matter" a new life, imprint upon it new and fruitful images. This is very nearly the language of the existentialists, who likewise left the future open, while at the same time viewing history as tragedy, as also did Malraux. Karl Jaspers, for example, as one might expect of an existentialist, rejected any sort of "contemplative forecast" of the future. For such a forecast expressed a desire to know without any active participation on the part of the thinker. Destiny did not decree the end of a civilization. This was only a possibility, subject to what man himself willed to do. "I myself will what is going to happen, even though the end of all things be at hand."[31]

As this last asseveration indicates, none of the champions of free-

[30] André Malraux, *Les Voix du Silence,* Galerie de la Pléiade, Paris, 1951, pp. 628–629. Italics are mine.
[31] Karl Jaspers, *Man in the Modern Age,* Eden & Cedar Paul (trans.), Henry Holt, New York, 1933, p. 239. This book was first published in 1932, with the title *Die geistige Situation der Gegenwart.*

dom, any more than the champions of destiny, underestimated the difficulties of the future. For Jaspers, for example, the power of apparatus was all too apparent, and men would be fortunate, indeed, ever to become its master. He insisted only that "it is possible" for "the conscious will" to do something positive, through political activity and education, but mainly through a rediscovery of man's true being. This was, indeed, one of the chief marks of European philosophy of history in the twentieth century: confidence in future progress was replaced, by and large, by gloom—or alternatively by modest hope—though possibly the latter grew somewhat with each year following World War II. Thus, Bertrand Russell, who despaired of England and Europe in 1931, had hope in 1951. Perhaps Ortega's concluding statement fits best the mood of those who rejected destiny, and yet saw all the problems. In comparison with the nineteenth century, the contemporary world, he wrote, had become "scandalously provisional," and no one knew toward what center it would gravitate in the near future. This was said in 1930, with much worse times ahead for Europe and the world than even Ortega could have imagined. But Russell was saying substantially the same thing twenty years later, without Ortega's special emphasis on mass culture, namely that the next half-century lay wide open, for man to rebuild a manageable world, or else to fall back into a tragic fate "like characters in a Greek drama."[32] If there was any consensus among those whom we may call, collectively, humanists, it was that European civilization, if it was to survive, had to discover new roots, a new center for creative life. "Things fall apart: the centre cannot hold" (Yeats). Traditions that had once united a great civilization had gone. From this "filthy modern tide" Yeats sought refuge in a dream of Byzantium, of a City outside time. But others sought answers in history: in the building-up of Europe into a great liberal state, to counteract both fascism and communism (Ortega); in the possible construction of the world state (Russell, Toynbee); in working out a compromise between free enterprise and socialism (Toynbee), and others. Jaspers cut deeper. Civilization would be reconstructed only if and when man—individual man—discovered his selfhood, and thus gained the perspective and the power to resist dominion by apparatus. The social sciences were wrong in regarding man as an object or a

---

[32] Bertrand Russell, *New Hopes for a Changing World* (1951). Compare with an earlier, more pessimistic, statement of 1931, *Autobiography of Bertrand Russell*, Little, Brown, Boston, 1951, Vol. II, p. 232.

result, about whom data could be collected, with the aim of modifying man through institutions. "The best laws, the most

> admirable institutions, the most trustworthy acquirements of knowledge, the most effective technique, can be used in conflicting ways. They are of no avail unless individual human beings fulfil them with an effective and valuable reality.[33]

Hence, for Jaspers at least, hope of public improvement lay ultimately, not in expertise, but in "the very being of man," and in the widening of his horizons by a return to metaphysics or "transcendentalism." Jaspers was not alone in saying that for civilization to be creative again, becoming (represented by apparatus, a feeling of impotent perplexity or fate, or whatever) had somehow to be connected again to being.

[33] Jaspers, op. cit. (see note 31), p. 185.

PART VI

Epilogue

The "Decline of the West" is hardly the note on which I would wish to end a book about modern European thought. True, the second Thirty Years' war, as Winston Churchill called it, bled Europe white intellectually, as in every other way, and understandably stimulated talk about decline. Yet all through her "time of troubles," Europe continued to give off intellectual sparks, igniting the creative imagination everywhere, including America. Partly, no doubt, she was living on accumulated intellectual capital; it is noteworthy that most of Europe's creative intellects were born and educated before 1900, or at least before the Great War. She also drove away much irreplaceable talent, especially after 1930. But there were also new quanta jumps, new intellectual movements of great power, which *started* during that period and were actually evoked by the crisis of the twentieth century. Whether Europe could, or can, remain "the great creative continent," as Max Lerner has called her, is, of course, debatable. Fortunately, intellectual leadership does not depend altogether on economic and political power, though one might argue that the latter can contribute much to it. It depends, certainly, on freedom. Without freedom there can be no real interchange of ideas, or "speculative adventure." It depends on an intellectual tradition of long standing, on respect and support for that tradition in the community, and on the intellectual discipline that comes only from a rigorous educational system. All of these precious resources remained, if not exactly intact, at least available, in Europe, after attempts to belittle and destroy them had failed and the rage of irrationalism had passed.

Shortly after World War II, André Malraux, soon to become France's minister of culture, observed that many people were contemplating "the death of Europe." "But it is far from certain that Europe is dead," he told the delegates assembled for the opening sessions of UNESCO in Paris. He reaffirmed his belief in "the will to discovery and awareness," which, he may be excused for saying, was "peculiarly and exclusively European." Malraux found that will in Europe's great art, science, and literature. It was true that Europe, like other civilizations in the past, had recently bowed her neck under the "destiny" of death.

> But it is no less true [he concluded] that, century after century, in this tract of earth that we call Europe—and in it only—men bowed beneath the yoke of destiny have raised their eyes to probe unwearyingly the darkness, to wrest a meaning from the vast confusion of the universe.[1]

But it is just this last point—the ability to wrest a meaning from the universe—that makes one wonder about intellectual Europe's prospects. For intellectual leadership also depends, surely, on the sort of inspiration that derives from belief in meaning, or the possibility of meaning. There must be alertness to change, to new ideas, to possible new interpretations of the world, to prevent a civilization from sinking into a Byzantine routine. On the other hand, a radical becoming, dominating all intellectual and cultural life, can destroy an intellectual community's will to do more than to keep alive curiosity and to think critically and without illusions. That is quite a good deal, to be sure, but it is hardly the stuff of which the greatest thought is made. If this book has a moral, then, it is that intellectual creativity of the highest sort depends on a healthy mixture, or tension, between being and becoming, between the permanent (permanent ideals, even if one does not yet know what they are in any final or complete sense) and the impermanent. Intellectual Europe had this mixture up to the end of the nineteenth century, and even somewhat beyond, and may still have it again. But it will not be easy to recapture.

A few words may be said, in conclusion, about intellectual history, or the history of ideas, in general. It is better understood now than it

---

[1] André Malraux, "Man and Artistic Culture," in *Reflections of Our Age*, Columbia University Press, New York, 1949, pp. 96–98.

used to be, that history's province extends to man's intellectual and imaginative life, to what he has thought, as well as what he has done. Much of man's thought has been expended on plans for action, which may, or may not, ever be carried out. But it is perhaps still not sufficiently realized how very much of man's thought has been without any practical motivation, but has been devoted simply to knowing and understanding, to the discovery of self and the universe, to wresting a meaning from "the vast confusion." That is, indeed, partly what it means to be a human being: to think about meaning. That is why man has asked "perennial questions"—the stuff of intellectual history, as I see it—which have to do, not only with how best to organize the world of action but with God, and nature, and the nature and destiny of man. European history is rich in this kind of "pure" thought. It has gone on for generations, regardless of, though never unaffected by, the ever changing social milieu.

It follows that intellectual history is very much concerned about truth, that is, not only with *why,* historically, people have thought the way they have, but whether what they have thought is *true.* It is the intellectual historian's métier to plot changing fashions in ideas and to explain these ideas in their historical context. But he is also interested in the ideas themselves, in their validity as well as their history. But how, it may be asked, can intellectual history, the study *par excellence* of the changing, the relative, and the conditioned, contribute anything meaningful to a discussion of "the changeless amid change"? It can do so in several ways. First, it can show how certain ideas have not merely survived but helped to build what men have adjudged to be great civilizations, outstanding in the arts and sciences. Contrariwise, it can show that some other ideas have lived only briefly or been associated with decadence. The weakness of this argument is, of course, that it depends on a *consensus gentium.* Yet it would be unwise to ignore the fact that there is overwhelming agreement that certain ages of history have been "happy" in the quality of their ideas. Men throughout history recognize the ideas as true in some sense, and try to appropriate them for their own use.

Second, intellectual history can reveal, better than any other discipline, the many-sidedness of truth. It is true that progress has been made over the centuries in solving certain kinds of problems, and that answers to questions once thought to be final have been shown to be one-sided, oversimplistic, and even mistaken. At the same time, however, men have a way of forgetting and ignoring valuable perspectives and insights, won at an earlier date only after much thought, courage, and suffering. Intellectual history makes these past perspectives once more accessible to modern man, so that he may weigh them in his own pursuit of the truth. Pascal's conception of the nature of man, for example, is known today only to a few, and taken seriously by even fewer. What he said may seem remote or harsh at first, but on closer acquaintance may be seen to have a certain wisdom. At least it is worth considering (as is also Voltaire's rejoinder to Pascal) in our estimate of what man is, and we would not even have considered it but for the "archeological" work of intellectual historians. Why go back into the past, presumed by many people today to be dead and gone? We do so because the past opens up a rich lode of ideas about the great questions. Thanks to intellectual history, we can contemplate these ideas, hatched in earlier times and for different men, as in certain ways contributory to the truth.

But intellectual history does more. It postulates an integral relationship between the truth or validity, and the historical origins, of an idea. An idea should never be considered in the abstract, as though it were the product of thinking *per se.* It is that in part, but it is more. Every idea comes out of a particular environment and is the inspiration of an historical moment, of an individual or group's facing up to a unique set of problems. It is, in fact, in large part because of that environment, or moment in history, that the idea was conceived in the first place. Thus, if we are to understand the idea fully, grasp its logic, we must see it first in its original state, at the time when it was born and flourished. In short, every idea has its historical dimension, and this dimension *not only* helps to explain how it came to be but *what it is.* By not taking this dimension into account, we run the risk of mistaking the idea entirely. On the other hand, by making the effort to enter into the experience which made it possible in the first place, we see the idea as it was meant to be. It comes alive for us, as it was alive for its creators. In such ways as these, intellectual history brings the truth nearer. We are nearer to it, and wiser, for having thought some of the thoughts of Europeans from 1600 to 1950.

Bibliography

I have limited this bibliography to fifty-odd books. All are general books, not monographs, and should be available in good libraries. Some have been reprinted and are still purchasable. The first date refers to the first edition (in English, if translated), the second to a later, though not necessarily the latest, edition. The footnotes refer to many other books on special subjects.

General

BURY, J. B., *The Idea of Progress,* Macmillan, 1920; Dover Publications, 1960

BAUMER, FRANKLIN, L., *Religion and the Rise of Scepticism,* Harcourt, Brace, 1960; 1969

CLARK, KENNETH, *Landscape into Art,* J. Murray, 1949; Beacon Press, 1963; 1976

COLLINGWOOD, R. G., *The Idea of Nature,* Oxford University Press, 1945; 1960

COLLINS, JAMES, *God in Modern Philosophy,* Henry Regnery Company, 1959; 1967

COPLESTON, FREDERICK, *A History of Philosophy,* 8 vols., Newman Press, new rev. ed. 1963–1966

DAMPIER, SIR WILLIAM CECIL, *A History of Science and its Relations with Philosophy and Religion,* Cambridge University Press, 1929; 1958

Dictionary of the History of Ideas, 4 vols., Charles Scribner's Sons, 1973

LOVEJOY, ARTHUR O., *The Great Chain of Being,* Harvard University Press, 1936; Harper & Row, 1965

MAZLISH, BRUCE, *The Riddle of History; the Great Speculators from Vico to Freud,* Harper & Row, 1966; Minerva, 1968

RANDALL, JOHN H., *The Career of Philosophy,* 2 vols., Columbia University Press, 1962–1965

SABINE, GEORGE, *A History of Political Theory,* Henry Holt, 1937; Dryden, 1973

Seventeenth Century

BURTT, E. A., *The Metaphysical Foundations of Modern Physical Science,* Harcourt, Brace, 1927; Doubleday & Co., 1955

BUTTERFIELD, HERBERT, *The Origins of Modern Science,* G. Bell, 1949; Free Press, 1968

CLARK, G. N., *The Seventeenth Century,* Clarendon Press, Oxford, 1929; Oxford University Press, 1961

FRIEDRICH, CARL J., *The Age of the Baroque, 1610–1660,* Harper & Row, 1952

HAZARD, PAUL, *The European Mind, 1680–1715,* Yale University Press, 1953; World Publishing Company, 1967

JONES, R. F., *Ancients and Moderns,* Washington University Press, 1936; University of California Press, 1965

NICOLSON, MARJORIE, *The Breaking of the Circle; Studies in the Effect of the "New Science" upon Seventeenth-Century Poetry,* Northwestern University Press, 1950; Columbia University Press, 1960

POPKIN, RICHARD H., *The History of Skepticism from Erasmus to Descartes,* Assen, Van Gorcum, 1960; Harper & Row, 1968

WILLEY, BASIL, *The Seventeenth Century Background,* Chatto & Windus, 1934; Doubleday & Co., 1953

Eighteenth Century

CASSIRER, ERNST, *The Philosophy of the Enlightenment,* Princeton University Press, 1951; Beacon Press, 1960

CRAGG, GERALD, *Reason and Authority in the Eighteenth Century,* Cambridge University Press, 1964

FRANKEL, CHARLES, *The Faith of Reason,* King's Crown Press, 1948

GAY, PETER, *The Enlightenment,* 2 vols., Alfred A. Knopf, 1966; 1969

HAZARD, PAUL, *European Thought in the Eighteenth Century,* Yale University Press, 1954

HONOUR, HUGH, *Neo-classicism,* Penguin Books, 1968

MEINECKE, FRIEDRICH, *Historism,* Routledge & Kegan Paul, 1972

VARTANIAN, ARAM, *Diderot and Descartes,* Princeton University Press, 1953

VYVERBERG, HENRY, *Historical Pessimism in the French Enlightenment,* Harvard University Press, 1958

WILLEY, BASIL, *The Eighteenth Century Background,* Chatto & Windus, 1940; Columbia University Press, 1953

Nineteenth Century

BARZUN, JACQUES, *Romanticism and the Modern Ego,* Little, Brown, 1943; reprinted as *Classic, Romantic and Modern,* Doubleday & Co., 1961

BRINTON, CRANE, *English Political Thought in the Nineteenth Century,* E. Benn, 1933; Harvard University Press, 1949

CASSIRER, ERNST, *The Problem of Knowledge, Philosophy, Science, and History since Hegel,* Yale University Press, 1950; 1974

EISELEY, LOREN, *Darwin's Century,* Doubleday & Co., 1958; 1961

HOOK, SIDNEY, *From Hegel to Marx,* Reynal & Hitchcock, 1936; University of Michigan Press, 1962

HOUGHTON, WALTER, *The Victorian Frame of Mind,* Yale University Press, 1957

IGGERS, GEORG, *The German Conception of History,* Wesleyan University Press, 1968

LICHTHEIM, GEORGE, *Marxism: an Historical and Critical Study,* Praeger, 1961; 1965

LOVEJOY, ARTHUR O., *Essays in the History of Ideas,* Johns Hopkins University Press, 1948; G. P. Putnam's, 1960

MANDELBAUM, MAURICE, *History, Man, & Reason: a Study in Nineteenth-Century Thought,* Johns Hopkins University Press, 1971

MANUEL, FRANK, *The Prophets of Paris,* Harvard University Press, 1962; Harper & Row, 1965

WAGAR, W. WARREN, *Good Tidings: The Belief in Progress from Darwin to Marcuse,* Indiana University Press, 1972

WILLEY, BASIL, *Nineteenth Century Studies,* Chatto & Windus, 1949; Harper & Row, 1966

WHITE, HAYDEN, *Metahistory: the Historical Imagination in Nineteenth-Century Europe,* Johns Hopkins University Press, 1973

Twentieth Century

BARRETT, WILLIAM, *Irrational Man,* Doubleday & Co., 1958; 1962

ČAPEK, MILIČ, *The Philosophical Impact of Contemporary Physics,* D. Van Nostrand, 1961

ELLENBERGER, HENRI, *The Discovery of the Unconscious,* Basic Books, 1970

HEINEMANN, R. H., *Existentialism and the Modern Predicament,* Harper & Row, 1952; 1958

HUGHES, H. STUART, *Consciousness and Society: the Reorientation of European Social Thought, 1890–1930,* Alfred A. Knopf, 1958; 1961

LEVI, ALBERT W., *Philosophy and the Modern World,* Indiana University Press, 1959

LICHTHEIM, GEORGE, *Europe in the Twentieth Century,* Praeger Publishers, 1972

MACQUARRIE, JOHN, *The Scope of Demythologizing: Bultmann and His Critics,* Harper & Row, 1960; 1961

NOLTE, ERNST, *Three Faces of Fascism,* Holt, Rinehart and Winston, 1965; 1966

See also Iggers and Wagar, listed under Nineteenth Century.

Index of Proper Names

Index of Subjects

Absolutism (*see also* Divine Right of Kings, Enlightened Despotism, Sovereignty), 229; protest against, 106f.

Absurd, the, 414, 437

Académie des sciences, 29, 44, 148; Plate 6

Academies (*see also* Académie des sciences, Royal Society), 44, 122, 127

Addresses on Religion (Schleiermacher), 277–78

Aesthetics, eighteenth-century, 154f.

Agnosticism, 263, 353f.

Alienation, idea of, 315, 320, 446, 483; in Hegel, 316; in Feuerbach, 317; in Marx, 319, 482; cosmic, 414–15

America (*see also* Discoveries, overseas), Jan van Kessel's painting of, 32, n. 10; Plate 1; 108, 158, 266

American Revolution, 220, 229, 251

Ancients (*see also* Moderns), *vs.* Moderns, 122f., 243

Anglicans, 66, 69, 74, 182; on the nature of man, 82–83

Anxiety, 414–15, 448

Aristotelianism and Aristotelians, 49, 50, 51, 56, 57

Arts, liberal, mechanical, and fine, 148–49

Associationist psychology, 174–75, 183, 321

Atheism, and atheists, 65, 183, 191–92

Augustinianism and Augustinians, 81–83, 111, 135, 175; "secular," 83f., 91, 166

Baroque, the, 26, 39

Battle of the Books, 123

Becoming (*see also* Being, Being and Becoming), 265, 305, 485, 487, 492, 498, 503; Renan on, 264; Century of, 267; in nature, 281, 376; in romantic thought, 300–301; and social thought, 360; Bergson and Nietzsche, philosophers of, 376, 381; triumph of, 402f.; man as, 436

Behaviorism, 421–22

Being (*see also* Being and Becoming, Becoming), 492, 496, 517; Existentialists on, 436; Catholic philosophy of, 450–51

Being and Becoming (*see also* Being, Becoming), 20f., 517; in seventeenth century ideas of nature, 59–60; God, 78; politics, 96–98; in eighteenth century thought, 140, 143, 152f.

Biblical Criticism, 196–97, 315, 338, 354, 355–56, 396, 495

Benthamism (*see also* Utilitarianism, Utility), 362, 380, 387

Byzantinism, 395

Calvinism and Calvinists, 66, 81, 88–89, 198; on human nature, 82–83, 88

Cambridge Platonists, 121, 168, 175

Cartesianism and Cartesians, 30, 66, 450, 451

China, in eighteenth-century thought, 158